Worldly Wisdom

Worldly Wisdom

Great Books and
the Meanings of Life

James Sloan Allen

FREDERIC C. BEIL
SAVANNAH
2008

Published in the United States of America by
Frederic C. Beil, Publisher, Inc.
609 Whitaker Street
Savannah, Georgia 31401
http://www.beil.com

LIBRARY OF CONGRESS CATALOGING-IN-PUBLICATION DATA

Allen, James Sloan.
Worldly wisdom : Great Books and the meanings of life / James Sloan Allen
        p.   cm.
Includes bibliographical references and index.
ISBN 978–1–929490–35–6 (alk. paper)
1. Best books. 2. Literature—History and criticism.
3. Humanism. I. Title.
Z1035.A1A45 2007
011'.73—dc22
                                        2006103472

Manufactured in the United States of America

First edition

To Elizabeth
and
all who help us find
the meanings of life

Contents

Contents

Acknowledgments

Like every author, I owe many debts to those who have made this book possible. I owe the first of these debts to the authors whose works inspired this book and who have been my intellectual companions for most of my adult life. They are my true mentors.

But I have many other debts as well. These arose from the scholarly teachers who introduced me to many of these authors, from the academic colleagues and learned friends with whom I have engaged in a long conversation about books and ideas, from my generous sisters who gave me much thoughtful encouragement, from my daughters and grandchildren who give me hope for the future, and from the college students and adults who have made reading and talking about classic authors a stimulating and pleasurable vocation. I owe them all a happy debt that perhaps this book will in some small pleasure repay.

I also want to mention in particular the members of my Great Books group at the Mercantile Library in New York City who have brought an invigorating enthusiasm and abundant insights to the reading and discussion of many of the books represented here. I was prompted to launch that group after the events of September 11, 2001, which, among other things, raised many questions about how to live with tragedy and how to find "the meanings of life." I thought no source could be more helpful in answering some of those questions than classic writings of the world. This group of seasoned New Yorkers has confirmed that I was right.

I would also like to note the value to me of the lively discussions with colleagues in the Columbia University Seminar on Innovation in Education, where I have long benefited from how the pieties of educational principles get challenged, the practices of education get scrutinized, and all kinds of learning get encouraged.

Now, a word of thanks to Frederic C. Beil. An astute editor and courageous publisher, he is among the few determined to keep the great tradition of independent and high quality publishing alive in this country. American culture would be better than it is if we had more like him. I count myself fortunate to have worked with him on this book.

Finally, my wife, Elizabeth Cheresh Allen. I could not have finished this book without her persistent good nature, unwavering confidence, and endearing affection. Throughout the years of my on-and-off labors on it, she insured that it would be a labor of love on many counts. Her worldly wisdom has deeply affected me, and words cannot say how grateful I am to her for it.

I have presented parts of this book to especially interested audiences at the University of Notre Dame, the Aspen Institute, and the Columbia Seminar on Innovation in Education. And early portions of several of the chapters here have appeared in periodicals; I thank the editors for permission to republish them:

The Sewanee Review: Preface in "The Existential Reader: Or Reading, Rumination, and the Classics," vol. xcix, no. 1, Winter 1991; Chapter 20 in "The Storytellers of Marrakech," vol. civ, no. 4, Fall 1996; Chapter 18 in "Mrs. Dalloway and the Ethics of Civility," vol. cvii, no. 4, Fall 1999; Chapter 25 in "Nietzsche and Wilde: And Ethics of Style," vol. cxiv, no. 3, Summer 2006.

The Georgia Review: Chapter 2 in "The Mystery of the Smiling Elephant. In the Erotic Temples of Khajuraho," Summer 1999.

The New Criterion: Chapter 19 in "Tolstoy's 'What Is Art?'" December 1998.

Arts Education Policy Review: Chapter 19 in "Aristotle and 'The Blessed Life,'" vol. 103, May/June 2002 and "The Morality and Immorality of Art," vol. 104, Nov./Dec. 2002; Chapter 25 in "The Use and Abuse of Aestheticism," vol. 104, May/June 2003. All reprinted by permission of the Helen Dwight Reid Educational Foundation. Published by Heldref Publications.

Preface:
The Humanistic Meanings of Life

Have you been able to think out and manage your own life?
Our great and glorious masterpiece is to live appropriately.
Michel de Montaigne

Have you read Voltaire?
I've done better than that. I've put him into practice.
Honoré de Balzac

YOU DON'T HAVE to be a philosopher to think about the meaning of life. Everyone does it. Sometimes we think about the meaning of life itself—where it came from, where it is going, what is its purpose, and so on. But more often we think about the many smaller *meanings* of our own lives as we live from day to day. Ideas about these everyday meanings of life underlie virtually everything we do—from pursuing pleasures to choosing careers, from making friends to rearing children, from planning for the future to voting for political candidates. These ideas may not be altogether conscious. And most probably go unstated. But we cannot live without them.

There would not be any classic writings, or Great Books, of world civilization without these ideas either (at least outside of science). In one way or another, these writings all deal with how we find meaning in our lives—or how we *give meanings* to our lives. Classic authors just differ from other people by having more elaborate ideas on this subject, and by articulating their ideas more memorably. This is how classic writings give us what I will call "good ideas," and "useful humanism," and "worldly wisdom."

Good ideas are not quite the same as "great ideas." Great ideas tend to be overarching abstractions—like Truth and Beauty and Justice—that stir earnest philosophizing and industrious scholarship. Many Great Books contain such great ideas, of course, but they usually turn them into good ideas as well. Good ideas are more particular and concrete than great ideas, and more useful to people every day. For good ideas help us understand how human beings live in this world, and they give us advice about how to live well in it. Good ideas in this sense belong to everyone who tries to give meaning to his or her own life *in this world*, without depending on an afterlife in another world.

That makes these ideas amount to a kind of "useful humanism." This is not the secular humanism that wholly dismisses the otherworldly aspirations of religion. Useful humanism is more generous and less ideological than that. It does not deny the possible existence of things outside of this world, including God and an afterlife. Instead it adopts Shakespeare's cautious skepticism, spoken by Hamlet to Horatio (slightly altered here): "There are more things in heaven and earth than are dreamt of in our philosophy." But at the same time, useful humanism admits the possibility of otherworldly things only to make human life in this world better for its own sake, and not to justify making this life merely a preparation for another life to come. This humanism therefore says: whether or not otherworldly things exist, we still live *in this world* and must try to find meaning within it, not outside of it. That is how useful humanism gives us the "worldly wisdom" of this book's title.

Worldly wisdom is made up of the good ideas and useful humanism that help us understand our lives and give meaning to them in this world. In fact, I would say this worldly wisdom is the great humanistic tradition that has come down to us through history and across cultures from the earliest fables of humankind. For it offers us, in the plain words of the wise Renaissance thinker Michel de Montaigne, "knowledge of how to live this life well." And in our era of proliferating religious fundamentalisms—the antithesis of any humanism—we need all of the humanistic worldly wisdom we can get.

Every classic book, essay, story, play, and poem discussed in *Worldly Wisdom* belongs to this humanistic tradition in one way or another. Or, in any case, like the otherworldly *Bhagavad-Gita*, they can be read for what they contribute to it because they all give us very good ideas about how to live in this world. These ideas are not foreign to any of us despite our dissimilarities as inhabitants of disparate cultures and times and places, as members of separate genders, or as persons of different ethnicities. That is the universality of worldly wisdom—by any name. I have listed some of these good ideas at the end of each chapter. The lists are impressionistic to be sure, but the good ideas in them come from the heart of the respective classic writings, and they exemplify the kind of humanism that this book elucidates and commends, which is useful to anyone, anywhere, anytime.

Certain critics might complain that to read Great Books in this way for their good ideas, useful humanism, or worldly wisdom reduces them to something like "how-to-books." And anyone who reveres the classics as "texts" to be studied only for more academic purposes will judge that kind of reading to be vulgar or perverse. But I would respond that, to some degree, the classics always have been "how-to-books." For originally most of them were, among other things, meditations or tales about *how to live this life well*, concerned as they are with topics like these (which Montaigne, again, gathered together):

> . . . the uses and ends of hard-earned coin; our debt to country and to friends; . . . what we may justly wish; . . . what we now are, what destiny for us is planned; what it is to know and not to know, and what must be the aim of study; what are valor, temperance, and justice; what is the difference between ambition and avarice, servitude and submission, license and liberty; . . . what springs move us, and what is the cause of different impulses in us; . . . by what signs may we recognize true solid contentment; how much should we fear death, pain, and shame; what hardships should we avoid, what should we endure, and how.

Montaigne wrote these words (recast a bit here) four hundred years ago, drawing on classic authors who had lived as much as two thousand years before him. We all want to know such things today. People always will. That is because we all want to say *Yes!* to the essential humanistic question, in Montaigne's words once more: "Have you been able to think out and manage your own life?" If you can, Montaigne adds, "you have done the greatest task of all," since "our great and glorious masterpiece is to live appropriately."

Now, you might ask: What does it mean "to manage your own life"? or "to live appropriately"? or "to live well"? There are many answers to these questions, or many good ideas needed to form a suitable answer. And the answers will differ in some measure from person to person, just as they do from classic to classic. Bookstores today supply walls of self-help books that presume to answer these questions with an array of tidy formulas for success. But nowhere can we find as many fundamental, universal, and lasting answers as in the good ideas of the humanistic classics. That is why we should read Great Books—at least sometimes—as "how-to-books."

And I will go farther. Reading classic writings in this humanistic way not only lends them a practical, "how-to" quality. It also makes the "good ideas" in them more important than the whole works themselves. This will also seem blasphemous to reverential readers of the classics. But there are many ways to read a book or an essay, a story, a play, or a poem. There is the historical, which places a work within the context of a tradition and of its own times. There is the biographical, which seeks connections between an author's life and works. There is the philosophical, which analyzes the theoretical content and implications of a work and identifies logical links to writings by other thinkers. There is the social-scientific, which interprets a book within broad patterns of human creativity and behavior. There is the literary-critical, which elucidates and appraises the formal aesthetic properties of a work. And there are the kinds of reading typified by liberal arts education and Mortimer Adler's Great Books movement, which, with variations, celebrate the general expansiveness of mind and the understanding of a cultural tradition that study of the classics can bring.

All of these and other kinds of reading are valuable. And who could doubt that to comprehend any classic fully we must read it in every way? Still, the kind of reading that should come first, and should never be abandoned, is this: to read the classics for the good ideas that illuminate our lives and help us give meaning to them and to live them well. To do this, we must become what might be described as "existential readers." That is, we must be willing to pass over most bookish matters, important as these may be to other kinds of reading, and go for the good ideas, the useful humanism, the worldly wisdom in them, like the character in Balzac's *Lost Illusions* who answers the question, "Have you read Voltaire?" by saying: "I've done better than that. I've put him into practice."

I hasten to add, however, that this kind of reading does not require ignoring the logic and beauty, the spirit and design, the imaginative pleasures and intellectual stimulation of a whole work to settle for what the great historian Jacob Burckhardt, in a more ominous context, decried as the pernicious superficiality of "terrible simplifiers" (although we should also keep in mind that superficiality and simplification are loaded terms often wielded to exalt technical expertise over more general learning). Reading for good ideas on the humanistic meanings of life should actually lead us through the logic and beauty, the spirit and design, the imaginative pleasures and intellectual stimulation of the classics into the heart and soul of their universal human appeal and their enduring service to human life.

This is what *Worldly Wisdom* aspires to do. If it succeeds in bringing readers the delights and life-serving humanistic uses of some classic writings, it will have done its job. It will have done even better if it entices readers to take up those and other classic writings for themselves with the curiosity to find more of those delights and uses, as well as other rewards, on their own.

I SHOULD POINT OUT that during the last couple of decades the classics have sparked some sharp controversies among educators over what people should read and why. On one side, traditionalists have insisted that people should read the Western classics as superior intellectual and literary creations indispensable to a rigorous education and to a common culture. On the other side, antitraditionalists, led by feminists and multiculturalists, have argued that the Western canon of classics should be shelved as the worn-out baggage of dead white European males who ignored or condescended to anyone unlike themselves (although antitraditionalists often overlook how critical of Western culture many of the Western classics are), and some antitraditionalists have scorned the very concept of a classic as elitist snobbery.

Worldly Wisdom shares something with both sides. It shares the traditionalists' contention that classic writings do indeed rise above others in genius and in universal and enduring value. But it also shares the antitraditionalists' inclination to go beyond traditional views of what counts as a classic and of what people should read and why. *Worldly Wisdom* assumes that every culture has its classics, whatever their form, and that we should read any classic from anywhere for its universal humanistic uses, not just for more academic purposes.

I should also note that antitraditionalists would likely protest that the humanism represented by *Worldly Wisdom* is itself merely a Western idea elevated here to a universal principle. There would be some truth to this charge. But it is the same truth that accounts for the Western idea of "human rights" gradually becoming a universal standard of humane justice for human beings around the world. If such human rights arose as a largely Western idea, that does not make it a bad idea. And if Western culture has been more openly occupied with certain humanistic ideals than have other cultures, that does not make humanism a solely Western possession. Far from it. The non-Western classics explored in *Worldly Wisdom* not only demonstrate the universality of the humanism that this book reflects, they also contribute some distinctly non-Western good ideas to it.

This brings me to the selection of classic writings taken up here. Everyone should have a list of favorite classics—never mind that any selection will fall short of someone else's standard. My choices came, for the most part, from answering three questions: (1) Which classic works of literature, philosophy, and social thought (entire books or parts of books, essays, even poems and oral fables), including some from non-Western cultures, contain the most notable good ideas, useful humanism, and worldly wisdom? (2) Which of these works are the most accessible to readers in lucidity, import, and pleasure? (3) Which of these works have been most stimulating, enlightening, and humanistically useful to me and to the college students and adults I have taught for over thirty years?

All of the fifty or so principal classic works (and related writings) featured in *Worldly Wisdom* meet these criteria. Needless to say, others could have met these criteria as well. Many familiar but omitted classics will jump to any reader's mind. Other, less well-recognized works might also have been included. But while I have cast my net fairly widely, I have not tried to represent all of Western culture, much less all other cultures and peoples. Nor have I aimed to find fault with the works I have selected, leaving that to other readers with other purposes. I set out to do something more modest and yet, I think, more widely inviting—that is, to draw readers into the humanistic worldly wisdom of some of the most renowned writings of world civilization (primarily of the West) because these writings have much to teach us about "how to live this life well."

Although I have arranged the chapters on these classics under the three headings of "Human Nature, Ethics, and the Good Life," "Living in the Social and Political World," and "The Promises and Perils of Aesthetics, Imagination, Romance," the arrangement is somewhat arbitrary. Many of the titles could have fit under another heading. But placed where they are, roughly chronologically within each section, these writings often talk to each other more directly than they otherwise would have. At all events, readers should find the chapters independent enough to browse through them in any order, while also seeing agreements and disagreements among them throughout. The good ideas listed at the end of each chapter, as well as the general index of ideas and names, also reflect both that independence and those relationships.

A word on translations. It is never ideal to depend on translations, particularly with poetry or where the original language is ideographic. But I have relied on translations (consulting the original texts or several translations, often doing both, and slightly modifying some translations where I have thought appropriate) for two reasons. First, since the readers of this book will be English-speaking, I wanted them to feel comfortable reading the classics in that language. Second, and more significant, translations confirm a central point of the book: that the humanistic worldly wisdom of the classics bridges gulfs between languages, as well as between historical periods and cultures, creating an ageless and endless global conversation about *how to live this life well.* Thanks to this conversation—and to the translations that facilitate it—worldly wisdom can be said to be the universal humanistic philosophy of the world.

A final note: I have followed the current practice of designating dates as B.C.E. (Before Common Era) and C.E. (Common Era) instead of B.C. and A.D.

New York City
Tenants Harbor, Maine
Honolulu

Part I

Human Nature, Ethics, and the Good Life

I

The Tragic Sense of Life and the Dawn of Humanism

Homer: *The Iliad*

The destinies put in mortal men the heart of endurance.
I wish that strife would vanish away from gods and mortals.

Homer

Homer (eighth century B.C.E.) himself might be a fiction. By legend he was a blind poet who sang verses to listeners on the Ionian shores—now the Aegean coast of Turkey. And he survives in tradition through the two Greek epics that carry his name, the *Iliad* and the *Odyssey*. But the name "Homer" might have been invented for an anonymous author (or authors) who gave literary form to those oral epics and had them written down four centuries after the events that the books record. But whether he is fact or fiction, Homer holds a preeminent place in Western culture. For his name signals the birth of Western literature, and the two epics ascribed to him remain among the greatest literary works ever created.

The *Odyssey* tells an episodic adventure story about the Greek warrior Ulysses as he makes his long way back from the Trojan War in Ionia to his home in Ithaca, where his wife, Penelope, has waited faithfully for twenty years. The *Iliad* precedes the *Odyssey* chronologically, recording events in the Trojan War itself. And while the *Odyssey* is more popular with readers, the *Iliad* is more profound.

Set in the tenth year of the Trojan War, the *Iliad* vividly and majestically describes the horrors of battle and the emotions of warriors and civilians. The subject is actually not so much the war itself—although there is plenty of that—as it is the drama of human beings struggling with their plight and their pride and their humanity amidst the combat, the shenanigans of their gods, and the dictates of a fate that they cannot escape. The angry, injured pride of the Greek warrior Achilles drives the specific wartime drama that Homer portrays here. But within that drama Homer also depicts his characters turning from the war and the gods to embrace humane values—such as honor, empathy, and love—to give meaning to their lives and to create a culture of humanity despite the inhumanity of war and of Greek religion.

3

The *Iliad* is violent, but it is also humane; it is tragic, but it is also hopeful; it is pagan, but it also marks the beginnings of a humanism that would leave the selfish gods behind and bring us the best of the humanistic culture that we know today, as well as our hopes, for all humanity.

NO HUMAN LIFE unfolds without tragedy. Tragedy thrusts itself upon all of us at one time or another in hurtful, sometimes terrible, events that we cannot predict, or cannot avoid. These events may look like random accidents, or the fruits of our own folly, or the malevolence of evil forces, or the harsh tests of a paternalistic god, or the cruel acts of a fate beyond our powers. Wherever tragedy comes from, it causes trouble. And it can lead us to believe that tragedy will strike us no matter what we do. We might call this belief—or, perhaps, it is just a feeling—"the tragic sense of life," to use a phrase from the Spanish philosopher Miguel de Unamuno.

The tragic sense of life gives rise to a variety of moods, ideas, and actions. It can, for instance, arouse rage at our helplessness, or induce resignation at our hopelessness, or even throw doubt over the very purpose of human life. The great Greek tragedies of Aeschylus, Sophocles, and Euripides dramatized all of these effects. That is what makes those dramas so darkly *tragic*. Consider that supremely tragic character, Sophocles' Oedipus. Determined to foil an astonishing prediction that he would one day murder his father and marry his mother, Oedipus runs away from home. While traveling, he kills a man in a fight on the road and later marries a queen. When he discovers, in Sophocles' play *Oedipus Rex*, that these two people were in fact his true parents—who, to thwart the same awful prediction, had long ago sent him away to die as an infant in the mountains, only to have him fall into the hands of a kindly couple who had reared him as their own while never revealing his origins—Oedipus screams to the heavens and plunges out his eyes. Every action by Oedipus and his true parents to escape their fated tragedy had only played into it. His frightful discovery of the truth overturns Oedipus' world. Nothing is what he had thought it was. Even *he* is not who he thought he was. How could he not have gone berserk with horror and guilt? But in time a change comes over him. When we see Oedipus as an old man in *Oedipus at Colonus*, he no longer blames himself for the tragedy. He rather blames an impersonal and heartless fate for foisting it upon him, despite every human attempt to avoid it. Tormented by his helplessness, he denounces a universe—or a mythology—that denies human beings the power to govern their own lives. The tragic sense of life had stolen Oedipus' confidence in everything, and it had ignited his rage against having to live a life beyond his control.

The tragic sense of life can cause desolation and impotent rage in anyone. But it can also call forth more benign responses. A humane religion can be one of them. By providing beliefs that make sense of the tragedies that happen to us, such a religion can give escape from those tragedies in the promise of a better world to come, and in codes of behavior to get us through this world benevolently alongside our fellow human beings. Social ideologies are another, assigning blame for most tragedies to social and economic conditions and aspiring to head off such tragedies by changing those conditions (see Chapter 15). The philosophy of existentialism is still another, encouraging people to meet life's tragedies with the courage of freedom and responsibility (see Chapter 9). We can also observe the tragic sense of life at work in the humane convictions and heroic acts of individual historical figures, like the ex-slave Frederick Douglass and the Holocaust survivor Elie Wiesel (see Chapter 16), as well as in the secular ethics of fictional characters like George Eliot's Dorothea Brooke and Virginia Woolf's Clarissa Dalloway (see Chapter 18). It is in historical and fictional individuals like these that we find the most paradoxical, and the most life-affirming, of all human responses to the tragic sense of life. We can call it humanism.

It is not too much to say that Western culture, at least literary culture, begins with the tragic sense of life giving birth to humanism. That beginning comes with the West's first literary work, Homer's *Iliad*. For the *Iliad* shows the tragic sense of life, hardened by the horrors of the Trojan War, not only provoking rage and despair, but inspiring ideas and beliefs and actions that make life in this world worth living despite the tragedy. These are not religious ideas and beliefs. Quite the contrary. They defy religion. And replace it. For they are the ideas that create humanism as a kind of victory over tragedy, not by envisioning an afterlife in another world, but by affirming human life in this world.

Homer's humanism, born of a world engulfed by war and tragically tossed about by capricious gods and an implacable fate, points to a peaceful world that depends on no gods and accepts no fate. It is a world where the gods and fate have been supplanted by human purposes and humane ethics, by secular philosophy and the rule of law. Oedipus yearned for such a world (although this world was, in fact, taking form in Athens when Sophocles wrote his tragedies three centuries after Homer).

The *Iliad* is therefore the most venerable Western teacher of those who turn from the tragedies of life not to rage or despair or to escape in another world but to hope for humanity, and even happiness, in the human world itself. (The Mesopotamian *Epic of Gilgamesh* anticipated

5

some of the humanism in the *Iliad,* but was more Asian and did not spawn a tradition.) The *Iliad* leaves nothing more certain than this: if no human life unfolds without its share of tragedy, no human being should try to live without at least a touch of humanism—and no humane civilization can exist without a lot of it.

THE *ILIAD* hardly looks that humanistic and humane on the surface. It is, after all, an archetypal war story. War in the *Iliad* is hell for sure. Armies clash, soldiers scream, heads splinter, blood sprays, eyes fall out, fingers clutch the dust, hatred reverberates through the air, and death drenches the Trojan plain. And yet this war is also heroic, epic, grand, giving us the very adjective *Homeric.* Just reading Homer's "epic similes" of the pounding violence, the turbulent emotions, and the awful spectacle of war, likening events and warriors to superhuman forces, takes your breath away.

When the Greeks launch their first assault against the Trojans, for instance, they go like this:

> As a heavy surf assaults some roaring coast,
> piling breaker on breaker whipped by the West Wind,
> and out on the open sea a crest first rears its head
> then pounds down on the shore with hoarse, rumbling thunder
> and in come more shouldering crests, arching up and breaking
> against some rocky spit, exploding salt foam to the skies—
> so wave on wave they came, Achaean [Greek] battalions ceaseless,
> surging to war.

And when the armies engage each other, "the screaming and the shouts of triumph rose up together of men killing and men killed, and the ground ran blood. . . . Fear would have gripped even a man stouthearted . . . and Terror drove them, and Fear, and Hate whose wrath is relentless." As the battle rages, soldiers "fell as a tower falls," or "as when an oak goes down or a white poplar or like a towering pine tree which in the mountains the carpenters have hewn down with their whetted axes to make ship-timber." And they hit the earth "thunderously." In a decisive later incident the great Greek warrior Patroklos, "screaming a terrible cry, . . . swept in like something greater than human" to attack the Trojan hero Hector. But Patroklos is killed. And when his friend Achilles (or Achilleus), the central character of the book, goes to retrieve his body, the goddess Athena enfolds Achilles in an awe-inspiring appearance:

> swept about his powerful shoulders the fluttering aegis;
> and she, the divine among goddesses, about him circled
> a golden cloud, and kindled from it a flame far-shining.

As when a flare goes up into the high air from a city
from an island far away, with enemies fighting about it
who all day long are in the hateful division of Ares [god of war]
fighting from their own city, but as the sun goes down signal
fires blaze out one after another, so that the glare goes
pulsing high for men of the neighbouring islands to see it,
in case they might come over in ships to beat off the enemy,
so from the head of Achilleus the blaze shot into the bright air.

Who could fail to be moved by such a war and by such heroes? Homer's epic poetry makes the Trojan War at once terrible and larger than life, cosmically tragic and humanly ennobling. And in that tragic nobility lie the origins of Homer's humanism. We see the first sign of this humanism in the very emotion that opens the *Iliad* and runs through it to near the end. That emotion is anger.

Anger might seem an unlikely sign of humanism. But it can be—as Sophocles later dramatized with Oedipus' rage at fate in *Oedipus at Colonus*. Homer makes the tragedy he records flow from it. For anger in the *Iliad* gives humanistic aspirations a hostile voice, while also clashing with those aspirations. This anger is, in fact, the very subject of the story that Homer chooses to tell. He announces this at the beginning.

Homer's first words are: "Sing, goddess, the anger of Peleus' son Achilleus and its devastation." Achilles is the greatest Greek warrior, the son of the goddess Thetis and the mortal Peleus. And he is an angry man indeed. The "anger came on" him in the first place because Agamemnon, the arrogant leader of the Greek forces, had taken Achilles' beloved consort and "prize" of a previous victory, Briseis, for himself. Agamemnon had taken her, "blazing with anger," to replace his own consort and "prize," Chryseis—who had been abducted from her father, a priest of the god Apollo, but then reluctantly returned by Agamemnon after Apollo, "angered in his heart," had started killing Greeks for the impious act. Achilles' anger at Agamemnon causes him to behave at first more like a petulant child than a great warrior. He runs crying to his mother for help. Achilles "weeping went and sat in sorrow apart from his companions," then he begs his divine mother to grant him revenge against Agamemnon "since he has taken away my prize and keeps it." Seething and sniveling, Achilles withdraws from the battlefield to pout while his mother goes to rouse the enemy to make her son look good and Agamemnon look bad.

As Achilles pouts, the tide of battle does turn against his fellow Greeks. Eventually Agamemnon is humbled. But when Agamemnon apologizes and offers to restore Briseis and give Achilles riches if he will fight again, Achilles spurns the offer. Achilles' anger runs too deep to give it up that easily. Only when his dearest friend, Patroklos, falls to the Trojan hero Hector does Achilles change his mind (in the eighteenth of the *Iliad*'s twenty-four books), for he has now become angrier at Hector than at Agamemnon. But even killing Hector does not quench this new rage. "Bent on outrage," he savagely cuts through the tendons in Hector's feet, lashes the fallen hero to his chariot, and drags Hector's body away; later he will drag it repeatedly around Patroklos' grave. Achilles' wrath does not subside until Hector's father, Priam, the king of Troy, plaintively persuades Achilles to return Hector's body for burial. The final passing of Achilles' anger and the burial of Hector bring the *Iliad* to an end. From Homer's opening line, no more time has elapsed than several months in the tenth, and last, year of the war (Homer tells us little of the earlier events and only hints at events to follow that will bring the war to its inevitable climax, and he says nothing of the famed Trojan horse and the fall of Troy).

The events of the *Iliad* come from the anger of Achilles. But Achilles is not Homer's only angry character. Virtually everyone in the epic, including the gods, has "the heart within filled to the brim with anger." They get angry at insults and injuries. They get angry at disappointments and losses. They get angry at anger itself. Anger breeds anger like an infection throughout the *Iliad* (Dante punishes anger the same way in the *Inferno*—see Chapter 5). And that brings much of the human tragedy.

The Trojan War owes its very origins to anger. According to Greek myth, the goddess of love, Aphrodite, gave the beautiful Helen (wife of Agamemnon's brother Meneleos) to the Trojan prince Paris as a prize for ranking the beauty of Aphrodite over that of two other goddesses, Hera and Athena. This was the mythical "Judgment of Paris," or as Homer puts it, "the delusion of Paris"—in Fagels' translation: "Paris in all his madness launched the war." Jealous, enraged, and burning with "hatred for sacred Ilion [Troy]," Hera and Athena urged the Greeks to a war of vengeance against the city with their aid, leading Hera's husband, Zeus, to sigh, "the anger of Hera . . . is grown all out of hand."

From those origins a conflagration of rage engulfs both the human and divine realms as the Greeks fight furiously to get Helen back. Most of the gods take sides with the warring mortals, and against each other—Hera, Athena, and Poseidon, joining the Greeks, while Aphrodite, Apollo, and Ares support Troy; Zeus and other deities switch sides as their moods stir them. The mortals often feel like pawns in this Olympian war. But even the gods themselves sometimes feel beset by emotions and hostilities beyond their control—some of the gods even suffer physical injuries at the hands of mortals. Amidst this rampant wrath and carnage, the god of war himself, Ares, complains to Zeus about the violence that absorbs them all. "Father Zeus," he pleads, "are you not angry looking on those acts of violence? We who are gods forever have to endure the most horrible hurts, by each other's hatred, as we try to give favor to mortals." Not even the god of war can end the cycle of anger and its bloody toll—although Zeus scolds him for his own warlike nature as "the most hateful of all gods . . . forever quarreling" and fomenting "wars and battles."

Eventually the wrathful Achilles actually wants the cycle to stop. While preparing to slay Hector, he admits: "I wish that strife would vanish away from among the gods and mortals, and gall, which makes a man grow angry for all his great mind, that gall of anger that swarms like smoke inside of a man's heart." And on the newly forged shield that Achilles carries into his last battle, Homer displays graphic images contrasting worlds of anger and calm, war and peace—of which more later.

An epic tragedy of wrath and war, the *Iliad* takes us from the hot emotions that inflame anger through the violence that anger inflicts and on to a vision of a peaceful civilization where wrath and war are quelled at last. But while the anger of man against man, and of gods against gods and men, is the *Iliad*'s explicit theme and the driving force of the action, Homer also implies that much of the mortals' anger in fact springs not from actual conflicts, but from the tragic sense of life. The mortals are angry—as well as sad—that destiny has condemned them to this tragic war. No one wants to fight it. And yet, manipulated by the gods and ruled by fate, they know that their own wishes mean next to nothing in the vast scheme of things. Who could blame them for getting mad?

Homer's humanism starts here—with the tragic sense of life and the anger it breeds in human beings who feel unable to truly govern their own lives. Their anger expresses thwarted humanistic aspirations. But Homer takes humanism far beyond anger. He lets human beings get angry at their tragedy, but then he has them begin to find ways to leave both their anger and their tragedy, along with fate and the gods, behind. That is how the *Iliad* becomes the fountainhead of Western humanism, and an inspiration for the humanistic life anywhere, anytime. For it shows us how human beings can find meaning in their lives in this world, despite inescapable tragedies and without benign gods or a redemptive heaven. We see this happening first in Homer's very depiction of the gods and fate. In the *Iliad* they are not what you might think they are.

HOMER'S GODS ARE hardly godlike. Although they wield supernatural powers (if not omnipotence) and are immortal, these gods otherwise have all the lowly attributes of human beings. They are jealous, lustful, fickle, deceitful, violent, selfish, competitive, vain, and so on. There is no denying these gods would be hard to worship—and Plato denounced Homer's depictions of the gods for largely that reason (see Chapter 19).

They also meddle in human affairs to get their way. Apollo sends a plague upon the Greeks because he is angry over the abduction of his priest's daughter; Achilles' divine mother, Thetis, persuades Zeus to hurl the Trojans against the Greeks in order to give Achilles glory in his dispute with Agamemnon; Athena protects Meneleos from a Trojan's arrow; Aphrodite saves her adored Paris from Meneleos by whisking him from their battle in a mist and depositing him safely behind the ramparts; Hera acts to end a truce welcomed by both sides so that the war will resume and Troy will eventually fall; Poseidon moves the Greeks to battle with earthshaking antics; Apollo frightens the Greeks into retreat with his cries and induces Hector to fight Patroklos, then he helps Hector defeat Patroklos; Athena deceives Hector into his fatal confrontation with Achilles, and, after Achilles wins, Apollo and Aphrodite protect Hector's body from destruction by Achilles' outrage. And more.

The intrusions of the gods understandably convince the mortals that they themselves have no ultimate control over events. The gods call the shots, down to moving human limbs and ending human lives—Achilles describes Zeus manipulating human lives by drawing lots from either "an urn of evils" or "an urn of blessings." The human beings resign themselves to these divine machinations by chalking them up to the dictates of fate with the belief that the gods and fate work together. When, for example, Hector defeats Patroklos, the dying warrior groans: "You are only my third slayer," for "deadly destiny, with the son of Leto [Apollo] has killed me." Later, when confronting Achilles for the last time, Hector "knew the truth inside his heart" that "there is no way out . . . now my death is upon me" because "it must long since have been pleasing to Zeus." And with Hector dead under his sword, Achilles growls, "Die: and I will take my death at whatever time Zeus and the rest of the immortals choose to accomplish it"—but Achilles knows this will not be far away, since his mother has told him: "It is decreed that your death must come soon after Hector's." Hector spoke for every human being in the *Iliad* when he told his wife, Andromache, "As for fate, I think that no man has yet escaped it."

Because human wishes and actions mean nothing if the gods and fate go against them, human life can seem more pathetic than tragic in the *Iliad*, a dumb show of futile actions and inescapable misery. Zeus says as much when he looks down from Olympus and observes: "Among all creatures that breathe on earth and crawl on it there is not anywhere a thing more dismal than man is." And Achilles echoes Zeus, while blaming the gods for the human plight. "Such is the way the gods spun life for unfortunate mortals," he complains, "that we live in unhappiness, but the gods themselves have no sorrows." Achilles is wrong about the gods having no sorrows, but he voices the common human pathos. Ravaged by helplessness and stung by resentment, choked by anger and trapped in tragedy, Homer's human beings have a sorry lot.

And yet, they rise above it—in the spirit of humanism. For while Homer's heroes lament their impotence as pawns of the gods and fate, they suspect that these gods, for all of their power, are not truly worthy of worship or emulation. Those heroes also suspect that fate, for all of its inexorability, is not so subservient to the gods, or as random, as it sometimes seems. These suspicions take Homer's heroes from open rage at inevitable human tragedy to an irrepressible affirmation of human life.

How, you might ask, can people suspect that their own gods might be unworthy of worship or emulation? The answer is this: Homer's gods lack something big. And that is moral authority. Because these gods are who they are—jealous, fickle, selfish, and the rest, besides having supernatural powers and immortality—mortals cannot look to them for moral guidance or for value judgments overall. These gods are virtually amoral, acting like pranksters who vie with each other for status, and who play with human lives for their own willful purposes. Unlike the Hebrew god, for instance, who issued rules of religious faith and ethical behavior that created an ecclesiastical, moral, and social system, Homer's gods ask nothing of human beings except that they show respect for them with offerings and allegiance. These gods have no other moral code to give—although when Zeus nods his head to pledge his word, he regards that as a bond, which he honors in his fateful promise to Thetis to assure Achilles' glory.

They have no salvation to offer either. Homer has no heaven or Nirvana or any other redemptive realm for human beings to seek as consolation—or reward or escape—from the tragedies of life. The gods' own residence on Olympus is not a place of moral and spiritual exaltation like the Christian heaven or the Islamic paradise. It is simply where the gods live and frolic and fight and take their potshots into the human world to aggravate the human tragedy. When mortals die they do not go to join the gods there, for Olympus welcomes no mortals, not even demigods. They go instead to a shadowy existence below in Hades. Hades is not a painful place. It is not the Christian Hell. It does not exist to punish. It is just a vale of lifeless emptiness. "In the house of Hades there is something left," Achilles sighs as he mourns Patroklos, "a soul, an image, but there is no heart of life in it." Free of punishment and pain though it is, Hades offers neither the bliss of heaven nor the escape of Nirvana, and so it gives human beings nothing to hope for beyond this world—which prompted another of Plato's complaints against Homer: the afterlife should not be made to look so bad, Plato said, or people will fail to live as they should in this life. Plato could be right. If your god gives you no moral values to live by, and no promise of salvation or an enticing afterlife to seek, you might sink into despair or amorality. But that is not what Homer's human beings do.

And that is the moral paradox and epochal genius of Homer's humanism. Although Homer's human beings get angry at their tragic lives, and can find no solace in their gods, or an afterlife, they do not collapse into paralyzing despondency or run amorally amok. Instead, they courageously find inspiriting meaning and satisfying values in human life itself. Even Plato conceded admiration for this courage when he had Socrates, awaiting his own execution in the *Phaedo*, praise Achilles for fearlessly facing death without the consolation of a saving religion. We get a hint of this humanistic affirmation in Homer's very portrayal of fate. For fate in Homer is not, after all, as scholars have noted, altogether subject to the whims of the gods. It is more orderly than that. It is more rational. It is almost philosophical.

Although Homer's heroes often blame their "fates" on the gods, Homer's voice makes it clear that the gods do not actually determine fate. Fate is above them. The gods are its agents, acting in its name. The gods may sometimes choose the moment that fate strikes, but they do not dictate the choices of fate. Zeus can decide, for instance, when the warrior Patroklos will die, but Zeus himself complains that he cannot protect his own son Sarpedon from a fated death, since Sarpedon "is destined" to "go down under the hands" of Patroklos. What fate decrees cannot be undone, even when the gods would like to undo it. This gives fate—or the human explanation of events that Homer labels fate—a surprising semblance of rationality.

When you look closely at fate in the *Iliad*, you see that it actually lends a certain rational order to events. And that rational order amounts to a moral order. This rational-moral order has some analogies with the Hindu doctrine of karma. According to karma, morally good or bad actions in one lifetime inevitably bring happy or unhappy subsequent lives. Homeric fate works somewhat like that, but it is less religious and applies only to one lifetime. It is also more abstract and philosophical. We could describe Homer's fate as a system of cosmic order that holds everything that exists in balance, or insures that things will not fall out of balance for too long. Fate is therefore a system of proportion or equity. And that makes it a kind of justice. In judicial terms, we would today call it a system of distributive justice, which gives everything its due share, or in Homer's terms, its portion of good and bad fortune. So despite the selfish whims of Homer's gods, Homer's universe is orderly, even *just*.

The Greek concepts of *hubris* and *nemesis* serve this kind of justice. Hubris signifies an upsetting of the balance, an overreaching, an excess of anything, and it inevitably brings its nemesis, the consequences that redress the imbalance and put things back in order. Metaphorically, most of us have felt them both: hubris lifts us up too high; nemesis brings us down hard. Agamemnon acted from hubris when he took Briseis from Achilles, and then he met his nemesis in Achilles' withdrawal from the war and in the Greeks' battlefield reversals. The Trojan War is itself a drama of hubris and nemesis: the hubris of Paris in taking Helen, and of Troy in harboring them both, followed by the nemesis of the Greek invasion and of Troy's ultimate defeat. Hubris will always bring its nemesis. Fate will always restore an orderly balance to the world, whatever the cost to human beings. Achilles knows, for instance, that his own life must be short because it is glorious, or it could have been long and inglorious, but no life can be both glorious and long. And everyone in the *Iliad* knows how the war will turn out, and even when some warriors will die, but they all go on relentlessly. That is the justice of fate in the *Iliad*, and the human tragedy.

The identification of fate with order, and of order with justice, comes through Homer's very words (as the great classicist F. M. Cornford laid out long ago in *From Religion to Philosophy* [1912]). The Homeric term for fate, *moira*, indicates "a fixed order" or "orderly division" of things; and the word for justice, *dike*, betokens the balance that keeps the order together. Homer twice joins the two ideas in a concrete image when he has Zeus hold up a scale to settle two battles. This happens first in a clash between legions of Trojans and Greeks, and then again during the fight between Achilles and Hector. "The father balanced his golden scales," Homer says in both places, "and in them he set the two fateful portions of death, which lays men prostrate," one for the Trojans and one for the Greeks the first time, and "one for Achilleus, and one for Hector" the second time. The first weighing tilts against the Greeks, for their "death-day was heaviest." The second tilts against Hector because "Hector's death-day was heavier and dragged downward toward death." Zeus does not influence the outcome either time; he awaits it. The scales of justice decide the warriors' fates.

Because Homer treats fate as a rational, moral order of cosmic justice above the gods, both fate and the gods appear in the *Iliad* to be myths now crossing a threshold toward something else. That is toward philosophy and the rule of secular morality and legal justice among human beings (Plato's conception of justice in the *Republic* even recalls Homer's fate in its distributive order assigning everyone a proper place). Here the *Iliad* shows the tragic sense of life and the twilight of the gods implicitly giving birth to humanistic civilization.

HOMER'S HUMANISM surfaces unmistakably in what Homer's heroes care about most. While the gods cavort, and while the justice of fate keeps things in a rational-moral order, Homer's human beings find the essential values and vital purposes of their lives in life itself among other human beings. The first of these values and purposes is honor.

We could say that honor is the overriding humanistic "value" in the *Iliad,* just as anger is the dominant emotion. In fact, honor and anger often go together. For offended honor, or dishonor, is what causes anger from the outset of both the Trojan War and the *Iliad*. And that dishonor usually comes from losing a "prize."

It was to avenge their *dishonor* over the kidnapping of Helen by the Trojan prince Paris (who had previously dishonored Athena and Hera by preferring Aphrodite) that the Greeks had embarked on their angry war of reprisal in the first place. Then Apollo sets the stage for Homer's tragedy by siding with "his priest whom Agamemnon dishonored" by stealing the priest's daughter as a "prize." After Agamemnon yields to Apollo's wrath and returns the priest's daughter, he offends Achilles by taking the consort Briseis, as "a new prize . . . to atone for the girl lost." That is when Achilles erupts, launching the events of the *Iliad*, because "Agamemnon has dishonored me, since he has taken away my prize and keeps it."

The anger of dishonor in the *Iliad* is not edifying. And, to be sure, it displays itself in rather primitive bouts of masculine ego as men treat women as booty of war and symbols of male competition and status. But Homeric honor goes beyond masculine egoism (the egos of the Olympian goddesses are nothing to mess with either, as Hera and Athena fatefully proved). It also names a supreme social ideal. For, above all, honor spells respect in the eyes of others. And, for the Greeks, a prize was related to it.

In Greek, the primary noun for "honor," *timē*, connotes the "worth of a thing," and therefore social distinction, rank, and high value. The word for "prize," *geras*, also implies honor, since it is a public acknowledgment of honorable acts, or "a gift of honor," leading to the word "honoring," *gerasmios*. A second term for prize, *athlon*, denotes a specific "reward" for victory, "the prize of a contest," from which we get the English *athlete*. All of these terms share the social recognition and stature earned by honorable public acts or by victory. No wonder the ancient Greeks adored competitions, even at funerals, which were "the last honor of the dead," *geras thanontan*, and that they made competitive events out of all kinds of activities, culminating in the great *athletic* Olympiad. Competitions brought prizes, because prizes were a badge of public honor and social esteem, whether won in competitions or in war. We award prizes for largely the same reason today (the English word "prize," like its Greek predecessors, originally connoted *value* and *price*).

By the same token, a show of disrespect—like stealing a "prize"—brought dishonor, diminishing a hero's social stature. This is why the worst offense a Homeric hero could suffer was to be dishonored, and the sweetest revenge he could get was to dishonor the offender. Achilles ravages Hector's body for exactly this reason: he wants to disgrace and dishonor the killer of his friend Patroklos, to diminish Hector's worth. It may seem odd that Hector should suffer more dishonor by having Achilles drag his corpse around on the ground than he did by running away from Achilles during their last battle. But Homeric honor is not lost simply by succumbing to fear, any more than it is by yielding to tears—and many are the brave Homeric heroes who flee in fear and collapse in tears. Honor is lost by losing the respect of others—a respect Achilles retains despite his childish behavior, and that Hector keeps despite his fears and flight, and that the pusillanimous ladies' man Paris can never truly possess.

Homeric honor is most often attained in war by valor—expressed in the Greek word *aristeia,* denoting "exceptional behavior." *Aristeia* brings honor, and prizes. It is a mark of superiority, of being the best, *aristos.* These are the roots of the word *aristocracy,* which to the Greeks meant "rule by the best." The larger-than-life heroes in the *Iliad,* who weep prodigiously and fall thunderously, and whose every gesture is grand, have *aristeia.* They are the best.

The ideas of honor and *aristeia* create the very concept of virtue in Homer's world (a subject memorably elucidated in Werner Jaeger's classic, *Paideia: The Ideals of Greek Culture* [c. 1945]). The Greek word for virtue, *aretē,* signifies excellence. To have *aretē* is to be excellent at something. Therefore, to have the *aretē* of *aristeia* is to be "excellent at exceptional behavior," especially in war. It is to be a truly superior human being, excellent at being the best. These are not just Homeric ideals, either. They show up in many philosophical conceptions of human nature and "the good" in the West and elsewhere. Confucius had something like this in mind when he spoke of the morally "superior person" or the "gentleman" (see Chapter 10). And Aristotle derived his ethics from *aretē* in the *Nicomachean Ethics,* where he defines the excellent human being as one who fulfills human nature at its best (Aristotle also observes, adopting Homeric terms, that such a human being is "worthy of honor . . .

15

because honor is the prize of virtue; it is the tribute that we pay to the good" [see Chapter 4]). Later Friedrich Nietzsche turned this ideal of excellence into a model of the morality of the strong, up to the Superman (see Chapter 8).

The Homeric quest for honor may provoke anger and induce some unsavory acts, but it also inspires the admirable human aspiration to achievement, excellence, and earned respect. That is surely a humanistic virtue—if not, as the Greeks thought, the essence of virtue itself.

The Homeric pursuit of this kind of honor gives an ennobling purpose to life amid the tragedy of war and the dictates of fate in the *Iliad*. And it is an unmistakably humanistic purpose. For Homer's heroes do not seek honor to please the gods, they do it to gain glory and esteem in the eyes of other human beings, and to achieve the worldly fame that will give them immortality in human memory. Honor offers them a kind of secular salvation—as Hector says when fatalistically confronting Achilles at the end: "Let me at least not die without a struggle, inglorious, but do some big thing first, that men to come shall know of it." The gods have nothing to do with it, except for unintentionally inspiring Homer's heroes to value honor among themselves—and, of course, human as these gods are, they demand a share of honor and fame in the eyes of men for themselves, too.

Not all of the humanistic purposes and values in the *Iliad* are as exalted as honor, or as heroic as valor. Some are as common as friendship, as intimate as parenthood, as tender as pity, and as moving as mourning. These show how deep Homer's humanism goes. And they turn out to eclipse even honor and anger, eventually changing the course of Homer's drama and bringing it to its poignant conclusion.

The drama takes this turn when Achilles decides to fight again. Despite his offended honor and consuming rage, he will fight to avenge a slain friend. Achilles is not just the angriest of the Greeks. He is also the most profoundly bound by friendship. And this alone draws him back to the field—fuming with new wrath. Achilles returns to avenge Patroklos because he and Patroklos are friends of the heart who had grown up together.

Their friendship helps Achilles through his darkest hours. After the proud, dishonored, and angry Achilles has withdrawn from the war, Patroklos frequently keeps him company. In one affecting scene, Homer tells us that "Achilleus delighting his heart in a lyre, clear-sounding," was "singing of men's fame, as Patroklos was sitting over against him, alone, and in silence." A companionship both heroic and warm, it is shattered by Patroklos' death under the sword of Hector. When word of this reaches Achilles, he goes berserk. "The black cloud of sorrow closed on" him, and "in both hands he caught up the grimy dust, and poured it over his head and face, and fouled his handsome countenance, . . . and took and tore at his hair with his hands. . . . He cried out terribly, aloud . . . 'My dear companion has perished, Patroklos, whom I loved beyond all other companions, as well as my own life. I have lost him.'" At Patroklos' funeral Achilles "wept still as he remembered his beloved companion" and "let fall the swelling tears."

So shaken is Achilles by Patroklos' death that he switches his anger from Agamemnon to Hector: "We will let all this be a thing of the past," he says of his dispute with Agamemnon, "and for all our sorrow beat down by force the anger deeply within us. Now I shall go, to overtake that killer of a dear life, Hector." Achilles' friendship for Patroklos proves stronger even than his affronted honor and his anger at Agamemnon. Or rather, that friendship gives his affronted honor and anger a new purpose. He returns to the war, declaring "I stayed too long out of the fighting. . . . Now I must win excellent glory." Honor is still the goal, and anger still the prevailing emotion, but friendship is the underlying motive. And Hector is doomed.

Homer's drama is here changing directions in spirit as well as events. Humanism is plainly breaking through the tragedy. And this brings the *Iliad* closer and closer to us as a drama of the resilient human spirit. Achilles' new adversary, Hector, shares some of this human spirit, too. The greatest Trojan warrior, a giant among giants, fierce and hard—whose very name came to denote a bullying personality—known among the Trojans as "the breaker of horses," nevertheless displays a most unwarlike tenderness and affection with his family. In a famous scene during an interlude in the fighting, he tells his wife, Andromache, that he must go back to the battlefield, even if it means death—and he suspects it does. But before he returns, he "held out his arms to his baby, who shrank back . . . screaming, and frightened" at the fearsome war helmet on Hector's head. The "beloved father laughed" and, removing the helmet, he took "his dear son" and "tossed him about in his arms, and kissed him" and prayed to the gods that the boy one day become "'better by far than his father.'" Then, handing the boy to Andromache, who is "smiling in her tears," Hector puts on his helmet again and goes off to the field of blood and horror, while Andromache goes "homeward, turning to look back on the way, letting the live tears fall." Fate will bring Hector his death, but meanwhile he lives as much for the human bonds of family as for the Homeric honor of valor he must earn in battle. He is one of us. The love of family gives him reason to live, even while honor gives him cause to die. These are both humanistic values that can lend purpose to anyone's life.

Another episode of family feeling leads the *Iliad* directly from its bloody battles to its affecting conclusion. This episode features Hector's father, Priam, and Achilles. By now, the raging Achilles has killed Hector, railing at his dying enemy, "I wish only that my spirit and fury would drive me to hack your meat away and eat it raw for the things that you have done to me," and he has dragged Hector's body around again and again to mutilate and leave it for "the dogs and birds"—although Apollo protects it. But when Priam comes to plead with him to release Hector's body, Achilles undergoes a surprising softening of mood.

"In the words of a suppliant," Priam entreats Achilles: "Take pity upon me, remembering your father," who "is of years like mine, and on the doorsill of sorrowful old age," and "give [Hector] back." Unexpectedly touched by the appeal, Achilles "took the old man's hand . . . and the two remembered" their loved ones. "Priam sat huddled at the feet of Achilleus and wept for manslaughtering Hektor, and Achilleus wept now for his father, now again for Patroklos." Thinking of his father, Achilles laments, "I give him no care as he grows old," and he concedes to Priam that he can himself "bring nothing but sorrow to you and your children." Then "in pity for the gray head and beard," Achilles relents. "Take your beloved son back to Ilion, and mourn for him," he says, and he agrees to "hold off our attack for as much time as you bid me" so that Troy can properly honor its greatest hero. A sad and anxious, yet grateful, Priam will soon take Hector home. Meanwhile Achilles, his anger now seemingly quieted at last, goes off to sleep in his "strong-built shelter and at his side lay Briseis of the fair coloring."

After these words, we see and hear no more of Achilles in the *Iliad*. His heroic anger has yielded to humane pity for the suppliant. (It is true that Zeus had also commanded him, through his mother, to return Hector's body because the gods were angry at his refusal to do this; but while Achilles obeys Zeus, his pity for Priam is genuine and owes nothing much to the gods.) Achilles goes to sleep peacefully, alongside Briseis, the "prize" whose seizure by Agamemnon had ignited the anger that drives the story of the *Iliad*, and who was returned to Achilles when he resumed fighting. The terrible, enraged warrior, who cares for friendship as much as for honor, also abides by the sentiments of family, the urgings of compassion, and the entreaties of suppliants—those in need who humbly beg our help. How fitting it is that Homer should quell Achilles' anger through an act of supplication (although Achilles says his anger could still erupt again). For, among the most insistent social values in Homer's world, the obligation to help suppliants (more conspicuous in the *Odyssey*, where Ulysses, the wanderer going home from the war, repeatedly relies on it) is also among the most humanistic of those values. The aiding of suppliants brings human kindness into a tragic world. Even the Trojans expect Achilles to yield to Priam's supplications because "whoever begs his mercy he will spare with all the kindness of his heart." And because Homer's heroes gain no heavenly reward for their kindness to other people, that kindness can only strengthen the bonds among human beings, while making human beings more independent of their selfish and amoral gods.

Nowhere are the humanistic meanings of life more pronounced in the *Iliad* than in the lavish mourning rites and funeral festivities for fallen heroes. These rites have virtually nothing to do with the gods, or with preparing the dead for another world, except to usher the deceased into Hades lest their shades drift aimlessly. Since everyone in the *Iliad* knows that the shadowy afterlife of Hades offers nothing to look forward to—because, as Achilles has tellingly remarked, "there is no heart of life in it"—the rites of lost life and entry into Hades serve human beings, not the gods. These rites are a celebration of life *in this world*, not in the next.

The mourning ceremonies for Patroklos demonstrate this with spectacle. Here the emotions of loss, together with the celebrations of life, go on and on. First the Greeks circle the body, where "the sands . . . and the armour of men" were "wet with their tears." Then Achilles, sighing "there will come no second sorrow like this to my heart again," orders the Greeks to prepare "the gloomy feast" of mourning and to build a funeral pyre "a hundred feet long." Following the feast, Achilles places upon the pyre Patroklos' loyal dogs, as sacrifices not to the gods but to the dead hero. And as a final gesture of rage at the enemy, Achilles casts twelve Trojan warriors for the "fury of the fire to feed on." On the top goes Patroklos' body, which the Greek soldiers had covered "under the locks of their hair," alongside jars of honey and oil. After Achilles' last farewell, "Good-by, Patroklos," the pyre is lit "and a huge inhuman blaze arose." The flames roar all night. The next day mourners "gathered up the white bones of their gentle companion, weeping, and put them into a golden jar" that they placed in a tomb piled high with a mound of earth. Then Achilles calls for games—chariot races, foot races, boxing, wrestling, spear throwing, a virtual Olympic competition for *prizes* that he will bestow. The games go on all day, stirring such fierce rivalry that the competitors occasionally burst into anger, an emotion never far under the surface in the *Iliad*. But more than anger, the games rouse camaraderie and even laughter, prompting some of the winners to share their coveted prizes. They are very humanistic games after all.

When the funeral events conclude, the Greeks go off to "sweet sleep," and Achilles goes to a restless night of weeping and sorrow for his departed friend, whose unhappy shade can now enter Hades. The human world has finished honoring one of its heroes—celebrating his glorious life among mortals, not preparing him for a better life among the gods.

It is at this moment that Priam arrives to supplicate Achilles for the return of Hector's body. Then, after Achilles goes gently to sleep with Briseis, and Priam takes Hector home, it remains only for the Trojan hero to be buried to bring the epic to its close. Hector's funeral gets less space in the *Iliad* than Patroklos', but it is no less grand.

For nine days the Trojan mourning goes on. "Singers chanted the song of sorrows, and the women were mourning beside him," while each day men were "bringing an endless supply of timber" for the funeral fire. On the tenth day "they carried out bold Hektor, weeping, and set the body aloft on a towering pyre for burning. And set fire to it." Then, "when the young dawn showed again with her rosy fingers," they "gathered the white bones up, mourning, as the tears swelled and ran down their cheeks." They placed the bones "in a golden casket and wrapped this about with soft robes of purple" and "put it away in the hollow of the grave, and over it piled huge stones." Finally the Trojans "assembled in a fair gathering and held a glorious feast within the house of Priam. . . . Such was their burial of Hektor, breaker of horses." With these words, the *Iliad* ends.

What had started as a poem of wrath and war concludes as a poem of peaceful community and common humanity in rituals of mournful death and celebrations of human life. Here the gods are absent. It is a human world of shared needs and emotions, honoring human heroes who achieved human excellence, and who were lost in the tragedy of human life. Tomorrow the war will resume. More death will come—soon the death of Achilles, and later the destruction of Troy. But that will not be Homer's story to tell. Homer's tragedy is finished. And the story of humanism has begun.

The wages of anger and the horrors of war, the tragic sense of life and the aspirations of humanity, the twilight of the gods and the dawn of humanism, these are Homer's subjects. And Homer brought them all together in a single image. That is the shield of Achilles. The god Haphaistos fashions this shield to replace the one Patroklos had borrowed from Achilles for his battle with Hector and that had then been stripped away by Apollo and given to the victor. Achilles gets the new shield for his own climactic duel with Hector.

The shield Haphaistos creates for Achilles is a work of art, and more.

Molded with abundant human figures and complex scenes, it presents a panoramic parable of war and peace. On it we see "two cities of mortal men" representing contrasting ways of life. One is a walled city rather like Troy, besieged by "forces of armed men shining in their war gear." But its "people were not giving way," posting even women and children on the ramparts and sending soldiers into the field where the warring forces "fought with each other and dragged away from each other the corpses of those who had fallen. . . . And Hate was there with Confusion among them, and Death the destructive." This is a city engulfed in fear and hatred, violence and war.

The other city—together with related scenes—is very different. It glows with "marriages" and "festivals" and "a great multitude happily watching" dancers and singers and acrobats. Vineyards and fertile fields and robust flocks of animals flourish here. And when an argument breaks out, instead of resorting to violence, the people turn to "an arbitrator, to have a decision" about which side is right. The "elders" gather in a circle to hear arguments on each side, and they place on the ground in the center "two talents of gold, to be given" to the person "who in this case spoke the straightest"—or as "a prize for the judge who'd speak the straightest verdict." In this city, people resolve disputes not by fighting, or even by appeals to the gods. They do it by reasoning and debate and the rule of law and justice. This is a city of humanity and peace. Achilles himself yearned for just such a place when, before taking this shield into battle with Hector, he had sighed: "I wish that strife would vanish away from among the gods and mortals."

We might see in this city on the shield of Achilles a kind of Homeric utopia. Here rationality and law, compassion and the humane pursuits of social life bring an end to the irrational rule of human anger and violence, as well as to the caprice of the gods and the unforgiving dictates of fate. Homer's tragic sense of life has given birth to a hopeful vision of a humanistic civilization.

One of the world's most monumental epics of tragedy and war, the *Iliad* is therefore also among the greatest literary expressions of humanism. For it tells us that while tragedies can happen no matter what we do, we can rise above them by finding humane values and inspiriting purposes in this world to make human life ever more worth living amid peace and justice. That is Homer's humanism. And ours—if we have the imagination and the will to live up to it.

On the Tragic Sense of Life
and the Uses of Humanism

1. Human life is tragic because tragedies happen no matter what we do to prevent them.

2. The universe and the gods—if there are gods—can be indifferent to human tragedy.

3. Tears over tragedies need bring no dishonor—they often express a profoundly human tragic sense of life.

4. The tragic sense of life can cause tears, anger, and despair, but it can also give rise to affirmative humanistic meanings of life.

5. Humanistic meanings of life come from human life itself and give value to it.

6. Humanistic meanings of life give us humane values like courage, love, loyalty, honesty, honor, sympathy, generosity, justice, and peace.

7. A humanistic civilization makes human life in this world better by, among other things, causing rationality to prevail over anger, justice over conflict, benign sociability over blithe selfishness, and peace over war.

8. Human beings who live nobly in this world deserve honor, pride, and prizes.

9. Funerals should celebrate human life in this world and honor those who served human life well.

10. The meaning of life is to affirm human life in this world and live honorably and humanely, regardless of any gods or an afterlife.

2

Control Yourself

Hinduism: *Bhagavad-Gita*
Buddhism: *Dhammapada*

A man of disciplined mind who moves among the objects of sense
with the senses under control and free from attachment
and aversion—he attains purity of spirit.

Bhagavad-Gita

Our life is the creation of our mind.

Dhammapada

Hinduism arose in India around 1500–1200 B.C.E. from a sea of notions about the place of human life in the universe. Its earliest principles took form in the *Vedas*, scriptures and poems of devotion to myriad gods. This Vedic religion evolved into worship of a Supreme Being, a cosmic power personified in the early deity Indra and later in the three chief Hindu deities, Brahma, Vishnu, and Shiva, as well as in their many incarnations. Codified in the *Upanishads* (c. sixth century B.C.E.) and in the great historical epics, the *Rāmāyana* (c. 300 B.C.E.) and the *Mahābhārata* (400 B.C.E.–400 C.E.), Hinduism interwove a vast theology, a belief in reincarnation and karma, and a severe social caste system. The *Bhagavad-Gita* (500–200 B.C.E.) comprises a small section, and the spiritual heart, of the sprawling *Mahābhārata*, and it is the single most important Hindu text. Its twenty-eight chapters record the spiritual instruction of the prince Arjuna by the god Krishna during war. Krishna tells Arjuna how to attain Nirvana, where the cycle of reincarnated lives ends in sublime extinction and union with the Supreme Being. To reach Nirvana, Arjuna must master a regime of yogas, or mental and physical exercises, that will give him control over his body and mind and reveal the divine within himself. Arjuna takes Krishna's advice, and then returns to battle buoyed by a new sense of duty and the meaning of his life.

Buddhism grew out of Hinduism in the sixth century B.C.E. as a kind of heresy. Although retaining many Hindu beliefs about human existence,

23

including reincarnation and karma, Buddhism spurned Hinduism's complex theology, severe asceticism, and brutal caste system. Buddhism began when the Hindu prince Siddhartha Gautama (563–483 B.C.E.) announced that he had discovered the secret of human existence in a moment of contemplative enlightenment. That secret is, in short: we suffer because we have desires, and we can end suffering by controlling desires and following a path between self-indulgence and self-denial. Some two hundred years after Siddartha Gautama became the Buddha, the Enlightened One, a compendium of his teachings appeared in India as the *Dhammapada*. Its twenty-six short poetic chapters remain a classic statement of Buddhist doctrines, eloquently dwelling most of all on how our minds create our reality, and how by mastering our minds with the right way of thinking we can vanquish suffering. Both the *Bhagavad-Gita* and the *Dhammapada* point to Nirvana. But they also point very much to this world. For they show how nothing matters more in living this life than learning to control ourselves.

THE WORLD'S RELIGIONS and humanistic ideologies have sprung from two questions that everyone asks: Why do we suffer? and, How can we overcome suffering? This is as true of paganism as of Christianity, of Judaism as of Islam, of Homeric humanism as of existentialism, of Marxism as of psychoanalysis. The answers may diverge widely, but the questions are the same. And no religious or ideological traditions have asked these questions more insistently or answered them more sweepingly than Hinduism and Buddhism. Once you have looked at suffering—and life—through the lens of Hindu and Buddhist ideas you may never see anything quite the same again. Or you shouldn't.

Hinduism came long before Buddhism—in the second millennium B.C.E.—and Buddhism branched off from it in the sixth century B.C.E. But the two belief systems have always shared a few central doctrines—not unlike Catholics and Protestants. Both Hinduism and Buddhism begin with the premise that human life is mighty rough, roiling with torments and plagued by miseries—or, as Sigmund Freud, who created psychoanalysis from a similar premise, gently put it: "Life as we find it is too hard for us" (see Chapter 17). Both doctrines also contend that we live many cycles of these troubled lives as we are reincarnated again and again according to our karma, or accumulated good and bad deeds, until we reach Nirvana, the blissful extinction of these sad cycles in union with the divine that "good karma" eventually gives us. Hinduism and Buddhism also agree on some of the steps we must take to get good karma and to reach Nirvana. And here is where these two great Asian belief systems give us advice worth taking, whether we believe in Nirvana or not.

That advice begins where Hinduism and Buddhism can be said to begin, with the idea of suffering. Unlike the religions and ideologies that blame human suffering on original sin or on the caprices of existence or on evil people or on rotten social conditions, and then promise to end it through the grace of a beneficent god or by changing those social conditions, Hinduism and Buddhism take another tack. They say suffering is our own fault. We cause it ourselves, as individuals, and only we ourselves can end it. We bring it on with ill-begotten desires and wrongheaded attitudes. Specifically, we want too much in this life, and we care too much about our pleasures and pains. And so, Hinduism and Buddhism tell us, to end our unhappiness in life, we just have to stop wanting and caring as much as we do. Get a grip, as American slang would say. Or control yourself.

Hinduism and Buddhism send their call for self-control across the landscape of human life, leaving nothing alone, from the lowliest functions of the body to the loftiest flights of mind. This call demands mastery of everything—actions, sensations, feelings, thoughts. Not everyone can attain that kind of absolute self-control, or would want to. You might have to be a monk to achieve it completely. But even a portion of it can help us cultivate a power of mind useful in virtually anything we do, not only freeing us from suffering, but bestowing an imperturbable peace on the soul, strengthening the will to live, and even boosting the joy of life. Everyone can benefit from a bit of this power. And no one can enjoy life without some of it.

This self-control comes, first of all, from the mind. And, particularly among Buddhists, the mind remains its essence. For the mind decides how we experience everything—that is, how we think and feel about our lives. And because we cannot altogether govern what happens to us externally, deciding how we think and feel becomes our only recourse. When we master how we think and feel about life, or what happens to us, we master life itself—or what it means to us, which amounts to the same thing. This is how Hinduism and Buddhism lift us from the abyss of human misery and deliver us to a life of contentment. Both of them say that whatever our circumstances, whatever happens to us, we *can* control how we think and feel about our lives. If this sounds like Western existentialism, it is not so very far from it psychologically. Like existentialism, Hinduism and Buddhism insist that we are responsible for the lives we live and for our mental and emotional responses to life. Circumstances merely set the stage for us to respond.

But to take responsibility for how we think and feel and to gain the kind of self-control that Hinduism and Buddhism require, we have to do more than become existentialists. We have to start from scratch. We have to abandon all of our ready-made assumptions about how life works, and even about what is most "real." This can be pretty taxing for people bred on American "practicality" and common sense. But it is worth trying.

IN THE CITY OF VARANASI, India (long known as Benares), lies one of the holiest spots of Hinduism. It is a stretch of the Ganges River that daily attracts hordes of believers who bathe and pray in its hallowed, turbid waters at dawn, paying obeisance to their gods, particularly Shiva, whose city this is. Holy men sit still with ascetic rigor or float motionless on the river in trances. Crematoria send the Hindu dead drifting in wisps of white smoke off to other lives, and their ashes are strewn along the bank, amid the benign chaos of human beings worshiping in sacred slime under the Hindu heaven.

A few miles from Varanasi, at Sarnath, stands one of the holiest shrines of Buddhism. While the Hindus resolutely purify themselves and celebrate their many deities in ascetic exercises and ecstatic watery ablutions, the Buddhists quietly observe their faith within a pastoral setting almost beatific in its quietude. It is known as the Deer Park, where Buddhism was born with the first sermon of Siddhartha Gautama as the Buddha. No chaos of humanity here. In these manicured grounds Buddhists honor the founding of their philosophy with calm, detached contemplation, exemplified by the saffron-robed monks who sit in meditation all day on the grass near the spot where Buddha is said to have spoken.

This contrast may tilt a bit unfairly against the Hindus. Hinduism is too various to be wholly captured by the theatrical scene along the Ganges—since it is surely the world's most ecumenical religion, embracing every other faith, and has even largely reabsorbed Buddhism in India by adopting the Buddha into its own capacious pantheon. But the contrasting images of Hinduism on the Ganges at Varanasi and of Buddhism in the Deer Park at Sarnath aptly symbolize the different spiritual worlds that many Hindus and Buddhists have come to inhabit, despite their similar doctrines. And so the Hindu and Buddhist versions of life ask for rather different kinds of self-control.

Two little classics, the Hindu *Bhagavad-Gita* and the Buddhist *Dhammapada,* are the place to start. Uniting philosophy and poetry, theology and psychology, they introduce the Hindu and Buddhist visions of life more concisely and rapturously than any other writings. They do not exactly read like how-to manuals (although some devotees have made them that, such as Eknath Easwaran in his massive two-volume commentary, *The Bhagavad-Gita for Daily Living* [1996]), but they are practical guides no less than companions for the soul. The *Bhagavad-Gita* radiates much more religion, since Hinduism is far more of a religion than is Buddhism. (Buddhism is actually a secular philosophy of life that originally claimed no gods.) But the *Bhagavad-Gita's* religious ideas on self-control and how to make the mind work for us point to where Buddhism later took those ideas—and that is to where the mind is everything.

THE *BHAGAVAD-GITA* is a set of religious doctrines and instructions on how to live given by the deity Krishna to the warrior Arjuna during

HINDUISM

an interlude in the perpetual wars among descendants of King Bharata from 1400 to 1000 B.C.E. recorded in the epic Hindu history the *Mahābhārata*. Krishna plays the role of Arjuna's companion and chariot driver, and he is himself an incarnation of Vishnu, one of the three primary Hindu gods, along with Shiva and Brahma, who together personify the ultimate Supreme Being, Brahman. Hindu theology works like that. Hinduism's Supreme Being exists beyond, and is incarnated in not only its own pantheon of gods but every deity ever worshipped by anyone on earth, which allows Hinduism to embrace every religion with the ecumenical confidence that all religions are one. This is a benign theological idea (which Hindu fundamentalists ignore or pervert).

"My face is everywhere," the *Bhagavad-Gita* records Brahman saying, "there is no limit to my divine manifestations, nor can they be numbered." In the *Bhagavad-Gita* you can't miss Him—or *It*. For the *Bhagavad-Gita* is a thoroughly God-intoxicated book—the title is sometimes translated as the "Song of God." And just trying to grasp the character of this transcendent deity will stretch your mind and imagination. This is the God of Gods. A God who creates everything. Who precedes and follows everything. Who underlies everything. Who *is* everything. "Nothing animate or inanimate exists without me," this God proclaims, "I am the beginning, the middle and the end in creation. . . . I am the strength of the strong. . . . I am the purity of the good."

Philosophically, Brahman could be described as the Ground of Being that makes all existence possible, including thought and feeling. Brahman is the very Nature of Things. The Ultimate of Ultimates. The Absolute itself. And although this Ground of Being takes visible form in countless gods, male and female, and exists within everyone as the spiritual self, or *Atman*, and although Its formal name is Brahman, It is to be addressed only as "OM" or "AUM." This is a sound, not a name really, which invokes rather than identifies the divine Absolute. "I am the syllable OM," Arjuna learns, which is "absolute knowledge." You can hear this syllable emanating wherever Hindus live.

This God may not be so different from the Hebrew "I Am," or the Allah of Islam (see Chapter 20). You do not address them by familiar names either. But a closer affinity lies with something like the ineffable "Way" of Taoism, less a being than a sheer abstraction (see Chapter 10). Even to imagine the Absolute Absoluteness of Brahman will change you. Or so the Hindus believe. More important, though, for most of us, is the way of life that the *Bhagavad-Gita* promises will lead to this God. For that way of life teaches the discipline of self-control.

The *Bhagavad-Gita* describes its techniques of self-control as paths of spiritual existence or "yogas." The person who practices yogas all the time becomes a "yogi." Many of these yogas would tax the hardiest of us. And that is exactly what they are supposed to do. Just as the *Bhagavad-Gita*'s image of God should stretch our intellectual or spiritual imagination beyond conventional limits, so the practices of self-control leading to that God defy conventional behavior. No chummy advice here on winning friends and feeling good. The *Bhagavad-Gita* tells us to conquer ourselves completely.

We have to conquer ourselves to protect us, above all, from the deceptions of the senses and the tides of emotion that blind us to truth and that cause our ceaseless sufferings. Moralists of all cultures have, of course, warned against submitting to the seductions of the senses and emotions. But the *Bhagavad-Gita* goes farther. It says that to overcome suffering we must impose an almost superhuman restraint upon ourselves. A restraint that takes us out of this world. Physically, emotionally, mentally. Moderation will not do. You have to win out altogether. And to win out, you have to begin by getting a firm hold on what we label the mind or consciousness or the psyche.

In the *Bhagavad-Gita* this "mind" possesses several attributes. But we might divide these into two: let us call them the "power to know" and the "power to will" (the specific terms matter less than the concepts). Through the power to know (including consciousness, intellect, intuition, and so on), we acquire objective knowledge. Through the power to will we exercise discipline. The power to know should lead us to spiritual Truth—which in the *Bhagavad-Gita* means the divine within us, Atman, and then the divine itself, Brahman. But because the power to know can go astray, the power to will must exercise discipline over it, or over the pursuit of knowledge. In other words, our will power must control our knowing power for us to grasp the truth (Confucianists imposed a similar requirement by insisting that true learning depends on "sincerity of will"—see Chapter 10). "When the mind runs after the roving senses," the *Bhagavad-Gita* warns, "it carries away the understanding." So, "for the uncontrolled, there is no intelligence; nor for the uncontrolled is there power of concentration; and for him without concentration, there is no peace."

To gain control of "mind" in all of its attributes and to direct it toward Brahman, the *Bhagavad-Gita* prescribes the yogas. These can involve any kind of physical and mental self-discipline. Some yogis "withdraw all their senses from contact with exterior sense objects." Others "practice breathing exercises—inhalation, exhalation, and the stoppage of breath, . . . shutting off sense from what is outward, fixing the gaze at the root of the eyebrows, checking the breath-stream in and outgoing within the nostrils. . . . Others mortify the flesh by fasting to weaken their sensual desires, and thus achieve self-control. . . . Others set themselves austerities and spiritual disciplines." Others "study and meditate on the truths of the scriptures," and still others engage in "steady concentration, uttering the sacred syllable OM and meditating upon me."

These yoga exercises can take us out of this world. If we want to go. That is their spiritual purpose. But some of them can also give us more mastery of this world, too, or rather how we live in it. For, like any kind of exercise, they bring strength, and strength brings freedom. And that is the everyday use of Hindu self-control.

"The sage who has controlled the senses, mind, and understanding, who is intent on liberation, who has cast away desire, fear and anger—he is ever freed" from the weakness and desires and deceptions that perpetuate suffering. Once freed in this way—"free from attachment," even "from the delusion of 'I' and 'mine,'"—we are "no longer swayed by joy and envy, anxiety and fear," we remain "unmoved by good or evil fortune" and "indifferent to honor and insult, heat and cold, pleasure and pain." Then our "home is everywhere and nowhere," because we are "ever contented, self-controlled." This is close to Nirvana on earth. For "a man of disciplined mind, who moves among the objects of sense with the senses under control and free from attachment and aversion—he attains purity of spirit," and "this is the divine state."

That is the core advice of the *Bhagavad-Gita*. Physical and mental exercise bring strength of mind; this strength brings freedom from error; this freedom opens the way to truth; and truth leads to contentment—or to absorption in Brahman and then to the transcendence of life in Nirvana. As practical secular advice, this doctrine is not so far removed from the ideas of many Western moralists—parts of Rousseau and Nietzsche come to mind—who warn against the self-deceptions that breed sorrows. And although it would not do to wholly secularize the *Bhagavad-Gita* by ignoring its assumptions about the gods, reincarnation, karma, and social caste, we can extract secular practical advice from it. For the *Bhagavad-Gita* encourages a self-discipline that can reward anyone, Hinduism aside. And those rewards can be very much of this world.

Many Westerners have discovered this when searching for spiritual sustenance to counter the pressures of shallow materialism, the seductions of artificial desires, and the discontents of cold rationality. If you get no more from the *Bhagavad-Gita* than encouragement to think again about what matters most in life, and to discover the benefits of mental strength, and the freedom of self-control, you will be the better for it.

SIDDHARTHA GAUTAMA, the Indian prince who became the Buddha, derived from the god-intoxicated religion of Hinduism (although not from the *Bhagavad-Gita*, written after his time)

BUDDHISM

the makings of a secular philosophy of life that neither revered the gods nor respected social castes—although it retained the principles of reincarnation and karma. This is not to say that Buddhism has nothing to worship. It does. But this came later, after followers of Buddha largely deified him. Siddhartha Gautama himself had learned from no god how to solve the mysteries of life. He just thought long and hard by himself. And then he hit upon the simplest, yet most consequential, of answers.

The story of how Siddhartha Gautama made his discovery some twenty-five hundred years ago and became the Buddha is the stuff of legend. And it is through legend that we know of it. The legend says that when he first ventured out of his family's palace Siddhartha was surprised to see people living in squalor and misery, and he started asking himself the most universal of questions: Why do people suffer? and How can we stop it? Convinced that he would get no answers in the protective opulence of the palace, where he had probably also experienced some normal bad moods himself, he soon headed for the countryside. There for seven years he consulted Hindu sages and, on their advice, practiced ascetic yoga exercises of physical self-denial. But instead of attaining the promised Hindu satisfaction, he sank deeper into confusion, compounded by exhaustion and physical pains. So he abandoned that severe ascetic path and took another: he sat and meditated. Then the light went on. As tradition has it, in a blinding insight he suddenly saw both the cause and the cure of human suffering. Setting out to announce his revelation, he found the perfect place to do it in the peaceful Deer Park at Sarnath. There, to a handful of listeners, he gave his first sermon as the Buddha, the Enlightened One.

The Buddha explained how, following a Middle Path between the self-indulgences of worldly appetites and the self-abnegation of Hindu asceticism, we find the fundamental Four-Fold Truth of human life. The four parts are these: first, life is full of suffering; second, suffering is caused by desire; third, suffering can be ended by ending desire; and fourth, desire, and therefore suffering, can be ended by following the Eight-Fold Path: (1) correct understanding, (2) correct intentions, (3) correct speech, (4) correct action, (5) correct vocation, (6) correct effort, (7) correct mindfulness or attentiveness, and (8) correct concentration. Tradition also records that when he announced his discovery—not as "any ascetic, brahmin, god, Mara, Brahma," but as the Buddha—its truths reverberated throughout the universe: the "ten-thousand-fold world system shook, shuddered, and trembled, and a boundless great light appeared in the world surpassing the divine majesty of the gods." Buddhism was born.

All of Buddhism flows from those few ideas. It is not a theology. It is more of a philosophy or psychology. It says that we suffer not because circumstances cause us to suffer, but because we do not control the desires within us, for these desires determine how we respond to circumstances. Hinduism had said this too, but it demanded harsh rituals of self-denial in quest of extinction through divine union with the Supreme Being. Buddha says nothing of the divine. And he did not demand severe self-denial. No sackcloth and ashes for him. He said: take the Middle Way, embrace the Four-Fold Truth, follow the Eight-Fold Path, then you will know all you need to know, you will do all you need to do, to escape suffering.

Not that this is easy. The Eight-Fold Path requires plenty of self-discipline. That is the point. But Buddha and the tradition he inspired tended to emphasize self-disciplined ways of thinking more than physical exercises. If the mind is right, it will not only escape its fatal servitude to desire. It will also be free to think anew, to transcend the obvious, to see unimagined realities, and even to know joy in this world. That is why the Deer Park is a happy place.

ONE OF THE EARLIEST recorded versions of this Buddhist devotion to mental discipline, and among the most engaging of all Buddhist writings, is the *Dhammapada*. The title may be translated as "The Path of Perfection" or "The Path of Truth and Virtue." Its twenty-six short chapters eloquently lead us more or less along the Eight-Fold Path, dwelling especially on ways of thinking that deliver us to the ultimate self-control and therefore contentment.

"Our life is the creation of our mind." This is how the *Dhammapada* begins (in a particularly lucid translation), plainly setting its theme.

No equivocation here. It is not external circumstances or events that determine the nature of our lives. Everything depends on our minds and how we think (the exact opposite, incidentally, of Karl Marx's insistence that "it is not consciousness that determines life but life that determines consciousness"—see Chapter 15). Whether rich or poor, healthy or sick, strong or weak, we only suffer if we let ourselves suffer, and only feel joy if we let ourselves feel joy. After all, suffering and joy are both states of mind more than they are physical conditions (Western biochemistry might argue otherwise, but Buddhists, no less than Hindus, give mental activity preeminence, and demonstrate this preeminence by, for instance, mentally controlling pain). Everyone knows this to be true to some extent from everyday experience—our changing moods, even the degree of our physical discomforts, do not come from objective conditions alone. But we do not always make the most of this knowledge. Buddhism makes the *very* most of it. And that is the fascination—and the widest practical usefulness—of Buddhist ideas.

Think about it: *our life is the creation of our mind.* That says the mind makes us what we are. At the same time, it says that we are nevertheless responsible for how our minds work. "The mind is fickle and flighty," the *Dhammapada* cautions; "it flies after fancies whenever it likes: it is difficult indeed to restrain." That is the Buddhist version of desire—a tendency of the mind to flit here and there and to attach itself to the transitory, the extraneous, the insignificant, or to act like an untamed elephant who with its mighty force roams dangerously—a common Buddhist image, and the theme of Chapter XXIII of the *Dhammapada*. And a person of unrestrained or "impure mind" the *Dhammapada* explains, suffers as surely as "the wheel of the cart follows the beast that draws the cart"; whereas a person of restrained or "pure mind" finds that "joy follows him as his own shadow." Consequently "good is the control of the mind," the *Dhammapada* insists, "and good is the control of the whole inner life."

Gaining "control of the mind" and "the whole inner life" can be like training an elephant—awkward, troublesome, and a little scary. "This mind of mine," says the Buddha in the *Dhammapada*, "used to stray wherever selfish desire or lust or pleasure would lead it. To-day this mind does not stray and is under the harmony of control, even as a wild elephant is controlled by the trainer." But wresting this control is not a self-flagellating labor, as the Hindus tended to make it, sleeping on nails and that kind of thing. The *Dhammapada* shows how to achieve self-control with a few mental strategies. And these are accessible to anyone—not only as Buddhist practices, but also as common sense psychological exercises. Two of these strategies stand out, or rather can be drawn out, as the *Dhammapada*'s primary advice and practical psychological wisdom. They are: Be Awake, and Be Detached.

The Buddha was by definition the "Awakened One" just as he was the "Enlightened One." He was awakened to the "the four great truths"; and he stayed awake. His awakenness created Buddhism. "The followers of Buddha Gautama are awake and watch," says the *Dhammapada*, "and even by night and by day they remember the Truth." Being awake to the truth means keeping the mind always under control, never letting it slip away into inattentiveness and get lost in the labyrinth of desire.

This is not an esoteric rule. It is prudent advice. Consider what happens when you do not follow it. If you are not awake, if you do not constantly watch over your mind to see how it thinks and where it goes, if you fall asleep at the wheel of your thoughts, you will lose control. Then, instead of guiding your life, your mind lets life drag you around, from desire to desire, deception to deception. And that leads only to misery. So, stay awake to the tendencies of your mind, to the truths you wish to live by, to the wily temptations that induce mental inertia. "Find joy in watchfulness; guard well your mind," advises the *Dhammapada*, for "the wise man who by watchfulness conquers thoughtlessness is as one who, free from sorrows, ascends the palace of wisdom."

Staying awake and watchful, however, means more than just keeping your mental eyes open. You also have to think actively. And that can require special exercise. This exercise calls for the discipline of contemplation or meditation. Just as meditation brought Buddha's original "awakening" to the Four-Fold Truth, so meditation keeps us awake and alert to truth, protecting us from lapsing into error and desires and suffering. "Those who in high thought and in deep contemplation with ever-living power advance on the path, they in the end reach NIRVANA, the peace supreme and infinite joy."

You might picture here a Buddhist monk "in deep contemplation" under a tree, oblivious to the rest of the world. And you could find some (especially in the tradition of Ch'an, or the Japanese Zen, which originated in the fifth or sixth centuries C.E. and flowered in the eighth century, and which made meditation the central Buddhist activity). But you do not have to be a monk to use meditation. Focused meditation by itself develops a mental discipline that does a lot for the ordinary life. Meditation helps you put the body at rest, to relax its muscles and dissolve its tensions, and even to moderate its pains. Meditation also takes you a healthy distance from the pressures of material existence, and from the claims of other people. And meditation leads you outside of yourself, where you can gain salutary dispassion and contented quietude. In these ways meditation helps us conquer what Freud labeled the three sources of human suffering: nature, other people, and ourselves. In the Buddhist spirit, meditation works by awakening us to the true worth of everything in this transitory world. And it does this by helping us master the second, and psychologically most demanding and valuable Buddhist strategy of life: detachment.

Buddhist detachment does not require the denial of all impulses, shutting down the senses and the psyche or forsaking the ordinary life to go live in a cave—as some Hindu ascetics do. It means simply not allowing the mind to stray, or to get too attached to anything, or to care too much about anything—external or internal, objects or emotions, the world or the self. The detached mind attributes no fixed and lasting value to anything in life, either by embracing it too zealously or by rejecting it too fervently, whether it be pleasures or pains, self-indulgence or self-denial. The hair-shirted ascetic preoccupied with denying the flesh cares *too much* about the flesh and will not find peace any more easily than will a self-indulgent debauchee. "Neither nakedness, nor entangled hair, nor uncleanliness, nor fasting, nor covering the body with ashes, nor ever-squatting," says the *Dhammapada*, "can purify a man who is not pure from doubts and desires." To be truly "master of yourself," of your "inner life," you must "train yourself" to be "free from whatever may darken [your] mind." And all attachments, all preoccupations, all cares, darken the mind. Only by finding calm detachment from anything can you live *in* the world without being too much *of* the world, which means attributing to everything just the right measure of importance, and being contented to let anything go. And that includes the good things in life. We should learn to enjoy such things without living for them. "Even his manner of enjoyment is detached," as Yoshida Kenkō, the seventeenth-century author of the classic *Essays in Idleness*, said of the good Buddhist. "Although a man may wear fine clothing," the *Dhammapada* reminds us, "if he lives peacefully, and is good, self-possessed, has faith and is pure," he can remain awakened and detached, free from desire and suffering.

Far from a life-denying austerity, therefore, this liberating Buddhist detachment, falling between indulgence and asceticism, can be a rather worldly way of life (albeit not approved by all Buddhists), akin to Aristotle's ethics of the mean, which prescribes doing neither more nor less of anything than we should (see Chapter 4). For "he whose mind is well trained in the ways that lead to light, who surrenders the bond of attachments and finds joy in his freedom from bondage . . . even in this mortal world he enjoys the immortal NIRVANA." Take note of that! This says detachment can bring the transcendent freedom of Nirvana, or blissful release—call it what you want—*even in this mortal world*, every day, in everything we do. Just by thinking right. Don't let circumstances get you down. Don't let moods be your master. Don't let the world, or even your own sense of yourself, rule you. Set aside worry, get over injury, taste life's joys, savor them, and let them go.

Leaving the trappings of reincarnation aside, the central Buddhist ideas of "awakenness" and "detachment" create no religion. They come closer to a humanistic philosophy of healthy-mindedness promising something like secular salvation. Isn't that Nirvana on earth? No wonder the Deer Park is a happy place—and that many troubled souls in modern America turn to Buddhism as therapy.

The great Indian emperor Ashoka embodied this worldly appeal of Buddhism when, after a career of conquest in the third century B.C.E., he embraced such teachings as those in the *Dhammapada* around the same time as the book appeared. Far from becoming a monk withdrawn from the world, he set about creating a Buddhist empire, dedicated to promoting the material well-being of his subjects with new roads, canals, and other physical improvements. And he sought to teach them, in the words of one of his many edicts, the Buddhist virtues of "self-control, calmness of mind, and gentleness." Ashoka's edicts still stand, inscribed in stone and arrayed across northern India, monuments to the uses of Buddha's message for those living *in this mortal world*, not outside of it. And Ashoka himself remains one of world history's most benign and visionary rulers.

"Awakenness" and "detachment" make for a life of mental self-control, freedom, and serenity. And they prove that it is not circumstances or pains and pleasures that give life its meanings for us. These meanings come from how we think about those circumstances and our pains and pleasures, how we think about our lives. Rich or poor, powerful or powerless, we can be happy or miserable. Only by mastering how we think, and not granting false value to anything—object or incident, emotion or idea—can we rule our lives. Only then can we attain the joys that come from caring about the right things, and caring about them in the right way, and from being able to let go of everything, including the claims of our own egos, our own selves.

These are very good ideas that yield strength, and with that strength comes freedom, and with that freedom comes an invincible serenity. That is a bit of Nirvana on earth for sure.

THE BUDDHIST NOTIONS of mental control have traveled down many trails through the ages. From Buddha's original secular discovery that by conquering our desires we conquer suffering, Buddhism moved on in the *Dhammapada* to encourage the control of the mind as the pathway to all good things. At the same time, Buddhism engendered, through the dominant Mahayana ("The Greater Vehicle") tradition, an elaborate ethical and philosophical system. This complex system taught individuals not only to save themselves from suffering, but to save other people in a spirit of limitless compassion. It also produced some radical and arresting challenges to Western ways of thinking. It nurtured some extraordinary aesthetic sensitivities as well. All of these things belong to the Buddha's legacy, branches of a single tree. And they widen the uses of Buddhism in everyday life.

The teachings of Buddha inspired an ethics of compassion as the Mahayana tradition departed from the more monkish, spiritual practices of Theravada or Hinayana ("The Lesser Vehicle") and gave birth to the Bodhisattva. The Bodhisattva is a Buddhist devotee who, after mastering his or her own desires, steps back from the threshold of Nirvana to help others find the way. "When both myself and others / Are similar in that we do not wish to suffer / What is so special about me? / Why do I protect myself and not others?" asks Shantideva in one of the principal documents of this tradition (c. 700 C.E.). "Hence I should dispel the misery of others / Because it is suffering, just like my own, / And I should benefit others / Because they are sentient beings, just like myself." "This intention to benefit all beings," Shantideva adds, "Is an extraordinary jewel of the mind, / And its birth is an unprecedented wonder."

This humane ideal animated Ashoka. And, elaborated in many bafflingly complex sutras, or scriptures, it is widely reflected in Buddhist art, portraying many-armed Bodhisattvas living their infinite cycles of lives bringing enlightenment to an infinite number of "sentient beings" in infinite universes. If you find the Buddhist idea of the infinity of things—lives, beings, everything—and the artistic images expressing it a little puzzling, even bewildering, you should. That is their purpose. They should throw us off stride and make us feel small and insignificant. After all, self-assurance and feeling large and significant are in themselves just signs of fallacious attachments—to ourselves and to our knowledge, or rather to illusions of them. Detachment from these illusions is therefore the most difficult and liberating of all detachments to achieve. For from it comes the ultimate freedom, clarity, and contentment of mind that is Nirvana in this world. As *The Sutra of Hui-Neng* (more widely known as the *Platform Sutra*, said to be the words of the Chinese founder of Ch'an—Zen in Japan—who lived 638–713 C.E.) promises, "If we never let our mind attach to anything, we shall gain emancipations."

∽

We attain this highest liberation when the mind detaches itself not only from desires or attachment to things outside itself, but from all limiting ideas within itself and about itself—that is, conventional ideas of knowing, of truth, and of reality. This radical freedom (influentially formulated by the Japanese philosopher Nāgārjuna in the first and second centuries C.E., with his theories of illusion and unreality, and later closely identified with Zen) is not won easily. How could it be? It requires breaking out of every commonsensical and comfortable conception of truth and rationality (at least as known to the West). These, too, can be ties that bind, fetters on the mind and soul.

"Truth," declares the *Diamond Sutra* (an early source of this tradition, written in India in the fourth century C.E.), "is uncontainable and inexpressible. It neither is nor is not." Illogical? To be sure. The logical law of contradiction, which says a thing cannot be both itself and its opposite at the same time, does not hold here. It is not supposed to. You must free the mind from the bonds of *mere* logic to free it from itself. "We should get rid of pairs of opposites," declares *The Sutra of Hui-Neng*, for these bind the mind in "defiling conceptions." "A bodhisattva should develop a mind that alights upon nothing whatsoever," the *Diamond Sutra* explains; "the mind should be kept independent of any thoughts that arise within it." By detaching the mind from itself and from the ideas that arise within it, and from the temptation to hold fast to things as "true," we achieve the "idea-lessness" needed to see that "nothing is knowable" while still retaining "the concept of unknowability," or even claiming to know this. Then we escape not only from restrictive ideas of truth, but from the very bonds of *self-consciousness* that limit our range of thought. "Free from the idea of an ego entity, free from the idea of a personality, free from the idea of a being, and free from the idea of separated individuality"—which "are merely figures of speech"—our minds are at last truly unbound, unconstrained by any preconceptions. "All things—good or bad, beautiful or ugly—should be treated as void," *The Sutra of Hui-Neng* goes on, for "in all things there is nothing real." And with this freedom from "defiling conceptions" of reality we attain absolute, transcendent detachment—from everything.

Some dizzying notions dance here for anyone accustomed to Western common sense, conventional logic, and everyday experience. And they are supposed to dizzy us, spinning us out of constraining habits of thought. For until that happens, our minds cannot escape their blind bondage to error and come under our complete control. Of course it can be difficult to exercise this kind of radical mental freedom while living in our practical world. But then the world might not be what we think it is, and our minds might have powers that can be tapped only by fleeing every ordinary thought. We will never know unless we allow ourselves to "think" afresh in ways we are not used to. Look upon "this world as a bubble of froth," advises the *Dhammapada*, "as the illusion of an appearance," then you will see it truly. Or in the poetic words of *The Diamond Sutra*: "Thus shall ye think of all this fleeting world / A star at dawn, a bubble in a stream; / A flash of lightning in a summer cloud, / A flickering lamp, a phantom, and a dream."

These images of the world as a "bubble," an "illusion," a "fleeting" semblance, a "phantom, and a dream" run through the imaginative literature touched by Buddhism, where, as in the Japanese classic *The Tale of Genji* (see Chapter 21), all life passes with an illusory ephemerality, like "a floating bridge of dreams." And, as that literature memorably demonstrates, this Buddhist way of thinking not only detaches us from things; it can also, paradoxically—Buddhism loves paradoxes, because they keep us awake!—actually grant a heightened meaning to things, or rather to certain perceptions of things. We just have to perceive them in the appropriate way. And an appropriate way is nothing less—although it is also much more—than through aesthetic beauty.

As Yoshida Kenkō observed, once our minds escape "preoccupation with worldly desires" we can acquire a new "sensitivity to the beauty of things." And this sensitivity goes beyond the surface beauties caught by the senses. It goes to the very nature of things, revealing cosmic transience in a blossom, eternity in a rhyme, infinity in a cup of tea. So, paradoxically—again—although Buddhist doctrines can be dauntingly complex, this Buddhist "sensitivity to the beauty of things" points the other way. And that is to where it wins us with its beguiling aesthetics of simplicity.

The *Dhammapada* had hinted at this aesthetics in the chapter "Better than a Thousand," where it urges us, through another exercise of mental self-control, to dwell on single moments of truth and beauty instead of on abundance, lest we flounder in a sea of endless imperfection and error: "Better than a thousand useless words is one single word that gives peace. Better than a thousand verses is a single verse that gives peace. Better than a hundred useless poems is one single poem that gives peace."

Zen masters followed this instruction with mental exercises concentrating on perfection of form. These exercises at once facilitate the detachment of mind and bring some fine gratifications. Such is the tea ceremony, where every single gesture must be just so, and flower arranging, where no branch or petal can seem contrived or excessive, and poetry, which barely speaks but says so much to those attuned to its few words. Here is one Zen teacher's corrections of a student's poem after the student had written: "Hard by the forest in the middle of the deep snow a few plum tree branches last night opened their blossoms." The teacher made a slight change: "Hard by the forest in the middle of the deep snow *one plum tree branch* last night opened its branches." The singular says more than the plural. One is more than many. Another teacher taught the same principle in gardening. A student had immaculately prepared a garden down to sweeping its path clean. The Master said the path was not yet right, and, touching the branch of a tree, sent a few blossoms fluttering to the ground. Now, said the Master, the garden was finished—complete in its incompleteness. To the trained Buddhist senses, aesthetic perfection lies in less, not more, and in a subtle imperfection. You can learn to sense this perfection only by freeing your mind and detaching yourself. "When you're both alive and dead, / Thoroughly dead to yourself," writes the Zen poet Bunan, "How superb / The smallest pleasure."

Here the Buddha's insight into liberation from suffering and desires delivers the unexpected joys of aesthetic delight. These joys are won not by impulsively unleashing the senses, but by displaying them and directing them toward images that are at once subtle, beautiful, and philosophically resonant—granting those joys the importance they deserve, and no more. As Murasaki Shikibu wrote in *The Tale of Genji*, "the cherry blossoms of spring are loved because they bloom so briefly"—because beauty in this fleeting world is best encountered in the passing moment, and then let go.

HINDUISM AND BUDDHISM start out by trying to understand human suffering. They end in complex systems of self-discipline and philosophy that, however different, encompass all of life and lead to Nirvana. But they also give us strategies for mastering the everyday life.

Those strategies take many forms in the Hindu and Buddhist traditions. But self-control is their guiding principle. This principle can ask us to live almost entirely outside the world, denying virtually every normal human thought and impulse and sensation and pleasure. But this principle can also help us live very much in the world, even while detaching us from it. For self-control, in either the Hindu or Buddhist version, confers on us the power and the freedom of mind to care about the right things, and to care in the right way about them. And this ability to care about the right things and in the right way makes it possible to achieve contentment and serenity whatever our circumstances. No life can be good without that.

Then, with a parting paradox, this freedom and power of mind give us a final reward. That is the ability to perceive some of the finest beauties in the world around us, and therefore to enjoy some of the highest joys of being alive—without having to live for those joys alone. And this detached delight, bestowed by serene self-control, is surely among the surest signs of Nirvana on earth.

On Self-Control

1. Human suffering comes more from a way of mind than a condition of life.

2. Human suffering comes from unsatisfied desires.

3. We can overcome suffering by managing our desires.

4. To manage our desires we must exert self-control—physical, emotional, and mental.

5. The highest form of self-control is mastery of our minds.

6. To master our minds we must be constantly awake to seductive desires and deceptive appearances, and we must resist them. (Buddhism)

7. When we master our minds, we gain "detachment" from everything—that is, we become mentally free from the desires that attach us to everything, including ourselves. (Buddhism)

8. Detachment is the most difficult, and the highest, human virtue. (Buddhism)

9. Detachment does not require withdrawal from the world. (Buddhism)

10. When we achieve detachment, we escape both self-indulgence and self-denial. (Buddhism)

11. When we achieve detachment, we acquire an acuteness of perception and depth of feeling that gives beauty and meaning to the smallest and most fleeting of things. (Buddhism)

12. When we achieve detachment, we let many things make our lives good, and we can let all of them go. (Buddhism)

13. The meaning of life is to have self-control and detachment so we can live contentedly in this world and still let everything go.

3

What Do You Know? How Do You Know It? Why Should You Care?

Plato: *Euthyphro, Apology, Crito, Phaedo*

The really important thing is not to live, but to live well.

Are you not ashamed that you give your attention to acquiring as much money as possible, and similarly with reputation and honour, and give no attention or thought to truth and understanding and the perfection of your soul?

Socrates

Socrates (470?–399 B.C.E.) and **Plato** (427?–347? B.C.E.) were the original teacher-student team of Western philosophy. But Socrates—like those other great moral teachers, Confucius, Buddha, and Jesus—never wrote a word, or none that has survived. Most of what we know of Socrates and his ideas comes from Plato, who made Socrates the mouthpiece in nearly all of his own two dozen dialogues, even though Plato was only about thirty years old when Socrates died. So it is impossible to know for certain how the teacher's ideas differed from the student's. Scholarly convention has it that Socrates was more of a moral philosopher and Plato more of a metaphysical philosopher. But we commonly read Plato and Socrates as speaking in one voice (the other principal source for Socrates' life, Xenophon, was less intimate with the master).

Although the lives of Socrates and Plato remain sketchy, we know that Socrates lived in Athens during its remarkable cultural flowering in the fifth century B.C.E. He could have rubbed shoulders in the agora with many of the playwrights, architects, artists, and politicians who made Athens the matrix of Western civilization. But, after years of questioning his fellow Athenians about what they knew, and how they knew it, Socrates found himself accused of impiety and corrupting the young by his critics who had come to political power in 403 B.C.E. following Athens' long war with Sparta. Swayed by these critics, the court found Socrates guilty.

After Socrates' execution in 399 B.C.E., Plato became a teacher himself in his "academy," and he wrote the dialogues that made Socrates the father of Western philosophy (preceded only by a few "pre-Socratics"). The history of philosophy knows no more artful or influential writings than these—which scholars say have traveled down the ages virtually complete. And for most readers the most inspiring of Plato's dialogues are those that record the last days of Socrates' life: *Euthyphro, Apology, Crito,* and *Phaedo* (traditionally placed among Plato's "early" and "dramatic" writings). Here Plato shows Socrates first on his way to court to face the charges against him, then in court defending himself, later in prison after the court's verdict, and finally on the day he dies, philosophizing about the meaning of life and death. During these last days, Plato has Socrates unforgettably display his ennobling conviction that we should live, and die if necessary, for the True and the Good.

YOU DON'T HAVE TO like Socrates. Many of his contemporaries didn't. He ruffled too many feathers, rattled too many fixed ideas, and generally made a pest of himself. By his own admission he was a "gadfly," an insect that flits about wielding a noisome sting. He claimed that he simply wanted to know what is *true* and *good*. So he went around asking people what they knew to be true and good and how they knew it. But their answers disappointed him. For it seemed to him that nobody knew anything to be true or good for sure. They just thought they did. As he tried to make them see their ignorance, his dauntless philosophical questioning won him some loyal followers, most notably Plato. But it also earned him many powerful enemies. Finally, in the aftermath of Athens' wartime defeat by Sparta, and subsequently successful efforts to restore Athenian democracy, those enemies said: Enough! They put him on trial for religious impiety, for corrupting the young, and for being a general threat to the well-being of Athens, whose still fragile democracy they thought Socrates now threatened with his odd religious views and his seemingly disruptive and elitist ideas about how to think. Then they convicted him and sentenced him to exile or death. He chose death by a goblet of poisonous hemlock.

Socrates remained unflappable through all of this. He figured he was doing the right thing—despite his insistence that he didn't know anything—asking the most fundamental questions in our lives: What do we know? How do we know it? And why should we care? It troubled him that people didn't take those questions seriously enough. That is why he wouldn't stop asking.

Socrates' determination to press these questions got him condemned to death. But it also made him the exemplary idealist who has inspired countless readers ever since. By the time we read of Socrates downing the lethal brew to carry out the court's verdict, few of us can resist him. Or rather, few of us can resist his idealism. For it gives meaning to life through a vision of the True and the Good and other ideals as seen by the mind's eye. Socrates sometimes suggested that these ideals actually exist outside of our minds in a metaphysical realm of pure, abstract, ethereal perfection. This is where we get so-called "Platonic Ideas" (see Chapter 19). But those Platonic Ideas could have been Plato's own invention. In any case, Plato has Socrates concede more than once that he did not count on ideals to exist anywhere outside the mind. And this implies that what mattered most to Socrates was this: how our ideals of the True and the Good and other things give us our highest reasons to live *in this world*, and that we should expect nothing more from them. This is the idealism to live by. And we have Socrates, through Plato, more than anyone else, to thank for it.

How Socrates became the father of this life-giving idealism, despite provoking many of his fellow Athenians to judge him subversive, is the story of Plato's four dialogues—*Euthyphro, Apology, Crito, Phaedo*—taking us from the day of Socrates' trial to the hour of his death. Here we first see Socrates the pesky "gadfly" asking his endlessly irritating and irreverent questions of a young man, Euthyphro, who is also on his way to a trial at court. Then we see Socrates defending himself in court for asking these very kinds of questions. After that we find him awaiting death in jail to carry out the court's judgment, debating with Crito and other loyalists whether he should try to escape. Finally we see Socrates preparing to drink the hemlock, cheerfully explaining to Phaedo and other disciples why we should not fear death. From beginning to end, Socrates subtly and often ironically demonstrates how thinking about what we know and how we know it matters more than anything else, and how learning to see the True and the Good with our mind's eye shows us what makes life most worth living.

WE MEET SOCRATES in the *Euthyphro* loitering outside the court awaiting his trial. There he encounters a young man named Euthyphro, a distant admirer of his who is surprised to learn that Socrates has been accused of impiety for inventing "new gods" and "corrupting" the young. As it happens, Euthyphro is also readying for a trial. But he will not be the defendant. He will be the prosecutor. He is going to prosecute his own father for murdering a servant. And he is doing this because, as a presumed authority on religion and righteousness, he believes this is the "pious" and right thing to do.

This family drama astonishes and intrigues Socrates. How could anyone put his own father on trial, no matter what the charge? "Do you really believe you understand the rulings of the divine law," Socrates asks, "and what makes actions pious and impious so accurately" that "you have no misgivings" about proceeding in this way? ("Piety" and "impiety" translate *osion* and *anosion,* elsewhere sometimes translated as "holy" and "unholy.") Euthyphro confidently answers, "I shouldn't be worth much . . . if I didn't have accurate knowledge about that sort of thing." This confidence prods Socrates to dwell on Euthyphro's case. He sees an easy fish to catch. And he starts baiting Euthyphro in words dripping with what has come to be known as "Socratic irony." "Since you have this remarkable talent," Socrates says, "the best thing I can do, I suppose, is to become your pupil." For then, Socrates adds, he will be able to tell his own accusers in court that the religious "expert" Euthyphro is his teacher, and consequently they "must suppose that my beliefs are true, too, and drop [their] case against me." Euthyphro takes the bait. He begins enlightening Socrates about piety by answering Socrates' leading questions. But here, as usual when Socrates interrogates people, the actual subjects are: What do you know? How do you know it? And why should you care?

"Tell me," Socrates opens his ostensibly naive questioning of the self-assuredly wise Euthyphro, "how do you define piety and impiety?" Well, Euthyphro replies, "I say that piety consists in just what I am doing now: prosecuting a wrongdoer," and that it would be "impious not to prosecute such a person," whether the person is your father or not. As evidence, he cites the story of the god Zeus, who "put his father [Cronos] in chains" for devouring Zeus's siblings, just as Cronos had earlier punished his own father, Uranus, for previous crimes. Euthyphro figures that this mythological tradition settles the matter.

Socrates voices some doubts that such unseemly events ever occurred among the gods (in the *Republic,* Plato has Socrates fault Homer and other poets for contriving such un-godlike incidents—see Chapter 19), but he admits that these doubts had provoked some of the charges of impiety against him. And yet, Socrates goes on, whether true or false, Euthypho's stories of the gods are beside the point. For Euthyphro has merely cited particular examples of what he considers pious actions. He has not defined piety itself. To define piety precisely, Socrates says (Socrates and Plato frequently take the exact definition of words to be the measure of knowing what anything truly is), Euthyphro must "describe the actual feature" or "single characteristic . . . that makes all pious actions pious." Only when Euthyphro knows "what this characteristic is in itself," Socrates insists, will he "be able to describe any action . . . as pious if it corresponds to the pattern, and impious if it doesn't." Otherwise, Euthyphro is just guessing, and probably he is guessing wrong.

Socrates is doing here what he always does, trying to lead a self-professed wise man from complacent certainty to critical inquiry, and from particular examples to general principles. We cannot find truth, Socrates argues again and again, unless we question all of our assumptions and rise above particular facts to discover universal principles or ideals. For that is what truth is—universal and ideal. If we stop short of that, he says, and remain satisfied with easy assumptions and obvious particulars, we will never understand anything as we should. Although Socrates often professed to be a humble skeptic, he was pretty emphatic on this score. And we can learn a lot about how to pursue the truth in anything by following Socrates on his twisty hikes from particular facts to universal ideals. But we should not get carried away with this. For to use ideals in life we do not actually have to find perfect definitions or universal truths. We just need to think right. Socrates grants this, too, as we shall see.

Seeming to grasp Socrates' objections, Euthyphro tries again. All pious actions do have something in common, he concedes, as do all impious actions. It is this: "What is agreeable [or "pleasing"] to the gods is pious, and what is disagreeable [or "displeasing"] to them impious." Socrates likes this definition better than the first one because it is more general. But it still does not go far enough. In the first place, Socrates observes, the gods often differ over what *pleases* them. And in the second place, even if we could find acts that please all the gods, and that "they all love," we would not really know what piety is in itself. We would know only that pious acts please the gods and so the gods *love* them. Therefore, Socrates says, we have to ask: Is an act pious because it pleases the gods and they love it, or does it please them and do they love it "because it is pious?"

Socrates is playing here on a familiar conundrum that most of us have grappled with at one time or another. That is: Are actions morally good or bad in themselves, or do they become good or bad because a god (or some other authority) says they are—like actions that become legal or illegal only because human laws make them legal or illegal? It is no surprise where Socrates stands. He believes that moral good exists in itself apart from anything that any god or other authority says. And he tries to prove this to Euthyphro with a canny argument about how attaching a name to a thing cannot give it qualities because names can only label the qualities that a thing already has. Therefore labeling something "good" does not make it good. The question is: Why do we, or the gods, decide to call a thing good in the first place? When you can answer that, Socrates says, you know what good is. The answer cannot be merely arbitrary. And the logic applies to knowing anything—for instance, as the contemporary philosopher of art Arthur Danto observed in *The*

Transfiguration of the Commonplace (1981), just because an art museum exhibits a particular object does not make that object art; the museum curators must have discerned some artistic quality in the object that leads them to exhibit it in the first place.

It is easy to get tangled up here. And Euthyphro gets completely lost. "Whatever we put forward," he complains, "somehow keeps on shifting its position and refuses to stay where we laid it down." Socrates, of course, expects nothing less as he demonstrates that Euthyphro does not really know what he thinks he knows.

Seeing Euthyphro's certainties wavering, Socrates presses on. Euthyphro's second definition of piety will have to go. A pious action must be loved by the gods "because it is pious," Socrates insists; it is "not pious because it is loved" by the gods. "It seems so," Euthyphro wanly admits. All right, Socrates continues, it is time to "make a fresh start" and look for a true definition of piety. "Tell me without reserve," he needles Euthyphro, "what piety and impiety are."

Laying on the irony thicker now with every word, Socrates tells Euthryphro, "I myself will help you make the effort to instruct me about piety." Let's say, he suggests, that piety is part of morality in general. What part of morality is it? Going along, Euthyphro says that piety is the part of morality that gives attention or "tendance" or "service to the gods." Ah yes, Socrates responds. But what kind of attention or service is that? Is it the kind that benefits and improves the gods, like a doctor who heals a patient or an expert who trains horses? No, Euthyphro answers, the gods cannot be improved by lowly humans. Piety, he falteringly explains, as Socrates leads him through another maze of badgering questions, is rather the kind of service provided by "sacrifice and prayer." It doesn't help or improve the gods, but they "honor and esteem" it. For what "is pleasing to the gods, this is piety."

Alas, Socrates seems to sigh, not that again. "Don't you see," he says, "that our discussion has gone right around and come back to the point from which we started . . . saying that piety is what is pleasing to the gods?" Relishing the moment, he flatters Euthyphro while twisting the knife in him. "I am a passionate admirer of your wisdom," Socrates effuses. After all, "if you didn't know all about piety and impiety you would never have attempted to prosecute your father" because "you would have been too much afraid of the gods, and too much ashamed of what men might think . . . in case you should be wrong." But, Socrates goes on, since the roots of Euthyphro's wisdom are still hidden, "we shall have to start our inquiry about piety all over again from the beginning; because I shall never give up of my own accord until I have learnt the answer."

By this point Euthyphro has had quite enough. "Another time," he mutters, and beats a retreat for "an urgent engagement." Feigning hurt and disappointment with a final jab of irony, Socrates bemoans losing Euthyphro's expertise for use in his own trial, as well as for helping him to "live better for the rest of my life."

Euthyphro goes off to his father's trial as ignorant, if perhaps not quite as self-confident, as when he had started this futile conversation. And he has also possibly learned a bit about how exasperating the gadfly Socrates can be. But if Euthyphro has learned nothing much, Socrates has surely shed light for us on why we should not be satisfied with easy, uncritical certainties. For who, besides Euthyrphro, can come away from this conversation thinking that Euthyphro actually knows what he claims to know?—and that he can be truly pious if he does not know what piety is?

As Socrates shows us, to pursue the truth in anything we have to scrutinize our every assumption, question every authority, and think hard about what truth is and how we know it. Thinking like this is not easy, and it can be unsettling. It is fraught with false starts and deceptive byways; sometimes it leads to unwanted conclusions; and it will likely fall far short of the truth in the end. Socrates recognized all of this. But he believed that the difficulties of pursuing truth, and even the likelihood that we won't reach it, should not give us an excuse to sit back comfortably on our assumptions, or to blindly echo some authority, or to smugly presume to know what we do not know. For, as Socrates goes on to tell the court in his most oft-quoted words, "the unexamined life is not worth living" because the honest, ceaseless search for truth gives integrity to our very souls. Socrates does not explain this to Euthyphro. That comes later. And he lives in history because of it.

Euthyphro will never see these things. He will go blithely on his way, prosecuting his father and being the self-satisfied fellow he is, convinced that he knows what he is doing despite every argument to the contrary. We all know the type today. We might be the type ourselves—and if we are, we will not be able to see it until we learn to ask ourselves the kinds of questions that Socrates asks about what we know and how we know it. Socrates puts such questions to most dramatic use at his trial, where he takes them to their highest ends. Although the court will condemn him anyway, his defense remains the most moving argument for idealism in all of philosophy. For it shows us that Socrates' idealism does not tell us to find absolute truths. It tells us to use ideals to live well.

VEXED BY SOCRATES' nettlesome questions and his "independent thinking and unorthodox views," Socrates' accusers have brought a couple of specific charges against him at court. They claim, as Plato records in the *Apology*, that (1) he is "guilty of corrupting the minds of the young," and

(2) he believes "in deities of his own invention instead of the gods recognized by the state." But behind these specific charges, Plato points out, there lie more general and graver complaints about Socrates' very way of thinking. These are that "he inquires into things below the earth and in the sky, and makes the weaker argument defeat the stronger," and that he "teaches others to follow his example." Such intellectual arrogance and villainies made Socrates appear subversive to his more religiously orthodox and defensively democratic enemies.

Socrates' conversation with Euthyphro could have provided evidence on almost all of those counts. For Socrates questioned Euthyphro's conventional image of the gods; he tried to shake Euthyphro's confidence in the gods' authority; he implied that some other kind of truth and reality exist beyond those gods; he deployed tangled logic to make "the weaker argument defeat the stronger"; and in all, he probed everything "below the earth and in the sky" and encouraged Euthyphro to "follow his example." We can guess how Euthyphro would have cast his ballot had he been at Socrates' trial.

When Socrates rises to defend himself against both the specific charges and the more general complaints, he proceeds with the same ironic modesty he had used with Euthyphro. He has done nothing wrong, he says. He has only asked people questions about what they know. But he is not one of those "skillful speakers," he points out, who "try to educate people and charge a fee" for their clever coaching in rhetoric (he means the Sophists, whose verbal tricks he had often argued against). He had started asking his questions, he explains, simply to learn from other people what wisdom is—and to find out how he himself could possibly be wise, as the oracle at Delphi had mysteriously told him he was.

That sounds innocent enough. But it hadn't turned out that way. Socrates admits it. For his innocent questions had led him to a surprising discovery: people are not as wise as they think they are. They may know how *to do* something, he observes—poets can write poetry, orators can orate, craftsmen can make objects, politicians can make laws, and so on—but for all of their technical proficiency, they do not know the *truth* of anything in itself. They do not know, for instance, what goodness or beauty or justice or piety really are, even though they assume they do. This discovery had led Socrates to conclude that the oracle might be right after all: he might be the wisest of men solely because "I do not think that I know what I do not." In other words, Socrates alone had the only wisdom possible, which is to honestly recognize one's own ignorance. That dawning revelation, Socrates declares, had given him a "private mission." He would become like a "stinging fly" that stirs a lazy horse, "rousing, persuading, reproving everyone of you" for claiming to know things without truly knowing them and for failing to examine what knowledge and truth really are.

What is this but a confession by Socrates that he was indeed a troublemaker? He had tried to undo everyone's beliefs by proving that nobody knew what they thought they knew and that he had more wisdom than everyone else simply because he didn't claim to know anything. He even acknowledges that if people followed his example they would wind up like him with, at best, the faint "wisdom" of honest ignorance, which appears to Socrates' accusers as nothing but shattered convictions, corrosive skepticism, or pernicious error. Euthyphro had escaped these baleful consequences by fleeing Socrates with his self-satisfied certainties intact. And yet, if destroying people's *orthodox* beliefs with his irreverent questions and *unorthodox* views was all that Socrates had been trying to do, he would hardly have become the inspirational thinker he became. (*Orthodox* comes from the Greek *orthos*, for correct, and *doxa*, for opinion. Plato often dismissed *doxa*, as mere opinion, in favor of *epistēmē*, or true *knowledge*.) Socrates had more to say in his defense than confessing that he was a nuisance and a troublemaker. He would prove he was a true *philosopher* trying to do good for Athens.

Taking up the specific charge that he is "guilty of corrupting the young," Socrates lays out his proof by leading his accusers on a philosophical chase typical of him. Do you mean that "I do this intentionally or unintentionally?" he asks. "Intentionally," responds the chief prosecutor Meletus. Well, let's see, Socrates responds, since "bad people always have a bad effect, and good people a good effect upon their nearest neighbors, . . . by spoiling the character of one of my companions I shall run the risk of getting some harm from him," won't I? Who would do that *intentionally*? No sane person would. It would be self-destructive. Therefore, he continues, "either I do not have a bad influence" in the first place, or any bad influence must be "unintentional" and come from "ignorance." Consequently, if the court rules that he has corrupted people, it should provide him "instruction" to remedy his ignorance for corrupting them *unintentionally* rather than punishing him for doing it intentionally.

A facile argument. Just the kind that had enflamed Socrates' enemies. But while it fails to persuade Meletus, it does shift the focus of the case to where Socrates wants that focus to be: on his intentions. This is where his real defense lies. For now he can explain that, far from intentionally trying to corrupt people, he had always intentionally tried to do good. And the highest good possible at that.

"I set myself," he announces, "to do you individually what I hold to be the greatest possible service." This was "to persuade each one of you not to think more about practical advantages than of mental and moral well being" (or "perfection in goodness and wisdom") because these alone, he insists, are "of supreme importance."

Here is the heart of Socrates' defense. The irritating gadfly is actually a moral philosopher. For Socrates had not intended his questioning to breed amoral skepticism. He had intended it to inspire *philosophy*—the love (*philos*) of wisdom (*sophia*)—and lead to the supremely moral life. In this light, Socrates explains, his "mission" in life has been to urge everyone to "let no day pass without discussing goodness and all the other subjects about which you hear me talking and examining both myself and others," since a "life without this sort of examination" (or "the unexamined life") "is not worth living." It is not worth living because it would be lived for the wrong reasons—steeped in the trivial, blind to truth, and bad for our "mental and moral well-being." Pumping up the rhetoric, Socrates nails his point: "I spend all my time going about trying to persuade you, young and old, to make your first and chief concern not for your bodies nor for your possessions, but for the highest welfare of your souls" [*psychē*], and as "long as I draw breath and have my faculties, I shall never stop practicing philosophy and exhorting you" with the question: "Are you not ashamed that you give your attention to acquiring as much money as possible, and similarly with reputation and honour, and give no attention or thought to truth and understanding and the perfections of your soul?"

With this turn in his defense, Socrates comes forward as the moral idealist who lives in history—father to Don Quixote and others. That is, he says he has wanted above all to live his own life, and to encourage others to live their lives, for high-minded purposes in this world. And that means nothing less than perfecting the soul, or call it character, as the very meaning of life.

By the time Socrates wraps up his defense—arguing to the end that he has provided the citizens of Athens "the greatest service possible" by telling them to live for "what is of supreme importance"—he is ready with a plucky finale. "What do I deserve for behaving this way," he asks, "a poor man who is a public benefactor and requires leisure for giving you moral encouragement?" He answers with a flourish: "Nothing could be more appropriate for such a person than free maintenance at the State's expense." He cannot resist the ultimate irony of turning the court's accusations against it.

The court does not agree. By a small margin it convicts Socrates of all charges. Then it condemns him to death after he refuses to mend his ways or to accept exile. True to his *philo-sophical* character, Socrates shrugs off the judgment with aplomb. Why should he fear death? he asks. "To be afraid of death is only another form of thinking that one is wise when one is not" by assuming that death deserves to be feared. In any event, he adds, if tradition is correct and "all the dead" go "to some other place, . . . what greater blessing could there be" than to "spend my time there, as here, in examining and searching peoples' minds, to find out who is really wise among them, and who only thinks he is." Socrates just won't leave people alone—even dead people in the afterlife.

This, however, is what makes him who he is—not so much a gadfly of aimless skeptical questioning, or even a philosopher of absolute truth and Platonic Ideas, as a moral idealist who lives for what he believes to be the highest ideals. And he lives for these ideals not because they exist in a perfect world somewhere, or that he knows them to be absolutely true, but because they make this life most worth living. Socrates will say exactly this just before he drinks the fatal hemlock in the *Phaedo*. And although the Athenian court condemned him to death, the moral idealism that he lived by, and defended before that court, and then spelled out again to his disciples who visit him in jail while he awaits the day of his death, will never die. And we will always need it, for the welfare of our souls, and the good of our lives, in this world.

UNLIKE THE UNFLAPPABLE Socrates, some of his friends and pupils became so enraged by the court's decision that they decided to spring him from jail before the execution day arrived. One of them, Crito, goes to Socrates' cell proposing the escape. "It is still not too late to take my advice and escape," Crito pleads. And he tries to persuade Socrates that since "you profess to have made goodness your object all through your life," Socrates should now "make the choice of a good man and a brave one" and save his life for the sake of those who need his wisdom. Instead of packing his bags to leave, Socrates takes up Crito's plea as an intellectual challenge. He subjects Crito to another lesson in what it means to pursue our "mental and moral well-being," or "the perfection of the soul." This lesson makes a case for virtue and obedience to law that should echo in everyone's conscience. For it shows how, even if we can escape physical punishment for wrongdoing, we cannot escape the wounds of wrongdoing in our souls, or our moral character. Socrates makes this idea simpler than it turns out to be when we try to apply it, but he puts his finger on a fact of human nature and the moral life that we should not fail to see.

Socrates first treats Crito's appeal as he does any advice. He wants to find out if Crito truly knows what he is talking about. So, he asks, in effect: What do you know? And how do you know it?

Suppose, Socrates begins, we want to know what is the right thing to do in any particular situation or activity. Whose advice should we seek? Not just anybody's, because "some opinions should be taken seriously but not others." How do we know who will give us the right advice? We must, Socrates explains, find someone who knows what would be best for us in the situation or activity at hand. For instance, an athlete should seek advice from someone who has "expert knowledge" about the body and what is good for it and how to train it for competition. The same rule holds for a person trying to decide whether to escape from a court's death sentence. But here, Socrates points out, we would not turn for advice to someone with "expert knowledge" about the body. We need someone with expert knowledge about "the part of us that is injured by wrong actions and improved by right ones." That part is not the body but the soul, or character. And who knows more about this than Socrates himself?

"Is life worth living with this part ruined?" he probes. "Certainly not," Crito replies. Then that means, Socrates goes on in a very nice line, "the really important thing is not to live, but to live well." As Crito nods, Socrates follows up with another leading question. Doesn't "to live well" come down to "the same thing as to live honorably or rightly?" Again Crito agrees. Therefore, Socrates concludes, the fundamental issue is this: "whether or not it is right for me to try to get away." If it is right to get away, this will enable him "to live well"; but if it is wrong, this will ruin his character, and then his life will not be "worth living" at all. Crito concedes and sheepishly invites Socrates to explain to him "what we ought to do."

The tables have turned. Socrates now has Crito where he wants him. Crito has accepted Socrates' fundamental moral principles. These are: the "important thing is not to live, but to live well"; and we live well when we live "rightly" or "honorably" by nurturing "the perfection of the soul," as Socrates had put it to the court. Socrates now comes down from this lofty moral idealism to teach Crito a simple-sounding rule of life for living this way. It is a good rule, but not always easy to live by.

Socrates spells out this rule to Crito through another pair of questions: "Do we say one must never willingly do wrong, or does it depend on circumstances?" And "is it true, as we have often agreed before, that there is no sense in which wrongdoing is good or honorable? Or," he adds, jocularly, "have we abandoned all our former convictions in these last few days?" Crito could hardly disagree. The answer is clear. *Doing wrong is always wrong.* Circumstances make no difference.

Socrates is not exactly criticizing moral relativism or "situational ethics" here. He does that, too. But here he is punching a slightly different point—we must never *intentionally* do anything that we know to be wrong, whatever that may be, and whatever the circumstances. This again echoes his defense at court, where he had argued that he would never intentionally corrupt people. Here he takes up intentions as a key to character. We shape our own characters for good or ill, he says, with everything we think and do, and especially what we think and do intentionally. Doing wrong intentionally therefore "ruins" our character unequivocally.

Of course most people do not often intentionally do things that they know to be wrong. We all have our lapses, of course, as when we knowingly let our bad habits or self-indulgent impulses get the better of us. But we usually do what we believe to be the right thing. This no doubt clouds the very idea of intentions with ignorance and self-deception. And yet, convinced as Socrates was that wrongdoing ruins our soul or character, he implies that even unintentional wrongdoing can harm our souls. For instance, we might honestly think we are doing the right thing, but be wrong from innocent ignorance—as Euthyphro was when he "piously" prosecuted his father, or as Socrates said he himself might be in his ironic gambit at court, or as Meletus was when he accused Socrates of corruption, or as Crito appears to be by urging Socrates to escape from jail. Or, less innocently, we might modify our ideas of right and wrong to justify anything we choose to do. In either case, Socrates contends, we are lazily living an "unexamined life," satisfied with our ignorance or our rationalizations instead of questioning every assumption, received idea, and easy self-justification, to honestly search for the True and the Good. That is not good for the soul, or character. And it is why Socrates can say, "To do wrong is in every sense bad and dishonorable for the person who does it." But bad as it is for us to do wrong unintentionally, to do wrong intentionally is worse: it blights the soul and character to the core.

Take lying, for example. If we consciously tell a lie, knowing this to be wrong, we become liars in our souls. Even if we excuse a lie by saying it serves a good cause, we cannot deny that we have put some other value above telling the truth. That makes us at least *situational liars*, people who justify lying according to circumstances, rather than people who never lie on principle.

Socrates is very rigid about this. Perhaps too rigid. But he is not wrong. If we want to have a certain kind of character, we cannot *ever* do anything that would conflict with this character. For everything we do leaves a mark on us—a fact that Aristotle made a central theme of his *Ethics* (see Chapter 4) and that Dante made the measure of sin (see Chapter 5). As Plato put it in the evocative "Myth of Er" at the end of the *Republic*: "It should be our first care" to gain "the knowledge and ability to tell a good life from a bad one" because "each soul must assume a character appropriate to its choice" of a life—the responsibility "lies not with God but with the soul that makes the choice."

Applying these principles to his own situation in jail, Socrates asks:

Is it *ever* right to break the law, as he would be doing by escaping from jail, even if a person has been unjustly condemned, as he and his companions believe he was? He thinks the answer is obvious. His situation is irrelevant. "One must not even do wrong when one is wronged." So, if it is wrong to break the law, being unjustly condemned under the law doesn't matter. By breaking the law, whatever your situation or justification, you become a lawbreaker. And that, Socrates explains, damages the soul, or character, in two ways. In the first place, it makes you morally untrustworthy. In the second place, it makes you a threat to society (Dante designed his hell along these very lines).

Think about it, Socrates says. If you break a law because you decide it is an unjust law, or if you violate a ruling of the court because you believe it is a faulty judgment, you are attacking the very principle of obedience to law. Can a city "continue to exist and not be turned upside down," Socrates asks, "if the legal judgments . . . are nullified and destroyed by private persons" who break the law at their own whim? Of course not. Therefore, Socrates says, if he were to escape from jail, he would in effect be confirming the judgment of the court and telling the citizens of Athens: "Yes, I do intend to destroy the laws, because the state wronged me by passing a faulty judgment at my trial." After all, Socrates emphasizes, since he has long lived as a law-abiding citizen under the laws of Athens, and has benefited from the security and well-being that those laws had given him and his family, how could he legitimately try to "destroy" those laws now just because he doesn't like what the court has done to him in this particular case? He cannot, and he will not, do that. He will stay in jail. Living an "examined life" has led Socrates to the moral conclusion that he must die.

Besides, he adds, if he escaped from jail, no moral and law-abiding society would want to admit him because they would view him "with suspicion as a destroyer of law and order." Then he would have to live in lawless states or among people like himself—outlaws. Either way, he asks, would that "life be worth living?" Hardly. Remember, the "important thing is not to live, but to live well."

Our moral lives may not be as simple as Socrates describes them. We have too many ambiguous choices to make and too many conflicting "goods" to serve. Socrates was also not dealing with lives lived under oppressive political regimes, which he did not accuse Athens of being, despite the unjust court verdict. Such regimes test people's character in ways that Socrates encountered only in part and at the end. Twenty-five hundred years after Socrates, Martin Luther King, Jr., jailed under the "unjust laws" of racial segregation in America, would in fact invoke Socrates as a moral mentor punished for serving a noble good, even though King persuasively defended breaking unjust laws (see Chapter 16). But King would not have persuaded Socrates. For Socrates rejected the idea that a person could legitimately pick and choose laws to obey or disobey, however unjust a particular law may be. He had good reasons. At the same time, Socrates obviously cared less about social justice than he did about "the perfection of the soul" that comes from living "honorably" and seeking the True and the Good. That is because he believed the soul is where we find the meaning of our lives. And this is how he has inspired generations of readers to find meaning in their lives.

With these morally idealistic arguments ringing "so loudly in my head that I cannot hear the other side," Socrates tells Crito at the end to "give it up." Socrates has only one path to follow. He will cheerfully submit to the verdict of the court, living up to his principles by dying for them. He could not have done otherwise.

When we see Socrates for the last time, he is calmly conversing with his disciples as he awaits the hour of his death in the *Phaedo*. Although the conversation takes some heady flights into the metaphysics of idealism, it ends on the earthly plane of how to use moral ideals in everyday life. By the time Socrates drinks the hemlock, he has made this idealism hard to resist—not as abstract philosophy but as a way of life.

The conversation begins with, of all things, Socrates writing poetry. He is recasting some fables of Aesop, he explains, because he has begun to wonder if the oracle that had long ago told him to follow the muse of philosophy had actually meant the muse of poetry. Socrates is no doubt playing with irony again, since he distrusted poets for many reasons, especially because they do not know the truth about anything, but only know how to speak as though they do (see Chapter 19). At the same time, he is questioning himself again, living out to the very end his "examined life." Soon this dabbling in poetry yields to philosophizing on the subject of the moment: Socrates' impending death. And because his companions don't understand how he can face death so serenely, he poses the question: Should we fear death? He doesn't think we should. Not that he claims to know what comes after death. To do that, as he had said in court, would amount to presuming to know something he does not know. But he has found a good way to think about death. And this is a good way for anyone to think about it.

Socrates starts off with a kind of joke on this funereal subject. "It seems to me natural," he says, "that a man who has really devoted his life to philosophy should be cheerful in the face of death," for what is death but "the release of the soul from the body?" And since philosophy aspires to "the perfection of the soul," shouldn't getting rid of the body with its physical imperfections help? In short, Socrates quips, "true philosophers make dying their profession." From this cheery premise, Socrates sets out to prove that the soul does indeed exist and that it is immortal. Remote as that subject might seem from everyday life, it isn't. For Socrates shows how it can be a very useful ideal.

Socrates weaves a denser philosophical fabric in the *Phaedo* than in the previous three dialogues. But one thread runs through: the idea, or the ideal, of the soul. This is the thread to draw out.

Socrates "proves" the existence of the soul with one of his more ingenious intellectual games. It goes more or less like this. He says that two realms exist in the universe. One of these contains material things, and the other contains immaterial things. We know things in the material realm through our senses. And we know things in the immaterial realm through our minds. To demonstrate the existence of these two realms, as well as how we know them and what kinds of things exist within them, Socrates leads his companions down a twisty path with, as usual, a skein of questions. But it is a path worth traveling.

Does there exist, he begins, the "real nature of any given thing—what it actually is" in its "essence," such as "absolute uprightness or justice" or "absolute beauty and goodness?" "Of course," his companions assent (good students of Socrates that they are). Well, he goes on, "Have you ever seen any of these things with your eyes" or perceived them "with any other bodily sense?" "Certainly not," comes the emphatic reply. Then that must mean, Socrates points out, that these *absolute essences* exist as ideas, and that we can know them only through our minds with "pure and unadulterated thought." His disciples are with him all the way. All right, Socrates continues, if these absolute essences exist, and we can know them as ideas only through "pure, unadulterated thought," then they must belong to the realm of immaterial things, just like ideas and thought itself. By the same token, he adds, the things we know through the "bodily senses" must belong to the realm of material things, just like the body and those senses themselves. We might doubt this tidy conclusion, but Socrates figures this part of his case is conclusive. Socrates' listeners surely nodded their agreement.

Now Socrates widens his logical game. Everything in the material realm, he says, must have the attributes of material things, like the body. And everything in the immaterial realm must have the attributes of immaterial things, like ideas. For example, material things are concrete, particular, relative, changeable, destructible, and so on. And immaterial things are abstract, universal, absolute, changeless, eternal, and so forth. The existence of these logically opposite realms also means, Socrates adds, that things belonging to one realm cannot cross over into the other or acquire its attributes, any more than odd numbers can join the realm of even numbers or vice versa. To switch like that would create an impossible contradiction.

With this logical scheme neatly laid out, Socrates poises himself for the finish. Where, he asks, does the soul fit into the scheme? His disciples see the light. If the physical body as a material thing belongs to the material realm, then the soul as an immaterial thing must belong to the immaterial realm. And as an immaterial thing belonging to the immaterial realm, the soul must have all of the suitable attributes. As one of these disciples astutely observes, "The body is most like that which is human, mortal, multiform, unintelligible, dissoluble, and never self-consistent," whereas "the soul is most like that which is divine, immortal, intelligible, uniform, indissoluble, and ever self-consistent and invariable." Aha! Socrates might have exclaimed and commended the fellow for hitting the nail on the head.

Socrates' little game of logical opposites and contradictions has proved his case: just as ideas and essences exist in the immaterial realm where we perceive them through the mind, the immaterial soul also exists there, and like ideas and essences and all immaterial things, the soul is immortal. Everything fits together very nicely. So, Socrates concludes with a wink, far from fearing death, we should welcome it, because "if we are ever to have pure knowledge of anything we must get rid of the body and contemplate things by themselves with the soul by itself." This is why "true philosophers make dying their profession."

That is a Socratic joke, not a prescription for suicide. For Socrates has said all along that we should try to perfect our souls, or characters, in order to "live well" in this world. Here he adds a note, though, on how living for "the perfection of the soul" in this world could bring later rewards, too. If the soul is indeed immortal, he says, it "takes nothing with it to the next world except its education and training" (*paideia* and *tropha*). Teachers should love that line. And it is as inspiring a humanistic notion of the afterlife as you will find.

To be sure, Socrates carried "the perfection of the soul" to some ends that many of us would shy away from. And he lent support to religions that denigrate the flesh, dismiss this world, and exalt the spirit (the puritanical St. Paul, schooled in Greece, probably learned a thing or two from him), and he even hinted that he believed in reincarnation. But we do not need to follow Socrates everywhere he goes in his "Cloud-cuckooland" (as the comic dramatist Aristophanes dubbed the place Socrates inhabited in *The Clouds*) to see the good uses of his idealism. For these belong very much to our everyday lives. Socrates says this himself as his own end draws near.

Descending from his philosophical flights and lofty arguments about the immortality of the soul, Socrates admits to Phaedo and the others that "no reasonable man ought to insist that the facts are exactly as I have described them" about "our souls and their future." Certainty in such things is not, after all, possible in this life. And yet, Socrates emphasizes, the immortality of the soul is "a belief worth risking, for the risk is a noble one." And it is noble for no other reason than because it helps us "live well" in this life. "We should use such accounts to inspire ourselves with confidence," he urges, and to chase away "anxiety about the fate of the soul." If this belief makes life more worth living, it is a morally useful ideal, and that is all it needs to be (Cervantes had his idealist Don Quixote live just this way—see Chapter 22).

And that, in the end, is how Socrates says we give the highest meanings to our lives: we embrace ideals "to inspire ourselves." He says this in the *Republic*, too, when envisioning the ideal state (or Plato's version of it): "It makes no difference whether [the ideal state] exists now or will ever come into being," he remarks, but if we "contemplate it" we can become "its citizen" in our souls. The truth and reality of ideals need be no more than this, as Socrates knew. If that makes Socrates not only the father of Western moral idealism, but also something of a pragmatist—foreshadowing William James, who built a pragmatic moral philosophy on this very principle with essays like "What Makes Life Worth Living" and "The Will to Believe"—so much the better.

In this happy mood, buoyed by the moral idealism that has given meaning to his life in this world no less than it has given him hope for another life to come, Socrates cheerfully prepares to release his soul from his body. He will go to his death, he says, like the swans who, as the time of their death approaches, "sing more loudly and sweetly than they have sung in all their lives before," not "because they are sad . . . but because they know the good things that await them in the unseen world." Contemplating his own swan song, with reasonable hopes for "the unseen world," if no knowledge of it, and gently chiding his companions for their needless tears, Socrates downs the hemlock.

Then, while waiting for the poison to take hold, he recalls a rite of sacrifice made to the god of health, Asclepius, for curing an illness. He tells his old friend Crito, who has stayed with him to the end: "Crito, we ought to offer a cock to Asclepius. See to it, and don't forget." Socrates' soul will now leave his body to enter the "unseen world" in good health. He owes a cock to Asclepius for being cured—of the body.

Socrates died happy. And perhaps he was, as Phaedo said, "the bravest and also the wisest and most upright man." Whether Socrates' soul flew off like a swan to healthy immortality, no one knows. But who can deny that his life achieved an immortality of its own in this world? For the moral idealism he lived by, tirelessly questioning others, persistently seeking the truth, vigilantly cultivating his soul, and even happily drinking the hemlock, will not die.

As a GADFLY, Socrates could be a pest. And he could come across as smug and condescending. But everyone should get to know him. For he urges us to live not for the daily trivialities, deceptive appearances, fleeting appetites, material possessions, and moral compromises that can so easily consume our lives—and which threaten to do so more in our times than in his. We should instead live for what we most deeply are, which is what lasts within us if anything does: our character, our souls. This is not a religious idea, whatever Socrates' religious beliefs. It is a secular idea that asks human beings to live for the highest humanistic ideals in this life.

Of course, idealism can lead to arrogant ideologies and religious fanaticism. We see this all too often. But that can happen only if we ignore Socrates' admonitions to examine our lives honestly and ceaselessly, to keep always seeking the True and the Good, and to be wary of believing that we know anything absolutely for sure (an admonition that some critics, like Karl Popper, have accused the metaphysical idealist Plato himself of neglecting). That is a telling difference between metaphysical idealism and moral idealism. Metaphysical idealism leads us to assert absolute truths and universal realities; moral idealism tells us only to "live well" in this world by pursuing ideals and questioning ourselves. Socrates was, to the end, a moral idealist. That was enough for him, whether or not another life would follow this one. And, through Plato's words, Socrates gave us the immortal image of himself as the kind of soul, or character, that makes life in this world most worth living: always searching for the True and the Good, unwaveringly honest and honorable, a bit skeptical, and full of good cheer. Socrates' idealism asks no more of us than that—and no less.

On How to Think and to Live Well

1. The purpose of life is not just to live, but to live well.

2. We live well when we live for what is most important in life, not for what is transitory and trivial.

3. The most important thing in life is the lasting good of our soul, or our character.

4. To have a good character we must search always for the True and the Good.

5. To search for the True and the Good, we must honestly and ceaselessly examine our lives, question our assumptions, and avoid self-deception.

6. An unexamined life is not worth living.

7. We should be a bit skeptical of every claim to know the True and the Good.

8. We will never find the True and the Good in themselves, but we must keep searching.

9. We come as close to the True and the Good as possible when we see ideals of perfection with our mind's eye.

10. Ideals do not have to exist outside of our minds in order to be real.

11. To live well, we must never do anything wrong, because every wrong act—especially those we know to be wrong—taints our character and diminishes our humanity.

12. The meaning of life is to live for ideals of the True and the Good and always question ourselves—then we acquire good character, wisdom, and cheerfulness; and if there is an afterlife, we will take our good character, wisdom, and cheerfulness with us.

4
Living the Good Life

Aristotle: *Nicomachean Ethics*

The highest of all practical goods . . . is happiness, say both ordinary and cultured people, and they identify happiness with living well.
Aristotle

Aristotle (384–322 B.C.E.) left his native Macedonia in northern Greece around the age of seventeen to study at Plato's Academy in Athens. He stayed there as a leading disciple of his mentor until Plato died some twenty years later. Scholars say that backstabbing competitors in the original "academic politics" then likely drove Aristotle out. Whatever the cause, he left, and after a dozen years in other cities, including a period back in Macedonia, where he taught the young prince who became Alexander the Great, he returned to Athens and set up his own school, the Lyceum. Aristotle taught for another dozen years at the Lyceum before departing Athens again to live his last year on the island of Euboea.

Although Aristotle was Plato's most renowned student, he came to disagree with his teacher about most things. Less drawn than Plato to abstract ideas and absolute truths, Aristotle wanted to know how real life works in all of its earthy and practical particularities. And in lectures that his students inscribed, which are our chief source of Aristotle's "writings," he defined many of the academic disciplines that we have today, including botany, zoology, psychology, political science, physics, metaphysics, logic, ethics, poetics, and art education. His "scientific" ideas are out of date now, but others live on. And the most lively of them all are those at the heart of the book known as the *Nicomachean Ethics*.

Named by tradition for the Greek editor, Nicomachus, who compiled it (and to distinguish it from Aristotle's earlier, lesser work on ethics compiled by Eudamus), the *Nicomachean Ethics* touches on virtually everything we as human beings do in conducting our lives, from how we make everyday choices to how we find our highest happiness. We create our *ethics* through all of this. And Aristotle's advice on how best to do that with every choice we make gives us probably the world's first, and perhaps the wisest, self-help book on living the good life.

ARISTOTLE WANTED TO KNOW everything. And he succeeded. He also gave more good advice on how to live the good life than has any other philosopher. That may seem unlikely for a thinker who tramped the sunny shores of Greece nearly twenty-five hundred years ago. But Aristotle was no airy theorist. He cared about the real world and how people live in it. And he looked into all of it—physics and biology, astronomy and psychology, politics and ethics, metaphysics and education, logic and rhetoric, art and entertainment. Nothing on earth or in the heavens escaped him. He became a one-man library. And centuries of Europeans, including the admiring Dante in the *Inferno*, honored him as "the master of those who know." Aristotle's intellectual authority reigned on almost every subject in the West for some fifteen hundred years, inhibiting new ideas until the Renaissance, so his modern critics charge.

We no longer look upon Aristotle with such reverence. Modern science has seen to that (although Aristotle's partisans, like the renowned historian of philosophy John Herman Randall, Jr., give him credit for pointing toward modern experimental science as well). Still, what Aristotle accomplished was truly astonishing. Some of his writings (or lectures written down by listeners) continue to enlighten us and to serve as a standard of what we *should know* and *should do*. This rings true especially of his pioneering book on what he called "ethics." Most of this book is as instructive now as ever, and on the subject closest to us: *how to live the good life*.

You will not find in the *Nicomachean Ethics* (generally known as the *Ethics*) a philosophical quest for absolute truths, or a lot of moralistic talk about the eternal soul, as you do in the writings of Plato. Aristotle shuns such ethereal themes to pursue "prudence" or "practical wisdom" or "common sense" (*phronesis*) about "the good life generally." And, Aristotle observes, "we must be satisfied with a broad outline of the truth" instead of expecting absolute certainty, because this is all "the subject matter allows." After all, he emphasizes, "we are studying not to know what goodness is" as an abstract, absolute idea (à la Socrates and Plato) "but how to become good human beings" in practice, "since otherwise it would be useless." And common sense counts for more here than does high-flown philosophizing.

How to become good human beings in practice. That is the subject, or "practical aim," of the *Ethics* (Aristotle's term for "practical aim" is *pragmatia,* from which we get "pragmatic"). But Aristotle does not have in mind *ethics* as we commonly use the term in English today—that is, a code of selfless moral conduct toward others. He has in mind the Greek word *ēthos*, which denotes *character* overall. Aristotle's *Ethics* is not about a morality of treating others selflessly—or, as in the philosophies of Socrates and Plato, about cultivating the moral purity of the soul, *psychē*. It is about the practical *ethics* of how we can shape our characters to become "good human beings" and to live "the good life generally." Selflessness has nothing to do with it. To the contrary. Aristotle believed that we become "good human beings" by fulfilling ourselves as individuals and as human beings. That is how *ethics* leads us to *the good life*. So, if ever there was a how-to-book for everyone on living the good life, this is it.

THE FIRST THING any reader will want to know, of course, is just how Aristotle defines "good." He anticipates the question. "The Good," he says, "has been rightly defined as 'that at which all things aim.'" This might not strike you as much of a definition, but Aristotle thinks it is the place to start (reflecting as it does the teleology, or theory of how things move toward ends, that runs through all of his philosophy). "Good," as Aristotle uses the term here, is not therefore an abstract moral norm or truth. It simply labels the ends we seek in anything—we only pursue ends we consider good, don't we? (This is a definition of "good," by the way, that Socrates would never have accepted—see Chapter 3. Aristotle's most common term for "good" in this sense is *agathos,* and the superlative for it is *aristos,* denoting the "best" or the "supreme good.") That is plain common sense. And it introduces Aristotle's next common sense observation. If every end that we seek is good simply because we seek it, then what we all seek as the ultimate end must be, Aristotle says, "the highest of all practical goods" for human beings. When we ask what this highest practical good is, Aristotle doesn't hesitate. He declares that everyone agrees: "'It is happiness,' say both ordinary and cultured people," and they "identify happiness with living well." (Aristotle's word for "happiness," or "well-being," is *eudaemonia*.)

No fuss here. Aristotle is as plain as anyone could be. If you want to know what good is in practice, look at the ends you pursue. And if you want to know what the highest practical good in human life is, take a survey. Since people generally say they seek happiness as their end (there are exceptions, of course, but Aristotle was not interested in them), and they "identify happiness with living well," then the happiness of living well, or the good life, must be the highest practical good for human beings. Simple as that.

Well, not really. The work of the *Ethics* lies ahead. For while people might agree that they seek happiness as their ultimate end, Aristotle acknowledges that "when it comes to saying in what happiness consists, opinions differ." Quite so. Some of us think that happiness comes from pleasure. Others think it comes from wealth. Still others think it comes from fame or status or spirituality—even if they don't call it "happiness" by name—and so forth. Surprisingly, Aristotle says these opinions are all correct to some degree. Happiness comes from all of the things that we pursue as ends, which makes them all good in their way. That is human nature. Never mind the moralistic scoldings of Socrates against pursuing some of these things, Aristotle hints, since Socrates ignored the practical facts of human nature. However, Aristotle asks, if all of these good things can bring happiness, are they all equally good as ways to become happy? Or, rather, do they all lead to the best kind of happiness?

Here we meet the Big Questions of the *Ethics*, and of everyone's life: What is the best kind of happiness? And how can we get it?

To answer these questions, Aristotle doesn't just cheerfully philosophize about ideals. That is not his style. He furrows his brow and looks closely at human nature as he finds it and at human life as we commonly live it. Taking another jibe at Plato's lofty yearnings for transcendent truths, he says we should set aside abstract ideas and start with "what is known to us" as "fact." And the fundamental fact of human nature and of human life derives from the fundamental fact of all existence, as Aristotle sees it. Both of these "facts" have to do with Aristotle's definition of good. Namely: human beings pursue ends because all things and all activities in the universe naturally move from beginnings to ends. Everything therefore has an end, and every end is good. This may be a dubious fact based on circular reasoning, particularly when it comes to the world of nature, as modern science has shown. But it has a neat teleological coherence to it, and it holds some nice implications for human nature and ethics.

These implications start here: the end, or good, of any thing or activity, including human beings, is the natural purpose or function of that thing or activity. For example, Aristotle points out, the end or natural purpose "in medicine is health; in strategy, victory; in architecture, a building." What is more, Aristotle adds, when a thing or activity serves its natural purpose or function at its best, it not only attains its end, which is good, but it does so with excellence or virtue—the ancient Greek word for both excellence and virtue was *aretē*.

Now we see Aristotle's idea of good in a new light. The best kind of good is not just any end that a thing or activity might move toward. It is the one end that will fulfill the true nature, or the natural purpose or function, of that thing or activity at its best. When a thing or activity succeeds at this, it achieves excellence or virtue. "Any kind of excellence,"

Aristotle elaborates, indicates that a thing "perform[s] its function well." "The excellence of a horse," for instance, "makes him both a fine horse and good at running and carrying his rider," because that is what a horse is supposed to do. Playing on Aristotle's definition of good, and on the two English words for *aretē*—excellence and virtue—we could give some other examples, such as: a good doctor has the virtue of producing excellent health in the body; a good soldier has the virtue bringing the excellence of victory; a good violin has the virtue of producing an excellent sound; a good painter has the virtue of creating excellent paintings; and so on.

The same rule applies to the nature of human beings. As Aristotle puts it, "human excellence," or virtue, "makes one a good man and causes him to perform his function well" as a human being. Or, think of it this way: a good human being is one who has the virtue of performing the natural "function of human beings" with excellence.

Here is Aristotle's prescription for how we become good human beings at our best and find the highest happiness: we must perform our natural function as human beings *excellently.* That is a fine humanistic ideal. But it is bound to make us wonder what the natural function of human beings is. Aristotle has his answer ready.

Setting aside the physical attributes that all living things share, Aristotle locates this unique natural function of human beings in what he calls "activity of the soul"—*psychē energeia.* Activity of the soul is a pretty cloudy notion. And rather Platonic. But Aristotle is not talking about some spiritual vibration or mystical state. He is pointing to a kind of activity that the English language identifies with a variation on the Greek word for soul, *psyche.* This activity is psycho-logical, or mental. Specifically, it is the mental act of making choices, "implying a rational principle," which nothing but human beings can perform. Human "life is a form of activity," he explains, for "life is a thing to choose."

The mental activity of making rational choices in life—this, Aristotle says, is our unique natural function as human beings. For "our virtues [or excellences] are expressions of our choices." Consequently, when we perform this "activity of the soul," or mental act of choice, at best, "in accordance with its proper excellence [or virtue]" or highest purpose, we fulfill our natures as human beings at our *best.* And that brings the best kind of happiness (John Stuart Mill gave choice similar importance in shaping character—see Chapter 14).

Or we could phrase the idea this way: When we choose excellently in everything that we do from day to day, we acquire an excellent or virtuous character. And this makes us good human beings who will live the good life at its best and reach the "supreme good" of the highest happiness (translators use both "supreme good" and "best" for Aristotle's *aristos*). That is Aristotle's basic prescription for *ethics*: the shaping of character to attain the good life at its best. And it is his general answer to the question, What is the best kind of happiness?

But that is only his general answer. We still do not know what are the actual choices that will lead us to the good life and the best kind of happiness. So the next question is: How do we make the excellent choices that will lead us to the good life and to the best kind of happiness? Answering this question takes Aristotle to the heart of the *Ethics* where we get his best advice on how to live.

To BEGIN, Aristotle says, in order to make excellent choices we have to know what we are choosing, and then we have to choose it freely and on purpose. A person's choices will lead to the good life only if he "knows what he is doing, if he chooses it, and chooses it for its own sake." Aristotle splits a lot of hairs distinguishing types of choices that are "voluntary," "involuntary," and "non-voluntary," and the degrees of knowledge, intention, freedom, and responsibility that go with these types. But his fundamental idea is clear and, as usual, commonsensical, not to say simplistic. We can make excellent choices, he suggests, only if we know what we are doing and do it deliberately.

But Aristotle does not let it go at that. He also takes pains to show that the act of choosing—or "activity of the soul"—is not confined to the mind. It requires physical action in the world. When Aristotle says "life is a thing to choose," he means that we do not merely choose among ideas, we choose *actions*. And when we choose actions we also have to act on those choices or they don't amount to anything. For actions, not ideas, shape life, since "life is a form of activity." This is commonsense again, and it applies to anything that we want to be able to *do* rather than to just think about.

"Anything that we have to learn to do" in life, Aristotle explains, "we learn by the actual doing of it," not simply by thinking about it. If "we wish to be healthy," for instance, we must "choose things that will make us healthy" and act on those choices, unlike those "invalids who listen carefully to their doctor but carry out none of his instructions." That is plain enough—and who hasn't heard this from a doctor? The same rule obviously applies to learning any kind of skill, like playing a musical instrument or speaking a foreign language. We acquire skills only through action, not through thought. Aristotle applies this rule to ethics as well. "Our characters are determined by our choice of what is good and evil" and our actions on those choices, he points out, "not by our opinion about it," however correct that opinion might be (this is the difference, he notes, between the "moral virtues" of character and the "intellectual virtues" of thought itself). In other words, we *are* what we *do* in action, not what we think or feel. This is why, by the way, Aristotle says in the *Poetics* that plot is more important in drama than character—plot comes from actions, and actions, not words or ideas, both shape character and reveal it.

We might deny that this is true of our own character, since we often wish to be judged more by our words or good intentions than by our actions. But we seldom get that wish. For people usually judge us by our actions—professions of love, for instance, and even the feeling of love in our hearts, mean little to our loved ones if we do not demonstrate that love with appropriate actions. And the more regular and consistent our actions are, the more surely they will shape our character. For regular and consistent actions become habits, and habits lock us in a box, in a way of life, whether good or bad.

Aristotle makes quite a point of habits. In fact, he observes that only a "slight modification" separates the Greek words for habit, *ethos*, and moral virtue, *ēthikē*—both of which are linked to the word for character, *ēthos*. "It is a matter of no small importance what sort of habits we form from the earliest age," Aristotle declares, "it makes a vast difference, or rather it makes all the difference in the world." Over two thousand years after Aristotle, the modern psychologist William James echoed Aristotle's observations in his pioneering *Principles of Psychology* when he wrote: "Could the young but realize how soon they will become mere walking bundles of habits, they would give more heed to their conduct. . . . Every smallest stroke of virtue or vice leaves its never so little scar. [We] may not count it, and a kind heaven may not count it; but it is being counted none the less." Aristotle saw it long ago: we *are* our habits.

Choices–actions–habits. This sequence makes us who we are, giving us our *ēthos,* our character, our ethics. We might even say that our character (*ēthos*) comes from our habits (*ethos*) and that is how we become ethical (*ēthikos*). All wise parents try to teach something like this to their children. But, as Aristotle knew, and many parents overlook, you cannot teach by instruction alone the ethical "virtues" of making good choices and acting on them. To be sure, you can define good choices and identify good actions, but children must learn to make those choices and to act on them for themselves. No one can give us our character but ourselves, through our actions.

This fact renders us responsible for our every choice and every action and therefore, Aristotle says, for living the kinds of lives we live and becoming the kinds of people we become. We are largely responsible for our own health, for instance, Aristotle observes, because physical weakness often comes from "lack of exercise," and sickness is often "the result of incontinent living and disobeying [our] doctor's orders." How true. Nor is ignorance an excuse for a bad life or character, Aristotle argues, because at some point we could have chosen not to remain ignorant, just as drunkenness is no excuse for wrongdoing because we chose to get drunk in the first place. "It was at first open to the unjust and licentious person not to become such," Aristotle points out, but by choosing unjust and licentious actions such persons "have become what they are." For this reason, he concludes with a memorable image, the shaping of life and character is like throwing a stone: "When one has once let go of a stone, it is too late to get it back—but the agent was responsible for throwing it." If we throw the stone of our lives well, we will become good human beings. If not, we will become bad, or deficient, human beings and live bad lives. Either way, we are responsible for throwing it, and for where it goes, and for becoming who we are, in our choices, our actions, our habits, our character.

This all makes Aristotle sound rather like a modern existentialist—particularly Jean-Paul Sartre, who insisted that we bear absolute responsibility for every choice we make (see Chapter 9). But Aristotle was no existentialist. He believed too firmly in a fixed human nature for that. And yet, like the existentialists, Aristotle believed that, because to be human means to make choices, we bear responsibility for virtually every choice we make, even if we don't think we do. That was a good idea, then and now, Aristotelian or existentialist.

And here at last we reach the threshold of Aristotle's most invaluable down-to-earth advice on just how to exercise that responsibility and choose actions that will make us good human beings, give us the good life, and bring us the highest happiness. It is perhaps the best practical advice on these timeless subjects that anyone has ever given.

ARISTOTLE CONJURES UP this advice, as we would expect, not from abstractions or ideals but from the ordinary, commonplace particulars of human life, "for in matters relating to feelings and actions theories are less reliable than facts." And the facts he builds on here are what he takes to be the many everyday good things that we all need in life in order to live well. He loosely lumps these "goods" into three categories: "(a) external, (b) of the soul, (c) of the body." In his *Rhetoric* he ticks off a tidy list of what he thinks these particular good things are: "good birth, plenty of friends, good friends, wealth, good children, plenty of children, a happy old age, also such bodily excellences as health, beauty, strength, large stature, athletic powers, together with fame, honour, good luck, and virtue." Besides these "goods," he confidently concludes, "there are no others to have." And, lest we miss the mundane truth of the matter, he adds a couple of blunt illustrations in the *Ethics*: "A man is scarcely happy if he is ugly to look at" or "if he has children or friends who are quite worthless." That is plain-spoken enough. Aristotle then wraps up with another confident assurance: "Our definition seems to include all the required constituents of happiness . . . because what we have described is virtually a kind of good life or prosperity."

We smile when we read this. And we might question Aristotle's glib generalizations—Socrates would surely object, being himself a reputedly ugly man with a notoriously shrewish wife, who nonetheless claimed to be happy always, although Aristotle might retort that to feel this way Socrates had to idealize pure perfection outside this world. But Aristotle was simply using common sense again to describe human nature and human life as he found them, not as he or anyone else might imagine them. The good life, he says, is made up of all the good things of life that everyone knows. When we have all of the good things we need as human beings in body, soul, and external circumstances, we have a good life and are happy. When we don't have those things, we don't have a good life and not happy. Who, besides an inveterate idealist—or an ascetic like Simeon Stylites, who lived on top of a pole for thirty years, so vividly described by Edward Gibbon in *The Decline and Fall of the Roman Empire*—can argue with that?

But now comes the hard part. And the best part. What are the choices we should make to get these good things in life? It is not easy, Aristotle warns. Knowing that something is good or bad for us does not guarantee that we will make the right choices about it—remember, he says, ethics requires good actions, not just good thoughts. We can, for instance, Aristotle notes on a favorite theme, even cause our own ill-health and ugliness by lazily neglecting "exercise and care for appearance" even when we know better. Fundamentally, he explains, the question comes down to distinguishing between ephemeral *wants* and genuine human *needs*. Satisfying needs fulfills our nature and makes us truly happy, but satisfying wants gives us only transitory, if sometimes necessary, gratifications that can actually lead us away from true happiness.

To demonstrate this crucial, and very useful, distinction between wants and needs, Aristotle considers pleasure and amusement. Many people assume that pleasure brings happiness, he explains, since "pleasure is very closely bound up with human nature" and does have "a powerful influence upon virtue and the happy life." In fact, Aristotle remarks—contrary to those who judge pleasure to be a bad thing—a life without pleasure could not be good. For "pleasure perfects the activities" that we choose in life, "and so it perfects life," rather "like the bloom that graces the flower of youth." "Pleasure" and "life" are so "closely connected," he adds, that they "do not admit of separation." In this sense, pleasure is a *need*. Pleasure, however, is not in itself the same thing as happiness. "Pleasant amusements" prove it.

"Amusement," Aristotle explains, "is a form of relaxation," and "people need relaxation because they cannot exert themselves continuously." As he says in the *Politics*, the pleasures of amusement are rather like "taking a nap or having a drink" and "a kind of cure for the ills we suffer in working hard." But even though we may need pleasures of amusement as a reprieve from work, Aristotle cautions, "it would be paradoxical if the end were amusement" and "if we toiled and suffered all our lives long to amuse ourselves." For that would make the pleasures of passive "relaxation"—like watching television today—the very purpose of life, and it would turn "the good life" into nothing but rest. No one but an inveterate sloth (like the famous fictional lout Oblomov in Ivan Goncharov's novel of that title) would want this.

Therefore, Aristotle explains, although pleasure contributes to happiness, and we need some pleasant amusements as a kind of rest, we should beware of wanting more of these pleasant amusements than we need. For when we yield to that excessive want, the natural and salutary pleasure of relaxation fades into lethargy and boredom—as we all know from having too much diversion, or entertainment, or rest. There is no happiness there. So, Aristotle goes on, in order to live the good life, we must choose actions that best fulfill our genuine needs and that do not just indulge our transitory wants.

This brings us to Aristotle's straightforward advice for choosing those actions. It is Aristotle's most familiar, thought-provoking, and practical—if often misunderstood—advice on how to live the good life. That advice centers on Aristotle's so-called Golden Mean.

Actually, the term Golden Mean is not Aristotle's. And the cliché that it has become for "moderation in all things" even skews Aristotle's point. Aristotle's idea is this: we need the right amount of all the good things in life. When we ask what the right amount is, Aristotle answers with what sounds like a truism but turns out to be a subtle notion and the most useful, and not at all simplistic, single rule you'll ever find for living the good life. The right amount, he says, is neither too much nor too little of anything. Too much or too little of anything is the wrong amount and can never be good for us and make us happy. For excellence and virtue in anything, he explains, "are destroyed by excess and deficiency and preserved by the mean." That is how Aristotle gets to what tradition has labeled the Golden Mean (anticipated by Plato at the end of the *Republic,* where he extols the moral mean between extremes). Choosing the "mean" (*meson)* between too much and too little of anything comes down to choosing the right amount—but that is not the same as a moderate amount. Look at some of Aristotle's examples:

> Both excessive and insufficient exercise destroy one's strength, and both eating and drinking too much or too little destroy health, whereas the right quantity produces, increases and preserves it. . . . The man who shuns and fears everything and stands up to nothing becomes a coward; the man who is afraid of nothing at all, but marches up to every danger, becomes foolhardy. Similarly, the man who indulges in every pleasure and refrains from none becomes licentious; but if a man behaves like a boor and turns his back on every pleasure, he is a case of insensibility.

Aristotle proceeds to name a host of specific virtues, or excellent choices, that hit the mean, or the right amount, between the extremes of too much and too little in a variety of pursuits. "Temperance" (or "moderation") is the specific virtue that comes between "licentiousness" and "insensibility"; "courage" comes between "cowardice" and "recklessness"; "magnificence" comes between "vulgarity" and "pettiness"; "magnanimity" (self-esteem) comes between "vanity" and "pusillanimity"; "patience" comes between "irascibility" and "lethargy"; "wit" comes between "buffoonery" and "boorishness"; "friendliness" comes between "obsequiousness" and "cantankerousness"; and so on. All of these virtues, or excellent choices, help give us a good character, a good life, and the best happiness.

Once again, this may seem obvious and simplistic. But make no mistake. Striking the excellence or virtue of the mean between too much and too little of anything is not obvious or simple. For this does not come down to merely choosing a moderate, or relatively small, amount of all things. The right amount between too much and too little might be a lot. And so finding that right amount is tricky.

It is tricky for two reasons. In the first place, if the right amount of anything is the amount that satisfies our genuine human needs, then we had better know what those human needs are. In other words, we have to understand human nature in general. That is no small task. Books on the subject could fill a library. But Aristotle gives a rough sketch of human nature as he sees it with his idea of "activity of the soul," or making choices, and his list of the good things in life that we need. There is more to Aristotle's view of human nature than that, but for the sake of argument let us take this sketch to cover the essentials.

Now we approach the second reason why it is so tricky choosing the right amount of anything we need to reach virtue or excellence. For Aristotle's sketch of human nature does not show us how to choose the right amount of any of the good things we need. Even when Aristotle names the virtues that mark the right amount between too much and too little of these things, we still don't know which particular actions will give us that right amount. For instance, knowing that temperance is the virtue of self-restraint that falls as the mean between licentiousness and insensibility does not tell us which actions are temperate—is it temperate to have one glass of wine with dinner, or one candy bar in the afternoon, or is having three, or five, or ten? To answer such a question, we have to know more than the needs of human nature and that we should choose the right amount between too much and too little of them. Beyond this we have to recognize that the right amount or the mean, or virtue of anything, does not always fall straight down the middle in everything, like a fixed line that is the same for everyone, as the middling notion of "moderation in all things" implies. Aristotle's idea of the right amount is subtler than that.

Here is the second reason why it is so difficult to choose the right amount of anything: besides the needs of human nature in general that all people share, each individual has his or her own portion of those needs. Therefore, the right amount between too much and too little of anything differs from person to person. The right amount of food and exercise for an athlete, for example, will be greater than for a sedentary intellectual, just as the right amount of mental activity for an intellectual will be greater than for an athlete; and the right amount of playing music for a talented musician will be greater than for a politician, just as the right amount of political activity for a politician will be greater than for a musician. "Every knowledgeable person avoids excess and deficiency" and "looks for the mean and chooses it," Aristotle remarks. However, he adds, this is "not the mean of the thing, but the mean relative to us."

Not the mean of the thing, but the mean relative to us. This is Aristotle's final key to the good life. It opens the door to the *right amount* between too much and too little of anything that each of us truly needs. To use this key we must grasp at once the needs of human nature and the needs of our own individual natures, and then find the right amount for us. Aristotle knows well that this can be very difficult because there are many nuances or degrees between too much and too little of everything we need as both human beings and as individuals. And not only that. Compounding the difficulty, our needs change as we age, and with those changes the right amount for us changes too. As Aristotle notes at the end of the *Politics*, "What is possible and what is appropriate" in life are "different for different ages," and therefore "the happy man" differs over time. For these reasons, Aristotle cautions, throughout our lives "failure is possible in many ways" as we make choices among many options, "but success is only one." We reach this success only when we hit the mark of *virtue* and get the *right amount* of what we need with any choice we make.

Choose the right amount of everything you need. That is Aristotle's plain practical advice for how to live the good life and reach the highest happiness. Simple sounding, but not simple to do. None of us can make excellent choices in life and hit the mark of virtue in everything for ourselves all the time. We can only try. In a bit of philosophical whimsy, Aristotle does offer a portrait of what a person would be like if he or she could do it and become a completely excellent human being. Such a person, Aristotle says, would have "greatness of soul" (*megalopsychia*), or great capacities and correspondingly great needs to satisfy—that is, the "great-souled" person "claims much and deserves much." And this person would live out those capacities and satisfy those needs with "greatness in each of the virtues," unlike the "small-souled" (*micropsychē*), or "pusillanimous," person who lives a small life, and even claims less than he deserves. The great-souled person is therefore an "extreme as regards the greatness of his claims," but he (Aristotle assumes the masculine) embodies the "mean, because he estimates himself at his true worth." For him the *mean* is a lot. Aristotle's portrait, or caricature, of this great-souled, or "magnanimous," person can be amusing—"his gait is measured, his voice deep, and his speech unhurried." But chuckle as we might, this portrait illustrates how our needs vary according to our individual natures, and how the more fully we satisfy those needs the more truly fulfilled and happier we become.

Aristotle's caricature also suggests how with this fulfillment and happiness comes another quality of character that belongs to "the good life." This is an honest "self-love." "It is right for the good man to be self-loving," Aristotle explains, since "what makes existence desirable is the consciousness of one's own goodness." This is not self-righteousness or arrogance. That would be too much self-love. It is rather the right amount of self-love, which is a kind of healthy self-respect. One admirable sign of this self-respect, which everyone should surely emulate, is how the great-souled person would not get ruffled by criticism or harbor resentment, "because it is beneath a 'great-souled' man to remember things against people, especially wrongs." A self-love that holds no grudges is a virtue for sure (Friedrich Nietzsche spun a whole moral philosophy out of this virtue—see Chapter 8).

We can laugh at Aristotle's great-souled man. But we probably come close to his benign self-love when we feel good about ourselves and our lives. The caricature is worth remembering for this alone.

Leaving the great-souled person, Aristotle goes on to say, with a philosopher's bias, that the highest happiness anyone can attain lies in intellectual contemplation. But we shouldn't let this bias disappoint us. For Aristotle winds up his advice on living the good life very much in the everyday world of everybody, where he started. This is where we make our choices of how to live from day to day, and, Aristotle now points out, where we make these choices among other people. This last detail is vital to Aristotle. There is no living like a monk in a cave for him. He believes the good life is a social and political life.

Although "happiness . . . is found to be something perfect and self-sufficient," Aristotle explains, "by self-sufficient I mean not what is sufficient for oneself alone living a solitary life, but something that includes parents, wife and children, friends and fellow citizens in general." For "man is by nature a social being," he declares, and "naturally constituted to live in company." Some people will have greater social needs than others, according to their individual natures, but no human being can even survive childhood without other people. And we need other people for more than mere survival. We need them, Aristotle asserts, "to fulfill our own lives," since we learn to make good choices and we gain much of our happiness through our relations with other people. Aristotle takes friendship as a prime example, and he devotes two of the ten books of the *Ethics* to the subject.

"The happy man needs friends," Aristotle says, because friendship is "not only a necessary thing but a splendid one." "A friend," he elaborates, is actually "another self" who reflects our own character and helps to shape it. At best, therefore, people "become better . . . by exercising their friendship and improving each other; for the traits that they admire in each other get transferred to themselves." By the same token, "the friendship of worthless people has a bad effect." In short, we become like our friends, for the better and the worse. For this reason, choosing the right friends is among the most important choices we make in our lives. Every parent acts on this when steering children clear of the "bad influence" of bad friends. And we all follow it for ourselves when we choose friends who are good for us.

It is also through friendship, Aristotle continues, that good human beings create a good society. For "good men and friends are the same," and "friendship also seems to be the bond that holds communities together." With this idea, Aristotle carries the good life from the shaping of individual character through the uses of friendship to the making of the good society and the good state. And that is where he ends the *Ethics*—by pointing to politics.

"Assuming that we have given (in outline) a sufficient account of happiness and the several virtues, and also of friendship and pleasure," he summarizes, we must now consider "the best system of laws and customs" to make the good life possible for everyone. This is "the art of politics," he says—creating "laws and customs" to help people make good choices and to live the good life. For, as he had said earlier in the book, ethics deals with "what is good in the case of an individual" and politics deals with "the good for man . . . in the case of a people or a state." Hence, the sequel to Aristotle's *Ethics* is his *Politics*.

Toward the end of the *Politics,* Aristotle returns to the main theme of the *Ethics* with thoughts on how education can help us fulfill our natures as human beings and individuals through what he calls "civilized pursuits." We can engage in these pursuits—particularly the arts—when we are free from work and other cares and able to live "the blessed life" of "leisure." But take note: Aristotle does not think of leisure as an empty time to be filled with "amusement" or recreation or rest. It is a time for cultivating our highest human qualities. If this sounds *aristocratic*, it is—in the specific sense that Aristotle believes leisure gives us the freedom to fulfill our natures at our *best*, and therefore to become good human beings at their *best*.

Aristotle looked at human life very *pragmatically*—his word. He wanted to understand how human nature works in practice rather than how it might work in theory, or how it should work according to some moral ideal. And he discovered, very pragmatically, that people want to be happy and that they pursue happiness through the most distinctive human function of making choices in life. He concluded that making good choices gives us the good life and the highest happiness. The *Ethics* is as simple, and as complicated, as that.

Filling in the blanks, we might string together Aristotle's entire argument and advice like this. Begin with the notion that our ends are good simply because we seek them. Add the commonsense observation that because the one end, or good, that everyone seeks is happiness, this must be the highest practical good in human life. Go on to the equally commonsense idea that happiness comes from living a good life. Add the reasonable proposition that the good life consists in having the many good things we genuinely need as human beings—which is not the same as having what we want. Go on from there to the idea that we get these good things by making excellent choices in life. Then put in the principle that we make excellent choices to get the good things we need in life when we choose the right amount of them—not too much or too little—since the right amount is excellence or virtue. Grasp that in order to choose the right amount of the good things in life, we must understand both human nature in general and our own natures in particular. Include the fact that we make our choices in a world of other human beings. Now, at last, we see how choosing the right amount of what we genuinely need in life fulfills us and makes us good, excellent, virtuous human beings and gives us the best kind of happiness.

That, in a nutshell, is Aristotle's ethics of the good life. And after you think it through, and try it out, you will likely decide, if you can live up to it, that it is indeed the best advice on living the good life that you have ever read.

On Living the Good Life

1. Common sense tells us that all human beings want to be happy.

2. True happiness comes from having the things we genuinely need.

3. We must know the difference between genuine needs and mere wants.

4. The things we genuinely need—from physical health and material security to friendship and pleasure—fulfill us as both human beings and individuals.

5. The things we merely want satisfy only ephemeral desires.

6. We need pleasure because it enhances everything we do in life, but we might want more of it than we need.

7. Amusement gives us a kind of pleasure that is like rest from toil, but it cannot be the purpose of life any more than rest can.

8. Human beings are human because we make rational choices.

9. We are responsible for all of our choices if we could have chosen otherwise.

10. We are responsible for our character because we create it with every choice we make.

11. Making choices in life requires acting on those choices.

12. To fulfill ourselves as both human beings and individuals we must choose the right amount of everything we need.

13. To find the right amount of anything for us, we must know the genuine needs of human nature and our own genuine needs as individuals.

14. We choose the right amount of the things we need when we choose the mean between extremes, or not too much or too little of any of anything.

15. The right amount, or the mean, is not "moderation in all things," because the right amount differs from person to person, and it can be a lot.

16. When we choose the right amount of everything we need as human beings and as individuals, and then act wisely on those choices, we become good human beings.

17. A good human being is one who fulfills human nature at its best.

18. A good human being will live the good life and be happy.

19. The meaning of life is to choose the right amount of everything we need to be good human beings and to live the good life.

5

The Moral Landscape of Hell

Dante Alighieri: *The Divine Comedy: The Inferno*

We've reached the place I told you to expect,
where you will see the miserable ones
who have lost the good of intellect.
Dante

Dante Alighieri (1265–1321) left a lasting literary legacy to Italian culture and gave the world a masterpiece that should live forever. Born to a commercial family in Florence, Italy, Dante opened his literary career with a series of youthful love poems, *La vita nuova* (c. 1293), inspired by a woman named Beatrice, whom he first saw when he was nine years old and whom he idealized and adored until he died. Along the way, after becoming embroiled in Florentine politics and losing to opponents among the dominant faction of the Guelph party, he was exiled in 1302 for the rest of his life. But he used his exile well, for in those years he wrote almost everything that brought him his enduring fame. In *De vulgari eloquentia* (c. 1304–05) he freed the Italian vernacular from Latin and established the Italian language we know today. In *Il convivio* (c. 1304–07) he philosophized on a variety of moral and political themes. And in public letters, *Epistolae* (1310–13), and the treatise *De Monarchia* (n.d.), he praised God for giving order to the world through the authority of the church and monarchs. But Dante surpassed himself in the *Commedia* (c. 1308–21), written in vernacular Italian and known in English as *The Divine Comedy* (a title assigned to it in 1555). He called this great work a "comedy" not because it is funny, but because it has a happy ending, which according to tradition made it comic rather than tragic.

The Divine Comedy starts off grimly enough as a journey through hell in the *Inferno*, but it then goes on to a benign *Purgatory,* and it ends up happily in a blessed *Paradise*, thanks to the spiritual beauty, perfection, and guidance of the idealized Beatrice. Happy endings aside, the *Inferno* contains Dante's most provocative and profound ideas on human nature, good, and evil as it leads us down through a moral landscape of sins and punishments. Dante lays out this moral landscape quite surprisingly, judging murder, for example, to be less evil than lying, and condemning treachery as the worst sin of all. And once you see why he arranges hell as he does, you find that the *Inferno* is one of the most revealing books you will ever read on the nature of good and evil, and on the makings of a good society.

WHAT DO YOU DO for a mid-life crisis? Take a trip? That is what Dante did. At least in his imagination. Dante's "mid-life crisis" was not the kind that has become a cliché in our times for amorphous middle-aged discontents and yearnings. Driven from Florence by political enemies, and moving from one town to another while writing about morals, politics, and the Italian language, Dante had turned forty and was in a troubled and reflective frame of mind. He also had some scores to settle with those Florentine enemies. And he had a vision of good and evil to present to the world. So he went on his imaginative journey in *The Divine Comedy*. It is the world's most extraordinary travel book. For it records nothing less than an excursion through hell and up to heaven—in the *Inferno, Purgatory,* and *Paradise.*

The journey opened Dante's eyes to many things. And it can open our eyes to many things, too. Especially in Dante's travelogue through hell, the *Inferno.* For the *Inferno* contains much more than depictions of the damned and their punishments. It has plenty of these, to be sure, as it should. If hell exists, as in the Christian tradition, it exists to punish, and to deter us from acts that justify punishment. Dante's hell clearly belongs to that tradition. Sinners burn here, or they are torn apart, or they wallow in mire, or they are chased about by ravenous beasts, or they change forms again and again, or they freeze in ice, and so on. The punishments in Dante's hell are more various than most of us could imagine. And it is the variety and vividness of Dante's images of punishments that stick in most people's minds.

But when you travel through Dante's hell, besides an abundance of sinners suffering their grisly punishments you also find a moral landscape carefully laid out according to Dante's vision of good and evil. Dante lays out this landscape metaphorically, with sins descending from the least to the worst as they banish goodness and blight the human world. We might call this Dante's *moral psychology of good and evil.* And with it comes Dante's *moral psychology of punishment.* That is to say, through the first Dante shows how every sin corrupts the sinner and harms society, and through the second he shows how each sin then brings its own distinct punishment. On both themes Dante can surprise, and convert, us.

In the first place, Dante ranks many evils in a way that most of us probably would not—at least not before reading the *Inferno.* Why, we will ask, does Dante judge erotic lust to be the least of sins and treason to be the worst, with murder somewhere in the middle? This is not our common practice. But the moral psychology of good and evil in Dante's ranking makes sense of it all, and can change our way of thinking about both good and evil.

A second reason that Dante's hell can surprise us is that it is not very religious. And it is hardly Christian at all. For it is not the Christian God who casts Dante's sinners into hell and assigns them their penalties. This God does not even appear, although Dante indicates in Canto III that this God did create hell. Dante has sinners sent to their sorrowful fates by the long-tailed creature Minos, who hears their confessions and puts them where their sins belong. This idea owes more to Greek philosophy than to Christianity. Socrates and Plato had warned against wrongdoing because it impairs the soul. And Aristotle had spelled out how we shape our own characters with our every action. Hell meant nothing to these Greeks, of course. They could believe in the soul and an afterlife in Hades, but they were primarily humanists convinced that we ruin ourselves in this world by living bad lives (see Chapters 3 and 4).

Dante's hell works pretty much like that. Its writhing residents—historical and literary figures, as well as Dante's political foes—have *become evil* by *doing evil*, and that hurts them just as it hurts their victims. Dante does depart from the Greek philosophers and from humanistic ethics in general by making the wicked pay for their sins in the next world, and by placing some souls in hell for not being Christian. He also implies, of course, that the whole place reflects God's moral scheme. But the *Inferno* reads best—or at any rate most thought-provokingly and usefully—as a humanistic vision of the moral life. For it not only shows us how Dante viewed good and evil in his world, it also points to how we might well view them in ours.

With this in mind, we could read the inscription above the entrance to Dante's hell with a note of irony. "Abandon all hope, you who enter here," it says forebodingly. But Dante did not follow that command, and eventually he got out and was much the better for his trip. Literary travelers should do the same. Journeying down, down, down into this hell, we see a moral landscape that belongs very much to the moral and psychological world we inhabit today. And seeing this world through Dante's eyes can awaken us to consequences of both good and evil that we had not seen so clearly before. And this can make us much the better for the trip.

Dante prepares us for the rough road ahead by first metaphorically describing his mid-life crisis. "Midway in this journey of our life," he writes, "I found myself in a dark wood" where the "way was lost." Perhaps he had strayed into sin or into confusion about the purpose of his own life at middle age (although few people lived beyond fifty years in those days). In any case, he was lost. He tries getting out of the woods by climbing a mountain, but encounters three wild beasts in succession—a leopard, a lion, and a wolf, which likely symbolize moral weaknesses. Then he meets the Latin epic poet Virgil, who had portrayed the founding of Rome by former Trojans in the *Aeneid*, and whom Dante took as his poetic mentor. Virgil tells him that to avoid the beasts he must take another route. It won't be pretty, Virgil says, because it will go "through an eternal place" full of "souls in pain." But it will deliver him to where everything is bright and beneficent. Virgil offers to lead the way, and off they go, the lost and troubled Dante and his Roman guide on a trip through hell.

After some other preliminaries, they approach the entrance gate, where Virgil pauses to offer Dante a bit of information about the sorry sights he will see on the other side. There, Virgil explains, dwell the souls of those who had "lost the good of intellect" in life, and so they sinned, and now they are miserable. The good of intellect (*il ben de l'intelletto*) is not really a religious idea, whatever religious associations it might have. Scholars sometimes interpret it to mean the knowledge of God or of Divine Truth. But it comes from Aristotle. And although Dante might have got his Aristotle through Thomas Aquinas, Aristotle himself equated intellect with the rational mind, or soul, and regarded it as a defining feature of human nature. (Dorothy Sayers notes that in the *Convivio* Dante himself quotes Aristotle saying "truth is the good of intellect.") Practical-minded thinker that he was, Aristotle would have considered "the good of intellect" to be more or less knowing what is *good for us as human beings* (see Chapter 4). That also fits Dante's hell. It is a nasty place for people who have lost sight of what is good for them, whether that good came from God or secular ethics. And in Dante's hell the two go together.

While the good of intellect is an Aristotelian idea, it need hardly be said that Dante's hell owes other ideas and images to traditional Christianity. That is only too obvious. But it may astonish many readers to learn that it owes so few (*Purgatory* and *Paradise* owe more). Christianity shows up in the *Inferno* most conspicuously in the overall image of hell itself and in three types of "sinners" who failed to embrace Christianity, or who abandoned its truths.

The first of these types appears at the Vestibule of hell, where they dart about chased by bees, unable either to enter hell or to go to heaven because in life they had chosen neither God's way nor Satan's, neither good nor evil. Belonging nowhere, they envy even those who have a place in hell. Dante clearly despises such characters for being cowards and lacking the will either to choose faith or to reject it, and for trying to live without commitment to anything. He has Virgil command: "Let us not speak of them—look and pass by."

The second group lives in Limbo, which is the First Circle of the nine Circles that form Dante's hell. The souls in Limbo have not actually sinned. They are the virtuous pagans and non-Christians who lived too soon to become Christians and therefore can never be exalted. "Among these I am one," Virgil remarks, and so are the many honorable ancient Greeks, including Homer, Socrates, Plato, and Aristotle, who is identified only as "the master of those who know." Dante clearly admires these people, for they were as good as they could be without Christianity (or without preparing for it, like the Hebrew prophets, whom Dante lets go to heaven for believing in the right God), so they deserve no pain. But Dante hears among them "the sound of sighing."

The last of those whose moral failings directly involved Christianity are the heretics. We do not get to them until much later, down in the Sixth Circle. More sinful than those in the Vestibule who simply declined to choose between belief and disbelief, or those in Limbo who never knew Christian belief at all, the heretics rejected true Christianity and arrogantly followed their own spiritual paths, leading others into error with them. Now they burn inside heavy sepulchers, going nowhere.

And that is it. Those are the sins against Christianity itself in the *Inferno*. Dante also includes blasphemy as a sin against God, but he does not make it a particularly Christian sin, and he links it with a curious pair of secular evils, sodomy and usury, as we will see. Dante gives Christianity a relatively minor role in the *Inferno* because religion is not really his subject. His subject is largely the secular world, for that is where good and evil have human consequences, making life better or worse for human beings. And it is those consequences that Dante cares most about. He makes this clear in how he organizes the moral landscape of his hell. He even has Virgil pause in Canto XI to describe and explain this landscape in a kind of general guidebook to hell.

As Virgil explains there, this landscape consists of the Vestibule and nine descending Circles. Besides the First Circle of Limbo and the Sixth Circle of the heretics, the other seven Circles take us down through three general types of sins (which Virgil says loosely reflect Aristotle's *Ethics*). Circles Two through Five contain the first type: sins of incontinence (*incontenenza*), or self-indulgence and lack of self-control. Circle Seven holds the second type: sins of force (*forza*), or violence and destructiveness. And Circles Eight and Nine brim with sinners of the third type: those guilty of fraud (*frode*) or deception. Each of these three types contains many particular sins, and these sins worsen as they go down.

For they pass from sins of the flesh that affect mainly ourselves, to acts of violence that destroy things and values, to calculated deceptions that subvert the human world. And with this descent, we see the sinners themselves sinking into deeper corruptions of character and the soul.

That is Virgil's sketch of Dante's moral landscape, outlining its moral psychology of good and evil and punishment. By the time we reach the bottom of this vertiginous hell, we see how well Dante does indeed know good, evil, and human nature—and how much we can learn from him about them all.

Now we can begin the journey in earnest. After leaving those good pagans sighing in Limbo, we meet Dante's first type of true sinners, who fill Circles Two through Five. Here languish those who committed sins of the flesh or incontinence and self-indulgence. These are all sins of weakness, not malevolence, arising from a failure to control appetites rather than from evil intentions; most of the traditional Seven Deadly Sins are here. That Dante chooses to put all of these sinners into the upper Circles of hell, and that he gives them only four of the thirty-four Cantos of the *Inferno* (although four of the nine Circles of hell) tells you quite a bit about his moral priorities. As Dante has Virgil point out, "incontinence offends God less" than the "malice" and "mad brutishness" that lie below.

The first batch of these incontinent sinners are the lustful. Occupying Circle Two, they drift about in ceaseless winds, like the passions that had buffeted them in life. But of all the sins in hell, this one appears to offend Dante the least. He even lets his heart go out to one of these sinners (although some scholars question his emotions, just as they debate the import of almost everything else in the *Inferno*). She is Francesca da Rimini. And hers is perhaps the most famous scene in the entire *Inferno*. Tearfully she tells Dante her story. One day she and Paolo, her husband's brother, had sat together reading the story of the star-crossed lovers Lancelot and Guinevere. "More than once that reading made our eyes meet," she says, and "when we read how the longed-for smile was kissed by so renowned a lover," Paolo "trembling all over, kissed me on my mouth." Discovered in this act of passion by Francesca's jealous husband, they had no defense, and the husband killed them both.

Dante's tender retelling of this story, and his sympathy for Francesca and other victims of their own lustful passions, may puzzle some readers. But it gives us the first clear clue to Dante's moral vision. No thin-lipped Puritan, no fire-and-brimstone-slinging Christian moralist, Dante judges lust mildly because, we might conclude, he finds it to be a warmly human passion, uniting lovers as it does, and the most socially benign of sins. Dante lets Francesca feel this passion as love, *amor,* the emotion she invokes again and again. "Love," she says, "which absolves no one beloved from loving, seized me so strongly" that "love brought us to one death" and "as you see, it has not left me yet." "For pity," Dante says, "I swooned and down I fell as a dead body falls." To no other sin in hell does Dante show quite such compassion—although he displays an even warmer personal affection for the Italian Sodomites in Circle Seven, whom he judges seriously sinful, but whom he knew personally and liked as individuals. The journey ahead will show why: Dante evidently prizes human bonds above everything else.

Dante's heart hardens as he goes down in hell, although he weeps many times, occasionally prompting Virgil to chastise him for misplaced sympathy. That is how Dante's moral psychology of good and evil descends: from the warm winds of human passion near the top of hell to the ice pack of bitter treason at the bottom, the worsening sins have worsening effects on both sinners and their victims, as well as on the tourist Dante. It is an image to remember, although we can fully understand it only when we complete the journey.

Dante vividly illustrates this image as he descends on down through the other sins of incontinence and self-indulgence. Each is nastier than the one before it, as they grow more selfish and antisocial. The Gluttons in the Third Circle grovel in putrid mire under torrential rain, torn by the teeth of the three-headed hound Cerberus. As in life, where they had succumbed to selfish and ravenous hunger, so do they here. In Circle Four come the Hoarders and Squanderers, the Covetous and the Avaricious. Craving things, or clinging to them, or recklessly expending them, these sinners valued only their own insatiable desires for possessing and spending. And now they perpetually shove huge rocks against each other, shouting "Why hold so tight?" "Why cast away?" They are a distasteful crew who clouded "the fair world," as anybody does by being so driven by materialistic desires to hoard or spend, covet or acquire, that he or she cannot enjoy life, much less serve the lives of others. Virgil prods Dante to leave them for "more piteous woes."

Those next woes, in Circle Five, belong to the Angry and Sullen—those who either yielded openly to anger or let it seethe resentfully within them, remaining "sullen in the sweet air." The openly angry savagely fight each other with fists and teeth, head and heels. The sullenly resentful, steeped in mud, gurgle their rage. Both the Angry and the Sullen take self-indulgence beyond the appetites of physical lust and gluttony and the selfishness of hoarding and squandering, coveting and avarice. Self-indulgence has now become visibly mean, divisive, and antisocial, as self-indulgence tends to do. And Dante finds it infecting him when he gets angry at one of these sinners and wants to lash out at him. We've all seen this happen to ourselves when we indulge our own anger only to find that we have aroused it in others through no fault of theirs.

Here again, this is how Dante's moral psychology of evil works. Egregious evils can begin in the seemingly innocent indulgence of an appetite, for self-indulgence can grow increasingly coarse and even become vicious. Most of us have witnessed this in people who come to live for their selfish appetites alone—addicts prove this inexorably. In time such people can become indifferent to everyone else, and even cruel, and they can infect those around them with the same vices. This is why, while Dante views self-indulgence as a relatively minor sin in itself, he sees its potential to descend into inhumanity.

Now, departing from those who, having lost "the good of intellect," had succumbed to incontinence and self-indulgence, Dante takes us into Lower Hell. Here we first encounter those arrogant heretics mentioned earlier, who burn within sepulchers in the City of Dis (Circle Six). But, like the self-indulgent above them, the heretics are nothing compared to the sinners below. As Virgil explains in his neat schematic outline of Canto XI , from Circle Seven on down the sinners are now malicious. They not only indulged themselves, they did harm to others to serve themselves. Their sins and the consequences of these sins occupy only three of the Nine Circles of Dante's hell. But they take up over two-thirds of the *Inferno*. And with every step that we take down through the ranks of these malicious sinners, we learn more of evil and of its effects on sinners, victims, and the human world. And we see the more how Dante's moral psychology of good and evil is true.

IN CIRCLE SEVEN we meet Dante's second general type of sinners, the violent (*violenti*), whom Dante accuses of malevolent "force." They did not roil with rage or resentment in life like the sinners in Circle Five. But they destroyed things, laying waste to everything they came near, rather like wild animals, and Dante has them watched over by creatures of their kind, a bull-headed man, or Minotaur, and centaurs, who are half man, half horse. Sometimes they destroyed things with the force of physical violence. But more often they did it metaphorically by *doing violence* to the very value of things. We probably would not at first think of every act that Dante includes here as doing violence with such destructive consequences as he does. But we come to see that he is not off the mark.

Dante separates these violent sinners into three categories, arrayed on three rings of the Circle: (1) those who did physical violence to others, (2) those who did violence to themselves, and (3) those who did violence to God, or to God's creation, nature. The first of these is the most conventional—murderers and tyrants who used physical violence freely and viciously against other people. Dante has them (including Alexander the Great and Attila the Hun) swim in a river of boiling blood. But he surely condemns them not only for specific acts of murderous force. Besides those acts, he likely blames those villains for destroying the security of civilized life, because physical violence, or the threat of it, unravels our sense of physical well-being. Anyone who has suffered from violence in the streets, or in the privacy of a home, or has even been gripped by the fear of it, knows this unhappy feeling. Fearful of such violence against us, publicly or privately, we cannot live fully civilized and human lives. Political terrorists exploit this fact against their enemies at every opportunity.

Turning from the murderously violent to those who do violence to themselves, Dante divides these self-destructive sinners into two camps: the Suicides and the Profligates. This seems an odd pairing. But it throws a revealing light on some unexpected affinities that touch on our everyday lives more than we might guess.

Suicide and profligacy go together, Dante suggests, because they both cause self-destruction. They just take different forms. Through suicide we destroy ourselves physically—Dante represents the Suicides as trees that cringe in continuous pain and bleed as their limbs and leaves break. Through profligacy we destroy ourselves metaphorically by heedlessly using up our legacies from the past, and all that we have acquired in the material world, and ultimately all that we are in the social world as reputable people—Dante makes the Profligates bushes chased and torn apart by dogs. Even more than the self-indulgent spendthrifts above, the Profligates value nothing that they have—each one "gambles away and wastes his substance"—just as the Suicides do not value themselves. And because of this, they demean the worth of human life and the things that sustain it.

Suicide might not be a sin of self-destruction that tempts most of us very often. But profligacy is. For do we not live amidst a certain profligate devaluation of things today in our commercial and technological society, which encourages waste, and which readily destroys the old to make way for the new? Is ours not actually a rather profligate culture overall, breeding an indifference to the worth of anything that can be easily replaced? Advertising deliberately and constantly nurtures this profligate attitude, and many a parent has seen the poisonous effects on children as a result. We should think of Dante's Profligates when tempted to discard a usable possession just to get a new one because the old is less up-to-date than the new. And we should think of the perils of profligacy as we exploit the earth's natural resources, for if we use these resources up we will have nothing left when they are gone. That would be self-destructive for sure.

Remember the Profligates, too, as we go on to Dante's next sinners of "violence." For these are also metaphorical destroyers. And they are a peculiar lot. Dante lumps them under the heading of those who do violence to God or to nature.

Doing violence to God sounds like a religious sin. And it is, in the form of blasphemy among those who "hold God in disdain." But we might see here more than religious blasphemy, and Dante's examples are less Christian than classical. For Dante implies that blasphemy is the "pride . . . unquenched" that defies all higher things or ideals or values that could stand above one's own interests or claims to truth, whether these higher things amount to a divine being or just secular moral principles. (Although Dante finds "pride" in many sinners, he does not single it out for its own punishment as the discrete sin widely condemned in the Christian tradition.) Dante has those who do violence to God in this way lie naked on their backs in hot sand under a rain of fire, staring into the infinite heavens that they had "disdained." We should picture that rain whenever we tend to think that we know all we need to know, or conclude that there is nothing in the universe beyond human comprehension, recalling Shakespeare's Hamlet telling his dearest friend: "There are more things in heaven and earth, Horatio, than are dreamt of in your philosophy."

From this violence against God and all higher beliefs, ideals, and values, it is not far to violence against God's creation, nature. Dante represents this violence with two other rather oddly matched groups of sinners: those who violate nature by misusing the body, and those who violate nature by loaning money for interest. If the first of these sounds familiar enough, the second sounds very arcane. And the second *is* arcane, on the surface. But metaphorically it makes a lot of sense.

Take the familiar one first. Those who violate the body, Dante says, pervert its natural purposes and therefore demean its value. Dante points to the Sodomites—exhibiting his disapproval of "unnatural" sex, although he shows affection for most of the individuals he recognizes here—and he has them running about aimlessly on the sand. But homosexuality aside, Dante could include here anyone who misuses the body for unnatural purposes, such as employing any drug or cosmetic or medical procedure to alter the body in ways that diminish its natural worth and do it harm. Define it how you will, we can see how violating the body can do a kind of violence to nature.

But how does loaning money for interest do violence to nature? The idea is almost incomprehensible today. In fact, it wasn't altogether clear in Dante's day either. So Dante has Virgil go out of his way to explain it when describing the landscape of hell in Canto XI. But if at first this idea appears arcane and antiquated, its implications turn out to fit our world all too closely.

Virgil says that moneylenders, or usurers, play a peculiarly corrupting role in nature. This is how they do it. God created nature, Virgil explains, and within nature human beings learn the "art" of living. By "art" (*arte*) Virgil means the practical work that we do as we use nature, or "God's bounty," to sustain ourselves (reflecting the traditional meaning of "art"—see Chapter 25). Through both nature and art, or work, therefore, we earn our "bread and prosper." That is God's plan and the *natural* way to live. But, Virgil points out, "the usurer takes another path." Usurers do not rely on nature for sustenance or on the arts of productive work derived from nature. Their way is to loan money for a price. That price is *interest.* The interest that usurers charge allows their money to generate more money all by itself, and this gives money a value and power of its own apart from God's creation, nature, or the human "arts" of work. And ultimately, the independent value and the power of money become superior to both nature and work.

Moralists have, of course, always warned against making material wealth the supreme value in human life—Socrates did it every day among his fellow Athenians, and he based his defense in the *Apology* largely on his commitment to that very principle (see Chapter 3). But Dante does not object to material wealth in itself, any more than did his philosophical mentor, the practical-minded Aristotle (see Chapter 4). Dante rather objects to assigning money a value divorced from productive human labor. And he does this for reasons that should give us pause today.

We cannot nowadays share Dante's medieval hostility to money-lending for interest. Personal finances, the modern economy, and modern nations could hardly survive anymore without lending and borrowing for the price of interest. But we also know that when money becomes our primary value it can indeed debase the worth of everything else, including the realm of nature, the activity of practical work, and even moral character (Karl Marx wrote a diatribe on this theme in "The Power of Money"—see Chapter 15). We hear complaints about this nowadays from dismayed environmentalists who say that greedy developers deem the making of money to be more important than the preservation of nature. We also see evidence of it in the widespread craving for unearned wealth among investors, and much more of it in the pernicious manipulations of corporate scandals. For that matter, doesn't the market economy itself assign an economic "market value" to many things and activities and even to people that often far surpasses the value given to the actual labor and services that any of them provide to society? Just think of the wildly disproportionate incomes of top corporate executives, professional athletes, or entertainers compared to that of everyday working people. And yet, on whom does society most depend for its well-being and future? Not a handful of CEOs or ball players or movie stars. Dante's idea of how the *unnatural* power of money—through "usury" or other economic ingenuities—can eclipse the value of nature and work is not so arcane and antiquated after all. And his treatment of usurers should remind us how easy it is to let the power of money distract us from everything else that we might see: he has the usurers sit on burning sand, their arms thrashing about to lessen the heat, their eyes ever fixed on the empty purses around their necks.

LEAVING THE USURERS sizzling on the sand in Circle Seven for devaluing nature and work through the artificial power of money, Dante now descends from the region of "violence" and "force" to enter the last of the three principal moral divisions of hell. And here the *Inferno* gets really ugly, and revealing. For in Circles Eight and Nine, which together occupy almost half of the entire *Inferno*, Cantos 18–34, Dante places those he judges guilty of the gravest kind of evil. That evil is fraud (*frode*) or, more generally, deception.

Deception cuts deeper than the two other types of sin above—self-indulgence and violence—because it goes beyond mere incontinence or letting destructive animal instincts run free. Deception is selfishly, secretly, and purposefully malevolent. And as they work their self-serving malevolence in secret, deceivers do the greatest harm that people can do to the human world: they deprive it of *trust*. As Virgil explains, "the vice of fraud . . . severs the bond of love" and the "special kind of trust" that human beings must depend upon in all of their relations with each other. For in a world of fraud and deception nothing is what it seems, and anything or anyone can turn against us (spy novels and political thrillers have long played on this fact for tingling intrigue, just as totalitarian regimes have deployed it to control their citizens). This is not a world that any civilized human being would want to live in, or could live in long, as we have all discovered when we have found ourselves deceived, and, above all, betrayed. To live among deception undermines confidence in everything and everyone, and then it makes deception a way of life. That is the consummate corruption of the soul, and the death of humane society. Dante knows what he is talking about, and his cluttered landscape of deceivers is both enlightening and, at the end, quite literally chilling.

Dante puts most of the deceivers in the Eighth Circle (comprising Cantos 18–31). For they preyed upon people's confidence in human interactions and in the appearances of things, weaving their deceptions and fraudulence throughout the social and economic life. Dante identifies ten types of them, whom he places in ten concentric sub-circles forming trenches, or *bolgias*.

In the first of these bolgias, Panderers and Seducers race along whipped by "horned demons." Like the lustful near the top of hell, their sin comes from sexual appetite. But they differ from those who simply succumbed to their own natural lust. They exploited lust and wrapped it in deception. Panderers, or pimps, do this by turning other people's lust to their own gain, whetting sexual appetites, trading in flesh, and reducing human beings to objects of exchange in a sordid sexual marketplace. Deft at selling illicit pleasures, they pocket their profits at the expense of human weakness.

Seducers also deceptively traffic in lust, but they do it to satisfy their own insatiable and yet impersonal desires. Unlike the sweet sinners Paolo and Francesca, who yielded to a personal passion akin to love, seducers feign affection to conceal their cold, calculating, and malevolent hungers, then they indifferently go their way to seduce again, leaving their deceived and dejected lovers behind. Whatever our own sexual mores, we will surely agree that lust alone carries less evil than lust exploited through the deceptions of panderers and seducers.

Dante judges the deceptions of seduction to be close to those of flattery, since both rely on "fancy [or polished] words." And he puts Flatterers in the next bolgia, swimming in excrement. Their punishment fits their crime grotesquely well. By falsely lavishing praise on others to manipulate them for their own purposes, Flatterers debase glowing words into offal. And once you have experienced the deceptions of flattery—which we should not confuse with honest praise, although the English language has let the distinction blur—you never fully trust words of praise again. Recognizing these evils of flattery, Machiavelli later warned rulers in *The Prince* against heeding flatterers because false adulation can bring down a leader as easily as can political enemies. Remembering Dante's Flatterers swimming in excrement should be enough to bring a blush of shame to any of us for bestowing flattery, or for believing it.

Dante next rounds up the Simoniacs in the third bolgia. They share a kind of sin with the "Barraters" in bolgia five, so we can consider them together. The Simoniacs secretly sell ecclesiastical influence, while the Barraters secretly sell political influence—we now call it graft. They both pretend to serve the church or state, but in fact they serve only their own greed, and Dante has the Simoniacs sticking head down in rocks with their feet protruding in flames, while the Barraters writhe in a flow of boiling pitch. But we can be sure it is not their greed alone that bothers Dante. It is how their devious behind-the-scenes deal-making and string-pulling undermine the legitimacy of church and state and therefore dissolve trust in the very institutions that should most hold our allegiance for giving order and security to society. Today we might include here corporations and other powerful institutions that ask us to trust them. And when trust in any of a society's leading institutions dissolves, that society is in big trouble.

Nowadays we take pains to prevent the evil of graft and hidden influence in politics and elsewhere. We worry a lot about, for instance, how "special interests" and campaign contributions can subvert the legitimacy of the democratic political system by granting too much influence to certain people. And we have seen all too often how "insider" deals and crooked business practices can enrich a few, impoverish many, and undo public trust in corporations. Long before modern democracy and capitalism, Dante recognized the evil effects of such illegitimate influences in any institution. And anyone who would misuse his or her own influence, or try to induce others to misuse theirs, is doing just what Dante rightly condemns.

Between these two kinds of influence peddlers, Dante puts the Sorcerers, Soothsayers, and Magicians in bolgia four. Their deceptions lay in claiming to possess esoteric knowledge or powers that could affect nature, foresee the future, or pull rabbits from a hat. And because they dealt in trickery not truth, with their spells and divinations and "magic tricks" or "magical fraud" (*magiche frode*), they confused people's minds and obscured the "good of intellect" while exalting themselves as experts to be revered. Dante despises them on all counts. In hell, he has them walk backwards, their heads twisted around on their bodies, just as they had twisted truth. As he says of one of them who had purportedly predicted future events, "because he aspired to see too far ahead he looks behind and treads a backward path."

Today we do not judge sorcery and its related practices evil. Science has discredited them, although fortune-tellers still ply their trade, and magicians have become entertainers. But we could say that a vice akin to what Dante finds here exists in any claim to esoteric knowledge or unique powers of mind that illegitimately exalts "experts" and intimidates the gullible. For such claims set deceptive standards of truth that lead people astray. Voltaire's fictional Dr. Pangloss was one of these misleading authorities, and Candide was his gullible follower (see Chapter 12). We can see much the same thing now in overweening intellectuals, strident ideologues, self-righteous religious leaders, and charismatic gurus who summon naive followers—often spewing impenetrable jargon—with promises of cryptic insights, infallible certainties, sure-fire salvation, or simply privileged discipleship. These are the sorcerers of modern life.

And now the Hypocrites. They trudge slowly along bolgia six groaning under shiny leaden cloaks, for just as in life they had gleamed with outward displays of virtue while possessing no virtue inside, now, Dante says, "gilded and dazzling on the outside, within they are of lead." Dante knows the psychology of hypocrisy well: false virtue might bring public rewards, but its empty observance of rules hardens the soul. He also knows that all codes of righteousness carry temptations to hypocrisy through rules of behavior that make it easy to *appear* righteous outwardly, whatever we might be inside. Religious institutions often use such rules to keep people in line. But Dante reminds us that true virtue does not display itself in pious appearances. For when people believe that virtue resides in appearances, the pious deceptions of hypocrisy have free rein. Then true virtue withers. Hypocrisy therefore corrupts the very idea of virtue—as many a religious leader and politician has proved. Small wonder Dante casts hypocrites so far down in hell.

Thieves come next, in bolgia seven. It surprises readers today that Dante should put thieves where he does, down here among the frauds and deceivers and well below the murderers. But his reasons reflect his moral psychology. Dante regards murderers as destructive animals. Theirs is a sin of violence, not deception. If they used deception to do murder, the deception will earn them greater blame, as it does for some of the sinners yet to come. Thieves are different. Dante deems them more calculating, and their offense more insidious and deceptively evil, making them more like hypocrites than murderers. Just as hypocrites deceive people by confusing false virtue with true virtue, thieves deceive people by confusing themselves with other people. That might seem a curious description of theft, but follow the logic.

By stealing the property of other people, thieves cloud distinctions between people that personal property legally preserves. In this sense our property partly defines *who we are*. So thieves become *who they are not* by stealing what is ours. In Dante's scheme, this is a form of fraud or deception. As an apt punishment for this confusion of what belongs to one person and what belongs to another, Dante has the Thieves lose their own identities—some are stung by serpents and then crumble into ashes, repeatedly coming to life again, while others are seized by monstrous animals who meld with them until thief and beast become one. This metaphorical notion of personal property may be more Roman or medieval than modern, but we have a suggestive residue of it. After all, in our modern materialistic society many people do feel that they *are* what they *own*. Even short of that, we all feel that when thieves steal our property, they rob us of part of our identity and make it *theirs*—they possess part of who we are; they pretend *to be us*. They also rob us, in a way more fraudulent than violent, of the privacy and security of our personal lives, which we need in order to be wholly ourselves, as any victim of theft or of other invasions of privacy well knows. Thieves therefore steal more than *things*. They steal a measure of our trust that our lives are our own. Peculiar as it as first seems, Dante's psychology of evil here rings true again.

While thieves rob people of their personal security and identities, the sinners in the next bolgia deprive people of their good character. They do this by leading others to become deceivers. Dante enfolds these Counsellors to Fraud (Dorothy Sayers' label) in flames that conceal their deceptive natures, betokening how they had enfolded good men in acts of fraud. The most notable of these villains is none other than the crafty Ulysses of ancient Greece. For tradition has it that he had conceived the "stratagem of the horse" that had brought the defeat of ancient Troy by the Greeks—followed by the flight of the surviving Trojans to Italy, led by Aeneas, as recorded by Virgil in the *Aeneid*, where they became "the noble seed of Rome." A proud Italian like his mentor, Virgil, Dante views the Trojan Horse as a vile deception. But Dante puts Ulysses down here in hell not because Ulysses had deceived the Trojans on his own. Ulysses is here because he had persuaded other Greeks—including, presumably, the young villain Sinon, whom we meet later—to help him deceive them, and because he had committed similar, if less historic, acts of corruptive persuasion.

Dante concludes his case against Ulysses as a facile corrupter by having him tell the story of his last voyage. Many critics consider this among the most eloquent sections of the *Inferno*, and all critics speculate on its meaning. Here Dante has Ulysses admit that no feelings for his family or no duties at home "could overcome the fervor that was mine to gain experience of the world and learn about man's vices, and his worth . . . and to pursue virtue and knowledge." Charged with this wanderlust, Ulysses boasts that after a "brief speech" to his followers, "I had my companions so ardent for the journey I could hardly have held them back." So they had set off on their voyage, which had ended when "the sea closed over us" in a storm. Ulysses' words are so fine and life-affirming they could suggest that Dante identified himself with Ulysses, as some critics contend (and Lord Tennyson took Dante's words as inspiration for his renowned poem "Ulysses"). But closer to the truth is probably Robert Hollander's observation that Dante gives Ulysses such persuasive powers in order to show that he is just "a con artist." In any event, Dante condemns Ulysses as someone who dealt in deceptive persuasion and was proud of it. And Dante surely fears the damage to trust in that. For bad as it is to deceive, those who induce others to do it spread the contagion. And as deception spreads, we lose ever more of the trust that a civilized world depends upon.

The next deceivers also damage trust, but they do it deliberately by turning people against each other. They are devious troublemakers who, to serve their own perverse and pernicious ends, "sowed scandal and schism," fomenting conflicts and dividing families, friends, religions, or states against themselves. (Dante includes Mohammed here for breaking away from Christianity.) We all know the most common garden variety of the type: the gossips who maliciously spread rumors that disrupt human relationships, shatter loyalties, and ruin lives. Their deceptions and willful divisiveness earn these "Sowers of Discord," as Dorothy Sayers calls them, the punishment in Dante's hell of being hung by the heels and repeatedly sliced by a sword. A deserving fate. Let that be a warning. When vicious gossip rises to your lips, think of that sword and bite your tongue.

Finally, Dante gets to the bottom of the Eighth Circle in the tenth bolgia, where four groups of especially vile deceivers languish. In one way or another, he says, these are all Falsifiers (*falsador*). They shared the common sin of creating or purveying false appearances by making physical things or words become something other than what they seemed to be. Like the sickness of their souls, they suffer from a variety of diseases—plagues, gangrene, rabies, scabs, itches, fevers, madness, and more. Dante could have put some of these Falsifiers elsewhere in the Eighth Circle, since all deceivers and frauds traffic in falsehoods. But he puts them here to make a particular point about deception—that is, people who deliberately deceive us erode our trust in all other people, as well as our trust in our own judgment, and even trust in our own senses.

First among these Falsifiers are the alchemists, who transformed one physical thing into another, or masked one thing as another. Unlike sorcerers, soothsayers, and magicians, who make *false claims* to special powers or knowledge, the alchemists possess actual powers to change things—so Dante believed. And they play tricks with appearances for their own gain, subverting people's confidence that physical objects are in fact what they appear to be. Although the pseudoscience of alchemy itself holds no threat in our times, we might see a semblance of its evil in the artificiality of many physical things nowadays. After all, when virtually anything, from jewelry to food, can be manufactured out of all kinds of materials, how can we trust anything to be what it seems to be? To reassure ourselves, we now require the ingredients in much of the food we purchase to be identified on labels, but that doesn't help much when those ingredients are themselves artificial or synthetic. Who but the manufacturers know what these things are really? So the fact is, we may have greater reason to doubt that physical things are what they seem to be than Dante did. Technology is the alchemy of modern life.

Other Falsifiers are equally bad. Those who falsify money, the counterfeiters, undermine our trust in the monetary currency that honest economic exchange depends upon. That mistrust also weakens our confidence in the public authority that stands behind the currency. Economic life cannot survive amidst this kind of mistrust. We will meet one of these counterfeiters shortly.

The Falsifiers of persons cause similar harm. They wear disguises or don false identities to seem to be who they are not in order to defraud others. One of these falsifying impersonators in Dante's hell is Gianni Schicchi, later memorable from Puccini's comic opera of that title, who had impersonated a dead man in order to dictate a false will and get the inheritance for himself. Such falsehoods make us doubt that we can trust people to be who they appear to be. This may not be the problem today that it was in Dante's times, when personal identity was often uncertain for lack of documentary proof. But our very insistence nowadays that everyone be able to prove with multiple documents to be the person that he or she claims to be confirms Dante's worry—as do our anxieties over spies or terrorists among us pretending to be who they are not.

Most common and probably the most corrupting of Dante's Falsifiers are those who falsified words: the liars. All deceivers lie, of course, and Dante has already shown us how seducers and flatterers falsify and debase language with "polished" words. But here Dante shows how the calculating deceptions of false words from liars dissolve trust in all communications among people. Today we might excuse distortions of the truth, and even outright lies, by advertisers and politicians because we have come to expect them. But these distortions nonetheless instill a certain cynicism about what advertisers and politicians say, while fostering doubts about the very meaning of the words they use (George Orwell powerfully portrayed such abuses of political language in his unforgettable essay "Politics and the English Language," as well as in his chilling novel *1984*). The truth is, we cannot easily trust the words of anyone who has told us a lie. And human relations cannot thrive in a world of liars. This is why Dante casts these sinners down near the bottom of hell.

Rottenest of Dante's liars, by the way, is Sinon, "the lying Greek from Troy" who, with a string of lies and oaths of assurance, had persuaded the Trojans to take the wooden horse into their walled city as a tribute to Athena (as reported by Virgil in the *Aeneid*). Dante shows Sinon and a particular counterfeiter in hell trading accusations over which of them is the worst sinner—the one who had deceived with false money or the one who had deceived with false words. "If I spoke falsely, you falsified the coin," Sinon says, and "I am here for one offense alone," but "you for more than any other devil." The counterfeiter retorts: "You perjurer, keep the horse in mind . . . and may it pain you that the whole world knows." Then Sinon again: "And may you suffer from thirst that cracks your tongue" (the disease of dropsy). Back and forth their verbal assaults go. Falsifiers are bound to wrangle since they cannot trust each other. While these two carry on their quarrel, Virgil scolds Dante for listening, because "the wish to hear such things is base." So the travelers move on, leaving the manifold deceivers in the Eighth Circle behind. Now they enter the Ninth Circle, the pit of hell reserved for the most egregious evils and the lowliest sinners of all.

THE SINNERS in the Ninth Circle are deceivers, too. But they are not as various and abundant as those in the Eighth Circle. They share a single deception. They did not, like the deceivers in the Eighth Circle, just prey upon people's common trust in appearances and in human interactions at large. They preyed upon a specific kind of trust. And they had the most malicious of intentions for doing it. These are the outright traitors.

Traitors usually commit other crimes along with treason, to be sure, as do most of the sinners deep in Dante's hell. They have to lie, pretending to be what they are not, and they might murder, steal, and so forth. But Dante casts them to the bottom of hell because they deliberately betrayed those to whom they owed a specific allegiance. Here they exist frozen in an icy lake. For, unlike the unpremeditated, heated passions of the ill-fated lovers near the top of hell, which brought the punishment of perpetual drifting in the wind, betrayal is calculating and cold, bringing a punishment of ice. Treachery has no heart of human passion or affection in it. Nothing remotely close to love. It freezes emotions and breaks human bonds. It is the ultimate death of the soul, and of humane society.

As Dante walks among these treacherous deceivers, he sees four kinds of them, arrayed in concentric rings: those who betrayed their families, those who betrayed their countries, those who betrayed their friends or guests, and those who betrayed their lords or leaders. Most of them are locked in ice with their heads protruding. Some of the heads butt against each other, and one devours the head of another. Dante kicks one "vile traitor" in the face and pulls his hair. When another implores Dante to break the ice that covers his eyes with frozen tears, Dante agrees if the sinner will reveal his name and offense. But after this woeful soul confesses that he had deceived and murdered his younger brother whom he had invited as a guest, Dante goes back on his word. "Extend your hand and open my eyes," the traitor pleads, but, Dante reports: "I did not open them. And to be rude to him was courtesy." Just as anger breeds anger, and deception breeds deception, so betrayal breeds betrayal, and cold-heartedness breeds cold-heartedness. Where human beings have become "estranged from every virtue" and "crammed with every vice," Dante writes, who could be humane to anyone?

In this cold, inhumane mood, Dante meets the basest sinners in hell. They had pledged explicit oaths of loyalty to their leaders, and had then heartlessly betrayed those oaths, often for the very purpose of destroying the leaders. Here Dante discovers none other than Satan himself. Satan is here because (in Dante's theology), once an angel, he had betrayed his master, God, and been cast out of heaven. Frozen in ice to his waist, he chomps, with three ravenous mouths, on the frozen bodies of three infamous human traitors to their leaders: Brutus and Cassius (the two Romans who had betrayed Julius Caesar), and Judas Iscariot, the betrayer of Jesus. Dante's Traitors devour each other, as traitors tend to do.

This image of Satan chomping on the traitorous trio at the icy bottom of hell captures Dante's deepest moral outrage. Of all the forms of deception, betrayal causes the worst damage to the human world because it viciously exploits the trust in professed loyalty that the political and social orders require, and that the strongest human relations must rely on. You know that Dante is right if you have ever been betrayed by someone close to you whom you trusted completely. This is bad enough when, say, a friend carelessly does you harm. It is much worse when such a person deliberately hurts you. More villainous than simple lying, betrayal by those who have invited our trust and pledged their loyalty causes us to lose our bearings with everyone. We don't know whom to trust, or where to turn, or how to behave or even how to think clearly—remember Shakespeare's Othello, and what Iago, literature's most infamous betrayer, did to him; we know where Iago would wind up in Dante's hell (see Chapter 12). Bereft of trust in everyone, and in all oaths of loyalty, and even in our own judgment of people, we may then resort to betrayal ourselves. And why not? Trusting no one, we owe no one honesty. All we can hope to do is to survive by any deception or betrayal necessary, as has happened to people in every autocratic society where political deceptions and betrayals are the common coin of survival, and as spy novelists have shown to ingenious and disturbing effect.

Once lost through betrayal, our trust in people can take a long time to be restored. But without it there can be no lasting human bonds, no society, no civilization. This is why Dante's moral landscape of hell descends as it does to the cold inhumanity of treachery.

THAT IMAGE OF SATAN frozen in the lake is the last version of evil that Dante gives us in the *Inferno*. He and Virgil now continue their way downward alongside this "Emperor of the woeful kingdom," and then find themselves climbing up outside "to see again the stars." The world has turned upside down, and Dante's trip through hell is over.

The sign at the gate of hell had warned those who enter to abandon all hope. Dante did not abandon hope, of course. He was just a tourist. And his trip did its job. For it showed him not only the moral landscape of hell, it also revealed to him the moral landscape of the human world on earth. That is, it taught him how we human beings corrupt our characters through our own evil acts; how we can sink from acts of self-indulgence to acts of violence, then to acts of fraud and deception, and finally to acts of outright betrayal; how self-indulgence affects mainly ourselves, how violence destroys the value of things, and how deception undermines trust in all appearances and in the human world itself. But while revealing this gloomy moral landscape of evil and punishment, this journey also opened Dante's eyes to the makings of a brighter moral world of human goodness and a good society. Here people would live with a measure of healthy self-restraint; they would cherish their lives and the legacies they have received from others; they would respect nature and work and high ideals; and, above all, they would be honest and trustworthy and would strengthen human bonds in everything they do. This would be a world always warmed by the soft breezes of human affection and trust, and never chilled by the frigid winds of betrayal.

We can imagine this is the kind of world that Dante, the wandering exile, would have lived in if he could have. It is where we would all probably live if we could. And there is no better guidebook for envisioning it, or for guarding against its opposite, than Dante's travelogue through hell.

On the Moral Psychology of Evil and Good

1. Hell is a landscape of moral evil descending from the least evils to the worst.

2. Our evil acts bring their own punishments by corrupting our character.

3. Evil begins in self-indulgence, descends into violence or destructiveness, sinks into deception, and culminates in treachery.

4. Self-indulgence means losing control over our physical appetites, and it hurts mainly ourselves.

5. Acts of violence destroy or demean the value of things, from human life to moral ideals—for instance, profligacy is an act of self-destructive violence that wastes everything we have, and we *do violence* to the value

of human work and human life when we give too much importance to money.

6. Deception dissolves our trust in everything it touches.

7. Deception can take many forms, from presenting false appearances to lying and treachery.

8. The worst deception is treachery because it undermines our trust in everyone and undoes society.

9. Treachery is the greatest human evil; trust is the greatest human virtue.

10. We can learn what is good by seeing what is evil.

11. The meaning of life is to create a good society by restraining our appetites, respecting the value of people, things, and ideals, and strengthening human bonds by being honest and trustworthy in everything we do.

6
Growing Up Naturally
Jean-Jacques Rousseau: *Emile*

*God makes all things good; man meddles
with them and they become evil.*

Oh man, live your own life and you will no longer be wretched.

Rousseau

No author of the eighteenth century won more admirers and earned more
enemies than **Jean-Jacques Rousseau (1712–1778)**. A champion of the Enlightenment as well as a father of Romanticism, Rousseau touched nerves
with everything he wrote. And he wrote about many things. Born in Geneva,
Rousseau came to his expansive and explosive vocation when he saw a poster
on a country road one day announcing an essay competition on whether
the Arts and Sciences have helped or harmed humankind. He threw himself
down under a tree and wept at the shattering truth that hit him and that
would animate the rest of his life: the reputed advances of civilization had
done humankind far more harm than good. The essay he wrote for the competition, "A Discourse on the Moral Effects of the Arts and Sciences" (1750),
won first prize and launched Rousseau on the road to fame and infamy. A
second prominent essay, "On the Origin and Foundations of Inequality
among Mankind" (1755), further flogged the theme with its image of what
became known as the "noble savage" living in a blissful pre-civilized state of
nature. Then came a flood of writings, including *The Letter to M. d'Alembert
on the Theatre* (1758), assailing the immorality of art; the sensational sentimental novel, *Julie, Ou La Nouvelle Héloïse* (1761); the influential political
treatise, *The Social Contract*, and the revolutionary exploration of education,
Emile, both published in 1762; and a skein of autobiographical meditations
culminating in the epochal, posthumous *Confessions* (1782). Along the way,
Rousseau became a composer and a music critic who wrote articles for Denis
Diderot's great *Encyclopedia* denouncing dense baroque harmony and extolling natural melody.

   All of France sobbed over the sentimentality of *La Nouvelle Héloïse*. Then
during the French Revolution that erupted a decade after Rousseau's death,
the fanatical Robespierre misused Rousseau's political theory to justify his

own rule of people against their wills, and to lop off heads, until his excesses cost him his own head. But nothing that Rousseau wrote had more influence in its day, or later, than *Emile*. It was the first child-rearing handbook, and more. Tracing the development of a child from birth to adulthood—a novelty then—*Emile* looks not only at child-rearing and education, but at human nature and the panorama of culture. Rousseau did not like most of what he saw around him because it smacked of unnatural habits, self-deception, and unhappy lives. But he thought he knew how to fix it all: adapt education to human nature and you will save lives and culture. In his provocative way, he was right, even now.

———

JEAN-JACQUES ROUSSEAU lives in history as an adamant enemy of society, a zealous partisan of all things natural, and a dogged champion of the "noble savage." Voltaire kidded him about that after reading Rousseau's provocative early essay "On the Origin and Foundation of the Inequality among Mankind." "I have received, sir, your new book against the human species," Voltaire wrote. "No one has ever been so witty in trying to turn us into brutes: to read your book makes one long to go on all fours."

Rousseau thrived on this reputation in his day, during a century fascinated by the tensions between nature and culture and curious about how children grow up in society and how they would grow up among wolves, as some "wild" children were said to have done at that time. A fair number of people suspected wolves might be the better parents. Rousseau was one of them. No wonder he became the most avidly read author in Europe, his writings devoured by a generation hungry for understanding of the pre-social "natural man" and thirsting for new freedoms. Many people later hailed Rousseau as the spark of the French Revolution, so subversive did his ideas sound and so pervasive was their influence. Others have blamed him for that revolution's bloody violence and for virtually every subsequent epidemic of incivility in Western culture. And others still have honored Rousseau for being the first to teach us how to think clearly about the relations between human nature and culture, the individual and society, freedom and morality, and education and human fulfillment.

Rousseau brought together his many revolutionary and influential ideas on these subjects in one book that quickly became, and has remained, a classic: *Emile*. Every educated Frenchman of the eighteenth century read it. Everyone should read it now.

In a characteristically combative spirit, Rousseau uses *Emile* to assault common assumptions about human nature and to insult accepted practices in education and society as he searches for answers to the overarching question that persistently animated him about the tangled give-and-take between human nature and civilization. We might phrase that question like this: What in human life is natural, necessary, true, and good for us, and what is artificial, accidental, false, and bad for us? To answer this knotty question, Rousseau claws at every social appearance, personal habit, and masking rationalization to reveal what we are as people and how we got that way, and to show how we could be otherwise. We might reject Rousseau's answers, but we should ask his question if we want to know why the human world is as it is, and if it can be better.

ROUSSEAU'S FIRST LINE in *Emile* sets the theme: "God makes all things good; man meddles with them and they become evil"—or more literally, but less vividly, "Everything is good as it leaves the hands of the Author of things; everything degenerates in the hands of man." This famous claim has led many readers to conclude that Rousseau despised civilization and wanted to let nature run amok in us untouched. Hence the motto attributed to him: Back to Nature. But Rousseau was not so simpleminded as that, and he never used the phrase "Back to Nature" or its companion, "the noble savage." Far from wanting to undo civilization and rouse a flight back to the woods, Rousseau simply wanted to turn human "meddlings" to good rather than evil ends. We all want this. It is what child-rearing and education aspire to. But Rousseau thought people generally get child-rearing wrong. And we get it wrong because we do not understand what is natural, necessary, true, and good for human beings. Consequently we live our lives and teach our children and shape our society in ways that are more *artificial than natural*, more *accidental than necessary*, more *false than true*, more *bad for us than good*. And then amid the wreckage that results we cap our blunders with the crowning error of thinking that we've done the best we can, and that our failings result from an intractable human nature. How blind we are, Rousseau says, to what human nature really is and how it works.

To see ourselves through Rousseau's eyes, we have to start, of course, with nature and the natural. That is, we have to know, or have an idea about, what is natural to human beings before we can decide what is necessary, true, and good for them. Presumptuous as this may sound, Rousseau is not alone in taking this as his premise. All political and social philosophy implicitly comes from it. You must have opinions about human nature—even if unstated—before you can understand and nurture people, and create a good world for them. But nature and the natural are notoriously difficult terms to define. Rousseau is not altogether clear about them either. In fact, he is pretty murky, and sometimes downright contradictory. Still, a strong enough theme runs through his uses of the terms for us to draw it out here. It is a good theme, too, with ramifications throughout life. This is how Rousseau states it most directly: "I call nature within us," he says, the original "tendencies" or "dispositions" that we human beings bring into the world prior to the hardening of our acquired "habits" and "opinions" and "prejudices." How does he know what those natural "tendencies" or "dispositions" are? He looks where he has to look, at the dawn of life. There he finds two conspicuous "tendencies." We might describe the first of these as the elemental fact and feeling of unmet, self-centered needs. And the second is our elemental powerlessness to meet those needs ourselves. As Rousseau concisely puts it, "Man's first state is one of want and weakness" (*la misère et la faiblesse*).

But that is only the beginning. From here, Rousseau adopts a pioneering strategy to trace, as no one had done before, the pattern of what we now call developmental psychology. That meant following how the original "natural tendencies" of "want and weakness" in human beings evolve from a person's birth to fully formed adulthood. And it meant to him showing how those tendencies can evolve either naturally to our benefit, or unnaturally to our detriment. His contrast between "natural" and "unnatural" human development, and between the related types of education, made Rousseau an educational revolutionary. For it prompted people to start thinking about what in our upbringing, our education, and our lives is natural, necessary, true, and good, and what is artificial, accidental, false, and bad. We think about these things every day. Or we should.

Before following Rousseau down his pioneering path of developmental psychology and educational reform, we should note another of his ideas about human nature that underlies his educational philosophy, and with a teasing paradox. It has to do with the relation of human nature to society.

A purely "natural man," Rousseau says, would live "entirely for himself," satisfying only his own purely selfish needs, and he would be "the whole, dependent only on himself." This image of the self-sufficient natural man would seem to pit human nature against society. But it doesn't. For Rousseau believes human nature and society must fit together. The natural man must become social because, in the end, the social human being is, at best, the most truly human. That is what Rousseau set out to demonstrate in *Emile* by describing and philosophizing about the education from infancy to adulthood of "an imaginary pupil" named Emile. And it is quite contrary to the popular view that Rousseau promoted a return to "the noble savage."

In short, Rousseau's prescription comes down to this: take the inborn natural tendencies of children and nurture them according to their most natural pattern of development, then you will have a natural human being living in society. Everything in child-rearing, education, and good social institutions must therefore work in "harmony with these natural tendencies" to transform the natural man of instinct into a natural man of society. And that means, every child must learn "to exchange his independence for dependence, to merge the unit in the group, so that he no longer regards himself as one, but as a part of the whole." In other words, "When I want to train a natural man," Rousseau says, "I do not want to make him a savage and to send him back to the woods." Far from it. "Emile is no savage to be banished to the desert, he is a savage who has to live in the town." That is the teasing paradox. And it is Rousseau's ideal for educating the best kind of social human being: one living out human nature at its most *natural*, *necessary*, *true*, and *good* within society.

Here is how Rousseau proposes to bring us to that happy end. Go back again to the dawn of human life. "We begin to learn," he says, "when we begin to live." That is when our natural tendencies of want and weakness first meet the real world. So "our education begins with ourselves" as soon as we start acting on those natural tendencies and other people begin responding to us. For then we respond to their responses. Here, Rousseau observes, "is forged the first link in the long chain of the social order." That is because the way these two natural tendencies in us play out with other people over time makes us the kind of people we become, and it makes society and civilization what they are. That "first link" starts being forged, Rousseau now points out, when an infant cries.

"As man's first state is one of want and weakness," Rousseau proceeds, "his first sounds are cries and tears. . . . Is he hungry or thirsty? there are tears; is he too hot or too cold? more tears; he needs movement and is kept still, more tears; he wants to sleep and is disturbed, he weeps." What does an infant learn from an adult's response to his or her cries? Not what adults usually think it is. For one thing, the child learns that weakness in satisfying its wants *causes* suffering; and, for another, the child learns that this weakness can be overcome by gaining power.

Exactly how a child uses these lessons about weakness, suffering, and power depends on how he or she experiences the connection between weakness, suffering, and power. If an adult responds cruelly to the child's cries and inflicts more suffering, the child may learn that adult power expresses itself *naturally* in cruelty, and this may induce a hidden rage in the child that will find its victims when the child later gains power of his or her own—a syndrome seen today among victims of child abuse who become perpetrators of it or of other violence. By contrast, if the adult's response is too doting, a child likely learns something more complex. He or she learns that tears can themselves actually become an exercise of power to gain manipulative control over others. "The child's first tears are prayers," Rousseau explains, then he adds the caution: "Beware lest they become commands." For although the helpless child "begins by asking for aid, he ends by demanding service." This is how the psychology of manipulation and domination is born. "From his own weakness, the source of his first consciousness of dependence," Rousseau warns, "springs the later idea of tyranny and rule." A provocative notion, which all parents should keep in mind.

Rousseau does not blame children for wanting to control others. They deserve no blame. The "idea of tyranny and rule" does not come from them alone. It is not in human nature. It is learned. Children learn it from parents and caretakers, siblings and friends, teachers and preachers, then they teach it to others. How easy it is to unwittingly transform an infant's natural needs and weakness into manipulative behavior.

So this "first link" in the "chain of the social order" shows us how the natural, necessary, true, and good can give birth to the artificial, the accidental, the false, and the bad. By *nature* and *necessity* we are self-centered, needy, and weak; but to act on those attributes by manipulating and exploiting others is *artificial* and *accidental*—Rousseau clearly rejects the contrary claims of thinkers like Machiavelli and Hobbes. And although it may seem true and feel good to exercise this power over others to survive, it is false and bad for us to do it because that kind of power steers people away from the life that would be best for them, individually and collectively. In Rousseau's words, as soon as children "can think of people as tools to be used, they use them to carry out their wishes and to supplement their own weakness. This is how they become tiresome, masterful, imperious, naughty, and unmanageable." But do not be deceived, Rousseau warns, this is "a development which does not spring from a natural love of power, but one which has been taught them."

If we fail to see this, Rousseau continues, we will compound the folly of our ignorance by reaching false conclusions about human nature. After inadvertently teaching children to express their natural wants and weaknesses in the most unnatural and often pernicious ways, we are prone to blame human nature for our work. When such an unmanageably miseducated youth "is flung upon the world," Rousseau scolds, "and his helplessness, his pride, and his other vices are displayed, we begin to lament the wretchedness and perversity of mankind. We are wrong; this is the creation of our fantasy," for "when we have taken pains to make him bad," then "we lament his badness," but "the natural man is cast in a different mold." We, not nature, have created this monster. And we cannot see it. To our peril.

From an infant's tears to the rest of a child's behavior, it all grows out of want and weakness, self-interest and incapacity, whatever else it might seem to be. These origins are often difficult to detect because children's wants and weaknesses adapt to circumstances with wondrous flexibility. Children do not see their actions for what they are, since acting out their desires and compensating for their weaknesses feels to them only natural. And they all too readily learn that when they cannot satisfy their desires directly by themselves, it is just as natural for them to do it by manipulating adults with devious behavior. Here lies the touchiest part of educating children: because children live by want and weakness, self-interest and dependency, and adapt like chameleons to whatever serves their natural purposes, the best intentions of adults can have entirely unintended consequences.

Take an example. You wish to teach a child morals. So you forbid certain acts and threaten punishment for committing them. When the child commits a forbidden act anyway, say, to borrow one of Rousseau's illustrations, breaking a window, you ask if he did it. He says no. You ask again, offering evidence of his guilt. Finally he confesses. Then you punish him for the lie as well as the misdeed, and you threaten worse punishment if he repeats the offenses in the future. Now you think you have protected the windows and taught respect for the truth and for your authority. Well, you might have protected the windows for a while. But most likely you have merely taught the child to fear your power and to spare himself from it by not getting caught when he misbehaves. And far from learning the morality of telling the truth, he has learned a different lesson: namely, that adults want him to tell the truth so they can use it to wield power over him and to thwart his desires—he wanted to break the window for fun, and he still he does! How could the child fail to conclude from this that to do what he wants he must simply learn to tell more adroit lies, and to cover those lies with more lies? This causes trouble for both child and parent, and for society.

Rousseau neatly spells out the perverse moral sequence: "By imposing on [children] a duty which they fail to recognize, you make them disinclined to submit to your tyranny, and you turn away their love; you teach them deceit, falsehood, and lying as a way to gain rewards or escape punishment; then by accustoming them to conceal a secret motive under the cloak of an apparent one, you yourself put into their hands the means of deceiving you, of depriving you of knowledge of their real character, of answering you and others with empty words whenever they have the chance." And "what does it all come to?" Rousseau asks. Instead of nurturing a moral personality for a moral society, we have nurtured an immoral personality for an immoral society, fashioning liars and hypocrites for a culture that thrives on lying and hypocrisy.

To head off these malevolent consequences, and to teach morality successfully, Rousseau advises us to go back to the beginning and follow nature more wisely. When children choose immoral over moral acts, it is because we have inadvertently taught them that immorality serves their interests better than morality does. We must reverse the connection. That is, we have to lead children's natural tendencies of want and weakness toward moral rather than immoral ends. And the best way to do this is to show them that moral behavior gives them power. As Rousseau says, "All wickedness comes from weakness. The child is only naughty because he is weak; make him strong and he will be good; if we could do everything, we should never do wrong."

This may sound implausibly idealistic. But doesn't much of the evil and suffering in the world come from natural human weaknesses and from people's self-serving efforts to compensate for them to get what they desire? Rousseau surely goes too far in claiming that no one is born with an evil impulse. And Western culture has debated this point virtually from the beginning, weighing the relative importance of nature and nurture in shaping personality. Still, Rousseau is probably right to say that more evil comes from human nature gone awry under a misguided culture than from human nature itself.

In any case, if we want to teach morality, we would do well to follow Rousseau's advice and try to make moral acts serve a child's interests, and make immoral acts do the opposite. That requires, for one thing, being very careful with punishments. Punishments should always flow directly from the wrongful act, not from adult authority. If you have evidence that your child has lied, for example, do not bring your power down on him for lying. Punish him with cold distrust: let him feel directly the rejection and pain of being—unbelievable. This will change his attitude toward lying instead of just instilling envy of your power. For he will see his own dishonesty, not you, as the cause of his pain, and will come to know lying as a hurtful enemy, and honesty as an empowering friend. Only in such ways as this can a child's self-interest and weakness be led toward virtue and away from evil, instead of the reverse.

Even reasoning with a child about moral principles will likely do more harm than good. For while we pat ourselves on the back for teaching our children the principles of good behavior, children are actually learning something else. "Attracted by selfishness and constrained by force," Rousseau points out, "they pretend to be convinced by reason" when actually they may be learning to distrust it. Our well-intended rational arguments for our morality—which ask the child to deny his or her natural wants—may appear to the child as nothing more than another expression of our power through a manipulative rationalization of our own self-interest. "Do not try to make him approve what he dislikes," Rousseau warns, "for if reason is always connected with disagreeable matters, you make it distasteful to him, you discredit it at an early age in a mind not yet ready to understand it." The child will then view reasoning not as a path to truth and virtue, but only as another devious technique for serving self-interest.

The consequences of misguided instruction keep coming out the same: misperceiving human nature and misunderstanding how ingeniously it works, we try to teach one thing to children and wind up teaching another. "Foolish teachers think they are doing wonders," Rousseau exclaims, "when they make their scholars wicked in order to teach them what goodness is and then they tell us seriously, 'Such is man.' Yes, such is man as you have made him."

Rousseau knew: "The apparent ease with which children learn is their ruin." It is their ruin because the facile appearances of learning too easily conceal mental byways that misdirect the journey of education. "With every piece of precocious instruction which you try to force into their minds," he cautions, "you plant a vice in the depths of their hearts." These vices are both moral and intellectual.

Moral vices are bad actions that come from bad moral education. Intellectual vices are bad ideas that make us think wrong about everything. So intellectual vices are the driving culprit in miseducation. For whenever we teach a child anything, we teach not only the content—that is, a subject matter or a skill—we also implicitly teach the child how to think and how to learn according to our methods of teaching. Consequently, if we do not choose those methods carefully, anchoring them well in real life and human nature, we nurture a wayward growth of mind that can lead to bad ends—Voltaire's Dr. Pangloss and Dickens' Mr. Gradgrind vividly prove the point (see Chapter 13).

Look at what happens in the schools. We place a child in a classroom (Rousseau would be aghast at how early the practice begins nowadays) and require him or her to read and write and do mathematics. The child might see no evident use for these skills, since these prepare the student to meet some future, unimaginable need. Children live in the moment, only playfully fancying anything else. Instructed in some fact or skill, a child will therefore ask: "What is the use of that?" He wants to know how this bit of learning will serve his "present interest," not some possible later interest—Rousseau stresses this after infancy up to the age of twelve, but good teachers know it goes well beyond.

This practical bent leads Rousseau to cry, "I hate books!" and to lament that "reading is the curse of childhood!" Today that claim would make Rousseau seem like a crackpot. He wasn't. He was just overly emphatic. He does not reject reading altogether, merely the wrong kind of reading. Rousseau heartily encourages young people to read one book (and it is the single one he allows Emile). That book is *Robinson Crusoe*, the eighteenth century's favorite novel—before Rousseau's own *La Nouvelle Héloïse*. Rousseau commends it because it tells of a sailor stranded on an island who learns from practical experience in nature, rather than from books, how to make a life for himself. Of course a child must know how to read before taking up *Robinson Crusoe*. And Rousseau relies on practicality, or "present interest" here, too. To teach a child to read, Rousseau would cast aside all primers and textbooks. In their place he would use words written for a purpose directly connected to a child's life, like party invitations, which the child itches to decipher because their contents do indeed serve his "present interest."

Rousseau follows the same principle in every subject: he links the teaching directly to life—as in astronomy, where he would ignore text-book abstractions and teach the child how to find his way home in the dark guided by the stars. Some of Rousseau's pedagogical examples may seem trivial, even silly, and they produced some zany practices among followers who took Rousseau too literally—as did the teachings of that modern Rousseau, John Dewey, whose pragmatic ideas of "progressive education" became anti-intellectual nonsense in the hands of Dewey's too-literal-minded disciples. But the principle behind Rousseau's pedagogy is as sound today as when Rousseau expounded it. For the closer learning is to life the better, and the farther removed it is the more wayward it can become. That is because the self-interest of children can take some curious intellectual turns while they display an intellectual diligence and precocity that astounds and delights parents and teachers. Ask them to memorize facts and they will memorize facts; drill them in skills and they will acquire skills; make them repeat an idea and they will repeat it; promise them rewards and they will do whatever it takes to get those rewards. But the youth who appears so intellectually precocious, disciplined, and alert, so bursting with knowledge and readied with skills might be more proficient in "intellectual vices" than anything else.

That is what happens when children learn primarily by rote or by imitating those in authority or by responding to entertaining sensory stimulation (as with children's television). They can exhibit learning, but they do not likely think critically or expansively. A similar result comes from emphasizing tests and grades that purport to stimulate and measure intellectual accomplishment. Instead of stimulating genuine intellectual accomplishment, these measuring devices tend to become the very goal and purpose of education, inducing young people to gain recognition for being good at tests and grades (even justifying cheating), rather than to gain true education. When scores and grades and related rewards become the hallmark of intellectual achievement and the means of advancement, a young person's self-interest will pursue them, regardless of their educational value. "Just tell me what I need to know for the test," every teacher has heard students ask today. With the "intellectual vice" of rewarding test-taking more than overall education so much in the air today, it is only *natural* (if perverse) that we now have a whole profession, equipped with its own schools, to teach students nothing but how to take tests. It seems that education and test-taking have little to do with each other anymore. Rousseau saw this coming.

Rousseau's persistent argument surfaces again: in schools, as in life, a child's natural self-interest, shaped by want and weakness, is a wily player who always holds the trump card and wins every game. Young people—particularly children—learn through the many hidden strategies of this self-interest, no matter what parents and teachers try to teach them. And if adults do not see how this self-interest works, they are bound to miseducate it.

Further playing out this *natural* psychology of education, Rousseau draws a vital distinction between two types of self-interest. One type is truly natural, or innate. The other is unnatural, or acquired. And each type follows its own path through education. Natural self-interest, Rousseau says, pursues education through "man's natural curiosity about things far or near which may affect himself." This natural curiosity belongs to the innate, healthy "self-love" that serves the universal innate human need for survival. But this natural curiosity can give way to its opposite. And that is an artificial "zeal for learning which has no foundation other than to appear learned." This "desire to appear learned" merely serves unnatural self-interest, which thrives on appearing superior to others. In other words, our natural and benign self-love can sink into an artificial and malign "selfishness." Then education goes awry.

This distinction between the two forms of self-interest—*natural self-love* or *love of self* (*amour de soi*) and *unnatural self-love* or *selfishness* (*amour propre*)—lies at the root of Rousseau's ideas on education and miseducation, on a healthy personality and an unhealthy one, on the good society and the bad. It is a distinction to think about. "Self-love," Rousseau explains, is the only passion "which is born with man," and it "is always good" because it "concerns itself only with our selves" and "is content to satisfy our own needs." "Selfishness" is something else. It is not born of nature, but of a society that causes us to define ourselves by comparison with others. And "the first feeling excited by this comparison," Rousseau points out, "is the desire to be first. It is here that self-love is transformed into selfishness."

For unlike natural self-love, which is honest, innocent, and fosters a love of others for "the help and attention received from them," this unnatural selfishness is contrived, predatory, and insatiable. Natural self-love leads to healthy self-awareness, autonomy, and happiness because it helps us become our most complete selves. Selfishness leads to unhealthy self-deception, dependency, and discontent, because it makes us into someone we are not as we try to be superior to others. "Selfishness, which is always comparing self with others," Rousseau explains, "is never satisfied and never can be; for this feeling, which prefers ourselves to others, requires that they should prefer us to themselves, which is impossible. Thus the tender and gentle passions spring from self-love, while the hateful and angry passions spring from selfishness."

And this is the state of civilization as Rousseau finds it. People are hypocritical, greedy, cruel, and devoid of self-knowledge, incapable of autonomy, and unable to be happy. They got this way by learning—or mislearning—that human beings are not to be valued for themselves, but only for their comparative superiority to others. Constantly measuring themselves against others, depending on social approval, craving public praise, enslaved to the fleeting sensations of self-importance that come when the ego is stroked, such persons will perform any act that will yield these pleasurable sensations, be it hypocrisy, obsequiousness, or cruelty. This is the social self at its worst—the kind so despised by Moliere's Alceste (whom Rousseau praised in his *Letter to d'Alembert on the Theatre*—see Chapter 12): nothing but a social performer. "The man of the world," Rousseau observes of this type, almost always wears a mask: he "is scarcely ever himself; he is ill at ease when he is forced into his own company. Not what he is, but what he seems, is all he cares for." How could anybody be free or good or happy living a life that is so *unnatural*?

Rousseau was not wrong. We see this kind of person everywhere nowadays—we might be among them ourselves. The student who cuts corners to get the highest score; the narcissist who feels alive only through the fugitive attentions of others; the star-struck youth for whom celebrity is the highest achievement, however attained; the vacuous lover ever searching for satisfaction from behind a facade of charming performance; the social climber who grovels before those above and scorns those below; the maven of fashion always abreast of the new, whose eye delights in others' imperfections; the craven materialist who vies for status with possessions; the spoiled child who becomes a spoiled adult, unwaveringly demanding and inevitably dissatisfied. Such persons perpetuate a society of the artificial, the accidental, the false, and the bad. And yet it is a society blindly convinced that it is natural, necessary, true, and good. "It's human nature," the *Wall Street Journal* quotes a factory manager proudly justifying his desire to have a better car than his fellow workers. And the newspaper's reporter confidently adds, "It's natural for people to compare themselves with neighbors, co-workers and relatives." It's human nature to want a better car than someone else? It's natural for people to compare themselves to others and seek superior status? Hardly. Rousseau knew better. And so should we.

To UNDO THE MISGUIDED practices of this false education and set civilization on a more truly natural course, Rousseau offers some ideas useful to anyone. For these ideas give Rousseau's version of what everyone most wants to know. And that is "to know how to live and be happy" (*savoir vivre et se rendre heureux*), or in a particularly pleasing translation, the "arts of life and happiness." These "arts" cover everything we do, but Rousseau brings them down more or less to two: "self-knowledge" and "self-mastery" (*se connaître* and *tirer parti de lui-même*). He was offering no great discovery here. These two arts can be found in most of the world's wisdom on how to live well, from Confucius and Socrates on down. But Rousseau played upon them with his own unusual ingenuity.

We begin to learn these "arts of life and happiness," Rousseau explains, when we accept a simple rule: match our desires to our strengths and our strengths to our desires. In other words, we should not let ourselves want either more or less than we have the power to get. As Rousseau puts it, "That man is truly free who desires what he is able to perform and does what he desires." Our desires must rise to the level of our capacities for us to "enjoy our whole being," but if our desires surpass our capacities, we will "only be the more miserable."

This rule might be simple common sense. But, like many other seemingly common-sense rules, it is not easy to follow. Do not blame nature for that. Blame a society that constantly arouses artificial wants and insatiable desires that outstrip our natural powers and leave us feeling helpless, frustrated, and "the more miserable." "Society has enfeebled man," Rousseau declares, "not merely by robbing him of his right to his own strength, but still more by making his strength insufficient for his needs." Modern advertising feeds these soaring needs as a calculated strategy, keeping people feeling inadequate, dissatisfied, wanting more, and perpetually defining themselves through new possessions and the status possessions bring—as an early rationale for advertising put it (in the professional journal *Printer's Ink* of 1930): "Advertising helps to keep the masses dissatisfied with their mode of life." Rousseau saw this coming, too, and how the pursuit of excessive and artificial desires inevitably leaves us discontented. And he saw how this will most often happen when we "are dependent on the prejudices of others" (he also scolds imagination for pushing our desires beyond reality).

"Do you know the surest way to make your child miserable?" Rousseau asks. "Let him have everything he wants; for as his wants increase in proportion to the ease with which they are satisfied . . . he will want all he sets his eyes on." And then he is doomed to misery. For we cannot have everything. Something always lies beyond our reach—a more fashionable fashion, a more luxurious luxury, a more celebrated celebrity. So, young people who think their every wish must be satisfied are setting themselves up (or, rather, *we* are setting them up) for a fall. Eventually they become resentful and dejected over their disappointment. And some then become wicked in order to serve their misshapen and miserable selves. "As they cannot do everything, they think they can do nothing," Rousseau observes; then, "daunted by unexpected obstacles, degraded by the scorn of men," they likely "become base, cowardly, deceitful."

With these cautionary words, Rousseau gives his version of a psychology of happiness and unhappiness first advanced in Hindu and Buddhist philosophy (see Chapter 2), and later elaborated upon by the pioneering modern sociologist Emile Durkheim (who greatly admired Rousseau) with his seminal concept of "anomie," and then by other social scientists with ideas like "relative deprivation." Namely: happiness and unhappiness do not arise from objective circumstances or from external facts so much as from the relation within us of our desires to our powers. In Rousseau's words, we gain "true happiness" only by "decreasing the difference between our desires and our powers, in establishing a perfect equilibrium between the power and the will." And we can do this only by cultivating those "arts of life and happiness": self-knowledge and self-mastery.

We can cultivate self-knowledge and self-mastery in children by nurturing their every strength and cautioning their every desire from their first plaintive tears onwards. The guiding rule should be: never do for children what they can do for themselves.

With all of their natural weaknesses and needs, children must first of all have physical care and emotional devotion. Parents must provide these to lay the necessary ground of psychological security that children will build upon the rest of their lives (the influential developmental psychologist Erik Erikson called this "Basic Trust"). But if parental assistance goes beyond what a child needs, it becomes an unintended lesson in dependency and manipulation—as with a child's contrived tears. So, our child-rearing should diligently "discriminate between those desires which come from nature and those which spring from perversity" in order to insure a "natural" education. The first requirement of a natural education, beyond the necessary care and devotion, is therefore to help children "do more for themselves and demand less of others." This requirement also points to Rousseau's ultimate goal: to shape human beings who will possess the happiness of genuine independence and autonomy. This is a goal all parents and teachers should pursue.

Rousseau pursues that goal at every step. For the teaching of independence through the accumulation of self-knowledge and self-mastery can never stop, as many parents of grown children know all too well. But for children who have grown up and gained the physical strength of adolescence, Rousseau shifts his focus from natural physical dependency to the subsequent risks of unnatural social dependency. For here is where education can take that most fatal turn of letting natural, healthy *self-love* veer off into artificial, unhealthy *selfishness*. Selfishness is a symptom of unnatural social dependency because it shows that we define ourselves only in comparison with other people and by wanting to be superior to them. To guard against this danger, Rousseau advises that, above all, we prevent children from comparing themselves to others. "Let there be no comparison with other children," he declares, "no rivalry, no competition, not even in running races." All comparisons are recipes for selfishness and discontent. "I would far rather" that a child "did not learn anything," Rousseau adds, "than have him learn it through jealousy or self-conceit." No happiness can ever come from that. "Oh man," Rousseau cries, "live your own life and you will no longer be wretched." A nice line. It is Rousseau at his most Rousseauian.

No American parent could easily follow this advice today when athletic competitions have become part of every school curriculum. And not many of us tutor our children privately, as Rousseau does with Emile, although home-schooling is gaining popularity for some of Rousseau's reasons. But Rousseau has a point. Whatever else that children glean from competitions and comparisons with others, they learn to define themselves though their superiority or inferiority to others. No one can avoid some of those comparisons. And they may not always be a bad thing. But no one can master the "arts of life and happiness" who lives a life defined by such comparisons. And who could deny that young people today probably suffer more unhappiness—and commit more crimes—from exactly this cause than from any other? Adolescence has become a torment of comparisons.

Rousseau's warnings against the evil consequences of competition and having children compare themselves with others might call to mind Karl Marx, who also judged the modern competitive individualist to be neither natural nor necessary, neither true nor good. Marx believed that only a political, social, and economic revolution could rectify the wrong and restore human beings to their true nature in a communist society devoid of competitive selfishness (see Chapter 15). Rousseau was less sweeping. He hoped to bring change through education by teaching people how to be rationally autonomous, benignly social, and emotionally contented. That is to say, to become "the natural man living in society."

To lead us closer to this happy end, Rousseau reminds us of the idea at the beginning of the book and gives it new punch. In order to gain self-knowledge and self-mastery in society, people must not only avoid invidiously comparing themselves with others, they must also absorb what Rousseau takes to be the most fundamental truth of human existence: "Let [them] know that man is by nature good . . . ; let [them] see how men are depraved and perverted by society." When people absorb this truth, they can see the difference between what is natural, necessary, true, and good in society and what is not. And then they can understand at last that human beings live badly and suffer unhappiness not because "such is man," but because "such is man as you have made him."

But, like everything else in Rousseau's natural education, this fundamental truth cannot be taught as an abstract idea. It must be taught through everyday experience. To do this, Rousseau finally brings Emile into the social world between the ages of fifteen and twenty years. There Emile will see for himself how "external causes . . . turn our [natural] inclinations into vices," how the perverted "passions and prejudices of men" subvert natural goodness, and how the "specious appearance" of social status breeds selfishness and converts our natural human equality into artificial inequalities. He will therefore learn directly "what forces move [people], he must calculate the action and reaction of self-interest in civil society," and "he must estimate the results so accurately that he will rarely fail in his undertakings." In short, Emile will learn how "to live in the world" without succumbing to it.

The first thing that Rousseau wants Emile, and everyone, to see about society is that beneath social appearances human beings are all equal, sharing a natural weakness that dogs us all our days. Rousseau had stressed this earlier in describing young children. Now he has Emile learn it for himself in the arena of adult social life. This means discovering that "by nature, men are neither kings, nobles, courtiers, nor millionaires. All men are born poor and naked, all are liable to the sorrows of life, its disappointments, its ills, its needs, its suffering of every kind;

and all are condemned at length to die. This is what it really means to be a man, this is what no mortal can escape." Once Emile can see through the artificial differences of social appearances and discover this natural equality of human beings, he can understand how human nature is good in itself, and how it then becomes corrupted when our natural wants and weaknesses and innocent self-love get misled into artificial dependency and malevolent selfishness. From this time forward, life experience will inscribe these truths in Emile's heart.

Rousseau does not, to be sure, let that life experience unfold on its own. He is still educating Emile, not just tossing him into the world. So he has to teach Emile to learn the right, or natural things from life not the wrong, or unnatural things. Rousseau's instructions go like this.

Weakness, need, and self-interest, Rousseau had said, are the elemental ingredients of human nature. They are innocent and good, and they unite all human beings beneath the surface of social appearances. But they are also the source of unhappiness and evil because they can go awry into unnatural dependency and the exploitation of other people. Therefore, he had asserted, make people self-sufficient and they will be both happy and good. Now he adds another spin to the idea of natural weakness. Weakness, he says, is the seed of social virtue. "Man's weakness makes him sociable," Rousseau explains, for "our common sufferings draw our hearts to our fellow-creatures." Or put it this way: weakness makes possible that most social of emotions, pity or empathy. And from empathy, so Rousseau believes, come all the social virtues, such as kindness, generosity, justice, and gratitude, which nourish benevolent human relations. "We should have no duties to mankind," he remarks, "if we were not men" with common needs and weaknesses.

This was not a radical idea. Many other eighteenth-century thinkers suggested it with theories of the "moral sentiments" (and later the Romantic poet Shelley made empathy itself the emotional ground of morals in "A Defense of Poetry"—see Chapter 23). But it is a good idea, whatever its origins or variations. For remembering our common weaknesses and shared feelings helps us to treat others well.

And more than that. Because weakness and empathy induce our humane sociability, they also actually further happiness. "If each of us had no need of others," Rousseau says, "we should hardly think of associating with them." And from this need for association we learn nothing less than love and happiness. "I do not understand how anyone who has need of nothing could love anything," he concludes; "nor do I understand how he who loves nothing can be happy. . . . So our frail happiness has its roots in our weakness." This is far from a prescription for solitary savagery in the bush. It is an invitation to enjoy empathetic, affection-ate, social interdependency. This is how the savage who lives in town learns "the arts of life and happiness."

If Rousseau's endorsement of weakness, empathy, and sociability comes as a surprise from this champion of the natural man, the last steps Rousseau has Emile take on the path to becoming an autonomous, happy, and virtuous human being will surprise even more. To arrive at those steps, the grown-up Emile first has to travel the world because Rousseau wants him to observe disparate lands, varieties of life, and types of laws. He also wants Emile to grasp the difference between love and marriage. Love is a condition of the heart; marriage is a condition of law. Emile needs to fathom both before trying to join the two with his beloved Sophy (whose education occupies a section of the book that was innovative in its day but is dated now). Obediently Emile goes off to carry out this late phase of his education—as all young people should probably do before winding up their formal schooling and taking up careers and families.

When Emile returns, he announces that he is ready to embrace adult life to the full as an autonomous human being. For he thinks his educa-tion is complete and has prepared him to live freely and happily on his own terms wherever he chooses. "Rich or poor," he proclaims, "I shall be free. I shall be free not merely in this country or that; I shall be free in any part of the world. . . . What matters my place in the world? What matters it where I am? Wherever there are men, I am among my breth-ren; wherever there are none, I am in my own home. . . . Give me my Sophy, and I am free." Emile is confident that he has comprehended the whole truth of his teacher's years of tutoring: he thinks he understands human nature; he thinks he has mastered "the arts of life and happi-ness"; he thinks he has achieved autonomy; he thinks he has everything he needs; he thinks he is the natural man who lives in society as he likes.

But Emile is wrong. He has come far, but he still has another profound lesson to learn—a lesson most of us do not learn any more quickly than Emile has. For learning "the arts of life and happiness" calls for more than becoming self-aware and intellectually independent, being able to see through social appearances, and feeling self-sufficient and free to live your own life as you wish. It also calls for what is the last step in Emile's education, which comes with what might seem a most un-Rousseauian rule of life. It is this: to fulfill ourselves as natural human beings, we must acquire the self-restraint of living under a nation's laws.

Some people might think, as does Emile himself, that freedom and autonomy give us the power to choose our own lives, and that laws re-strict liberty rather than expand it. But they are mistaken. Freedom and autonomy require the highest form of self-mastery: the power of self-denial. And laws encourage this power by teaching each of us, as Rousseau says, "to fight against himself and to prevail, to sacrifice his own interest to the common weal." Hence, Rousseau concludes of Emile: "It is not true that [the laws] have failed to make him free; they have taught him to rule himself." Now he has the ultimate freedom and autonomy that come from self-knowledge and self-mastery. So Emile must settle in the land that had nurtured him under the laws that have helped to make him free.

With Emile's strong-willed submission to the laws of his land, he has finished his education at last, insulating himself against artificial dependencies, accidental habits, false ideas, and bad attitudes and behavior (never mind that Emile still wants his tutor's guidance). Now he can live as a happy savage in the town: enjoying natural independence, performing necessary duties, embracing true ideas, and doing what is good for himself and for others.

Here we get to Rousseau's surprising and paradoxical conclusion: the natural man in society is morally superior to the natural man in nature because he has attained full self-knowledge and self-mastery as a civilized human being. And this brings him not only personal autonomy but public virtue. The natural man could never have acquired these qualities living in the wilds. "Born in the depths of the forest," Rousseau speculates, Emile might have felt more spontaneous and lighthearted than he does in society, "but being able to follow his inclinations without a struggle, there would have been no merit in his goodness; he would not have been virtuous, as he may be now." Living in society makes Emile better because, Rousseau concludes, "he owes to it the most precious thing possessed by man, the morality of his actions and the love of virtue." Consequently "the public good, which to others is a mere pretext, is a real motive for him." Understanding what is truly natural in human beings and what is unnatural in society, and having learned the "arts of life and happiness" and acknowledged his debt to the laws and society, Emile will now not only live in the social world without succumbing to it. He will make it better. He might even become a teacher.

WHAT HAD BEGUN as a revolutionary manifesto against the follies of an unnatural civilization ends up as an affirmation of a beneficently natural civilization. There, instead of living in bondage to the artificial, the accidental, the false, and the bad, people would live freely according to the natural, the necessary, the true, and the good. It is Rousseau's utopia: the triumph of nature not *over* civilization but *within* it.

Like all utopian visions, this one is unattainable in details. Rousseau conceded that at the outset: "I am showing what we should try to attain, I do not say we can attain it." But, he adds, "I do say that whoever comes nearest to it is nearest to success."

That is good advice. For despite what we might consider Rousseau's overwrought hostility to society, and his blithe idealization of human nature, many of Rousseau's ideas are true enough to have become commonplaces of the social sciences, and to cast light on every life, and to alert us to impediments and opportunities on the pathway to the good life. Anyone who tries to apply Rousseau's ideas will likely agree: Rousseau can set us free from chains we did not even know held us. He did this to historic effect in the eighteenth century. He can do it still in the twenty-first century. For you can be sure there are many more clues to ourselves and our society yet waiting to be discovered in answering Rousseau's question: What in our lives and society is natural, necessary, true, and good, and what is artificial, accidental, false, and bad?

On Child-Rearing, Education, and Culture

1. Human beings are not morally bad by nature, they learn to be bad.

2. Children learn from everything that happens to them, from their first breaths.

3. People learn to be bad from a culture that causes them to misunderstand what is natural, necessary, true, and good in human life.

4. Human beings are naturally weak, needy, and self-interested, and they will necessarily act out these characteristics—that is benign natural self-love.

5. Children want to learn how to overcome their natural weaknesses and to satisfy their natural needs.

6. People learn to be bad as children when parents and teachers inadvertently teach them to act out their natural weaknesses, needs, and self-interest in accidentally bad ways—this turns benign natural self-love into malign accidental selfishness.

7. Children learn what serves their own interests at the moment, whatever adults might want them to learn for the future.

8. Children should be taught to overcome their weaknesses and satisfy their needs honestly for themselves—that is autonomy.

9. Autonomy should be the aim of child-rearing.

10. We achieve autonomy through self-knowledge and self-mastery.

11. We should be careful how we reward young people for learning—

rewards, rather than good education and autonomy, can easily become their goal.

12. Never do for children what they can do for themselves, or they will learn dependency and manipulation.

13. A child's first tears are prayers; beware lest they become commands.

14. Spoil a child and you create a dependent and unhappy human being.

15. When our desires exceed our powers, we lack autonomy.

16. When we lack autonomy, we are unhappy, constantly compare ourselves to other people, feel inferior, and yearn for superiority.

17. When we have autonomy, we are comfortable with ourselves, and we feel neither inferior nor superior to other people.

18. Autonomy involves living at once independently and virtuously among other people.

19. Empathy comes from natural human equality and is the source of morals.

20. Modern culture breeds dependency, evil, and unhappiness by inadvertently stimulating *artificial* rather than *natural* desires, rewarding *accidental* rather than *necessary* learning, teaching *false* rather than *true* ideas about life, and fostering selfishly *bad* rather than autonomously *good* behavior.

21. The meaning of life is to follow what is natural, necessary, true, and good in human life, and to avoid the artificial, accidental, false, and bad.

7

Enough? Never!

Johann Wolfgang von Goethe: *Faust*

*Freedom and life are earned by those
who conquer them each day anew.*

Man errs so long as he will strive.

Goethe

Johann Wolfgang von Goethe (1749–1832) belongs to that small handful of historical figures so gifted they hardly seem human. He could do everything well that he tried to do, and he tried almost everything. Brilliant, prolific, inexhaustibly curious, he held a reigning place in European culture from the publication of his youthful, wildly popular romantic novel *The Sorrows of Young Werther* (1774) to his dying day. He wrote influentially in many genres and on many subjects that animated his times, producing bushels of poetry, a library of criticism and essays, numerous plays, several novels (including *Elective Affinities* [1809] and the sprawling *Wilhelm Meister* [1795–1829]), and the autobiography of his youth, *Poetry and Truth* (1811–31). Not content to dominate German literature, in which he remains the national icon, Goethe also engaged in extensive scientific studies to prove that nature is "organic" (it *grows*, a new idea at the time) rather than "mechanistic"; and he became a minister of state to boot. His death was an international event, and signaled the end of an era.

Today most people know Goethe as author of the poetic drama *Faust*, written over the course of his long adult life and published in two parts separated by nearly twenty-five years (Part I, 1808; Part II, 1832). The legend of Faust appealed to Goethe for its subject: an unhappy thinker swaps his soul to the devil for aid in doing whatever he wants. And what Faust wants is to gain power over nature and to follow his whims. But unlike the traditional versions, Goethe's Faust bets his soul that the devil, or Mephistopheles, can never make him contented. The wager struck, Faust exploits Mephistopheles' services to indulge his insatiable desires and ignore others' sufferings, to commit crimes and escape punishments, to manipulate nature and dally with the supernatural. It is all wild and reckless, and some of it pretty mysterious (especially in Part II). In the end Goethe lets Faust win his bet by having God save him with an unusual idea of good. Thanks to Goethe's God, Goethe's *Faust* turns out to be a moral fable that celebrates nothing so much as the creative energies of life itself, lived insatiably.

———

WORLD LITERATURE knows many unhappy characters. For that matter, it knows few truly happy ones. This may be because life brings more grief than joys. Or because contentment is harder to write about than adversity. Plato suspected this long ago when he complained that the "calm life" does not inspire art, while conflicts and troubles set creativity soaring (see Chapter 19). Whatever the reason for the many discontents in literature, no literary character has more intense, or instructive, discontents than Goethe's Faust.

The legend of Faust goes back to a peculiar character of the Renaissance steeped in the occult who was said to consort with the devil. Repeated in many literary versions, that legend made Faust familiar as a restless intellectual who tires of book learning and sells his soul to the devil for a lifetime of boundless excitement. Goethe follows this line with a distinctive turn. Introducing his own provocative ideas of good and evil, he gives Faust unique motives for wanting excitement and then takes him through some weird and often muddled adventures to a quizzically happy end. At the same time, beneath the adventures Goethe makes Faust less the satanic figure of legend than a character of life as we know it. We can therefore learn much from Goethe's Faust, even if we do not want to be like him. And what we learn begins with his unhappiness—just as what we learn from, say, Aristotle, Wordsworth, and Virginia Woolf's Clarissa Dalloway begins with happiness (see Chapters 4, 23, 18).

Goethe's Faust was "the most somber human character who has ever represented evil and unhappiness," wrote the nineteenth-century critic Alfred de Musset in *Confessions of a Child of the Century* (1835). Nothing pleases Faust, everything vexes him. He despises life and taunts death. He hurls curses at the heavens and brazenly courts hell. What is wrong with him? What does he want?

Simple explanations will not do. The agonies and anger of Goethe's Faust, as well as his desires and his dealings with the devil, baffle simplicity. Yet with all of his vexations and enigmas, Goethe's Faust is not alien to us. His unhappiness is ours. Or perhaps we should say that our unhappiness is always a bit Faustian. And so are our desires. For unhappiness is a child of desire.

Goethe's Faust is a creature of desire, even more than he is a cauldron of misery. His desires are as soaring as his despair is abysmal. How he manages those desires makes him who he is, miseries and all. This could, of course, be said of everyone (Freud certainly said that—see Chapter 17). We *are* what we wish, and what we do with those wishes. And while our wishes give us direction, they also fuel our discontents. When we cannot get what we want, we hurt. Recognizing this, many sensible people (including influential thinkers like Siddhartha Gautama and Jean-Jacques Rousseau—see Chapters 2, 6), have recommended curtailing desire. This is good advice. If we do not take it, we will pay a stiff price. But it also just might be a price worth paying. Goethe thought so.

Instead of condemning Faust's insatiable, tormenting desires as the formula for a botched existence, Goethe finds in them a supreme affirmation. This affirmation springs from desire itself, from a hunger that cannot be satisfied, a thirst that cannot be quenched, an endless yearning for things to be better—or merely different—than they are. Dangerous, for sure. No contentment lies down this road. But vitality does. And creativity. And perhaps the meaning of life. For these reasons Goethe lets this curious affirmation, amid all of Faust's agonies, resonate to the very heavens, where Goethe's God Himself applauds it.

That is the tangled truth of Goethe's *Faust*. *Faust* at once dramatizes the psychology of unhappiness, or frustrated desires, and celebrates the energies of desire, the spirit of creation, and the will to live, even at the cost of unhappiness. We should learn caution from that psychology. But we should also join in that celebration. For it shouts the Faustian *Yes!* to life—a *Yes!* that may make life less safe, but that also keeps it from getting dull.

FAUST'S DESIRES and unhappiness grow from a frustrated craving for knowledge. Not just any kind of knowledge. Faust has studied everything. But that was not good enough. "For all our science and art we can know nothing," he laments. Faust wants more. He demands the knowledge that brings power.

When Francis Bacon penned the often-quoted line "knowledge itself is power" (in *Meditationes Sacrae* [1597]) near the time of the historical Faust and the early writings about him, Bacon was urging us to act on our knowledge, not just think about it. That is what Faust wants: knowledge to act on. For him, this means above all knowing the "secret" or "the inmost force that holds the world together," for force is energy; force is power. And he thinks that knowing this force will give him control of it—possibly, as he says, to "better mankind," although he shows no signs of doing that, until the end.

Relentlessly pursuing this potent knowledge, Faust turns from book learning to magic. For the rapturous prospects of magic can both reveal nature's "inmost force" and give power over it. Not bound by the laws of logic or of cause and effect that limit normal science, magic can do anything with its "mysterious potency." Most of us do not take up magic like Faust, but we often turn to a kind of magical thinking to transform ourselves through the products we buy and the nostrums we imbibe, the religions we embrace and the therapies we follow (as the American historian L. Jackson Lears has demonstrated). Magical thinking always promises quick fixes and transcendence of everyday limitation. Faust throws himself into magic to gain nothing short of god-like omnipotence.

"Am I a god?" he cries as he tries to summon the "inmost force" of "creative nature." When this appears in the form of a "Spirit," Faust ardently professes himself "your peer." Then—poof! The Spirit vanishes, leaving Faust bruised and humbled. He is not this Spirit's "peer," after all, only a lowly mortal with high ambitions. "Not yours?" Faust calls out plaintively in the Spirit's wake. "Whose then?" Reeling from the blow to his desires and his pride, Faust rails against his impotence:

> I am not like the gods! That was a painful thrust. . . .
> I, image of the godhead, that began
> Exulting on the heavens' brilliant beach
> As if I had stripped off the mortal man . . .
> [And] shared the creative joys of God's domains—
> Presumptuous hope for which I pay in pains.

Dashed expectations sting most in that part of us where we forge our hopes and chart our lives. There we define ourselves and experience failure as a defeat of who we are, or who we think we are, or who we want to be. With his vaulting ambitions to godlike powers, Faust had a long way to fall, and disappointment brought him down hard. "I'm like the worm that burrows in the dust," Faust growls, "who, as he makes of dust his meager meal, is crushed and buried by the wanderer's heel." How deflating that our highest aspirations can be so easily dashed, usually by our own incapacities. Then former hopes become depression, despair, and rage. We have all been through this. Some of us never recover. Faust recovers—and in boldly Faustian style. We can, too, if we have the Faustian will to do it.

Unsatisfied by conventional learning, taunted by failed magic, tortured by his own impotence, Faust now hurls his rage at life itself. What is life, he asks, but a series of denials? "You must renounce! You ought to yield! That is the never-ending drone which we must our life long hear." Every day is but another insult to our desires. Awakening each morning, Faust wishes he "had tears to drown the sun and check the day that soon will scorn my every wish—fulfill not one."

This is one bad mood. And it gets worse. We could blame Faust for bringing it on himself with his "every wish," or, like Flaubert's Emma Bovary, by living for his every fantasy (see Chapter 24). But he will have none of that. He accuses human life of causing us grief by its very nature.

In the first place, Faust complains, life is ridden with "care." Care (*Sorge*) is another name for the burdens of everyday existence that weigh us down, as well as for the troubles we know as worry, anxiety, sorrow, fear, illness, pain, and death. Care, Faust observes, arises from the things we love in life, like children, no less than from those we dread, like disease. For the things we love cause us constant care—we worry about them and sacrifice for them, even as we gain joy from them. Every parent knows this well. Care also taints our moments of happiness with its sad intimations that all might be lost, that in the end probably all *will* be lost, because we cannot entirely control our fates. No one can escape the ever-present and everyday anxieties of care. "Deep in the heart," Faust sighs,

> there dwells relentless care
> And secretly infects us with despair;
> Restless, she sways and poisons peace and joy
> She always finds new masks she can employ:
> She may appear as house and home, as child and wife,
> As fire, water, poison, knife—
> What does not strike, still makes you quail,
> And what you never lose, for that you always wail.

Near the end of Faust's long life, Care appears personified as a character who "sneaks . . . in through the keyhole" to haunt Faust's final hours. "In all forms, at every hour," Care tells Faust, "I wield the most cruel power. . . . He whom I have conquered could own the world and not feel good." Faust reacts defiantly: although "you persecute the human race with a thousand miseries," Faust cries, "yet your power, Care, creeping and great, I shall refuse to recognize." Recognize it or not, Faust cannot escape it. And at that moment, Care proves its power by striking Faust blind.

Inescapable as are the pangs of care, something else afflicts Faust more. That is the futile longing not only to defeat care, but to surpass the very limitations of human nature. Why, Faust wonders, do we want what we cannot possibly get? Why do we have unattainable desires? Why do we keep yearning beyond our powers? These are Faust's most agonizing torments—and often ours.

And these torments reveal to Faust the seeds of discontent at the core of human existence. These seeds take root in a cruel paradox. We are by nature finite beings, he observes, hedged in on all sides by constraints and incapacities, and yet we manage to have consuming desires and infinite longings. How unfair that is. Either we should have powers matching our desires, Faust thinks, or desires befitting our powers (exactly Rousseau's prescription for happiness, by the way). Otherwise, we can never be satisfied. "It is inborn in each of us," Faust complains, "that our feelings should soar upward and away, when over us, lost in the azure space the lark trills out her glorious song; . . . the eagle soars, and over plains and over lakes the crane returns to homeward shores." If birds can fly, why can't we? Or if we cannot fly—or play the violin or achieve greatness or do anything that we fervently wish we could do—why does our nature let us want to? We are cursed by being desiring animals, always reaching, always looking beyond ourselves. How galling, Faust complains, that "the god who dwells in my breast can deeply stir my inmost being, [but] though he deeply bestirs [me within], all my powers can move nothing outside of me." We feel so much, Faust sighs, imagine so much, want so much, and yet we are so impotent. "If I but think of any pleasure," he protests, "bright critic day is sure to chide, or diminish, it, and to hinder the creative forces in my breast with a thousand of life's mockeries." Our inadequacies thwart us at every turn—at least for anyone moved by Faustian ambitions, as most people are now and then.

Torn between soaring desires and stingy powers, between the "two souls . . . in my breast"—one bound to the mundane earth, the other poised for flight—Faust lashes out at everything. The enticing illusions, the seductive wishes, the false hopes that fill our days and unsettle our nights now fall under Faust's impassioned curses:

> I now curse all that would enamor
> The human soul with lures and lies,
> Enticing it with flattering glamour
> To live on in this cave of sighs.
> Cursed above all our high esteem,
> The spirit's smug self-confidence,
> Cursed be illusion, fraud, and dream
> That flatter our guileless sense!
> Cursed be the pleasing make-believe
> Of fame and posthumous life!
> Cursed be possessions that deceive,
> As slave and plough, and child and wife!
> Cursed, too, be Mammon when with treasures
> He spurs us on to daring feats,
> Or lures us into slothful pleasures
> With sumptuous cushions and smooth sheets!
> A curse on wine that mocks our thirst!

> A curse on love's last consummations!
> A curse on hope! Faith, too, be cursed!
> And cursed before all be patience!

Dwelling in a living hell of unfulfillable desires, where "existence is . . . a burden" and "life is . . . hateful," Faust welcomes any change, wherever its goes. That angry, reckless state of mind brings him to the most perilous of adventures. He decides to "tear open the eternal portals, past which all mortals slink in dread" and "not to tremble," but to "brave that passage around whose narrow mouth burn the flames of hell." And he vows to "take this step with cheerful resolution even though at the danger of flowing into Nothingness." This is a man ready to deal with the devil if ever there was one.

Enter Mephistopheles. Any moralist or psychotherapist could have warned Faust that his desolate state made him an easy prey for evil tempters, maybe for Satan himself. This would not have mattered to Faust. It did not matter to Goethe either. He does not tell Faust's story to purvey conventional wisdom about living a prudent life. He tells it to show us something very different. And this brings on stage Mephistopheles, Satan's top recruiter of troubled mortals in the Faust legend.

The traditional versions of Faust's story—such as the Renaissance play *Doctor Faustus* by Christopher Marlowe and the modern novel of this same name by Thomas Mann—present Mephistopheles as a collector of souls: he comes proffering Faust certain services for a period of time in exchange for Faust's eternal soul. Marlowe says little of Mephistopheles' character, or of the evil he embodies, although Mann intriguingly depicts him as an agent of demonic artistic creativity. Goethe's Mephistopheles is different. He represents a very specific kind of evil. And the deal he strikes with Faust is far from a straight trade.

The Mephistopheles who suddenly materializes in Faust's study out of a poodle carries the evil of sheer destruction and negation (by contrast to Mann's Mephistopheles, who promises Faust spontaneous artistic creativity). "I am the spirit that negates," he proudly announces himself. "And rightly so, for all that comes to be deserves to perish wretchedly; 'twere better nothing would begin." No mere collector of souls or builder of a diabolical kingdom, Goethe's Mephistopheles is not driven to accumulate or create. He destroys just to destroy. He does harm for harm's sake. He is the enemy of life.

This kind of evil defies easy comprehension because we tend to think of evil as rapacious selfishness—like that of, say, street thugs, or tyrants. But *selfless* evil like that of Goethe's Mephistopheles is different. It is the evil of an absolute villain—and few they are (let us hope), like Shakespeare's Iago—bent on causing grief not so much for gain to themselves, but to bring others down. That is Mephistopheles' entire vocation. He is the supernatural downer. He gleefully seeks to undo all that exists, to dissolve the bonds of law and loyalty, to stifle every humane feeling, to extinguish any spark of creativity, to negate everything. What will he get out of it? Nothing more than the satisfaction of seeing his life-denying negation triumphant. You can think of this as a selfish gratification if you must. But that misses Goethe's point. Goethe's Mephistopheles is the antithesis of creation and of existence itself. He is the Destroyer, the Spirit of Negation, the Lord of Nothingness, the embodiment of Nihilism.

Mephistopheles appears in Faust's study to perform a task typical of him: to destroy Faust by leading him into eternal damnation and Nothingness—although, as Mephistopheles admits, Faust seems well along the way already. But destroying Faust is not Mephistopheles' only purpose. He is there to win a bet. A bet he has made with God.

Goethe's God is every bit as peculiar as is his Mephistopheles. There is no God quite like Him. He will puzzle you, possibly offend you, and not likely make a believer of you. But He is well worth thinking about, if for no other reason than that He can shake us out of what the philosopher Immanuel Kant in another context once described as "dogmatic slumbers."

Just as Goethe's Mephistopheles is no garden variety corrupter and collector of souls, so Goethe's God is no smiling savior of obedient spirits and pious do-gooders. Neither the Hebrew God, who demands subservience, nor the Christian God, who requires faith and love, Goethe's God values something else. He prizes action, striving, risk. "Man errs so long as he will strive," God tells Mephistopheles in the "Prologue in Heaven" that precedes the play. Human error or corruption or sin or whatever you want to name it is incidental. Error is a cost of striving, of action. And so Goethe's God readily forgives it. What counts is exertion, deeds, doing *something* rather than *nothing*.

Looking down upon Faust, God therefore sees not an arrogant disbeliever demanding "from heaven the fairest star and from earth the highest pleasures" and ripe for the devil's taking. He sees instead a man driven by insatiable desires, always hungering for new stimulation, constantly searching for ever-greater powers. This is a man, God says, who serves Him "confusedly" through a "dark urge," but he is a man who serves this God nonetheless. For Faust is a man of striving and action—Faust had even retranslated the biblical line "In the beginning was the Word" to read: "In the beginning was the Act."

God's confidence in Faust entices Mephistopheles. Convinced that he can wholly corrupt the anguished Faust and enlist him in the devil's ranks forever, Mephistopheles puts a brash proposition to God: "What will you bet?" on Faust. Goethe's God is a gambler, too. He takes that bet. But He takes it not like the God in the biblical story of Job, who bet with Satan on Job's invincible purity. Goethe's God does not care about Faust's purity or whether Faust succumbs to temptations. This God's moral standard is energy, action, and creation. And He thinks Faust will live up to it.

Here we find the direct moral conflict between Goethe's God and Mephistopheles: Mephistopheles, the Lord of Nothingness, meets in Goethe's God not only a game opponent but his moral opposite, the Lord of Creation. This God values striving and action not for themselves but because these are the makings of things, the engine of invention, the energy of creativity. Just as "the gardener sees even in the growing tree the flowers and fruits that will adorn its later years," Goethe's God sees in dauntless aspiration and perpetual activity the source of growth and productivity. Inactivity and rest may be benign and innocent, but they produce nothing. And now this God sees in the bet with Mephistopheles not only good odds for himself, but a way of actually helping Faust to be more Faustian. By letting Mephistopheles entice Faust with his services, God insures that Faust will keep moving from desire to desire, act to act, deed to deed. And ironically, this will make Mephistopheles, the nihilistic Spirit of Negation, the Lord of Nothingness, an unwitting agent of creation. "Man's activity can all too easily abate," God explains, "he soon prefers uninterrupted rest; therefore, I gladly give [Faust] this companion who activates and agitates and must even as Devil create."

God sends Mephistopheles to his task, declaring that the "true sons of God" always pursue the "process of growth and change that eternally works and lives." They might fail, but they must strive. This God, accepting error but expecting exertion, disdaining rest and demanding action, tolerates many failings. Even vices. Even sins. He sounds like an awfully good sport. But He may not be so easy to serve after all.

Of the conceptions of God you have come across, have you ever encountered one as open to life's temptations and one asking so strange a service? Never stop desiring. Never tire. Change. Create. At any cost. Piety? Forget it. Worship? Never mind. Just make something happen! Bring something into being. Make it new. Leave the world changed for your having been in it. Could you believe in such a God? Exhilarating, perhaps. But there is danger here. Faust's story proves it, as Faust careens from desire to desire, from action to action, leaving a wake of sorrow—including the torment of his lover Gretchen and the deaths of her mother, brother, and child. Goethe's God forgives even that. This could be the God of our times—the God of power, the God of action, the God of ceaseless change. For good *and* ill.

Goethe's God and Goethe's Faust have much in common, although Faust does not know this as he assails existence and prepares himself to deal with the devil. Mephistopheles doesn't know this either. And having struck a bet with God over Faust's character, Mephistopheles confidently places a second bet on the same thing. This time the bet is with Faust himself.

In the traditional Faust legend, the bargain struck between Faust and Mephistopheles is a straightforward trade: Faust swaps his soul for twenty-four years of Mephistopheles' services. Goethe is more ingenious than that. His Faust makes no crude exchange. He makes a bet.

The transaction does not start out that way. Mephistopheles comes with the standard pitch: his services in return for Faust's soul. But Faust rejects him. Gripped by hopelessness, Faust can think of nothing that the devil could possibly do for him worth the trade. "What would you, poor devil, give?" he snarls. Then an idea hits him, and he presents Mephistopheles a proposal of his own. And an extraordinary one it is.

He does not ask for anything. Certain that he can never be satisfied, Faust challenges Mephistopheles to try to give him satisfaction. "This bet I offer," he says: "If ever I lie calmly on a bed of sloth," if ever "in myself I find delight," if ever "to the moment I should say: Abide, you are so fair," then "put me in fetters on that day, I wish to perish." But, Faust adds, if he never finds this blissful moment, if he is never satisfied, if he never says to any moment, "Abide, you are so fair," then he will win the bet, and he will have had Mephistopheles' powers at his disposal for a lifetime without paying for them with his soul.

Surprised at Faust's terms, Mephistopheles cannot at first grasp them. "You are welcome to whatever gives you pleasure," he repeats, "but seize me and don't be stupid." After all, he adds, for everyone "the time comes when we would recline in peace and feast on something good." Faust recoils: "Do you not hear? I have no thought of joy! The reeling whirl I seek, the most painful excess. . . . Plunge into time's whirl that dazes my sense, into the torrent of events! And let pain and pleasure, annoyance and success exchange with one another as they can." When Mephistopheles continues to press the enticements of sweet satisfaction, Faust spells out his terms again. It is not satisfaction he wants. It is not happiness. He wants incessant activity whatever the price. If "I grow stagnant, I shall be a slave," he insists. And, he assures Mephistopheles, "cured from the craving to know all," he now wants to let his "passions drink their fill," and to let nothing stand still: "Show me the fruit that rots before we pluck it and trees that daily renew their foliage" because "restless activity makes the man." Far from seeking ultimate gratification, Faust reemphasizes, to never cease "striving with all my force is exactly what I have promised."

Who could fault Mephistopheles for being confused at Faust's bizarre proposition? Faust's despair cries out for remedy. We would expect Faust to ask for joy and peace at last. But no. Although he fulminates against the burdensome "cares" and the paralyzing confinements that thwart his yearnings, Faust now asks not to escape those cares and fulfill those yearnings, but to have more of them both. He wants a life freed not from discontent, but from all constraints upon experience, come what may.

This is the Faustian personality—restless, energetic, excessive, insatiable, tormented, undaunted. It is a personality poles apart from that marked by the healthy-minded virtues of restraint and self-control. These virtues insure a safe life, one of cautious desires and modest satisfactions, wholesome pleasures and quiet contentment. Without a share of these virtues we cannot be happy, as thinkers from antiquity to the latest self-help gurus have told us. Yet the Faustian personality disdains precisely this. Prudence, contentment, and happiness all spell stagnation to him. Goethe had the proto-Faustian hero of his novel *The Sorrows of Young Werther* deride such sober-minded "worthy" people for being fit to "head a committee," but being incapable of "passion," or "art," or "genius," or anything worth living for. Who can create when contented? Who would change the world when happy?

And that is what both Goethe's God and Goethe's Faust want us to understand: you cannot have a life of energy, activity, and creativity without a portion of discontent (Freud said the same thing from another point of view). This is a positive, not a negative, idea. It is the Faustian *Yes!* to life. Do not let frustrations and unhappiness get you down. Let them move you to act. To change. To make yourself and your life anew. It takes will and strength of character to do this. But if you do not turn your discontents to advantage, they can consume you with despair, or drive you into escapes that can diminish rather than enhance your life.

Because of his insatiable restlessness, Faust seems characteristically modern and Western, suited to a culture that feeds on change. It is no surprise that the Faust legend originated in the European Renaissance, when individuals were breaking the fetters of communal traditions; and that Romanticists, whose appetites were grand and from whose midst Goethe's Faust sprang, took this Faust as a hero, spurning contentment and craving action; and that Friedrich Nietzsche later saw in Faust a forerunner of his Superman, and that many modernist authors made a certain Faust-like agony a badge of honor and the rough road to truth—as Dostoevsky put it in the modernist credo of *Notes from Underground*: "Which is better, cheap happiness or noble suffering?" Renaissance individualist, Romantic hero, emblematic modern man—Faust is our brother, in his desires, in his discontents, and in his zeal.

"Restless activity makes the man," Faust told Mephistopheles. And it is his inexhaustible energies, however tormenting, that cause Faust to bet his soul that he will never say to a moment: "Abide, you are so fair." But does Faust win the bet? The outcome of this wager brings to light yet another bracing quality of the Faustian personality.

A long life of adventures, beginning with a witch's potion that makes him young, and running through selfish pleasures, wild thrills, and many mysterious doings (in Part II, largely passed over here), as well as injury and death to others, eventually brings Faust to his last days as an old man, and still he has not uttered the forbidden words inviting a sweet moment to remain. These last days are typical of him. Having "stormed through life . . . with might and main" from desire to desire, action to action, Faust is now master of a territory that he has diked from the sea. True to himself, he is a restless master. "My realm is endless for the eye," he boasts. But there is still a cottage belonging to an old couple, a stand of trees, and a small church that are not his, and he growls: these things "that are not mine reduce the world I own to gall." He never has enough of anything. So he tells Mephistopheles to take these over, too, and relocate the people—an assignment Mephistopheles sends his henchmen to accomplish, which they do by burning everything and letting the people die.

Now Faust possesses everything in sight. But even this is not enough. He decides to transform the landscape. Although struck blind at this very moment by Care, he exults, "inside me there shines a brilliant light," and he commands his workers to carry out his latest design: "Up from your straw, my servants! Every man! Let happy eyes behold my daring plan. Take up your tools, stir shovel now and spade. What has been staked out must at once be made . . . to make the grandest dream come true."

The plan is to dredge a large marsh and extend the dikes to create more land for the habitation of "many millions." These millions will form nothing less than a Faustian nation inspired, Faust proclaims, by "the highest wisdom that I own." This wisdom amounts to a Faustian moral ideal—Faust turns out to have ideals and not just appetites. That moral ideal is this: "Freedom and life are earned by those who conquer them each day anew." In other words, we are free, and life is worth living, only when we strive energetically every day to overcome obstacles and become masters of our lives.

To insure that this nation lives up to his ideal, Faust has chosen to locate it on land diked against the sea, because here people will have to strive constantly to fend off the hungry waters. There can be no complacent contentment here. No cheap happiness. The inhabitants will "live, not secure but with free activity." And as the dikes "are licked by raging tides," and as the sea "threatens to rush in with force, a common will" gathers to turn it back. Here, "surrounded by such danger each one thrives, childhood, manhood, old age, lead active lives." Unlike Rousseau, who equated the free and good life with wanting only what you can get and getting what you want, Faust binds freedom and the good life to endless dangers and ceaseless action. A Faustian nation could not be otherwise.

But as Faust rhapsodically envisions this new nation, hearing "the spades' lusty clanking . . . putting a bond around the ocean," he lets himself go too far. He delights in that vision too much. He allows himself to frame in his mind the fatal words: "Such a multitude I would like to see, and to stand with a free people on a free land. Then to the moment I might say: abide, you are so fair." Imagining "a happiness so high," he says, "I now enjoy the highest moment."

With these thoughts in his mind, Faust dies, the vision of his Faustian nation bright in his blind eyes, the sounds of excavation ringing in his ears. Mephistopheles stands by rubbing his hands and ready to carry off Faust's soul, smiling at the wicked irony of Faust's last wish: Faust had thought he heard the sounds of his Faustian nation under construction; in fact, these were the sounds of Mephistopheles' minions digging Faust's grave.

Confident that Faust has lost the bet by framing the forbidden words, Mephistopheles relishes a double victory. Not only did Faust lose the bet, Mephistopheles muses, Faust lost it for *nothing*, his final bliss merely a pathetic illusion. Although "he sturdily resisted all my toil," Mephistopheles gloats, "the poor man wishes to hold fast . . . the final, wretched, empty moment." This is a delicious triumph. Despite Faust's ceaseless activity and hopeful visions of creation, Faust's life added up to what Mephistopheles lives for: *nothingness*. "Why have eternal creation," Mephistopheles asks, "when all creation sinks into nothing?" It pleases him to think that all creativity is futile. "I should prefer," he says, "Eternal Emptiness." Mephistopheles the eternal naysayer savors his satisfaction as the shadow of negation falls across the corpse of the failed yea-sayer Faust.

Gleefully clutching the document Faust had signed gambling away his eternal life, Mephistopheles prepares to transport Faust's soul to the realm of perpetual negation. But Mephistopheles has another bet to settle first. That is the bet with God.

And God looks at Faust's last moments very differently from how Mephistopheles looks at them. God sees in Faust a man who never, not even at the end, abandoned the ideal of striving and creating. For even as Faust drew his last breath he was envisioning a new creation, and he had phrased the forbidden words in the conditional terms of a future possibility: he "would like" (*möchte*) to see and stand among a free people on the free land he has created; then he "might" (*dürft*) ask the moment to remain, proud that "the traces of my earthly days would not in eons disappear."

Faust died as he had lived, keeping his mind's eye on the future, always looking beyond the moment toward tomorrow and the making of things. In the end God decides that this persistence wins the bet for both Him and Faust. God therefore allows Faust's soul to be saved. With Mephistopheles' curses resounding in the background, the angels bear Faust's soul to heaven, intoning God's credo: "Whoever strives with all his power, we are allowed to save."

Goethe's God would have it no other way. Striving, acting, creating will always prevail over negation in His universe. For they cause things to grow and improve. Without them there is only stasis, sloth, and ultimately—nothingness. Mephistopheles can stir things up, but he cannot rule. And his very efforts can wind up serving God's cause, as they do with Faust.

The triumph of creation over nothingness fills the poem's last lines: "What is passing is but appearance; Insufficiency becomes efficacy; The indescribable is realized; The Eternal Feminine leads us ever upward." What began with God's confidence in Faust's restlessness, despite Faust's abysmal despair, ends in an affirmation of the energies of life. Aspiration and creation—symbolized by the Eternal Feminine—will always triumph.

Faust suffered from his strivings, his appetites, his desires, as he had to. But in time these led him out of despair and self-indulgence into the happy vision of a free people in a good society. Given time enough, Faust would not only have built his Faustian nation. He would probably have become a socialist, or something like it.

But socialist or not, Faust converted his discontents into creativity and an inspiring social ideal. And for this he deserves our praise. For we all have Faustian discontents—as long as we have desires. We can let these discontents make us angry, despondent, and enervated. Or, like Faust, we can draw from them the will to act, to change, to make a world where "freedom and life are earned by those who conquer them each day anew."

Johann Wolfgang von Goethe: *Faust*

The Faustian life is not easy. But it is never dull. For all of its discontents, it thrives on energy and will, risk and strength, affirmation and creation, and, at its best, it fills the future with promise. Humanism knows many gentler ways of life than this, but none more vital or invigorating—or modern.

On the Insatiable Hunger for More in Life

1. Evil means negation and destruction; good means creation.
2. Satan negates life; God creates it.
3. Human beings naturally tend to want more in life than they can ever get.
4. Wanting more than we can get causes unhappiness, but it can also make us strive and change and create.
5. A life without a hunger for more is gray and dull.
6. Freedom comes from striving to conquer life anew each day against all resistance, and against all odds.
7. Striving can bring errors and sorrows, but a life without striving goes nowhere.
8. History moves forward because of human striving and the energies of creation and change.
9. To create a good society of free people we must strive together to defeat danger and make life better.
10. God forgives the errors of those who strive because they create life.
11. A life of ceaseless striving is both exhilarating and dangerous.
12. The meaning of life is to live life with aspiration, energy, daring, and creativity.

8

From the Maggot Man to the Superman

Friedrich Nietzsche: *On the Genealogy of Morals*

There are no moral phenomena at all,
only a moral interpretation of phenomena.

One thing is needful: 'Giving style' to
one's character—a great and rare art.

Nietzsche

Friedrich Nietzsche (1844–1900) started his career as an obscure scholarly philologist and ended it as a crusading cultural revolutionary. Born in Prussia, he became a professor at the University of Basel, Switzerland, where he wrote his first book, *The Birth of Tragedy* (1872), a defiantly unconventional interpretation of ancient Greek culture that puzzled other scholars. Then, increasingly offended by what he judged to be the mendacity and hypocrisy of his times, Nietzsche embarked on a campaign against these evils. Declaring himself the adamant enemy of self-deception, the herald of God's demise, and champion of the "Superman," he spewed forth abundant philosophical essays and books from the mid-1870s to the late 1880s, including *Untimely Meditations, Human All-Too-Human, The Gay Science,* the powerful volumes *Thus Spoke Zarathustra, Beyond Good and Evil, On the Genealogy of Morals,* and the more summary *Twilight of the Gods, The Antichrist, Ecce Homo,* and *Nietzsche contra Wagner.* Then in 1889 he fell silent. And for the rest of his life he lived as an invalid, his mind undone by the ravages of disease (probably syphilis). But his reputation was mounting, especially among a younger generation champing at the bit of Victorian constraints and attracted by Nietzsche's ideas of tough-mindedness, moral rebellion, and exalted will. Nietzsche remains today one of the supremely provocative and illuminating thinkers of history.

Nietzsche's words are bold and clear, but his ideas are notoriously difficult to grasp firmly. We can blame this in part on Nietzsche's aphoristic style, which communicated thoughts in pithy phrases that Nietzsche knew needed "rumination" to be understood fully. That style also let Nietzsche deal in contradictions that could justify conflicting interpretations of what he intended. The one book that comes closest to a sustained, logical presentation of Nietzsche's most important ideas is *On the Genealogy of Morals* (1887). There Nietzsche forcefully lays out his critical thoughts on what is wrong with the world and how to set it right. Interpreting moral judgments as expressions of strength or weakness, Nietzsche extols the morality of the strong and excoriates that of the weak. His argument is twisty and fraught with paradoxes. But it reveals much about us, whatever our morality. And it leads to as inspiring, if risky, a humanistic view of life as you will ever find.

FRIEDRICH NIETZSCHE was the most outrageous thinker of his or probably any other time. He turned his guns on everything in sight. He took no prisoners. Not society. Not culture. Not morality. Not rationality. Nothing.

This outrageousness gave him wide appeal in the late years of the nineteenth century and the early years of the twentieth when many people had a fervid taste for this kind of thing. These years were, after all, the heyday of modernist revolution and experimentation in the arts and ideas and in social and psychological life. No convention was safe.

But if the rebellious temper of those times had not won Nietzsche a following, the zealous promotions of his sister, Elisabeth, probably would have. While she cared for her brother in his last three years, mentally debilitated as he was, she published a bowdlerized edition of his works attractive in audacious snippets to anti-Semitic, jingoistic fanatics like herself and her husband, Bernhard Förster, and later to the Nazis. Adolph Hitler presented a set of these perverted works to Mussolini. Hitler also supported the Nietzsche archives in Weimar, tended by Elisabeth until her death in 1935. Then he and other Nazi dignitaries attended Elisabeth's funeral, and construction soon began there on a shrine to Nietzsche—complete with a statue of Dionysius, symbol of Nietzschean exuberance, contributed by Mussolini.

By this time Nietzsche's reputation had risen perilously high among Nazis who likened themselves to the "blond beasts" that Nietzsche had pictured surging from the forests to save a sickly civilization from itself. But the Nietzsche celebrated by these barbarians was not Nietzsche—or not the "real" Nietzsche. Nietzsche had wanted nothing to do with his sister's ideology. "People like my sister," he had said, "must be irreconcilable enemies of my thought and my philosophy," for she was, as he told her, "almost the opposite of what I am." Even she conceded that his "entire philosophy goes against my grain." Had he been able, Nietzsche would certainly have damned the version of his ideas that Elisabeth presented to the world. He would also have taken aim at the Nazis themselves, slaves as they were to their own Teutonic bluster and obsession with enemies. The Nazis were not Nietzschean supermen. They only wanted to be. They were closer to the "maggot man" Nietzsche execrated.

It was to jolt people out of such self-serving delusions that Nietzsche, in his words, had "to philosophize with a hammer." He took that hammer to every false conception and comfortable assumption he could find. "I am challenging humanity as a whole with my terrible accusation," he wrote to his sister, adding with characteristic bravado, "I hold, quite literally, the future of mankind in the palm of my hand." But upon nothing did he wreak more havoc than upon morality.

Nietzsche made morality his primary target because he detected morality in everything human. To know why people believe what they believe and do what they do, to know why cultures are what they are and why they rise and fall, to have any chance of guiding the future, you must understand morality in all of its confident self-righteousness and subtle masquerades.

This is what Nietzsche set out to do in *On the Genealogy of Morals*. He would track the wiles of morality back through the overgrown trails of Western civilization to their origins. He would lay bare the secret judgments, the hidden wishes, the guilty lies that mold cultures and move history. And in doing this he would send the prevailing Western morality to its grave, preparing the way for a new morality, a new civilization, a new kind of human being. Everything Nietzsche wrote rushed toward these ends. But nowhere were his purposes clearer and his hammer-blows harder than in this book. And nothing anyone ever wrote springs more revelatory surprises and delivers more eye-opening truths about how we think and who we are. In short, reading Nietzsche will change your life.

NIETZSCHE'S PREMISE is this: we make choices all the time, and every choice is moral. Choices are moral because they are value judgments: we choose one thing over another because we value it more. And we value it more, Nietzsche says, for one reason: because it is good for us and our kind.

We tend to ignore this elemental fact of human life, Nietzsche explains, by thinking that our everyday choices are simply pragmatic and morally neutral, and that our conscious moral decisions come from some objective truth or standard of good established by God or nature or ethics. Not so, says Nietzsche. Everyday choices and conscious moral decisions come down to the same thing: they originate *in us*, and they express our very natures. "Our ideas, our values, our yeas and nays, our ifs and buts," he writes, "grow out of us with the necessity with which a tree bears fruit." Nietzsche was referring specifically to philosophers here, but the observation applies to anyone. And because we do not feel this growth happening, caught up in it as we are, we should all the more try to stand outside of ourselves and be on the watch.

Seen in this light, our choices and our ways of thinking take on a new look. They are value judgments that at once "grow out of us" and lend order to our experience. These judgments are therefore, Nietzsche says, a way of answering the questions: "'What really was that which we have just experienced?' and moreover: 'Who are we really?'" This is to say that all of our judgments, our choices, our morality, are an interpretation of what happens to us, a way of giving meaning to our lives. We may think that this meaning, and our morality, come from outside of us, but they do not. "There are no moral phenomena at all," Nietzsche declares, "only a moral interpretation of phenomena." And we are the interpreters, in everything we think and do. This is Nietzsche's wake-up call. Everything else he says follows from it.

Nietzsche's moral relativism may be unsettling. But what comes next is downright jolting. If morality (or the choices, preferences, and judgments that make up morality) is only an interpretation of experience, and often a blind interpretation at that, then our morality can—and here Nietzsche rubs his hands—be wrong! Suppose, Nietzsche asks, that our very definition of "good" were wrong! Suppose that, instead of this "good" being beneficial to us, "the reverse were true?"—that what we thought was good for us was actually bad and destructive? What if our "good," our morality, were actually "a seduction, a poison, a narcotic, through which the present was possibly living at the expense of the future?" (as Karl Marx believed religion to be—see Chapter 15). "What if a symptom of regression were inherent in the 'good,'" a going backwards, a decline? Then it would not be "good" at all. It would be the opposite; it would be "the danger of dangers." If we discovered this to be so, if we came to see that morality works as a "mask, as illness, as tartufferie, as misunderstanding," then all our previous values would be overthrown. Nothing would be what we thought it was. We would not be who we thought we were.

Nietzsche throws down the gauntlet of these provocative ideas to start us thinking from scratch and looking at ourselves from the other side of the mirror. For only then can we understand "the genealogy of morals"— and ourselves. As Nietzsche charts this genealogy, it is no mere history of conventional moral ideas. That would be a misleading history of appearances. Nietzsche goes after the root of moral ideas: why we choose *this* rather than *that*, why we value what we value, what is the *"value of these values themselves,"* the meaning of the meanings we give to things. By seeing into these depths, we learn things about ourselves that we could not otherwise have imagined and that we might want to change.

Digging into the roots of our morality, Nietzsche finds what he is looking for. Those roots lie tangled and embedded in psychological needs. The "good" is what satisfies those needs. But suspecting that those needs and their satisfactions—and therefore what is "good" for us—are not the same for everyone, Nietzsche links them to personality types. He reduces these types to two. The one type is the strong, for whom energy, exertion, and affirmation are the breath of life. The other is the weak, for whom passivity, cunning, and denial are everything.

From these personality types flow two moral traditions. The tradition of the strong (which Nietzsche associates first with the aristocratic warrior and the savage "blond beast") prizes all things in which there reigns "a powerful physicality, a flourishing, abundant, even overflowing health, together with that which serves to preserve it: war, adventure, hunting, dancing, war games, and in general all that involves vigorous, free, joyful activity." Within this tradition, the value judgment "good" names everything that feeds vitality, power, superiority (Aristotle defined "good" quite like this in the *Ethics*—see Chapter 4). And "bad" is but a dismissive term for incapacity, weakness, baseness, and so forth. The strong do not pay much attention to the "bad" and to the people who embody it, since they are merely low, inferior, insignificant. How could the strong be other than indifferent to what is so far beneath them?

The tradition of the weak is more complicated. It began, so Nietzsche imagines, among the priestly class, which valued restraint and purity and the manifold secret and quiet qualities of the inner life. "It was on the soil of this essentially dangerous form of human existence, the priestly form," Nietzsche says, "that man first became an interesting animal." Human beings became "interesting" because they passed beyond the simple value judgments that had labeled strength "good" and weakness "bad," and produced a new morality, born of inwardness, inactivity, and denial. This was a subtle and complicated morality, and a dangerous one. It was the morality of the weak themselves, the slave, the mob, the herd, the morality of all people who are deficient in strength and will, energy, and capacity, but who interpret these deficiencies as what else but—"good." This is how the lowly qualities that the strong had labeled "bad" became the very measure of "good" to the weak. The weak wanted to feel good about themselves, and so they called themselves "good." This idea "grew out of" the weak, like fruit from a tree. But this fruit was defective, containing the seeds of a lie.

Unlike the morality of the strong, which "develops from a triumphant affirmation" of their own natures, the morality of the weak originates not in genuine affirmation of themselves, but in denial of what differs from them. "In order to exist," Nietzsche explains, "slave morality always first needs a hostile external world . . . its action is fundamentally reaction." Lacking a nature worthy of affirming directly, the weak can only react negatively to what they are not, denying it value, and then affirm themselves indirectly. Their "morality from the outset says No to what is 'outside,' what is 'different,' what is 'not itself'; and this No is its creative deed." And so they comfortably tell themselves, "Let us be different" from the others; let us be "good" in our own way.

Nietzsche graphically depicts this "transvaluation of values," as he sometimes calls it, in the "workshops" where the ideals, or morals (or lies), of the weak are made:

> There is a soft, wary malignant muttering and whispering coming from all corners and nooks. . . . A saccharine sweetness clings to every sound. Weakness is being lied into something meritorious, no doubt of it . . . , and impotence which does not requite into "goodness of heart"; anxious lowliness into humility; subjection to those one hates into obedience. . . . The inoffensiveness of the weak man, even the cowardice of which he has so much . . . here acquire flattering names, such as "patience" . . . ; his inability for revenge is called unwillingness to revenge, perhaps even forgiveness. . . . They also speak of "loving one's enemies" . . . and sweat as they do.

And as the weak christen their deficiencies and inferiorities "good," they do something else to the qualities of abundance and superiority that characterize the strong. The weak could not simply dismiss the attributes of the strong as "bad." For the weak cannot look down on the strong and disdain them as insignificant. The strong are above them, superior, powerful, threatening. No, "bad" would not do. Another term, and another moral idea were required.

So it was that the strong and their strengths, the very qualities that were "good" for the strong, and that aroused fear in the weak, were condemned by the weak not as "bad" but as—"evil." "According to master morality, it is precisely the 'good' who inspire fear," Nietzsche observes, "while the 'bad' man is judged contemptible," the antithesis of fearful. But "according to slave morality, the 'evil' inspire fear," for "power and danger were felt to exist in evil, a . . . strength which could not admit of contempt," and which called for moral ingenuity in response. This ingenuity made a virtue of being "different from the evil, namely good." And "good" as only the weak could be: "He is good who does not outrage, who harms nobody, who does not attack, who does not requite . . . who keeps himself hidden as we do, who avoids evil and desires little from life, like us the patient, humble, and just." This was a cunning move by the weak—and *cunning* is itself another of their virtues, secret and sly. Oh, how much more virtuous are the "good" than the "evil."

Nietzsche concluded that overturning the values of the strong by the weak was an epochal event. Its consequences inspired Nietzsche's most jarring observations of modern culture and many of his most compelling ideas. These observations and ideas slash and destroy, but they also clear the air. And they can alert us to our own weaknesses, and arm us against them.

First among these ideas is resentment. Everyone should know what resentment is. It infects most of us at some time. And it does us only harm. If we do not diagnose and at least try to cure it, resentment can consume us like a cancer.

Nietzsche did not invent the idea of resentment, or *ressentiment*. It goes back at least as far as the French moralists of early modern times—Montaigne, La Bruyère, La Rochefoucauld (Dante had seen a version of it in sullen anger—see Chapter 5). But it was Nietzsche who made resentment paramount to understanding value judgments and the genealogy of morals. For he recognized resentment as the very soul of psychological weakness and of our deceptive self-justifications.

Weakness gives birth to resentment when it keeps us from doing what we want to do, such as fulfilling an ambition or redressing a grievance, often both. Then weakness compounds our frustration by igniting a peculiar emotion. This emotion combines hatred and envy. In the grips of this emotion we do not blame ourselves for our frustrations, our failures, our hurts. We blame others, and we hate them for thwarting us even while we envy them for succeeding. Yet instead of acting directly against these others—weakness, after all, cannot act directly—we remain silent, holding our pains and frustrations within. There they fester, intensifying our hatred and envy, which do not wane until we gain our satisfaction, through revenge. Whether the offending incident is great or small, intended or accidental—a failed aspiration, a competitor's success, an injury suffered, an unintended slight—the effect outsizes the cause, for it is heated by a cauldron of seething, impotent rage. This hatred and envy, this impotent rage, this is the cancer that is resentment. And it is not a pretty sight.

Except to the resentful themselves, of course, who feed on resentment and make a virtue of it. "The slave revolt in morality," Nietzsche says, "begins when *ressentiment* itself becomes creative and gives birth to values." This perverse creativity fueled those workshops where the new morality was being forged. And in its various manifestations it typifies the psychology of weakness and holds a mirror up to all of us in our moments of impotence and resentment.

Start with the idea of enemies. Because resentment springs from weakness and reaction, the psychology and morality of resentment revolve around enemies. Nothing happens in a world of resentment without enemies. Enemies are everywhere. Enemies give the resentful the very purpose of their lives: revenge. "I suffer," they complain, "someone must be to blame for it." And, blind to the truth that "*you alone are to blame for yourself,*" they seek vengeance against "the enemy" for their misfortunes. They will take anyone as their enemy, whom they dub "*the Evil One.*" "Whoever is dissatisfied with himself," Nietzsche observes, "is always ready to revenge himself therefore; we others will be his victims." And the resentful never cease plotting reprisals, all of which make them feel deliciously righteous.

Just as the morality of resentment springs from reaction and fastens onto enemies, it thrives on lies. How else can people of resentment transfigure their own incapacities, their envy, their hatred, and their unseen self-contempt into an elevating moral system, except by lying? The creative deed of resentment, the surreptitious "No" murmured to all that is unlike itself, and the consoling "Yes" whispered to its own inadequacies, these are all lies. Nietzsche's older contemporary, Henrik Ibsen, had a character in *The Wild Duck* defend what he called the "Life Lie" as a medicinal self-deception that shields us from hurtful truths. The lies of resentment work like this, although they are not benignly medicinal. At least Nietzsche did not think so. For the lies of resentment spin a vicious web of fraudulent virtue with "the sublime self-deception that interprets weakness as freedom and thus-and-thus as a *merit.*"

Nietzsche usefully discriminates here between two kinds of lies: the honest lie and the dishonest lie. An honest lie knows itself for what it is, a conscious piece of invention that masks facts for deliberate purposes. A dishonest lie is not so honorable; it does not know itself as a lie, but takes itself as truth, its provenance and purpose remaining unknown to its maker. Dishonest liars cannot abide actual truth. Yet their unconscious lies let them feel virtuously truthful. "A real lie, a genuine, resolute, 'honest' lie," Nietzsche says, "would be something far too severe and potent for them; it would demand of them what one may not demand of them, that they should open their eyes to themselves that they should know how to distinguish 'true' and 'false' in themselves." The people of resentment are "utterly incapable of confronting any matter except with dishonest mendaciousness—a mendaciousness that is abysmal but innocent, true-hearted, blue-eyed and virtuous."

Persons thriving on dishonest lies, on lying to themselves, are blind to objectivity. They will not open their eyes—to logic, facts, or to themselves. These people include most conspicuously the bigots and fanatics who are impelled by a simpleminded need to feel superior. But we all lie to ourselves when we embrace ideas that protect us and make us feel comfortable and "virtuous" without our acknowledging these enticements. Sentimentality is one such dishonest lie (look at Emma Bovary—see Chapter 24) and so is smug self-righteousness. Addicted to this self-serving mendacity, "the man of *ressentiment* is neither upright nor naive nor honest and straightforward with himself. His soul squints; his spirit loves hiding places, secret paths and back doors, everything covert entices him as his world, his security, his refreshment." He is an insect who lurks in dark places, licking his wounds and watching for his chance.

And there, wrapped in dishonest lies, people of resentment remember "how not to forget." Just as they cannot exist without lying, the resentful can never forget an injury. The memory, shaped by dishonesty, possesses them, guiding their perceptions, commanding their judgment, inspiring their reactive morality. Patiently, cunningly, secretively, they remember. And wait.

By contrast, the strong, who always meet life head-on and openly, respond to an affront by avenging it promptly or dismissing it altogether. Either way, it is gone. "To be incapable of taking one's enemies, one's accidents, even one's misdeeds seriously for long—that is the sign of strong, full natures in whom there is an excess of the power to form, to mold, to recuperate and to forget." Such a person "shakes off with a single shrug many vermin that eat deep into others." This is one of Nietzsche's sharpest and most life-serving insights: that "shrug" can spare us more emotional discontent than almost any other psychological act we can perform (Aristotle had also observed this in the *Ethics*—see Chapter 4). When we learn to give that shrug, we conquer resentment, with its ubiquitous enemies, dishonest lies, and consuming hunger for revenge. And we acquire a strength that can serve us in uncountable ways.

For that strength involves a severe control of mind extending from past to present and into the future. We cultivate it first by exercising "active forgetfulness," which "is like a doorkeeper, a preserver of psychic order, repose, and etiquette." This doorkeeper is what makes healthy-mindedness possible. "Without forgetfulness," without that control of our thoughts and feelings about the past, "there could be no happiness, no cheerfulness, no hope, no pride, no present." We would be captives of the past—as we are when suffering resentment—we could not live our own lives. (Freud derived psychoanalysis from similar observations about memory and forgetting—albeit not all positive—and he admitted refusing to read Nietzsche lest he find all of his ideas already there.) If you can truly forget, you can be strong and free and move on.

And here appears another telling and instructive difference between the weak and the strong. This has to do with discipline and self-mastery as such. Because the strong alone have mastery of their memories, minds, and emotions, they alone can rightfully claim "mastery" over themselves and over "circumstances." That power enables them not only to honestly manage their lives with "active forgetfulness," but to shape the future by sheer strength of will. And this ability to shape the future gives them alone "the right to make promises," for they can fulfill any vow they make—another sign of honesty. The weak have none of this. Creatures of impotence, seething with resentment, steeped in mendacity, incapable of "active forgetfulness," the weak have no true control over their minds or emotions, themselves or their lives in the past, the present, or the future. Therefore they have no right to make promises. Their promises become lies.

The weak think, of course, that they exhibit strong self-mastery through their morality of self-denial, patience, forgiveness, turning the other cheek, and the like. But this only masks impotence, reaction, resentment, and lies. The weak have nothing much within themselves to exercise self-mastery over, no fount of energy to hold back, no imperious will to constrain. In truth, only the strong contain forces that could call for restraint. And by forcefully harnessing their powerful energies and turning these inward, Nietzsche explains, the strong win strength from strength and shape events. The so-called self-mastery of the weak can only breed weakness from weakness. And then, devoid of honest self-mastery, the weak despise it in others and chafe at it in culture, lying to themselves and to everyone.

Punching the point, Nietzsche asks: Who will prove best at following and exercising the law, the strong or the weak? It might seem to be the weak since they extol self-denial, obedience, and submission. But in fact it is the strong. They, not the weak, Nietzsche contends, created "the institution of law" and the state. For they alone, these "artists of violence and organizers who build states," welcome the imposition of discipline and form upon surging energies, the conversion of subjectivity into objectivity, the wresting of order from chaos. And along with the law and the state, they invented justice, that "piece of perfection and supreme mastery on earth," which supplants "the predominance of grudges and rancor"—that is, resentment—with an "impersonal evaluation of the deed." Justice then made possible that most surprising of Nietzschean virtues—"*mercy*," the "privilege of the most powerful man." Who else could grant mercy besides those with the power to waive the objective authority of justice and go "beyond the law" for no reason other than to be merciful? Rooting through the underbrush of human psychology and morality, Nietzsche finds all kinds of things. Some ugly, some delightsome. Law and justice and mercy are delightsome, like most of the attributes of the strong.

The psychological qualities of law and justice and mercy could never belong to the weak and resentful. Alien to harsh self-discipline, and opposing "everything that dominates and wants to dominate," the weak resent authority—although they will abase themselves before it and then mercilessly exercise it if given the chance. They spread that peculiarly modern malaise "misarchism," Nietzsche says, "to coin an ugly word for an ugly thing," which disrespects hierarchy, authority, and constraint. For the weak want no one above them, no interference with their feeble natures. Fearful of what is different from and superior to them, they value nothing but themselves, their own comforts, their own ease, their own anxieties, their own hatreds, their own kind. And they deem the others, those who admire superiority, those who insist upon the strenuous exertion of will, those who subject themselves to an impersonal discipline, all of these the weak regard as enemies, and *evil*. "What gives greater offense" to these self-deceived and self-righteous people of resentment, Nietzsche asks, "than to reveal something of the severity and respect with which one treats oneself? And on the other hand—how accommodating, how friendly all the world is toward us as soon as we act as all the world does and 'let ourselves go' like all the world!" Harsh self-discipline bespeaks a strength of will that the weak cannot achieve and so they cannot abide. Consequently they welcome its absence with warm affection. "It is only human," we commonly say of our weaknesses and fallibilities, and we expect sweet understanding and kindly acceptance. Nietzsche knows.

He also knows that the weak will be as imperious in victory as they are obsequious in defeat. And, irony of ironies, paradox of paradoxes, for all of their deficiencies and self-deceptions, Nietzsche declares, the weak have prevailed. "The slave revolt in morality" triumphed! The "morality of the common man has won," Nietzsche announces. "The people have won—or 'the slaves' or 'the mob' or 'the herd' or whatever you like to call them. . . . The 'redemption' of the human race (from 'the masters,' that is) is going forward; everything is visibly becoming Judaized,

Christianized, mob-ized (what do the words matter!)." Nietzsche's hammer blows are unapologetically elitist. This may not appeal to every reader. But these blows produce more useful clues to our psychology and our culture than an encyclopedia of humanitarian ideals. Take a further look.

Although Nietzsche thinks the slave revolt succeeded in part by sheer numbers—because the weak outnumber the strong, as inferiors outnumber superiors—numbers do not tell the whole story. Certainly not the most important part of the story. More significant, and revealing of human nature, is Nietzsche's observation that the strong actually contributed to their own defeat by living out their own natures: they ignored the weak, and forgot them.

After all, it is a sign of strength not to take one's opponents or lessers seriously for long, and to exhibit "a bold recklessness whether in the face of danger or of the enemy" with an "indifference to and contempt for security, body, life, comfort." Without these attributes, the strong would not be the strong. But these same attributes make the strong peculiarly vulnerable—"there is indeed too much carelessness, too much taking lightly"—to such dangers as the devious strategies of those inferior beings preoccupied with enemies and bent on revenge.

The paradox produced tragedy: the psychology of the strong let the weak gain their insidious ascendancy, Nietzsche says. And so the weak transformed Western civilization in their image through a "transvaluation of values" that supplanted potency with impotence, affirmation with resentment, honesty with mendacity. In Nietzsche's eyes this victory imposed a cruel hoax on the West. For it brought the reign of moral ideals which, in the name of advancing mankind, have retarded it.

This is what Nietzsche meant at the beginning by a "good" that turns out to be false, wrong, harmful, a morality that is "regressive," a "narcotic," a "misunderstanding." For this "good," wrapped as it is in weakness and self-deceptive lies, has, Nietzsche argues, actually diminished respect for human beings. A civilization shaped by the weak will judge itself "better" than its predecessors because it is more humane. But in denying the virtues of strength and individuality and superiority, such a civilization will have accomplished a terrible deed: it will have robbed human life of all higher values. And "this is how things are," Nietzsche asserts, "the diminution and leveling of European man constitutes our greatest danger, for the sight of him makes us weary.—We can see nothing today that wants to grow greater, we suspect that things will continue to go down, down, to become thinner, more good-natured, more prudent, more comfortable, more mediocre, more indifferent, more Chinese, more Christian—there is no doubt that man is getting 'better' all the time."

Good-better-best. By this perverted declension, so Nietzsche believes, civilization has gone down, down, down. What can we genuinely admire and honor—by contrast to mendaciously judging as "good"—when everything is low and deficient, when we can never raise our eyes to gaze on anything different, greater, higher, superior? "Who would not a hundred times sooner fear where one can also admire," Nietzsche asks, "than not fear but be permanently condemned to the repellent sight of the ill-constituted, dwarfed, atrophied, and poisoned?" Who indeed? The weak, that is who. "And is that not our fate?" Nietzsche continues, "that we no longer have anything left to fear in man; that the maggot 'man' is swarming in the foreground; that the 'tame man,' the hopelessly mediocre and insipid man, has already learned to feel himself as the goal and zenith, as the meaning of history, as the 'higher man.'"

Nietzsche clearly relished his rousing denunciations of the world around him, as did many of his late nineteenth- and early twentieth-century readers—among them Gabriel D'Annunzio, George Bernard Shaw, and José Ortega y Gasset—who found in Nietzsche's words both a diagnosis of their culture and a remedy for its ills (Ortega's *The Revolt of the Masses* [1930] presents a penetratingly Nietzschean interpretation of modern culture). Few readers today will altogether share that relish. Western civilization, most would say, is not all that bad. Nevertheless, Nietzsche's condemnation of the culture of his day should not be dismissed. For it challenges us to look closely at ourselves and our "values," and at how we can make our culture thrive or decline. Nietzsche also brings to light here a peculiar attribute of modern culture, which he sees as both the culmination of the sorry genealogy he has traced and as a signal pointing beyond that genealogy to his own buoyantly affirming vision of the future. This attribute is nihilism.

Nihilism is the judgment that nothing that exists has ultimate value, whether that judgment is deliberate or implied. Nietzsche blamed modern nihilism on the morality of the weak (Charles Dickens, also detecting nihilism as a prevailing modern malaise, blamed it on the dehumanizing cult of facts—see Chapter 13). For what can we truly value when weakness reigns, when everything is base, when human beings spurn self-mastery to feed on lies and denial? "Here precisely is what has become a fatality for Europe," Nietzsche rails, "together with the fear of man we have also lost our love of him, our reverence for him, our hopes for him, even our will to him. The sight of man now makes us weary—what is nihilism today if it is not that?—We are weary of man." This is how the morality of the weak becomes "the danger of dangers." It turns morality against itself—that is, it makes a value of impotence, of worthlessness, of negation, of *nothing* (Goethe's Mephistopheles would relish this—see Chapter 7).Then life itself loses meaning. Even if people do not openly admit this, as few people ever would, they can still think and act as if they believed it.

No wonder Nietzsche happily greeted "all signs that a more manly, more warlike, age is about to begin," when "the beast of prey, the splendid blond beast prowling about avidly in search of spoil and victory" will return from the forest to raze the culture of resentment and redeem the human race from "the great nausea, the will to nothingness, nihilism." And no wonder Nietzsche became the mentor for a generation of European males around the turn of the twentieth century. They, too, yearned to smash the old decadent culture with an explosion of animal energies. World War I erupted with Nietzschean phrases on the lips of soldiers in every country: let us have war, they cried, "war, the hygiene of the world," as Filippo Marinetti put it in the *Futurist Manifesto*. After that war Fascists renewed and intensified the campaign, with the Nazis promising to cleanse the world of the likes of Nietzsche's "maggot man" by extinguishing inferior peoples and establishing a thousand-year reign of the strong.

But notwithstanding his elitism and images of violence, Nietzsche was not calling for Fascists and Nazis, as noted earlier. He had another remedy for weakness and nihilism. This was "the great health," a bracing affirmation of life that could energize anyone—even now.

"Grant me the sight," he writes, "but *one* glance of something perfect, wholly achieved, happy, mighty, triumphant, something still capable of arousing fear! Of a man who justifies man, of a complementary and redeeming lucky hit on the part of man for the sake of which one may still *believe in man!*" How can human beings inspire and justify this belief? Strength is necessary, to be sure, but not strength to crush others—that would be a motive born of resentment. The strength needed is to rule oneself. For only the "severity and respect with which one treats oneself" can nurture the will, the integrity, the beauty, and the cheerfulness that bring "the great health."

Nietzsche gives a prescription for "the great health" in a memorable passage of *The Gay Science* applicable to everyone. "One thing is needful," he says: "'Giving style' to one's character—a great and rare art! It is exercised by those who see all the strengths and weaknesses of their own characters and then comprehend them in an artistic plan until everything appears as art and reason and even weakness delights the eye."

These words contain Nietzsche's finest contribution to the art of life. For they translate Nietzsche's paean to the strong into a formula for shaping character—with all of its "strengths and weaknesses"—through honesty, imagination, and will. Who can do it, and who cannot? "It will be the strong and domineering natures who enjoy their finest gaiety in such compulsion, in such constraint and perfection under a law of their own. . . . Conversely it is the weak characters without power themselves who hate the constraint of style." Nietzsche could not have thought otherwise. We shouldn't either.

To equate character with style is not to reduce ethics to aesthetics, or to prescribe a "life-style," that cheap shibboleth of late twentieth-century popular psychology and consumerism. It is to highlight the interrelations among strength, character, and artistic form. The strong create their morality, their character, by subjugating vast unruly forces to the discipline of style or form. In a lyrical passage of *Thus Spoke Zarathustra*, Nietzsche says: "One must have chaos within to give birth to a dancing star." The chaos is powerful energies; the star is energies formed. This imposition of form is an artistic act. "This secret self-ravishment, this artists' cruelty, this delight in imposing form upon oneself as a hard, recalcitrant, suffering material," this is the shaping of a star, the making of the character of the strong. It is also art itself and all "imaginative phenomena." And it is law and justice and the state. It is mercy. It is an invigorating culture. In sum, it is "an abundance of strange new beauty and affirmation" that are human life and civilization at their zenith.

Nietzsche proclaims that those who can impose this rigorous form on themselves will create "a bridge, a great promise," from the low to the high, from impotence to potency, from the "maggot man" to the "Superman." They will be "preparatory" beings, "higher men," who are what all of us could be: "characterized by cheerfulness, patience, unpretentiousness, and contempt for all great vanities, as well as by magnanimity in victory and forbearance regarding the small vanities of the vanquished." This is indeed the image of a strong person, free from petty passions and meanness of spirit. It is a person "possessed of keen and free judgment concerning all victors and the share of chance in every victory and every fame"; a person who swiftly avenges offenses or shrugs them off, and who lives confidently, artfully, cheerfully, a life of "greater danger, more fruitful, and happier!" than that of less courageous and imaginative people.

Who could resist this invigorating portrait of "the great health" and "higher men"? Only those whose feeble natures begrudge constraint and shrink from risk. For the psychology of the "great health" of "The Higher Man" (as Nietzsche entitles a chapter in *Zarathustra*) calls for testing oneself, challenging received ideas, skirting the easy path, pressing to the limits. "The secret of the greatest fruitfulness and the greatest enjoyment of existence," Nietzsche says, "is to *live dangerously*! Build your cities under Vesuvius! Send your ships into uncharted seas! Live at war with your peers and yourselves!" Only those who can live dangerously will seize the highest joys from life—whether or not they prepare the way for a still superior type of being, the human above the human: the *Übermensch*, the Superman.

But never mind the Superman. That was a burst of Nietzsche's exuberant optimism (which inspired some of George Bernard Shaw's brilliantly didactic intellectual dramas, like *Man and Superman*). No one need embrace Nietzsche's philosophy whole to learn from its warnings against resentment and to gain from its ideal of the "great health." For Nietzsche saw more clearly than anyone before him, or since, that no truth of human nature is more decisive than this: "A human being" must "attain his satisfaction with himself"—whatever the means—and "whoever is dissatisfied with himself is always ready to revenge himself therefore." Countless personal sorrows and public tragedies have sprung from this dissatisfaction. And nothing we do can more efficaciously secure our own satisfaction than, as Nietzsche says, by "giving style" to our character—that is, honestly seeing who we are and then imposing an artistic form on our entire being, "until everything appears as art and reason and even weakness delights the eye."

With this consummate achievement of imagination and will, we can confidently answer Nietzsche's opening questions: "'What really was that which we have just experienced?' and moreover: 'Who are we really?'" The answers are: What we have experienced is life itself. And who we are is those who have imposed style on our characters and who therefore enjoy the great health. We are the strong, the truthful, the cheerful, the model of a civilization to be proud of. To no truly better end could the genealogy of morals lead.

On Morality, Weakness, Strength, and Health

1. Our moral ideas serve our interests, often in disguise.
2. Our moral ideas could be wrong, and even harmful to us.
3. The morality of the strong openly serves strength, and the morality of the weak secretly serves weakness.
4. The morality of the weak is harmful to human character.
5. The morality of the weak feeds on self-deceiving lies and thrives on resentment.
6. Resentment turns feelings of weakness and self-contempt into moral righteousness and blame of the strong.
7. The resentful never forget a hurt, and they secretly crave revenge.

8. Beware of those who crave revenge—they will blame anyone for their discontents.

9. We can fight resentment in ourselves by not blaming others for our discontents, and by forgetting the injuries done to us.

10. The power of active forgetfulness is a sign of strength that brings freedom from the past and confidence in the future.

11. The right to make promises belongs only to the strong because they can fulfill their promises, as the weak cannot.

12. The strong impose *style* on their characters—a great and rare art—through penetrating self-knowledge and severe self-discipline.

13. By imposing style on our character, we honestly mold both strengths and weaknesses into *the great health* that delights the eye.

14. The meaning of life is to have the honesty and strength to stifle resentment, and the imagination and will to impose style on character and achieve *the great health*.

9
Condemned to Be Free

Fyodor Dostoevsky: "The Grand Inquisitor"
Jean-Paul Sartre: "Existentialism"

*Nothing has ever been more insufferable for man
and for human society than freedom.*

Dostoevsky

*Before you came alive, life is nothing; it is up to you
to give it a meaning.*

*You're free, choose, that is, invent.
We are condemned to be free.*

Sartre

Fyodor Dostoevsky (1821–1881) grew up in Moscow and St. Petersburg, Russia, on ideals of social justice, personal heroism, and romantic love. But he lost most of his idealism after a decade (1849–58) of imprisonment and forced military service for politically subversive activities. He had written a couple of short novels—*Poor Folk* and *The Double*—and a few stories, including "White Nights," before this time. Now, in a darker frame of mind, he embarked on a literary career in earnest with a string of powerful works in the 1860s: *Notes from the House of the Dead, Notes from Underground, The Gambler, Crime and Punishment,* and *The Idiot.* The next decade brought the novels *The Possessed, A Raw Youth,* and his masterpiece, *The Brothers Karamazov.* In all of his mature fiction Dostoevsky explored the subjects that had come to occupy his life—especially conflicts between rationality and irrationality, good and evil, freedom and constraint. And he condensed a host of these subjects into one chapter of *The Brothers Karamazov* that has become a classic in itself. It is "The Grand Inquisitor," a story told by one of the brothers about why people do not truly want to be free, and why it is the role of authority to help them escape from freedom. Disturbing as this tale is, it says things about freedom and human nature that ring hauntingly true for most, if not all, of us.

Jean-Paul Sartre (1905–1980) says in his autobiography, *The Words* (1963), that he spent his middle-class childhood in Paris reading and thinking. Insular, intellectual, and inventive, he went on to study phenomenology in Germany and later became the most renowned philosopher of his times as the voice of existentialism. Following the success of his novel *Nausea* (1938), he elaborated his theory of existentialism during World War II in *Being and Nothingness* (1943). After the war he issued a steady stream of novels, stories, plays, essays, biographies, and philosophical works on the existentialist themes of alienation, freedom, and responsibility. He was awarded the Nobel Prize for literature in 1964, but declined it for ideological reasons. Although Sartre grew increasingly, if idiosyncratically, Marxist—reflected in the hefty tome *Critique of Dialectical Reason* (1960) and in his vast speculative biography of Gustave Flaubert, *L'Idiot de la famille* (1971–72)—his name will always stand for existentialism. His thoughtful essay known in English as "Existentialism" (1946) shows why. It lucidly explains how existentialism is a boldly affirming humanism that grants an inescapable freedom, an unflinching integrity, and an inspiriting individuality to our lives.

THERE ARE MANY KINDS of freedom, or many ways of thinking about it. We might think of freedom as the absence of bad things that impair our lives, as in the freedom *from* hunger or oppression. Or we might think of it as the presence of good things that help us live better lives, as in the freedom of opportunity *to do* what is best for us. We might think of freedom as an abundance of choices that we can choose among. Or we might think of it as a selection of only good choices that point the way for us. We might also think of freedom as an independent way of life we value enough to die for. Or we might think of it as a burden of choice that we try to escape at any cost. However we think about freedom, everyone has some idea of it.

In the eighteenth and early nineteenth centuries, defining the political freedom of democracy occupied much of Europe and America (see Chapter 14). But shortly after the middle of the nineteenth century, Fyodor Dostoevsky abandoned his own thwarted desires for political freedom in Russia to become a novelist occupied with other kinds of freedom. His political hopes crushed by a decade of imprisonment and exile, and his ideal of humanity abandoned amidst his exposure to human depravity, Dostoevsky now delved into the dark irrationalities of human nature and the murky ambiguities of free will. These became persistent themes of his writings thereafter.

In *Notes From Underground* (1864) Dostoevsky portrayed an eccentric, and self-described, "anti-hero" who proves to himself that he is free by committing zany, irrational, self-destructive acts. After all, he says, if you always follow "rational self-interest" you are predictable and have no more freedom than a "piano key." The Underground Man is a nut case, on principle, opposing "rational self-interest" and self-restraint as enemies of human freedom. And yet, as we may remember from our own youthful rebelliousness—or as we may discover in mid-life crises—most of us have on occasion done reckless things just to feel free, not so unlike him.

Later, in his greatest novel, *The Brothers Karamazov* (1879–80), Dostoevsky looked at freedom from another angle. There he has Ivan, one of the three Karamazov brothers (a fourth brother is illegitimate) and the philosophical voice in the novel, tell a story about how most people actually do not want to be free to think or to make choices at all, whatever they may say to the contrary. They would rather let others think and choose for them. This story, "The Grand Inquisitor," is probably the world's most profound, disturbing, and unforgettable literary work on human freedom and the desire to escape from it. The Inquisitor's argument that most human beings do not want freedom, and that it is the role of institutional authority—especially in religion—to help them flee it, might revolt us. But when we think about what he says, and look at history and at ourselves, we cannot easily refute him—although Dostoevsky would likely want us to try.

A century after Dostoevsky, the French philosopher Jean-Paul Sartre wove a philosophy of human life around the idea that human beings have absolute freedom of choice whether they want it or not. Popularized as "existentialism," this philosophy had widespread, if often confused, influence over the generation of postwar youth in the West who modeled themselves on the likes of Sartre's antihero in the novel *Nausea*, a creepy character absorbed in his own consciousness and estranged from the world. Although existentialism has long since gone into eclipse, its idea of human freedom deserves to endure. For this idea is among the most intellectually thought-provoking, psychologically challenging, morally demanding, and useful of any notion of freedom the world has known—and it is among the most humanistically inspiring.

The ideals of freedom that occupied Dostoevsky and Sartre have become rather lost nowadays among cries of wounded psyches assigning blame to others for every hurt and discontent, as though no one is responsible for his or her own life, as well as among social scientific theories and therapeutic ideologies that encourage such attitudes. Both Dostoevsky and Sartre would sadly understand this. For they knew that the escape from freedom, and from responsibility for our lives, can take many forms, and wear many disguises. They also saw that in one way or another we are all constantly choosing either to embrace freedom or to run from it, and that there is always a spark of freedom in every choice we make. If we do not see this fundamental truth of human nature and the responsibilities that go with it, they say, we are lying to ourselves and denying our humanity.

DOSTOEVSKY sets Ivan's tale of the Grand Inquisitor in sixteenth-century Seville, Spain, during the infamous Inquisition of the Catholic Counter-Reformation, which executed countless

DOSTOEVSKY

errant believers for heresy. One day a charismatic stranger enters the congested city square, sending murmurs rippling through the crowd. The murmurs say the stranger is Jesus, come again as he had promised to redeem the world. The curious gather around him as he moves among the throng bestowing blessings. Then the Grand Inquisitor appears on the scene and soon instructs his guards to escort the stranger away—to prison. That night the Inquisitor visits the prisoner in his cell. And in a long monologue he tells the man whom he believes to be Jesus, the Son of God, why he intends to burn Him at the stake as "the most evil of heretics."

The Inquisitor says he must execute Jesus again for the sake of humankind. That is because Jesus' teachings are all wrong and have done only harm to the world. The Inquisitor's accusations will strike many readers as offbeat at best. But they give Dostoevsky an occasion to make a powerful case about the fallibilities of human nature and the ambiguities of freedom.

You "acted as if you did not love [human beings] at all," the Inquisitor charges Jesus in laying out his indictment, for "you demanded too much." If Jesus had truly loved human beings, the Inquisitor explains, he would have ministered to human weakness. Instead, Jesus had expected "everything that was beyond men's strength." "I swear," the Inquisitor declares, "man is created weaker and baser than you thought him."

The Inquisitor has a specific human weakness in mind—that is the fear of freedom and its responsibilities. Rather than serving this weakness and allaying this fear, as the Inquisitor thinks Jesus should have done, Jesus had assumed people would want to become stronger. So Jesus had asked them to think freely and choose their lives and their beliefs on their own, with no guidance. But human beings don't want that kind of freedom, the Inquisitor argues, and it was cruel of Jesus to expect them to want it.

The Inquisitor bases his indictment on certain incidents in the New Testament indicating that while Jesus could have spared human beings this burdensome freedom, he had refused to do it. In particular, the

Inquisitor points out, Jesus could have spared human beings by giving them what they most need in life: ample food to fill their stomachs, and absolute truths to fill their minds. Jesus had declined to use his divine powers to satisfy these needs, the Inquisitor accuses, because he had wanted people to choose their lives and embrace faith freely, without the seductions of easy handouts or the sway of heavenly revelations. That was Jesus' crime.

Whether the Inquisitor gets Jesus' story right here is irrelevant. Dostoevsky's subject is not Jesus or Christianity. These are only pretexts or metaphors. Dostoevsky's actual subject might be put as this question: Which do human beings want most, freedom or security? Or, to put it another way: Do people want the *active* freedom to choose their lives and their beliefs for themselves, or do they want the *passive* freedom of not having to choose? We answer these questions with virtually every decision we make, from the religions we profess and the politics we adopt to the careers we pursue and the child-rearing practices we use. As Dostoevsky ingeniously plays upon these questions, the Inquisitor's argument proves to be more insightful than many readers might imagine. Some readers even find themselves siding with the Inquisitor in the end. For the Grand Inquisitor knows human nature all too well.

The Inquisitor makes his own answer to the questions above very clear: "Nothing has ever been more insufferable for man and society than freedom." By ignoring this fact of human nature, he says, Jesus had set Christianity on the wrong course and had caused people grief by asking them to choose their lives and beliefs freely. So the Church, the Inquisitor says, has worked to put Christianity right. "With us everyone will be happy," he explains, because the Church lets people trade the hard active freedom of choice for the easy passive freedom of not having to choose. As he states it, instead of forcing people to suffer the "terrible torments of personal and free decision" in a cruel world, "we shall convince them that they will only become free when they resign their freedom to us, and submit to us." This gives human beings what the Inquisitor believes they need most: freedom *from* choice and responsibility through the security of thoughtless certitude and abject dependency.

Don't quarrel with the Inquisitor's slanted portrait of Christianity and the Roman Catholic Church. What matters is his idea of authority in general. It is an idea that most of us have met at one time or another, in one guise or another, although probably not as baldly as here. We have met it in parents, in preachers, in teachers, in politicians, and possibly in ourselves. Usually it sounds benign, as in a paternalistic desire to protect a child, just as the Inquisitor tries to make it sound. Perhaps it is benign— that hinges on whether the Inquisitor is right about human nature.

The Inquisitor supports his own benign version of authority with a portrait of human nature accentuating the human needs that Jesus had refused to satisfy, and showing why most human beings readily abandon the freedom of choice. In the first place, he says, people will spurn freedom to follow anyone who gives them "bread" or helps them survive, since the freedom to choose is worthless if you are starving. In the second place, even if they are not starving physically, they have a consuming psychological craving to know "what one lives for," or the meaning of life, and they will follow anyone who can satisfy this craving. And no one satisfies it more thoroughly, the Inquisitor contends, than the Church. For the Church deploys three irresistibly persuasive powers: "miracle, mystery, and authority."

By miracle the Grand Inquisitor means physical demonstrations of supernatural powers that win people's spontaneous assent and unquestioning submission. "Man seeks not so much God as miracles," he explains, because God remains remote and unperceivable, whereas miracles happen before our eyes. For instance, when the rabble had shouted for Jesus to come down from the cross, the Inquisitor says, they were demanding a miracle—"then we will believe." But Jesus had resisted, the Inquisitor charges, because "you did not want to enslave man by a miracle, and thirsted for faith that is free, not miraculous." This had left His divinity in doubt for those who demand palpable certainty, not "faith that is free." And that is most people. But the Church has done better for them, the Inquisitor boasts. It has given needy human beings abundant miracles over the years to soothe their anxious psyches and to supply them contented certainties. It has also supported those miracles by using the second persuasive power that brings ready psychological comfort—the beguiling truths of "mystery."

Mystery is a hidden truth that defies fact and rationality. It is what makes miracles possible. Mystery cannot be explained. It cannot be understood. It cannot be disproved. It is beyond all of our logical powers of comprehension. We must believe in mysteries without questioning. And that is exactly what the Inquisitor says most human beings seek. "It is not the free choice of the heart that matters," he argues, "but the mystery, which they must blindly obey." Almost no one wants "to decide for himself, with a free heart," between the true and the false or "what is good and what is evil." People want to be told, with the assurance of divine mystery. For then they bear no responsibility to think or judge for themselves, even to judge the validity of their senses when they encounter miracles. Mystery can justify anything. That is its genius, and its persuasive power. And here is where "authority" comes in.

Authority can manage mysteries, as well as conjure up miracles and provide bread. Whatever people claim to the contrary, the Inquisitor says, they want nothing more than to submit to authority and have security, in body and soul. For "as long as he remains free," suffering the "terrible torments of personal and free decision," a person will have "no more ceaseless or tormenting care . . . than to find someone to bow down to" who can grant release from the responsibilities of free choices. What is more, the Inquisitor adds, that release feels best when it is shared with other people, because then it satisfies not only a personal craving "to know what one lives for," but "the need of mankind for universal and general union" among submissive believers huddled under an authority's wing. Not that anyone admits to submitting in this way or for these reasons. But, the Inquisitor implies, we are submitting in these ways and for these reasons all the same whenever we let any authority do these things for us, and we are inviting others to submit like this whenever we use authority to do these things for them.

"We have corrected your deed," the Grand Inquisitor confidently concludes to Jesus. By wielding "miracle, mystery, and authority," the Church has given human beings what they need, as Jesus would not do. "Have we not, indeed, loved mankind," the Inquisitor asks, by "so lovingly alleviating their burden . . . ?" For "mankind rejoiced that they were once more led like sheep." And now, he taunts Jesus, just watch how eagerly people will "heap hot coals around your stake" when the Inquisitor executes Jesus again "for having come to interfere with us."

In response to this long monologue, Jesus says nothing. He only rises and kisses the Inquisitor. The Inquisitor shudders, and the kiss "burns in his heart." Then the Inquisitor has a change of mind. He will let Jesus live. Ivan Karamazov does not say why. But we have to suspect that Ivan's Inquisitor has decided that Jesus no longer poses a threat, because, after all, Jesus' insistence on the terrible freedom of choice will ultimately fall on deaf ears amidst the Church's enticing invitations to "escape from freedom" (a phrase popularized in the mid-twentieth century by the psychologist Erich Fromm to characterize the totalitarian systems of Fascism and Communism). The Inquisitor opens the prison door and says to Jesus: "Go and do not come again . . . do not come at all . . . never, never!"

In telling this chilling story, Dostoevsky is obviously assailing a particular kind of religious authority. But more important he is probing human nature, the meaning of freedom, and all kinds of authority. For he subtly lets us see that the Grand Inquisitor plays two different roles. In one role the Inquisitor appears as a sympathetic authority figure who genuinely understands the weaknesses of human nature, and who honestly and humanely tries to make life better for human beings by trading their anxious freedom of choice for calm security in a troubled world. This is, of course, how the Inquisitor wants us to see him. In the other role the Inquisitor appears as an ingenious spokesman for all of those in positions of authority, from parents to preachers to politicians, who promise certitude and security to people in exchange for their submission—and the Inquisitor hints that he actually speaks for the devil in making his case. But the truth is, whenever we exercise any kind of authority that relieves people of responsibility, we are performing in one, or possibly both, of the Inquisitor's roles. We might honestly be serving people's needs, but we might also be inviting them to escape from freedom into submission, whether we admit it or not—the act of submission can be pretty much the same. So we should weigh carefully the consequences of ever giving up our freedom of choice, or asking others to give up theirs.

Religious zealots play both of the Inquisitor's roles with a deceptive solicitude, promising to save people by telling them how to think and act, and assuring them that this is God's will, and that a reward for their submission awaits in heaven. But any doctrinaire or ideological way of thinking can lead us down that path. For these ways of thinking encourage people to swap the freedom of critical judgment and open-mindedness for authoritative answers to every question—remember that fictional paragon of glib philosophical certainty, Dr. Pangloss in Voltaire's *Candide* (see Chapter 13), or Marxists in their heyday, or rigid academic theorists and fervent political ideologues of any stripe today. The intentions of anyone or of any authoritarian religious, intellectual, or ideological system can be as humane as the Grand Inquisitor claims his to be. But even the most humane of these intentions can induce the escape from freedom. Every advocate or follower of any authority or system of thought—and even every well-meaning parent—should be aware of this.

It is likely that Dostoevsky intended "The Grand Inquisitor" to alert us to the blandishments of authority that help us rationalize our escapes from freedom. Still, the Inquisitor is surely right in saying that to be happy people must trade a measure of freedom for security, or trade a measure of the active freedom to choose for the passive freedom from having to make choices all the time—what would marriage, for instance, be without such a trade? The question is how much freedom, and what kind of freedom, does the trade ask that we give up? In any case, Dostoevsky's tale prompts us to ponder what it means to be free: to think about what freedom can do for us, and what it costs us; to think about how we can balance the competing needs for freedom and for security; to think about how we can distinguish between legitimate and illegitimate submission to authority; to think about how we can escape from freedom without even knowing we are doing that; and to think about how we judge the price to our character and our lives of letting that escape from freedom succeed. In short, "The Grand Inquisitor" makes us think about freedom and security as probably never before.

LIKE DOSTOEVSKY's Grand Inquisitor, Jean-Paul Sartre recognized that, whether people admit it or not, they do not always want to be free. But, unlike the Grand Inquisitor, Sartre concluded that, **SARTRE** try as we might, we cannot ever truly escape from this freedom and the responsibilities it brings. For better or worse, he asserted, we are "condemned to be free" no matter what. That idea is the heart of existentialism.

It is a provocative, paradoxical, and perplexing idea. And as Sartre elaborated it, he made existentialism the most radical philosophy of human freedom possible, and the most "popular" philosophy of the mid-twentieth century. Existentialism has more to it than its idea of freedom, but this is the bedrock for everyday purposes, and it is both a true idea and a useful one.

Sartre explained what he meant by the phrase "condemned to be free" at arduous length in *Being and Nothingness* (1943), his wartime metaphysical treatise. He had previously intimated the idea in his provocative prewar novel *Nausea*, and he later played upon it in many postwar works of fiction and drama, as well as in abundant essays—often published in his own periodical, *Les Temps Moderne*—and in philosophical biographies of Jean Genet and Charles Baudelaire (most of his later writings strike a more Marxist tone). But wading through Sartre's dense and rather formless philosophizing can be daunting and unrewarding. And his didactic existentialist fiction, such as the three-volume novel *Les Chemins de la Liberté* (*The Roads of Liberty* [1945–49]—a projected fourth volume never appeared), can be dreary and unpersuasive. Sartre could, to be sure, write brilliantly. He did this in many places, including *Nausea*, the story "The Wall," the play *No Exit*, his evocative autobiography, *The Words*, and in numerous engaging essays.

One of these essays stands out for evocatively summarizing the chief and best ideas of existentialism. Published in English simply as "Existentialism," this essay originated as a speech to a conference of clergymen just after World War II during the rising tide of existentialism's vogue. First published in French as *L'Existentialism est un humanisme* (1946), it skirts metaphysical thickets and abstruse philosophizing to describe how, as the French title says, "existentialism is a humanism." Existentialism is, in fact, Sartre says, the most elemental humanistic philosophy there can be. For it is *the* philosophy of human freedom and responsibility. He was probably right. And if we can see human freedom as Sartre does, this can affect how we think about every choice we make—as well as about the choices we choose not to make.

Existentialism might not seem to have this everyday practicality when we first meet Sartre's idea of freedom. But hang on. Sartre likes to provoke reactions, and then he leads the way to some enlightening conclusions. He does this in the essay "Existentialism" better than anywhere else.

Sartre explains there that man is condemned to be free because, in the first place, human beings have no fixed and given "human nature." How is that possible? we might ask. This is Sartre's answer: human beings were not created by a god who gives them a soul and a purpose in the universe, nor are they mere animals driven by inborn instincts, nor are they objects manufactured in a factory to serve specific functions. Human beings are simply "thrown into the world," Sartre says (echoing his philosophical mentor Martin Heidegger), with no predetermined or fixed nature or plan of existence programmed into them. Consequently "there is no determinism" of any kind that applies to human beings. This means they *exist* with free will, which nothing else in the universe has. In fact, Sartre adds, human beings do not just possess free will: "Man *is* freedom." That is to say, freedom exists nowhere else in the universe except in human beings as they make choices to live. Aristotle had made the act of choice the defining quality of human beings, too (see Chapter 4). But Sartre goes farther. He says that human freedom is absolute because human existence is absolutely free.

If these claims for human free will seem beyond common sense—and certainly alien to religion and social science—wait to see where Sartre goes with them. Some very good ideas will come, even some moral common sense.

To begin, Sartre makes an important distinction about human nature. Although he insists that human beings have no fixed "human nature" or "universal essence" or predetermined purpose that they bring into the world with them, he observes that they do share a "universal human condition." This human condition consists in the fact that human beings exist as they do. Namely, that they are "thrown into the world" with no nature or set purpose, and that they live and die among other free and mortal human beings like themselves. However—and this is the point to grasp most firmly—it is precisely because we have to make free choices in this human condition that each of us alone gives purpose and meaning to his or her own life through those choices. As Sartre puts it, "the first principle of existentialism" is that "man is nothing else but what he makes of himself"—"you are nothing else than your life."

This radical freedom to choose our lives and to create ourselves makes existentialism the ultimate humanism. It also makes existentialism a very challenging way of life indeed. For if we are condemned to be free to create ourselves with every choice we make, we must live up to that freedom and its responsibilities. To clear the way for us to live up to it, Sartre banishes any conception of human existence that could compromise our absolute existential freedom of choice in the human condition.

That is why he starts by rejecting "human nature." It is also why he throws out God. Because we are condemned to be free in the human condition, he explains, "we are alone," with "no excuse behind us, nor justification before us," such as a predetermined human nature or a transcendent God would provide. Sartre does grant that a person might still believe in God if that God remains remote and silent, as in the religious existentialism of Gabriel Marcel and Paul Tillich. But Sartre considered religious existentialism to be rather illogical because it required too many philosophical gymnastics to preserve true existential freedom with God in the picture.

Be that as it may, Sartre does not stop with discarding human nature and God. He also "rejects the hypothesis of the unconscious" asserted by Freudian psychoanalysis, as he had said in *Being and Nothingness*. For if the unconscious lives in us as the irresistible subliminal force that Freud said it was, it would determine our conscious choices beyond our control, as Freudian psychoanalysts and many other psychotherapists have counseled generations of patients. That would limit the pure existential freedom of the human condition. Sartre won't have that, since existentialism "recognizes nothing *before* the original upsurge of human freedom." Existentialist therapists have followed Sartre's lead. These therapists tell patients not to blame the unconscious for their troubles, but to get over them and start taking responsibility for their lives because everyone is always existentially free, unconscious be damned.

And Sartre goes even farther than this. He not only rejects the unconscious. He questions the very influence of the emotions themselves on our freedom of choice. Sure, we feel emotions, he says, and they can sway us. But that does not limit our existential freedom of choice. "The existentialist does not believe in the power of passion," he states unequivocally. For the existentialist "will never agree that a sweeping passion is a ravaging torrent which fatally leads a man to certain acts and is therefore an excuse." Whatever our emotions may be, Sartre insists, we *choose* either to resist them or to yield to them. Either way, we are making a choice.

Again, Sartre does not deny that many influences, both internal and external, impinge on our choices. To the contrary, he knows—and often vividly wrote about—how our emotions can roil us and how our circumstances can gravely limit our options for choice, leaving us with nothing good to choose. But none of this, Sartre repeats over and over, reduces our existential freedom of choice itself in the specific act of choosing one course of action over another. Emotions, circumstances, and so on just create what Sartre calls a "situation"—as well as a "predicament," a term that gained currency in popular existentialism. These situations and predicaments extend, Sartre explains, from "man's fundamental situation in the universe"—that is, the existential human condition—down to the particular circumstantial difficulties that envelop individual choices. "Choice always remains choice within a situation," Sartre says, and any situation can carry its own particular predicament. But whatever our situation and predicament, the act of choice is ours alone, here and now, in the moment of choosing. And with every choice we make, we are choosing at once to create ourselves.

That is the tough truth of existential freedom: we are condemned to be free no matter what, and so we are responsible for our every choice. Sartre applies this principle to everything we do. For he says that always and everywhere, in our hearts and minds, or rather in our consciousness (and Sartre lends pure consciousness a significance akin to that attributed to it by his his French philosophical predecessor René Descartes, who had famously asserted: "I think therefore I am"), we are existentially deciding for ourselves to do one thing instead of another—to resist an emotion or yield to it, to fight circumstances or submit to them, to live this way or that. Whatever our temperament or past experience (whether we had a happy childhood or suffered abuse, whether we are educated or ignorant, whether we are strong or weak), and whatever our circumstances (whether we are rich or poor, whether we run a corporation or someone is holding a gun to our head), in the moment of choice none of that counts. In that moment, in the conscious act of choice, we are free despite our situation and predicament. Because it is we alone who choose to do one thing instead of another. No one else does that for us. We can choose to tell the truth or to lie, to be courageous or cowardly, to vote for this candidate or that, to marry one person or another, to do what someone with a gun at our head demands or to let him shoot us. We can even choose not to choose. But we are always choosing. And we always have existential freedom in the moment of choice.

This can be a hard notion of freedom to understand, much less to embrace. And Sartre may take it farther than common sense and conventional wisdom want us to go. But that is not necessarily to our credit, or to the credit of common sense and conventional wisdom. For when we admit that whatever our situation and predicament, in the moment of choice we are acting with a raw existential freedom, we thus see our lives, and our responsibilities to ourselves and to others, in a new and chastening and enlivening light. That light is the ethics of existentialism. And it is as demanding an ethics as the world has ever known.

It is also a paradoxical ethics. After all, since existentialism banishes God and human nature and everything else that could compromise our freedom of choice, how can it assert an ethical standard of behavior?—as Dostoevsky's provocative protoexistentialist Ivan Karamazov argued, if there is no God, then everything is permitted. Sartre confronts the paradox head on. Although existentialism recognizes no preordained ethical standards, he says, that does not mean it recognizes *no* ethical standards. Existentialism simply contends that no ethical standards exist until we invent them. We human beings have to create our ethics as we go along, just as we create our lives and ourselves. This fact, Sartre points out, makes ethics like art. A work of art comes into existence only when the artist makes aesthetic choices and acts on them to create that work of art. In the same way, ethics come into existence only when we make choices and act on them to create our ethics. "What art and ethics have in common," Sartre explains, "is that we have creation and invention in both cases. . . . 'You are free, choose, that is, invent.' No general ethics can show you what is to be done."

Take one of Sartre's examples. A young man must decide whether to go to war for his country or to stay home and care for his ailing mother. Which is the ethically right choice? Does it come from God, or from some universal moral rule? Neither. The ethically right choice does not exist until the young man acts. He creates the ethically right choice, just as he creates himself, by choosing within his own particular situation and predicament. His choice defines his ethics. Go to war or take care of your mother, Sartre says, the choice and the ethics are yours to make—and to live by.

No wonder moral critics of existentialism, like the clergyman in Sartre's audience, objected: Hold on! Ethics as art? We invent ethics for ourselves? That's a prescription for moral chaos. But this was just Sartre's provocative gambit. He was heading toward the ultimate existentialist ethics. That ethics works like this.

We must "want but one thing," Sartre declares, "and that is freedom as the basis of all values." Therefore, we "may choose anything if it is on the grounds of free involvement." And this means that because "man is nothing else but what he makes of himself," he is ethically "responsible for everything he does." Everything. Always. No exceptions. No excuses. Ever. Anyone who denies this absolute ethical responsibility by resorting to some kind of "determinism," Sartre warns, is "a dishonest man" living in "bad faith," and one of the "liars," "cowards," and "stinkers" of humankind. Sartre doesn't mince words about it. He slings these epithets again and again in his writings. Consequently, Sartre announces, "existentialism's first move is to make every man aware of what he is, and to make the full responsibility of his existence rest on him." That is no prescription for chaos. It is a heavy ethical burden indeed.

And Sartre adds still more weight to it. Although we make our choices freely and alone, he says, those choices do not affect only us alone. They have implications for all human beings. Here existentialism becomes not only an ethics of personal responsibility, but an ethics of public responsibility as well.

"When we say that a man is responsible for himself," Sartre explains, "we do not only mean that he is responsible for his own individuality, but that he is responsible for all men." We bear that universal responsibility because "in creating the man that we want to be, there is not a single one of our acts which does not at the same time create an image of man as we think he ought to be." In other words, with every choice we make, we define not just ourselves and our own humanness, but that of all human beings. This is what Sartre means by the existentialist catch phrase "existence precedes essence"—first we *exist* in the human condition, then we make choices, and these choices define the *essence* of our humanness or humanity.

"In choosing myself," Sartre says, "I choose man." And so, he concludes, "for every man, everything happens as if all mankind had its eyes fixed on him and were guiding itself by what he does." There is no slack here, and no ethical relativism, either. This is the heaviest ethical burden possible—and the ultimate humanistic ethics (although it has some kinship with Immanuel Kant's "categorical imperative," which says we should act only in ways that we can expect of everyone).

Sartre elsewhere pointed to the antihero of Albert Camus's novel *The Stranger* (1942) as the exemplary existentialist for living up to that ethics in a peculiarly courageous way. After shooting someone by accident on a beach—because the sun had glinted in his eyes—this antihero, an emotionless cipher named Meursault, calmly accepts responsibility for his actions with no excuses or quibbles. He hadn't intended to shoot anyone, he says, but he admits that he had pulled the trigger himself. It was his act alone. And he is willing to pay the price for it. He looks forward to his execution with existentialist honor.

Camus wrote his famous essay "The Myth of Sisyphus" (1942) on this same uncompromising existentially ethical theme. But here he comes to a very upbeat conclusion. According to the ancient Greek legend, Sisyphus had tried to cheat Destiny and had been punished by having to roll a great rock up a mountain and then let it tumble down, and then having to roll it back up again, repeating this act endlessly, and miserably. But in Camus's version, Sisyphus is not miserable. To the contrary. He embraces his fate as his own existential situation and predicament: "His fate belongs to him. His rock is his thing." For "the struggle itself toward the heights is enough to fill a man's heart. One must imagine Sisyphus happy."

No liars, stinkers, or cowards trying to escape from freedom and responsibility, Camus's Meursault and Sisyphus are good existentialists. But the existentialist creed that they embody—accepting the existential freedom and responsibility of human beings in every choice and action, whatever the situation and predicament—gave rise to the quip that existentialism is a philosophy born of war and best suited to slaves. That is not how Sartre saw it. He was certain that existentialism—despite its dour notions of the "absurd," "forlornness," "anguish," "despair," and the like—was, after all, an "optimistic . . . doctrine of action." In fact, Sartre declares, "there is no doctrine more optimistic." For just as existentialism tells us that "you are nothing else than your life," it also tells us that "action is the only thing that enables a man to live." This does not just come down to the austere ethics of Meursault taking blame for his pistol shot or of Sisyphus rolling his rock. It is a humanistic affirmation of life. "You are free," Sartre cries, "choose, that is, invent" as a human being who creates a life and takes responsibility for it.

These principles actually turn out to be not so far removed from the ethics of Aristotle, despite Aristotle's assumptions about human nature. Like Sartre, Aristotle judged the act of choice to define humanity, and he considered human beings responsible for virtually all of their choices, down to creating their own character through these choices. Or go back before even Aristotle to Homer's *Iliad*. There we see human beings largely estranged from their gods and ruled by an impersonal fate and embracing human life in this world as the source of all value. This was the birth of Western humanism—and a kind of existentialist humanism at that (see Chapter 1).

We could say that Sartre completed what Homer had begun. Discarding the gods and fate and all other deterministic possibilities, Sartre sees human beings thrown into a universe that has no meaning except the meaning that human beings give to it by making choices and creating human life. "There is no universe other than a human universe," Sartre proclaims, because "before you come alive, life is nothing; it's up to you to give it a meaning." Therefore, "man's destiny is in himself" since "things will be as man has decided they are to be" while "man makes himself" and "will fulfill himself as man" in the "human universe." That is the finale of Sartre's "existentialist humanism." And the history of humanism knows no greater affirmation than that.

SARTRE's existentialist humanism should leave us energized and hopeful, even if it gives us heavy responsibilities. For there is a bracing honesty and an invigorating vision of life in it that we find nowhere else. Being "condemned to be free" is not a bad thing after all. It can be the very inspiration of our lives, and the making of our humanity.

Dostoevsky had not gone as far as Sartre toward existential freedom. But he had implied in "The Grand Inquisitor" that when we passively obey authority, or when we trade hard choices for easy security, we are choosing to escape from the freedom of choice—even if, as the Grand Inquisitor would have it, we excuse making that escape as a forgivable weakness of human nature. Dostoevsky could forgive such human weaknesses more generously than Sartre, since Sartre reproached anyone who made excuses for human nature. But Dostoevsky also respected the strength and courage of those who do not succumb to such weakness. And he, too, encouraged us to be free, even if we do not want to be.

We might doubt that Dostoevsky and Sartre truly understood human freedom and that they were fair to burden us with so much responsibility. And we might justify our doubts by pointing to the transcendent power of God or to the elemental forces of human nature, or to any of the other so-called "influences" that we nowadays typically detect at work in human life, and that we believe inevitably curtail our true freedom of choice. But we should not let it go at that. Dostoevsky and Sartre should awaken us to stubborn truths about our *freedom of choice in the moment*, and how we often try to escape from that freedom down myriad paths, but how we should instead honestly accept it with all of its responsibilities (whether we believe in God or other "influences"). For this freedom and its responsibilities give us the most uncompromisingly honest and completely *human* life possible. And that is as humanistically affirming as life can be.

On Freedom and Responsibility

1. The freedom to choose makes us human.
2. The freedom to choose brings responsibility for our choices.
3. Responsibility for our choices is a burden that many people do not want to bear.

4. To escape the responsibilities of freedom, people will trade the active freedom to choose for the passive freedom of not having to choose.

5. We trade the active freedom to choose for the passive freedom of not having to choose when we let others make choices for us.

6. We also try to escape from freedom and responsibility when we blame other people or circumstances for our choices.

7. We should beware of people who invite us to let them make our choices for us because they want our submission.

8. Human freedom exists in the act of choosing to do one thing instead of another, even if we choose not to choose. (Sartre)

9. In the moment of choosing, we are always free and alone—that is existential freedom. (Sartre)

10. Existential freedom exists in us regardless of anything that preceded our act of choice or the situation that surrounds us at the time. (Sartre)

11. If we think we are not existentially free, we are lying to ourselves. (Sartre)

12. There is no divine plan or fixed human nature that prescribes human existence, only a human condition of mortality and free choice. (Sartre)

13. There is no preordained ethics—we create our ethics with every choice we make. (Sartre)

14. We create our lives and ourselves with every choice we make. (Sartre)

15. We define "humanity" with every choice we make. (Sartre)

16. The one universal standard of ethics is to recognize our existential freedom of choice and accept the responsibilities that go with it. (Sartre)

17. The meaning of life is to embrace human freedom, whatever its worldly risks and limitations, and to create our own lives with imagination and courage, accepting full responsibility for the consequences.

Part II

Living in the Social and Political World

10

Find the Right Way,
Do the Right Thing

Confucianism: *The Analects, The Great Learning, The Doctrine of the Mean*
Taoism: *Tao Te Ching, Chuang Tzu*

There is nothing I can do with a man who is not constantly saying,
"What am I to do? What am I to do?"
Confucius

When equilibrium and harmony are realized to the highest
degree, heaven and earth will attain their proper
order and all things will flourish.
The Doctrine of the Mean

Can the Way be learned? Goodness, how could that be?
Chuang Tzu

Although their intellectual origins go back to dim antiquity, **Confucianism** and **Taoism** arose as full-fledged doctrines amidst that extraordinary flowering of world culture in the sixth and fifth centuries B.C.E., which also brought us Buddhism and Greek philosophy. Confucianism and Taoism gave China two intellectual-religious traditions that ran parallel to each other, intersected at points, and also veered off in different directions. And they have endured ever since.

Confucianism came from a sage first known as Master Kung and later, in the West, as **Confucius (551/52–479 B.C.E.).** Inspired by the wisdom of the "ancients" and the mysterious metaphysics of the ancient *I Ching,* Confucius became an oral teacher, rather like Socrates soon afterwards, urging his listeners to live wisely instead of thoughtlessly. And for him, living wisely meant applying an earnest mind and a keen sense of moral responsibility to everything from the personal life to government. Confucius' wise sayings were compiled—probably including other Confucian proverbs—over centuries until more or less codified in *The Analects* (c. 200 B.C.E.–200 C.E.), the first of the four official Confucian "classics." A disciple of Confucius named **Mencius (371–289 B.C.E.?)** expanded upon Confucius' philosophy, mainly in the direction of an idealistic humanism seasoned with a dose of Taoism, in a volume known as *Mencius*, which became the second, and longest, of those classics. Two other documents of uncertain authorship and date, *The Great Learning* and *The Doctrine of the Mean*, completed the canon of classics established in the twelfth century by the Confucian philosopher Chu Hsi. Differing in an emphasis here and there, the four classics all shape a single Confucian vision of the personal, moral, social, and political life. It is a vision that we in the West could well use to temper our proud individualism.

Sharing certain origins and assumptions with Confucianism, while claiming older roots, Taoism shunned moralism and practicality for the essence and mystery of things. The book that lends its name to the doctrine, the *Tao Te Ching* (attributed to **Lao Tzu**, probably an elder contemporary of Confucius in the sixth century B.C.E.), makes a poetic excursion into that essence and mystery, or the *Tao*. Next to the *Tao Te Ching*, the most important Taoist writing is a book named for one of its several likely authors, **Chuang Tzu (c. 369–286 B.C.E.)**. A collection of engagingly quirky vignettes, *Chuang Tzu* demonstrates with as much wit as philosophy the Taoist Way to think and live. But mysterious as it can be, Taoism also gives hints for a way of living in the everyday world. And it is a Way that, like Confucianism, has more good uses today than one might expect.

T HE TERSE AND OFTEN CRYPTIC sayings of Confucianism and Taoism often sound like fortune cookie philosophy. And they do in fact sometimes show up on those little strips of paper tucked inside fortune cookies in American Chinese restaurants. But Confucianism and Taoism cannot be reduced to phrases baked in cookie dough. These doctrines amount to much more than commonplace pieties and inscrutable notions. They are ways of life. And though their origins in ancient China may be remote from us, those ways of life consist of the same kinds of principles and practicalities that occupy everyone today. Such as: How do we know the truth, and how should we use it? How should we manage our personal lives? What are the roles of individuals and families in society? What are the obligations of public life? What is the place of morality in politics? What is the relation of sincerity to morality? And how do we create a good society and achieve world peace?

To be sure, some of what Confucianism and Taoism say on these subjects is very foreign to modern Western ideas and experience. But much of it is not foreign at all. Foreign or familiar, the ideas of Confucianism and Taoism can be useful. And they are likely to be increasingly drawn upon as a global culture forms, and as people and institutions everywhere search for new sources of inspiration, new bearings in a sea of historical change, something firm to hold on to, something satisfying to believe in, and ways to make human life more livable and to make the world better.

Many Westerners have turned to the teachings of Hinduism or Buddhism for such purposes, particularly for discipline of mind and solace for the soul. Confucianism and Taoism offer some of this, too. But they also attend very much to the public life and the everyday world. Not that Confucianism and Taoism agree with each other. Far from it. At first glance, Confucianism and Taoism appear to be entirely at odds. Confucianism tends to be objective, rational, practical, and institutional. Taoism is the opposite—subjective, intuitive, mystical, and amorphous. And the ways of life they represent exhibit all of these differences. Yet, despite the contrasts, Confucianism and Taoism share closely related histories, and a fundamental assumption about how the universe works. That assumption is this: within the maelstrom of existence that engulfs us, there lies a "Way," or path (*Tao* in Chinese), of essential truth that leads from the good of individuals to the good of all. We must find that Way and follow it if we wish to get the most from life for ourselves, and to make the public world work as it should.

As the word *Taoism* suggests, Taoists believed this Way to be the essence of reality itself, and they devised a philosophy concentrating on how to think about it—how to find and follow the essential *Tao*, or rather, how to enter into it. This philosophy gave Taoism a tendency to irrationality and mysticism and made for some odd notions. The Confucian conception of the Way is more down to earth and pragmatic. It comes closer to the ordinary American notion of the *right way* to do something, or the *right way* to be, or the *right way* to live, individually and collectively (which to the early Confucianists often meant the *ancient way* of their forefathers). And this secular, pragmatic slant gave Confucianism its sober rationality and earnest worldliness, as well as its tone of philosophical humanism.

Although Confucianism and Taoism traveled along their separate "Ways," they also sought a common end. And that was a peaceful harmony encompassing all things. To reach that end, they had to journey down most of the pathways of life as we know it. Find the right Way, they say, and you will do the right thing.

We might not want to go with them all the way along their Ways— English inevitably plays on the words. That would ask us to accept some assumptions about the nature of things that most Westerners would question. But traveling with Confucianism and Taoism takes us through a terrain we all live in, where we try to organize our lives successfully, alone and with other people, and to do things well, and to create a good society. Confucianism and Taoism navigate this terrain with ingenuity and with considerable wisdom, pointing out landmarks and pitfalls. Confucianism does it with strict instructions and careful steps. Taoism does it with poetic evocations and twists and turns, and some laughs. But both Ways show us sights that everyone should see, and learn from.

FIND THE RIGHT WAY and do the Right Thing. Every ethical thinker urges this. And everybody wants to succeed at it. Confucius, the quaint, laconic Chinese sage of twenty-five

CONFUCIANISM

hundred years ago, is the father of them all. "There is nothing I can do," he says, "with a man who is not constantly saying, 'What am I to do? What am I to do?'" Whether in private life or public, as child or parent, individual or politician, to follow Confucius you must ceaselessly search for the right thing to do. And, being the sober-minded sort they are, Confucianists make that search as methodical as they can. Step follows step along the Confucian Way from the cultivation of personal character to the harmony of the universe. Whether we care about the harmony of the universe or not, we should look at the Confucian steps. Because they chart a very clear, quite inviting, and notably humanistic path through the landscape of private, social, and political life.

For almost two thousand years, down to the early twentieth century, China lived under the guidance of Confucian precepts about doing the right thing. Those precepts were not just a venerable philosophy; they became formal state doctrine: from the seventeenth to the twentieth centuries, Chinese state bureaucrats had to pass examinations on the four canonical Confucian classics—*The Analects*, *Mencius*, *The Great Learning*, and *The Doctrine of the Mean*. In recent decades some Asian politicians and intellectuals, led by Singapore's philosophical former senior minister, Lee Kuan Yew, have pointed to that Confucian heritage as an ethical, social, and political model of "Asian values" superior to "Western values." They say that while the West has prized untrammeled individualism and material progress, it has also scanted the claims of morality, authority, and social order. The Confucian tradition, they emphasize, is quite different. It prizes moral responsibility, respect for authority, social interdependence, and cultural stability. The differences, they go on, have led Western culture—especially America—to pay for its individualism and material progress with social discontents and lawlessness, while the best of Asian societies promise to be both prosperous and stable. They might be right. But it is also true that Confucian principles can create a certain hardening of the cultural arteries and justify political authoritarianism and abuses of human rights, as it has in some of these same Asian societies. That is the danger of any stringently moralistic politics.

And yet, notwithstanding the political promises made in its name nowadays, and its tendency to rigidity and authoritarianism, Confucianism is indisputably one of the most idealistic social philosophies ever conceived—the equal of Marxism without the Communist trappings. For it tells people how to live together harmoniously and how to govern themselves wisely. Confucius also believed these ends achievable for one of the same reasons that Karl Marx believed in Communism: both thought that human nature is inherently social, not individualistic. If people seem more individualistic than social, Confucius said, again like Marx, this is simply because they have forgotten the truth and picked up bad habits. "Men are close to one another by nature," Confucius asserts, and "they diverge as a result of repeated practice." And that is their peril.

Like most Confucian sayings, this one lends itself to various interpretations—and to use in fortune cookies. But the central idea is clear: human beings are by nature interdependent. And to Confucius, this interdependence belongs to the very nature of things as well. For Confucianists believe that everything in the universe is interrelated. Nothing stands alone. Not individuals. Not families. Not society. Not rulers. Not the state. Not nature. They are all interwoven. So, everything depends on and influences everything else. The diminutive classic *The Great Learning* spells out this holistic vision and the Confucian mode of thinking that goes with it in a few lines that constitute most of the text:

> Those who wished to bring order to their states would first regulate their families. Those who wished to regulate their families would first cultivate their personal lives. Those who wished to cultivate their personal lives would first rectify their minds. Those who wished to rectify their minds would first make their wills sincere. Those who wished to make their wills sincere would first extend their knowledge. The extension of knowledge consists in the investigation of things. When things are investigated, knowledge is extended; when knowledge is extended, the will becomes sincere; when the will is sincere, the mind is rectified; when the mind is rectified, the personal life is cultivated; when the personal

life is cultivated, the family will be regulated; when the family is regulated, the state will be in order; and when the state is in order, there will be peace throughout the world.

That other slender classic, *The Doctrine of the Mean,* adds to this sequence: "When equilibrium and harmony are realized to the highest degree" everywhere, "heaven and earth will attain their proper order and all things will flourish."

Heaven and earth will attain their proper order and all things will flourish. That is how the Confucian Way ends. Not in social order for its own sake. Or in goodness for religious purposes. Or in other-worldly salvation. But in the flourishing of all things that exist. This may seem an impossibly utopian ideal, reaching as it does from an orderly personal life to the harmony of the universe. Yet it took hold of China for nearly two millennia (also spilling over into Japan, where it ruled the official Heian court, for example, in the days of Murasaki Shikibu, author of *The Tale of Genji*—see Chapter 21) as a tutored way of thinking and of life. And it took hold because it has practical applicability no less than idealistic aspirations. It can teach us on both counts.

It teaches us, as *The Great Learning* describes, by linking everything together step by step, up to the highest end. For "things have their roots and branches," *The Great Learning* explains, in an emblematic Confucian image, and "there is never a case when the root is in disorder and yet the branches are in order." Or as Confucius had put it, "once the roots are established the Way will grow therefrom."

We have to take all of the steps along the Way to reach the end. And, because everything depends on everything else, the steps go back and forth. But the step that matters most is what *The Great Learning* calls the "cultivation of the personal life." The person who has done this well makes everything else possible. "He cultivates himself," says Confucius, "and thereby brings peace and security to his fellow men." So, "from the Son of Heaven down to the common people," says *The Great Learning*, "all must regard cultivation of the personal life as the root or foundation." And what Confucius and his followers have to say about how to cultivate the personal life offers good advice for anyone who cares about shaping an ethical character.

That advice begins by telling us that shaping an ethical character depends on both intellectual and moral discipline. "Devote yourself to learning," Confucius says, and "abide to the death in the good way." This sweeping prescription answers that echoing Confucian question "What am I to do?" But applying it properly proves to be demanding, entwining several Confucian philosophical and moral principles. Untangling them, we can identify three of these principles that stand out as the most prominent in Confucianism, as well as probably the most useful in the common life today. We might call them *learning, sincerity,* and *objectivity.*

Confucius and his followers prescribed that we pursue learning (even those Confucianists who considered human beings inherently good, like Mencius, required that) for two closely related reasons. The first is to fathom "the principles of all things"—in the words of Chu Hsi, who canonized the four Confucian classics in the twelfth century and edited *The Great Learning,* adding a commentary traditionally taken to possess virtually the same authority. That is, we must understand how everything is interrelated, from individuals to the universe, from root to branch. To reach this understanding, we can therefore never be satisfied with only a part of the whole. We have to learn *everything.* "Learn without flagging," Confucius urged. "When there is anything not yet studied," *The Doctrine of the Mean* elaborates, "or studied but not yet understood, do not give up. When there is any question not yet asked, or asked but its answer not yet known, do not give up. When there is anything not yet thought over, or thought over but not yet apprehended, do not give up." The Confucian life is a life of ceaseless learning.

But Confucianists ask us to continue learning not just to accumulate knowledge about the interdependent "principles of all things." A second reason is equally important. It is that continuous learning keeps our quest for virtue honest. Without sufficient learning, we can all too easily lose sight of what virtues truly are, and then we slide through error and self-deception into vices, thinking these are virtues. Confucius ticks off an instructive list of how this can happen: "To love benevolence without loving learning is liable to lead to foolishness. To love cleverness without loving learning is liable to lead to deviation from the right path. To love trustworthiness in word without loving learning is liable to lead to harmful behavior. To love forthrightness without loving learning is liable to lead to intolerance. To love courage without loving learning is liable to lead to insubordination. To love unbending strength without loving learning is liable to lead to indiscipline." These warnings convey a wisdom about human psychology as pertinent today as it was in ancient China.

This wisdom reminds us that the pursuit of virtue itself requires intellectual and emotional discipline to protect us against the subtle, detrimental influence on our thoughts of emotions or self-interest or other hidden biases. As Chu Hsi remarked in his commentary on *The Great Learning,* "when one is affected by wrath . . . fear . . . fondness . . .

worries and anxieties, his mind will not be correct." Then the search for truth of any kind will go awry into ignorance, arrogance, complacency, and the host of self-deceptions that prey upon us. That is what "rectifying the mind" guards against: it makes sure our minds are "correct" so we can think clearly and honestly. And this is where *sincerity* comes in, as *The Great Learning* said: "Those who wished to rectify their minds would first make their wills sincere."

Sincerity is a familiar idea in the West. In early modern times it was a commonplace of European literature and life. Europeans at that time thought of sincerity as mainly a social virtue. It meant being consistent in your motives and actions—being at heart what you *seemed* to be in public, so you could be trusted. And insincerity, or not being at heart what you seemed to be in public, and therefore being untrustworthy, was often judged the most vicious wickedness, which is why Dante put traitors at the pit of hell (see Chapter 5).

Some of those early modern Europeans also detected that sincerity could be more than a social virtue. It could also mean being inwardly true to ourselves. That was the obvious point of Shakespeare's pompous Polonius in his widely quoted advice to his son: "To thine own self be true," and "thou canst not then be false to any man." And being inwardly true to ourselves is as much a psychological or intellectual virtue as a social one. For it requires, above all, that we see ourselves and our motives honestly, or as honestly as possible—which Michel de Montaigne found to be so difficult, and Molière's Alceste in *The Misanthrope* could never do (see Chapter 12). But this requirement can actually lead away from the social virtue of sincerity into an ethics of sheer self-awareness, or "authenticity," being true to oneself for its own sake, social consequences be damned—as happened in Western literature with, for example, Denis Diderot's eccentric and amoral but dauntlessly self-aware title character in *Rameau's Nephew* (c. 1774) and Dostoevsky's Underground Man, who justified his antisocial behavior with claims of psychological integrity, and which gave the critic Lionel Trilling the subject of *Sincerity and Authenticity* (1972).

The Confucian ideal of sincerity was also more of a psychological or intellectual virtue than a social virtue. But it did not stray off into an ethics of "authenticity." Confucius maintained that sincerity is the self-knowledge that keeps us honest as we learn, insuring that we have the right motives and act on them. If we do not know the truth about ourselves, our minds will not be "correct," our "will" will go astray. Then true learning will elude us, and we will likely misperceive or misuse every truth—as in Confucius' list of derailed virtues. This makes sincerity an indispensable link in the chain binding character to learning: we cannot develop character without learning, and we cannot learn anything truly without a "rectified mind," and we cannot "rectify the mind" without the sincerity and honesty of knowing ourselves. There it is. The passage from sincerity through learning to character—and back—becomes clear.

"To think how to be sincere," says *The Doctrine of the Mean*, "is the way of man," for "only those who are absolutely sincere can fully develop their nature." Mencius echoes this principle in a burst of enthusiasm, "There is no greater joy for me," he says, "than to find, on self-examination, that I am true to myself." It can even be said, *The Doctrine of the Mean* goes on, that "sincerity means the completion of the self," because sincerity "is that by which all things are completed." And "the completion of all things means humanity" and "wisdom." Sincerity therefore both opens the path to knowledge and good character and completes that path. "It is due to our nature that enlightenment results from sincerity," and "it is due to education that sincerity results from enlightenment." That circle "completes the self" in Confucian wisdom and goodness.

Confucius described this ultimate wisdom in terms quite similar to those of Socrates in Greece a generation later, equating it with a kind of intellectual honesty and modesty. "Shall I tell you what it is to know[?]" Confucius asks, and answers: "To say that you know when you know, and to say you do not when you do not, that is knowledge." Also like Socrates, but without Socrates' irony, Confucius *sincerely* claimed to know very little, even while he kept on learning. A bit of his intellectual modesty would do most of us some good.

One thing Confucius did know was that to be sincere or honest with ourselves takes constant effort and vigilance. For there is no wilier foe than that secret enemy of sincerity and integrity and knowledge: self-deception. Self-deception is the opposite of true learning, and it works so subtly and imperceptibly, and in so many guises that feel like truth, that it is sometimes almost impossible to detect—as in, again, Confucius' list of aborted virtues, and in every state of mind from simple ignorance to self-righteousness to fanaticism. Alerting us to these wiles and evils, Confucianists advise that to be truly sincere and honest with ourselves, we must never let down our guard. And that means a person must take special pains to "always be watchful over himself when alone." For that is when the temptations are greatest to lapse into those most comforting of self-deceptions: the belief that we know all we need to know, and that we are all we need to be. If we want to be sincere and honest with ourselves, we can never succumb to that deceptive belief or kid ourselves about anything, especially when no one else is looking.

↬

Learn all you can, and do it with sincerity. That is good Confucian advice. It also points to the third Confucian principle implicit in the search for truth and the making of character. Confucius does not specify this principle by name—unlike learning and sincerity—but it has signposts along the Confucian Way. We might call this principle *objectivity*.

Bound up with the ideas of learning and sincerity, the principle of objectivity says that truth itself exists beyond ourselves. It is not just in our minds. It is not a mystery. It does not come from a whispering spirit, either. Truth is *out there*, in the real world, and for Confucianists this truth and the world it inhabits are largely rational and completely moral, because in the Confucian universe everything fits together—the branches grow from the roots, and "enlightenment results from sincerity." "The intelligent mind of man is certainly formed to know," Chu Hsi explains, since "there is not a single thing in which its principles do not inhere." That is to say, the "principles of all things" exist in both the external universe and in the human mind. This is not a mystical union, as in Taoism. It is more like Western mathematics or the laws of physics, which enable the human mind to comprehend the workings of the physical world. Consequently, we must not, Confucius says, be misled by those who claim that truth cannot be known, or that it is irrational or subjective. Rational, objective truth actually exists, and it is the same for everyone. If you pursue it diligently and sincerely, you can find it.

The Confucianists prized objective truth so highly that during the European Enlightenment Voltaire extolled Confucius as the very model of sober rationality, and as the antithesis of irrational superstition. In his *Philosophical Dictionary* under the heading of "Fraud," Voltaire has a Confucianist dispute with an Islamic fakir over the nature of truth and virtue. The fakir says that people are basically irrational and therefore must "be deceived" with tricks and fictions if they are to be made virtuous. "We teach them errors, I confess," he says, "but it is for their own good," just as "the supreme Being . . . surrounds us with errors that suit our nature"—like the deceptions of the senses—to win our obedience. "Do you think that one can teach the common people truth without sustaining it with fables?" he asks. Voltaire's Confucianist scoffs. People are more "rational than you might believe," he says, and they possess the "good sense" to see truth and goodness on their own terms. "We should never deceive anybody," he goes on, because that only teaches error and immorality. "The surest method of instilling justice into all men," the Confucianist insists, "is to instill them with a religion free from superstition" and with ideas "about which human reason is in agreement" and which are "honest, probable, useful to everybody." Voltaire's Confucianist clearly has enough confidence in objective truth and in human reason to be convinced that human beings can rationally learn virtue and not need to be manipulated with irrational ploys or childlike escapes. He is Voltaire's kind of philosopher—reasonable, practical, humanistic, and honest.

Whether Voltaire got Confucianism altogether right here—to say nothing of Islam—he captured a quality of Confucian rationality that set a high standard of intellectual honesty and objectivity worth remembering. For if we do not accept the possibility of objective, rational truth, and if we do not have the discipline of mind to pursue that kind of truth, whether we can reach it or not, then truth is anybody's guess, or anybody's subjective conviction, and anything goes. And if we do not sincerely aspire to achieve objectivity, we easily fall victim to all kinds of self-interest and self-deception. The contemporary world, beset at one extreme by rabid religious fundamentalism and at the other by blithe relativism, could use a healthy dose of this objectivity.

WHEN YOU HAVE CULTIVATED your personal life and character through learning and sincerity and objectivity, you are well on your way to the Confucian goal. Confucius called this goal the "superior person" or "gentleman." It is a person who lives out the root and branch of Confucian virtues and so attains the highest "goodness" of human beings. Confucius did not think of this goodness as a narrowly moral idea—being nice to other people, and so on. As translators explain, the Chinese word for "goodness," *jen*, is one of the most important, complex, and weighty words in the language (often translated as "benevolence," it is also the word for "humanity" or "human being"). Originally, as the renowned translator and scholar Arthur Waley points out, *jen* identified human qualities attributed only to members of one's own tribe or clan. Over time, *jen* became linked to individuals who exemplified the characteristics most admired by the clan, or the social group. The individuals who possessed *jen* were said to be superior. The Confucian term for this "superior person" (*chün-tzu*) is frequently rendered by British translators as "gentleman." This translation reflects the British social ideal that grew out of the Latin word for clan, *gens*, into "gentle," "gentility," and "gentle person," terms denoting refined and high-born members of society bred to rule and be fastidiously moral. The Confucian "gentleman" is all of this. He or she (although Confucius assumed male) is also close to what Aristotle defined as the "good" or "excellent" human being and the "great-souled man"—that is, a person who has fulfilled the highest potential of human nature (see Chapter 4).

Confucius was himself too modest to claim that he or anyone could fully possess the qualities of the superior person. This modesty is itself, of course, an attribute of "goodness," a sign of sincere self-knowledge and the unceasing search for truth. "It is these things that cause me concern," Confucius admits, while cataloging his own weaknesses and identifying what we should all rise above: "failure to cultivate virtue; failure to go more deeply into what I have learned; inability, when I am told what is right, to move to where it is; and inability to reform myself when I have defects." Always trying to find the right way and do the right thing, Confucius humbly recognizes that the perfection of goodness is beyond the best of us. "The gentleman," he adds, "is troubled by his own lack of ability, not by the failure of others to appreciate him." The "gentleman's" sincere self-knowledge gives him no room for vanity.

The Confucian pursuit of "goodness," or excellent humanity, brings many rewards both to the "gentleman" and to the world. The first rewards go to the "gentleman" himself, who acquires a calm sense of purpose and invincible self-assurance. Because "superior men have got hold of what is of major significance," Confucius says, "while inferior men have got hold of what is of minor significance," the "gentleman" is "easy of mind . . . while the small man is always full of anxiety." For "what the gentleman seeks he seeks within himself; what the small man seeks, he seeks in others." Inferior, small-minded people can therefore never know the truth or be sincere or be comfortable with themselves. They merely clamor for external gratifications—attention, wealth, power—and do no one any good. And this is why "the gentleman is at ease without being arrogant; the small man is arrogant without being at ease." Aristotle and Nietzsche praised a similar type. And it is one to emulate.

Although Confucian "goodness" gives many rewards to the superior people who can achieve it, it also bears on other people as well. That is the Confucian Way—everything fits into the whole. The individual and society, the private and public, the family and the state, the moral and the political are interdependent. And "goodness" is the bond that ties everything together in the human world from the personal life to universal peace. So Confucianism is nothing if not a philosophy of the good society.

"Make it your guiding principle," Confucius demands, "to do your best for others." This means not only adopting the Confucian Golden Rule, namely, "Do not impose on others what you yourself do not desire," but engaging actively in public life. "Not to enter public life," Confucius warns, "is to ignore one's duty." The Confucian superior person is by definition a public person.

Public life originates with the family. Confucius was the true father of "family values." For it is in the family that we learn "the proper regulation of old and young" and "the duty between ruler and subject, and everything else follows from that." If the family is not in order, which is to say, if children do not suitably respect their parents, and if husbands and wives do not fully respect each other and manage their children well, then no foundation exists for a stable society or a secure state. Consequently the superior person will take it as a *political* responsibility to "regulate" the family. For, as *The Great Learning* says: "When the family is regulated, the state will be in order."

Once the family is "regulated," the superior person turns to the state. Here Confucius might raise some eyebrows with his assumptions about how political life works. And no doubt those assumptions belong more to a traditional Confucian society than to the twenty-first-century democratic nation-state. But the differences make Confucian ideas the more worth thinking about, especially in a time of accelerating historical change, multiplying moral uncertainties, and ascending global consciousness and anxieties.

As we would expect, the Confucianist governs in the same way he lives: by being *good*. Uniting the personal and the political life and setting an example of goodness in governing, he insures goodness and stability throughout the state. "What the gentleman holds on to is the cultivation of his own character," Mencius says, "yet this brings order to the Empire." So, "in administering your government," Confucius advises, "just desire the good yourself and the common people will be good. . . . Rule over them with dignity and they will be reverent; treat them with kindness and they will do their best; raise the good and instruct those who are backward and they will be imbued with enthusiasm." Or as Mencius puts it, "when the prince is benevolent, everyone else is benevolent; when the prince is dutiful, everyone else is dutiful." According to the Confucian Way, people will *be* good if they *see* good, because goodness is the same in public life and politics as it is in private life and character. This makes the Confucian state a moral state through and through, like the Confucian universe—the root and the branch, the personal life and world peace, depend on each other.

This is about as far as you could go from the view of political life set forth in that seminal modern Western political manual, Machiavelli's *The Prince*. Machiavelli would say that Confucius was just imagining human nature and politics as he *wanted* them to be rather than seeing them as they actually *are*. Convinced by experience that human beings are neither fundamentally rational nor social nor moral, Machiavelli believed morality and politics conflict more often than they coincide, and so he concluded that in order to survive, political leaders must learn "not to be good" (see Chapter 11). Most modern Western readers would probably take Machiavelli's side against Confucius. The Confucian assumptions about human nature, morality, and truth can seem to us too idealistic. The world does not work that way, we might say. Its layered complexities, competing interests, and social diversity, as well as its outright villainies, defy any single standard of goodness, much less making possible the moral unity of the universe. Perhaps we would be right. But we could be wrong.

Imagine what a successful modern Confucian society would be. It would be a society where both prosperity and security reign, where learning, sincerity, and intellectual honesty thrive, where the private good and the public good fit together, and where even amidst change people believe in their benign interdependency and in a good society and in an order of things greater than any of them alone. That is the kind of society many people in this restless modern world hunger for. And it is an ideal that Confucianists will not, to their credit, abandon. We should learn anything we can from it.

When you turn from the Confucian Way to the Taoist Way, you take a strikingly different path—if to a somewhat similar place. The Confucian Way leads over the high road of objective rationality, disciplined character, and public responsibility.

TAOISM

The Taoist Way leads through the undergrowth of subjective irrationality, mystical intuitions, and metaphysical whimsicality. Some Taoists played upon the differences by ridiculing Confucius himself as pompous, proud, and misguided. Chuang Tzu, the Taoist philosophical wit, described Confucius as a man "with a long body and short legs, his back a little humped and his ears set way back, who looks as though he were trying to attend to everything within the four seas." And he scathingly reproached the great sage for missing the true Way: "Don't you have the sense to understand the situation?" or "Are you just naturally a boor? . . . Get rid of your proud bearing and that knowing look on your face and you can become a gentleman."

This burlesque captures the contrasts. These were not just a matter of style, either. They came from conflicting ideas of what is real and how we know it, and how we should live. The clash could be said to begin with the Taoists' disdain for the Confucian claim that objective, rational truth exists. This claim is sheer presumption, the Taoists say. The Way exists, sure enough, but sober Confucian rationality will never find it. The Taoist Way, the true *Tao*, does not reveal itself like that. It cannot be "learned" like the Confucian Way. "Can the Way be learned?" asks Chuang Tzu, "Goodness, how could that be?" As the *Tao Te Ching*, the philosophical fount of Taoism, announces, "If one looks for Tao, there is nothing solid to see; if one listens for it, there is nothing loud enough to hear." What is the Tao then? Well, Chuang Tzu explains, "The Way has its reality and its signs but is without action or form. You can hand it down but you cannot receive it; you can get it but you cannot see it. It is its own source, its own root. . . . It was born before Heaven and earth, and yet you cannot say it has been there for long; it is earlier than the earliest time and yet you cannot call it old." Or in the poetic words of the *Tao Te Ching*, "The Way itself is like something / Seen in a dream, elusive, evading one. / In it are things like shadows in the twilight. / In it are essences, subtle but real, / Embedded in truth."

With this murky notion of the Way, an elusive shadow lying beyond rationality, defying all claims to know it or describe it, Taoists had to take some peculiar mental turns, and sometimes perform some mental acrobatics, even to talk about it. Chuang Tzu was their virtuoso. "Suppose I try saying something," he teases, "what way do I have of knowing that if I say I know something I don't really know it? Or what way do I have of knowing that if I say I don't know something I don't really in fact know it?" Come again? we respond. Chuang Tzu would relish our puzzlement. He thrives on it. In a famous parable, playing further upon the impossibility of our knowing anything, he asks (as paraphrased): If you dream you are a butterfly, and then you awaken to discover you are a person, how do you know whether you are a person who dreamed you were a butterfly or a butterfly dreaming you are a person? Well, you don't. And, glibly remarking, "there must be some distinction," Chuang Tzu happily leaves it.

What about Confucius' earnest need to answer the question, "What am I to do?" and the Confucian certainty that "a man . . . has no way of judging men unless he understands words"? Forget it! Rational truth and coherent language go out the window together. "The way I see it," Chuang Tzu says, "the rules of benevolence and righteousness and the paths of right and wrong are all hopelessly snarled and jumbled. How could I know anything about such discriminations? . . . If right were really right, it would differ so clearly from not right that there would be no need for argument." Only fools think otherwise. He goes on: "The stupid believe they are awake, busily and brightly assuming they understand things." But they are merely dreaming—like everyone else. "Confucius and you are both dreaming. And when I say you are dreaming, I am dreaming, too." At least Chuang Tzu is consistent enough to admit his own confusion—and his love of mocking paradoxes won an admirer in Oscar Wilde (see Chapter 25).

But where does this leave us? "Perception and understanding have come to a stop," Chuang Tzu declares. And yet, it is only now, he says, after banishing the demands of logical coherence and expectations of rational truth, that we can start to find the true Way. "Forget distinctions," he cries. "Leap into the boundless and make it your home."

These loopy puzzles and irreverent slaps at Confucian rationality, the mocking of logic and the insults to common sense, make Taoism a curious affair—and gave Taoists a reputation as oddballs, as you can see, for example, in the great Chinese novel by Cao Xueqin, *The Story of the Stone* (1763). At the same time, these antics do not leave the Taoist without guidance. Taoism is, after all, a cult of the one true Way, a discoverable path to somewhere. You just have to leave conventional learning and rationality behind in order to find and follow it. You have to "leap into the boundless" and give yourself over to mystical flights and intuitive vibrations. Then you can approach the unknowable: "Touch ultimate emptiness," says the *Tao Te Ching*, for "The world may be known / Without leaving the house; The Way may be seen / Apart from the windows. The further you go, / The less you will know." So the wise man, Chuang Tzu advises, "just lets things be and doesn't try to help life along."

Once you "forget distinctions" and "leap into the boundless" and "let things be," you can at least travel on the mysterious Taoist Way. But you travel toward a kind of virtue and harmony of all things that is not altogether different from those of Confucius. "Cultivate the Way yourself," says the *Tao Te Ching*, "and your Virtue will be genuine. / Cultivate it in the home, and its Virtue will overflow. / Cultivate it in the village, and the village will endure. / Cultivate it in the realm, and the realm will flourish. / Cultivate it in the world and Virtue will be universal." Here the Taoist Way, no less than the Confucian Way, unites all things from the self to the world. But, again, the signposts here are different, inviting passivity not duty, quiescence not diligence. "So long as I do nothing," says a sage in the *Tao Te Ching*, "the people will of themselves be transformed. / So long as I love quietude, the people will of themselves go straight. / So long as I act only by inactivity the people will of themselves become prosperous." A vision of unity and universal good thus pervades both the Confucian and the Taoist Ways. The guidebooks to those Ways just chart alternative roads to that end—although these roads can appear so dissimilar that they make the end seem different, too.

Following the Taoist Way down its twisty trails can take us to some strange places, among them a mystical union with the Tao itself, where we quietly lose ourselves in otherworldly transcendence. But Taoism can also take us to where we acquire a sense of intense engagement with anything we do. For while the Tao invites us to enter into it as the very essence of existence, it can also awaken us to the singular Tao in every object and activity.

Everything has its own Tao, or essence and guiding principle, by virtue of its own nature or how it uniquely works—there is the Tao of flowers and of stones and of animals, and the Tao of painting, of singing, of archery, of physics, of selling, and so on (and bookstores now offer many books on just such subjects). To know anything well, or how to do anything expertly, we must therefore discover its Tao. But doing that requires that we go beyond logical thought and deliberate consciousness. Finding and following the Tao of anything is more an act of transcendent intuition, or mind-bending concentration, almost mystical identification. It resembles what science fiction writers describe as a benign power within us that can take over, like "The Force" in the popular *Star Wars* movies: when "The Force," or the Way, is with you, you can, as Chuang Tzu said, "let yourself go," and it will inevitably guide you to your end. This is also rather like what athletes and performers and anyone concentrating on a task speak of as being "in the flow" or "in the zone," where everything they are trying to do comes together as if magically. As Chuang Tzu puts it, "a good swimmer" has "forgotten the water." Everyone should experience that near-mystical unity with some activity. It brings an enthralling sense of efficacy and elation, and makes things work.

So, for all of its subjectivity, irrationality, and whimsy, inspiring mysticism and justifying downright silliness, Taoism has valuable practical uses. These can pay off in everyday life, in many everyday *ways*.

CONFUCIANISM AND TAOISM traveled down the centuries along their parallel Ways, often as adversaries, but also as allies. Taoist writings, for instance, commonly honor rather than ridicule Confucius by depicting him espousing Taoist principles; and Mencius openly absorbed into Confucianism a good deal of the genial Taoist spirit. And both have much to give us today in Ways of thinking.

For Confucianism and Taoism ask us above all to consider how all the parts of life fit into a whole, how everything is related, and how the ends we pursue follow from everything else that we do. They also tell us that we need a certain mental concentration to see the whole, and to direct our lives to the best ends. Confucianism does this by encouraging us to see how the parts of life are linked in an ethical and largely rational unity, and how learning and sincerity can lead us to good character, a good society, and a peaceful world. That is the Confucian Way. Taoism urges us instead to discover how the Tao runs deeply and invisibly through everything, and how, by consuming concentration, we can enter into it and "go with the flow," where everything falls into place and we gain a power otherwise unknown. That is the Taoist Way.

We should welcome both Ways becoming more widely known, and more traveled along, as the peoples and cultures of the world increasingly turn to each other, searching for common ways to make the personal life more fulfilling and the political and social life more harmonious. For Confucianism and Taoism can help anyone find the right Way and do the right thing.

On the Ways of Life

1. Everything has its own Way, or essential principle and nature.
2. There is a right Way to do everything.
3. There is a right Way to live.
4. Never cease searching for the right Way.
5. The Way is an objective and rational truth. (Confucianism)
6. The Way is a subjective and mysterious truth. (Taoism)
7. We find the Way though constant learning, rectifying our minds, sincerity, and cultivating our character. (Confucianism)
8. We find the Way through mental paradoxes and intuition. (Taoism)
9. When we find the Way in anything we do, we become one with it, we feel in the flow, and we can accomplish anything. (Taoism)
10. Humanity or goodness is the Way of human beings. (Confucianism)
11. When we have humanity or goodness to the full, we become superior persons. (Confucianism)
12. Superior persons are learned and wise, self-aware and sincere, strong and modest, restrained and responsible. (Confucianism)
13. Good character leads to good families, good families lead to the good society, the good society leads to the good state, and the good state leads to the good of all people. (Confucianism)
14. All things that exist can be properly connected like root and branch through the right Way, from personal life to world peace, for nothing exists on its own.
15. When all things are connected and in harmony they flourish.
16. The meaning of life is to find the Right Way in everything we do.

II

How to Succeed in the Business of Life

Niccolò Machiavelli: *The Prince*

Men use various methods in pursuing their own personal end . . . and yet everyone, for all this diversity of method, can reach his end.
Machiavelli

Niccolò Machiavelli (1469–1527) has fame today for writing the ingenious and, some might say wicked, little book *The Prince*. But in his day Machiavelli enjoyed a successful career for nearly twenty years as a hardworking government official and an influential adviser to leaders of the Italian city-state of Florence. Then power changed hands and he was ousted, suspected of disloyalty to the new regime. Settling on a small farm with politics on his mind, he soon wrote two books that would make his name: *Discourses on the First Ten Books of Titus Livius* (c. 1513–17) and *The Prince* (1513). The *Discourses* lengthily presents Machiavelli's strong support for the reasonable and humane principles of republican government. But the tempestuousness of his times also led Machiavelli to question whether human beings possess the rationality to live together harmoniously, or the selflessness to be humane. These doubts inspired *The Prince* and furnished the theme of Machiavelli's deft comic drama, *The Mandrake* (1518), and they marked other writings that occupied his remaining years, such as his *History of Florence* (c. 1525). Although Machiavelli never regained an important political position, he will never be forgotten for *The Prince*, if nothing else.

The Prince baldly displays Machiavelli's dark view of human nature as it advises rulers how to survive amid untrammeled competition for power. Laying out examples from history, Machiavelli illustrates how some rulers have succeeded by using power cautiously, others by using it ruthlessly, and how still others have failed by not using it cautiously or ruthlessly enough—the point, Machiavelli says, is to use power effectively so you can keep it in your hands. From these examples he derives many acerbic judgments about human irrationality and selfishness, and he offers the political advice that seems to justify doing anything to hold power. But when you read *The Prince* carefully, you see that it is not simply about how to survive in politics at all costs. It is about how to succeed at *anything*—and how you might have to be very unlike a ruthless ruler to do that.

THE NAME MACHIAVELLI evokes images of unscrupulous politicians, insidious self-promoters, and callous backstabbers. And no wonder. Machiavelli made heroes of such characters in the first how-to-book of power politics, *The Prince*.

Machiavelli wrote *The Prince* as political advice for rulers in sixteenth-century Italy, hoping that the current Florentine ruler, Lorenzo de' Medici (grandson of Lorenzo the Magnificent), to whom he dedicated the book, would give him a job on its merits. Machiavelli had been politically isolated for some time and needed money—he was also in the same kind of dark midlife mood that had prompted his fellow Italian author Dante to write *The Divine Comedy* two centuries earlier (see Chapter 5). Moved by dejection and spurred by ambition, Machiavelli laid out in this little volume the tough-minded strategies and cold-blooded tactics for succeeding in politics that won him infamy as the philosophical father of the sinister political principles now labeled "Machiavellian"—although it did not get him a job. But *The Prince* is not just about how to succeed by sinister means in the business of politics. It is also about how to succeed in the business of life. And there doesn't have to be anything sinister about it.

This is not to suggest that *The Prince* contains a set of instructions for success in the manner of, say, a manual on how to set up a personal computer or have good sex. Instructions like these lead us through every step and show us how to take them. They do not ask us to think. They do the thinking for us. *The Prince* is different. It shows us how to think: how to think about succeeding in politics, and how to think about succeeding at anything we do.

Machiavelli openly passes from politics to life in general only toward the end of *The Prince*. Until then, in a couple of dozen brief topical chapters, he guides us through a treacherous political terrain extending from antiquity to his own times, with an eye to why some leaders have succeeded and others have failed, why some states have survived and others have vanished. Along the way he gives us a catalog of power struggles and sly maneuvers, wily deceptions and brutal violence, prudent moves and fatal miscalculations, all punctuated by the pithy observations on human nature and the cold precepts on success and failure that not only gave the name to "Machiavellian" but make *The Prince* so much more than a political book.

Machiavelli's rendering of this rough landscape is not intended to please. It is instead intended to be unapologetically accurate. For while Machiavelli grants that what he shows us may not be how things *should* be, he has no doubt that what he shows us is how things *are*. Machiavelli describes "things as they are in real truth," he explains, "rather than as they are imagined," because "the gulf between how one does live and how one should live is so wide that a man who neglects what is actually done for what should be done learns the way to self-destruction not self-preservation." This gritty realism sets the very premise of the book: success in politics or life depends on a firm grasp of plain reality, not on the pursuit of ideals; and on knowledge of facts, not on the speculations of theory. *The Prince* tells us how to succeed in the real world, not in our fantasies (Emma Bovary should have read it rather than her romances—see Chapter 24).

And it tells us this through a few simple rules of thought and action. Machiavelli does not state these rules explicitly. He rather lets them emerge implicitly through abundant historical facts and the patterns he discerns in them, and through his practical advice, first to politicians and then to everybody. In brief, his rules are these: (1) clearly identify your ends, (2) fully comprehend your circumstances, (3) choose only means to pursue your ends that your ends justify and that fit your circumstances, and (4) be willing to use *any means* to achieve your ends that those ends justify and that your circumstances require. Or, to put it succinctly: Know your ends, know your circumstances, and do whatever those ends and circumstances tell you to do.

These rules apply to everything we do. If we follow them, we will, like all successful people, become *good* Machiavellians. That is, we will know how to think about succeeding in life, no less, and perhaps more, than in politics. And we don't have to be amorally Machiavellian to do it. To see how these rules work, we should first draw them out of *The Prince* and look at them conceptually, then we can see how Machiavelli applies them to politics in particular and to life at large.

To SUCCEED AT ANYTHING, we have to begin with the end. Hence rule number 1: clearly identify your ends. Ends come first because ends show us what kinds of means, or actions, can logically lead us toward those ends, and which cannot. We must therefore clearly identify our ends, or goals, before we can even think about choosing means. Any uncertainty about our ends will lead to confusion about means, and confusion about means leads to failure. For our ends and means must fit together.

This is how our ends *always* justify our means. Don't let the term "justify" throw you. It merely signals that some ends and some means are logically compatible, and other ends and means are logically incompatible. For example, we cannot hold on to power by giving it to someone else, or become healthy by abusing our body, or be loved by being unlovable. Those ends do not justify those means because they are logically incompatible with them. Although Machiavelli did not use the phrase "the ends justify the means," he commonly gets blamed for making it an amoral political doctrine. That blame is unfair. We all live by this principle most of the time, whether we admit it or not. For we all choose means that we think will take us to our ends. And those ends therefore *justify* our means. Or we could say that these ends just help us choose our means. Aristotle derived his *Ethics* from exactly this commonsense truth (see Chapter 4). And it is not an amoral truth at all.

But imperative as it is to identify ends before choosing means, Machiavelli says almost nothing about the ends of politics in *The Prince*. This is because he takes the ends for granted. Those ends come down to one thing: holding on to political power. Political power in *The Prince* is not a means to other ends, like the public good. It is an unalloyed end in itself. Everything else is a means to it. And everything that Machiavelli says about politics in *The Prince* assumes this.

There are plenty of people today who take power as their end, too, whether in politics or a profession or personal life. For them *The Prince* could indeed be a very useful—and amoral—how-to-book about holding power. But when we follow Machiavelli's argument, we see how *The Prince* can serve us in pursuing any end, and how moral we may need to be to succeed.

This starts to become evident as soon as Machiavelli takes up the subject of "means." Although ends come first and justify our means, Machiavelli does not think that ends alone can dictate any specific, surefire means of achieving them. "Ends" are abstractions, aspirations, intentions, ideals, mission statements, what is hoped for, not what *is*. But "means" are concrete actions in the here and now, made of fact and practicality. And if our means fail to reach our ends, it doesn't matter what those ends are. The good intentions that cause hurt, the lofty principles that bring ruin, these ends and their like have no merit in Machiavelli's eyes. The means make all of the difference. For our ends are only as good as the means we choose to reach them.

So, how do we know which means will achieve a particular end? *The Prince* amounts to a detailed answer to this question, or rather it offers good advice on how to think about answering it. When we look for the practical means to achieve our ends, Machiavelli says, we have to scrap our abstract theories and dig into the facts of things as they really are, not as we would like them to be. And the facts that matter most in determining our choice of means are those that define our circumstances. This is where Machiavelli's second rule comes in: Fully comprehend your circumstances.

Whatever our ends, success is won or lost within particular circumstances. Even if our ends would in principle justify almost any means whatsoever—as Machiavelli figures that the end of holding political power does for the prince—our circumstances will not permit us to use any means whatsoever. Our ends justify any means that can reach our ends, but our circumstances determine which particular means will succeed. We must therefore be as flexible in our choice of means as our circumstances are various. So we cannot know which means to choose until we know our circumstances.

Those circumstances include everything that bears on what we want to do—the physical, historical, cultural, political, social, human realities through which we chart our paths to reach our every end. We must see these circumstances clearly or we will stumble, get lost, and fail. This is why Machiavelli loads up *The Prince* with historical facts. These facts defined the circumstances in which historical leaders chose their means to hold power. And Machiavelli opens *The Prince* with a list of specific political circumstances that he says a prince should be aware of in choosing his means to that end. These opening sentences sound dry and rather dense, but they show the Machiavellian way of thinking, and they spell out exactly how Machiavelli proposes to analyze political success and failure in *The Prince*.

"All the states," he begins, "under whose authority men have lived in the past and live now have been and are either republics or principalities. Principalities are hereditary . . . or they are new. The new are completely new . . . or they are like limbs joined to the hereditary state of the prince who acquires them. Dominions so acquired are accustomed to be under a prince, or used to freedom; a prince wins them either with the arms of others or with his own, either by fortune or by prowess." Then, declining to discuss "republics" (because he treated them in *The Discourses*), Machiavelli concludes this opening by promising to "follow the order set out above, and debate how these principalities can be governed and maintained."

Here is Machiavelli's explicit subject. It is not how to get power, or how to govern a republic where leaders are elected (although Machiavelli's rules for success also apply to these cases). His subject is how a *prince*—Machiavelli's term for any political leader who is not elected—can govern and maintain, or hold power, in a "principality" once he has power in his hands. The means that a prince uses to reach this end should come from his political circumstances. For instance, did the prince obtain power by inheritance or seizure? If by seizure, was it with his own soldiers or with foreign help? Is the principality old or new? If it is new, were his subjects previously accustomed to democracy or autocracy? If the prince does not distinguish carefully among such circumstances and fit his means of holding power to them, he will fail. He will create enemies needlessly; he will misjudge his friends; he will ignore his weakness and overestimate his strength; and so on. Then he will lose power.

The point to get here is not these circumstantial details in themselves—reading Machiavelli, we should not get bogged down in the morass of historical facts. We should instead let these facts remind us that if we want to succeed at anything, we had better know our circumstances well. Again, whatever our ends, our circumstances must supply us with the means to achieve those ends. And this brings us to Machiavelli's third rule: Choose only means to pursue your ends that your ends justify and that fit your circumstances.

Remember, our ends justify our means simply by indicating which means can logically lead to our ends. Therefore, we must make sure that the kinds of means we choose are logically compatible with our ends. If power is your sole end, as it is for the prince, you must always act to strengthen your power and do nothing to weaken it. If that requires skulduggery or ruthlessness, so be it. If wealth is your only end, you should consistently make your wealth grow and do nothing to diminish it. If that entails penny-pinching or exploiting people, fine. If survival is your single end, you must do anything to survive. If that involves murder or betrayal or flight, do it. By the same token, if having a flawless moral character is your preeminent end, you must always act morally and never act immorally. If that requires compromising your career or even sacrificing your life, you must make the sacrifice—as that eminent moralist and *good* Machiavellian Socrates did when he chose to drink the fatal hemlock rather than escape from jail (see Chapter 3).

But whatever means our ends might justify as logically compatible with those ends, our circumstances tell us which means will actually take us to those ends. For means, or strategy and tactics, that work in one circumstance might not work in another. The French Maginot Line, for instance, might have held back the German armies of World War I, but it failed in the circumstances of World War II. To avoid the Maginot Line Fallacy, we must do what suits the actual circumstances, not just what might have worked in the past or what some abstract theory or personal preference inclines us to do. We must be bold when boldness is called for, but be temperate when time is on our side; we must fight battles when we need to, but also play for the long term to win the wars, and so forth. That is why we must not only choose means that our ends justify, we must also choose means that fit our circumstances.

And now we come to Machiavelli's fourth rule. This is the one that has especially given Machiavelli a bad name. But is also the one we can learn the most from. Be willing to use *any* means to achieve your ends that those ends justify and that your circumstances require. This rule smacks of sheer amorality. And it sanctions some very unsavory acts in *The Prince*. But it does not need to do that. In the first place, to be willing to do anything that our ends justify and that our circumstances require to achieve our ends is not the same thing as being willing to do anything whatsoever. (Even the esteemed scholar Leo Strauss missed this when he asserted that "Machiavelli's teaching is immoral and irreligious" largely because it reflects "the Machiavellian principle that the good end justifies every means.") Our ends and our circumstances will always curtail our means. But if we shrink from doing anything that our ends do justify and that our circumstances do require in order to achieve our ends, then we probably don't know what our true ends are.

In fact (and this is among the chief rewards of following Machiavelli's rules), we might only discover what our true ends are by deciding which means we are willing to use and which we are not. For making this decision can open our eyes to what we most care about. Are we willing to lie, for example, when our circumstances require it in order to get what we want? If not, then we don't really want the ends that lying can give us. And if Machiavelli's prince will not do what his circumstances require to maintain political power—to deceive his allies and slaughter his enemies, feign piety and exploit the populace, bestow rare kindness and spare no cruelty—then political power is not his true end. He might have ends other than power, such as the rule of law; or he might have ends in addition to power, such as the public good; or he might be uncertain of his ends. In any case, he won't have power for long. And this rule holds for every end we pursue.

Our lives are, of course, more various and complicated than the single-minded power politics of *The Prince*. As individuals and as a society we have diverse, sometimes tangled, and often conflicting ends, and we live amidst complex circumstances ranging from our personal lives to our public responsibilities. But Machiavelli's practical rules nonetheless apply. And even keeping these rules in mind can help us think about our ends and means as we pursue success in anything.

❧

As we now turn to Machiavelli's application of his rules to princely politics, we see that he thought the end of political power could justify some mighty dreadful means, and that circumstances could often require among the most dreadful of them. This is not because Machiavelli had a taste for villainy. It is because he thought that besides the specific historical circumstances that rulers must understand in choosing their means for holding onto power, a more generic circumstance always plays a prominent role. That circumstance is human nature. And Machiavelli's version of human nature is not pretty. But anyone who has ever tried to rule or lead or influence other people—even to benign ends outside of power politics—knows that it is all too accurate. (James Madison viewed human nature not so differently as he helped establish America's democratic system—see Chapter 14.)

"One can make this generalization about men," Machiavelli asserts with assurance: "they are ungrateful, fickle, liars, and deceivers, they shun danger and are greedy for profit." More instinctual than rational, more selfish than selfless, more self-deceived than self-aware, they are basically animals, usually predators, sometimes cornered beasts, always bent on their own survival. No sentimentalist, Machiavelli thinks he sees people for what they are, not as we might want them to be, or as they say they are. Perhaps he fastens onto the worst in them. Call him a cynic. But do not dismiss him.

Occasionally evident in everyday life, the bestial qualities that Machiavelli discerned in human beings become blatant in power politics. That is why Machiavelli uses images of animals to represent what a prince, or perhaps any politician, must be to succeed. The prince should have "the qualities of a ferocious lion and of a very cunning fox," he says. As a lion and a fox, a prince can both intimidate and entice, dominate and betray, kill and con. And as the model of this versatile bestiality, Machiavelli holds up Cesare Borgia, who, for instance, assigned a bloodthirsty lieutenant to brutally subdue an intractable town and then had him murdered so that Borgia himself could emerge at once as the town's benefactor and its secure ruler (an implied piece of good Machiavellian advice here: if you do someone's dirty work for them, you become dispensable and will likely become another victim). "I know no better precepts to give a new prince," Machiavelli says, "than the ones derived from Cesare's actions." Machiavelli's politics is nature in the wild, where power and survival are everything.

Machiavelli's unforgiving portrait of human nature engenders many pungent maxims in *The Prince* on how to succeed in politics, and in human relations generally. For instance: "Men must be either pampered or crushed because they can get revenge for small injuries but not for grievous ones."—"The wish to acquire more is admittedly a very natural and common thing; and when men succeed in this they are always praised rather than condemned."—"Whoever is responsible for another's becoming powerful ruins himself."—"One can be hated just as much for good deeds as for evil ones." Machiavelli weaves such pithy thoughts throughout *The Prince*. They may offend or amuse, but they are not frivolous or false.

Machiavelli's maxims ring true mainly because, as Machiavelli never tires of illustrating, human beings are invariably motivated by self-interest and easily seduced by self-deception. He is not wrong here either.

Consider force and fear, by contrast to persuasion and love, as means of exercising authority. Persuasion and love are soft and inviting, but unreliable. Force and fear are hard and insistent, but reliable. People want to be led by the first pair so they can act on their own desires, but they will always yield to the second because they want to survive. "The bond of love," Machiavelli explains, "is one which men, wretched creatures that they are, break when it is to their advantage to do so; but fear is strengthened by a dread of punishment which is always effective." Therefore leaders who "use persuasion," Machiavelli warns, "always come to grief," because "the populace is by nature fickle" and are only to be trusted when "they can be made to believe by force."

Machiavelli overstates his case here, since he knows that force and fear do not always work, even in princely politics, because different historical circumstances require different tactics. And he cautions that untempered force can actually provoke hatred strong enough to bring a ruler down. Still, he is surely correct to observe that no one, whether politician, parent, or anyone else, can exercise authority effectively unless gentle appeals to the heart and mind are somehow supported by power. Just notice, for instance, how a child torn between battling parents will usually cling to the parent who offers love backed by power—such as money, influence, strength of will—over the one who offers love alone. People can even feel love for those who have used force to dominate them—think of some kidnap victims—because, human nature being what it is, power can inspire love. Self-interest and self-deception run that deep. "This is why," Machiavelli observes in one of his often-quoted aphorisms, "all armed prophets have conquered, and unarmed ones have come to grief."

Just as self-interest inclines us to follow those with the power to use force and fear, even if we desire persuasion and love, so self-interest induces us to follow those who exercise power successfully, almost regardless of how they do it. We rarely condemn those in power who serve our interests, whatever their means, and we seldom forgive those in power who fail to serve our interests, whatever the causes. If we must choose between, for example, a leader who remains fastidiously honest but who cannot serve our ends and one who serves our ends but compromises honesty, the choice is predictable: honesty loses. We will grumble that leaders are not honest, and all else being equal we will choose honest over dishonest ones. But ultimately we will forgive a leader almost anything except failing to serve us. By the same token, we do not credit their successes for long. "What have you done for us lately?" we demand, letting yesterday's service be forgotten among today's wants and tomorrow's expectations, as many once-acclaimed but subsequently defeated leaders could attest.

Because Machiavelli finds human beings driven by self-interest and blinded by self-deception, he reaches a most unsettling conclusion about politics. It is this: to hold power, a political leader cannot be altogether morally good. That is because he or she would then have to pursue only moral ends and choose only moral means. Political leaders cannot limit their options this way. They must be willing to use immoral means if circumstances require it. As Machiavelli says, "A prince must learn how not to be virtuous, and to make use of this according to need." Any political leader who would, for instance, refuse on moral grounds to lie or to kill an enemy who threatens his country would be too moral to survive as a leader. The country would lie in ruins, and his own people would denounce him. Because "good deeds are your enemies" when they thwart your ends, Machiavelli warns, a leader is "often forced not to be good." And when survival is at stake, few people would disagree or complain.

But here Machiavelli adds a telling twist on the role of morality in politics. Although at bottom we do not want our leaders to *be* morally good if that will prevent them from serving our interests, he says, we do expect them to *appear* morally good. "The common people are always impressed by appearances and results," Machiavelli remarks. "A prince, therefore, need not necessarily have all the good qualities . . . but he should certainly appear to have them. I would go so far as to say that if he has these qualities and always lives accordingly he will find them ruinous; if he only appears to have them they will render him service."

That is an amoral Machiavellianism for sure. It overturns our most cherished notions about expecting our leaders to be what they seem to be. Don't be virtuous in fact, Machiavelli advises politicians, just learn to use the appearances of virtue to advantage. Politicians should wear a mask of virtue because that is what people want to see. And not only that, it is better for both the leader and the people if the leader's virtue is only a mask, since if his virtue were genuine it would inhibit his actions.

This is probably more true of politics in America today than we would like to admit. We want our political leaders to display all the signs of "good character," morality, and even religiosity. But we also want them to do whatever is necessary to serve our interests. Machiavelli saw the potential contradiction and self-deception here, even if we don't. He knew human nature better than we do. In our age of mass communications and ubiquitous television, politicians—whether in democracies or tyrannies—use appearances more than ever to sway the public. And we convince ourselves that a politician's appearance of good character and the like will somehow serve our interests. This is, in fact, one of the dominant circumstances of contemporary American politics, and any politician who does not fit his or her means to it will surely fail to gain power or hold on to it.

Because he so freely sanctions necessary immorality in politics, Machiavelli may seem wholly to divorce morality from political life. He comes close, but he doesn't quite do that. He rather recognizes that morality and politics have conflicting ends more often than not, especially in principalities. Circumstances might allow a leader to be moral and to still succeed in holding power. If this can happen, Machiavelli says, so much the better. But no one who sets political power, either personal political power or the political survival of the state, for that matter, as the end should count on it, or scruple to care. (All of this departs dramatically from the moral politics of Plato and Aristotle, and it is the political antithesis of Confucianism—see Chapters 3, 4, 10, 19.)

Politics in *The Prince* is a bestial arena where holding power is the only end, and where playing to the instinctual selfishness and irrationality of human nature, within diverse political circumstances, supplies the means. Who succeeds at holding power depends on who best understands the generic circumstance of human nature and the historical circumstances of politics, and who plays to them most effectively. There are no sure things in politics, of course, or in anything else. No one can know enough about the complex circumstances of the human world to guarantee success in pursuing any ends. But our best chance comes from following Machiavelli's rules as deftly as we can. And to do that, Machiavelli now adds, we must also learn how to deal with what he calls "fortune" (*fortuna*).

"Fortune" amounts to the shifting winds of circumstance that we cannot predict. Fortune can bring good luck, but it can also undo the best-laid plans and choices of means—as it did to Machiavelli's hero, Cesare Borgia, who lost power mainly because he fell ill and his father and chief ally, Pope Alexander VI, died. To help us respond to fortune,

Machiavelli adds a corollary to his four rules of success. And with this he moves from politics to life in general.

Life in general is not quite the jungle of savage beasts that Machiavelli makes of politics. But it is no less an arena where to succeed at anything we must know our ends, understand our circumstances, and do anything that those ends justify and that those circumstances require. At the same time we must try to conquer fortune. That is to say, we must "cope not only with present troubles but with ones likely to arise in the future, and assiduously forestall them."

Fortune is a shifty and dangerous adversary, for when "circumstances change," Machiavelli warns, anyone "will be ruined if he does not change his policy" (or "mode of procedure"). But we can conquer fortune if we are savvy and strong enough. As Machiavelli puts it in a couple of bold metaphors: fortune is "one of those violent rivers" that must be harnessed before it overflows its banks; and "fortune is a woman, and if she is to be submissive, it is necessary to beat and coerce her." Beyond the macho Renaissance rhetoric, Machiavelli goes on to explain that to conquer fortune we need a "policy" that anticipates changes of circumstances with "prudence" (*prudenza*) while preparing us to respond to those changes with "audacity" (*audacia*), even "impetuously" (*impetuoso*). "Men prosper," he declares, "so long as fortune and policy are in accord, and when there is a clash they fail" (or men "are successful so long as [their] ways conform to circumstances"). In other words, we succeed when the means that we choose to pursue our ends fit the circumstances that fortune throws at us and we can adapt to the changing "demands of the times." And although we need both prudence and audacity to do this, Machiavelli remarks that it is often "better to be impetuous than circumspect" in order to "beat and coerce" fortune into submission.

Prudence and audacity, or we could say foresight and decisiveness, these are the ways to conquer fortune. Anticipate changes of circumstance with foresight and prudence, then meet them with audacity, even impetuousness, and decisiveness—that is Machiavelli's corollary to his rules of success.

Applied to holding princely power in sixteenth-century Italy, this Machiavellian way of thinking sanctioned an amoral politics. But, as Machiavelli knew, his rules can work anywhere for anyone who has the *virtù*—a term he uses frequently, connoting prowess, courage, and practical wisdom—no matter what his or her ends. Machiavelli says as much when he concludes that although people have different ends and disparate circumstances in life, and must therefore use different means to attain their ends, they can all nonetheless succeed. "Men use various methods in pursuing their own personal end," he explains. "One man proceeds with circumspection, another impetuously; one uses violence, another stratagem; one man goes about things patiently, another does the opposite; and yet everyone, for all this diversity of method, can reach his objective." The results, Machiavelli adds, depend on "the extent to which their methods are or are not suited to the nature of the times."

Machiavelli's rules of success are certainly easier to apply to brutal power politics than to, say, morals or child-rearing or to life as a whole, where we have multiple, sometimes conflicting, ends and live complicated lives. But if we think about our lives as Machiavelli advises—that is, clearly identifying our ends; fully comprehending our circumstances; doing anything that our ends justify and that our circumstances require; and anticipating changes of circumstances with prudence, then meeting these changes with audacity—we are more likely to succeed than not in anything that we try to do. Nobody wants to be a loser. *The Prince* is the classic how-to-book for winners. Whatever the game—even the game, or the business, of life itself.

On How to Succeed at Anything

1. To succeed at anything we must first know our ends.

2. After knowing our ends we must understand our circumstances.

3. Once we know our ends and understand our circumstances, we must choose means that will logically lead to our ends and that fit our circumstances.

4. Our ends justify our means by pointing to the kinds of means that will logically lead to those ends, and to the kinds of means that will not.

5. Our circumstances, not our ends, give us the particular means we need to achieve our ends.

6. Our ends and circumstances together will always limit our choice of means.

7. Our ends are only as good as our means of achieving them.

8. To achieve our ends we must be willing to use any means that our ends justify and that our circumstances require.

9. If we are not willing to use any means that our ends justify and that our circumstances require in order to achieve our ends, then our ends are not what we thought they were.

10. Pursuing a single end, like political power, makes choosing means easier than if we pursue multiple ends, like power along with goodness.

11. When we clearly identify our ends and fully comprehend our circumstances, and then do anything that those ends and circumstances tell us to do—while anticipating changes of circumstances with prudence and foresight and meeting those changes with audacity and decisiveness—we will likely succeed at anything.

12. The meaning of life is to know all of our ends and use the right means to achieve them.

12

So It Seems

William Shakespeare: *Hamlet, Othello, King Lear*
Molière: *The Misanthrope*

Seems, madam? Nay, it is. I know not "seems."

Men should be what they seem.

I pray you, father, being weak, seem so.

Shakespeare

Be sincere, and never part with any word that isn't from the heart.

Molière

William Shakespeare's life (1564–1616) took him from the rural English town of Stratford-upon-Avon to the London stage, where he performed with a leading theatrical troupe, became an owner of it, and wrote poetry and plays. Then he returned to his home town to die a wealthy man. He seems to have been an able actor and an adroit manager. But his writings are so eloquent and erudite that some critics have credited them to other figures of his day better educated than a mere actor-manager. Be that as it may, what we know as Shakespeare's twelve comedies, eleven tragedies, nine histories, four romances, and twenty-two sonnets remain an unsurpassed treasure in the English language of beauty, wit, and wisdom on all kinds of subjects. And no theme winds through Shakespeare's plays more tragically and comically than the confusions of appearances and realities, particularly of people not being what they seem. This theme appears most powerfully in the late tragedies, *Hamlet* (c. 1600), *Othello* (c. 1604), and *King Lear* (c. 1605). For in these renowned dramas of a son's troubled vengeance for his father's murder, a good man's ruin through deception and jealousy, and a kingdom's disintegration from an old man's folly and his children's perniciousness, Shakespeare shows us how tragic life can be when we cannot see that people are not what they seem—whether they be friends, family, or even ourselves.

Molière (1622–1673)—the pen name of Jean-Baptiste Poquelin, the son of a professional craftsman in the French court of Louis XIII—was, like Shakespeare, an actor who won lasting fame writing plays. He wrote a lot of them, most no longer performed. But a few continue to tickle and enlighten audiences by playing upon the moral conflicts between social appearances and underlying motives amid the dandified manners of seventeenth-century France. The best known of these moral comedies are *Tartuffe* (1664–69), *The Misanthrope* (1666), and *The Bourgeois Gentleman* (1670). And it is in *The Misanthrope*, a wry comedy about a man who condemns the social hypocrisies around him while unwittingly deceiving himself, that Molière most cleverly and profoundly explores the morality of manners, the ambiguities of sincerity, and the self-deceptions that can entangle us even when we try to be what we seem.

"ALL THE WORLD'S A STAGE, and all the men and women merely players." So goes Shakespeare's familiar line from *As You Like It*. And who would deny its truth? Everybody knows that social life is a kind of theater. In it we play many roles, present many appearances, wear many masks. We *seem* to be many things, or many *persons*—a word descended from the Latin *persona,* for mask—to many people. And we are. Every social encounter comes with theatrical demands, asking us to behave or perform according to the social conventions that will make us understood. We smile, we speak, we emote, and do other things as role-players communicating our wishes to others, our audience. These roles, or appearances or seemings, can be either true or false to the motives behind them and to the emotions inside of us. And it can be hard to detect from the outside whether they are true or false. To convincingly tell the truth, for instance, or to convincingly tell a lie, a person has to act the same way. As the Hollywood mogul Samuel Goldwyn once reportedly said, "The most important thing in acting is honesty; once you learn to fake that, you're in." So, we can use the roles we play to deceive others, or we can use them to be true. We can use them either to our advantage or to our disadvantage. And other people can perceive them accurately or inaccurately. But whether we embrace or rue these facts of social life, we should not ignore them. For then we fail to understand how we live in a social world.

And when we fail to understand the social world, we cannot understand all kinds of things about ourselves. For the truth is, we feel emotions, embrace ideas, adopt manners, exhibit morals, shape our characters, fashion our lives, and even look at ourselves, almost always through our relation to other people. And that means through social performance. We might think that we are the persons who we are by nature, or because that is who we are in our heart of hearts. But stepping outside ourselves, we see that, whoever we are by nature or in our heart of hearts, much of who we are comes from the roles we play on the stage of social life. (In the eighteenth century, Denis Diderot turned this fact into a revelatory comic psychology and philosophy in *Rameau's Nephew,* whose title character plays every kind of role and demonstrates to others that everyone plays roles almost all the time.) Erving Goffman, the renowned sociologist of role-playing, got it right when he said, echoing Shakespeare: "All the world is not, of course, a stage, but the crucial ways in which it isn't are not easy to specify."

Role-playing so pervades our lives that the fragile bridge between our inner selves and our social appearances has long been not only the making of morals, but the stuff of gossip, the brunt of comedy, and a driving force of tragedy. At the dawn of modern times in the West, Dante pictured hell as a place to punish false appearances more harshly than any other evils—frauds, hypocrites, deceivers, traitors, and the like, these were Dante's most abominable sinners (see Chapter 5). Later, amidst a growing historical concern in the Renaissance over determining personal identity—the invention of the passport in the sixteenth century reflecting this concern and foreshadowing things to come—dramatists seized on the theatrical possibilities of people not being who they seem. Long before this Sophocles had played memorably on that theme in the tragedy of Oedipus, but no one ever exploited it more than Shakespeare, and no one turned it to cleverer effect than Molière.

Shakespeare made the deceptions of social appearances and their connections to inner realities a central cause of laughter in his comedies and of sorrow in his tragedies. Molière fastened onto the same subject, spinning comedies of manners where tensions between social roles and inner selves burst on the stage in farces bearing pointed truths. Shakespeare and Molière show us how tangled is the web of our appearances and realities in the worldly theater of role-playing, where we all must perform. And how confusing it can be to try to untangle that web. Yet how necessary it is to try.

SHAKESPEARE was the king of seemings. His comedies roil with confusions of identities, where funny things happen when characters are not who they seem. Many of his tragedies also

SHAKESPEARE

turn on these confusions, but they show terrible consequences caused by the same thing. And nowhere did Shakespeare more forcefully dramatize the ambiguities and perils of false seemings than in the three great tragedies, *Hamlet*, *Othello*, and *King Lear*. These are tragedies of false seemings, among many other things. Most of the principal characters in these plays are not what they seem, or they prove to be both what they seem and not what they seem, or you can't tell quite which they are. These muddles, or efforts to unravel them and learn whether the seemings are true or false, drive the tragedies' very plots. And after following their unhappy twists and turns, we cannot easily ignore in life around us the theatrics that cloak virtually all social relations in performances of truth and falsehood. For interpreting these theatrics does much to define the social, the psychological, and the moral life. As the king of seemings knew so well.

Take *Hamlet*. Here the melancholy prince of Denmark so distrusts seemings that he makes a crusade of unmasking them. Hamlet sets this theme at the outset when his mother, Gertrude, seeing him moping about, asks: "Why seems it so peculiar with thee?" He responds irritably: "Seems, madam? Nay, it is. I know not 'seems.'" Deeply mourning his lately deceased father, the king, Hamlet explains that the "forms, moods, shapes of grief . . . indeed seem, / For these are actions that a man might play; / But I have that within which passeth show." Hamlet refuses merely to *seem* sad; he is playing no role. His feelings for his father run deeper than that, so deep that he believes they can never reveal themselves fully in mere appearances. And he resents the suggestion that his feelings could be any less, that he could ever simply play a role and only *seem* to be what he feels. Hamlet respects the depths. He almost always finds social appearances a bit suspect. They can be too easily contrived.

But Hamlet is no naive moralist. He knows that seemings can reveal as well as conceal. The trick is to tell which is which. So even as he scolds his mother for her insensitive question about his *seemings,* he condemns her for failing even to try to *seem* sorrowful over her husband's death herself. He expects her at least to display signs of loss, whatever her true feelings. But she doesn't. She grieved too little, and remarried too soon after her husband's death. "A beast . . . would have mourned longer," Hamlet growls under his breath. Unintentionally she revealed to Hamlet that she did not care enough for Hamlet's father even to feign sorrow. Hamlet reads her appearance as saying: she has that within which shows itself too well, and it is—nothing.

Disgusted at his mother's evident lack of feeling for his father, Hamlet then discovers a harder truth. From his father's very ghost, Hamlet learns that Gertrude's new husband, the dead king's own brother, Claudius, had in fact murdered the king to seize his crown and marry his widow. Hamlet feels himself sinking in a sea of evil seemings.

"Smiling, damned villain!" Hamlet curses Claudius. How ghastly, how terribly wrong, "that one may smile, and smile, and be a villain." Claudius' deceptively benign appearances rile Hamlet as much as his father's death pains him. And he resolves to unmask those appearances to reveal the murderous truth. So he lays an ingenious plan. He will ask a troupe of traveling players to present a play containing "something like the murder of my father." Then, Hamlet thinks, when Claudius unexpectedly sees his own misdeeds dramatized before him he will unwittingly drop his guard and betray his true self. For "I have heard," Hamlet explains, "That guilty creatures, sitting at a play, / Have by the very cunning of the scene / Been struck so to the soul that presently / They have proclaimed their malefactions." Claudius should do the same. "I'll observe his looks," Hamlet says; "if he but blench, I know my course." So, he exclaims, "The play's the thing / Wherein I'll catch the conscience of the King." Setting the players to perform "The Murder of Gonzago," with some lines written by himself, he invites his friend Horatio to watch with him for the clinching evidence: "Observe my uncle," he urges, for signs of hidden or "occulted guilt." "Mine eyes," he adds, "will rivet to his face, / And after we will both our judgments join / In censure of his seeming."

The ploy works. Claudius, at first discomfited and then disquieted by what he sees, suddenly leaps to his feet, halts the performance, and flees the room. "Did'st perceive?" Hamlet prods Horatio. "Very well, my lord," replies his friend. Hamlet calls for music to celebrate the triumph. He has caught the conscience of the king in an unsuspecting confession. The villain, so long masked behind a lying smile, had been unmasked by the guilty *seemings* that had suddenly surfaced from his own tarnished soul.

Later, in a moment of remorse, Claudius confesses to God that although he knows his guilt will glare openly in the next world, where we are "compelled even to the teeth and forehead of our faults to give evidence," he cannot repent because "I am still possessed of the effects for which I did the murder." So he plots to protect himself against the prying Hamlet—who had happened on to the confession, but had declined to take his revenge while Claudius was in a pious mood that might have gained him grace in the next world. Claudius first enlists Hamlet's hapless friends, Rosenkrantz and Guildenstern, to escort Hamlet to England with a letter secretly sealing his death by naming him to a hired killer. Offstage Hamlet foils this plot by replacing his name in the letter with theirs, quipping to Horatio in another dramaturgical allusion: "They had begun the play," but he had finished it.

Undaunted, while Hamlet continues to delay revenge, Claudius sets up the climactic scene of the drama with a "friendly" duel—complete with a poisoned sword tip and poisoned wine—between Hamlet and Laertes (whose father, Polonius, Hamlet had earlier skewered through a curtain in an uncharacteristically impulsive move, possibly thinking he was Claudius). The scene ends in bloodshed and mayhem, with the dying Hamlet at last slaying Claudius for the "treachery" of his last false seemings in the deceptions of the duel. Hamlet himself dies urging Horatio to "report me and my cause aright" so that people will learn the truth—namely, that Claudius was not what he seemed, but that Hamlet was indeed what he had seemed: a loyal son moved to revenge by deep and honest feelings of grief and injustice.

Hamlet repeatedly tried to unravel the tangle of appearances and realities that enmeshed him. He wanted things and people to be what they seem. He could have echoed the pompous Polonius' famous advice to Laertes: "To thine own self be true, / And it must follow as the night the day / Thou canst not then be false to any man." But Hamlet also knew that being true to yourself gives no assurance that this "self" is good. He saw this in both his mother and Claudius. In the revealing moments when they had seemed to be what they truly were, they were no good. Still, like most of us, Hamlet feared deception more than overt evil, because if outward appearances accurately mirror inward realities, at least no one is deceived. Hamlet could not save himself from falling afoul of false appearances, but he did learn some of their wiles. He was Shakespeare's student of seemings.

HAMLET was a probing student of seemings. Othello was a naive victim of them. Noble, trusting, resolute, Othello kills his beloved wife and himself because he is deceived. And he is deceived by the character who stands out in all of Shakespeare, and perhaps all of literature, as the most thoroughly and maliciously evil character—as Lionel Trilling pointed out in *Sincerity and Authenticity*, this is the only character that Shakespeare labeled a "villain" in the first folio of his works. This is Iago. Iago makes Claudius look like a boy scout. Surely no other character in literature is so calculatingly, so unrelentingly, so malevolently *not* what he seems. There is no doubt where Dante would put Iago in hell: at the icy bottom with the traitors.

It is clear from the start that Iago's treachery is the very subject of the play *Othello*. Iago proclaims this himself when he steps forward and announces his intention to destroy Othello in order to avenge some vague grievance. He grumbles that Othello promoted his rival, Cassio, over him, and he also alludes to a rumor of Othello's having slept with Iago's wife—although he concedes this unlikely. But Iago passes over these accusations quickly, as though fishing for justification. And that is what gives Iago's malevolence its peerless viciousness, and its fascination: Iago's evil has no convincing cause. Iago plots Othello's destruction with an obsessiveness arising far more from the pure desire to do harm than from any reasons he can conjure up. So Iago is that strangest and most frightening of characters: the person who does harm for harm's sake. If you ever meet one, you will be confused and curious almost as much as you will be dismayed—and you had better run the other way.

To bring off his devilish designs against his boss, Iago decides to become the consummate deceiver. He knows that only by *seeming* to be good can he effectively do the evil he wants to do. "Though I do hate him as I do hell pains," he confides, "I must show out a flag and a sign of love," not "for love and duty, / But seeming so." For if he were to display his true feelings, to "demonstrate the native act and figure of my heart," or to "wear my heart upon my sleeve," he would be found out. Iago caps his perverse ambitions with a consummate motto of false seemings: "I am not what I am."

Iago's skill at being "not what I am," at concealing his malevolent heart while "seeming" loyal and honest to Othello, makes for some heavy ironies. Othello's usual epithet for him is "honest Iago," since "a man he is of honesty and trust." And as "honest Iago" weaves his invisible, lethal web of lies around Othello, he relishes extolling the moral ideal to which he seems so true, but is so false: "Men should be what they seem," he insists to Othello; and what could Othello reply but: "Certain, men should be what they seem." The irony is thick enough to slice.

Iago launches his villainy first by trying with innuendo to turn people against Othello. Failing at that, he looks for another strategy. "To get [Cassio's] place, and to plume up my will in double knavery," he muses, "How, how?—Let's see." Then, remembering that "the Moor . . . thinks men honest that but seem to be so," he plots to use this naïveté and trust against him. He will induce Othello to believe that Cassio is betraying him with his wife, Desdemona.

Proudly unscrupulous, Iago plays Othello, Cassio, and Desdemona off against each other, feigning loyalty to each with false confidences and loaded advice that inexorably lure them all into his trap. "When devils will the blackest sins put on," he says smugly, "They do suggest at first with heavenly shows, / As I do now." And so, once his machinations have aroused Othello's suspicions of Cassio, he advises the unsuspecting Cassio to seek Desdemona's help in winning back Othello's inexplicably lost trust. Then to tighten the noose around Othello's neck he plants doubts about Desdemona herself. Reminding Othello that she "did deceive her father, marrying you" against her father's wishes, he adds:

"when she seemed to shake and fear your looks, / She loved them most," proving that even one "so young, could give out such a seeming" of false innocence that it approached "witchcraft." All of Desdemona's seemings are now suspect.

After planting his evil seeds, Iago cultivates them into bitter fruit, helped along by Desdemona's misplaced handkerchief, which Iago lyingly persuades Othello she had given as a gift to Cassio. As Iago gleefully watches Othello's jealousy deepen into frightful rage, he glibly warns against its ravages: "O, beware, my lord, of jealousy! It is the green-eyed monster." Iago doesn't miss a trick of manipulative pretense.

When at last the truth of Iago's plot comes out, after Othello's jealousy has erupted in the crazed murder of Desdemona, Othello is as baffled as he is furious. He feels what Dante said the betrayed always feel: confusion about what is real and what is not—"honest Iago" turns out to be anything but honest, and those Othello had believed to be dishonest are in fact true. Cursing the "villain," Othello demands to know "why he hath thus ensnared my soul and body." Iago, coolheaded and coldhearted as ever, will not give him the satisfaction. He says only: "What you know you know."

With this laconic utterance, Iago falls silent, refusing to the end ever to "wear his heart upon his sleeve." And yet here, in a final twist of irony, perhaps he is truly for the first time what he *seems* to be. Because he refuses to give a motive for his evil deeds, he seems to have been motivated by nothing more than the grotesque satisfaction of doing evil for itself. He *seems* to be purely evil. And he is.

Iago should give us chills. And make us wary. His virtually motiveless evil will stop at nothing, while it thrives on false seemings. Beware of anyone who will never wear his or her heart upon a sleeve.

Hamlet deals in the detection of seemings, true and false. *Othello* is steeped in the evil of false seemings. *King Lear* plays upon the ambiguities of seemings, true and false, and the sorrows that misperceiving seemings can bring.

King Lear opens with an official social performance of seemings that goes awry. Lear stages this performance to have his three daughters profess their affection for him, and then to divvy up his kingdom among them according to those professions. "Which of you shall we say doth love us most," he explains, "that we our largest bounty may extend." In other words, the daughter who performs best, professing the most love, will get the most land.

If ever a child had reason to fake filial devotion, this was it. And Lear's two older daughters, Goneril and Regan, unabashedly play their roles to the hilt. But the youngest daughter, Cordelia—who had been Lear's favorite, and whom he had (unfairly) intended to grant the largest portion of land—cannot bring herself to play her expected role. Like Hamlet, who has "that within which passeth show," Cordelia thinks: "My love's more ponderous than my tongue." So when Lear asks, "What can you say to draw / A third more opulent than your sisters'?" she bluntly responds: "Nothing." What?! Impossible! her father thinks. Pressed to say more, she concedes that her feelings do not lend themselves to words, and she won't pretend otherwise. "I cannot heave my heart into my mouth," she swears, and goes on to assure Lear that she loves him as much as a daughter can or should, but not without limits, since one day she will have a husband and family of her own to love as well. "But goes thy heart with this?" Lear asks in disbelief. "Ay," she replies, for that is simply "true." More determined to be plainly honest than to play the public role of devoted child, Cordelia refuses to make herself *seem* for her demanding audience, her father, to be what she truly is within—a genuinely loving child. At all events, she has a lot to learn about the power of social appearances. Affronted by what he takes to be cold indifference, Lear angrily condemns Cordelia for the "pride which she calls plainness," and abruptly divides her portion of the kingdom between her sisters, dismissing Cordelia as a "little seeming substance," now having no dowry to give in marriage.

No sooner has Lear disinherited his favorite daughter for *seeming* not to love him, than he banishes his most loyal ally, the Duke of Kent, for intervening on Cordelia's behalf and urging Lear not to let "flattery" outweigh "plainness." Lear will hear none of this. Kent *seems* unloyal to Lear, too, and so he unhappily departs under the cloud of his misperceived seemings.

"Most strange," says the visiting King of France about the whole spectacle—and he then gallantly takes Cordelia as his wife. Even the triumphant and loathsome Goneril and Regan are troubled by how "rash" their father is. "He hath ever but slenderly known himself," Regan observes, and now, with "the infirmity of his age," he is getting worse.

Lear is vain and impulsive, no doubt about that. But it is not vanity and impulse alone that undo him. It is his insistent misreadings of social appearances. He sees people only as his mood demands—fawning flattery is to him devotion, candor is callousness. And, insistently misreading social appearances as he does, he persistently misjudges almost everyone around him.

Lear's tragedy begins right there. And Shakespeare lets it unfold through one muddle of appearances and realities after another in a drama where no one is quite what he or she most visibly seems. The seemings can also be difficult to interpret, layered as they are with truths and falsehoods. For example, when the Duke of Kent returns in disguise to serve the king, Lear asks who he is, and Kent replies: "I do profess to be no less than I seem, to serve him truly that will put me in trust, to love him that is honest." He does not *seem* to be Kent, but, as Lear says, he *seems* "a very honest-hearted fellow." And so he is. Ironically, in disguise, Kent both is and is not what he seems.

A subplot about another family torn apart like Lear's turns on the same ironies. Here the evil son Edmund pretends to be good while spinning lies that set his father, the Duke of Gloucester, against Edmund's half-brother, the virtuous Edgar. Forced to flee for his life, Edgar takes up the disguise of a wandering madman, who then winds up serving his father by *seeming* to be someone he is not. The parallel plots run through a maze of seemings, eventually converging in the play's tragic climax, which leaves none other than the two benign masqueraders, Kent and Edgar, to pick up the pieces. As Hamlet discovered, appearances both reveal and conceal. It is all in knowing how to read them.

Lear's misperceptions begin turning against him when he goes to stay with Goneril and her husband. She receives him ungraciously, instructing her servants to "put on what weary negligence you please," and refusing to receive his entourage of a hundred men. Confounded by the dishonor to his kingly self—he has retained the stature of king despite the division of his kingdom—Lear cries, "Does any here know me?" And then he pleads, "Who is it that can tell me who I am?"

These pathetic words poignantly recall another slightly dotty figure of literature, Don Quixote (see Chapter 22). Both are aging gentlemen, on the road, and a little mad, and people say of them both that they do not know themselves. But Don Quixote, who fashioned his own bizarre persona for himself, emphatically insists, "I know who I am." Lear, the king without a kingdom, is reduced to imploring: "tell me who I am." Don Quixote, inspired by one kind of madness, invented an identity and lived it out. Lear succumbed to another kind of madness when his kingly identity got lost.

Insulted by Goneril's insolence, Lear hurls ferocious curses at her and then heads for Regan's castle. But he gets an even colder reception from her (meeting her at Gloucester's residence rather than her own in one of Shakespeare's unexplained narrative turns). Unapologetically Regan tells her father to *seem* to be what he is, a frail old man: "I pray you, father, being weak, seem so." Go back to Goneril's castle on Goneril's terms, she demands. At that moment Goneril herself arrives, and the two sisters toss their father's wishes back and forth, subtracting each time from the number of his entourage that they will agree to entertain.

"What need you five-and-twenty? ten? or five?" asks Goneril. "What need one?" chimes in the steely Regan. This undoes Lear for good. He yells: "O, reason not the need. . . . Allow not nature more than nature needs, / Man's life is cheap as beast's."

Clinging to his hundred knights as the last emblem of his identity as king, Lear defends them also as the very symbol of human culture by contrast to rough nature. "Nature needs not what thou gorgeous wear'st," he points out to his daughters. And yet without appearances such as lavish clothing and knightly entourages, we are, so Lear believes, but brutes of nature. These *seemings* make civilization, and they make us human. Decrying both of those "unnatural hags" for demeaning him, civilization, and humanity, he runs out screaming: "I shall go mad."

Lear gets swiftly swallowed up in a storm raging outside, which echoes his own tumultuous mood. He likens this storm to the anger of the gods wreaking vengeance on the guilty—and the guilty are none other than those who have done evil "under covert and convenient seeming." There, amidst the "cataracts and hurricanoes," in the company of the disguised Kent and Edgar, as well as Lear's alter ego the Fool—who is wise despite seeming to be a fool—Lear vents the full force of his ire and madness. In time, Gloucester joins them, wandering the heath after being blinded by Regan's ghastly husband, bringing all of the play's victims of deception together in a pathetic company. Eventually Cordelia also arrives, along with the French army poised to fight for Lear against the evil forces of Goneril, Regan, and Edmund. But it is too late. Lear and Cordelia are captured. Cordelia is hanged. And, half-repentant, half-deranged, Lear clutches her body to him, dying himself with a hopeless litany on his lips: "Never, never, never, never, never."

But Shakespeare does not end the play on a note of hopelessness. The villains are slain—most of them by each other—and the two honorable deceivers, Kent and Edgar, step in to "rule in this realm and the gored state sustain." Edgar himself fittingly brings down the curtain on this preeminent tragedy of muddled seemings with the words: "The weight of this sad time we must obey, speak what we feel, not what we ought to say." The tragedy of *King Lear* has come full circle. What had begun with an ill-fated staged performance of professed emotions ends with a wish to supplant mere performance with truths spoken from the heart. False—and misunderstood—seemings have torn Lear's kingdom apart and destroyed the royal family. In the end, hope lies only with those who will truly be what they seem.

Hamlet, Othello, and *King Lear* seethe with the tensions and mirror the ambiguities that link social appearances to the psychological realities beneath them. Most of the social appearances in these plays are not altogether what they seem. Shakespeare knew that what *seems* to be true may be false, and what *seems* to be false may be true. He also knew that these tangled seemings do not just make it hard for us to understand other people; they also make it hard for us to understand ourselves. And who would say that Hamlet, Othello, and Lear really understand themselves?—they all believe themselves to be, at least in part, what we learn they are not: Hamlet thinks himself a conscientiously vengeful son; Othello views himself as a good judge of character; Lear boasts of being a generous, noble king. Shakespeare does not show us how to get it right when looking at others or at ourselves. But he does show how good and evil can turn on our being, or not being, what we seem. He even makes trying to tell the difference a matter of life and death.

Molière also takes these tangles of seemings as his subject in *The Misanthrope*. Not as tragedy, but as comedy—a comedy of manners that laughably lays open social performance in both its follies and its virtues. And amid the laughter, we also find clues to the very nature of society and morality, psychology and character, contentment and discontent—clues that people nowadays pay to get from psychotherapists. And so while *The Misanthrope* is justly famous for its comedy, it also comes to us with the makings of a sociology, a morality, a psychology, and a philosophy of life.

IT IS NOT SO SURPRISING a thing for someone to despise the human race. Philosophers have done it. Novelists have done it. Most people do it now and then. We all have moments when the selfishness, irrationality, or everyday nastiness of other people leads us to think that we would be better

MOLIÈRE

off living alone in a cave. Molière's Alceste in *The Misanthrope* is the model of us all in those moments.

Alceste is literature's monumental misanthrope. He hates humanity, finding no redeeming quality in the lot (except, to his chagrin, in the coquette Célimène, whom he judges to be as bad as the rest, but whom he cannot resist). Eventually he spurns civilization altogether, vowing to live by himself in the howling wilderness. But Alceste is more than a curmudgeon who gives up on humanity. He is a comical philosopher of consistent principles—if inconsistent in applying them. And the debates his principles arouse with defenders of humankind are not trivial. These debates swirl around the appearances of social life—their truths and deceptions, their morality and immorality—as well as around the intractable desires and sly disguises of psychological life. And through it all we see again how complex and potent *seemings* are, in society and in our lives.

The curtain rises on *The Misanthrope* with Alceste and his principles poised for battle. Repelled by an effusive greeting from an acquaintance of his, Philinte, lavished upon someone Philinte hardly knows, Alceste snarls the deliciously vicious insult: "By God, you ought to die of self-disgust.... If I caught myself behaving in such a way, I'd hang myself for shame without delay." And he supports his scorn with philosophy. People are wrong, Alceste says, "To falsify the heart's affections.... I'd have them be sincere, and never part with any word that isn't from the heart." To which Philinte gently replies: "But in polite society, custom decrees that we show certain outward courtesies.... When someone greets us with a show of pleasure, it's but polite to give him equal measure."

Sincerity and *politeness*. Between these two poles of the social, moral, and psychological life, the comic battles of *The Misanthrope* sway. And as Alceste and Philinte clash over their contradictory positions, they throw light across the wide stage of human relations. What, after all, do we mean by sincerity? What do we mean by politeness? Must they conflict? Which of them best reflects human nature? Which best serves society? Which is best for us? And how do we *seem* to be one or the other? Listening to Alceste and Philinte, we have to laugh. But we should also take another look at ourselves.

For his part, Alceste has no doubts: sincerity is the highest social and moral good. And by sincerity he means nothing less than making our every word, our every gesture, our every action directly reveal the thought or feeling behind it with no pretense, no contrivance, no compromise, no *politeness*. Otherwise it is insincere, a mere seeming, spreading falsehood and breeding wickedness. "We should condemn with all our force," Alceste insists, "such false and artificial intercourse. Let men behave like men; let them display their inmost hearts in everything they say."

Animated by this morality, Alceste assaults insincerity in every form. And he finds it everywhere (this was, after all, the socially ostentatious, periwigged France of Louis XIV and Versailles). For he thinks insincerity corrupts not only public morals, but personal character and the whole of culture as well.

What happens to actual affection or admiration, for instance, Alceste asks, when extravagant expressions of affection fill the air? We lapse into a "promiscuous esteem" that demeans every human relationship and debases the language of social intercourse, while *seeming* to elevate them.

"To honor all men is to honor none," Alceste tells Philinte, so "the friend of mankind is no friend of mine."

While debasing language and social relations, insincerity also perverts our very perceptions and judgments of people. For in a culture of insincerity, it does not matter what we truly think or feel, or even what we do behind the scenes (as the infamous hypocrite Tartuffe says in Molière's play named for him, "there's no evil till the act is known." It matters only how we appear, how well we play our social roles. Appearances become reality, social manners become morals, aesthetics becomes ethics. To *seem* good is to *be* good (see Chapter 25).

Like Shakespeare, Alceste knew that this can be a parlous state for morality. By subordinating morals to manners, or rather, by turning manners into morals, we can not only let "good manners" conceal evil intentions, we can let them sanction evil actions. For then the reigning moral code will be: all actions are acceptable if the manners are impeccable. You may injure people in private, but you must not lose public poise; you may ignore or even cause human suffering, but you must dress properly; you may lie indiscriminately, but you must speak graciously.

A viciously polite exchange between the rival ladies Célimène and Arsinoé wittily exhibits the principle, and the style. Detesting each other thoroughly, they engage in a decorous exchange of barbed insults masked as considerate reports of malicious rumors about each other—"To bring you, as your friend," they say, "some information about the status of your reputation." They never cease smiling as the venom drips from their lips. Iago would have loved it.

Alceste hates it. And he carries his loathing of this kind of artiface over into a criticism of art. For Alceste knows that when social appearances eclipse psychological realities, when manners become morals and aesthetics become ethics, then art too will fall into affectation and mannerism bereft of honesty. Seized by his fury, Alceste savages a flowery poem written by the fop Oronte, taking the occasion to blast the entire artistic culture. "This artificial style that's all the fashion," he complains, "has neither taste, nor honesty, nor passion; it's nothing but a sort of wordy play, and nature never spoke in such a way." Artificiality is to art what insincerity is to morals: the death of integrity. "What, in this shallow age," Alceste ruefully asks, "is not debased?"

Alceste's antipathies do not, of course, belong to him alone. Plenty of social critics have shared them over the centuries—think of Jean-Jacques Rousseau, who lengthily extolled Alceste's singular virtues in his *Letter to d'Alembert on the Theatre*, or Friedrich Nietzsche, or the many fiery modernists who hungered for a culture of emotional honesty and aesthetic purity. And almost no one nowadays would say that Alceste was altogether wrong. But the extremity of Alceste's wrath also prompts curiosity. Just why exactly, we might ask, does Alceste hate mankind so much? Why would anyone? If you think this is because a misanthrope like Alceste believes human beings are hateful by nature, think again. Far from believing human beings are inherently and irredeemably evil, Alceste believes them capable of the highest good. That is precisely why he hates them so much—it is not nature that makes them hateful; they make themselves hateful by being corrupt. And they do it chiefly by donning phony manners, false social seemings.

Alceste's misanthropy mirrors a common paradox: scratch a misanthrope, or a nihilist, or a person of any consuming bitterness—or any of us in such moments—and you will find an idealist almost every time; that is, someone who believes the world should be better than it is (remember Flaubert's Emma Bovary—see Chapter 24). Alceste's story is therefore a tale of idealism gone sour. But not only that. Casting blame for his disappointment becomes an obsession for Alceste. And that obsession should give us doubts about whether Alceste is as sincere as he thinks he is—or, in other words, whether he is the person he *seems* to himself to be. These doubts might also lead us to ask ourselves whether we are quite what we seem to ourselves to be, especially in our feelings and convictions of righteousness.

THIS IS HOW PHILINTE sees Alceste: the misanthrope who scarcely knows himself. And while Alceste proves to be an embittered idealist and self-deceived moralist, Philinte steps forward as a candid, good-natured, rather cynical realist who may well understand society and psychology better than Alceste ever could.

A genial, unflappable courtier who flatters and fawns with the best of them, Philinte dismisses Alceste's misanthropy with a desultory wave of his lacy handkerchief. Alceste, he says, is a boor who takes people too seriously and expects too much of them. "I take men as they are, or let them be," he tells Alceste, "and teach my soul to bear their frailty." For "there's no greater folly, if you ask me, than trying to reform society." And he adds with panache: "My phlegm's as philosophic as your spleen."

My phlegm's as philosophic as your spleen. Here Philinte hits the mark. The dispute between him and Alceste over sincerity and politeness is at heart a quarrel over human nature. While an injured and unforgiving idealism about human nature breeds in Alceste an angry misanthropy, the opposite of this, a resigned and undemanding realism about human nature, etched with a trace of pessimism, gives rise in Philinte to a benign acceptance of human behavior—we could almost call it "philanthropy," a love of mankind.

Philinte chides Alceste for expecting people to be perfect and then despising them when they fall short. The most we can reasonably expect of people, Philinte argues, is those "outward courtesies" that make people *seem* good. For without these courtesies we have only our raw human nature (as perhaps King Lear saw), which Philinte thinks is not good at all. By nature, "Man's a beastly creature," he says, and we should accept the plain fact—"it's no more a matter for disgust that men are knavish, selfish, and unjust, than that the vulture dines upon the dead, and wolves are furious, apes ill-bred." It's human nature. So we must not ask "too lofty a perfection" of human beings. We should instead ask them to conceal their imperfections, that is, to *seem* good by donning good manners. "It's often best to veil one's true emotions," Philinte explains, because "wouldn't the social fabric come undone if we were wholly frank with everyone?" Manners fight human nature, true enough, but only to protect us from each other.

Like Machiavelli, who advised dealing honestly with human nature as the bestial thing it is rather than pretending it is otherwise (see Chapter 11), Philinte expects manners to bridle our innate selfishness and harness our feral impulses so that we can live together amicably. And through the protection of manners, Philinte believes, we also create the only morality possible. For if people were good by nature, "If honesty shone forth from all men's eyes, if every heart were frank and kind and just," we would have no need to improve ourselves. And more, "each human frailty," he goes on, "provides occasion for philosophy," or "virtues," whose very purpose is none other than to help us endure "the villainies of men without despair." In Philinte's mind, philosophy and virtue teach us to understand human nature and to live with false seemings. It is no surprise that Rousseau took Alceste's side—although Rousseau's version of virtue at the end of *Emile* actually comes close to Philinte's (see Chapter 6).

This debate over manners and morals penetrates to the very foundation of social life. Alceste's high expectations of human beings cause him to view society as an arena for the honest expression of human nature, a place where emotions do "not mask themselves in silly compliments." Alceste could therefore never see manners as anything but lying pretense. He allows social life to have no rules or purposes or benefits of its own. He thinks all social behavior should mirror our natural selves. That is, we must, as Kent demands at the end of *King Lear*, "speak what we feel, not what we ought to say." Anything else is "insincere."

By contrast, Philinte's low expectations of human nature lead him to see social life from the other side. Social life has its own rules and purposes, quite apart from the spontaneous expression of emotions. It is, indeed, a stage where we communicate through role-playing—gestures, words, and actions that say: "These are my intentions," "These are my feelings," "I am trustworthy," "I understand," and so on. Philinte would agree with sociologist Erving Goffman that society "is in truth a wedding" where, imperfect as we are, we continually celebrate our shared desire to live harmoniously—and where we might even have to learn how to *seem* sincere in order to convince people that we *are* sincere.

It is true that Philinte does not grasp how his view of social life can grant too much importance to some appearances, letting manners rule arbitrarily, enabling social sham to flourish, and allowing villains, like Iago, to succeed by adroitly manipulating those appearances. But Philinte nonetheless reminds us that human nature and society are not so opposed to each other as Alceste believes. Human nature itself is after all—who can deny it?—partly a creation of social life, or social interdependency. It is only too obvious that what we think and feel comes, in no small degree, from our relations with other people (if not as completely as some sociologists, like the pioneer Emile Durkheim, have believed). So manners do not simply conceal thoughts and emotions. They also create them. The Italian playwright-novelist Luigi Pirandello cleverly depicted this truth in the novel *The Old and the Young (I Vecchi e I Giovani* [1913]), where a couple who were betrothed as children by their families prove to be woefully incompatible as a married couple, and yet they are prohibited by law from divorce. Resigned to living together, they grudgingly enter into manners of strained cordiality, followed by gestures of simple kindness, then acts of genuine appreciation, and finally they fall in love with each other's social performances: the love impossible for them by natural inclination blossomed through manners. Philinte could have understood this. Alceste could never have imagined it.

This points to another reality of social life quite lost on Alceste, which should not be lost on us—namely, *manners themselves can be sincere.* Manners are not mere appearances. They are not just phony conventions and tools of social status. Manners can express genuine feelings that can surface no other way. "Good manners" can signal a true desire to please others, sometimes to protect them from hurt, if we perform properly and others interpret us accurately. We perform all kinds of gracious social acts in order to make other people feel good, and perhaps to feel good about us—like Virginia Woolf's Clarissa Dalloway, with her "network of visiting, leaving cards, being kind to people, running about with bunches of flowers, little presents" (see Chapter 18). Or take the grand party scene near the beginning of Tolstoy's *War and Peace*. There an argument over Napoleon threatens to disrupt the entire evening until a guest dissolves the dispute by intruding into the conversation with a rambling, irrelevant story that makes him look foolish and sends his listeners drifting quizzically away. Although seemingly unmannerly to those listeners, he has, at his own expense, deliberately saved the party from the argument, to the grateful relief of the hostess, who has anxiously watched his sacrificial social performance.

Manners are never simply manners. They are almost always also about some genuine feelings and honest morals, and, as Philinte says, about philosophy, too—as well as politics. For they do not just mask reality with falsehoods—although they can do that sure enough. At best they raise us above our ourselves, softening our selfishness, attuning us to each other, shaping common ends, and enabling us to perform the arts of social life. Without those arts, human relations—from politics to marriage—would be pretty base, and very hard to figure out.

ALCESTE, like any self-righteous moralist who despises human foibles and the caprices of society, denies all of this in the name of the unalloyed virtue of sincerity. But this denial blinds him not only to the necessities—and virtues—of social life. It also blinds him to truths about himself. If Alceste had understood social manners better, he would also have understood himself better.

Being the vehement moralist he is, Alceste thinks he knows himself very well indeed. After all, this champion of sincerity speaks nothing but the truth. As he boasts, "My one great talent is for speaking plain"—although he does fudge his words at first when Oronte asks for his opinion of the poem. But how well does Alceste really know himself? And if you do not know yourself, how sincere can you be?

Not very sincere—Confucius knew this long ago (see Chapter 10). Alceste's odd actions with the lady Célimène prove it. Célimène embodies all the qualities Alceste most deplores. She is a coquette who flirts and flatters and feigns affection, secretly adoring every suitor's attentions. And yet despite all this Alceste loves her. He even admits the inconsistency, conceding in a rare confessional outburst that "love's irrational and blind; I know the heart's not subject to the mind." But this confession hardly justifies the moral compromises that follow. Before long, Alceste has all but abandoned his cherished principles for love. And he doesn't see it.

Discovering to his dismay that Célimène has bestowed her affections on Oronte as well as on him, Alceste behaves oddly, to say the least. When he confronts her with the charge, she readily admits that "I welcome [Oronte's] intentions with delight." But instead of respecting her honesty, Alceste recoils: "Could anything be more inhuman?" he cries, "She won't deny her guilt; she glories in it!" Far from admiring her sincerity and resigning himself to the hurtful truth—as his principles require—he goes on to do quite the opposite. He begs her to lie, to play a dishonest role, to *seem* to be what he wants her to be rather than what she is! "Pretend, pretend, that you are just and true" (literally, "force yourself here to appear faithful"—*efforcez-vous ici paraître fidèle*), he pleads, "and I shall make myself believe in you." Capping the irony, Célimène indignantly refuses. How dare Alceste ask her to be insincere just to save his self-respect? "Why should I pretend?" (*feindre*) she exclaims disdainfully. "What could impel me to stoop so low as that?" and not display feelings with "sincerity."

Alas! Alceste's unreasoning heart has compromised his imperious principles. Some truths, however sincere, are just too painful for Alceste to bear. Unsatisfied love is one of them.

An affront to his pride is another. After extracting hints of contrition from Célimène, and then even winning her consent to marry him, Alceste stumbles into another indignity. Buoyed by his romantic triumph, he wants Célimène to embrace his misanthropic life and "fly with me to that wild, trackless, solitary place in which I shall forget the human race." But she sharply refuses: "What! I renounce the world . . . and die of boredom . . . ?" Her refusal leaves Alceste both crushed and enraged. "I could excuse everything else," he says, "but since you thus refuse to love me wholly, . . . I reject your hand and disenthrall my heart from your enchantments." Alceste must have exclusive affection or none. And so he vows once and for all to "flee this bitter world where vice is kind, and seek some spot unpeopled and apart where I'll be free to have an honest heart" (or rather, "to be a man of honor," *être homme d'honneur*).

These are not the words and actions of someone moved solely by "an honest heart" or "honor," as Alceste thinks he is. They come from one desperate to feel superior to others. This makes Alceste's boastful sincerity and sweeping misanthropy less the fruit of moral principle than an expression of moral self-aggrandizement. And because Alceste does not recognize the self-serving motives for his angry claim of moral superiority as the *one sincere man*, he could never be the very things he most *seems* to himself to be—knowing and sincere. None of us could be. Self-righteousness can never be knowing and sincere. It has too much self-serving egotism in it. Self-righteous people, like all self-deceived people, are never truly what they *seem* to themselves to be.

HAMLET SCRUTINIZED the psychology and morality of seemings. Othello fell victim to their malevolent duplicity. Lear got fatally entangled in their ambiguities. Philinte put on seemings like a suit of clothes, winking at the social show. And Alceste wrongly thought he knew all there is to know about how false the appearances of people can be. All of these characters dramatize how, whether we like it or not, the human world is indeed a stage where role-playing *is* reality, and where to be or not to be what we seem takes many forms and brings many consequences. It is also where, for better and for worse, in the meeting of individuality and social life, our very selves are born.

Thinkers from Confucius and Socrates through Shakespeare and Molière and beyond have seen that if we do not know ourselves quite well, we can be many things, but not sincere. As pointed out in Chapter 10, that makes sincerity both a psychological, or intellectual, virtue and a social virtue. As a psychological virtue, sincerity gives us the intellectual discipline and integrity to pursue objective truth and to shape an honorable character (as Confucius contended). And as a social virtue sincerity gives us the moral discipline and integrity to present honest social appearances. Overall, we might say that sincerity means having the self-knowledge to truly feel what we seem to feel, to think what we seem to think, to be what we seem to be (the English word "sincere" comes from a sixteenth-century French term connoting "pure" and "unfalsified").

But we should also see that the self-knowledge of sincerity does not grant us license to just "be ourselves," releasing every impulse, venting every feeling, voicing every thought. True sincerity is not so self-indulgent. For, as Alceste could not see, sincerity—genuinely being what we *seem* to be as social no less than as psychological beings—lies not outside the rules of intellectual life and the manners of social life. It is among the best of them.

On Being What We Seem

1. We should be what we seem.
2. We are what we seem when we have the motives and feelings that we appear to have.
3. When people are not what they seem, we cannot trust them.
4. Society depends on people being what they seem.
5. Sincerity is a name for being what we seem.
6. Sincerity is both a psychological and a social virtue.

7. We cannot be sincere if we do not know ourselves.

8. Social life is made of social roles or performances—sometimes they are sincere, sometimes not.

9. Manners are social performances—sometimes they are sincere, sometimes not.

10. Manners are sincere when they express honest motives and genuine feelings.

11. Some feelings can never fully surface as social performance.

12. Some feelings should not be allowed to surface.

13. We may have to learn the rules of social performance in order to seem to be who we honestly think we are.

14. We may not be who we think we are.

15. We become who we are in large part by playing social roles.

16. The meaning of life is to know who we are, to be what we seem, and to make human relations honest and benign.

13
The Price of Miseducation

Voltaire: *Candide*
Charles Dickens: *Hard Times*

*It is demonstrable that things cannot be otherwise than they are;
for, as everything is made for an end, everything must
necessarily be made for the best end.*
Voltaire

*Now, what I want is, Facts. . . .
Facts alone are wanted in life.*
Dickens

No pen name in history is better known than **Voltaire (1694–1778)**. The wittiest and most versatile member of that remarkable brotherhood of eighteenth-century *philosophes* who gave us the Enlightenment, Voltaire, or François-Marie Arouet, was an upper-class Parisian by birth, a genius by nature, and a crusader by conviction. He wrote plays, poetry, philosophy, history, criticism, and propaganda urging people to search for factual truth and to use practical rationality and good sense instead of relying on superstition, arbitrary political power, and bad ideas. Among Voltaire's voluminous writings, the *Philosophical Letters* (1734) staked out his wide critical and satirical terrain; the tale *Zadig* (1747) spelled out his enduring themes of inexplicable evil and imponderable stupidity; *The Age of Louis XIV* (1751) explored patterns in cultural history as no one had done before; and *The Philosophical Dictionary* (1764) displayed his lucid, ecumenical, witty intellect at serious play. And yet, for all of Voltaire's prominence in his times, few of Voltaire's works are read in America nowadays. Except for one that almost every student reads at some time, or at least knows about. This is *Candide, or Optimism* (1759). A short comic novel that makes fun of a foolish philosophy and of prejudice in general, *Candide* follows the title character and his teacher, Dr. Pangloss, and a large cast of characters through tribulations that prove the need to eschew bad education, to learn from experience, and to think for yourself. It is a sustained and unforgettable joke—with punch, and a lot of wisdom.

226

Charles Dickens (1812–1870) was the most capacious comic genius in English literature. And he was a social critic who let no folly of Victorian England escape his eye. Through his many novels and stories, beginning with the first hit, *Pickwick Papers* (1836–37), and running down a long list of now-familiar titles—for example, *Oliver Twist* (1838), *Nicholas Nickleby* (1839), *The Old Curiosity Shop* (1841), *Martin Chuzzlewit* (1844), *Dombey and Son* (1848), *David Copperfield* (1850), *Bleak House* (1853), *A Tale of Two Cities* (1859), *Great Expectations* (1861), *Our Mutual Friend* (1865)—Dickens created a rogues' gallery of unforgettable characters who embody all kinds of moral and social attributes of Victorian society and capitalist culture. The public avidly awaited every chapter from his pen, published serially in magazines. Mingling ribald wit and scalding reproach, teary sentimentality and grisly muckraking, Dickens' writings cast a revealing light on his world. Nowhere did that light fall more harshly than in *Hard Times* (1854). It is a portrait of the hard times that Dickens lived in. These hard times came from both the industrial system—a favorite Dickensian theme—and, even more, from foolish ways of thinking. Here Dickens embodies that system in dreary Coketown, and that foolishness in the frightful educator Mr. Gradgrind. But he also shows us our own hard times, along with remedies for them.

THE PRICE OF EDUCATION is high. Today it is higher than ever. But the price of miseducation is higher still. It always has been. Not in money, perhaps, but in other things. Including the quality of our lives, and of civilization.

During the eighteenth century Jean-Jacques Rousseau gained fame and infamy by fervently assailing the child-rearing and educational practices of his day for perverting human nature and creating a wayward culture. He proposed recasting those practices to nurture human nature at its best (see Chapter 6). Voltaire kidded Rousseau, unfairly, for wanting to send humankind back to its childhood. Voltaire disapproved some of the same practices and consequences as Rousseau, but, unlike Rousseau, he could laugh at what he loathed, while giving reasonable advice, often between the lines, on how to make things better. He wrote *Candide* for this purpose, to poke fun at misguided education and wrong ways of thinking, and at anything else that caught his keen critical eye, while also pointing wisely toward ways of thinking that can improve our lives. *Candide* is a philosophical comedy on a tragic theme.

Charles Dickens could also laugh at what he loathed. Blessed with an inventive literary imagination second in English only to that of Shakespeare, and with a satiric genius and an understanding of society second to none, Dickens took on his entire age. His copious novels and stories amount to an encyclopedia of social types in Victorian England, most of them caricatures, many of them comic, all of them representing varieties of good or evil in the modern world. The price of miseducation worried him, too, and many of his writings trace the troubled paths of youths coming of age amid the perilous ascendancy of modern commerce, industry, and science. Almost exactly one hundred years after Voltaire wrote *Candide*, Dickens published a novel, *Hard Times*, which carried forward Voltaire's assault on miseducation. But unlike *Candide*, *Hard Times* is not very funny. Although amusing enough in places, it nevertheless lives up to its title. And it argues that the hardest parts of these hard modern times plunge us from folly to downright dehumanization.

Candide and *Hard Times* tell us that the price we pay for miseducation is the highest price that can be paid, because we pay it with our hearts and minds, and with the whole conduct of our lives. Voltaire and Dickens vividly portray all of this, evoking both smiles and tears, by playing on the errors of two famous fictional teachers, Dr. Pangloss and Mr. Gradgrind. Pangloss and Gradgrind are literature's worst teachers. They are comical to watch, caricatures as they are (respectively sending up two noted philosophers, Gottfried Wilhelm Leibniz and James Mill). But their influence is not mere comedy. For they teach submission to the kinds of intellectual habits that thwart thought and diminish lives while promising to do the opposite. We know such teachers today, inside schools and out. Instead of cultivating open-minded curiosity, critical inquiry, and intellectual honesty, they instill knee-jerk responses and inscrutable jargon, overreaching ideologies and intellectual arrogance, self-satisfied rectitude and self-deceived ignorance. Pangloss and Gradgrind are not just jokey parodies of their times. They are emblems of all miseducation that has the effect of closing rather than opening minds, of confusing rather than liberating the spirit, of constricting rather than enhancing lives. This also makes them reminders of what education ought to be, and why. Pangloss and Gradgrind give us some good laughs. Then they should leave us braced to challenge any pat way of thinking, whether in teachers or preachers, in intellectuals or ideologues, in institutions or cultures, in others or in ourselves.

VOLTAIRE WROTE *CANDIDE* in the aftermath of a cataclysmic earthquake that leveled the city of Lisbon, Portugal, in 1755, killing thirty thousand people or more. Moved by the human tragedy, Voltaire was also vexed at the tendency of Europeans to explain such events with religious superstitions or philosophical abstractions. This tendency troubled him because he saw how it prevented people from learning the truth about the real world

VOLTAIRE

and how to live reasonable and responsible lives. *Candide* gives Voltaire's satiric response to that fallacious bent of mind in a tale of tragedy and folly, where error follows error and disaster follows disaster. But *Candide* is also a tale of promise and a parable of true education finally wrested from false education. And it is the funniest such tale ever told.

On its surface *Candide* wittily recounts the story of a simple, innocent, "candid" young man who, along with a cast of luckless characters, stumbles through an astonishing series of adventures and misadventures. And at every turn and every stumble we hear the voice of Candide's teacher, Dr. Pangloss, instructing Candide how to think about what has happened to him. Which means how to think about life, and how to think about anything.

Pangloss is one of those singular characters in literature, like Don Quixote, who embodies an idea or trait so vividly that he becomes a symbol of it—he gave us the derisory adjective "Panglossian." Pangloss symbolizes a way of thinking that bears his own peculiar stamp, but it also points beyond that. Voltaire labels Pangloss' philosophy "metaphysico-theologo-cosmolonigology," which amounts to what it sounds like: nonsense. But the nub of the Panglossian philosophy lies in that now well-known phrase, "all is for the best . . . in this best of all possible worlds." Candide's miseducation follows from this idea, as Voltaire parodies the philosophical optimism of Leibniz as popularized by Alexander Pope in his *Essay on Man*.

Pangloss never tires of reiterating variations on the phrase. He means by it, as he explains to Candide near the beginning with his typical intellectual gymnastics, that since "there is no effect without a cause," everything that happens is the effect of some cause and is the cause of some effect. Therefore, everything happens in a chain of cause and effect going back to the beginning of time. And this means that nothing could happen otherwise than how it does happen; and everything has to be just as it is. So, the cheery Pangloss concludes, to understand why any event occurs or anything exists in this world, we need only see how it follows from its cause. That cause is the "sufficient reason" for it happening. Proudly labeling this theory the principle of "sufficient reason" (another parody of Leibniz), Pangloss adds his own (or Pope's) philosophically optimistic slant. "Since everything is made for an end," he says confidently, "everything is necessarily made for the best end." In other words, since everything must be as it is in the cosmic chain of cause and effect, everything must be for the best—there simply are no alternatives possible in this scheme of things. And that comes down to saying that if the world we live in is *the only possible world*, then it has to be the *best of all possible worlds*.

We might arch our eyebrows with doubt or outright incomprehension at all this. But Pangloss doesn't miss a stride. Guided by his tidy circular logic, he piles up evidence proving his case as he demonstrates to Candide how to think like he does. "Observe that noses were made to wear spectacles," he points out, "and so we have spectacles. Legs were visibly designed for breeches, and accordingly we wear breeches; stones were formed to be quarried and to build castles, . . . pigs were made to be eaten," etc., etc. A gullible pupil, "Candide listened and believed innocently." His miseducation has begun.

From this day forward Candide reels from one catastrophe to another, always hearing Pangloss' maxim in his ear—this is the best of all possible worlds. The saga is both tragic and comic, as well as instructive, anticipating many of the fallacious ways of thinking that afflict us today (Panglossian optimism aside). Just look at what happens.

Expelled from his home in a baron's castle for an indiscretion with the baron's daughter, Cunegonde, and now wandering penniless and alone, Candide takes refuge with soldiers of the Bulgarian army. Feeling secure, he decides these unhappy events must be part of the Panglossian scheme of necessary causes and effects. But then he is forced to fight alongside the Bulgarians, and afterwards they flog him to the brink of death. Somehow escaping to peaceful Holland, where he expects to find kindness, he meets none until a gentle fellow named Jacques takes him in. Relieved, Candide again concludes that "Doctor Pangloss was right in telling me that all is for the best."

While in Jacques' company, Candide meets a disease-ridden beggar who turns out to be Pangloss himself. Pangloss relates how the Bulgarians had overrun the castle and killed Cunegonde, and how he had fled carrying an infection caused by "love"—which, in a bit of wild-eyed history, he traces back to the explorations of Columbus and judges to be a good thing because otherwise "we should not have chocolate." Do not search for logic here. You won't find it, except in Pangloss' tortured version of it that justifies venereal disease by the acquisition of cocoa beans in the New World. Concluding his report, Pangloss confidently affirms, "It was all indispensable."

Candide, Jacques, and Pangloss then embark on a voyage to Lisbon, during which a storm breaks out, the ship sinks, and everyone dies except Pangloss and Candide (and one cruel sailor). Consoling Candide for the loss of Jacques, Pangloss proves that this part of the sea near Lisbon "had been expressly created" for Jacques to drown in. And then, after reaching safety in Lisbon, when they are engulfed in the great earthquake, Pangloss still doesn't bat an eye. "This earthquake is not a new thing," he explains. "The town of Lima felt the same shocks in America last year; similar causes produce similar effects." And since "it is impossible that things should not be where they are . . . all this is for the best."

And so it goes. Misadventure follows misadventure: Pangloss is executed by hanging, Candide is beaten, their companions are slain, and virtually everyone whom Candide meets has further sagas to relate of injuries incurred and miseries endured. Everyone's life appears to be mainly a succession of horrors, and most people prove to be liars, cheats, and scoundrels. Even those who seem happy aren't—among them a vivacious Venetian lady, whose inviting appearance conceals her identity as a miserable harlot, a seemingly contented monk, who secretly seethes with rage against his fate, and the genial aristocratic Venetian Pococurante, who has everything one could desire but aches with boredom.

At the same time, Voltaire gives Candide's story more comedy than tragedy, and he lets some of the tragedies turn out to be less tragic than at first they seemed. For instance, several characters written off as dead show up later not dead at all. Candide's beloved Cunegonde is one of them, surviving her rape and reported murder by the Bulgarians and later recounting to Candide that such "accidents are not always fatal"— although she goes on to further misfortunes, including becoming the mistress of the Inquisitor who hangs Pangloss. Pangloss, in turn, survives this hanging, keeping his philosophy intact.

Besides making light of many tragedies, Voltaire also gives us glimpses —and one detailed description—of what a better life would be. He arranges these, incidentally, outside of Europe, whose reigning ways of thinking and behaving Voltaire unrelentingly derides. Voltaire is no "Eurocentric" thinker. Quite the contrary. One of these glimpses comes in a scene of some monkeys chasing girls in a distant jungle. Instead of being terrified, as Candide expects, the girls are having a wonderful time, prompting Voltaire to remark that European moral standards are neither universal nor necessarily superior to others. Voltaire gives an elaborate version of a culture much superior to that of Europe with his depiction of the mythical Eldorado—a utopia in the Americas often imagined by Europeans after the voyages of Columbus.

Voltaire has Candide arrive with his valet in Eldorado on a journey "to a new world," which he hopes "is the best of all possible worlds" since "it must be admitted that one might lament a little over the physical and moral happenings in our own world"—an early hint that Candide is beginning to question Pangloss' philosophy. There Candide and his valet cannot believe what they see. There is no money. Children use gold and gems as toys. Other European institutions and attitudes are missing, too. There is no church. Instead, the people just revere a benign

God without asking Him for anything. And although a king reigns, the citizens do not abase themselves before the crown; they simply respect the king's political authority, just as they respect each other. No disputes occur either, and no courts or prisons exist. No one needs to work, and yet everyone is industrious and intellectually vigorous. And, prizing neither opulence nor possessions, neither power nor status, they take the highest pride in the likes of their "palace of sciences," an institution devoted to advancing secular learning.

Candide and his companion remain in Eldorado for a month enjoying the warm hospitality and marveling at the bounteous surroundings, the disregard for material things, and the common decency. Then they grow restless. And a European restlessness it is. Imbued with European egotism and materialism, they simply cannot be contented in a place where everyone is equal, free, and indifferent to wealth. Candide wants to take some of that wealth back to Europe, where it will make him superior to other people. Only then will he truly feel at home. "If we remain, we shall be like everyone else," he complains to his valet, "but if we return to our own world with only twelve sheep laden with Eldorado pebbles, we shall be richer than all the kings put together." A fatal European error (also derided by Rousseau in *Emile*). And so they depart on a machine built to transport them by "three thousand learned scientists," bearing the treasure and assisted by the bewildered but generous Eldoradans. Candide soon loses most of the booty in another series of troubles, but the remaining gems carry him through the rest of the story.

Eldorado is Voltaire's utopia—a place indifferent to material riches, devoid of egotistical competitiveness, free of irrational authority, alive with intellectual inquisitiveness, and infused with benign humanity. But Candide cannot understand any of that, any more than he can understand the tragedies of life. For he is captive to his own European desires and to Pangloss' optimistic maxim about cause and effect that speciously explains everything. Consequently, despite his eye-popping experiences, Candide sees none of them accurately, and therefore he learns nothing from them. Or almost nothing.

VOLTAIRE has much fun at Candide's expense as he satirizes the prejudices of European culture and the errors of Pangloss' foolishly abstract way of thinking. But the satire also leads toward Voltaire's own ideals and practical advice. This is evident not just in the description of Eldorado. It also comes out explicitly in the wisdom of an old Turk whom Candide meets near the end. The Turk is the last of several characters Voltaire inserts as foils for European prejudices and Pangloss' follies.

The sober-minded Jacques is the first of these. Jacques had judged

Pangloss a fool, but was not inclined to philosophize himself—a hint of Voltaire's own modest skepticism. The practical philosopher Martin, whom Candide selects from a crowd of unfortunates as his traveling companion for the trip back to Europe from the New World, is another. Martin is as pessimistic as Pangloss is optimistic. Lumping all existence into the two Manichean categories of good and evil, Martin actually finds little good anywhere. The world was created "to infuriate us," he says, and human beings are far more disposed to evil than to good. Martin's pessimism may be closer to reality than Pangloss' optimism is, but Martin has not much more to teach Candide than does Pangloss. For even though Martin has learned from experience, what he has learned has given him a view of life nearly as fixed as Pangloss'.

The old Turk is different. By the time he appears, the tragedies have taken their toll on Candide and the others, and now virtually the whole cast of principal characters live together on a small farm in Turkey, nursing their wounds and tending their scars—Candide, Pangloss, Martin, Cunegonde, Cunegonde's old long-suffering maidservant, as well as the monk and harlot from Venice, who turn out to be persons Candide had met earlier in the story. But none of them has learned much from their troubles. Instead they sit around complaining about their sufferings and speculating about why life is so wretched. Then one day Pangloss and Candide encounter the old Turk, who invites them into his well-kempt and flourishing garden. He tells them how he has managed to keep his family happy: we all cultivate the garden together, he says, for "work keeps at bay three great evils: boredom, vice, and need"—*ennui, vice, besoin.*

This humble truth hits Candide. When they return home, he suggests to Pangloss that they follow the old man's example. "You are right," Pangloss says, "for when man was placed in the Garden of Eden . . . " And he goes on to apply once again his goofy theory of inescapable cause and effect. Martin surprisingly butts in on Candide's side: "Let us work without theorizing," he says, "it is the only way to make life endurable."

"The whole small fraternity" decides to give it a try. They all go to work, each in his or her own way. And, to their astonishment, they all become productive and reasonably contented. None of them delights in this surprising consequence more than Pangloss. For he sees it clinching his theory. Puffing up his chest, he interprets for Candide their entire saga down to that moment: "All events are linked up in this best of all possible worlds; for, if you had not been expelled from the noble castle, by hard kicks in your backside for love of Mademoiselle Cunegonde, if you had not been clapped into the Inquisition, if you had not wandered about America on foot, if you had not stuck your sword in the Baron, if you had not lost all your sheep from the land of Eldorado, you would not be eating candied citrons and pistachios here." To which Candide shyly replies, in the now-famous last line: "'Tis well said, but we must cultivate our garden."

Pangloss is indeed incorrigible. But Candide seems to have learned something at last. And he has learned it because he has finally come to grips with experience on its own terms. This is exactly what Pangloss and his teachings could never do. And that is Voltaire's point. Pangloss is trapped in his theories, his fixed ideas, his ideology, his beliefs, his prejudices; and this causes him to dogmatically interpret experience rather than open-mindedly learning from it. Consequently, he knows nothing but what he sees in his cage. We could say this of any ideologue, orthodox thinker, doctrinaire exponent of fashionable academic ideas, and those who spout impenetrable jargon or mindless clichés, as well as fundamentalists of any religion or creed—"fanatics," as Voltaire scornfully labeled the lot in his *Philosophical Dictionary*. They all think—or rather *feel*—that they have the truth. But they do not. They do not actually *think* at all. They rely on a form of prejudice, or prejudgment, that tells them automatically what to think and say about everything.

Long before Voltaire, Francis Bacon had faulted this crippling way of thinking as submission to what he called "Idols of the Theater" and "Idols of the Cave." The first are abstract intellectual systems that account for everything, and the second are comfortable patterns of received ideas that take the place of thought. And Bacon warned: "Whatever [the] mind seizes and dwells upon with peculiar satisfaction is to be held in suspicion." For this kind of mental satisfaction *feels like thought* and nourishes prejudice to do our thinking for us. Rousseau's *Emile* plays upon a host of kindred intellectual errors that stymie understanding. Later, Fyodor Dostoevsky gave us another and more disturbing version of Bacon's Idols and Voltaire's Pangloss in his Grand Inquisitor, who entices people to submit to religious authority in order to obtain mental comfort and escape the need to think for themselves (see Chapter 9).

Candide had to escape from Pangloss' way of thinking—or not thinking—before he could learn from experience and think for himself. We can see him doing this slowly as he begins to question whether experience really confirms Pangloss' theory. How could so much evil and suffering in this world be for the best? he asks. Finally, the old Turk's explanation of evil and suffering suggested an answer. For the Turk modestly observed that no abstract theory could account for the world being as it is, whether good or evil. So, neither Pangloss nor Martin could be right. And this implies, as Voltaire surely intends, that the world is neither good nor evil in itself, whatever any theory says. "Good" and "evil" are value judgments that we derive from experience. We judge some experiences good, and some bad—usually depending on how they affect us. We cannot control all of our experience for the best, but we can try to understand it. And by understanding it on its own terms and judging it for ourselves, we can influence it for the better—which a Panglossian dogmatist of any kind could not do.

The old Turk's understanding was plain and simple: if we want to have more good experiences than bad, we must avoid the three primary sources of human unhappiness—boredom, which comes from inactivity; vice, which comes from boredom; and need, which comes from failing to provide for yourself. The cure for all three is work. If we cultivate our gardens, we will have no time for boredom, and we will therefore have no tendency to vice, and we will have no needs unsatisfied. To the Turk, that was not an abstract idea, not an ideology. It was a practical truth of real, everyday life as he had come to know it .

Candide paid a high price for his miseducation. Not only in many mishaps and much suffering, but in his inability to learn from events and shape them for the better. Pangloss paid this price too, as did the other victims who guided their lives by prejudice instead of practice, by received ideas instead of critical judgment. Voltaire skewers all of their errors, not least the proud satisfactions of European culture itself, while also indicating how miseducation can persist within even the most exalted and revered claims to truth—and often especially in these claims. *Candide*'s tale of stubborn ignorance and bumbling tragedy is funny. But it should make us wince whenever we see ourselves growing cozily comfortable with our beliefs and clinging to dogmas at the expense of rigorous intellectual honesty and learning from experience. (Confucius had warned against just such a fate, and Voltaire praised him for his rationality—see Chapter 10.) It is easier to slip into Panglossian ways of thinking than we might suspect.

DICKENS' *HARD TIMES* gives a darker picture of miseducation and prejudice than *Candide* does. We laugh at Pangloss and Candide caught up in

DICKENS

their bizarre misadventures and in the absurdities of Pangloss' logic. And we chuckle at Dickens' typically brilliant caricatures throughout *Hard Times*. But no reader can fail to see that *Hard Times* is very serious indeed. We sadly shake our heads almost as much as we laugh at many of Dickens' characters and their world here: the rigid educator Mr. Gradgrind and his wilting wife and unfortunate children Louisa and Tom, the execrable industrialist and banker Mr. Bounderby, the busybody housekeeper Mrs. Sparsit, the luckless mill worker Stephen Blackpool, the amoral suitor James Harthouse, the benevolent naïf Sissy Jupe, and others; only the horseman and circus master, Mr. Sleary, gives hearty comic relief—although he, too, has a serious role to play.

Hard Times is the most modern of tragedies. Dickens subtitled the novel "For These Times." And you cannot read it today without looking at our own times through it and seeing how, if not as dark as the Victorian world Dickens portrays, our times can be mighty hard, too. And for some of the same reasons that troubled Dickens. But while *Hard Times* presents a modern tragedy, it also brings a certain hope.

The novel's opening line waves the flag of modern culture and education as Dickens saw them. "Now, what I want is, Facts. Teach these boys and girls nothing but Facts. Facts alone are wanted in life. Plant nothing else, and root out everything else. You can only form the minds of reasoning animals upon Facts: nothing else will ever be of any service to them." These infamous words come from Mr. Thomas Gradgrind, a school administrator and "a man of realities" who is instructing a teacher, aptly named Mr. M'Choakumchild, how to conduct a class according to the needs of contemporary society. Dickens makes no pretense of subtlety here or anywhere else in the book. His satire slashes with vicious excess. And he saw nothing in modern life more worthy of that satire than the insidiously evil way of thinking that Gradgrind and his fellow philosophers championed. That way of thinking reduced everything, both in school and outside, to quantitative facts and pseudoscientific rationality (critics say Dickens modeled Gradgrind on the Utilitarian philosopher James Mill, whose own overwrought education of his son, John Stuart Mill, led to a mental crisis in the young Mill cured only by poetry—see Chapter 23).

Gradgrind goes on to demonstrate his pedagogical principles with a classroom exercise. Selecting a student, "girl number twenty," he says: "Give me your definition of a horse." She is Sissy Jupe, who has grown up in a circus and knows horses well. But she is "thrown into the greatest alarm by this demand" to *define* a horse. She cannot speak, and Gradgrind sniffs: "Girl number twenty possessed of no facts in reference to one of the commonest of animals." Then a sycophantic lad named Bitzer jumps in with his definition: "Quadruped. Graminivorous. Forty teeth, namely twenty-four grinders, four eye-teeth, and twelve incisive. Sheds coat in the spring; in marshy countries, sheds hoofs, too.

Hoofs hard, but requiring to be shod with iron. Age known by marks in mouth." Gradgrind gloats: "Now girl number twenty, you know what a horse is." Does she? Bitzer's typological textbook definition says nothing about what Sissy knows a horse to be—what a horse *does* in real life, and how to use it. But that means nothing to Gradgrind. He demands disembodied "facts."

Gradgrind predictably finds this pedagogical principle confirmed by a visiting school official. "Would you paper a room with representations of horses?" the official asks the class. When the children split on the question, he presses the point: "Do you ever see horses walking up and down the sides of rooms in reality—in fact? Of course, no," he booms. For "you are not to see anywhere, what you don't see in fact." And this means, he goes on to extrapolate from empirical science to aesthetics, that "what is called Taste, is only another name for Fact."

There it is. All one needs to know about life and art comes down to observable facts and abstract ideas derived from facts. Imagination be damned (a dismissal that the poet Shelley blamed on modern science a generation before *Hard Times*—see Chapter 23). Triumphant in the classroom, Gradgrind firmly applies his principles outside the classroom as well—notably, to the theory of child-rearing and to his own children in particular. "From their tenderest years," Dickens says, Gradgrind had coached his son Tom and his daughter Louisa (his three other children, Adam Smith, Malthus, and Jane, are barely mentioned, and that mainly for a laugh) in the Philosophy of Fact, along with the intellectual exercises of quantitative calculation and inductive logic. He made them "replete with facts" and taught them how, "by means of addition, subtraction, multiplication, and division," they could "settle everything." They learned "Ologies of all kinds, from morning to night," their proudly befuddled mother observes. And, bent as he was on "educating the reason without stooping to the cultivation of the sentiments and affections," Mr. Gradgrind added a corollary rule to the Philosophy of Fact: "never wonder . . . Fact forbid!" Accordingly, "no little Gradgrind had ever known wonder" on any subject or in any form. They had never, for instance, "seen a face in the moon" or learned "the silly jingle Twinkle, twinkle, little star; how I wonder what you are!" Or at least they were not supposed to. Nothing but brute facts and mathematical rationality. Endorsing these practices without grasping their meaning, the feeble Mrs. Gradgrind, who looks "like an indifferently executed transparency of a small female figure, without enough light behind it," frequently sends her children off to do their studies with the dotty charge: "Go and be somethingological directly."

Gradgrind advises Louisa about marriage in just this fact-bound, aridly abstract manner. Certain that he has equipped Louisa "to view everything from the strong dispassionate grounds of reason and calculation," he presents a proposal of marriage from the loathsome Mr. Bounderby. "Consider this question," he tells her, "simply as one of tangible Fact." And the "Facts of this case" are primarily these: "You are, we may say, in round numbers, twenty years of age: Mr. Bounderby is, we will say in round numbers, fifty." Because "the statistics of marriage" show this "disparity in your respective years" to be the rule rather than the exception, it "almost ceases to be a disparity." Add to this neat calculation the facts that Bounderby is also socially respectable and financially well off, and the case is closed. There can be no reasonable, calculable objection to the marriage. And when Louisa asks her father if either he or Mr. Bounderby believes that she loves Bounderby, or if she *should* love him, her father dismisses the question as "a little misplaced" and irrelevant to the transaction. Finally, conceding that "you have trained me so well" to deny "tastes and fancies . . . aspirations and affections," she agrees to the marriage: "Let it be so," she sighs, "What does it matter!" Predictably, "Mr. Gradgrind was quite moved by his success."

Success, alas. A success that drives more nails into Louisa's coffin. And a success mirrored everywhere in *Hard Times*. We see it in the triumph of the recently invented railroad, celebrated in Parliament, where "the excellence of the whole system" is demonstrated by the impressive statistics of an accident that injured thirty-two people and killed five others and a cow. We see it in Mr. M'Choakumchild's quantitative definition of England's "National Prosperity" as a large quantity of money in the country—which is as alien to Sissy Jupe as was the definition of a horse, since she fails to understand how a large quantity of money in a nation's banks or in the hands of a few people can define "National Prosperity" when so many citizens have little or no money at all. And we see it in the success of Coketown itself, the perfectly organized, rational, productive, industrial city where the story takes place.

Gradgrind is the very personification of Coketown, and Coketown embodies all of Gradgrind's principles. "Coketown," Dickens announces, "was a triumph of fact. . . . Fact, fact, fact, everywhere in the material aspect of the town; fact, fact, fact everywhere in the immaterial." Everything is orderly. Everything is efficient. Everything is "severely workful." Every building looks alike. Reckoning Coketown's productivity, Bounderby even praises the factory smoke as "the healthiest thing in the world," and mill work as "the pleasantest work there is." Lest we miss the obvious, Dickens points out the "analogy between the case of the Coketown population and the case of the little Gradgrinds." We hardly need the instruction. The mirror image is blatant. And it advertises the pervasive hardness of hard times, not only in material conditions but in the condition of the mind.

GRADGRIND's—and Coketown's—Philosophy of Fact has effects more far-reaching and woeful than those of a Dr. Pangloss. The Panglossian way of thinking imprisons the mind in pure theory or pat ideology, which falsely explains every experience, and which learns from none. Although Gradgrind's way of thinking claims to do just the opposite—to learn everything from experience, or facts—it winds up making facts as impossible to learn from as any theory. For it divorces facts from real life and turns them into disembodied data and floating abstractions (remember Bitzer's horse). And worse. The reign of disembodied facts, factitious calculations, and bloodless rationality creates a world that people cannot truly examine analytically, or judge, or imagine alternatives to, or change. They must submit to the so-called *facts* (or a Gradgrindian version of them).

This "thoughtless" state of the world under the Philosophy of Fact has many unhappy consequences in *Hard Times*—and in our times. But they come down to the dehumanization of human beings by subordinating them to the quantative facts of material life, which leave nothing to believe in beyond these facts, except perhaps soulless self-interest, as Tom Gradgrind and James Harthouse exemplify.

Those unhappy consequences lock people into what the pioneering sociologist Max Weber later called an "iron cage." That cage is "the modern economic order," dominated by "machine production" and controlled by rules of "rational conduct." "The peculiarity of modern culture," Weber went on in another place, "demands this very 'calculability' of results" everywhere "without regard for persons," imposing quantitative value, or "rational" measures of worth, on ever more human activities, and thereby rendering them "dehumanized." "The fate of our times," he declares, is therefore "characterized by rationalization and intellectualization, and, above all, by the 'disenchantment of the world.'" If you doubt that Weber was right, just take a look, for example, at higher education today, where students are increasingly viewed as "customers," where "enrollment managers" "recruit" and "retain" them as numbers, and where learning is "assessed" as a quantifiable "consumer product." Mr. Gradgrind would be pleased.

Like Dickens, Max Weber judged these conditions of life to be among the most damaging inventions of modern times. Both of these critical observers also saw here the makings of human tragedy. As the world falls under the sway of fact and quantifiable efficiency in its purposes, and becomes more "rationalized" and machine-like in its operations—Weber saw bureaucracy as the pernicious model—human beings can lose their very capacity to rise above this world and find higher meanings in life. That is what Weber meant by "the disenchantment of the world." In a rationalized world, he says, "the ultimate and most sublime values have retreated from public life," and with them go a large part of our common humanity. Or, as Dickens envisioned even more frighteningly than Weber, with them can go our very ability to imagine such higher values, much less to judge life by them.

We should know this Dickensian fate well enough nowadays, but we easily forget it. Quantifiable facts do not in themselves carry value. They are just facts. They can be observed, calculated, explained. But they acquire value for us only when we give it to them by judging them. And we do that when we decide what matters most to us, what those facts mean to us, how we wish to use them, and to what ends (a point William Wordsworth stressed often and well—see Chapter 23). Facts of physics, for instance, can tell us how to make a bomb and how to use it, but they cannot tell us whether we *should* make a bomb or use it—as many of the scientists who produced the first atomic bomb learned to their dismay. Facts of biology can tell us how to prolong life or end it or even create it, but not whether we *should* do any of these things. Facts of industrial production can specify quantitative efficiency, but they cannot tell us whether industrial production is good or bad. As a result, when facts and calculations rule our lives divorced from higher value judgments, what is there to believe in except those facts and calculations? And isn't that about the same thing as believing in no higher values, or believing in nothing at all? As Louisa said to her father after he had cited the "facts" pertaining to Bounderby's proposal of marriage: "The question I have to ask myself is, shall I marry him?" But then she could only conclude, "What does it matter!"

Gradgrind's philosophy and Coketown's reality proudly boast all of these triumphs of Fact. And they make for a very "disenchanted" and dehumanizing world indeed. It is also a world still very much with us, if subtler in its workings and softer in its effects than that portrayed by Dickens. We just have to look more closely at our times to see it, from child-rearing and schooling to careers and politics.

Gradgrind's own children, Tom and Louisa, are conspicuous victims. Far from opening the doors to life, their emotionally stifling and intellectually vacuous education holds those doors tightly shut. Frustrated by his failure to pry them open, young Tom Gradgrind recoils: "I wish I could collect all the Facts we hear so much about," he tells Louisa, "and all the Figures, and all the people who found them out; and I wish

I could put a thousand barrels of gunpowder under them, and blow them up together!" Short of this revenge, he seeks satisfaction elsewhere. Grudgingly going to work for Bounderby, he later wantonly steals from Bounderby's bank. Then, after his guilt becomes known, Tom gets a perverse pleasure in justifying his illegal act to his father by using the Gradgrind philosophy: "So many people are employed in situations of trust," he says, "so many people, out of so many, will be dishonest. I have heard you talk, a hundred times, of its being a law. How can I help laws? You have comforted others with such things, father. Comfort yourself!"

Tom is mocking his father. But he is also sorry proof of Gradgrind's teaching. Tom has learned to wield facts without learning to judge them, other than to follow his selfish impulses. More pathetic than wicked, Tom is a helpless child. "It was very remarkable," Dickens writes, "that a young gentleman who had never been left to his own guidance for five consecutive minutes, should be incapable at best of governing himself; but so it was with Tom." This is Dickens' sobering caution to every parent and teacher (a caution Rousseau and Voltaire had also urged): if you do not teach children how to think for themselves, and to make value judgments, they will never learn to know themselves or to live independent, responsible lives. Instead of leading Tom toward an intellectually independent and morally responsible life, his father's teachings have stunted his mind, enervated his will, and thwarted his self-control. Tom has nothing reliable to guide him; he drifts on a sea of meaningless facts and rudderless self-indulgence.

Louisa suffers an equally sad and predictable fate. Emotionally starved and morally confused by her loveless marriage to Bounderby (a figure of cold heart and hard rules who causes or compounds many hardships in Coketown, including those of the factory worker Stephen Blackpool, an honorable man ostracized by the workers for refusing to join their union and falsely accused of Tom Gradgrind's theft, and whose bathetic story weaves like a fraying thread through the novel down to his fatal fall into a black pit), she slips under the influence of a dashing reprobate, James Harthouse. He decides to seduce her. Feeling a strong emotion for the first time, she fears she cannot resist him. She knows she has neither firm judgment nor strong will. But before succumbing to Harthouse, she runs to her father, imploring him for guidance. "This night," she confesses, "my husband being away, he [Harthouse] has been with me, declaring himself my lover. This minute he expects me. . . . I do not know that I am sorry, I do not know that I am ashamed, I do not know that I am degraded in my own esteem. All I know is, your philosophy and your teaching will not save me. Now, father, you have brought me to this. Save me by some other means!"

Like her brother, Louisa Gradgrind is helpless to govern her life. Her father had given her a set of rules about learning that were supposed to bring truth and guidance. They did neither. Instead of educating her and Tom to become self-reliant and morally disciplined adults, Gradgrind had created perpetually dependent and disoriented children—as many parents do, despite themselves (a consequence laid out in telling detail by Rousseau in *Emile*).

Dickens accentuates Louisa's tragedy, and Gradgrind's impotence in the face of it, as he drops the curtain on the scene of Louisa's wrenching confession. Louisa's pleas echoing in his ears, Gradgrind stands paralyzed. His "face was ashy white, and he held her in both his arms. . . . He tightened his hold in time to prevent her sinking on the floor, but she cried out in a terrible voice, 'I shall die if you hold me! Let me fall upon the ground!' And he laid her down there, and saw the pride of his heart and the triumph of his system, lying, an insensible heap, at his feet."

"The triumph of his system" lies at Grandgrind's feet, lost in ignorance, helplessness, and fear. When confronted with hard questions of judgment and value, that system is useless. Because it has created a world where no one can say that anything has more value than anything else, except by quantitative calculation, and where the needs and yearnings, the weaknesses and strengths of human beings have no place. That is the world Louisa fears to live in, where she has nothing to live by, and nothing to live for. But it is a world made expressly for the likes of her slick, predatory suitor, James Harthouse.

Harthouse is one of the consummately devilish characters in literature. Not a conventional melodramatic villain who lurks in shadows to destroy his prey, he is rather a sly modern rogue moved by nothing more than idle caprice and chilling insensitivity. "Indifferent and purposeless," Dickens tells us, Harthouse is like "the drifting icebergs setting with any current anywhere, that wreck the ships. . . . Whither he tended, he neither considered nor cared." Harthouse admits as much himself. "I am not a moral sort of fellow," he says glibly, "and I never make any pretentions to the character of a moral sort of fellow. . . . I have had no particularly evil intentions," but "I am as immoral as need be." He has merely "glided on from one step to another," casually allowing, Dickens adds, "what will be will be."

But make no mistake. For all of his moral indifference, Harthouse has a philosophy. And it is the twin of Gradgrind's. Both Gradgrind and Harthouse live for fact and disdain value. Harthouse exploits this affinity in his seductive overtures to Louisa. Hungry for "a new sensation," he allies himself with "the hard Fact fellows," to persuade Louisa that she can have no good reasons to resist him. "None of us believe," he explains, "in any moral sort of fellow whatever." Besides, he goes on, the moral fellows who profess "*virtue or benevolence*, or philanthropy . . . do not believe themselves" actually, because they have no ground of fact to stand on. "The only difference between us" (the amoralists) and "the professors of virtue or benevolence or philanthropy—never mind the name—" he assures her, "is, that we know it is all meaningless, and say so; while they know it equally well and will never say so."

It is all meaningless. This is as bald a statement of nihilism—the belief that nothing has meaning or value—as you could find. And it is the logical conclusion of Gradgrind's philosophy. Facts in themselves have no value or meaning. Value and meaning come from ideas and judgments. When facts reign, both value and meaning are lost. The Philosophy of Fact, whether in Gradgrind's version or Harthouse's, says: "What will be, will be. . . . It is all meaningless." Period.

Instead of being repelled by Harthouse's nihilistic philosophy, Louisa is won over by it. How could she help it? After all, she has been taught the essentials of this philosophy since childhood. "It was not so unlike her father's principles," Dickens again leads us by the hand. "What was the difference between the two schools, when each chained her down to material realities, and inspired her with no faith in anything else?" Hungering for feeling in her desiccated life, and defenseless against a nihilist's arguments, Louisa was a ready victim of the "Harthouse philosophy." "Upon a nature long accustomed to self-suppression," Dickens continues, "the Harthouse philosophy came as relief and justification. Everything being hollow and worthless, she had missed nothing and sacrificed nothing. What did it matter, she had said to her father, when he proposed her husband. What did it matter, she said still. With a scornful self-reliance, she asked herself, What did anything matter—and went on."

What did anything matter? It is all meaningless. That is the ultimate nihilistic triumph of the Philosophy of Fact, or of a philosophy that denies any value but fact: nothing matters. From here, Louisa travels inexorably down the path—or down the staircase envisioned by Bounderby's jealous housekeeper, Mrs. Sparsit, who takes malign pleasure in watching Louisa's perilous descent, hoping Harthouse will ruin her—that delivers her in a despondent heap at her father's feet.

Harthouse's nihilism is that of an age of fact and disenchantment, of dehumanizing calculability and abject materialism. It is dangerous. For when nothing in this world matters, anything is permissible—as history has witnessed over and over, down to suicide bombers of the twenty-first century bent on destruction for its own sake because they find nothing in this world worth living for. Can miseducation cost more than that?

WITH THESE BITTER FRUITS of Gradgrind's philosophy, Dickens offers bleak forebodings of the future. And yet, he also holds out a hope. That hope lies in his conviction that human nature will never wholly submit to the modern cult of fact and quantification. Human nature has too much feeling, fancy, and wonder in it, or as Dickens summed up, too much "mystery" to be altogether crushed. For who knows what hidden powers of humanity this mystery holds?

Dickens detects these powers as he contrasts the dehumanizing system of modern industrial society to the deeply human character that still resides in the regimented mill workers. "It is known, to the force of a single pound weight, what the engine will do," he observes, "but not all the calculators of the National Debt can tell me the capacity for good or evil, for love or hatred, for patriotism or discontent, for the decomposition of virtue into vice, or the reverse, at any single moment in the soul of one of these, its quiet servants, with the composed faces and regulated actions. There is not mystery" in any engine or in any calculation, but "there is an unfathomable mystery in the meanest of them, for ever." And from the depths of this mystery, and its feelings and fancy and wonders, human beings will eventually, Dickens assures us (anticipating Freud—see Chapter 17), resist domination by any dehumanizing system. They might even erupt violently, since "closely imprisoned forces rend and destroy." That resistance can cost them dearly—as Gradgrind's children prove. But human beings will do it anyway.

Gradgrind himself first recognizes this elemental humanity when Louisa collapses at his feet. Perhaps "there is a wisdom of the Heart," he ruefully admits, as well as "a wisdom of the Head. . . . I have not supposed so; but I mistrust myself now." Then he learns the lesson for good after Tom Gradgrind's theft, when he implores Bitzer, now Tom's underling at Bounderby's bank, not to ruin his son by reporting him. "Have you a heart?" Gradgrind begs. Bitzer solemnly replies, as he had been taught: "No man, sir, acquainted with the facts . . . relating to the circulation of the blood, can doubt that I have a heart." And he goes on to refuse Gradgrind's pleas on the grounds that "the whole social system is a question of self-interest . . . as you are aware"; and since he will now get Tom's job, he has no other rational choice than to turn the thief in. Bitzer, Gradgrind's prize student, has learned the Grandgrind philosophy too well—he has become a variation of Harthouse. And Gradgrind, broken by the cruelly ironic success of his own teachings, and by the unhappy fates of his children, at last abandons his philosophy altogether and devotes himself thereafter to "Faith, hope, and charity."

The Philosophy of Fact all but destroyed the Gradgrind family, while largely dehumanizing Coketown. Human nature resisted, but not to very happy ends. Except in one corner of the Coketown gloom. That is the circus. Mr. Gradgrind had, of course, deplored the circus and scolded his children for straying into its corrupting arena. For the circus represents everything Gradgrind opposes. It is the home of "fancy" and play, of feeling and frivolity. And the leader of the circus, Mr. Sleary, has a philosophy to go with it.

Sleary, an uneducated horseman with a heavy lisp and a "game" eye that wanders off, governs his circus troupe with hearty affection and a slightly tipsy brain. But he exhibits a rough, humane wisdom. Sleary comes into the story from time to time as comic relief—once offering a laughable speculation on how lost dogs return to their masters by forming a communications network with other dogs. He also tries to enlighten Gradgrind on the importance of the circus. The circus serves a vital human need, he explains with his distinctive lisp. "People mutht be amuthed. They can't be alwayth a learning, nor yet they can't be alwayth a working, they a'nt made for it. You muth have uth, Thquire. Do the withe thing and the kind thing too, and make the betht of uth; not the worht! . . . I lay down the philosophy of the subject when I thay to you, Thquire, make the betht of uth not the wortht."

People must be amused. Make the best of us, not the worst. This is the "Sleary philosophy." And to "make the best" of the circus means to let it lighten hearts, delight fancy, and rouse a bit of joy. Or, to put it another way, it means to let the circus play upon the human "mystery" within us. This was the mystery that Louisa reproached her father for denying to her: the entire "immaterial part of my life, the spring and summer of my belief, my refuge from what is sordid and bad in the real things around me . . . the sentiments of my heart . . . the graces of my soul." Sleary played to them all.

In his last appearance, near the end of the novel, Sleary aims his philosophy directly at Gradgrind's. "There ith a love in the world not all Thelf-interetht after all, but thomthing very different," he explains, and "it hath a way of ith own calculating or not calculating" that is "ath hard to give a name to" as how a lost dog comes home—as Sissy's late father's dog does. This love is another of those incalculable mysteries of the human heart that must be honored. And it belongs with those other reasons why, Sleary concludes, "You *muth* have us."

Here Dickens prepares to leave his readers, Sleary's philosophy resounding in our ears. But Dickens saves the very end of the novel for that most heart-wrenching victim of Gradgrind's philosophy, Louisa, and her redemption, in no small part by that other creature of the circus, Sissy Jupe—she who could not define a horse for Gradgrind at the beginning. Daughter of a circus performer with a dancing dog, Sissy has lived with the Gradgrinds since her father left the circus. Mr. Gradgrind had welcomed her in hopes of educating her properly in the Philosophy of Fact, but he had finally given up because she had "something in her which could hardly be set forth in a tabular form." That "something" made Sissy the one source of warmth in the Gradgrind household and a devoted companion of Louisa, whom she saved from Harthouse by driving him away, and who, by her example, taught Louisa how to feel, and to imagine, and to live. While so many people in Coketown pay a lastingly heavy price for the miseducation of the Gradgrind philosophy —Tom sinking into amorality and dying in exile, Bounderby alienating everyone and expiring ignominiously, Gradgrind himself failing as a father and becoming a sorrowful convert to charity—Sissy Jupe grows up to happily raise a family. And Louisa remains close to her.

Louisa does not marry again. But she comes to be much loved by "happy Sissy's happy children" and by "all children." For she becomes something of a teacher in her own right. Not in a classroom, but in the world. And she does this with a philosophy of her own, born of her silent tutelage by Sissy, as well as by her own sorrows and her rejection of the Gradgrind philosophy. Her philosophy is: "Thinking no innocent and pretty fancy ever to be despised; trying hard to know her humbler fellow-creatures, and to beautify their lives of machinery and reality with those imaginative graces and delights, without which the heart of infancy will wither up" and "the sturdiest of physical manhood will be morally stark death." Louisa Grandgrind embraced and shared all of these things "simply as a duty to be done." Who could doubt that this was Dickens' philosophy, too?

SISSY JUPE, insulated from Gradgrind's miseducation, learns to be a servant of those in need and a happy mother. Louisa Grandgrind, repelling that philosophy, learns to be an exponent of feeling and fancy and wonder, and of all those mysterious parts of us that Dickens saw most threatened by the rationalization and dehumanization of life in these modern hard times. These might be sentimental caricatures—Dickens never shrinks from sentimentality. And yet, as survivors of hard times and as kindly antidotes to them, Sissy and Louisa exemplify the kind of parents and teachers many of us have had the good fortune to know. The kind who, unlike Pangloss and Gradgrind and their ilk, learn from life as it is lived most humanely, and teach us to think openly and without arrogant ideology, and to live joyously with respect for the "mystery" in us, and with a generous sense of "duty to be done." They also exemplify the kind of person whom Dickens' contemporary George Eliot extolled at the end of her great novel of modern secular sainthood, *Middlemarch*, where she wrote: "The growing good of the world is partly dependent on unhistoric acts, and that things are not so ill with you and me as they might have been, is half owing to the number who lived faithfully a hidden life, and rest in unvisited tombs." Eliot imagined this of her heroine Dorothea Brooke. It could be said of Sissy Jupe and Louisa Gradgrind.

We might also imagine Louisa and Candide together. They both eventually escape the intellectual prejudices and tyranny of misguided teachers, becoming free to think and feel for themselves, to learn from their own experience, and to work with conviction and good cheer to save themselves and others from boredom, vice, and need, and from miseducation in many forms. We can picture Louisa and Candide dutifully cultivating similar gardens.

And we might join them, if we have the intellectual courage to shun the enticements of ideas that make us feel important, of ideologies that give us easy explanations of everything, of beliefs that we cling to because we fear to let go, of any habit of mind that takes the place of thought, and of any way of life that denies more understanding of life than it gives. For only then can we avoid the heavy price of miseducation. Only then can we learn from thought and feeling and experience. Only then can we nurture the life-giving, incalculable "mysteries" of humanity.

On Education and Miseducation

1. The price of miseducation is one of the highest prices we can pay.

2. Miseducation teaches prejudice and dependency instead of teaching how to learn wisely and independently from experience.

3. If we do not learn wisely from experience, we cannot think for ourselves or govern our lives well.

4. To learn from experience means to respond rationally to what happens in the real world rather than learning only disembodied facts or adopting pat theories and ideologies.

5. Adhering to theories or ideologies can amount to prejudice as much as can ignorance or clinging to naive biases. (Voltaire)

6. Preoccupation with facts can lead to a life devoid of human meaning or value. (Dickens)

7. We need to cultivate the emotions and the imagination, and to enjoy many delights in order to fulfill our humanity. (Dickens)

8. Evil and unhappiness come from prejudice, boredom, vice, and need. (Voltaire)

9. Work helps us to fend off boredom, vice, and need. (Voltaire)

10. To be happy and to change the world for the better, we must learn from experience and do productive work. (Voltaire)

11. The meaning of life is to learn wisely from experience, judge values with imagination and rationality, work productively, and satisfy the human needs of both heart and mind.

14
Democracy as a Way of Life

James Madison: *Federalist Paper #10*
Alexis de Tocqueville: *Democracy in America*
John Stuart Mill: *On Liberty*

The instability, injustice and confusion introduced into the public councils, have in truth been the mortal diseases under which popular governments have everywhere perished.
Madison

The taste which men have for liberty, and that which they feel for equality, are, in fact two different things.
Tocqueville

The only freedom which deserves the name, is that of pursuing our own good in our own way, so long as we do not attempt to deprive others of theirs.
Mill

James Madison (1751–1836) stood just five feet four inches tall, but he rose to the stature of "Father of the Constitution," author of the Bill of Rights, and fourth president of the United States. Born to a leading Virginia land-owner, Madison became a partisan of democracy, but he also feared that democracy could devour itself. So he advocated a relatively strong central, or "federal," government rooted in a representational, or "republican," legislative system tempered by many protections against majority rule. To promote ratification of the federal constitution, Madison joined two fellow champions of the "Federalist" cause, Alexander Hamilton and John Jay, in writing a series of newspaper articles published as *The Federalist Papers* (1787–88). Together, these eighty-five papers form the strongest defense of "republican democracy" ever written. Perhaps the most forceful of these papers is #10, composed by Madison. It explains how democracy must protect itself from people who think it should serve only their own selfish interests. Madison's words apply to everyone in every democracy today—and they go to the heart of democratic pluralism everywhere as a way of life.

The French aristocrat **Alexis de Tocqueville (1805–1859)** cast a wary eye on democracy and deplored the upheavals of the French Revolution of 1789. But he became a cautious liberal in his day, and he saw the exuberant French Revolution of 1830 as proof that, for good or ill, democracy had history on its side. The next year, at the age of twenty-five, he traveled to America with a friend to observe the first modern democracy for himself. He was awed by what he saw. For nine months he observed and recorded how in only fifty years democracy had become not only a settled political system in America but a novel way of thinking and feeling. His detailed account in *Democracy in America* (1835–40), spiced with mordant judgments on the foibles of the democratic mind and prescient predictions on the future of democratic life, remains a classic on the culture of democracy.

John Stuart Mill (1806–1873) had the misfortune to be born the genius son of a philosophical father determined to make him fulfill his gifts from birth. By the age of ten the young Mill was steeped in the Greek and Latin classics. Then he took up economics, political philosophy, and practically every other subject. At seventeen he entered government service, while launching an intellectual career as a prolific author. But at twenty-one he sank into an enervating depression, which lasted for years and got cured only with strong doses of emotive poetry. After that he entered into an en-livening, if Platonic, relationship with a married woman, Harriet Taylor, whom he married twenty years later when her husband died. Meanwhile, although Mill continued writing voluminously on many political and philosophical subjects, his interests gravitated from the coldly calculating Utilitarianism of his youth to a more humanistic individualism. In this spirit—and badgered by rumors about his long, unconventional relation-ship with Harriet—Mill wrote the book for which he is best known today, *On Liberty* (1859). An impassioned declaration of the right of people to live their own lives as they choose, it is history's greatest—and most controver-sial—tribute to the democratic freedom of individuality as a way of life.

THE IDEA OF DEMOCRACY is probably as old as civilization, and it is as fresh as the latest debates over public legislation and personal liberties. It is also gradually bringing the world under its sway—perhaps. But widespread as democracy has become, it is not easy to put into practice, as every fledgling democracy discovers. For democracy is more than a set of political arrangements for "government by the people." Democracy is also a culture, a way of thinking, and a way of life. And nothing defines that culture, and way of thinking, and way of life more fundamentally than what we might call *the freedom of equality.*

The freedom of equality has won more and more converts since the American Revolution triumphed in its name near the end of the eighteenth century. But it has also aroused enemies who see in it a threat to all traditional culture, ways of thinking, and ways of life. Its enemies—like the religious fundamentalists who claim God's law should rule, assigning everyone his, or, more insistently, *her*, place in this world—are not wrong. And even its advocates continue to disagree over just what the "freedom of equality" means. For to declare that human beings are equal is one thing. To define that equality and to inscribe it in law are quite another.

When Thomas Jefferson asserted in the *Declaration of Independence* that it is a "self-evident" truth that "all men are created equal," what did he (and Benjamin Franklin, who gave him some of the words) have in mind? He certainly did not mean that human beings possess equal aptitudes. He must have meant, in general, as he said in the next line, that "they are endowed by their Creator with certain unalienable Rights," and "among these are Life, Liberty and the pursuit of Happiness."

But, then, what is an *equal* and *unalienable right* to such things as *Life, Liberty, and the pursuit of Happiness*? American democracy still debates this question. And some of the answers go beyond anything Jefferson and his eighteenth-century contemporaries could have imagined—such as the use of Jefferson's own words to defend the "Right to Life" of an unborn fetus. But when Jefferson wrote the *Declaration* he had no time to split hairs. He was issuing a battle cry born of a radical political idea. That idea was "equal rights." And it engaged many of the best minds in Western civilization during the eighteenth century. Then, toward the end of that century, as a battle cry it ignited a series of political revolutions, beginning in America, that swept across the Western world.

The idea of "equal rights" had explosive effects in the eighteenth century, and it has had reverberations ever since, because it made some truly revolutionary claims about human nature. All political ideas reflect some notion of human nature, of course. But the idea of equal rights overturned age-old assumptions about differences among human beings, and about the legitimacy of traditional social and political hierarchies (notwithstanding the lingering persistence in many places even today of legal discrimination against some groups of people). For it declared that human beings are by nature elementally equal, despite apparent differences, and therefore they have a *natural equal right* to govern themselves politically—and by implication they have the same right to social and economic equality as well, or so the Socialists concluded.

The theory and practice of Marxism would play out this radical egalitarian idea of human nature with promises of absolute political, social, and economic equality in a Communist utopia. But Marxism added a claim about human nature that most eighteenth-century theorists of equal rights would have rejected. Marx claimed that human nature is essentially social and collective, rather than individualistic, and so when human beings possess complete political, social, and economic equality under Communism they will all be cooperative and good (see Chapter 15). The early champions of democratic equal rights were not so optimistic. In fact, many of them cautioned that while human beings should be allowed to govern themselves politically under the democratic doctrine of equal rights, human nature has selfish and irrational streaks in it that clash with democracy and can destroy it. Those wary "democrats" therefore argued that while democracy should insure the equal political rights of people, it must also protect itself from the natural selfishness and irrationality of those same people. That is the paradox of democracy.

That paradox is as alive today as ever—in America, where democracy is older than anywhere else but still defining itself, and in countries where democracy is young and struggling to establish itself. That paradox, and the concerns about it, will probably always persist, because democracy will always have to balance the freedom of equality against the nettlesome antiegalitarian inclinations of human nature. At least that is what the wary early democratic thinkers believed.

Three of these thinkers speak to us about the paradox of democracy and about their worries over its future with especially timeless insights. They are James Madison, Alexis de Tocqueville, and John Stuart Mill. These three clearly recognized the difficulties that democracy must continually surmount, and they offered some of the best advice in history for helping it do just that. It was practical advice too, born of democratic experience, not of abstract theory. For Madison, Tocqueville, and Mill addressed the paradox of modern democracy head-on. If democracy is to thrive, they said, it must be protected from itself—or, rather, people in democracies must be protected from each other and from themselves. And as it has turned out, the kinds of protections they recommended, no less than the principle of equality itself, have shaped modern democracy not only as a political system, but as a culture, a way of thinking, and a way of life.

AMONG THE MOST BRILLIANT founders of American democracy, James Madison became known as "Father of the Constitution" because the Constitutional Convention of 1787 largely adopted the framework he set forth in his Virginia Plan as its model for the Constitution of the United States. And nothing marked Madison's vision of the Constitution more conspic-

MADISON

uously than his concerns over how democracy can consume itself. It can do this, he warned, by concentrating too much political power in too few hands, and by granting popular opinion—especially local and parochial interests—too much influence over national legislation.

These concerns prompted Madison to propose a relatively strong *federal* government—making him a *Federalist*—to offset the more parochial power of the states, and to prescribe separating the executive, legislative, and judicial powers within the federal government to prevent any one of these from wielding too much authority. These constitutional arrangements, he believed, would diffuse power at all levels of government. And this diffusion of power would make political compromises constantly necessary. These compromises would in turn protect the democratic liberties of individuals and of minorities from any persons or groups wishing to impose their own interests on everyone else. The success of American democracy owes much to these arrangements—and the world's young democracies ought to study them carefully.

After the Constitutional Convention adopted many of Madison's proposals in the summer of 1787, Madison joined fellow Federalists Alexander Hamilton and John Jay to write the series of essays we know today as *The Federalist Papers*, explaining the federal and democratic principles of this new constitution and urging its ratification by the states. Published in 1787 and 1788, these essays should be a touchstone of all democracies everywhere.

Federalist #10 (1787), one of the twenty-nine written by Madison himself, stands out for its penetrating scrutiny of how the democratic principle of *equality* can be perverted, and for its adroit protections of democracy from that perversion. But *Federalist #10* is not just about politics. This pithy essay captures the essence of democracy as a way of life in politics, culture, and personality. And everyone living in a democracy, or aspiring to, should take its message to heart.

Madison's scrutiny of democracy and his prescription for protecting it start where all political ideas start—with human nature. And like many outright opponents of democracy (as well as that mentor of all modern power politicians, Machiavelli—see Chapter 11), he thumps the two chief foibles of human nature well known to everyone: selfishness and irrationality.

It is "in the nature of man," Madison says, to think and act from "self-love" and "passion." And these tendencies set people against each other whenever people's interests conflict. Traditional governments headed off such conflicts among people at large through fixed social hierarchies and autocratic political authority. But democracy cannot use either of these methods. For it grants all people the equal right to govern themselves. And this gives the natural "self-love" and "passion" of people a loose rein. That poses many dangers. For "as long as the reason of man continues fallible, and he is at liberty" politically, Madison observes, people will often think they are free to act on their selfishness without restraint. And this produces the divisive "mortal diseases under which popular governments have everywhere perished." In other words, by liberating all people from traditional political constraints, democracy can unleash a monster—human nature—which can turn democracy against itself.

A similarly dim view of human nature has led many thinkers, from Plato onwards, to disdain democracy altogether. But not James Madison. He vowed to find "a proper cure" for the "diseases" that democracy spawns and that can kill it.

To find that "cure," he first conceded a stubborn truth: we cannot change human nature. "Self-love" and "passion," as well as the "different and unequal faculties" of people are here to stay. After all, Madison points out, people cannot be made to have "the same opinions, the same passions, and the same interests." In fact, he says, "the protection" of people's differing "faculties is the first object of government." That is the principle of pluralism, which Madison believed essential to democracy—and he was right. At the same time, because Madison recognized that these inevitable differences among people are also bound to cause conflicts rooted in our elemental selfishness and enflamed by our tendency to irrationality, he cautioned American democracy to keep its guard up.

Anticipating Karl Marx's claim that economic selfishness arises with private property (also echoing Rousseau in his essay on the origin of inequality), Madison notes that "the most common and durable source" of selfish conflict is "the distribution of property." But unlike Marx, Madison did not think that private property actually caused human selfishness or that eliminating private property would put an end to it. Human nature goes deeper than that. So, Madison says, we should forget about trying to uproot the natural selfishness and irrationality of human beings that cause the "diseases" of democracy. We should instead go after the pernicious effects of those "diseases" in the democratic political system.

Examining these effects up close, Madison discovered that it is not actually the natural "self-love" and "passions" of *individuals* that most threaten pluralistic democracy. Individuals alone do not have the power to impair the democratic political system. But groups of individuals who share the same selfish interests and passions do have that power. Madison calls these groups "factions." And he was convinced that they pose the greatest danger to democracy. That is because when factions become large enough they can exploit the self-government of democracy, through elections and legislation, in their own interests to the detriment of other people.

"By a faction," Madison explains, "I understand a number of citizens . . . united and actuated by some common impulse of passion, or of interest, adverse to the rights of other citizens, or to the permanent aggregate interests of the community." Outwardly, factions endorse the democratic principles of self-government and majority rule. But they use those principles exclusively to serve their own ends. Madison labels this practice "the mischief of faction." And it can crop up whenever anyone's claim of an "equal right" to things like "life, liberty, and the pursuit of happiness" conflicts with anyone else's *equal right* to the same thing. We see plenty of factions like this today in groups that want to impose their own self-serving religious, economic, or social interests on everyone by law, irrespective of the conflicting interests of other people.

This "mischief of faction" might not be so bad when a faction amounts to a small minority, like the fanatical groups that rattle around the edges of democratic society. A minority faction "may clog the administration" and "may convulse the society," Madison says, but it cannot "execute and mask its violence under the forms of the Constitution" as legislation. However, when a faction grows into a majority, look out. For then, in the name of democracy, it can impose "its ruling passion or interest" on everyone through "the form of popular government" regardless of "both the public good and the rights of other citizens." This is the *tyranny of the majority* pure and simple, and the death of true democracy. For true democracy, Madison emphasized, respects the principle of pluralism—or the rights of diverse interests—as much as it honors the principle of majority rule. But "factions," especially in young democracies, fail to see this—as do religious fundamentalists and domineering groups everywhere.

The prospect of such an *undemocratic* democracy frightened Madison, as it should frighten anyone. Thus it was to "secure the public good, and private rights, against the danger" of faction that Madison offered his prescription to save democracy from itself. He knew this prescription would not wipe out the threat of faction because self-love and passion would persist in human nature. But it would "cure the mischief," or the worst of it, that factions can cause politically.

Madison proposed to "cure the mischief of faction" with a particular kind of political system. In the first place, he would for the most part thwart direct democracy—that is, a democracy that allows all citizens to enact laws directly. Direct democracy might seem to be the ideal or pure democratic system—and democratic radicals have often demanded it for that reason. But Madison knew better. For under direct democracy, factions flourish. They flourish because when people make laws for themselves rather than through elected representatives, they tend to fashion laws that serve only their own selfish interests. And this enables large factions to extinguish the pluralism of diverse interests under the heel of its own interests parading as democratic majority rule—we often see this tendency in local politics and committees.

To prevent these ill-effects of direct democracy, Madison advocated a representative democracy, or a republic, dividing local and national political authority and requiring citizens to elect representatives to legislate for them. "The great and aggregate interests" of the entire country, he explained, should fall to the "national," or federal, government, and the "local and particular" interests should belong "to the state legislatures." On the national plane, legislators would have to represent many people and therefore a wide variety of interests and factions to serve the "public good" of the nation as a whole, while on the state and local levels, they could represent fewer people and interests closer to home. Madison thought that the larger a legislator's constituency, and the more diverse the interests that a legislator represents, the better. For when legislators represent many diverse interests, they have to compromise. And compromise, Madison maintains, is what the democratic process is all about.

"The regulation of these various and interfering interests," he contends, "forms the principal task of modern Legislation." Hence, "extend the sphere" of a legislator's constituents "and you take in a greater variety of parties and interests," making it "less probable that a majority" will "invade the rights of other citizens." That is to say, once again, democracy must accommodate a plurality of interests, not just serve the interests of a few, or even of a majority. With this in mind, Madison also urged people to rise above their own interests and elect national legislators who can "discern the true interest of the country" rather than merely serve the local interests of their constituents. For he knew that the "mischief of faction" can infect even the most carefully organized democracy. How right he was we see everyday.

A few decades after Madison tried to cure that "mischief," Alexis de Tocqueville saw some of Madison's worries about factions becoming unhappily confirmed even under Madison's constitutional protections. "A custom is becoming more and more general in the United States," Tocqueville wrote in the 1830s, "which will in the end do away with the guarantees of representative government: it frequently happens that the voters, in electing a delegate, lay out a plan of conduct for him and impose upon him a certain number of positive obligations from which he can in no way deviate. It is as if, except for the tumult, the majority itself were deliberating in the public square." Tocqueville was describing the buoyantly populist America of Andrew Jackson in the 1830s, which smacked of direct democracy. But his words have a ring of truth in America today. Few voters nowadays ask political candidates to serve diverse interests and the common good. Most demand that candidates serve only those voters' own parochial interests. The spirit of faction is alive and well.

Still, despite the enduring spirit of faction, the national political system that Madison and his fellow founders devised has in fact largely held in check the worst "mischief of faction": the outright tyranny of the majority (although the legality of slavery and the persistence of racial segregation long after the federal Constitution was ratified proved that this mischief could flourish on the state level—see Chapter 16). Madison deserves much thanks for that.

Madison also deserves our thanks for alerting us to something else about faction. That is how the "disease" of faction can infect not only the political life but our individual lives, and how we should fight this disease in ourselves by seeing beyond our own selfish interests to the interests of others, and by accommodating the differences among us with a democratic spirit of compromise, not only in politics but in all human relations. The disease of faction may have roots in the self-love and passions of human nature, but we do not have to succumb to it. And as true "democrats," we won't.

Democracy as Madison describes it in *Federalist #10* is therefore more than a political system. It is indeed a way of thinking and a way of life. It is not an easy way of thinking and of life, as Madison well knew. For it asks us to restrain our natural self-love and passions in order to insure the pluralism of equal rights for everyone. This makes Madison's democracy—or republic—a humanistic way of thinking and of life that must grow with democracy everywhere if the world is ever to share the true democracy of "human rights" for all people.

NEARLY HALF A CENTURY after James Madison and his colleagues wrote the *Federalist Papers* advocating a strong federal constitution to shield American democracy from itself, the

TOCQUEVILLE

young French aristocrat Alexis de Tocqueville arrived on America's shores to witness this democracy in action. Born in 1805, Tocqueville had rued the social disorder and war in France that had begun with the Revolution of 1789 and had lasted until Waterloo in 1815. He was no reactionary. He actually leaned toward a moderate political liberalism. But his heart clung to the virtues of a traditional aristocratic social order. And during the post-Waterloo restoration of the Bourbon monarchy, he developed political ambitions of his own. Then, when a new revolution overthrew King Charles X in July 1830, and installed the constitutional monarchy of Louis Philippe, Tocqueville found his ambitions thwarted. Influenced by the eminent contemporary historian François Guizot, he concluded that democracy was, for better or worse, historically inevitable. So he decided to learn more about it at the source—America—in hopes of finding clues to how the worst in it could be avoided.

As it happened, when Tocqueville reached America in May 1831 with his companion Gustave de Beaumont—officially to study the American prison system—the presidency of Andrew Jackson was in full swing. Country folk with coonskin caps and populist principles from the outback of Tennessee had taken over the White House, and a vibrant democratic culture was spreading across the land. It was a good time to observe the youthful American democracy in action.

For nine months Tocqueville and Beaumont toured the country from Boston and New York to Michigan and New Orleans, although they spent most of their time in the northeastern states. After returning to France, they prepared a book about the prisons, and then Tocqueville wrote the book we know in English as *Democracy in America*. The first part appeared in 1835 and the second in 1840. It quickly became what it remains today: the classic study of modern democracy as a culture, a way of thinking, and a way of life. For Tocqueville wanted to know both how democracy works politically and what it does to people when it pervades their lives, and what democracy could mean for the future not only of America and France, but of the world.

"In America I saw more than America," Tocqueville announces near the outset. For "I sought there the image of democracy itself, with its inclinations, its character, its prejudices, and its passions; in order to learn what we have to fear or to hope from its progress." Much of what Tocqueville observed has, to be sure, long passed from the scene as hallmarks of American democracy. But his observations and his interpretations of what he saw continue to fit our democracy remarkably well, and many of his predictions are right on the money. He could repeat his words were he traveling the country today.

Tocqueville's wide-ranging, astonishingly accurate, sometimes disturbing insights into the culture of democracy surprise every reader. But these insights all come from a single discovery. As Tocqueville puts it, the "fundamental fact" of American democracy "from which each other fact seems to issue," and the "central point at which all of my observations came to an end," is this: "the equality of condition among the people." The "influence of this fact extends far beyond the political character and the laws of the country," he goes on, for "it creates opinions, gives birth to new sentiments, founds novel customs, and modifies whatever it does not produce." In short, the "equality of condition" shapes democracy as a culture and a pervasive way of life.

Equality of condition (or *conditions*). That is the engine of democracy as Tocqueville came to understand it. He did not mean simply the eighteenth-century political idea of "equal rights," which advocated the political liberty of individuals. He meant that democracy in Jacksonian America had extended the idea of equal rights into a new kind of equality outside of politics. This was *social equality*. And the world had never seen it before. That is because, unlike France and other European countries, which had preserved hereditary aristocratic social hierarchies even after democratic political revolutions, America had never possessed such established social hierarchies. Americans appeared to Tocqueville to be equal in the fundamental social conditions of their lives—no one had legal superiority over anyone else (at least no one among the white male population). This was an "equality of condition" far more encompassing and penetrating than political equality could ever be.

Tocqueville judged this democratic equality of condition to be not only unprecedented in scale, but a rising historic tide portending the whole future of humankind. The "development of the principle of equality," he declares, is "a Providential fact" as inexorable as if decreed by fate. "It has all the chief characteristics of such a fact: it is universal, it is lasting, it constantly eludes all human interference, and all events, like all men, contribute to its progress." The democratic equality of condition has history on its side, and nothing can hold it back. "The whole book," Tocqueville confesses, was "written under the influence of a kind of religious awe in the author's mind by the view of that irresistible revolution."

Aristocrat that he was, Tocqueville viewed this democratic social equality rather skeptically, to say the least, even as he respected democratic political liberties. And the closer he looked at how the equality of condition was shaping American culture and character, the more troubled he became about its potential to change the world for the worse. For he detected an inner conflict in democracy that was yielding disturbing consequences. This conflict set the democratic principle of *liberty* against the democratic principle of *equality*. Tocqueville's account of this conflict and its consequences, more than anything else, makes

Democracy in America the revelatory guide to life in democracy that it is. Here is how Tocqueville's account goes.

Modern democracy arose through the American and French revolutions with battle cries of "all men are created equal" and *"Liberté, Egalité, Fraternité."* These battle cries led people to believe that the *liberty of each individual* and the *equality of all people* go together as two sides of the same coin. But Tocqueville learned in America that the desire for liberty and the desire for equality do not always amount to the same thing. In fact, they can clash. "Although men cannot become absolutely equal without being entirely free," he points out, "the taste that men have for liberty, and that which they feel for equality, are, in fact two different things, and I am not afraid to add that among democratic peoples they are two unequal things."

The two democratic principles of liberty and equality begin to conflict, Tocqueville explains, precisely when democracy, in effect, moves from politics to social life, as had happened in America. For then the democratic ideal of political liberty, which promises everyone an equal right to political self-government, and the democratic ideal of social equality, which promises everyone the right to equal social conditions, converge at the expense of another kind of liberty. This is personal liberty, or individuality (John Stuart Mill would call it "social liberty"). For people living under democracy turn out to want social equality more than they want individuality, and they will use their political liberty to get that social equality at all cost. In Tocqueville's lucid and dramatic words, "Democratic peoples have a natural taste for liberty. . . . But for equality, they have an ardent, insatiable, eternal, invincible passion; they call for equality in liberty; and if they cannot get that, they still call for equality in slavery."

That is a melancholy conclusion. But as Tocqueville supports it by pointing to an array of practices that he witnessed among Americans, and that he found rooted in a peculiar democratic psychology, we see how close to the mark he was even today. Tocqueville dubbed this democratic psychology "individualism."

Nowadays, individualism is so familiar and positive an idea that we cannot easily imagine the world without it. But before the nineteenth century neither the idea nor the word as we know it existed. Tocqueville himself brought the term to life, or at least gave it currency (the first recorded English usage comes from Henry Reeve's translation of *Democracy in America*, published shortly after the book's appearance in France). *"Individualism,"* Tocqueville writes, "is a recent expression arising from a new idea." It differs from the individuality of people's personalities, and from the natural human selfishness that, he notes, is "as old as the world." For "individualism is of democratic origin," he asserts, "and it threatens to develop as conditions become equal."

Get this: individualism threatens to develop as conditions become equal. That sounds odd and contradictory, since we assume that individualism makes people different from each other, enhancing their individuality in contrast to their equality. Our assumption that individualism enhances individuality comes from the likes of Jakob Burckhardt, who contended in his classic history *The Civilization of the Renaissance in Italy* (1860) that the Italian Renaissance gave birth to individualism as the modern self-assertive character type that had by the nineteenth century come to dominate Western culture—Karl Marx denounced this kind of individualism near the same time as the evil creed of the self-aggrandizing capitalist bourgeoisie. But that was not Tocqueville's original idea. Writing before Burckhardt and Marx, Tocqueville said that individualism comes with social equality and breeds not vigorous individuality or self-assertion or self-aggrandizement, but myopic self-absorption and blinkered social conformity.

"Individualism," Tocqueville elaborates, "proceeds from an erroneous judgment rather than from a depraved sentiment." It is the conviction of individuals in democracy that they "owe nothing to anyone" because "their whole destiny is in their own hands." This "erroneous judgment" blinds people to their debts to history and to other people, as well as to their obligations to the future. "Individualism" therefore "disposes each citizen to isolate himself from the mass of those like him and to withdraw" where "he willingly abandons society at large to itself." This leads each person into "himself alone and threatens finally to confine him wholly in the solitude of his own heart." That makes democracy sound like a culture of social alienation and personal isolation—a prediction widely confirmed in the late twentieth century by social scientists and social critics who observed a proliferating loss of community among Americans. But more surprising than this prediction is Tocqueville's conclusion that by inducing people to withdraw into themselves under the equality of condition, democratic individualism actually promotes the sameness of people, diminishing the liberty of individuals and true individuality.

Among "aristocratic peoples," Tocqueville points out, "each man is nearly fixed in his sphere; but men are prodigiously unalike; they have essentially different passions, ideas, habits, and tastes. Nothing changes, but everything differs." Kings are kings. Nobles are nobles. Knights are knights. Peasants are peasants. It may not be fair, but it makes for a colorful cast of characters as people conduct their own lives within these disparate "spheres." "In democracies, on the contrary," Tocqueville continues, the equality of condition insures that "all men are alike, and do things that are nearly alike." Even the constant changes that beset modern democracies make no difference. While "American society is animated because men and things are always changing," Tocqueville points out, "it is monotonous because all these changes are alike." An overstatement perhaps, but not unreasonable. For when people become socially equal, and believe they can create their own lives with no obligations to anyone because they have their "whole destiny in their hands," they can wind up imitating each other without seeing it. That is another paradox of democracy—we could call it "egalitarian individualism."

Tocqueville predicted that the homogeneity of egalitarian individualism would arise wherever the equality of conditions takes hold. And he suspected that this would one day be everywhere. He didn't like it. For "variety," or individuality, "is disappearing from the human species," he complains, and one day democracy will cause "the same ways of acting, thinking, and feeling" to be "found in all corners of the world." Tocqueville wrote this in the 1830s. What would he say today looking at the mushrooming uniformity of America's main streets, strip malls, neighborhoods, sartorial fashions, social fads, and mass entertainments, and at how this uniformity is molding much of the world in its image? No doubt, he would shake his head knowingly at the spread of sameness in the name of individualism and offer a sad refrain on what he said then: "When I survey this countless multitude of similar beings, amidst whom nothing rises and nothing falls, the sight of such universal uniformity saddens and chills me, and I am tempted to regret that state of society which has ceased to be."

We might quarrel with Tocqueville's definition of individualism or with his pessimism about the loss of individuality, but we should not discount Tocqueville's perception of what the equality of condition does to people, and how it does this. Consider what he says about the American appetite for wealth and material things, which he found conspicuous even in the 1830s.

Where social status comes from birth within a hereditary social hierarchy, as in aristocratic societies, Tocqueville remarks, material things largely go with that hereditary social status. The castle and its opulent possessions belong to kings and queens, the manor and its fine furnishings belong to lords and ladies, the cottage and its humble artifacts belong to commoners and peasants. Property does not change hands, and neither does social status. As Tocqueville said, in such traditional societies "nothing changes, but everything differs." At the same time, within these societies, material things have no power to alter social status. No amount of wealth could turn a commoner into a lord.

But in a democracy all of that ends. When hereditary social status yields to the principle of equality, wealth and material things virtually determine social status—and prominent commoners can even become lords, as they do nowadays in England. This might seem to be a boon, since it grants everyone an equal opportunity to rise socially—the more wealth and expensive things we possess, the higher our social status. But it also puts everyone at risk, for when wealth and material things determine status no one can be secure. And people become preoccupied with that fact. When "distinctions of ranks are obliterated and privileges are destroyed," Tocqueville explains, "the longing to acquire [material] well-being haunts the imagination of the poor, and the fear of losing" that "well-being" occupies "the minds of the rich." Everyone becomes absorbed in "pursuing or preserving those gratifications so precious, so incomplete, so fugitive."

As a result, people living under the equality of condition suffer a perpetual hunger for wealth and material things, coupled with a certain anxiety over the insecurity of it all. As Karl Marx later put it, egalitarian, capitalist times have created a "power of money" that determines the very value of human beings—we *are* what our wealth and possessions make us (see Chapter 15). And, as Tocqueville witnessed, these material-istic hungers and insecurities can yield some curious social and psycho-logical consequences.

One of these consequences Tocqueville calls the "hypocrisy of luxu-ry." It thrives today, but we do not readily recognize it. "In aristocracies," he observes, the handicraftsmen work "for only a limited number of fastidious customers," namely, monarchs and nobles, who "derive from their superior and hereditary position a taste for what is extremely well-made and lasting." This aristocratic esteem for "perfection" of "work-manship" influences "the general way of thinking" about "the arts," so that "even the peasant will rather go without the objects he covets than procure them in a state of imperfection." But with the rise of egalitar-ian individualism—along with machine-made products—the refined taste for excellent workmanship wanes. As "the number of consumers increases," Tocqueville argues, those traditional "opulent and fastidi-ous customers become more scarce." And this "induces the artisan to produce with great rapidity many imperfect commodities, and the consumer to content himself with these commodities." For instance, Tocqueville notes, "when none but the wealthy had watches, they were almost always very good ones; few are now made which are worth much, but everyone has one." Sound familiar? Democracy encourages quantity without quality, and few people know the difference, or want to know.

And that is not all. With this vulgar preference for quantity over quality, Tocqueville goes on, comes an inclination of people in democratic culture to prize "all commodities" that enhance social status, including those exhibiting "attractive qualities which they do not in reality possess." That is to say, egalitarian individualism leads people to accept artificiality, and outright fakery, because the mere possession of fancy things in themselves, real or fake, brings status. This is the glaring "hypocrisy of luxury."

Just as moral hypocrisy is a display of false moral appearances designed to earn moral status, the hypocrisy of luxury is a display of false material appearances fashioned to win social status. And it belongs "particularly to the ages of democracy." For "in the confusion of all ranks" that democracy brings, Tocqueville observes, "appearance is more attended to than reality" since "everyone hopes to appear what he is not, and makes great exertions to succeed in this object." Why do they do this? To be the best among equals, that is why. Or to guard against losing their equality with someone else. And because people in a democratic culture at once lack a taste for excellence and depend on possessions for their social status, they eagerly adopt this hypocrisy of luxury as a way of life, surrounding themselves with artificial objects, imitation art, and fake luxuries of any kind—like the stately columned houses along Manhattan's East River that impressed Tocqueville until he discovered they were made of brick and wood constructed and painted to look like marble European villas. Tocqueville even predicted that someday democratic culture would purvey "false diamonds" and take them for granted. How true.

The culture of democracy, Tocqueville laments, can bring human beings to this. A life of desperate status-seeking through ersatz luxuries and debased aesthetic judgments that make people more alike all the time. (At the end of the nineteenth century the pioneering economist Thorstein Veblen identified a variation on these consequences of democratic materialism with his idea of "pecuniary standards of taste," in *Theory of the Leisure Class* [1899]).

Look at American homes and the possessions in them. Do we not live amidst the hypocrisy of luxury, where imitations abound? Tocqueville's aristocratic disdain for such depravities of democratic culture led him to conclude that America would likely never engender great artistic or intellectual works. He was wrong about this. But he was not wrong about how the hunger for both equality and individualism can bring anxious status-seeking, craven materialism, and unconscious conformity. Throw in modern consumer capitalism and the mass media and you have the makings of the restless discontents, insatiable acquisitiveness, and the cult of inane celebrity among many Americans today.

But Tocqueville's keen and cold observations of democratic culture led to more ominous predictions than that of the hypocrisy of luxury. Eventually, Tocqueville warned, the conflict within democracy between liberty and equality could end in a wholesale victory of social equality over individual liberty. Tocqueville lays out this sorry scenario with some depressing speculations. And he comes closer to describing our democratic culture than you might at first think.

Since people in democracy tend to identify liberty with equality and then to exalt equality over liberty, Tocqueville says, they will expect their government to insure equality at any cost. This will bring ever more uniform legislation covering ever more of life, and it will necessitate an expanding central government to manage everything in the service of equality, from commerce to education, from diversions to morals. As Tocqueville characterizes it, this will be "a sole tutelary, and all-powerful form of government, but elected by the people," who can "console themselves for being in tutelage by the reflection that they have chosen their own guardians." That is, people might no longer be free to live their lives as individuals, but they will feel free because they have chosen a government to take care of them. Tocqueville views this as the death not only of individual liberty, but of humanity itself. For it brings "a species of oppression . . . unlike anything which ever before existed in the world. . . . The old words despotism and tyranny are inappropriate: the thing itself is new." He describes this novel oppression in aching words:

An innumerable multitude of men, all equal and alike, incessantly endeavoring to procure the petty and paltry pleasures with which they glut their lives. Each of them, living apart, is a stranger to the fact of the rest. . . . Above this race of men stands an immense and tutelary power, which takes upon itself alone to secure their gratifications, and to watch over their fate. That power is absolute, minute, regular, provident, and mild. . . . It covers the surface of society with a network of small complicated rules, minute and uniform [through which] it provides for [peoples'] security, foresees and supplies their necessities, facilitates their pleasures, manages their principal concerns, directs their industry, regulates the descent of property, and subdivides their inheritances: what remains, but to spare them all the care of thinking and all the trouble of living?

"Such a power," Tocqueville concludes, "does not destroy, but it prevents existence, it does not tyrannize, but it compresses, enervates, extinguishes, and stupefies a people" as it "gradually robs a man of all the uses of himself" and strips "each of them of several of the highest qualities of humanity," until "each nation is reduced to be nothing better than a flock of timid and industrious animals, of which the government is the shepherd."

That is a grim utopia. No wonder enemies of big government view Tocqueville as a mentor—alongside that father of classical conservatism, Edmund Burke, who had detected sources of these wayward democratic tendencies early in the French Revolution. Tocqueville's words did indeed anticipate the paternalistic features of all modern democracies that have advanced the equality of condition through social legislation. We could also say that those words hinted at the horrific campaigns against individual liberty perpetrated in the guise of the equality of condition by many a Communist regime during the twentieth century, from Stalin's Russia and Mao's China to Pol Pot's Cambodia. Tocqueville's bleak vision also foreshadowed fictional utopias like Evgenii Zamyatin's *We* and Aldous Huxley's *Brave New World*. No one had imagined democracy in quite these ways before Tocqueville. No thoughtful person could fail to imagine it, at least occasionally, in these ways since.

Fortunately, Tocqueville does not leave us there peering into the dismal future of a benignly oppressive democracy that has snuffed out the personal liberty of individuals through a dehumanizing equality of condition. He offers tentative hopes to offset his anxious fears. "I firmly believe that these perils are the most formidable, as well as the least foreseen, of all those that the future holds," he writes. But, he adds, "I do not believe them insurmountable." Tocqueville's hope lies in the possibility of democracy evolving "with that salutary fear of the future that makes one watchful and combative . . . in favor of men's freedom." For "I say," he declares, "that, to combat the evils that equality can produce there is only one efficacious remedy: it is political freedom."

Political freedom. That is Tocqueville's overarching remedy for the foreboding conflicts between the personal liberty of individuals and the social equality of condition. By political freedom, Tocqueville meant thoughtful political activity. That is to say, democracy should encourage individuals to make choices for themselves and participate in public life directly, rather than mindlessly expecting government to do everything for them under the aegis of the equality of condition.

This sounds almost like an appeal to the direct democracy that Madison had warned against. It isn't. But Tocqueville saw that Madison's representative political system does not necessarily keep people from equating liberty with living like sheep under a government that serves their selfish interests. He wanted people to save themselves from this pathetic fate. And he believed that they could do this by taking an active role in the affairs of society and politics. He even discerned many hopeful signs of this in America.

In the first place, he remarks with some surprise, that instead of entirely withdrawing into isolating individualism, "Americans of all ages, all conditions, and all dispositions, constantly form associations" for "commercial and industrial" purposes and "a thousand other kinds: . . . to give entertainments, to found seminaries . . . hospitals, prisons, schools . . . to build inns, to construct churches, to distribute books," and so on. Tocqueville admired these kinds of "associations" because they engage people directly in public life, limit the intrusion of government into life, and nourish the liberty of individuals. His admiration was justified. Just think of all of the associations most of us participate in, from our neighborhoods to our churches to our professions to our political organizations, all of which lend vitality and immediacy to the democracy we live in. The activities of such diverse political, social, and economic associations have given currency in recent years to the idea of "civil society" as the network of public and private, political and nonpolitical organizations of citizens that collectively make democracy work. Tocqueville saw the virtues of democratic "civil society" possibly before anyone else did.

Besides these associations, Tocqueville also says that to protect the liberty of individuals from the dangers of equality and individualism, nothing is more important than a free press. "As men become more equal, and individualism more to be feared," he says, "newspapers become more necessary." For "equality isolates and weakens men, but the press places a powerful weapon within every man's reach," enabling each person "to call to his aid all his fellow citizens" and to join together "wandering minds, which had sought each other in darkness." The press also alerts individuals to their common interests, encourages the activities of associations, and counteracts the tendencies to political centralization. "The empire of newspapers should therefore grow as men become equal," Tocqueville proclaims, because "freedom of the press . . . alone cures most of the ills that equality can produce." Thus "the press is the chief democratic instrument of freedom," and is necessary to "maintain civilization" itself. Nowadays we often fault our free press for its excesses, as Tocqueville had also forecast, but no one can deny that political and social liberty in some measure depend on it for alerting us to realities beyond our own lives and for stimulating us to think politically in order to make informed political decisions.

Tocqueville identifies other antidotes to the evils of democratic equality and individualism as well. These include a strong judiciary, respect for social "forms," or manners and propriety, a vigorous religious life (which he saw in America and credited to the insistent separation of church and state), and what he labeled "self-interest rightly understood." Tocqueville described "self-interest rightly understood" as a way of thinking that he hoped would supplant narrow self-interest with a wise understanding of how to serve our own interests by serving the interests of other people. It is a way of thinking that at once benefits individuals and strengthens democracy.

Tocqueville saw some of these antidotes at work in America more than others. And in the end, he concludes *Democracy in America* on an ambiguous note about the future of democracy. "The nations of our time cannot prevent the conditions of men from becoming equal," he says, "but it depends upon themselves whether the principle of equality is to lead them to servitude or freedom, to knowledge or barbarism, to prosperity or wretchedness." That is, democracy can use the liberty of individuals to guide the growth of equality for everyone, or it can let equality for everyone crush the liberty of individuals.

We still try to balance the competing claims of this liberty and this equality every day. That is what democracy as a way of life often comes down to. After reading Tocqueville, we should be able to balance those claims more ably, or at least be more attentive to what those claims are and to what is at stake in choosing between them—not only in politics, but in our hearts and minds, where democracy as a way of life eventually takes hold, for the better or the worse.

DURING THE FOUNDING of the American republic, James Madison set out to defend the democratic liberty of individuals from "factions" that would use democracy to impose their own interests
MILL on everyone. Close to fifty years later, Alexis de Tocqueville delved into what he judged an even more pervasive danger to the liberty of individuals: the democratic passion for equality that could turn everyone into clones. Another twenty-five years on, John Stuart Mill saw modern democracy in mid-nineteenth-century England threatening the liberty of individuals in ways akin to those perceived or foreseen by both Madison and Tocqueville. Mill also judged those threats to be as grave as anything Tocqueville had imagined, although he found them to be if anything more insidious. In *On Liberty*—published in 1859, the same year that Tocqueville, Mill's contemporary, died—Mill made a case for shielding the liberty of individuals that remains one of history's

most profound, and controversial, works on the culture and psychology of democracy. And it is surely the most powerful and influential book by anyone on the liberty of individuals as the inspiration of democratic legislation and as an inspiriting way of life.

Mill started out from the same historical observation that had troubled Tocqueville, whose work he admired: modern democracy tends to make everyone the same. But whereas Tocqueville had blamed this gray homogeneity on the democratic equality of condition that kills off the vigorous individuality known to aristocratic societies, and he had worried that a paternalistic government would likely emerge to insure this, Mill shifted the focus a little. He did not lament the loss of aristocratic individuality, and he did not worry as much about an all-powerful government arising to impose homogeneous equality. His fears fastened onto the potential decline of civilization and ultimate loss of humanity from another source. That was the overweening social pressure to conform, whether that pressure gains the authority of law or not. Mill wrote *On Liberty* to warn against this democratic evil, and to offer a formula for saving the liberty of individuals and the very future of humanity from it.

Mill's formula is simple and now well-known. It supplies a credo for democracy as a way of life that we all live by to some extent, although we do not always live up to it. For Mill's formula can be difficult to apply—and it has prompted Mill's critics to denounce it as a prescription for moral anarchy. But Mill gives us the best of reasons to live up to it—for the sake of our own individuality, and of humanity.

Mill sets the stage for presenting this formula by identifying the particular type of liberty that concerns him. "The subject of this essay," he states at the beginning, is "Social Liberty." This is not the same thing as political liberty. Political liberty grants people the right to self-government. And Mill was confident that by the middle of the nineteenth century England had established political democracy well enough that political liberty did not need defending. But this democratic political liberty had turned out not to protect social liberty, just as Tocqueville had predicted in different terms. This is therefore Mill's subject. Actually, Mill defines social liberty in a rather backhanded way as "the nature and limits of the power which can be legitimately exercised by society over the individual." But let us think of it more plainly as the freedom of individuals to live as they wish within the limits of society. Mill considered this social liberty to be more at risk than ever before because in democracy the pressures of social conformity can be both subtle and penetrating and can aim at nothing less than total victory over all individuality. In this light, Mill declares, besides "protection against political despotism," we need "protection also against the tyranny of the prevailing opinion and feeling" and "the tendency of society to impose, by other means than civil penalties, its own ideas and practices as rules of conduct." For this kind of "social tyranny," Mill warns, is worse than any political tyranny could ever be, because it leaves "fewer means of escape and penetrates much more deeply into the details of life, and enslaves the soul itself." Mill was clearly no less worried than was Tocqueville about the fate of humanity under democracy.

These worries prompted Mill to come up with some kind of protection against social tyranny. "The vital question of the future," he announces, is this: How do we define "the nature and limits of the power which can be legitimately exercised by society over the individual"? Or, to put it another way, where do we draw the line between "individual independence and social control"? Mill hit the nail on the head. These questions about the relation of individual liberty to social authority go to the crux of democracy as a way of life. They resonate in every piece of social legislation, moral debate, and cocktail conversation that touches on the nexus between individuals and society.

Mill answers these questions with a formula for protecting individual liberty that many people now know by rote, even if they do not know where it came from, or agree with it. That formula is: individuals should be free to do anything they want to do, as long as they do not hurt other people. Here is Mill's emphatic, if prolix, version:

> The object of the Essay is to assert one very simple principle, as entitled to govern absolutely the dealings of society with the individual in the way of compulsion and control, whether the means used be physical force in the form of legal penalties, or the moral coercion of public opinion. That principle is, that the sole end for which mankind are warranted, individually or collectively, in interfering with the liberty of action of any of their number, is self-protection. That the only purpose for which power can be rightfully exercised over any member of a civilized community, against his will, is to prevent harm to others.

This is a reasonable formula. It is even common sense. But reasonable and sensible as it is sounds, it can be deceptively difficult to apply (rather like Aristotle's ethics of the so-called Golden Mean—see Chapter 4). Mill recognized the difficulties. And he grapples with them throughout *On Liberty*, anticipating many of his critics. This makes the book both an exuberant tract and a probing exploration of the rough terrain where individual liberty and social control meet in democracy.

And it is indispensable reading for anyone who cares about the liberty of individuals to live as they choose.

Being no fool, Mill foresaw that critics would, of course, first target his idea that individuals and society can be separated as far as he said they can. He even baited critics with bold statements like: "The only part of the conduct of anyone, for which he is amenable to society is that which concerns others. In the part which merely concerns himself, his independence is, of right, absolute." He knew his critics would say in response, as they continue to do today, that nothing an individual does ever "merely concerns himself," for we live among other people, and we affect each other with virtually everything we do. True enough, Mill goes on, "no person is an entirely isolated being," and "whatever affects himself, may affect others *through* himself." But, he emphasizes, we must make a crucial distinction. "When I say only himself, I mean directly and in the first instance," whereas to "affect others *through*" one-self affects them only *indirectly*. And any action that affects others only indirectly through oneself does not warrant limiting the liberty of individuals. Trying to clarify the point further, Mill adds: "To individuality should belong the part of life in which it is chiefly the individual that is interested; to society, the part which chiefly interests society," and "as soon as any part of a person's conduct affects prejudicially the interests of others, society has jurisdiction over it."

We might scratch our heads here still straining to see the lines Mill is drawing. And even if we were to accept his general distinction between acts that chiefly affect the individual and those that chiefly and directly affect society, how would we decide when a person's action crosses the line and "affects prejudicially the interests of others," giving society "jurisdiction" over it? These words are so hazy that we cannot get hold of them. Sensing this, Mill tightens his focus. All right, he says, let's put the idea of "harm to others" like this: any act of a person that causes a "perceptible hurt to any assignable individual except himself," or that causes "definite damage, or a definite risk of damage, either to an individual or to the public," removes that act from "the province of liberty" and puts it under the "social control" of "morality or law." But any act of a person that falls short of causing such a "perceptible hurt" or "definite damage, or a definite risk of damage" to "an individual or to the public" should be tolerated, because then it causes only "inconvenience" to others, or frustrated "preferences," and "society can afford to bear" such minor consequences "for the greater good of human freedom." (Mill includes as "definite damage," by the way, the harm done to others by violating "any specific duty to the public," like the duty of parents to care for their children or of soldiers to obey commands.) That is as clear as Mill's formula for liberty gets. And it contains Mill's most provocative challenge to us as we try to draw a line between "individual independence and social control."

That challenge is not to confuse the inconvenience or frustrated preferences of anyone with perceptible hurts or definite damage or even definite risk of damage. If we do confuse them, we will wind up extending the reach of social control over everything that people do. And this will eventually crush human freedom and all individuality under social tyranny. The demands made along these very lines in our day by both right-wing religious zealots and left-wing crusaders for "political correctness" take us straight back to Mill's warnings. To prevent this social tyranny from rising, Mill would make the realm of harm to others through perceptible hurts and definite damage or risk of damage as small as possible in order to minimize social control, and he would make the realm of tolerable inconvenience and frustrated preferences as large as possible, in order to maximize social liberty. If you don't trust this disproportion, Mill says, you don't trust liberty or individuality. And many people don't.

To drive home his point, Mill names two areas of our lives that he believes so thoroughly concern chiefly ourselves that within them we could never cause "perceptible hurt," or even "definite risk of damage," to others, whatever "inconvenience" or frustrated "preferences" we might cause. These are: (1) "the inward domain of consciousness," or "thought and feeling," along with the expression of those thoughts and feelings; and (2) the ways we live our personal lives, or the "tastes and pursuits" we choose in "the plan of our life." What is more, Mill says, because these are the very areas in which we think and feel and create our own lives, it is also here that we shape our individuality. Hence, not only can we do no harm to others through freedom in these areas, we need as much of that freedom as possible to develop ourselves as individuals.

Mill gets very intense about this kind of freedom because it is what inspired him to write *On Liberty* in the first place. People should be free to have "different opinions," as well as to "lead different lives" with "different experiments in living" and "different modes of life," he insists, because this is how they cultivate their own aptitudes and nurture their individual personalities. If people do not have the freedom to think for themselves and to choose among various ways of life, Mill writes, "they neither obtain their fair share of happiness, nor grow up to the mental, moral, and aesthetic stature of which their nature is capable." Therefore, he proclaims, capping this idea with a bold statement worth remembering: "It is good there should be differences" among people, "even though not for the better, even though, as it may appear . . . some should be for the worse."

It is good there should be differences among people, even though not for the better. If this appears radical, it is. Many people would recoil at it because they want everyone to be *good*, as they define the term. But Mill was convinced that without differences among people—even if "for the worse"—we can make no choices among ideas and ways of life. And if we have no choices of these kinds to make, human life stagnates (Aristotle, incidentally, pointed to the act of choice as the defining quality of human beings). "It is only by the collision of adverse opinions," Mill says, that "the truth has any chance of being supplied," and that people can learn to think for themselves beyond "prejudice" and to shape their "character and conduct" as their own. That is how making choices about how to think and how to live creates individuality. And individuality is what gives rise to civilization, spurs progress, and elevates humanity. "The initiation of all wise or noble things comes and must come from individuals," Mill asserts. For people with a vigorous sense of their individuality have the "desires and impulses" and "energy" that generate "character," "originality," "moral courage," and "genius." It is these individuals who bring the pursuit of truth, the ideal of excellence, and the achievements of civilization into the world and that make "the human race" vital and hopeful and progressive. Mill takes social liberty that far. And he exalts individuality that high.

Plenty of readers have faulted Mill for taking individual liberty too far and for exalting individuality too high. They say his invitation to throw open society to all kinds of ideas and all kinds of lives—including lives that are "not for the better" and may even be "for the worse"—gives license to moral anarchy in the name of individuality. If society allows this, these critics (like the neo-conservative scholar Gertrude Himmelfarb in *On Liberty and Liberalism* [1974]) protest, morally pernicious influences will run amok, and that will adversely affect the "interests" of people who live more reputable lives. How, for instance, the critics ask, can parents rear children to be good among other children who are allowed to be bad? They can't. Good people must protect themselves and their children against the "damage" that Mill's liberty would cause through the moral depravity of others and the disorder of society. After all, the critics conclude, democracy bestows on us the *right* to protect ourselves from that damage by allowing us to live among people who agree with us and share our way of life.

These are familiar complaints nowadays from those who decry the depravities of modern society that threaten their well-being. Anticipating such criticisms, Mill launches a defense of his radical idea of liberty that attacks the basic principle underlying them. It is a defense that anyone who values the liberty of individuals and individuality should know well, and that everyone else should at least have to deal with.

When we claim that other people's ways of thinking or modes of life cause damage to our interests and should therefore fall under social control, Mill says, we not only confuse *indirect* with *direct* effects and "inconvenience" with "perceptible hurt" or "definite risk of damage." We also advocate a spuriously democratic doctrine. Mill calls this the doctrine of "social rights." The doctrine of social rights, Mill explains, asserts "the absolute social right of every individual" to have "every other individual . . . act in every respect exactly as he ought," and "that whosoever fails" to act properly "in the smallest particular violates [our] social right, and entitles [us] to demand from the legislature the removal of the grievance." This, Mill stresses, comes down to claiming the right to impose our own convenience and preferences and tastes and mode of life on everyone else. Whether we do this through social intimidation or legislation, it is Mill's worst nightmare. It should be one of ours.

The doctrine of social rights, Mill continues, is in fact "so monstrous" that "there is no violation of liberty which it would not justify" to insure conformity to the convenience and preferences of "prevailing opinion." And it would require a "moral police" to enforce. Democracy, Mill warns, could sink that low. And in his most pessimistic mood he saw this happening all around him. Just read his melancholy words:

> In our time, from the highest class of society down to the lowest, everyone lives as under the eye of a hostile and dreaded censorship. . . . I do not mean that they choose what is customary in preference to what suits there own inclination. It does not occur to them to have any inclination except for what is customary. Thus the mind itself is bowed to the yoke: even in what people do for pleasure, conformity is the first thing thought of; they like in crowds; they exercise choice only among things commonly done: peculiarity of taste, eccentricity of conduct, are shunned equally with crimes: until by dint of not following their own nature they have no nature to follow: they become incapable of any strong wishes or native pleasures, and are generally without either opinions or feelings of home growth, or properly their own. Now is this, or is it not, the desirable condition of human nature?

Mill possibly overstated the facts here. But he was on to something. The spurious and pernicious doctrine of social rights as he describes it lives wherever people believe democracy grants them the *right* to protect their interests from damage by having everyone around them accept their ideas and ways of life. Partisans of racial segregation in America wrapped themselves in this right for decades, and religious fundamentalists claim this right all the time—although they do it under the mantle of a higher authority than democracy. We might even see the doctrine of social rights at work in the proliferating gated communities across this country that offer model homes for model people to lead model lives—the perfect American town, Disney's theme-park style Centennial, Florida, was designed with just this social ideal in mind, down to the last detail of the town's immaculate, wholesome, uncompromising purity.

Whatever form it takes—and however apparently legitimate its application—the doctrine of social rights clashes with the liberty of individuals to think for themselves and to choose their own lives (while providing an escape from that liberty for people who do not want it—see Chapter 9). This, Mill laments, amounts to "robbing the human race" of the very attributes it most needs to thrive—the attributes of vigorous individuality. Society should do everything possible to nurture that individuality, Mill demands, and do nothing to restrain it that is not absolutely necessary.

Consequently, Mill cautions, before society acts to "interfere" with an individual's liberty, it should ask "whether the general welfare will or will not be promoted by interfering." In other words, will society gain more or lose more by permitting a particular liberty or by curtailing it? Mill had no doubt: in the long run, society will nearly always gain more, and lose less, by permitting individuals to exercise liberty than by limiting them. And he took pains to show that even when society must necessarily curtail the liberty of individuals through social control it should preserve as much of that liberty as possible. He knew this can often be very complicated because many actions "lie on the exact boundary line" where the liberty of individuals, or social liberty, meets a need for social control. We see how correct he was whenever we try to draw that line in democratic legislation, as well as in our own lives. Drawing this line wisely, Mill says, is the primary challenge of democracy. Consider a few of Mill's examples.

Should people be free to sell and buy poison, Mill asks, since poison clearly holds "a definite risk of damage"? Yes, Mill answers, they should be free to sell and buy it because it also has a useful purpose. But, he adds, the law should require that packages of poison carry warnings of the "definite risk of damage" that the contents can cause so that buyers can make a rational choice in using it—which is precisely the rule that led to warnings on cigarette labels in America. By the same logic, Mill goes on, foreshadowing another issue in American politics nowadays, a person should be allowed to commit suicide if he or she does it through a rational choice and will not be violating any explicit "duty to others"—today the Hemlock Society echoes Mill, as do exponents of assisted suicide. Individuals should also be free, Mill proceeds, to indulge in private vices, if these are regulated to discourage the excesses that can cause damage to others. We should permit the sale of alcohol, for instance, but should limit its availability and tax it to inhibit overuse. Gambling should work the same way: society should allow gambling, but should restrict and manage the opportunities to do it. Even sexual behavior falls under the rule: let private sexual activity go free as a mode of life, Mill advises, but don't permit illicit sex to be promoted publicly as a business through prostitution. Mill did not approve of vice. He just believed that the best way to restrain people from indulging in vices, while still protecting their personal liberty, was to make it a bit difficult for those who wanted to indulge in them.

Mill's examples go on and on. Some of these are quite complex, and most are very familiar to us. And they all reveal how much our democracy reflects Mill's idea of social liberty—whether we got this idea from Mill or, more likely, from democratic experience itself. For debates continue over how much personal liberty we should permit, and how much social control we require, in all kinds of activities, from expressing political passions and pursuing personal pleasures to permitting abortion and protecting gun ownership. These are the kinds of debates that democracy as a way of life depends upon—at least for those who truly believe in the liberty of individuals.

Mill adds a final bit of advice on how to help individuals make the most of that liberty. It is a rather unexpected bit of advice, too. He says that "states should require and compel the education, up to a certain standard of every human being who is born its citizen." This might appear to contradict Mill's insistence on the freedom of thought and of choice by making everyone go to school. But it doesn't. Compulsory education does not limit the freedom of thought and choice, Mill explains. It makes that freedom possible. For the freedom to think and choose grows from the ability to weigh different opinions, evaluate different ways of life, and make rational decisions. Education cultivates that ability. Therefore, Mill says, no one "should be free not to be free" by choosing to remain ignorant and incapable of exercising rational and responsible judgment. Children must be forced to become free. The growth of individuality demands it.

For this reason, Mill concludes, democratic government should take as its overriding social obligation to promote "the activity and powers of individuals" through education and other incentives to "individual exertion and development." The future of civilization is at stake. By the same logic, government should not do for people what they can do themselves or it will wind up thwarting individuality and fostering a society of "small men" where "no great thing can really be accomplished." Anything that promotes individuality is good, and anything that lets it wither is bad. On that cautionary note—echoing Tocqueville's warnings about paternalistic government—and with his hymn to education as the matrix of individuality, Mill ends *On Liberty.*

When we close the book, we have read the most impassioned and influential testimony to the social liberty of individuals ever written. And we should see more clearly than ever how we can use democracy either to encourage that liberty or to inhibit it. The difference hinges on whether we ask democracy to grant people the freedom to make their own choices and to live their own lives—even if not for the better—or we ask it to extend social control in the name of social rights. We might not at first agree with Mill that nothing less than the future of civilization and humanity is at stake here. But when we think about it, and observe life today in parts of the world where social rights and social control dominate, and where the liberty of individuals gets condemned as the enemy of all that is good, we will probably side with Mill.

JAMES MADISON, Alexis de Tocqueville, and John Stuart Mill found themselves engulfed by the most sweeping political, social, and cultural transformation in human history. This was the rise of modern democracy. They agreed that the strengths of democracy lay in the unprecedented liberty that it granted individuals to govern themselves. They also agreed that its weaknesses lay in the tendency of these same individuals to subvert the liberties and pluralistic spirit of democracy by trying to shape society in their own image through the misguided democratic claims of faction, egalitarian individualism, and social rights.

These eighteenth- and nineteenth-century worries might seem almost quaint in twenty-first-century America, where we are surrounded by galloping multiculturalism, widespread moral relativism, and a tolerance of individuality that may seem to have no bounds. But when people opposing these conditions strive to reform America to embody their own more restrictive social and moral values, those old worries gain new resonance. For these worries remind us that democratic liberty cannot be defined by any one group's interests or beliefs or ideology. True democratic liberty can thrive only when people have extensive freedom to think and to live as they choose, even if they do not like what other people do with that freedom. This rule may make democracy as a way of life untidy and, in Mill's term, "inconvenient." But it is a way of life that goes with democracy if democracy is to exist at all. And it makes democracy a humanistic way of life for sure.

On Democracy as a Way of Life

1. Democracy is not just a political system, it is a way of life.

2. Democracy as a way of life shapes our thoughts, feelings, and relations with others.

3. Democracy as a way of life does not give us a right to always get our own way.

4. Democracy does not mean just rule by the majority; it means respect for differences among people.

5. Democracy does not give us a *social right* to be surrounded by people only like ourselves. (Mill)

6. The selfishness and irrationality of human nature put democracy at constant risk.

7. Democracy can bring many kinds of tyranny—the tyranny of the majority, the tyranny of equality, the tyranny of public opinion, the tyranny of conformity, the tyranny of paternalistic government.

8. To protect liberty from the tyranny of the majority, we must fight the disease of faction. (Madison)

9. When we expect democratic politics to serve our own interests despite the interests of other people, we are acting out the disease of faction. (Madison)

10. Democratic liberty and democratic equality are not the same thing, and they can conflict. (Tocqueville)

11. Democracy can lead people to value social equality, or equality of condition, over the liberty of individuals. (Tocqueville)

12. Equality of condition tends to produce both individualism and conformity, or egalitarian individualism. (Tocqueville)

13. Egalitarian individualism makes people feel like individuals while nevertheless making them the same. (Tocqueville)

14. The love of equality can lead to a tyranny of paternalistic government. (Tocqueville)

15. To protect liberty from the tyranny of equality and paternalistic government, we must take active political responsibility for our own lives. (Tocqueville)

16. To protect the liberty of individuals from the tyranny of public opinion and conformity, we must allow people to be free to think and to do anything they want, as long as they do not hurt anyone else. (Mill)

17. We should not confuse an actual hurt to anyone with an inconvenience or a thwarted preference. (Mill)

18. To develop our individuality, we must make choices about how to live. (Mill)

19. To make choices, we must encounter various ideas and modes of life. (Mill)

20. There should be differences among people, ideas, and modes of life, even though not for the better. (Mill)

21. We gain more as individuals and as a society by expanding the liberty of individuals than we do by expanding social control over that liberty. (Mill)

22. The meaning of life is to live freely as we choose and to develop ourselves as individuals, while nevertheless compromising our own interests to help serve the interests of others.

15

Through a Class Darkly

Karl Marx and Friedrich Engels: *The Communist Manifesto*

Life is not determined by consciousness, but consciousness by life.
Marx

Karl Marx (1818–1883) was born in Prussia and nurtured on radical ideals of historical truth, human freedom, and social justice. These fed dissatisfaction in him with the world as it was, and he expressed both his ideals and his dissatisfactions in abundant writing of the 1840s. Some of these (notably the *Economic and Philosophical Manuscripts of 1844* and *The German Ideology*), shedding Marx's early Hegelianism for materialism and marked by lofty philosophizing and socialist humanism, went unpublised until the twentieth century, when they became influential among Marxist intellectuals. Others, often in the form of journalism and pamphlets, had the stamp of propaganda for political and economic change. Chief of these was *The Communist Manifesto* (1848)—written, like *The German Ideology*, with Marx's longtime collaborator, Friedrich Engels (1820–1895). The timing of the *Manifesto* was right. Within weeks of its publication, smoldering discontents erupted in revolutions across Europe. But these radical upheavals generally lost out to conservative forces, and Marx was one of the losers. He then took up exile in England, where he lived thereafter with his wife and children, partially supported by Engels. But he did not give up the fight. Night and day he poured his energies into new writings to further his cause, most notably the monumental *Das Kapital* (vol. I, 1867) laying out the historical inevitability of Communism. Although Marx did not live to complete this sprawling work, he left an intellectual and political legacy that shook the world.

The Communist Manifesto bridges Marx's early ideals and some of his later theories. Scanning Western history, it explains how ruling classes have always exploited those below them through economic power and manipulative ideologies. It also points to the triumph of Communism, after which property will be shared, class conflict will disappear, government will wither, and truth will prevail. But Communism aside, the *Manifesto* shows us something we should see when, through the lens of social class, it examines how our ideas and views of the world arise from our social and economic circumstances, and how this can breed self-deception and social conflict unless we learn to see ourselves and our circumstances clearly.

THE COLLAPSE of the Soviet Union in the late twentieth century convinced many people that Communism failed there because it was bound to fail, and is best forgotten. Well, let Soviet Communism go unmourned, perhaps, but let the humane aspirations and intellectual insights of Communism—or Marxism, the theory of Communism devised by Karl Marx—not be forgotten.

Whatever we might think of its historical fruits in the twentieth century, Marxism, and Socialism in general, gave humankind a great hope. This was the hope for a world of cooperative, productive, prosperous, happy human beings. So inviting was this aspiration that in barely a century after its origins Marxism gained sway over more of the globe than any other body of ideas outside of the great religions.

The historical parallel with religion was not merely coincidental. Marxism won over so many people because it made the same kinds of promises as religion. Like most of the world's religions, Marxism guaranteed a remedy for universal human suffering, complete with a sublime realm where human beings will dwell together peacefully and contentedly forever. But Marxism parted company with religion by putting that remedy in the hands of human beings instead of God, and by placing that sublime realm on earth for the living instead of in heaven for spirits—dismissing the very beliefs in God, heaven, and spirit as illusions. Marxism was not a religion. At its best, it was a humanistic alternative to religion, despite those zealous Marxists who disdained "humanism" itself as a deceptive piece of bourgeois ideology. And notwithstanding its failures in practice and the assaults of its current enemies (including religious fundamentalism, ethnic nationalism, market economics, and capitalist individualism), Marxism represents an ideal of shared humanity and common well-being that we should not banish from our minds. Utopian? Yes. Impossible? Maybe. But let us keep at least some of its hopes alive for a good society—for everyone.

While we should remember Marxism's humane aspirations, we should also learn from Marxism's intellectual insights. For these have uses that will last whether Marxism as a political and economic system vanishes completely from the earth or not. These uses come from Karl Marx's sweeping efforts to explain why we think and feel and act as we do.

Many thinkers have tried to explain these things. Some have partially succeeded. Marx, a stranger to intellectual modesty, thought he had got hold of the whole truth. He hadn't. But he had got hold of something. Looking into our thoughts, feelings, and actions to discover the causes behind them, Marx believed he had detected, or unmasked, the deepest truth of human character, culture, and history. That truth is the influence of social and economic, or "material," interests. Marx took his unmasking truth too far, reducing virtually everything in human life and history to it. Nevertheless—like the other great influential "unmaskers" of our ideas and actions, Jean-Jacques Rousseau, Friedrich Nietzsche, and Sigmund Freud (see Chapters 6, 8, 17)—Marx gave us a very useful way of looking at human beings and our world indeed. If you are not a Marxist in this sense, you fail to see many things, whatever your politics.

MARX'S UNMASKING truth boils down to this: how we manage to survive in this world gives us our economic and social, or "material," interests. And these material interests shape everything else about us. Marx formulated this idea before he and Friedrich Engels wrote *The Communist Manifesto*. And he stated that idea in a phrase that became a motto of Marxism: "Life is not determined by consciousness, but consciousness by life." In other words, how we live and work from day to day shapes our thoughts and feelings more than our thoughts and feelings shape how we live and work. This is not just an abstract notion. It has far-reaching consequences for thinking and for living.

If how we live and work shapes how we think and feel rather than the other way around, then thoughts and feelings have no independent existence of their own. They do not *cause* anything. They are just reactions to, or reflections of, our lives and our material interests—"reflexes and echoes . . . phantoms formed in the human brain," as Marx puts it, "by the real life-process." But people don't see this.

Here is how it all happens: First we work to live; then we think about how we live; then we form beliefs and fashion culture to explain and organize how we live; then we convince ourselves that those beliefs, and our whole culture, are rooted in universal truths, moral principles, abstract ideas, and so forth; finally, we generally conclude that those truths and ideas, and other mental things, are the primary reality and the driving force of history. Marxists call this sequence "historical materialism": material life produces everything; then people lose sight of this fact and settle into the self-deception that mental life rules.

In the light of this historical materialism, Marx explains, "morality, religion, metaphysics . . . as well as their corresponding forms of consciousness, thus no longer retain the semblance of independence. They have no history, no development." They simply mirror and help sustain our material lives. So you cannot understand ideas, actions, culture, or any part of the human world if you look at it by itself. You must examine the material conditions that surround it and the material interests or purposes it serves. To understand why we embrace any idea, or even feel any feeling, we must therefore discover where in the "real world" it came from, and what it does for us in "real life."

This requirement has become a commonplace nowadays among intellectuals for whom no idea or argument goes unanalyzed to unmask the material or other selfish interests it serves. This practice can go so far as to discredit almost any idea as a self-serving rationalization. Marx deserves much of the credit—or the blame—for that. But we should not be dissuaded by the excesses of some Marxists and intellectuals from making use of Marx's good ideas for ourselves And when you think about it sensibly, historical materialism is a very good and useful idea.

Marx was not, of course, the first to tie thoughts and feelings to material conditions. Plenty of thinkers before Marx had recognized that economic and social interests play a prominent, sometimes predominant, role in shaping people's minds and guiding their lives. Jean-Jacques Rousseau, for one, had claimed that private property created social inequality, and he had warned in *Emile* against letting any material interests control the way we think; James Madison, for another, had also seen that private property shapes peoples' interests, and he contended that American democracy could succeed only by constitutionally mitigating the effects of material interests in politics (see Chapter 14). Marx did not think he had made an altogether new discovery either. "Does it require deep intuition," he asked, "to comprehend that man's ideas, views, and conceptions, in one word, man's consciousness, changes with every change in the condition of his material existence, in his social relations and in his social life?" But Marx made more of this insight than anyone before him.

Curiously, no one knows exactly what Marx had in mind on this subject. Did he believe that material interests literally *determine* thought and culture, like a physical reflex, or just *influence* them? (The German term Marx uses, *bestimmt*, can mean both the stronger and the weaker action.) This question ignited disputes in Marx's day, prompting Friedrich Engels to set the record straight after Marx's death with a memorable answer. Marx did not mean, Engels wrote in a letter, that economic and social interests mechanistically determine mind and culture in every detail at every moment, but that a pattern of cause and effect appears over time. And Engels quoted Marx saying, in reference to followers who had taken the doctrine of historical materialism too literally: "All I know is that I am not a 'Marxist.'" Marx was not repudiating his own doctrine, only the deterministic pedantries of "Marxist" ideologues.

The uncertainty of Marx's precise meaning and the excesses of his followers aside—including those who today mobilize Marxist arguments to assail the very possibility of objective truth—Marx was surely right to emphasize our material interests. However free, independent, spontaneous, or deliberate we take our ideas and emotions to be, they are always influenced by (to use the soft version) and serve our economic and social well-being: they always have links somehow, somewhere, to money and status. The noblest moral codes can turn out to be simply the manners of our social class or clique—like those of the European nobility who set the very standard we know as "noble." The highest elation can swell from nothing more than getting a financial windfall. The cheeriest *joi de vivre* or spirit of independence can dissolve with financial decline. We educate our children, choose our friends, pick our political candidates under the pressure of financial and social circumstances. Heeding this does not require changing what we think and do—although Marx thought it should. But it does make us better able to understand ourselves and our world.

MARX CARRIES OUT his unmasking strategy against the backdrop of his utopian socialist ideals most boldly in *The Communist Manifesto*, or *The Manifesto of the Communist Party* (Engels would pardon giving Marx authorial credit, since he never claimed intellectual originality for himself), one of the most famous and infamous political documents of modern times. Some people have refused to read the *Manifesto* from contempt for its Communist doctrines. They miss the point. The *Manifesto* tells us about Communism, all right. In its few loaded pages it sketches Marx's version of history as class conflicts, the characteristics of social classes, types of Socialist programs, and the inevitable Communist revolution to come. But most revealing, it looks at everything in the light that illuminates how material interests affect the way people think and feel, especially members of the middle class—a light that also shows why middle-class readers might not want to read it.

Before getting to Marx's argument, we should recall that the *Manifesto* was, in the first place, a battle cry raised when life was bleak for the downtrodden amidst burgeoning industrialization and buoyant capitalism in Europe. As a battle cry, the *Manifesto* has affinities with the American *Declaration of Independence*. Both demand radical, even revolutionary, political action to end oppression of the majority by the powerful few and to establish an egalitarian society. Both justify their demands with claims about human nature, and about how existing institutions abuse it. And both conclude with calls to arms: the *Declaration* pledging "our

Lives, our Fortunes and our sacred Honor" to insure that "these United Colonies are, and of Right ought to be Free and Independent States"; and the *Manifesto* proclaiming: "The proletarians have nothing to lose but their chains. They have a world to win. WORKING MEN OF ALL COUNTRIES, UNITE!"

The Declaration of Independence, with its fine eighteenth-century assumptions about self-evident truths and divine providence, provided the rationale for a host of political revolutions that overturned monarchical rule and aristocratic privilege and established democratic institutions grounded in the principles of equal rights and individual liberty. *The Communist Manifesto* supplied the rationale for upheavals of a rather different sort. These aimed at the absolute equality of all people in political, social, and economic life, and a consequent transformation of consciousness that would unite all human beings in common interests and shared ideas once and for all.

Few readers today are likely to hit the streets waving slogans of the *Manifesto* and calling for a Communist revolution. That day seems to have passed. But we should take Marx's conception of historical materialism seriously. For it touches on how we think and feel and act as members of a social class. And that is how the argument of the *Manifesto* begins—with the dominant reality of the human world as Marx saw it: social class.

"The history of all hitherto existing society is the history of class struggles." A familiar first line. But it says more than its words. The words say that history is nothing but one class conflict after another. The gist is something else, and more consequential. That is: individuals do not make history, social classes make history. Individuals act only as members of social classes. A person is rich or poor, freeman or slave, lord or serf, aristocrat or peasant, owner or worker, or in Marx's terms, bourgeois or proletarian. There are no individuals. History is therefore the history of social classes.

Setting social class at the center stage of history, Marx goes on to portray that history as a bloody drama of ceaseless conflict between the haves and the have-nots, the empowered and the unempowered, "oppressor and oppressed." These conflicts have ever raged, Marx says, because the ruling class of society cannot hold its place without exploiting those below it, squeezing them dry of both economic and human resources. But during the course of history, the oppressed have repeatedly overthrown the oppressors. Then, alas, they have only become new oppressors. Now, Marx says, in modern industrial society the oppressors and the oppressed stand off against each other as the only two social classes remaining in history: the bourgeoisie, or middle class, and the proletariat, or working class.

A lot has changed since Marx and Engels wrote the *Manifesto* in the late 1840s, and neither the bourgeoisie nor the proletariat is quite what they described, certainly not in twenty-first-century America. Still, Marx's central idea of material and class interests can apply to how we live now.

Marx's theory says that the future lies with the proletariat, whose triumphant revolution will be the last act in history. History will then end because once the proletariat eliminates the bourgeoisie, the proletariat will be the only class left, with none below it. When only one class exists, oppression will end and class conflict will cease. And with no class conflicts there can be no history, or no history like that of all "hitherto existing society." From that moment, the Communist utopia will reign.

Although the future belongs to the proletariat in Marx's theory, the present belongs to the bourgeoisie. And as the ruling class in the final combative episode in history, the bourgeoisie is both a hero and a villain in the *Manifesto*. Marx's very idea of Communism and his summons to revolution in its name spring from his vision of the bourgeoisie—its historical creativity, its unprecedented productivity, its malevolent character, its inevitable doom. And despite the distance separating Marx's times from ours (when, unpredicted by Marx, the middle class, not the industrial working class, is becoming the only one), Marx's vision accounts for many traits of American society today. For that vision points to the historical debt we owe to the bourgeoisie, and to how some of our most cherished ideas—are they only bourgeois ideas?—came to seem so true.

"The bourgeoisie, historically," Marx announces, "has played a most revolutionary part. . . . It has been the first to show what man's activity can bring about. It has accomplished wonders far surpassing Egyptian pyramids, Roman aqueducts, and Gothic cathedrals; it has conducted expeditions that put in the shade all former Exoduses of nations and crusades." Marx admires the bourgeoisie not only for its unprecedented material productivity. Equally significant was its own revolution in consciousness or ways of thinking. Without this mental revolution, Communism could not even have been imagined. It could not have been imagined, Marx says, because before the bourgeoisie took over, human beings could not see the real cause of their own suffering. They couldn't see it because they had perceived reality through veils of comforting illusions. The thickest of these veils was religion.

When Marx wrote the well-known phrase, religion is "the opium of the people," he did not mean, as many assume, that religion is a dangerous drug that besots minds and blights lives. He meant that religion is an anesthetic invented by human beings to assuage their pain. "Religion," he said, is "the expression of real distress and also a protest against real distress. Religion is the sigh of the oppressed creature, the heart of a heartless world. It is the *opium* of the people." Marx wanted to banish religion, and he took the "criticism of religion" as "the premise of all criticism," not because religion harms people, but because it conceals the cause of their troubles, misguiding their diagnoses of human suffering and making it impossible for them to find an effective cure.

If you are sick, and a doctor prescribes a painkiller, you might feel better for a while, but that will not cure you. You need more than an anesthetic for the symptoms. You need a genuine cure for the disease. To find that cure, you must discover the causes of the symptoms. Religion, according to Marx (as well as to Jean-Paul Sartre and Freud, by the way—see Chapters 9 and 17), falsely reads symptoms and then prescribes a dose of medicinal beliefs that work like a narcotic to make the pain bearable in a haze of artificial security. You have to cast these beliefs aside to have any chance of truly getting well. "The abolition of religion," Marx asserts, will replace "the *illusory* happiness of the people" with "a demand for their real happiness." And "real happiness" can exist only in the real world, not in illusions. So, the call for people "to abandon their illusions about their condition is a *call to abandon a condition which requires illusions*"—that is, a condition so painful that they need drugs or illusions to endure it.

Marx thanks the bourgeoisie for paving the way out of this illusory state of affairs. The bourgeoisie did not intend to do this. But that was the result. For the bourgeoisie thrust that "condition which requires illusions" into the historical spotlight, where its ugly reality could finally be seen for what it is. That reality, the true cause of human suffering, is economic exploitation.

The bourgeoisie, harboring no deep reverence for religious illusions and the "idyllic relations" of traditional society that had long masked and sustained economic exploitation by the aristocracy, stepped onto the stage intoning the creed of individualism and "naked self-interest" and "callous cash payment." That act changed everything. "Whenever it has got the upper hand," Marx explains, the bourgeoisie "has drowned the most heavenly ecstasies of religious fervor, of chivalrous enthusiasm, of Philistine sentimentalism"; it "has stripped of its halo every occupation hitherto honored and looked up to with reverent awe" and "torn away from the family its sentimental veil." Thus "all fixed, fast-frozen relations with their train of ancient and venerable prejudices and opinions, are swept away. . . . All that is solid melts into air, all that is holy is profaned." Now, economic exploitation would become brazen, undeniable, unapologetic. "For exploitation veiled by religious and political illusions," the bourgeoisie "substituted naked, shameless, direct, brutal exploitation." And this brought the epochal change: "Man is at last compelled to face with sober senses, his real conditions of life, and his relations with his kind." There was left "no other nexus between man and man than naked self-interest, than callous cash payment." And, as Marx said in "The Power of Money in Bourgeois Society," when "money is the supreme good . . . its possessor is good."

But, by thrusting the "real conditions of life" that cause human suffering into the open, the bourgeoisie also ironically pointed to the true cure for that suffering: the bourgeoisie itself must go, overthrown by the ever-growing proletariat. "What the bourgeoisie therefore produces," Marx wraps up with a flourish, "are its own gravediggers." And when the gravediggers bury the bourgeoisie, they will be burying not just a class of exploiters, but a kind of consciousness and a culture. Everything that people think and feel and do as members of the middle class will disappear. That is the Marxist revolution in consciousness—an effect of economic and social revolution, mind you, not a cause; consciousness itself does not cause anything.

Marx got the future wrong here. The burial has not taken place, and probably never will, so agile has the capitalist middle class been in maintaining and extending its dominance and absorbing into its ranks much of the former industrial working class, which has dwindled rather than grown. But that fact does not lessen the value of learning what it could mean—intellectually, culturally, psychologically—to be a member of the middle class, or bourgeoisie, that Marx marked for extinction. It could actually make it more valuable to learn about this. For the capitalist middle class is becoming the ruling class of the world.

To SEE WHAT IT MEANS to be a member of this class as Marx perceived it, we return to the idea of the individual, which Marx implicitly threw out at the beginning of the *Manifesto*. When we think of who we are today, most of us (especially Americans) probably think of ourselves first as individuals. We do not think of ourselves immediately as members of a social class; and our other group identities, like gender, family, race, ethnicity, nationality, and religion, probably come to mind even before social class. We also tend to assume that individuality lies at the root of human nature, and that individuals create society, and that strong individuals drive history. That is to say, we believe in "individualism."

But Marx scoffs: that is merely a middle-class bias, and the elemental middle-class bias to boot. The very idea of "individualism," Marx says, is itself a middle-class idea, part of bourgeois ideology (Alexis de Tocqueville, who gave the term currency, said it was a creation of democracy, although he defined it differently from Marx—see Chapter 14). Even the middle-class *individual* himself or herself, Marx adds, is nothing but an invention of that social class. How, we might ask, can this be? Well, Marx explains, like other bourgeois ways of thinking, the idea of the individual grows out of the material and social conditions, and works to the benefit, of that class. In other words, it pays off for members of the middle class to be independent individuals rather than *inter*dependent persons, and to believe in individualism rather than Socialism.

Now, if we find ourselves quickly rejecting these assertions as vulgar Marxist clichés, we might stop to ask ourselves honestly how much of that rejection—as well as what portion of our social status, profession, education, manners, and the like—might in fact come from our belonging to the middle class. Then we can better learn from Marx not only how individualism can be a middle-class idea, but how all bourgeois ways of thinking work, and where they come from, and what they do for us.

Individualism and other middle-class ideas, Marx says, come from nothing so much as the one fundamental fact, or condition, of middle-class life: private property. But this private property is not personal possessions, like your toothbrush or your shoes. It is income-producing property, like land and factories. Income-producing property is "capital." And capital produces wealth and power. Consequently, only those who own capital, or private property, have power. Only they have full control of their lives. You do not need to be a nineteenth-century factory owner or a corporate magnate today to feel this independence. Simply investing in the stock market, or owning a house, or even having money in the bank, can give you a taste of it. This confident sense of independence, Marx argues, leads the owners of private property, that is, the capitalist middle class, to believe that they prosper largely because they are superior, self-reliant *individuals*, and that the poor are poor mainly because they lack sufficient self-reliance and individuality. That, in a nutshell, is how Marx figures the middle class came to exalt individualism as the supreme value—together with the other middle-class ideas that "are but the outgrowth of the conditions of bourgeois production and bourgeois property."

But the middle-class exaltation of individualism is not only a class bias, Marx says; it is an egregious error that obscures the fundamental reality of human nature. "By individual," he says scornfully, "you mean no other person than the bourgeois, than the middle-class owner of property" constantly competing for economic power. The human reality, Marx insists, is something else. Human beings are by nature not *individuals* in this sense. Strip away the trappings of class and they are "social beings," interdependent and cooperative, not individualistic and competitive. The triumph of bourgeois individualism has insidiously obscured the truth. Get rid of private property and the truth can come out. And so Marx declares: "The theory of the Communists may be summed up in the single sentence: Abolition of private property." Once private property goes, human beings will abandon the spurious middle-class ideal of individualism, along with other false class notions and the abuses they breed, and will become genuinely *human* at last. "Communism," Marx affirms, is therefore the "transcendence of *private property*, or *human self-estrangement*" and "the complete return of man to himself *as a social* (i.e., human) being" with his "*human*, i.e., *social*, mode of existence."

Don't worry about the jargon. Here is the crux of the Marxist cultural revolution, the jugular thrust that has scared, and inspired, so many people: Marx openly vows to supplant one way of life and of thinking with another—namely, to replace what he takes to be the self-deceptive and exploitative individualism of the bourgeoisie, and all that surrounds it, with a truly social humanism. From the middle-class point of view, of course, as Marx concedes, that revolution spells the end of "individuality and freedom." But, Marx points out, to eliminate "individuality and freedom," along with private property, does not extinguish these things in themselves, only the bourgeois definitions of them. Marx makes no bones about it: he expects "the abolition of bourgeois individuality, bourgeois independence, and bourgeois freedom," and even the bourgeois individual as such: "The middle-class owner of property: this person must, indeed, be swept out of the way, and made impossible."

The end of bourgeois private property, freedom, and individuality will bring the extinction of the middle class and its entire exploitative culture. The members of this class will resist, to be sure, fearing a descent into barbarism. For, as Marx says, they equate their own culture with culture itself and view its possible disappearance to be "identical with the disappearance of all culture." And they are convinced of this because they take their own ideas of the individual and of freedom, as well as their ideas of justice, truth, humanity, and so on, to be "eternal truths" that are "common to all states of society." But, Marx declares, like all ruling classes, the middle class has only "transform[ed] into eternal laws of nature and of reason" its own material self-interests. Middle-class ideas and culture work to the advantage of the middle class; for everyone else, Marx concludes, they are "a mere training ground to act as a machine."

Small wonder that the aspirations of Communist revolution aroused such fierce opposition among the prosperous and powerful middle class while stirring worldwide appeal among the downtrodden. That revolution would eliminate the capitalist middle class and its culture and deliver the world to a utopia of the oppressed, where people will no longer be mere pawns of class conflicts; where they will live *human*, not *class*, lives; where no selfish individualism will exist; where no competition between people will occur; where the masks of self-serving and self-deceptive ideas will fall away forever; and where no powerful government will be needed to serve a ruling class and keep public order. "In place of the old bourgeois society, with its classes and class antagonisms, we shall have an association in which the free development of each is the condition for the free development of all."

IN THE EARLY TWENTY-FIRST CENTURY, with Communism still retreating and free-market capitalism spreading across the globe, it appears that Marx's prophesies are doomed. But whether Marx's Communist utopia is even possible in principle depends ultimately on one thing: whether Marx was right or wrong about human nature. Every political theory rests on a theory of human nature, but none more insistently than Marxism. If Marx was right, then human beings are inherently social (an idea Marx shared with Aristotle and Confucius, by the way—see Chapters 4 and 10), and they become selfishly individualistic only through private property, class conflict, and false ideas. Therefore, a Communist utopia is possible in principle, since it would allow human beings to live out their fundamental social selves amidst the common ownership of property. But if Marx was wrong, and human beings are innately more individualistic than social, then Communism is impossible in principle, and every Communist, or even Socialist, experiment will inevitably crash against the shoals of humankind's inherent individualism. Nowadays many champions of capitalism gloatingly point to the historic failures of Communism in the Soviet Union and elsewhere as proof that Marx was wrong. But who knows for sure?

In any case, whatever the virtues or failings of Marx's image of human nature and his revolutionary aspirations, we would do well to make wise use of Marx's ideas about the influence on us of material interests and social class. This does not mean adopting those ideas as Marxist ideology, for an ideology of any kind tells us what to think rather than asking us to think for ourselves (as Voltaire's Dr. Pangloss comically demonstrated—see Chapter 13), and Marxism certainly took on that ugly ideological form in the twentieth century. Making wise use of Marx's ideas means asking ourselves where our own notions and self-assured assumptions about individuality, freedom, justice, humanity, and our other ideas, values, and judgments came from, and whose interests they serve, and whose interests they do not serve. For regardless of Marx's oversimplifications, and his error in denying any formative influence to ideas and beliefs, if we are to understand ourselves and others accurately, and if we are to organize human society justly, we must take a cue from Marx and learn how our perceptions and value judgments, our very thoughts and feelings, are affected in the subtlest ways by our economic and social interests. In short, we must unmask ourselves.

On the Influence of Our Material Lives on Our Minds

1. Our lives shape our thoughts and feelings more than our thoughts and feelings shape our lives.

2. To understand why we think as we do, we must understand the social and material interests of our lives.

3. Our social and material interests make us members of a social class.

4. Freedom, justice, ethics, and other ideas mean different things to different social classes.

5. People turn to religion when it serves their social and material interests—as a painkiller for suffering.

6. The idea of competitive individualism serves primarily the social and material interests of the capitalist middle class because that class thrives on the moneymaking power of competitive individuals.

7. Human beings are by nature more cooperative than competitive and more social than individualistic, but modern capitalism has obscured this by making them competitively individualistic.

8. Under capitalism, money itself gains the power to determine the very worth of human beings.

9. In an ideal society, wealth and economic resources would be shared, divisive social hierarchies would not exist, individuals would cooperate instead of compete, people would work for the good of all, and everyone would be secure and fulfilled as human beings.

10. The meaning of life is to recognize the social essence of human nature, understand how material conditions influence our ideas, and unite in our common humanity to work for the common good of all human beings.

16

We Shall Overcome

Frederick Douglass: *Narrative of the Life of Frederick Douglass*

Elie Wiesel: *Night*

Martin Luther King, Jr.: "Letter from the Birmingham Jail"

I have found that to make a contented slave it is necessary to make a thoughtless one, . . . and he can be brought to that only when he ceases to be a man.
Douglass

Humanity? Humanity is not concerned with us. Today anything is allowed. Anything is possible.
Wiesel

Any law that degrades human personality is unjust.
King

The son of a slave mother and an unidentified white father, **Frederick Douglass (1817–1895)** escaped from slavery in Maryland at the age of twenty one to gain freedom in New England, where he became an eloquent abolitionist. Then, after spending two years in England crusading for that cause, he settled in Rochester, New York, in 1847 to publish his own antislavery newspaper. Intelligent, articulate, and increasingly prominent, Douglass became an adviser to Abraham Lincoln during the Civil War, and subsequently held a variety of official positions, including consul general to Haiti. But it was his autobiography as a slave—*Narrative of the Life of Frederick Douglass. An American Slave. Written by Himself*, originally published in 1845—that secured his place in history. Unsurpassed as a record of the sufferings of slaves, and, more chillingly, of the dehumanized cruelty of slaveholders, it is also an uplifting testimonial to the liberating powers of education and strength of will, and to the necessity of humane values for everyone.

Romanian-born **Elie Wiesel (1928–)** had his consciousness permanently seared by the horrors of the Jewish Holocaust during World War II, especially by his own experience in the concentration camps Auschwitz and Buchenwald during the last year of the war. Later educated in France, he would in time devote himself to writing many novels and other books inscribing the Holocaust in modern memory. These include *Dawn* (1961), *The Jews of Silence* (1966), *Souls on Fire* (1972), *The Oath* (1974), *The Testament* (1980), *Evil and Exile* (1990), *The Forgotten* (1989), two volumes of memoirs (1995, 1999), and *Reflections on the Holocaust* (2002). In 1986 he was awarded the Nobel Prize for Peace as a tribute to his work. But his first book, the short memoir of his own youthful Holocaust experience, *Night* (1958), stands out as perhaps the preeminent eyewitness account of this historical nightmare. For Wiesel's description of the evolving Holocaust reveals how unbelievable human inhumanity can be, while it also shows us that we may need this dark knowledge to preserve our own humanity.

Martin Luther King, Jr. (1929–1968), scion of a Baptist preacher, rose from his own ministry to become the emblematic leader of the American civil rights movement in the 1950s and 1960s. His crusade earned him the Nobel Prize for Peace in 1964, and got him assassinated in 1968. A forceful speaker and a disciple of Gandhi's doctrine of nonviolent protest, he was jailed many times for openly breaking racially segregationist laws. During one of those incarcerations, he wrote a philosophical defense of his illegal actions: "The Letter from the Birmingham Jail" (1963). In this letter to a group of fellow ministers he thoughtfully explained why we should not obey "unjust laws"—including the laws of segregation—and why a humane civilization depends on "just laws." No one has made the ideas of justice and injustice more straightforward and compellingly true than he.

H ISTORY FLOWS with the blood, and is littered with the corpses, of what we have come to lament as "man's inhumanity to man." We wonder why. Why do human beings heap so much misery upon each other? We hope it will end. Perhaps someday it will. If it does end, we will owe thanks for this in part to those who have endured some of history's worst human horrors and have then become witnesses to them, testifying to how inhumanity can trammel all civilized constraints, and how it can surpass all imaginings, and how it can dehumanize both villains and victims, and how it can happen anywhere, anytime.

Among these witnesses, Frederick Douglass, Elie Wiesel, and Martin Luther King, Jr., rise above most of the rest for the force of their observations, the power of their words, and the wisdom of their judgments. Their respective accounts of what they saw and suffered during American slavery, the Jewish Holocaust, and racial segregation in America take us through a Dantesque hell of human inhumanity. Once we read their words, we cannot forget them. We also see life and human beings more fully, if more sadly, but also perhaps a bit more hopefully. For these witnesses—and judges—not only describe dark historical episodes of inhumanity, they cast light into that darkness, illuminating causes of inhumanity and brightening prospects for ending it, or at least for creating a more humane world where inhumanity would not be tolerated, or could not be so easily masked in the guises of a "higher humanity" or religious truth, as it often has been, from antiquity to the present. The future could wrest no better legacy from the inhumane past than that.

These three witnesses do not present this happy prospect through lofty philosophizing about good and evil. They do it with plain and simple words and sobering reflections on life as they knew it—and images that can stick in our minds of how misguided and cruel human beings can be, and how human beings might learn to be better.

NEARLY A CENTURY after American slavery ended at the cost of a civil war, the Nigerian author Chinua Achebe recreated in the historical novel *Things Fall Apart* (1959) events of the kind that

DOUGLASS laid the ground for Frederick Douglass' life story. Achebe tells the tragic tale of how slavery came to his homeland, and how the Nigerians at first did not believe it possible, and how it then destroyed their culture and drove one heartbroken Nigerian to suicide instead of submission. Achebe's novel is a vivid work of the literary imagination. Frederick Douglass' autobiography of his early years, *Narrative of the Life of Frederick Douglass. An American Slave. Written By Himself*, is the more vivid for being a memoir of remembered fact.

The *Narrative* retells events of Douglass' life as a slave during the 1820s and 1830s (within which time, incidentally, fell Alexis de Tocqueville's journey to America and observations of democracy's triumph here—see Chapter 14). Although scholars have noted errors in Douglass' account of slavery, and some have faulted its limited perspective on the slave experience, that does not diminish the power and human significance of Douglass' portrayals of what he saw and what he endured. For in Douglass' pages, we see slaveholders trying literally in every way they could to dehumanize slaves into animals. And we see how this actually dehumanized those masters more than the slaves, and prompted Douglass to escape from slavery and become an articulate witness to its horrors. So, we see the kinds of things that can erode a person's humanity, as either slave or master, victim or villain, along with the kinds of things that can preserve it. Douglass deserves credit for this.

Douglass tells us that the slaveholders' efforts to dehumanize slaves began with methods for denying the slaves a sense of themselves as human beings. This started at a slave's very birth. No record of a slave's birth was kept, or at least none that the slave ever knew (as far as Douglass was aware). "I do not remember to ever have met a slave who could tell me of his birthday," Douglass writes, so "slaves know as little of their ages as horses know of theirs." The masters refused to record or to reveal such facts, Douglass explains, in order "to keep their slaves thus ignorant." And the masters regarded a slave's inquiries on the subject to be "improper and impertinent, and evidence of a restless spirit." The most that a slave could do to learn of his or her origins and age was to pick up clues from random incidents, like remarks by the master—from such a remark Douglass himself later estimated his own age when he wrote his memoir in 1845 to be twenty-seven or twenty-eight years old.

Obviously the presence of parents could have helped. But this, too, the masters contrived to thwart. For the slave system, as Douglass knew it, also tore apart family bonds to deprive slaves of both a family identity and the emotional attachments of family life. It was, Douglass says, "a common custom" where he lived in Maryland, "to part children from their mothers at a very early age, frequently, before the child has reached its twelfth month." And "the inevitable result" was to "hinder the development of the child's affection toward its mother, and to blunt and destroy the natural affections of the mother for the child."

Douglass recalls seeing his own mother only a few times as a child and then only at night when she was able to travel from her master's plantation to see him at his (although he lived for a time with his grandmother). Before long, his mother died. He never even knew who his father was, but, like many slaves at the time, he did hear from rumor that his father was white. Possibly it was the master himself. Douglass says his mother gave him the name Frederick, which he clung to as "a sense of my own identity," but that he changed his last name several times after he became a free man until he settled on the one we know. We could say that Frederick Douglass actually created an identity for himself as a free man, even in name—a commendable quixotic act (see Chapter 22).

Whether by design or by its heartless nature, the slave system tried to deny slaves the human sense of themselves that comes from lasting bonds of affection and interdependence among families, among friends, and ultimately among a community of hopeful human beings. For they were bought and sold, traded and transported, like animals at the whim of the master. "A single word from the white man was enough," Douglass records, "—against all our wishes, prayers, and entreaties—to sunder forever the dearest friends, dearest kindred, and strongest ties known to human beings." While collectively treated like a herd of animals, each slave was also alone.

These attempts to stifle the slaves' sense of their humanity extended to giving slaves phony "holidays." Or so Douglass came to understand. These holidays offered slaves a reprieve from forced labor and a taste of freedom and community. But instead of serving truly humane ends, Douglass says, these holidays were "part and parcel of the gross fraud, wrong, and inhumanity of slavery." Their actual and perfidious purpose was "to carry off the rebellious spirit of enslaved humanity" in "dissipation artfully labeled with the name of liberty." For the slaveholders aimed "to disgust their slaves with freedom" by "plunging them into the lowest depths" of stupefying excess, promoted by drinking contests. And so "when the holidays ended," he says, "we staggered up from the filth of our wallowing . . . feeling, upon the whole, rather glad to go, from what our master had deceived us into a belief was freedom, back to the arms of slavery."

The behavior of slaves during these "holidays" confirmed to slaveholders that the slaves did not truly deserve or even want to be free, since given a little liberty, they would only run amok and then eagerly return to bondage. The slaveholders did not see the truth here, of course, but they were exploiting a fact of human nature that Douglass learned from them. That fact is: to use freedom well—and to be truly free—human beings must be able to exercise self-mastery (Jean-Jacques Rousseau concluded his entire plan of education in *Emile* on just this point—see Chapter 6). And the slaveholders did not want slaves to have this kind of self-mastery, any more than they wanted them to be free. The slave holidays supplied an insidious device to undermine both.

The sad inhumanity that Douglass detected in the spurious freedom of the slave holidays he also heard voiced in the slaves' songs. The slaveholders chose to believe that slaves sang as "evidence of their contentment." But, Douglass says, "it is impossible to conceive of a greater mistake." Far from being music of contentment, "the songs of the slave represent the sorrows of his heart . . . and a prayer to God for deliverance from Chains." They express good feelings "only as an aching heart is relieved by its tears." Hearing those songs, he goes on, "always depressed my spirit, and filled me with ineffable sadness," for they betrayed more about "slavery than the reading of whole volumes of philosophy on the subject." "To these songs," Douglass adds sorrowfully, "[I] trace my first glimmering conception of the dehumanizing character of slavery." Here was the birth of the blues.

While the slaves' songs first suggested to Douglass the profoundly "dehumanizing character of slavery," what most unmistakably dramatized that character, and the troubling self-righteousness of the slaveholders, was the practice of physical cruelty. Douglass' record of this is revolting in its details, and unforgettable in its implications for how deeply self-righteousness can corrupt anyone.

The slaveholders used physical cruelty frequently, randomly, and savagely as punishment for any perceived infraction of a slave's duties. And these infractions were virtually impossible to avoid. With some masters, Douglass says, "to escape punishment was to escape accusation, and few slaves had the fortune to do either," since the accusations were as capricious as the punishments were harsh. Although some masters dealt out more physical abuse than others, none whom Douglass encountered did their dehumanizing work without it. And many practiced it with malicious and lascivious zeal.

Douglass' first master was one of these. He seemed "to take great pleasure in whipping a slave," Douglass observes, and he often brutalized one particular female slave, who happened to be Douglass' aunt. "I never shall forget it whilst I remember anything," Douglass writes, how this beastly master "used to tie her up to a joist, and whip upon her naked back till she was literally covered with blood." And "the louder she screamed, the harder he whipped. . . . He would whip her to make her scream and whip her to make her hush; and not until overcome by fatigue would he cease." Such callous cruelty lays bare the abysmal inhumanity to which slavery could sink. And sometimes it led to murder.

Douglass blood-curdlingly recalls one such killing. An imperiously vicious overseer—whom Douglass describes as "artful, cruel, and obdurate . . . just the man for such a place, and it was just the place for such a man"—coolly turned from the whip to the gun when one slave fled into a river to escape a beating. After halting the terrified escapee by demanding that he return or die, the overseer calmly blew the slave's brains out, and "his mangled body sank out of sight." "Killing a slave," Douglass remarks, "or any colored person, in Talbot County, Maryland, is not treated as a crime." There could be no crime against the subhuman—as the Nazis would also claim of their treatment of Jews.

Douglass' accounts of the physical cruelties of slaveholders are so prolific, prolonged, and graphic that they can make you sick. But he does not detail them simply for dramatic affect. He does it to show us a pair of disturbing truths about human nature that lay at the heart of the slave system. The first of these truths is that slavery, like any kind of inhumanity, dehumanized the masters even more than it dehumanized the slaves. As Douglass says of that first master who relished whipping Douglass' aunt, "He was a cruel man, hardened by a long life of slaveholding." This becomes a wrenching refrain in Douglass' story: human beings lose their own humanity by treating others inhumanely.

Douglass describes this happening among even the most moderate of slaveholders. A kindly mistress, for instance, who had started teaching him to read in his youth, lost her kindness after her husband reproached her for treating Douglass as a human being. It only took "some training in the exercise of irresponsible power," Douglass reports, "to make her equal to the task of treating me as if I were a brute." And yet, he observes, from then on "slavery proved as injurious to her as it did to me," and "soon proved its ability to divest her" of her "heavenly qualities," for "under its influence the tender heart became stone."

Douglass records another instance when this bitter moral consequence of slavery again struck him to the core. It was at a slave auction where "men and women, old and young, married and single, were ranked with horses, sheep, and swine. There were horses and men, cattle and women, pigs and children, all holding the same rank in the scale of being, and were all subjected to the same narrow examination." He knew the slaves had no choice but to submit physically to this inhuman condition. But what shocked him more was that the slaveholders had actually made themselves inhuman by choosing to treat other human beings like animals. "At this moment," Douglass recalls, "I saw more clearly than ever the brutalizing effects of slavery upon both slave and slaveholder." Who can doubt that the masters, "hardened by a long life of slaveholding," had become even less human in their hearts than the slaves?

To be sure, the slaveholders claimed the most honorable moral motives for their dehumanizing deeds. And this came to trouble Douglass as much as anything he witnessed. For it disclosed to him the second, and most disturbing, truth of human nature underlying the slave system: human beings can all too easily justify anything they do, including acts of abject inhumanity, with self-deceiving feelings of moral rectitude.

This unhappy truth has prompted many thinkers over the centuries to revile the use of religion and morality as masks of hypocrisy and evil. Dante classed hypocrites among the vilest sinners in hell (see Chapter 5). And Voltaire spent much of his long literary life exposing how religious piety and inhumanity work together all too readily in the dark chambers of the human heart, and how they have done this all too often in human history (see Chapter 13). But perhaps never in history did this unholy alliance parade as overtly, perplexingly, and heartrendingly as it did in the union of the Western slave system and Christianity. This, more forcibly than anything else, told Douglass how slavery could exist even in a "civilized" and religious society.

We might assume that because the Christian ethic prizes love and charity, it would mitigate, if not prevent, brutality among Christian slaveholders (just as it inspired many Northern abolitionists). But that was not to be. In fact, Christian beliefs often intensified that brutality by fueling it with feelings of moral and spiritual rectitude (just as the fifteenth-century Portuguese had launched the Western slave trade in the first place to bring African heathens to Jesus: the court chronicler Gomes Eanes de Zurara reported that when the first shipload of African slaves arrived on Portuguese shores, the king, known as Henry the Navigator, "had no other pleasure than in thinking that these lost souls would now be saved").

A godless slaveholder, Douglass remarks (and in his experience these were few), merely "relied upon his own depravity," but once converted to Christianity "he found religious sanction and support for his slaveholding cruelty." And "of all slaveholders with whom I have ever met," Douglass declares, "religious slaveholders are the worst." For they were "the meanest and basest, the most cruel and cowardly, of all the others." "One of the many pious slaveholders" would, for example, "tie up and whip" a lame female slave, causing the "warm blood to drip," and then, "in justification of the bloody deed, he would quote this passage of Scripture—'He that knoweth his master's will and doeth it not, shall be beaten with many stripes.'" Such characters give religion a bad name (and remind us why Mark Twain had Huckleberry Finn fear that he would go to hell for helping the slave Jim escape to freedom).

While the slave system hardened the hearts of slaveholders, Christianity handed them a cloak of false righteousness to wear. Douglass is unambiguous about this. "I assert most unhesitatingly, the religion of the south is a mere covering for the most horrid crimes—a justifier of the most appalling barbarity—a sanctifier of the most hateful frauds—and a dark shelter under which the darkest, foulest, grossest, and most infernal deeds of slaveholders find the strongest protection." For anyone who might question this assertion, Douglass provides a scalding appendix on Christianity as the "*slaveholding* religion." This was not true Christianity, he says, but it was the Christianity he saw all around him. And it included Christian ministers who, themselves often slaveholders, aided slavery with doctrine, the church, and the lash alike. "I am filled with unutterable loathing," Douglass exclaims,

☙

when I contemplate the religious pomp and show, together with
the horrible inconsistencies, which everywhere surround me. . . .
The man who wields the blood-clotted cowskin during the week
fills the pulpit on Sunday, and claims to be a minister of the meek
and lowly Jesus. . . . We have men sold to build churches, women
sold to support the gospel, and babes sold to purchase Bibles for
the *poor heathen! all for the glory of God and the good of souls!* The
slave auctioneer's bell and the church-going bell chime in with each
other, and the bitter cries of the heart-broken slave are drowned
in the religious shouts of his pious master. The slave prison and
the church stand near each other. The clanking of fetters and the
rattling of chains in the prison, and the pious psalm and solemn
prayer in the church, may be heard at the same time. . . . Here we
have religion and robbery the allies of each other—devils dressed
in angels' robes, and hell presenting the semblance of paradise.

There is an indictment of self-righteous and self-deceiving religiosity
if ever there was one. And his shocked revulsion at how Christian piety
sustained the worst inhumanities of slavery gave Frederick Douglass his
mission to become a witness to those kindred evils. That mission also
made Douglass a chastening conscience for anyone who would embrace
piety and power together.

Douglass embarked on that mission as he came to understand the slave
system's most essential strategy for dehumanizing slaves and keeping
them suppressed. This was illiteracy.

Douglass discovered this strategy inadvertently when he overheard
his master reproaching that once kindly mistress for teaching Douglass
how to read. Douglass never forgot that moment—and he possibly em-
bellished it in the telling. "Learning would *spoil* the best nigger in the
world," he quotes the master berating his wife. "A nigger should know
nothing but to obey his master," and "to do what he is told to do." And,
referring to young Douglass himself, the master concluded, "if you
teach that nigger how to read, there would be no keeping him. It would
forever unfit him to be a slave. He would at once become unmanageable, and of no value to his master."

The incident struck Douglass, then at the dawn of adolescence, as an
epiphany. "These words sank deep into my heart," he says, "and stirred
into existence an entirely new train of thought. It was a new and special revelation, explaining dark and mysterious things, with which my
youthful understanding had struggled. . . . I now understood what had
been to me a most perplexing difficulty—to wit, the white man's power

to enslave the black man." That power was none other than control of the slaves' minds through ignorance. "To make a contented slave," Douglass now grasped, "it is necessary to make a thoughtless one. It is necessary to darken his mental and moral vision, and as far as possible, to annihilate the power of reason. He must be able to detect no inconsistencies in slavery; he must be made to feel that slavery is right; and he can be brought to that only when he ceases to be a man."

Here, Douglass recognized, was the ultimate dehumanization of slavery (as it was to be the ultimate triumph of the totalitarian state in George Orwell's *1984*). When you control peoples' minds, you can control them completely because then they cannot see their own oppression. But Douglass also recognized here the paradox that the slave system tried to conceal: namely, that slaves were indeed human beings whose minds had to be chained even more tightly than their bodies or they would begin to think and then they would break free. As Douglass' master had said, educate a slave and he or she will be a slave no longer. If that secret got out, slavery would be finished.

With this discovery, Douglass reports, "I understood the pathway from slavery to freedom"—it was education. And he was determined to take it: "I set out with high hope, and a fixed purpose, at whatever cost of trouble, to learn how to read."

He pursued the skills of literacy in any way he could, sometimes by inducing white people to help him without sensing his purpose. Then he shared his knowledge with other slaves, even holding his own secret "Sabbath school," where at one time he had "over forty scholars" who "came because they wished to learn," and were willing to risk a beating for it. "The work of instructing my dear fellow-slaves," he recalled of those days, "was the sweetest engagement with which I was ever blessed." For it gave him a sense of unity with his comrades born of both common suffering and common hope. "We were linked and inter-linked with each other," he says, and "I loved them with a love stronger than any thing I have ever experienced since." Here Douglass saw a human sense of community among slaves taking form, despite the masters, through the common quest to *learn*.

Teaching his fellow slaves to become free in mind by reading and thinking then emboldened Douglass to try to "live *upon free land*" himself. After some failed attempts, he managed in 1838 to escape to the North, where he not only found his physical freedom, but created his new identity as "Frederick Douglass." Learning how to read and write did in fact quite literally emancipate Douglass. It emancipated him first from his intellectual submission to slavery. Then it prompted him to gain physical freedom. Finally it gave him his identity as the free man

Frederick Douglass whose eloquent voice helped emancipate all slaves. Douglass' life story therefore goes from the dehumanization of slavery to an ennobling affirmation, and historical proof, of how education can humanize and literally set human beings free. The *Narrative* closes with an account of the day when this new man, the truly free Frederick Douglass, was born.

This occurred at an abolitionist gathering in Nantucket, Massachusetts, in 1841. Urged to address the gathering, Douglass was at first intimidated, because "the idea of speaking to white people weighed me down." And "the truth was," he admits, although legally free, "I felt myself a slave." Nevertheless, girding his courage, he stood up, and after speaking "a few moments," surprisingly "felt a considerable degree of freedom, and said what I desired with considerable ease." That freedom of speaking in words that flowed from his heart and gained form from his agile mind opened his new life as a witness and an advocate, "pleading the cause of my brethren."

Four years later Douglass published *Narrative of the Life of Frederick Douglass. An American Slave. Written by Himself.* Unlike some other "slave narratives," this was no mere collection of sensational stories written to enflame abolitionist passions. It was and remains a moving and eye-opening testimony to how human beings can treat other human beings like beasts, and can even do this in the name of religion, but that in the end those who try to dehumanize others dehumanize themselves more than their victims. It is also a monument to how, through intellectual awakening and moral courage, victims of inhumanity can become champions of humanity. If we are ever to put an end to inhumanity in our world, Frederick Douglass will be one of those who showed us how to do it.

THE KIND OF HEART-WRENCHING inhumanities that the young Frederick Douglass witnessed in American slavery, Elie Wiesel saw taken to even more grotesque and horrifying extremes in the night-
WIESEL
mare of the Jewish Holocaust. And, like Douglass, Wiesel would devote the rest of his life to bearing witness to what he saw and suffered.

Wiesel's little memoir, *Night*, the first of his many books, strikingly resembles Douglass' *Narrative* by recalling with spare eloquence epochal horrors of a youth that made Wiesel the man he became. But, unlike Douglass, Wiesel refrains from retrospectively interpreting the events he records. He lets his frightful story tell itself. The bits of commentary in it come from the voices of other people and from memories of his own emotions. Wiesel remembers these words and emotions because they taught him the deepest meanings of the Holocaust, as people responded to its monstrous realities first with stubborn disbelief, then with consoling skepticism, and finally with dumbfounded resignation. The most indelible of these words came from his own father, who gasped when he and Elie entered Auchwitz: "Anything is possible, even these crematories."

Anything is possible. We commonly use that phrase to spark hope, spur confidence, and inspire commitment. Wiesel turns it into a warning against unimagined evil. That is what his father's words taught him about the Holocaust. He now understood the tragic truth that "anything is possible"—a truth that might call to mind the pained words of Shakespeare's King Lear upon seeing his kingdom fall apart: "It is not the worst so long as we can say 'This is the worst.'" For if we convince ourselves that the *worst* is over, we can let even worse things occur. And that is the revelation of *Night*, making it an instructive companion to Douglass' *Narrative*. Both of these memoirs of inhumanity ruefully remind us that for all of the righteous principles of religion, and for all of ethical ideals of secular philosophy, and for all of the progress of civilization, *anything is possible. Alas.* Bleak as this idea is, it belongs in everyone's understanding of the human world—as does the hope of one day ending the evil of inhumanity for good.

Wiesel graphically records how even the victims—most remarkably the victims—of the Holocaust awakened to this idea only very slowly. Perhaps this should not surprise us. Believing the unbelievable, or anything never before imagined, is challenging, to say the least. Religions know this well, asking us to have faith in the supernatural. Samuel Taylor Coleridge gave the idea a secular spin by urging a "willing suspension of disbelief" when we encounter the unimaginable and unbelievable in art. But how do we respond when unbelievably terrible things happen before our very eyes, or even to us? First, we disbelieve them, distrusting our very senses. That is logical. But we do this at our peril. For this disbelief can allow terrible things to continue, and to happen again. And possibly to get worse. That is Elie Wiesel's nightmare.

From the outset, *Night* records the disbelief, denial, and then gradual awakening of Jews to the nightmare that was enfolding them. Wiesel remembers how the first news of what was happening reached his home town of Sighet, Transylvania (now Romania), in 1942. It came from a resident known as Moshé the Beadle, who had been deported with other foreign-born Jews earlier that year. Townspeople had explained the deportations at the time as an unfortunate expedient of war. Now, several months later, Moshé returned. He was a changed man. With "no longer any joy in his eye," Wiesel writes, he "went from one Jewish house to another" telling how the Nazis had slaughtered the whole trainload of deportees, and how he had escaped, wounded and left for dead. But people's reaction to him was almost as painful to him as the tale he told them. They "refused not only to believe his stories, but even to listen to them," Wiesel recalls. "'What an imagination he has!' they said." Moshé the Beadle's story was literally unimaginable and therefore *unbelievable*.

The young Wiesel knew Moshé personally because the two of them had often talked about their shared interest in Jewish mysticism. "Why are you so anxious that people should believe what you say?" Wiesel asked him, and Moshé answered: "I wanted to come back to warn you. . . . So that you could prepare yourselves while there was still time." But it was no use. No one *could* believe him. "I did not believe him myself," Wiesel admits. Unheeded, Moshé the Beadle grew "weary of speaking" and eventually "wandered in the synagogue or in the streets, with his eyes down" in silence. And "life returned to normal" in Sighet.

Over the next year and more, the Jews of Sighet received, with the same comforting disbelief, further news of terrible events occurring elsewhere. A flurry of disturbing rumors would arise, Wiesel says, "but not for long. Optimism soon revived." Then, when German soldiers arrived and settled into the town, they were viewed as "distant, but polite" residents, and "the Jews of Sighet continued to smile." Even when the Germans arrested Jewish leaders and began restricting the lives of Jews in Sighet—curfews, mandatory wearing of the yellow star, enclosing the Jewish ghetto in barbed wire—still few grave worries surfaced. "The general opinion was that we were going to remain in the ghetto until the end of the war. . . . Then everything would be as before."

That deceptive optimism confronted unsettling new realities when the Nazis forced the entire Jewish population of the town onto trains in the summer of 1944 for travel to an unknown destination. But once again, Wiesel heard only assurances that *this is the worst*. As a youth of fifteen, he might have been protected by well-meaning adults from their own bleaker forebodings and fears. But he remembers only repeated expressions of disbelief and denial among the Jews of Sighet about the night descending upon them as their trains pulled out of town.

They carried this disbelief with them to the concentration camp itself—although one woman on the train kept crying out along the way that she could see furnaces and flames, but she was generally dismissed as deranged. When they reached their destination, Auschwitz, they beheld what lay before them with blank bewilderment. "Surely it was all a nightmare," Wiesel remembers wondering, "an unimaginable nightmare?" For "flames were leaping up from a ditch, gigantic flames";

a truck "drew up at the pit and delivered its load—little children. Babies! Yes, I saw it with my own eyes." And yet, Wiesel could not believe what his eyes perceived. "I pinched my face. Was I still alive? Was I awake? I could not believe it. How could it be possible for them to burn people, children, and for the world to keep silent? No, none of this could be true. . . . Humanity would never tolerate it."

None of this could be true. Humanity would never tolerate it. How tragically wrong those humane expectations were. It was at this moment that Wiesel's father voiced his dire discovery: "Humanity? Humanity is not concerned with us. Today anything is allowed. Anything is possible, even these crematories." Here the young Elie Wiesel found the tragic enlightenment that changed his life.

"Never shall I forget that night," he writes, "the first night in camp, which has turned my life into one long night." That image of *night* gave him the meaning of the Holocaust and of his life thereafter: the truth that *anything is possible. Alas.* And that he must never cease testifying to it.

From that first night in the camp in the summer of 1944 until the liberation in April 1945, Wiesel witnessed and suffered a system of dehumanization such as the world had never known before. Frederick Douglass and other slaves had experienced something like it. But the Jewish Holocaust of the Nazi concentration camps defied all precedent in physical scale and inhuman purpose. And it tells us more disturbing truths about human nature and inhumanity.

Like the American slave system, the Nazi concentration camps tried to dehumanize their victims by eradicating human personality. The camps replaced names with numbers, they broke up families, they herded human beings like animals, and they deployed physical brutality frequently and capriciously. But American slavery had had a human purpose, however perverse. The slaves were productive property that served the economic ends of their masters. By contrast, the Jews in the camps had no human value at all. They were there only to be destroyed. They were detritus. "What have you come here for?" a hysterical prisoner shouted at a group of new arrivals in Auschwitz: "Don't you understand anything? You're to be burned. Frizzled away. Turned to ashes."

With death as their very purpose, the camps themselves, Wiesel remembers, took on an irrationally surreal air. Prisoners were shunted about aimlessly. They were forced to work endlessly. They were starved. They were subjected to brutalities at once abject, random, and indifferent. They were executed en masse because they were said to be less than human and did not deserve to live. It all defied common rationality and reality no less than it denied the Jews' humanity.

Bent on reducing human beings not only to animals but to ashes, the dehumanization of the Jews in the camps was unbounded and unrelenting. And it did reduce some of its victims to the base animal instinct for survival. In one depressing scene Wiesel describes a cluster of prisoners clashing over food like "wild beasts of prey," and he recalls another prisoner attacking his own father for a piece of bread.

And yet, as in Douglass' account of slavery, nothing in Wiesel's record of the concentration camps ultimately shakes us more than the dehumanization of the masters. How could anyone behave as the Nazi masters did? They proved capable of inhumanities that surpass all normal understanding. These masters might justify themselves with the Nazi ideology of racial superiority—like the perverted Christianity of Douglass' slaveholders. But Wiesel also shows them acting from more of what Hannah Arendt famously discerned in the Nazi villain Adolph Eichmann: "the banality of evil." They could herd and torture and kill human beings with a dull, unreflecting impersonality. Either way, they seem less human than their victims.

The dehumanization of the Nazis themselves in the death camps, like that of the worst slaveholders, is more troubling than it is surprising. It is troubling because it proves not only that human beings are capable of any evil, but that the humane values of modern Western civilization did not restrain these Nazis from committing any evil. We like to think that cultural refinement and education and religion and so on in one way or another make us more human and humane. But Wiesel, like Douglass, discloses the hard truth that none of these, and not even all of them together, necessarily do that. Both authors also confront us with an even harder truth, which history has demonstrated again and again—and which Thomas Mann identified particularly with art (see Chapter 25). That truth is: civilization and education and religion and cultural refinement can actually make us less humane than we otherwise might be. Christian slaveholders could piously quote Scripture while whipping slaves, and the Nazis could send Jews to the gas chambers with moral superiority, and possibly while humming Beethoven's "Ode to Joy"—just as troops of the Marxist Pol Pot could murder millions of their Cambodian countrymen in the 1970s while invoking humanistic social philosophy, and just as religious fanatics of any stripe readily destroy human lives for spiritual truth. Inhumanity can occur not only despite lofty ideals, but sometimes because of them.

And this returns us to the idea at the center of *Night*, the idea that has haunted Wiesel since the events the book records: anything is possible. With these words Wiesel warns us that we should never let our religion or education or cultural refinement or anything else convince us that these elevate us above the moral claims of common humanity or that the worst inhumanities of humankind lie in the past. For human beings will remain capable of inhumanities we might not yet have imagined and might not believe possible. This, as Wiesel vowed to keep saying, we should never forget.

Discovering this unhappy truth made Wiesel actually question his own religious convictions. For, in a world where "anything is possible, even these crematories," God, if there is a God, indifferently permits anything to happen (Dostoevsky's Ivan Karamazov anticipated Wiesel's very words when picturing a universe with no God). "My eyes were open," Wiesel says, "and I was alone . . . without God and without man." And from there he began to see his humanistic mission. "I was no longer capable of lamentation," he explains. "On the contrary, I felt very strong . . . stronger than the Almighty to whom my life had been tied for so long."

The Russian novelist Alexander Solzhenitsyn had his fictional prison camp victim, Ivan Denisovich, turn from God to himself for similar reasons in *One Day in the Life of Ivan Denisovich* (1963). And the Western humanistic tradition has seen many others do much the same thing, from Homer in the *Iliad* to Virginia Woolf in *Mrs. Dalloway* to Jean-Paul Sartre in existentialism, to name only these (see Chapters 1, 9, 18). With his mournful voice, Wiesel joined this long tradition. Instead of becoming a Jewish mystic and scholar as he had intended, he became a witness to how, in this world, God or no God, ideals or no ideals, inhumanity can flourish, and human beings must do anything they can to prevent this.

So, besides urging us to imagine the unimaginable and prepare to believe the unbelievable, Wiesel—like Douglass—reminds us that whatever religious or cultural ideals we live by, if we are to prevent inhumanity, in ourselves and others, we must embrace the humane values of our common humanity. When we think about what these kinds of humane values are, we might call to mind the so-called Golden Rule of Confucius and Jesus, which tells us to treat others as we wish to be treated. Or, we might think of something more philosophical, like Immanuel Kant's principles that we should always treat human beings as an end, not a means, and that we should act only in ways that we could make into a "universal law" for everyone. Or we might think of the empathy that Rousseau and the poet Percy Bysshe Shelley considered the source of all morals (see Chapters 6, 23). Wiesel was not so explicit. He conveys his humane message in *Night* simply through stark reports of the dehumanization of the Nazi masters, and through poignant renderings of human beings serving human life, as in the love he shared with his father, who died one night in the bunk above him, and in his gratitude to another prisoner who beautifully played a violin into the night just before that prisoner was killed.

We might therefore conclude from *Night* that to thwart inhumanity, to be truly humane, we must, among other things, embrace the likes of kindness and charity, generosity and gratitude, honesty and responsibility, and tolerance and respect for the humanity of all human beings. Such are the humane values of a truly humanistic civilization. And the last of these values brings us to Martin Luther King, Jr.

No one has spelled out the principle of respect for all human beings more concisely and persuasively than Martin Luther King, Jr. He did this while in jail on one occasion during the American civil

KING

rights movement of the 1960s, when—a little over a century after Frederick Douglass had escaped from slavery and written his autobiography—the legacy of slavery persisted in racial segregation. King had taken it upon himself to uproot that legacy. But his methods got him into hot water because, among other things, those methods called for openly breaking segregationist laws.

On this occasion, King had landed in jail for leading an illegal protest in Birmingham, Alabama, to pressure local merchants and politicians into abolishing the city's systematic discrimination against black people —segregationist ordinances, prejudicial court rulings, racist signs, and unpunished racial violence. A group of fellow clergymen had criticized King for deploying the wrong tactics. Although they did not dispute his goals, they said he should not be so impatient for change, and he should certainly not break the law. He replied in a letter that set forth the reasons for his actions.

But King's "Letter from the Birmingham Jail" did not just explain and defend his tactics for winning the civil rights battle. That is the least of it. King used this occasion to go to the core of what civil rights are— or "human rights," as we think of them more generally today—and why civilization must protect these rights at all cost.

Invoking Socrates as a mentor who got jailed for trying to liberate people from "the bondage of myths and half-truths," King describes in a few short lucid pages how he was trying to do much the same thing. In particular, he wanted to free African-Americans from segregationist laws. But the issue was bigger than that. King argued that it was nothing less than the difference between justice and injustice. And to make his case he set out to draw a clear and convincing distinction between a "just law" and an "unjust law."

The fact that a democratically elected legislature has enacted a law, King points out, does not make that law just. And if a law is unjust, it is not binding. That is the nub of King's case for his own law-breaking tactics. "One has not only a legal but a moral responsibility to obey just laws," he explains, but "one has a moral responsibility to disobey unjust laws." That is a bold declaration. And it could grant anyone license to decide that any law they don't like is unjust and therefore unbinding, as many of King's critics charged—and as Socrates himself had warned his friends in *Crito* (see Chapter 3). But King has a good defense against this charge. He contends that the difference between a just and an unjust law is not merely a matter of opinion. It reflects a universal standard—Socrates would like that. That standard is: "Any law that uplifts human personality is just," and "any law that degrades human personality is unjust."

This may be a fine humane principle for promoting the legal respect for people. But it is mighty vague. What does "human personality" mean? And who is to say what "uplifts" or "degrades" it? Answering these questions, King adds more detail. "A just law," he goes on, "is a code that a majority compels a minority to follow and that it is willing to follow itself." This, he adds, is "*sameness* made legal." By contrast, "an unjust law is a code that a numerical or power majority group compels a minority group to obey but does not make binding on itself." This is "*difference* made legal." In other words, King defines "human personality" as the elemental humanity of all human beings—including physical, intellectual, social, and emotional needs—that must be respected and "uplifted." A law that respects and uplifts this humanity in all people is therefore a just law. But a law that intentionally disrespects and "degrades" that humanity in some people while uplifting it in others is an unjust law. That is King's universal standard. And it is a good one.

Universal sameness made legal, or hierarchical difference made legal. That contrast goes back to the days of the American Revolution and the founding of American democracy. It strikes the crucial democratic distinction between legitimate equality and illegitimate privilege. But crucial as this distinction is, American democracy has been slow to live up to it. By making it the measure of just and unjust laws, whether those laws are democratically enacted or not, Martin Luther King, Jr., raised the stakes for democracy and human rights. After all, as he notes, "everything Adolf Hitler did in Germany was 'legal,'" permitting the Nazis to "degrade" the "human personality" of millions of people. American slavery was legal, too, as Fredrick Douglass knew all too well. And so were the laws of racial segregation that King vowed to uproot. Although technically democratic because they were legislated by a majority (in a triumph of "faction" such as James Madison had inveighed against in

Federalist #10—see Chapter 14), these segregationist laws had as their very purpose, King emphasized, to give "the segregator a false sense of superiority and the segregated a false sense of inferiority." And this instilled in the "segregated" a "degenerating sense of 'nobodiness.'" King wanted everyone to see not only the misuse of democracy in this, but the very degradation of "human personality."

For these reasons, going to the core of human rights, King explained to his fellow clergymen that to endure unjust laws, however enacted, amounts to enduring inhumanity. No human beings should have to do that. Not in the name of legality. Not in the name of democracy. Not in the name of patience. And not, he might have added, in the name of any purportedly higher principles, like religious truth. Therefore, King concluded, if negotiation fails to undo unjust laws, justice "must be demanded by the oppressed" through all kinds of "direct action" like his own: protests, marches, openly violating unjust laws, and so on, anything short of violence—Gandhi, not Christianity, had taught him this. Pay the price of imprisonment or death if necessary, he says, as many fighters for freedom and justice have had to do. But do not pay the price of enduring the inhumanity of legal degradation and "nobodiness."

The history of civil rights in America largely played out King's principles. And if the campaign for human rights around the world is to succeed, more and more people must also adopt those principles. People must agree that justice consists in universal sameness made legal because this respects and elevates the humanity of everyone. And they must agree that injustice consists in hierarchical differences made legal because this disrespects and degrades the humanity of some people while elevating the humanity of others. But even agreement on these principles does not, of course, make them easy to legislate. We frequently debate how to put them into law. And, to be sure, there are still plenty of people in this world who see these principles as a threat to cultural traditions that, often for religious reasons, assign people different places and privileges in society. But if it is humanity we wish to serve, and inhumanity we wish to end, the principles of justice and injustice in King's "Letter from the Birmingham Jail" must be among those to guide us.

THE ACCOUNT OF AMERICAN SLAVERY by Douglass, and of the Jewish Holocaust by Wiesel, and of racial segregation in America by King disclose much that is disturbing about human nature and civilization. As witnesses to some of history's worst inhumanities—so far—they prove that the human capacity for inhumanity is frightening, and that despite, and sometimes because of, religion and ideology, education, and cultural refinement, this capacity can go unconstrained. But we can also draw from these witnesses an appreciation of the kinds of humane values—including charity, kindness, generosity, gratitude, honesty, tolerance, and respect—that can protect us from inhumanity in ourselves, as well as in others. So, if besides learning from Douglass, Wiesel, and King about the worst in human nature we also learn to cultivate such values in ourselves and to nurture them in others, we will owe those authors a great debt. We might even one day owe them the greatest debt of all: helping humankind to put an end to inhumanity for good.

On the Causes and Cure of Inhumanity

1. The human capacity for inhumanity knows no bounds.

2. Anything is possible—alas. (Wiesel)

3. People become inhumane when they exalt themselves and dehumanize others.

4. Inhumanity thrives on the self-deceptions of moral superiority.

5. Religion, education, idealism, and cultural refinement can justify, and even intensify, inhumanity rather than prevent it.

6. Inhumanity dehumanizes the masters even more than the victims.

7. To prevent inhumanity, we must make it known wherever it occurs.

8. To prevent inhumanity, we must replace unjust laws with just laws. (King)

9. Unjust laws intentionally elevate the dignity of some people and degrade that of others—this is difference made legal. (King)

10. Just laws respect the dignity of all people—this is sameness made legal. (King)

11. To prevent inhumanity, we must recognize it and learn to be humane.

12. To be humane, we must live by humane values like charity, generosity, gratitude, honesty, tolerance, and respect, no matter what else our education or religion or philosophy or culture teaches us.

13. The meaning of life is to embrace humane values in every form and fight inhumanity everywhere.

17

The Psychology of Everyday Life

Sigmund Freud: *Civilization and Its Discontents*

Life, as we find it, is too hard for us.

There is no golden rule which applies to everyone: every man must find out for himself in what particular fashion he can be saved.

Freud

Sigmund Freud (1857–1939) started his career as a medical doctor in nineteenth-century Vienna and died in London on the eve of World War II as one of the most influential thinkers of the twentieth century. Moving beyond medicine and his early studies of hysteria and of its then-innovative cure, hypnosis, Freud offered his own revolutionary theory of the psyche in *The Interpretation of Dreams*, published as the new century dawned in 1900. This theory revolved around the idea that virtually everything we think and do serves psychological purposes, and that these purposes can be heavily disguised because "psychic reality"—conscious or unconscious—often takes precedence over physical reality for us (fantasy over fact, repression over desire). Freud's theory also included the unconventional claim that much of what people think and do involves sex. But Freud did not think of sex as only a biological urge. It was eros, the libido, the creative energy of life. Freud soon elaborated on these ideas in *The Psychopathology of Everyday Life* (1904), *Three Essays on the Theory of Sexuality* (1905), and other writings. By 1909 his theories of "psychoanalysis" were sufficiently recognized in the fledgling science of psychology that he was invited to the United States to explain them before a gathering of American psychologists in lectures later published as *The Origins and Development of Psychoanalysis*. Freud spawned many disciples, and saw several of them defect, but he never doubted that he had discovered the deepest secrets of human nature.

Freud went on to expand his theories of psychoanalysis along increasingly far-reaching and philosophical lines in many articles and books, such as *Totem and Taboo* (1913), *Beyond the Pleasure Principle* (1920), *The Ego and the Id* (1923), *The Future of an Illusion* (1927), and *Moses and Monotheism* (1939). And in *Civilization and Its Discontents* (1930) he synthesized his chief ideas as they had evolved. This book shows us, through Freud's eyes, our lives in all of their desires and disappointments, fantasies and necessities, energies and pathologies. It also shows us why civilization exists as it does and why we must honestly understand ourselves to the depths if we are to be healthy-minded and to make civilization good for us.

FEW THINKERS, if any (there is always Aristotle), have said so much about so many of the twists and turns in human life as Sigmund Freud. Nothing that people do or think or feel was a stranger to him (even truer of Freud than of Aristotle). He wanted to understand it all—how every action and idea, every feeling and fantasy, every conscious act or unconscious desire, comes to be, and why. From this ambition came the minute observations, the probing analyses, the ingenious interpretations that created psychoanalysis as a theory of human nature that has no equals in the height of its ambitions and the depths of its explorations.

Freud may be best known today for his dramatic accounts of roiling sexual appetites, rending Oedipal struggles, and weird pathological behavior. But it is not these accounts that make Freud most worth reading for most people. It is rather what he had to say about the ordinary life with its everyday exertions and frustrations, its normal joys and sorrows, its common hopes and fears, even if he saw this ordinary life beset by psychological pitfalls.

Although trained as a physician to diagnose and cure physical illnesses, Freud proclaimed in the year his revolutionary *The Interpretation of Dreams* appeared—which had miniscule sales until Freud had gained renown—that he was less a physician or a scientist than a "conquistador by temperament, an adventurer" of the psychic frontier. And in exploring that frontier Freud increasingly left cure behind to conquer bolder terrain. "I am not basically interested in therapy," he confessed to a colleague. In fact, he explained to another, serving "therapeutic needs . . . is not the main or even the essential aim of psychoanalysis. The chief aim is to contribute to the science of psychology and to the world of literature and life in general." And later he would say: "My discoveries are not primarily a heal-all; my discoveries are the basis for a very grave philosophy." This was nothing less than a philosophy of life.

With his expansive intellectual vision, his genius for psychological interpretation, and his talent for evocative prose, Freud wrote about everything from toilet training and slips of the tongue to the making of civilization. A decade before his death, Freud wove together his sweeping conclusions about all of this in a little volume known in English as *Civilization and Its Discontents*.

Freud says there that he wrote the book after the novelist Romain Rolland criticized his book on religion, *The Future of an Illusion*, for failing to perceive "the true source of religious sentiment." That source consists, Rolland had said, in "a peculiar feeling . . . a feeling as of something limitless, unbounded—as it were 'oceanic.'" Conceding to Rolland that this feeling might exist, although he could find no traces of it in himself, Freud began reflecting on where such a feeling could come from and how it is related to other feelings. Typical of him, Freud wanted to know how this or any other *feeling* can matter so much to us, and can even give meaning and purpose to our lives.

Starting from here, Freud went on to ask: How do people find meaning and purpose of any kind in life, and what do these meanings tell us about human nature and human culture?

This is the central subject of *Civilization and Its Discontents*. It is an age-old subject. But Freud's explorations of it are distinctly his own. And they take us beyond the Freud of sexual pathology to the Freud of the psychology of everyday life. *Civilization and Its Discontents* is therefore about everyone, everywhere. Most of us can find ourselves in it pretty easily, as we pursue our wishes, manage our desires, suffer our hurts, and generally mold the lives we so imperfectly and yet so hopefully live. And it is to learn more about how to do these things well that we should read this little book on its big subject.

FREUD BEGINS WHERE ARISTOTLE had begun that first Western book on why people live as they do, the *Nicomachean Ethics* (see Chapter 4). That is, with the common-sense observation that people want to be happy. What do people "show by their behavior to be the purpose and intention of their lives?" he asks. "The answer can hardly be in doubt," he replies: "They strive after happiness." But whereas Aristotle had taken this as an unassailable fact because that is what "ordinary and cultured people" say, and he had then laid out a practical plan for getting happiness, Freud looks deeper. He wants to know what happiness itself really is, why it can take such various and even peculiar forms, and why it is so difficult to find. This curiosity led Freud to the discoveries that he believed unlocked the most hidden and profound secrets of human nature and culture.

Freud found such significance in our pursuit of happiness because he learned that happiness is not just a nice feeling that comes over us when, say, we are in a good mood or when we get something that we want. Freud's conception of happiness is more complicated. "A feeling can only be the source of energy" or satisfaction, Freud says, "if it is itself the expression of a strong need." Therefore, "what we call happiness in the strictest sense," he explains, "comes from the (preferably sudden) satisfaction of needs which have been dammed up to a high degree."

This definition seems rather mechanistic. And Freud often tended to describe human beings as hydraulic contraptions moved by needs and energies, restraints and releases. But he does not stop at such descriptions. Freud was too much a poet at heart for that. He goes on quickly to equate happiness with "strong feelings of pleasure." And he hastens to point out that we can't get this pleasure without restraint. "We are so made," he declares, "that we can derive intense enjoyment only from a contrast and very little from a state of things." In other words, pleasure depends on pain, and it can never last long. Consequently the pursuit of pleasure can never entirely work for us. Although "an unrestricted satisfaction of every need presents itself as the most enticing method of conducting one's life," Freud says, this "method" is bound to fail because every satisfaction "soon brings its own punishment" as the psychic pendulum swings back to dissatisfaction. These discoveries led Freud to the doleful conclusion that, if the essence of happiness is pleasure, and if pleasure is fleeting and depends on pain, we're going to have difficulty making happiness "the purpose and intention" of our lives.

And that is exactly what Freud takes to be the fundamental truth of human life. Asking himself a question that has surely agitated human beings from the beginning, "Why [is it] so hard for men to be happy?" Freud ruefully answers: "One feels inclined to say that the intention that man should be 'happy' is not included in the plan of 'creation.'"

The "plan of creation" is flawed indeed when it pits natural human needs against natural human impossibilities. This was the angry complaint of Goethe's Faust, driving him to team up with the devil (see Chapter 7). But Freud is not as outraged as Faust. He does see some hope for happiness, or rather for getting enough of something like happiness to make life worth living. This hope turns out to lie not in pursuing pleasure itself—which many a thinker has warned against, if not for Freud's psychological reasons—but in going the other way: protecting ourselves against pain, or, as Freud says, in the "avoidance of unpleasure." We avoid "unpleasure," Freud explains, when we "moderate [our] claims to happiness" and learn to be "happy merely to have escaped unhappiness or to have survived suffering." This is an attenuated, even negative, happiness, to be sure, if it is happiness at all. But Freud figured it is the most we can get—as Hindus and Buddhists, and even the ancient Epicureans, had also decided (see Chapter 2).

With this idea of attenuated happiness, Freud readied himself to probe the psychology of everyday life in detail, where he suspected that, whether we know it or not, we try to avoid "unpleasure" more often than to pursue pleasure. And he handily identified two overarching strategies that we all follow either to pursue pleasure or to avoid unpleasure.

Freud called the first strategy "the Pleasure Principle." This is the "primary" and infantile urge of human beings to sate every hunger, slake every thirst, crave every comfort, act on every desire, and expect immediate satisfaction all the time. No restraint or compromise. A life lived wholly under the Pleasure Principle would be a straightforward and rather childlike affair: nature untamed.

The second strategy Freud called "the Reality Principle." A life lived under the Reality Principle is much more complex than one lived under the Pleasure Principle. That is because the "avoidance of unpleasure" is more subtle and ambiguous than the straightforward pursuit of pleasure, just as adulthood is more complicated than childhood, and long-term satisfactions more difficult to achieve than immediate delights. In leading us through the treacherous terrain of a world where pain threatens us from every side, the Reality Principle gives our lives the bewildering diversity, both normal and abnormal, that continually surprises us, and that makes civilization what it so variously and inventively is. For the Reality Principle constantly grapples with that saddest of all truths, which Freud spelled out in plain words: "Life, as we find it, is too hard for us; it brings us too many pains, disappointments and impossible tasks." The Reality Principle tells us why this is so, and what we can do about it.

Not one to shrink from bold claims, Freud launches his explanation of how the Reality Principle works by first describing life as a struggle against three causes of pain. "We are threatened with suffering from three directions," he says: "from our own body, which is doomed to decay and dissolution and which cannot even do without pain and anxiety as warning signals; from the external world, which may rage against us with overwhelming and merciless forces of destruction; and finally from our relations to other men." The body, the material world, and other people. A tidy accounting of the enemies of happiness.

Freud counts the Reality Principle's techniques for avoiding these pains, or for pursuing "happiness in the reduced sense in which we recognize it as possible," just as neatly. Although "every man must find out for himself" how best to live, Freud observes, the options fall into three general categories: "how much real satisfaction he can expect to get from the external world; how far he is led to make himself independent of it; and, finally, how much strength he feels he has for altering the world to suit his wishes." In other words, however we live our lives, we are always doing one or more of these three things: adapting ourselves to the world as we find it, going outside of that world, or trying to change it. And usually we are doing some of all three.

Simplistic? Maybe. But look at what this idea helps us see about the patterns of our lives. Politicians, for example, adapt themselves to the world by working with other people, but they also try to change the world through legislation. Scientists adapt themselves to the world by trying to discover how nature works, but their discoveries can also change the world; at the same time, scientists may be happiest when lost in the mental activity of science itself, which takes them outside of the world. Lovers adapt themselves to the world by attaching themselves to a beloved companion, and they may change the world by having children, but they also take themselves outside of the world by living for the transports of romantic love itself. Then there are those who try to live almost entirely outside of the world in order to escape its pains, rather than even attempting to adapt to it or to change it. Among these are ascetics, who deny the flesh so they won't suffer from its physical pains, and hermits, who sever themselves from the social world to skirt the emotional injuries caused by other people—Molière's Alceste, the misanthrope, vowed to do just that (see Chapter 12). Freud also put here those people who live for religious feelings of the kind Romain Rolland had described. By steeping themselves in the "oceanic feeling," Freud argued, religious believers feel at one with a benign universe and a beneficent god, and therefore they feel "saved" no matter what happens to them in this world (for kindred reasons, Karl Marx dubbed religion an opiate: an emotional painkiller for a deprived life—see Chapter 15).

Crude as these sketches may be, they indicate the surprising and diverse turns that the tactics of the Reality Principle can take as people try to avoid pain—more than to pursue pleasure—by adapting to the world, going outside of it, or trying to change it. Always complex, often entangled, these tactics largely make us who we are in our multivarious ways. As Freud says, invoking religious language for our pursuit of happiness, "There is no golden rule which applies to everyone: every man must find out for himself in what particular fashion he can be saved."

Thanks to these tactics of the Reality Principle, human beings have also won many battles against the three primary causes of pain. Many of these victories have come from changing the world through advances in civilization. We have scored successes against sufferings of the body by anesthetizing its hurts, curing its illnesses, and prolonging its life. We have gained triumphs against the forces of nature, or the material world, by controlling their powers and harnessing their energies. And we have achieved advances against troubles from other people by prescribing ethics to restrain selfish impulses, and establishing the rule of law and the reign of justice to pacify conflicts.

At the same time, Freud emphasizes, along with these defensive victories against the three sources of pain, the Reality Principle has also given rise to a most refined mode of human satisfaction, one that links the Reality Principle with the Pleasure Principle to protect us from pains and deliver some pleasures. This is the kind of satisfaction that occurs in what Freud called the "internal, psychical processes"—namely, mind and imagination.

Of the many achievements of the Reality Principle, Freud judged none so momentous as this. For it was by cultivating "satisfaction in [the] internal, psychical processes" of mind and imagination that human beings first learned to understand the world as it is and then to change it. Philosophy, science, law, and psychoanalysis itself were among the creations of mind and imagination that brought these benefits. But, along with these benefits in changing the world, the "satisfactions" of mind and imagination also give us a gratifying escape, or *psychological independence*, from the world. And Freud believed that the best of these worldly benefits, as well as the best kind of psychological independence from the world, come with that most fecund and rewarding of the "internal, psychical processes," *sublimation*.

Today sublimation is commonly thought of as channeling one kind of energy and pleasure into another—such as transfering the energies and pleasures of sex into those of athletics. But originally, and in Freud's usage, "sublimated" pleasures were not simply substitute pleasures. They were "finer and higher," more elevated (as connoted by the Latin word *sublimis*, meaning "lifted above," which is the root of the English words "sublime" and "sublimation," as well as the German *Sublimierung*). Some sublimation may occur in most of the work we do because work not only helps us defend ourselves against the sources of pain in the world, it also often lifts us above the world—Freud mentions Voltaire's *Candide* in this light for its conclusion that we should cultivate our gardens. Still, Freud considered sublimation to be primarily the "psychical and intellectual work" of mind and imagination, and he suggested that its "finer and higher" pleasures can be attained only by those endowed with "special dispositions and gifts." In any case, Freud was convinced that without sublimation, civilization would not even exist because human beings would still be living like animals in nature. "No feature seems better to characterize civilization than this," Freud writes: the "esteem and encouragement of man's higher mental activities—his intellectual, scientific, and artistic achievements—and the leading role that it assigns to ideas in human life." At its best, therefore, civilization is the child of sublimation.

Through the ingenuities of sublimation, we produce our finest achievements and can gain our loftiest satisfactions (although these may be "mild" compared to the pleasures of "our primary instinctual impulses" that "convulse our physical being"). But Freud saw another "psychical process" that developed along with sublimation, too. This also belongs in part to both the Reality Principle and the Pleasure Principle. It provides psychological independence from the world, but its chief purpose is to yield immediate pleasure. This "psychical process" is fantasy. And we all use it regularly—sometimes more than we should.

As civilization has increasingly removed human beings from the world of nature into the psychical world of culture, Freud contends, fantasy has ascended in importance. The pleasures of fantasy can be aroused by artistic creations, including entertainment, but they come most often in the sheer play of imagination. Be they artistic or merely imaginative, the pleasures of fantasy take us out of this world. And they do this by fulfilling wishes inside of us, free of the restraints of external reality. The Reality Principle helped create the realm of fantasy to make us independent of the world, but in that realm, the Pleasure Principle reigns, because there we can be free of the Reality Principle's practical demands. Whether playfully as children building castles in the sand, or longingly as adults building castles in the air, whether in daydreams or night dreams, we get immediate pleasures from our fantasies that real life must deny or defer—in our fantasies, we are anything we want to be.

Fantasy is a good and necessary thing, granting many innocent pleasures that are generally fleeting, conscious, and benign escapes into imaginary wish-fulfillment. We go in and out of them at will as instructed by the Reality Principle. Freud points out that artists do this all the time, turning their fantasies into artworks that earn money to help them live in the real world. But Freud also warned that fantasy can eclipse reality if it flies too far away from the Reality Principle. When it does that, as in neurosis and psychosis, or even in an obsession with some ideal or desire or pleasure, we lose mastery of our lives in the real world—as some people accuse Don Quixote of doing, and as Flaubert's Emma Bovary surely did (see Chapters 22, 24). Those unhappy consequences of fantasy actually inspired Freud's creation of psychoanalysis in the first place, first as a therapy for people whose fantasies, Freud concluded, had pathologically taken over their lives, then as a psychology of everyday life for anyone seeking the happiness that can be ours through the tactics of the Reality Principle. Like sublimation, fantasy is a gift of human psychology nurtured by civilization. But we must use it well or it will lead us astray.

Sigmund Freud: *Civilization and Its Discontents*

As CIVILIZATION HAS EVOLVED through the tactics of the Reality Principle, human beings have gained much. We have improved our material conditions, harnessed forces of nature, achieved a measure of social justice, attained the knowledge of science and the insights of ideas, and created the beauties of art. But we have lost something, too. For the rewards of the Reality Principle exact a price. And it is paid in the restraint of our animal appetites or "impulses," which Freud loosely labeled the id (in contrast to the rational ego and the judgmental superego). When we ask if the strategies of the Reality Principle have enhanced the pleasures of our animal impulses, Freud answers with a resounding NO! And there, Freud says, lies the cause of the "discontents" of civilization.

To get the benefits of civilization, Freud says, human beings had to curtail, deny, repress, or sublimate many instinctual desires that could run free outside of civilization. In a manner of speaking, they had to "denature" themselves. This is, of course, an old idea. Jean-Jacques Rousseau won notoriety in the eighteenth century for extolling the precivilized "natural man"—although he also argued that this natural man must be "denatured" by society in order to become the higher type of "natural man in society" (see Chapter 6). And not long before Freud, Friedrich Nietzsche had foreshadowed him by observing that human beings became "interesting" when social life forced their instinctual energies inward, making those energies "creative" in forming morality and culture (see Chapter 8). But Freud went beyond his predecessors in devising the psychoanalytic theory of how human nature and civilization constantly make war and peace with each other. Human beings became psychologically complicated and culturally creative, as well as fraught with discontents—and therefore primed for psychoanalysis—as the very civilization they produced compelled them to thwart part of themselves.

At first Freud interpreted these discontents, or the various pathologies presented to him, as symptoms primarily of the sexual repressions conspicuous in the late Victorian years of the nineteenth century when he formulated his theories. But by the time he wrote *Civilization and Its Discontents* he had detected other kinds of symptoms arising from restraint of an instinct or energies other than sex or the more general desire for libidinous pleasure. That was the instinct to aggression. With this discovery that aggressiveness is as natural to human beings as sexuality, that the urge to death and destruction is as innate as the desire for pleasure and life and creation, that in our souls eros has enemies, Freud added a disturbing feature to his portrait of human nature, prompted in part by the violence of World War I. (The instinct to aggression derives from, but is not identical to, the "death instinct" that Freud first murkily defined in *Beyond the Pleasure Principle*.)

Was he right? Thinkers have debated the notion for centuries. Those who claim that human nature is inherently vicious, like Machiavelli and Hobbes, take Freud's side. Those who insist that human beings are innately benign and only learn to be vicious, like Rousseau and Karl Marx, take the other. Right or wrong, Freud drew some typically provocative conclusions from his point of view. And these shed light on much that we think and do.

"Men are not gentle creatures who want to be loved," he asserts, "and who at most can defend themselves if they are attacked; they are on the contrary, creatures among whose instinctual endowments is to be reckoned a powerful share of aggressiveness." This aggressiveness "constitutes the greatest impediment to civilization," Freud goes on, because it "reveals man as a savage beast to whom consideration for his own kind is something alien." By nature, human beings would rather kill each other than be kind. So their aggressiveness must be controlled, and therefore social virtues must be learned, if civilization is to exist.

Freud saw us imposing this control and learning these social virtues through many devices of civilized life. One of them is what he calls "psychical reaction-formations." These are ideals that induce us to behave as though the instinct to aggression, or the urge to vicious selfishness, did not exist. The Christian injunction to "love one's neighbor as oneself" is among them. The central doctrines of Communism—flourishing when Freud wrote—are another, asserting that "man is wholly good . . . but that the institution of private property has corrupted his nature." Freud concedes that these are appealing ideals. But he contends they are fallacious. For whatever "paths the development of civilization" takes, he warns, "one thing we can expect . . . is that this indestructible feature of human nature," aggressiveness, "will follow it there." And yet Freud's very point about such humane ideals is that we need them all the more precisely because they are purely ideal and deny the bestial streak in human nature. If human beings were naturally good, we would not need ethical ideals at all. Ethical ideals are "really justified," Freud insists, by "the fact that nothing else runs so strongly counter to the original nature of man." (Molière's Philinte wittily makes the same case in *The Misanthrope*—see Chapter 12.)

Perhaps we do, as Freud says, create the "psychical reaction-formations" of ethical ideals to convince ourselves that we are something we are not—kind instead of cruel, selfless instead of selfish. At all events, human beings seem to need ethics in order to be good. And when this doesn't work, we have other techniques. Among them are, of course, public laws and legal punishments. Not so obvious, and therefore more interesting to Freud, are what amount to psychological laws and punishments. The most effective of these involve the inner pain of conscience that we feel as *guilt*.

The "sense of guilt," Freud says, is self-punishment inflicted on us by our own aggressive energies turned inward through the restraints of civilization—just as benign sublimation and pathological symptoms come from the restraint of sexual energies. Be that as it may, guilt strikes when we hear a voice inside chastise us for failing to meet any of civilization's demands. We commonly call this voice our conscience. Freud called it the superego.

Whether Freud is correct about our inborn aggressiveness—he might have modified his opinion if he had known about testosterone—Freud's theory of how the superego functions is among the best and most useful of Freud's ideas. For practical purposes, we might reduce the theory to this: When civilization wants us to do something, it not only sets standards of behavior, imposes explicit restraints, and metes out punishments, it also insinuates all of these into our very psyches, and that creates the superego.

The superego speaks inside of us first for our parents, because they are the ones who originally taught us rules and punished us for breaking them. But through our parents and other persons of authority it speaks for civilization, which established the rules. And it speaks not just as an echoing voice. It also acts as the law, the judge, and the agent of punishment. When we fail to live up to the demands of civilization, we might escape physical punishment with lies and cunning or just by running away. But if the superego has been well developed in us, we cannot escape its punishments from the inside. They go wherever we go. The superego sees our every failing. Not just moral lapses either. Failure to meet any standard of behavior, like parental expectations of achievement, has the same effect—which is why children of high-achieving parents often feel guilty for not living up to their parents' standards. The superego inscribes standards within us, and if we fail to meet them it punishes us with inescapable self-reproach, or with a disquieting feeling of inadequacy, or even "a sort of malaise, a dissatisfaction" (Freud's word is *Unbehagen*, translated in the title as "Discontents"). It is all guilt.

Bear in mind that the superego and the punishment of guilt depend on subtle, psychological nurturing. This means using psychological rather than physical punishments—such as a parent punishing a child by withdrawing love or expressing disappointment instead of spanking him or her. In fact, physical punishment tends to work against the fostering of guilt. Children who experience frequent physical punishment do not learn to internalize rules and self-punishment, and they often become unruly, even violent and criminal—and a pattern of physical child abuse can be passed down through generations. But by the same token, parents who try too hard to instill guilt with repeated reminders of failure and severe psychological punishments can cultivate guilt-ridden, self-denigrating children—Franz Kafka, the epic storyteller of this most civilized malaise, showed how consuming, perverse, and debilitating this guilt can be. Or it can also happen that parents lose moral authority over their children by attempting to "guilt" them into too much obedience. The superego must be nurtured carefully or it will turn against us and civilization.

Whatever its form, the "sense of guilt" is a most deft invention of civilization for getting its way with us through the superego—or, more accurately, it is a way for us to deal with each other according to civilized standards of behavior. But while Freud considered the psychology of guilt a necessary condition of advanced civilization, just as are the "psychical processes," he also considered it "the most important problem in the development of civilization." For guilt gets stronger as civilization tightens its control over us, primarily, so Freud believed, over our aggressive impulses.

Following Freud, some anthropologists distinguished between cultures that have relied on shame as a punishment, and those that have relied on guilt. Shame cultures, typically premodern or tribal, shape behavior through the external devices of explicit, rigid rules and the harsh public punishments of shame—like the scarlet letter worn for her adultery by Nathaniel Hawthorne's Hester Prynne. Guilt cultures shape behavior through the internal devises of exacting, sometimes implicit, expectations, and the subtle psychological punishments of guilt. But however potent the punishments of shame can be, an offender can escape these punishments just by fleeing the village. Not so with guilt. Because it is internal self-punishment, it travels with us. Modern civilization is a guilt culture, just as it is a culture of the superego and sublimation and fantasy. It builds physical prisons only for people in whom it has not cultivated a sufficient "sense of guilt" to punish themselves in psychical prisons. For everyone else, the pain of guilt is indeed prison enough.

The superego names a cluster of interrelated psychological acts that do much to make us who we are, and to make civilization what it is. Morality comes from the superego, as do all ideals and high standards of achievement, along with the sense of inadequacy or guilt over failure. If we understand and use the superego well, it can make our lives and our relations with other people both easier and better for everyone. If we use the superego badly, it can breed weakness, rebellion, or a malaise of self-contempt. All parents should keep this in mind. And everyone should try to understand and master the workings of the superego for themselves.

THE WORKINGS OF THE SUPEREGO, with the psychology of guilt, bring us to the final brush strokes in Freud's panorama of civilization and its discontents. Much in this panorama can be rather disheartening. As Freud says, "If civilization imposes such great sacrifices not only on man's sexuality but on his aggressivity, we can better understand why it is hard for him to be happy in that civilization." But instead of telling us to resign ourselves to these troubles, Freud asks us to courageously pursue a salutary humanistic goal. That is the goal of psychological honesty and tough healthy-mindedness.

To reach that goal, Freud cautions, we must first be sure to avoid one tempting byway: the road promising perfect happiness. It can lead only to more sorrow. For anyone bent on ending all discontents and gaining immediate, unalloyed happiness will find nothing but transient delights and worsening pains, while all higher joys and remedies for pain will be unreachable. A world of such people would not even be civilized—no self-discipline, no law, no ethics, no science, no medicine, no art, no ideals, no material progress, no hope for the future. The gurus of a happy consciousness, like the social critic Theodore Roszak in *Person/Planet: The Creative Disintegration of Industrial Society* (1978), vowing to end the "Tyranny of Excellence" and "The Culture of Guilt" and usher in a regime of invincible bliss, are no friends of Freud. He would hear them as voices of seductive illusion summoning us away from reality, not toward it. And he would probably be right.

Freud's road to emotional honesty and tough healthy-mindedness promises no such utopia. That road rather leads to where we consciously adapt ourselves to reality when we should, change it when we can, and rise above it when we need to. Freud adds something else as well. To be truly healthy-minded, we must ask civilization to moderate the very demands it makes upon us. Civilization can demand much of us, but not too much. And Freud, doctor to victims of sexual repression, faulted his own civilization for demanding too much. "In the severity of its commands and prohibitions," Freud says, civilization "does not trouble itself enough about the facts of the mental constitution of human beings. It issues a command and does not ask if it is possible for people to obey it. On the contrary, it assumes that a man's ego is psychologically capable of anything that is required of it, that his ego has unlimited mastery over his Id (instincts). This is a mistake; even in what are known as normal people the Id cannot be controlled beyond certain limits."

Freud's ideal of a healthy-minded civilization therefore calls for restraint on the part of civilization no less than of individuals. For if civilization asks too much of us, human beings will crumble or resist, crack or rebel (Charles Dickens portrayed a version of this in *Hard Times*—see Chapter 13). And this truth points to another of Freud's ideals of healthy-mindedness. It amounts to the ethics of psychoanalysis, which is, as Philip Rieff nicely put it in *Freud: The Mind of the Moralist* (1961): "The Ethics of Honesty." This is the psychological honesty to look into ourselves and our culture and to see what realities are there—what needs must be satisfied, what wishes cannot be granted, what conflicts can be avoided, what pains must be endured, what we owe to the past in hurts and kindnesses, and what we can give to the future in healing and hope.

W. H. Auden movingly described this ethic of honesty in his elegy to Freud, "In Memory of Sigmund Freud" (1939). There Auden observed how much Freud gave the modern world simply by asking people to know themselves as people had not known themselves before, and to live with themselves as honestly as they can, and to cherish the energies of eros as the fount of life and joy.

Freud was not the dogmatic father of a pseudoscientific sexual ideology, as his critics maintain—or he was not only that. He was a generous humanist belonging to that venerable company of thinkers who have searched for the true and the good and the path to happiness in this world ever since civilization began. This is a Freud who prized the energies of creation no less than he warned against the psychological forces that can wound and destroy. And it is a Freud who speaks to anyone yearning for a healthy-minded life. That is, anyone with the courage to search the night of our souls for its secrets and to bring them into the light of the day, and anyone able to face the worst in us and to create the best in civilization. Yes, Freud was surely right: the often competing claims of human nature and culture, of our desires and our denials, of our truths and our falsehoods, of our realities and our fantasies, are the stuff of which not only dreams and pathology are made, but also civilization, and the healthy and honest, if not altogether happy, humanistic psychology of everyday life.

On the Psychology of Everyday Life

1. Life is too hard for us because it causes us suffering from the body, from the natural world, and from other people.

2. We give meaning to our lives with everything we do to gain pleasure and to avoid pain—that is the psychology of everyday life.

3. We often find more reliable happiness in avoiding pain than in pursuing pleasure.

4. When we pursue immediate pleasure we are living by the Pleasure Principle, and when we try to avoid pain we are living by the Reality Principle.

5. The Reality Principle gives us three methods of avoiding pain and gaining lasting satisfaction: adapt to the world, become psychologically independent of it, or try to change it.

6. We create all of the good things of civilization—science, medicine, justice, morality, ideals, art, etc.—as we use the methods of the Reality Principle.

7. Psychological reality—mind and imagination, fantasy and sublimation—can be more important to us than physical reality, for both good and ill.

8. Psychological reality belongs to both the Pleasure Principle and the Reality Principle.

9. Fantasy belongs mainly to the Pleasure Principle because it gives us immediate gratifications, and it can do that to the detriment of our lives in the real world.

10. Sublimation belongs to the Reality Principle because it channels physical pleasures into productive activities, especially those of the mind and imagination.

11. Sublimation can make us psychologically independent of the world in mind and imagination, but it can also help us adapt to the world, and to change it for the better.

12. Human nature has both erotic and aggressive energies.

13. Civilization requires us to restrain and rechannel both erotic and aggressive energies.

14. Civilization makes its demands on us through the superego, which acts as the conscience that tells us to live up to high standards and that punishes us with guilt when we fail to do this.

15. Human beings cannot be completely contented in civilization because it makes demands on us biologically and psychologically.

16. The meaning of life is to be psychologically honest with ourselves, to use the Pleasure Principle and the Reality Principle well, and to reconcile the needs of our natures and the demands of civilization.

18

It's Party Time:
The Ethics of Civility

Virginia Woolf: *Mrs. Dalloway*

She always had the feeling that it was very, very dangerous
to live even one day.

In her own mind now, what did it mean to her, this thing she called life?

Virginia Woolf

Virginia Woolf (1882–1941) eagerly left her stifling Victorian youth behind (as the daughter of the eminent Victorian intellectual Leslie Stephen) to breathe the bracing air of modernism shortly after the twentieth century began. Soon becoming a founder of that band of adventurous artists and thinkers in London known as the Bloomsbury Group (including her future husband, Leonard Woolf), she went on to write innovatively, abundantly, and splendidly—criticism, essays, memoirs, novels, plus the pioneering feminist tract *A Room of One's Own* (1929). She also fashioned an evocative, stream-of-consciousness literary style that gave her fiction a psychological subtlety and verbal elegance unsurpassed in English. Following her early conventional novels *The Voyage Out* (1915), *Night and Day* (1919), and *Jacob's Room* (1922), she played out this style to probe personalities and human relations in her great novels of the 1920s: *Mrs. Dalloway* (1925) and *To the Lighthouse* (1927). She went on in the subsequent novels *Orlando: A Biography* (1928), *The Waves* (1931), *The Years* (1937), and *Between the Acts* (1941) to travel down various paths into art and life that this style opened up to her. Then, shortly after completing that last novel, fearing the onset of another bout of the debilitating psychotic depressions that recurrently plagued her, Virginia Woolf stuffed a rock in her pocket and walked into the Ouse River to drown.

Although critics have generally judged *To the Lighthouse* to be Virginia Woolf's masterpiece for its lapidary style and feminist psychology, *Mrs. Dalloway* is more intellectually ambitious and profound. Unexcelled as a psychological novel with wide social resonance, *Mrs. Dalloway* deftly portrays human life as a dense pattern of tragedies and trivialities, anxieties and ethics as it follows a middle-aged woman through one day. We observe her activities, hear her conversations, and enter her thoughts as she vacillates between a fear of life's fragility and a dedication to social graces while she prepares for a party. When people cross her path directly or indirectly—husband, acquaintances, and strangers, including a deranged war veteran who appears again and again—we enter their thoughts, too. The seamless narrative passes back and forth from mind to mind, from the external to the internal, from past to present, letting many rivulets flow smoothly into a single stream. Finally, the lives floating in that stream pool together at Mrs. Dalloway's party, where we see the hostess as heroine and social alchemist, bringing people together to defeat tragedy with civility and to form a civilized society.

EVERYONE SHOULD GET TO KNOW Clarissa Dalloway. She one of the great—and greatly underestimated—characters in literature. It is true that Virginia Woolf can be hard on her, telling us that Clarissa Dalloway "knew nothing; no language, no history"; she "could not think, write, even play the piano"; she "talked oceans of nonsense: and to this day ask her what the Equator was, and she did not know." But this severe portrait (in the narrator's account of Clarissa Dalloway's own self-reflections) is hardly fair. Clarissa Dalloway knows and thinks about many things, if not about the equator. And she follows her thoughts wherever they lead. Clarissa Dalloway also does one thing very well: she gives parties.

This is the bare subject of the book: a day in the life of Clarissa Dalloway as she prepares for and hosts a party. She shops. She talks. She frets. She reflects on her past, and on her moods, and on what matters to her. She sets her party in motion. That is the drift. Yet as it unfolds in Virginia Woolf's intricate, eloquent, "stream-of-consciousness" narrative, Clarissa Dalloway's day also contains a rich cast of characters and virtually every consequential theme of literature and life: love and death, human nature and society, manners and morals, desire and denial, joy and despair, and so on (although you would not know this from most portrayals of Clarissa Dalloway in criticism, fiction, and films). While writing the novel, Virginia Woolf confided to her diary in June 1923 that "in this book I have almost too many ideas. I want to give life and death, sanity and insanity; I want to criticize the social system, and to show it at work, at its most intense." And in her literary manifesto, "Mr. Bennett and Mrs. Brown" (1924), she said that this is the panoply of life that every fictional character should embody. We could in fact read *Mrs. Dalloway* as a fictional companion to Freud's *Civilization and Its Discontents* (published in English five years later by Virginia Woolf's husband,

Leonard, at his Hogarth Press—see Chapter 17), so probingly and ambitiously does it explore the patterns of disparate lives, their psychological composition, their social reverberations, and how they weave the fabric of civilization. By looking very closely into Clarissa's own life, *Mrs. Dalloway* shows above all how often artful and always fragile is the balance within Clarissa between her needs and her sorrows, her fears and her joys, her nature and her culture, and how that balance holds a model for anyone. For Clarissa Dalloway, a woman in her early fifties, personifies the psychologically complicated, emotionally resilient, and ethically responsible adult who affirms life despite its tragedies, and who makes civilization work. And much of how she does these things revolves around her parties. We can learn a lot from her reasons for giving them.

Clarissa Dalloway lives to give parties. At least other people say this of her. And many of them wonder why she does it. Peter Walsh, her early love, whom she had rejected to marry Richard Dalloway, and who re-enters her life on this day, leaves her house after an emotional reunion with her invitation ringing in his ears: "My party tonight! Remember my party tonight." He will remember. But, "Oh these parties, he thought; Clarissa's parties. Why does she give these parties?" Clarissa feels his disapproval and imagines: "Suppose Peter said to her, 'Yes, yes, but your parties—what's the sense of your parties?'" Peter Walsh answers his own question, with a hint of resentment: perhaps, he thinks, "these parties . . . were all for him," her husband, the respected public servant, "or for her idea of him" as a member of the English establishment. Whatever their purpose, Peter Walsh thinks Clarissa may be wasting her life: "She frittered her time away, lunching, dining, giving these incessant parties of hers, talking nonsense, saying things she didn't mean, blunting the edge of her mind, losing her discrimination."

Richard Dalloway questions Clarissa's parties, too. As he talks to his wife at midday during her party preparations, he says to himself, "It was a very odd thing how much Clarissa minded about her parties." And, as if she had heard him, she thinks he would say they are "childish." When Richard returns to the House of Commons that afternoon, her mind follows him. There he will help "the Albanians, or was it the Armenians?" And she confesses to herself that "she cared much more for her roses than for the Armenians"—the roses Richard had brought her that midday as silent testimony to his love, and as consolation for her not having been invited to a particular society luncheon. Most of all, she cares for her parties.

Then, at this moment, Clarissa's mood darkens. The pleasures of preparing for the evening fade, and she sinks into thought. "But—but—why did she suddenly feel, for no reason that she could discover, desperately unhappy?" She retraces the day's events. "It was a feeling, some unpleasant feeling, earlier in the day perhaps." She sorts through her memories: "Something that Peter had said, combined with some depression of her own, in her bedroom, taking off her hat; and what Richard had said had added to it, but what had he said. There were his roses. Her parties!" The light goes on: "That was it! Her parties! Both of them criticized her very unfairly, laughed at her very unjustly, for her parties. That was it! That was it! Well, how was she going to defend herself?"

How can Clarissa defend herself, and her parties? That becomes a theme of her day. She must defend her parties and the entire pattern of her life. And this pattern is far more complex and substantial than others see. Clarissa gives parties, but she winces from criticism of them; she likes her life, but she often feels uncomfortable with it; she frequently savors joy, yet a current of anxiety flows deep within her; she knows herself quite well, but she doubts herself profoundly. Why does Clarissa Dalloway live and feel the way she does? And why does she give these "incessant parties"? When we answer these questions, we know not only Clarissa Dalloway. We know something vital about society, and civilization, and how to live in them. We do not all give parties as Clarissa Dalloway does. But we must have our version of them if we are to learn from our hurts and fears how to live with resilient cheer.

START WITH THIS NOTABLE FACT: despite her internal conflicts, Clarissa Dalloway is that rarity in literature, especially modern Western literature: a conspicuously happy person. It is invigorating just to be with her. "What a lark! What a plunge!" she exults as her day begins. And she plunges into the maelstrom of the London streets to be carried on "waves of that divine vitality which Clarissa loved" and to absorb every sight and sound with delight. "Heaven only knows why one loves it so," she thinks. "In people's eyes, in the swing, tramp, and trudge; in the bellow and the uproar; the carriages, motor cars, omnibuses, vans, sandwich men shuffling and swinging; brass bands; barrel organs; in the triumph and the jingle and the strange high singing of some aeroplane overhead was what she loved; life; London; this moment in June." Her urban spirit is as exuberant as it is rare in literature.

In the eighteenth century Samuel Johnson memorably remarked: "When a man is tired of London, he is tired of life." That was before commerce, industry, and mass populations gave cities a bad name and furnished modern writers their images of urban dehumanization—like T. S. Eliot's glum rendering of London in *The Waste Land* (published three years before *Mrs. Dalloway*). Samuel Johnson would have liked

Clarissa Dalloway. Her London is no modern wasteland, desolate and alienating, nor is it a seductively decadent metropolis like the Paris of Charles Baudelaire. It is an enlivening place where even "the veriest frumps, the most dejected of miseries sitting on door steps" signal no blight: "They love life," or so Clarissa Dalloway believes. And as for the pastoral countryside so dear to William Wordsworth and generations of English artists, it cannot compete with the city: "I love walking in London," Clarissa effuses; "really it's better than walking in the country."

Clarissa Dalloway's affection for London grows out of her very being. "She enjoyed practically everything," Peter Walsh observes; "it was her nature to enjoy." "Nothing could be slow enough" for her, she thinks, "nothing last too long," for "what she loved was this, here, now, in front of her . . . simply life." And she wants to tell this to people. She wants them to know, before it is all gone, "how unbelievable death was!—that it must end; and no one in the whole world would know how she had loved it all; how, every instant. . . . "

Clarissa Dalloway's happiness is undeniable. Not for her the fashionable modernist anguish over the meaninglessness of existence, or even the spiritual vacancy of Sinclair Lewis' George Babbitt (another literary character of the 1920s), who celebrates cities and the gospel of business while aching with emptiness. Clarissa Dalloway is genuinely, viscerally glad to be alive in London in the 1920s.

Clarissa's happiness is the first quality in her to see, but it is far from the last. There is also something amiss in Clarissa Dalloway, an underlying disquietude that is as much a part of her as is her obvious joy. This makes that joy the more significant, and her the more worth knowing. And it brings her closer to us, because while we may pursue happiness above everything else (as those two preeminent students of human nature, Aristotle and Freud, assumed), we often feel happiness most keenly against some pain or sorrow (as Freud was convinced).

Clarissa's disquietude arises partly from doubts about her own worth, doubts fed by those who criticize her. "People would say," she imagines, "'Clarissa Dalloway is spoilt,'" a shallow socialite ignorant of the world. She wishes she could have been someone else, someone more substantial, someone more like a man. "Oh if she could have lived her life over again! she thought"; she "could have looked even differently! She would have been . . . slow and stately; rather large" and "very dignified, very sincere." She would have been "interested in politics like a man"; and she would "have been one of those people like Richard who did things for themselves," rather than one who "did things not simply, not for themselves; but to make people think this or that," such as "that people should look pleased as she came in; perfect idiocy she knew."

Clarissa worries that she is in fact what other people—especially the men—seem to believe her to be: frivolous, superficial, inconsequential. She loves her life, but she questions its worth because others belittle it. It sinks into insignificance compared to those of the men close to her, so adventurous, intense, weighty, carrying the fate of nations. And she asks herself, "Could any man understand what she meant . . . about life?" They could not, of course, caught up as they are in inflated passions, like Peter, or in sobering political responsibilities, like Richard. Adrift in these thoughts while shopping for the party, "she had the oddest sense of being herself invisible, unseen; unknown; there being no more marrying, no more having children now, but only this astonishing and rather solemn progress with the rest of them, up Bond Street, this being Mrs. Dalloway; not even Clarissa any more; this being Mrs. Richard Dalloway."

Clarissa cannot comfortably be who she is, or who she feels herself to be. This is not allowed her, not by the men who condescend to her, nor by the women she knows either, if only implicitly—her old friend Sally Seton, her social rival Lady Bruton, and Joyce Kilman, the tutor of her beloved daughter, Elizabeth, and competitor for Elizabeth's allegiance, all of whom exemplify professional, political, or intellectual interests and aptitudes so unlike hers. Clarissa Dalloway differs strikingly from each of these women in ways peculiar to herself, which causes her occasional pangs of inferiority. Yet, if she could be free of their spoken or silent reproaches, these are differences she would relish.

But Clarissa's discomfort with the life she lives and the person she is comes not solely from the criticism she senses from others. Clarissa also suffers from deeper sorrows, and struggles with darker demons. Many of these beset her in the secret recesses of her emotions—secret because she wants them to be.

Clarissa distrusts emotions, her own and other people's. This distrust guides her life as much as anything. For all of its joyousness, Clarissa's life is also a network of defenses against emotional vulnerability. We all have such defenses. We need them to protect us from injurious memories and future injuries, as well as to insure some satisfactions. Sometimes we protect ourselves by simple denial, refusing to admit pain; at other times we do it with cautions that steer us clear of dangers; and at yet other times we do it by engaging in creative acts that yield safe mental pleasures or by doing good works that improve the world. These are the kinds of things that shape both our character and our culture. Freud wrote *Civilization and Its Discontents* about them. Clarissa Dalloway knows them all.

It was to defend herself against potentially threatening emotions that Clarissa had rejected Peter Walsh's early romantic affections. He had wanted too much—passion, intimacy, *all of her*. "With Peter," she says, "everything had to be shared; everything gone into. And it was intolerable." She could not bear his love. "What's your love? She might say to him. And she knew his answer; how it is the most important thing in the world and no woman possibly understood it." But she thinks she understands it all too well. It is a "horrible passion!" she grumbles, a "degrading passion!" It pretends to please, then leaves you desolated. "Love . . . that monster," ruined "everything that was fine, everything that was true"—Clarissa Dalloway is no Emma Bovary (see Chapter 24).

Clarissa had perhaps felt something like this "degrading passion" once. But not for Peter. And it wasn't degrading. It was for Sally Seton. "Had not that, after all, been love?" she asks herself, recalling how in their youth Sally had "kissed her on the lips," and it was "the most exquisite moment of her life." Yet this was not, she thinks, the kind of passion Peter revels in. "It had a quality which could only exist between women, between women just grown up." It was "completely disinterested" and "protective," since it "sprang from a sense of being in league together, a presentiment of something that was bound to part them (they spoke of marriage always as a catastrophe)."

This was a youthful affection with a frisson of sexuality. "The strange thing, on looking back," Clarissa thinks, "was the purity, the integrity, of her feeling for Sally." It was a guarded love, between females, the only kind Clarissa could allow herself. And she fleetingly allows herself to taste its delectations still. For "she could not resist sometimes yielding to the charm of a woman, not a girl." At these times, she admits, "she did undoubtedly then feel what men felt. Only for a moment; but it was enough. It was sudden revelation, a time like a blush which one tried to check and then, as it spread, one yielded to its expansion, and rushed to the farthest verge and there quivered and felt the world come closer, swollen with some astonishing significance, some pressure of rapture" and then "it was over—the moment." She did feel these things. But never for a man. That kept her safe.

In Clarissa's relations with men, including her husband, "she could never dispel a virginity preserved throughout childbirth which clung to her like a sheet." She had married Richard in part because he posed no threat to that virginity. So unlike Peter, Richard keeps his distance. "Richard gave her, and she him . . . a little license, a little independence," such as "people living together day in and day out" require. Richard loves Clarissa. But he does not wear emotions on his sleeve. He hardly expresses them at all. "It was a miracle that he should have married Clarissa," he thinks as he hastens across London in mid-afternoon with flowers to give her, vowing repeatedly "to tell Clarissa that he loved her, in so many words." When he arrives, he presents the flowers, "(But he could not bring himself to say he loved her; not in so many words)." And that was fine with her. "She understood without his speaking." It was better for her than if he had spoken. For Richard gives Clarissa what she most wants from him: emotional ease and security. Anything more would disquiet her.

Clarissa's distaste for heterosexual erotic love has a partner in her loathing of religion. "Love and religion!" Clarissa mentally exclaims: "How detestable, how detestable they are!" Both breach emotional defenses, invading our interior spaces and filling them with someone else's desires and needs and ordering vision, and extinguishing what we so singularly are, or wish to be. Yes, "love and religion would destroy that, whatever it was, the privacy of the soul."

Taking love and religion as twin emotional enemies, Clarissa identifies Peter Walsh with the one, and the tutor Doris Kilman with the other. For just as Peter had wanted to get too close to Clarissa, Kilman uses religion, larded with self-pity, as a weapon in her silent struggle with Clarissa over young Elizabeth's maturing character. Clarissa had escaped Peter's emotional demands, but she can only cautiously combat Kilman's influence, while feeling at an intellectual disadvantage.

Besides love and religion, Clarissa identifies still another enemy of "the privacy of the soul." And she sees this embodied in the person of the psychiatrist William Bradshaw, a therapist called upon to treat that sorriest of the book's characters, the psychological war-wounded Septimus Warren Smith. Neither Bradshaw nor Smith's physician, Dr. Holmes, would have earned much admiration from Sigmund Freud, since they believe, in Holmes's words, that "health is largely a matter in our control," and therefore they focus their related treatments on persuading patients always to adapt, or submit, to the world as it is. Bradshaw confidently calls this adaptation acquiring a "sense of proportion," for "health is proportion." And he diagnoses Septimus Warren Smith, victim of paranoid delusions and suicidal despair, as simply lacking it. Get hold of yourself, man! Put things in perspective! Find your "sense of proportion"! See things as I do! This is Bradshaw's therapy.

Clarissa Dalloway doesn't like it. For it advances a principle related to love and religion, but even more invasive and pernicious. That principle is the "sister" of "Proportion," and "Conversion is her name." Conversion leaves nothing alone, nothing free. Conversion is the most insidious exercise of power, acting not by force or intimidation but "under some plausible disguise; some venerable name; love, duty, self-sacrifice," and by bestowing "her blessing on those who, looking upward, catch submissively from her eyes the light of their own." Here Virginia Woolf steps forward from Clarissa's apolitical persona to blast not only Bradshaw's therapy but Britain's colonial policies and domestic politics for exploiting conversion to dominate the human spirit. "Conversion," she writes, "feasts on the wills of the weakly, loving to impress, to impose, adoring her own features stamped on the face of the populace," whether "in the heat and sands of India, the mud and swamps of Africa, the purlieus of London, wherever in short the climate or the devil tempts men to fall from the true belief which is her own."

For Virginia Woolf, this spelled the death of the soul. And the death of culture. And so it does for all of those who regard independence of mind and heart and will as the matrix of character and the energy of culture. Clarissa Dalloway is high among them (and John Stuart Mill is their patron political philosopher—see Chapter 14). We know where she would stand in the cultural wars raging between secularism and religious fanaticism in our world today.

William Bradshaw is all that she most heartily detests and determinedly resists. Yes, alas, Clarissa thinks, "worshipping proportion, Sir William not only prospered himself but made England prosper." Through conversion, he would extinguish independent personality in anyone, as he had done in his own wife and in every patient, who "naked, defenseless . . . received the impress of Sir William's will."

When Bradshaw brings news of the suicide of Septimus Warren Smith to Clarissa's party, where he and his wife are guests owing to his social prominence despite Clarissa's distaste for him, Clarissa thinks that if Septimus Warren Smith went to Bradshaw seeking help, he went to the wrong place, and he must "have said (indeed she felt it now), Life is made intolerable; they make life intolerable, men like that." Then, strangely, as she absorbs the rude shock of this suicide so inappropriately introduced into her party—"What business had the Bradshaws to talk of death at her party?"—she begins to feel a curious affinity for Septimus Warren Smith, whom she had never known. "She felt somehow very like him—the young man who had killed himself." And she was glad he had done it.

How could this be? How could Clarissa Dalloway, the joyful stroller on the London streets, the decorous hostess, the wary manager of her emotions and protector of her soul's privacy, identify herself with a shell-shocked suicide and be glad he had killed himself? To escape from Bradshaw was part of the reason. But the surprising affinity has another source, and it casts light on something in Clarissa that is more troubled than anything yet seen. It lies beneath the happiness and the sociability, beneath even the doubts about her own worth, and beneath her emotional self-protectiveness. Beneath all of these, Clarissa is beset by a lurking fear. A fear that holds revealing secrets to her life—and ours.

"There was in the depths of her heart an awful fear," we are told when she learns of the suicide; "there was the terror; the overwhelming incapacity, one's parents giving it into one's hands, this life." This fear is not Clarissa's alone, or so she believes. It belongs to the nature of life itself, the very life she loves so much. "This late age of the world's experience," she reflects, "had bred in them all, all men and women, a well of tears." It is in the war-torn soldiers and the sad survivors, in the glittering social-ites and the hard-working laborers, in an old woman across the court-yard whose solitary existence Clarissa observes and admires from time to time—and whom she glimpses through the window during the party: "There! the old lady had put out her light! the whole house was dark now with this going on, she repeated, and the words came to her [words gently evoking death, from Shakespeare's *Cymbeline*, seen earlier that day in a shop window]: 'Fear no more the heat of the sun.'"

This trepidation before the day, this undercurrent of anxiety that induces Clarissa to identify herself with this curious, withdrawn, etiolated old woman—and with the suicide intruded into her party—runs insistently through Clarissa's life, surfacing now and then, being suppressed yet again and again. Henry James called it "the imagination of disaster," a vague portent that amidst the joys and security and serenity of civilization, the worst can happen. Even as she walks the London streets loving every sight and sound and minute, Clarissa Dalloway is gripped by dread intimations: "She always had the feeling that it was very, very dangerous to live even one day."

She always had the feeling that it was very, very dangerous to live even one day. This is not the commonplace modernist "despair" awash in cosmic alienation. Clarissa's anxieties have a more prosaic cause—and a more rewarding effect, for her and for her readers. The cause also binds Clarissa closer to the hapless, deranged Septimus Warren Smith than she knows: Clarissa Dalloway and Septimus Warren Smith had both suffered injuries of the soul in tragic human losses.

Septimus Warren Smith had never recovered from the ravages of what was then known as The Great War, which had ended a few years earlier, and particularly from the death in battle of his friend Evans. The shock had shut down his feelings. He could not stand the pain. This denial of emotions became his psychosis: "The sin for which human nature had condemned him to death; that he did not feel. He had not cared when Evans was killed; that was the worst." Eventually, possessed by delusions and literally pursued by Dr. Holmes, who is bent on curing him, Septimus Warren Smith had flung himself from a window ledge onto the pikes of a fence below.

Clarissa Dalloway had undergone a shock in her youth quite—terribly—like that of World War I and of Evans' death for Septimus Warren Smith. She had seen her sister killed in an accident.

"Sylvia's death—that horrible affair," Peter Walsh recalls as he ponders Clarissa's character. "To see your sister killed by a falling tree . . . before your very eyes, a girl too on the verge of life, the most gifted of them, Clarissa always said, was enough to turn one bitter." In Septimus Warren Smith, such a tragedy was enough to block his emotions, shatter his sanity, and provoke his suicide. In Clarissa Dalloway, it cast a shadow across her life, leading her, too, to deny emotions, and to suspect dangers everywhere, as well as to fear death—she is also said to have a bad heart and lately to have been ill. And yet, for all of this, Clarissa Dalloway did not, like Septimus Warren Smith, succumb to the tragedy. She even turned it to advantage. It became her inspiration.

AND WITH THIS INSPIRATION, Clarissa Dalloway proves her emotional resilience, her strength of will not to condemn life for its tragedies and for her anxieties, but to overcome those tragedies and anxieties by enhancing life. Tragedy cannot claim her. She defeats its claims with creativity and benevolence—not unlike the humanism born of tragedy in Homer's *Iliad* (see Chapter 1). We may never entirely recover from a tragedy; but Clarissa Dalloway shows us how we might be the better for it.

"Possibly she said to herself," thinks Peter Walsh, who despite his criticism often seems a good judge of her character, and who here surely gets it right: "As we are a doomed race, chained to a sinking ship . . . as the whole thing is a bad joke, let us, at any rate, do our part; mitigate the sufferings of our fellow-prisoners . . . ; be as decent as we possibly can. Those ruffians the Gods, shan't have it all their own way—her notion being that the Gods, who never lost a chance of hurting, thwarting and spoiling human lives were seriously put out if, all the same, you behaved like a lady."

To behave like a lady—"that network of visiting, leaving cards, being kind to people; running about with bunches of flowers, little presents"—this is for Clarissa an ethical calling. She may have doubts about its significance in a masculine world of imperial ambitions and Armenian crises. But when she permits herself to accept her life as it is, she delights in its brilliant moments and takes pride in what she has been called to do with it. "Not for a moment did she believe in God; but all the more, she thought . . . one must repay in daily life to servants, yes, to dogs and canaries, above all to Richard . . . one must pay back from this secret deposit of exquisite moments." Or as Peter Walsh puts it: "She evolved this atheist's religion of doing good for the sake of goodness." And that is to behave like a lady—and to give parties.

What is a party? A frivolity? A diversion? An escape? Richard Dalloway and Peter Walsh say so. They chalk up Clarissa's parties to the most trivial of motives: "They thought, Peter at any rate thought, that she enjoyed imposing herself; liked to have famous people about her; great names; was simply a snob in short. Well, Peter might think so. Richard merely thought it foolish of her to like excitement when she knew it was bad for her heart"—or so Clarissa imagines.

Clarissa thinks that "both of them criticised her very unfairly, laughed at her very unjustly, for her parties." They "were quite wrong" about her. But "how was she going to defend herself" when "she could not imagine Peter or Richard taking the trouble to give a party." Then it strikes her: "What she liked was simply life. 'That's what I do it for,' she said, speaking aloud, to life." Catching herself again, she asks, "Could any man understand what she meant . . . about life?" And pausing "to go deeper," she betrays her own uncertainty as she wonders: "In her own mind now, what did it mean to her, this thing she called life?"

As Clarissa searches for that particular quality of life that her parties capture and celebrate, she sets aside the things she has so fondly enumerated before, such as the animated London streets, a summer day, her roses. Something more about life summons Clarissa Dalloway to give parties. "Oh, it was very queer," she thinks. "Here was So-and-so in South Kensington; someone up in Bayswater; and somebody else, say in Mayfair. And she felt quite continuously a sense of their existence; and she felt what a waste; and she felt if only they could be brought together; so she did it." She would bring them together in—a party.

By giving parties, Clarissa Dalloway was, for one thing, playing upon what she considered "the supreme mystery" of life (Peter Walsh once called this her "transcendental theory"). This mystery lies in how everyone is connected by "odd affinities" through "the unseen part of us," and how this "unseen part . . . spreads wide" and is "somehow attached to this person or that," and that "the unseen might survive" death, giving us all a kind of immortality. Yes, "somehow in the streets of London," she thought, "on the ebb and flow of things, here, there, she survived" because "it spread ever so far, her life, herself." Playing upon this mystery, Clarissa Dalloway therefore wanted "to kindle, to illuminate; to give her party" because "it was her gift," her way to "pay back from this secret deposit of exquisite moments" what she owes to life. But Clarissa's parties were more than this too. They were also a way of thwarting the gods, of wresting from life's tragedies and fears an elevating purpose with "an offering; to combine, to create" nothing less than society and civilization.

And this, above all, is what Clarissa's parties do. They create society and build civilization, bringing people together to interact as social beings. "She made her drawing room a sort of meeting place," Peter Walsh observes. "Over and over again he had seen her take some raw youth, twist him, turn him, wake him up; set him going." Peter Walsh himself, who has so belittled these parties and has made Clarissa feel trivial for giving them, even he could not stay away. "Here he was starting to go to a party, at his age, with the belief upon him that he was about to have an experience. But what?" Then he decides: it would be "beauty anyhow"—the beauty of social life, refined and warming. As he approaches Clarissa's street, he feels swept along on a buoyant current flowing toward her house: "Cabs were rushing round the corner, like water round the piers of a bridge, drawn together, it seemed to him because they bore people going to her party, Clarissa's party." No more than anyone else can the romantic, idealistic, critical Peter Walsh resist Clarissa's parties.

There he would join in the making of society and civilization under the guiding hand of Clarissa Dalloway. "For there she was . . . prancing, sparkling," talking, laughing, glowing, greeting the Prime Minister, "all with the most perfect ease and air of a creature floating in its element," having about her "an inexpressible dignity; an exquisite cordiality; as if she wished the whole world well."

And she does wish the whole world well. Clarissa Dalloway is, as Peter Walsh has remarked (with misplaced disdain), "the perfect hostess." She does what good hosts and hostesses do: they make guests feel good about themselves as social performers—like the hostess who covers a dinner guest's gaffe in etiquette by unostentatiously repeating it herself. And Clarissa knows that this calls for a distinctly seductive charm, a subtle social performance, a special art. The Renaissance author Baldesar Castiglione, whose *Book of the Courtier* remains a catalog of wise instructions on social behavior, dubbed this art *sprezzatura*, the "art which does not seem to be art," the skill of making every action, every gesture, seem natural and not artificial, spontaneous, not consciously artful. "She did it genuinely," muses Peter Walsh, "from a natural instinct." To be sure, Clarissa Dalloway makes her "offering" to life, as a hostess, with *sprezzatura*.

Clarissa Dalloway's offering does this by setting the stage for her guests to cultivate the manners or arts of social life for themselves. These are not false arts, as some people nowadays complain. Society depends on them. For they ask us to be better, not worse, than our instinctual and everyday selves, to perform well in the eyes of other people and to treat them with gracious social care. "Every time she gave a party," Clarissa reflects, "she had this feeling of being something not herself, and that every one was unreal in one way; much more real in another. It was, she thought, partly their clothes, partly being taken out of their ordinary ways, partly the background, it was possible to say things you couldn't say anyhow else, things that needed an effort; possible to go much deeper." Parties make us go deeper? This contradicts common assumptions about socializing.

Yet what is social life if not this: that we act out an ideal of ourselves which is as real to us and as important as are the personalities with which we are born; that we manage to find in others' perceptions of ourselves a confirmation of how we wish to be; that we establish the ties to others that form society? And what would social life be without parties to crown social performance? Molière's *The Misanthrope* amusingly echoes such questions in its profound comedy of manners (see Chapter 12). Clarissa Dalloway answers them in her philosophy of parties.

And a substantial philosophy it is. For it converts the nagging insecurities and subterranean anxieties of Clarissa's life into the virtues of emotional courage and social civility. This puts that philosophy firmly in the tradition of humanism going back to Homer (and prominently including Frederick Douglass, Elie Wiesel, and Martin Luther King, Jr.—see Chapter 16), in which human beings valiantly rise above the tragedies and sorrows of life by embracing humane values and trying to make human life in this world better. It also links that philosophy to a more recent tradition that advocates the civilities and civic interactions of citizens as the makings of a "civil society" and the hallmark of democratic culture.

So, we may think of Clarissa Dalloway's life as a bastion of defenses against pain. We may think of it as a web of sublimated satisfactions. We may think of it as defiance of "those ruffians the Gods." We may think of it as a victory over the dangers "of living even one day." We may think of it as a celebration of civilized social life. But we may not justly think of it as insignificant. If we choose to feel regrets for Clarissa Dalloway, it should be not because she has frittered away her life, but because she has been denied the honor she deserves.

We need Clarissa Dalloways. They grace life with refinement and beauty, and people it with civilized human beings who skillfully perform together on the stage of society. The sociologist Erving Goffman once said that "the world, in truth, is a wedding," a "celebration" of social life, a "party . . . where reality is being performed." This is Clarissa Dalloway's vision, and her mission. To her, society is a party, and parties are society. For they bring out the best in us—without parties and social civility, as Clarissa Dalloway might put it, "one could not be a lady."

And that is Clarissa Dalloway's triumph over tragedy, her thwarting of the gods—by being "a lady." Summoning "courage and endurance; a perfectly upright and stoical bearing," as she had admired other people for doing, she becomes an exemplary humanist, a social philosopher, and a model of civil society. She surely deserves to be among those whom George Eliot honored at the end of *Middlemarch* for contributing to "the growing good of the world" by performing many "unhistoric acts." Make no mistake. Clarissa Dalloway is no mere socialite. She *is* society and civilization—at their best. And her story is the surpassing novel of the ethics of civility.

On the Ethics of Civility

1. It is dangerous to live even one day because tragedies can happen to anyone anytime.

2. We should respond to the tragedies of life by striving to make life better for human beings in this world.

3. We should give something back to life for the good things it has given us.

4. Civility brings social benevolence into the world and gives human beings a victory over tragedy.

5. Civility means acting with sincere manners, gracious refinement, social generosity, and bringing people together to nurture humane social life.

6. Humane social life gives us a defense against life's sorrows.

7. A party is an act of civility and an offering to life that creates social bonds and a humane society.

8. Parties can bring out the best in us—our ideal social selves.

9. A good hostess makes other people feel good about their social selves.

10. All people are connected through a web of common life, anxieties, and humanity.

11. Beware of those who invade the privacy of the soul with intrusive emotional demands, therapeutic manipulation, or efforts to convert us wholly to their view of the world.

12. The meaning of life is to rise above tragedy and sorrows and make life better for ourselves and others by nurturing the social bonds, beauties, and benevolence of gracious civility.

Part III

The Promises and Perils of Aesthetics, Imagination, Romance

19

The Morality and Immorality of Art

Plato: *Republic*
Aristotle: *Politics, Poetics*
Leo Tolstoy: *What Is Art?*

We must issue . . . orders to all artists and craftsmen, and prevent them portraying bad character, ill-discipline, meanness, or ugliness in pictures of living things, in sculpture, architecture, or any work of art.

The object of education is to teach us to love what is beautiful.

Plato

Poetry is concerned with Universal Truth.
Aristotle

Art is not a pleasure, a solace, or an amusement; art is a great matter.
Tolstoy

Plato (see Chapter 3) distrusted the powers of art, and he distrusted artists almost entirely. But he wrote philosophy with peerless artistry. And he wrote about art and artists again and again—for example, in the *Republic, Laws, Apology, Ion, Phaedrus, Symposium*—usually warning of their wiles and evils, occasionally extolling their virtues. He devoted many pages of the *Republic* to explaining why he would censor art in his ideal city, and much of what he says there resembles public controversies over art today. But he also touched on the good that art can do, and he rhapsodized in the *Symposium* about the uses of beauty. Western debates over the powers and dangers, as well as the virtues, of art began with Plato, and we can be sure those debates will never end.

    Aristotle (see Chapter 4) took art just as seriously as Plato did. Both of them placed it at the heart of politics and education. But, more open-minded and practical than the idealistic and moralistic Plato, Aristotle believed art plays various useful roles in our lives. He described these roles in the

345

Politics and the *Poetics*, explaining how art goes from shaping moral character to providing a crowning pursuit of life. We still use art in the many ways Aristotle described. And we can still learn much from him about how to use art well in all of them.

Leo Tolstoy (1828–1910) comes to mind as the author of the monumental novels *War and Peace* (1863–69) and *Anna Karenina* (1875–77), and perhaps a few brilliant stories, such as "The Death of Ivan Ilych" and "The Kreutzer Sonata." But he was also a Russian aristocrat who became a zealous cultural critic after his religious conversion in 1877. From then on he wrote increasingly didactic tales, including the novel *Resurrection* (1899), and issued a stream of hortatory essays berating Western culture, professing a noninstitutional Christianity (for which he was excommunicated from the Russian Orthodox Church), and idealizing a spiritual, pacifist, peasant society. Tolstoy's greatest achievement as a cultural critic is *What Is Art?* (1898). Bold and eccentric, controversial and eye-opening, it assails most of the art of Tolstoy's day and advocates a moral "art of the future." Its conclusions might make few converts nowadays, but after reading it, we cannot think about art quite the same as we did before, nor should we.

EVERYBODY LIKES ART. People always have, although not always as "art." "Art" as we commonly use the term (and its cognates) nowadays is fairly new. Modern Western culture invented it by largely removing art from the rest of life, beginning in the eighteenth century, and loading it with unique aesthetic and imaginative attributes unknown to most cultures. Before that, art denoted "craft," as derived from the Latin *ars* for technical skill in making things or in performing difficult tasks (see Chapter 25). But the semantics of "art" aside, art objects, by whatever name, were among the first cultural creations of humankind. And they were probably created to give human beings power.

The earliest creators of art objects likely believed those objects possessed magical powers over nature. The prehistoric figurines of bulbous, profusely breasted females molded some thirty thousand years ago were probably fashioned to promote fertility, and the paintings of animals adorning cave walls that appeared about fifteen thousand years later were possibly thought to assist the hunt. In time, artworks would be used to placate and honor the gods, to prepare the dead for an afterlife, and to edify and educate people, as well as to decorate and entertain. But whatever the uses of what we call "art," people seem to have always assumed that art has some kind of power. No idea in human history is older than that—and none is more current.

The power of art was among the first subjects of Western philosophy, too. Plato and Aristotle made it a central theme of their theories of human nature and politics. A good state depends on good character, they said, and good character depends on good education, and no part of education, they agreed, shapes character more deeply than art. Therefore, they concluded, a good state needs good art education, along with art that is good for people and censorship of art that is bad for them. Plato and Aristotle did not altogether agree on what good art is, or how art wields its power to do good or ill, or how we should use that power. But their agreements and disagreements sparked a debate that continues today in controversies over the proper social, political, and moral role of art in our lives.

Two millennia after Plato and Aristotle, and at the dawn of the mass artistic culture we now inhabit, Leo Tolstoy entered the debate over the nature and proper uses of art with another testimonial to art's power. He came in more or less on Plato's side (notably preceded by Jean-Jacques Rousseau in his *Letter to d'Alembert on the Theatre* [1758]), distrusting art more than Aristotle did, if for somewhat different reasons than Plato. But no one since Plato and Aristotle has said more thought-provoking things about the power of art to shape our lives and civilization. Today, when the arts surround us, and when as entertainment they threaten to pervade our culture and to become our principal standard of value, we can learn as much as ever—perhaps more—about the power and the morality and immorality of art from Plato, Aristotle, and Tolstoy, whether we agree with them or not.

PLATO SET HIS SIGHTS on art early in the *Republic*. While thinking about how to create an ideal state, he figured that the first step should be to

PLATO

educate its leaders, or "guardians," to have good character. And since he believed that art possesses unique powers to shape character for the better or the worse, especially in the young, he decided that this education should start with art in order to harness those powers early for the better. This led him to advise that the education of the state's leaders should therefore begin in childhood with the kind of art that most affects children: stories. Nowadays we might not think of educating the future leaders of an ideal state with children's stories, but we often tell stories to our children for many of Plato's reasons.

Plato starts with stories because they belonged to the part of Greek schooling occupied with "educating mind and character," or the "soul," in contrast to the other part occupied with "physical training" of the body. The Greeks called this soulful part of education *mousikē*—sometimes misleadingly translated as "music," the particular art that did in

347

fact play the most prominent role in Greek schooling, but only one of the "arts" of the muses, among them philosophy and history, included in *mousikē*. And within *mousikē*, Plato said, "we begin by telling stories to children" in order to make an "impression" and help "form opinions" while people are young.

"Stories" come in "two kinds," Plato explains: "true" and "false" or "fiction." (Plato's term for stories in general is *logos* or its derivatives, which could include any narrative or discourse. But his most common term for stories is *mythos*, which implied the inventions of myth and fable. His term for "false" is *pseudos*, denoting lies but also connoting the kind of fiction found in *mythos*.) "Our education must use both" true stories and fiction, he asserts, but it should "start with fiction," or stories that "are, in general, fiction though they contain some truth"—in other words, suitable fables that convey edifying truths. And we must take this "first step" very carefully, he cautions. For "it is of the utmost importance . . . when we are dealing with those who are young and tender" and "easily molded" that "the first stories [*mythos*] they hear shall aim at encouraging the highest excellence of character." The "first business" of education should therefore be not to "allow our children to listen to" just "any stories made up by anyone," but "to supervise the production of stories, and choose only those we think suitable, and reject the rest." Then "we shall persuade mothers and nurses to tell our chosen stories to their children, and by means of them to mould their minds and characters." That is the moral foundation of Plato's ideal state in the *Republic*: wholesome children's stories.

Most people today (short of rabid religious fundamentalists and pie-eyed ideologues) would likely shrink from Plato's proposal "to supervise the production of stories." But most would also agree that children should not be allowed to hear every kind of story—or to watch everything on television or to see every kind of movie. Prudence and common sense require this. However, Plato is just getting going. He not only declares that "we shall have to reject . . . the greater part of the stories current today" in favor of "our chosen stories" for children. He goes on to say that "we must compel our poets to tell them similar stories when they grow up." Here Plato unveils himself as the scolding father of artistic censorship. But make no mistake. He owes this reputation as much to his high respect for the powers of art as to his deep fears of those powers. Every censor of art since Plato has shared a measure of that respect, along with many of those fears.

Plato brusquely rejected most "stories current today" for miseducating children and adults alike with a host of errors. First, he says, the stories, or fables, that poets (notably Homer and Hesiod) tell are "quite untrue," and they teach bad lessons to boot. If, for instance, we "permit stories of wars and plots and battles among the gods" to circulate, adults no less than children will assume "that anyone who commits horrible crimes . . . is doing nothing out of the ordinary but merely what . . . the gods have done before." How can anyone be virtuous if the gods themselves are not? If this sounds like an antiquated worry, just consider how you would feel if your children grew up on versions of your God anything like Homer's version of his gods—contentious, deceitful, devious, unscrupulous, and vain?

Plato also condemns these storytellers (*mythologos*) for their portrayals of human beings as irrational, self-indulgent, and immoral. "If our young men listen to passages" that represent heroes that way, he says, "they are hardly likely to think this sort of conduct unworthy of them as men, or to resist the temptation to similar words and actions." Then "they will feel no shame and show no endurance" or other virtues (although in the *Phaedo* Plato lets Socrates admire Homer's account of Achilles' courage in facing death). Plato won't have that. "We must therefore put a stop to stories of this kind," he insists, "before they breed in our young men an undue tolerance of wickedness."

Plato carries this moral censorship beyond literature as well. "We must issue similar orders to all artists and craftsmen" (or "skilled workers," *demiourgos*), he insists, "and prevent them portraying bad character, ill-discipline, meanness, or ugliness in pictures of living things, in sculpture, architecture, or any work of art." (Plato does not use a noun for "art" here, but rather the verb *empoiein*, for anything that a skilled craftsman "causes," "makes," or "produces.") That puts artists on a pretty short leash. And many a moralist and ideologue of both the Left and Right has wanted to do just that—and more. Some have succeeded, if only for a time.

But Plato faults not only the immoral contents of art. He distrusts the very artistic skills of artists. For these skills give artists the power to represent deceptive fictions as truth, and to induce people to act on those deceptions. Artists do this, Plato elaborates, by imitating common reality adroitly enough to convince people that their artworks accurately mirror that reality. At the same time, they enfold these imitations in artistic inventions that subtly distort reality while deceptively and enticingly appearing to be true. This is the Great Lie of Art, Plato complains. And it is the chief source of art's corrupting power. For when art deceptively imitates life, people gullibly imitate art.

Many moralists have tended to agree with Plato. But others object that people are not this naive about art imitating life or about life imitating art. And over the last hundred and fifty years it has become common for partisans of art to say that art and life, or morality, have nothing to do with each other, and therefore artists should be free to do what they want to do, and we should value all art simply for its own sake. Plato, the fervent moralist, would scorn this last argument above all. He would say that any philosophy removing art from life and morality misjudges the very nature and power of art. For art by its very nature imitates realities and truths, and therefore it has the power to influence people's lives, and more often than not, it leads them astray. To make this case, Plato spins an ambitious theory of reality and truth that only Platonists embrace. But it is probably the most renowned theory in the history of philosophy —and it has begotten many a popular reference to "Platonic Ideas." It can also illuminate how art does indeed work some of its effects on us. The theory, in brief, goes like this.

True reality and real truth exist only in the ideal realm of pure, universal ideas—the ideas of goodness or of justice, for instance, or even the idea of an object like a bed. We can picture these ideas with our mind's eye in their pure ideal form, but they can never exist in the everyday world like that. We can bring them into this world only by producing particular, concrete examples of them, like a judge who issues individual just rulings based on the universal *idea of justice*, or a carpenter who builds individual beds based on the universal *idea of a bed*. These concrete examples of universal ideas possess only the secondhand reality of imperfect particular things that we can see or use in this world, since universal ideas alone have the firsthand reality of perfection in their own ideal realm outside of this world—nature itself falls short of this true Platonic reality.

Now to artists. They take us even farther from true reality. For they go from the secondhand reality of imperfect particular things to produce thirdhand "imitations" or "representations" of the mere "appearance" of these particular things. Having "no grasp of truth," artists imitate these "appearances" because appearances are "easy to produce without any knowledge of the truth." And that makes "the art of representation" or "imitation" (*mimesis*) a "third remove from reality" and "a long way removed from truth."

But at the same time, Plato warns, adept artists can imitate appearances well enough to deceive people into believing that their artworks do in fact reflect reality and truth. "So great is the natural magic of poetry," Plato observes, that the poet "can persuade people who are as ignorant as he is, and who judge merely from his words, that he really has something to say about shoemaking or generalship or whatever it may be," just as the "scene painter and conjurer" can "with magical effect" trick the eye into seeing what does not exist. In other words, artists are clever liars.

That is roughly Plato's theory of art in the *Republic* anyway (Plato was more generous in *Ion* and *Phaedrus*, where he concedes that artists can convey truth in art, although he says they do this without understanding the truth they convey because they act through "divine madness," "possession," or "inspiration" outside of all "reason" and "knowledge"). And we do not have to accept the ethereal reality of "Platonic Ideas" to see that Plato was at least partially right about how the representational arts exercise their power. For that power always comes in part from art's freedom *not to be true* to life even while *seeming to be true*. Unconstrained by literal truth, and gifted with the talent at once to represent things as they are and to invent imaginary worlds, a good artist can seize our imagination and take us to where we can believe that anything is possible. Aristotle praised poetry (or the literary arts) in the *Poetics* for doing just that when it shows us truths of possibility. And every art lover has relished flights into those imaginary worlds for some of these very reasons. That may be a commonplace. But Plato didn't go for it—even though, as anyone who reads his dialogues can see, he wrote philosophy in that same artful spirit.

Plato moves on from the deceptive misrepresentations of truth in art to warn of a related artistic villainy. This is also as familiar now as it was then, and it is surely more widely exploited. It is the tendency—and the power—of art, especially the popular arts, to appeal to our easiest emotions, which Plato judges to be the basest part of us.

"On what part of the human being," Plato asks, does the artistic "process of representation . . . exercise its power?" He answers that it is the lowest, "irrational" part, which makes us self-indulgent, "recalcitrant," "lazy and inclined to cowardice," and keeps us "bemoaning . . . our sufferings" and hungering for pleasure. By the same token, he says, artists shy away from "the highest part of us" because that is the realm of "reason," where we learn "restraint" and to "obey the direction of principle," and to guard against art's deceptions.

"Possessed" imitators and manipulative opportunists that most artists are, Plato argues, they reap several advantages from working on this low irrational level instead of on the high plane of reason. First, irrationality supplies artists more "material for dramatic representation" than do reason and restraint. Second, artists "find it easy to represent a character that is unstable and refractory," whereas "the reasonable element and its unvarying calm are difficult to represent." Third, people respond to art irresistibly on the irrational level—through emotions and sensations—whereas on the rational level things are "difficult to understand," and so people must use thought and judgment and the very "restraint" that artists try to discourage.

Plato may have been ungenerous to artists and art lovers alike here, but no one attuned to modern entertainment can honestly say he was wrong. Just look at almost any Hollywood movie or television series today. Intense emotions and human conflicts give these entertainments a richer trove of dramatic subjects to portray than do the contentments of the orderly life. Those subjects also lend themselves to arresting visual representation. And who can doubt that the more emotional and sensory power these entertainments deploy, the more irresistible—if not enduring—their effects, because then they get inside us without engaging our rational judgment, or they overwhelm that judgment?

We could argue against Plato that such emotional powers of art are actually a good thing. Aristotle thought that these powers can act on us benignly by helping us release unsettling feelings through *katharsis*. Much later, Romantic poets like Wordsworth and Shelley prized art's emotional powers for taking us out of ourselves, giving us empathy with others, sparking morality, and revealing to us what is most important in life (see Chapter 23). And most of us have gained many gratifications from the emotional powers of art that we would not want to lose.

But not Plato. He was convinced that the more art "gratifies and indulges the instinctive desires," the more it corrupts us, because then "it waters" the passions "when they ought to be left to wither, and makes them control us when we ought . . . to control them." This emotional nourishment "strengthens the lower elements in the mind to the detriment of reason, which is like giving power and political control to the worst elements in a state and ruining the better elements." These worries led Plato to conclude that besides morally suitable children's tales and "similar stories" for adults, "the only poetry [or literature] that should be allowed in a state is hymns to the gods and paeans in praise of good men." For "once you go beyond that and admit the sweet muse of lyric or epic," or any art that acts on people too emotionally—or any "innovation" in the arts and education, for that matter—"pleasure and pain become your rulers instead of law and the rational principles commonly accepted as best." Then "disorder" sets in, undermining "morals and manners," infecting "business dealings generally," and spreading from there "into the laws and constitution . . . until it has upset the whole of private and public life." No wonder Plato wanted to banish most artists from the state. They can be downright politically subversive, not just by corrupting people morally through their dishonest representations, but by fomenting general disorder through their infectious irrationality.

Plato's crude censorship would make for a very thin artistic culture indeed (detailed more in the *Laws* without the ingratiating style of the *Republic* or the enlivening presence of Socrates). But it is a price Plato says must be paid. Art should make people better, not worse, he insists, from their first children's stories onward. And that means making them restrained, rational, and responsible. Hence we cannot allow immoral and emotionally subversive art in a state any more than we can allow politically subversive people—as authoritarian governments, religious fundamentalists, and conservative cultural critics have agreed. Most of us would reject this point of view today, but we should not fail to understand the reasons for it—namely, that art has the power not only to move us and to please us, but to change us, for the better and the worse. That is Western culture's original rationale for artistic censorship, but it is also the original mandate for art education.

Plato does not carry out that mandate, as Aristotle would come closer to doing, but he does not leave art there confined to moralistic fables, inspiring hymns, and images of rational composure. Despite his wish to chase virtually every artist out of town, Plato wraps up his ideas on art in the *Republic* with some ambiguous remarks on how art might do more good than harm, after all.

If anyone can prove, he says, that art "brings lasting benefits to human life and human society"—he refers specifically to poetry—"we will gladly" give it "a place in a well-run society." Plato doubts that anyone can supply this proof, but he leaves the subject open and ends the *Republic* with nothing less than a story, or *mythos*, of his own. This is the evocative "Myth of Er." Here Plato depicts a realm where immortal souls choose the lives they will live—and therefore the moral characters they will possess—"for happiness in this life" and "for a journey from this world to the next and back again." It is a "tale" to "remember," Plato concludes, for it reminds us that the lives and characters we choose for ourselves will be ours forever. Be that as it may, it is an artistically told and morally inspiring *myth* if ever there was one.

The "Myth of Er" recalls Plato's words on the moral inspiration of children's stories near the opening of the *Republic*. And it suggests not only how good stories can shape the character of children for the better, and can constrain the irrationalities of adults for the good, but also hints at how art can lead people to heights of virtue. We reach these heights, Plato believed, when we see ideals of perfection with our mind's eye. There is a kind of artistry in that, for this is an imaginative use of mind. Plato even admits that the *Republic* itself is an imaginative creation intended to inspire us in just that way. "It doesn't matter," he has Socrates say of the ideal state that he has taken such pains to describe, "whether it exists now or will ever exist." For anyone who "can see it" with the mind's eye can "establish it in his own heart." That makes the *Republic* an ideal myth to think about and to live by. And this idea points to the highest ideal of all that Plato urges us to see. This is none other than the ideal of beauty itself.

Beauty meant a great deal to Plato, as it did to his fellow Greeks. The Greek language itself united beauty and good. The word *kalos* denoted both beauty in appearance and good in function, and it implied the morally beautiful. A well-constructed road, for example, was said to be *kalos* because it was both beautiful in form and good to use. But Plato went farther. He made beauty the very ideal of all perfection—in form, function, morality, and character. For he saw in beauty all the qualities that good people must have: rationality, restraint, order, harmony, and the like. And he assumed that a person touched by beauty would acquire these qualities. Such a person will "rightly dislike and condemn . . . anything ugly" in "works of art or nature" for being inharmonious, disorderly, and the rest, and "will welcome gladly . . . anything beautiful" and "make it his own and so grow in goodness of character." With this in mind, Plato comes right out and says in the *Republic*: the "object of education is to teach us to love what is beautiful." We might think of that as a nice motto for art education. But Plato would have had it inscribed over every classroom door, whatever the subject of the class.

Plato does not spell out how to teach the love of beauty. But he crowned that love in the *Symposium*, a lyrical dialogue devoted to it. Although he rhapsodizes there, through the words of one of his liveliest characters, Diotima, about how the attraction to beauty throbs with the desires of *eros,* he takes this attraction to distinctly moral ends. "The person who sees absolute beauty in its essence" with "the faculty capable of seeing it" (the mind), he declares, "will be able to bring forth, not mere reflected images of goodness but true goodness" of soul and character. This makes beauty at once the highest moral ideal and the supreme moral educator. And it shows how far Plato was willing to go from where he had started with children's stories: art can lead us to true beauty, and true beauty can make us good.

Most of us in Western culture do not think of beauty like this today. Our culture has divorced the beautiful from the good—or, to be more up-to-date, it has removed aesthetics from ethics, except among moralists bent on artistic censorship. Whether this is good or bad for us stirs continual debate. But Plato was certain. And despite the censorship of art in his ideal state, Plato's praise of beauty has inspired many an artist—including that most infamous modern aesthete, Oscar Wilde—to take Plato as a mentor.

Plato even has Socrates himself turn to art and start writing poetry while in prison awaiting the hour of his death. As Plato relates this unex-

pected event in the *Phaedo,* Socrates explains to his astonished companions, who had heard him reproach artists many times, that he has taken
up poetry, and is adapting some fables of Aesop, because he might have
misunderstood the dream that had long ago told him to "practice and
cultivate the arts [*mousikē*]." He had thought the dream was instructing
him to follow the muse of philosophy, "because philosophy is the greatest of the arts," but now he wonders if instead the dream had intended
him to follow the muse of poetry and to start "composing verses," or
rather to be a "poet" and "compose stories" in "verse." (More literally,
Socrates thinks that as a "poet" [*poieten*] he should "make myths" [*poien
mythos*], but not being a "maker of myths" [*mythologikos*] he borrowed
some myths or fables from Aesop and "turned them into verse" [*epoisa*].)
Socrates might have been indulging in a bit of his typical irony here.
But it would not be wrong to hear in his words a reminder that Plato
believed *mousikē* could shape character through all of the arts, and that a
good character is always *beautiful.*

Plato might have been a thin-lipped moralist preoccupied with the power of art to do harm. But he was also an idealist who hailed the power of
art and beauty to do good. It is no mere coincidence that no one has ever
wrwritten philosophy with more eloquent artistry, more vivid imagery,
and more memorable stories than he. For besides his ardent moralism
and lofty metaphysics, Plato knew that truths, no less than the lies he
accused artists of telling, sway us most compellingly when delivered on
the wings of art.

And, curmudgeonly censor that he could be, Plato nonetheless deserves our thanks for asking enduringly provocative questions about
the morality and immorality of art. Nowadays, when art in its various
forms, most conspicuously as entertainment, is all but ubiquitous, those
questions may have more resonance than ever. For how easily we can
take art for granted and ignore its powers. And how easily we can submit
to those powers without knowing it. And how easily we can then let
those powers serve ends far from the beautiful and the good. If you do
not think this can happen, or that it matters, read Plato.

PLATO'S MOST CELEBRATED STUDENT, Aristotle, shared his teacher's respect for the power of art, although he did not share Plato's worst fears
of it. Like Plato, Aristotle gave art a central place
in his political theory, devoting a sizable portion

ARISTOTLE

of his *Politics* to the subject. And he advised
limiting some kinds of art for much the same reasons as Plato did. But
Aristotle was more broadminded than Plato. After all, Aristotle wanted

to know everything—how things work and how to use them. So he dwelled less on the harm art can cause than on the good it can do when we use it well. While Plato became the father of artistic censorship, Aristotle became the father of art appreciation and art education. And we live out Aristotle's ideas on both of these subjects every day.

Along with Plato, Aristotle put the arts into people's lives near their beginning, in childhood, to shape "a certain kind of character." And Aristotle shared Plato's wariness over how to do this. He recommended that we carefully choose the "kinds of stories and legends children . . . are to hear" and that we expose the young to no "unseemly talk." We should also forbid "debased paintings" representing "unseemly actions" and insure that all "tunes and modes" and instruments used in education "have *ethical* value" and no "orgiastic and emotional" effects, because "hearing such sounds does indeed cause changes in our souls."

Aristotle's constraints on art in education sound as quaint today as Plato's. But Aristotle was only warming up. From there he goes on to describe the many benefits of art, and to conclude that we need art to fulfill ourselves as human beings. Between cautiously using art education to instill good character, and loftily promoting art appreciation to fulfill human nature, Aristotle gave art many roles to play. It plays most of those roles for us still—when we let it. Looking back at Aristotle, we can see why we should get the most we can out of those roles, not the least.

Begin with what Aristotle calls "amusement." Aristotle saw good uses for amusement, and he expected the arts—he often did specifically mean *music*—to give it to us. "Amusement," he says, supplies "relaxation" and "refreshment," rather like "taking a nap or having a drink," and is therefore "a kind of cure for the ills we suffer in working hard." Everybody needs amusement, just as we need physical rest and renewal. But, Aristotle cautions, useful and necessary as they are, we should not "make amusements an end in themselves." For that would be like making physical rest the purpose of life.

To punch the point, Aristotle draws a line between "amusement" and "civilized pursuits" or "noble activities." Because amusement gives us a necessary reprieve from work in pleasant rest, its rewards come effortlessly. But "civilized pursuits" require "a certain amount of learning and education" to prepare us for the "best kind of enjoyment." We draw the same line today between Low Culture and High Culture, or entertainment and art. The entertainment of Low Culture comes easily and makes us *feel* good. The art of High Culture takes effort and helps us *be* good, or more civilized—at least that is the age-old assumption going back to Plato. We might wonder what Aristotle would say of our times, when so many people "make amusements an end" that entertainment now threatens to become the very purpose of life. He would probably say (and he would not be alone or wrong) that our culture of entertainment is not fulfilling human nature, but diminishing it with too much lazy relaxation—"amusing ourselves to death," as the social critic Neil Postman complained in a prominent book of that title in the 1980s. Aristotle considered "civilized pursuits" an antidote for excessive amusement, giving us the highest purpose of "leisure"— not just providing rest and relaxation, but completing our lives.

While Aristotle would likely fault our overuse of amusement, he would not complain about it as much Plato would. Plato condemned all art that plays to easy emotional responses because it exploits the low, "irrational" part of us and induces us to act out those emotions. Aristotle knew better. He saw that when art stirs our emotions, we do not simply act out these emotions. For one thing, if art education has done its job, Aristotle says, people become "completely immune to any harm that might come to them from such spectacles" as raucous comedies and other amusements. And for another thing, when emotive art—including "orgiastic" music—moves us deeply, we discover another of art's important uses. This is to provide us "a way of working off the emotions." It short, art brings *katharsis*.

Nowadays almost everybody knows about artistic *katharsis*. And many know that the idea came from Aristotle. In fact, Aristotle says very little about *katharsis*. He introduced the notion in the *Politics,* promising to elaborate on it later in the *Poetics*. But then he seems to have forgotten his promise, since in the *Poetics* he refers only in passing to the *katharsis,* or "purgation," of "pity and fear" through tragedy. Despite his cursory treatment of the idea in both places, *katharsis* has had a long and eminent career ever since. And for good reasons.

By borrowing the term *katharsis* from medicine and applying it to art, Aristotle broke with Plato's confining moral theory of art. For *katharsis* protects us from the emotionally subversive powers of art that Plato most feared—and that many people still worry about. Thanks to *katharsis*, Aristotle explained, art (he had music and tragedy specifically in mind) can arouse strong emotions in us and yet not lead us to act them out because *katharsis* allows us to experience those emotions while sitting in our chairs and then let those emotions go. As Aristotle puts it, when we experience "pity and fear, for example, but also excitement . . . or any other emotion," even "orgiastic effect[s]" through art, we feel as if we "had undergone a curative and purifying treatment" that leaves "a sort of pleasant purgation and relief," and "an elation which is not at all harmful." Then we can go on to conduct rational and responsible lives.

So that is *katharsis*. It might not always work. And Aristotle did not expect it to work in children because we need education and maturity in order to go through *katharsis* fully, just as we need them to appreciate all of the higher purposes of art as a "civilized pursuit." We could place *katharsis* among those higher purposes. And it gives us one good reason not to banish or censor artists who move us emotionally. As Aristotle says, we should just learn to use their art properly. Art educators, art lovers, and moralists—like everybody else—should not forget this.

The workings of *katharsis* also hint at another vital role that Aristotle says art can play. In this role, art actually teaches invaluable truths. These are not disembodied abstractions like Plato's ideals of Truth and Beauty and Goodness. They come much closer to home. These truths amount to knowledge of human life as we actually live it, and as we might live it. The hint of these truths in *katharsis* is this. *Katharsis* occurs, Aristotle suggests, when something happens in a drama unfolding before us to bring about a "discovery" or "recognition" of an impending tragedy. This recognition stimulates the "tragic pleasure" of "pity and fear" in the audience, followed by "purgation of such emotions." The sequence implies that *katharsis* results from discovering both the causes of tragedy and the reasons for our tragic emotions, a knowledge that helps us purge those emotions. Something like this takes place when we discover the origins of any unsettling emotion in us and then feel freed from that emotion, or able to master it—psychoanalysis tries to do exactly this as a remedy for neurosis through the "talking cure." We could therefore conclude that art provokes *katharsis* by prompting our recognition of the emotional meaning of the events being represented before us. And this delivers a kind of truth, which is insight into events and into how events arouse our emotions. Anyone who has experienced *katharsis* knows that Aristotle was right—and anyone who has not does not yet know how to use art well enough.

Aristotle implies this sequence of emotions–recognition–*katharsis* rather than laying it out. But he explains in some detail how art manages to provide us with more general insights into life even without *katharsis*. In the first place, Aristotle says, art (including some kinds of music) can represent or imitate reality very accurately. And, taking a slap at Plato, who cast a wary eye on artistic representations as distortions of reality, Aristotle declares that not only can art imitate reality accurately, but imitation (*mimesis*) is a good and necessary thing in both art and life. "The instinct for imitation is inherent in man," he observes, "the most imitative of creatures." For human beings learn almost everything they know through one kind of imitation or another. That is why, Aristotle elaborates, people "enjoy seeing representations or likenesses," since "in doing so they acquire information (they reason out what each represents, and discover, for instance, that 'this is a picture of so and so')." That is the commonsense Aristotle for you. He is convinced that the imitations of art—mainly those in tragedy, which represent "action and life," "happiness and unhappiness"—honestly reflect the world we live in instead of deceiving us, as Plato had complained, and that anybody can "reason out" how this works.

But Aristotle also believes art gives us even more than that. It can take us beyond everyday reality to "universal truths." These are not Platonic abstractions in "Cloud-cuckoo-land" (as Aristophanes joked), either. Aristotle's truths always belong to life in this world. "By universal truths," he explains, "are to be understood the kinds of thing a certain type of person will probably or necessarily do in a given situation." That makes them practical human truths, or truths of "possibility and probability" in "the kinds of thing that might happen." Perhaps these truths are what we discover in those moments of recognition that bring *katharsis*. In any case, we surely find them when we encounter things in art that we have not encountered in life but that bring the enlightenment of "possibility" and "universality." "For this reason," Aristotle concludes (emphasizing the literary arts), "poetry is something more philosophical and more worthy of attention than history," for history deals in the "particular facts" of "what has actually happened" whereas "poetry is concerned with universal truths" of "possibility and probability." Historians will object here, but everyone has probably found that art can indeed awaken us to what *might* be—and perhaps *should* be—whether we label these universal truths or not. Is this not an attribute of all great works of art, and perhaps even one of art's highest purposes? Aristotle had no doubt.

Now we can see clearly why Aristotle makes art one of those "civilized pursuits" that we need in order to complete ourselves as human beings. Art goes with "leisure." And it is during leisure that we most fulfill ourselves. Leisure is not a time for mere rest or amusement. It is a time for "enjoying oneself in the right way" through "the best kinds of enjoyment from the finest sources." And since art can spark the emotional release of *katharsis*, yield insights into life, and even reveal universal truths of "possibilities and probabilities," it must be one of the "best kinds of enjoyments" (although, as a philosopher, Aristotle judged no enjoyment to be quite as high as contemplating truth and goodness). So we should take the time to learn how to enjoy art—at its best. That is what it means to engage in "civilized pursuits during leisure," or, more literally, "to leisurely occupy our time with noble and good purposes." (Aristotle's phrase is *scholazein dynasthai kalos*, which denotes being able to devote one's time of leisure to noble, good, and beautiful purposes.) Art gives us many of those "noble and good purposes."

And this brings us to Aristotle's last piece of advice on how to make the best uses of art. It is a good piece of advice, although many people won't like it. Aristotle says that everyone (meaning for him the privileged class, but let that pass for now) should learn not only how to appreciate art passively, but how to create and perform artworks. He would have us learn how to play music, as well as just listen to it, how to paint paintings, as well as just look at them, how to write poetry, as well as just read it, and so on. This is not an odd notion. Schools act on it every day as they teach our children all of these arts. But Aristotle also adds a caveat. And this is what many people won't like—particularly professional artists, and those who aspire to become professional artists, along with parents who want their talented children to become professional artists.

Valuable as artistic training is, Aristotle cautions, it should stop short of "professional education"—he refers specifically to music. For "in this kind of education the performer does not perform in order to improve his own virtue" and gain fulfillment through the civilized pursuit of the arts. Instead, he or she converts a single civilized pursuit into *work*.

Here Aristotle strikes the vital distinction between professional and amateur artistry, surely more pronounced in our times than it was in his. For he was certain that while amateur artistry as a "civilized pursuit during leisure" helps complete our humanity, professionalism thwarts that humanity. Professionalism does this by making "the mind preoccupied" (literally, "without leisure," as the translator notes) and "unable to rise above lowly things" to the higher purposes of art. To ward off the danger, Aristotle would exclude from education any music or musical instrument (such as music for the "pipes" and the "lyre") that "requires the skill of the professional"—he was thinking of "sensational pieces" exhibiting flamboyant skills and performed in artistic competitions and "spectacles."

Aristotle's cautions against professional artistry may be archaic and betray a bias toward an aristocratic social class having no need to work and enjoying abundant leisure to cultivate themselves at their best (in Greek, *aristokratia*, or "aristocracy," meant rule by the best). But we should not dismiss his cautions on those accounts. After all, what can happen to any civilized pursuit when we convert it into nothing but work and a career? Instead of fulfilling our lives, it can indeed harness us to technical skills and consume us in careerist ambitions. To be sure, nowadays we expect professional expertise in many activities—who would want to go to an amateur doctor? But we also know that when we live for any single pursuit, however fine, we lose at least a little of our humanity. And when we do this in the arts, we also sacrifice the unique rewards that art as a civilized pursuit can bring. No one knew this better than Aristotle.

Artists and ardent art lovers might forget, or deny, that art can do us harm in this or other ways because they prize the powers of art so highly. But that does not protect either artists or art lovers from the harm that art can do. The novelist Thomas Mann made this a recurring theme of his fiction—down to depicting in the novel *Doctor Faustus* a composer who trades his soul to the devil for artistic creativity (see Chapter 25). But anyone can misuse the arts by taking them too seriously, or by not taking them seriously enough, or by succumbing to their lesser attractions and failing to use their life-fulfilling powers. Aristotle was among the first to tell us not to let this happen, and why. And he was the first to show us how many good uses art can have—from shaping moral character to providing the necessary pleasures of amusement to granting the insights and emotional release of *katharsis* to revealing the universal truths of possibility and probability to fulfilling our humanity through civilized, or "noble, good and beautiful," pursuits during leisure. Argue with Aristotle on this point or that if you like. But in the end, most of us will probably agree with him that when we use art at its best, it does indeed help us to find, as he says, not only pleasure and happiness, but "the blessed life." ("The blessed life" is *makarios*, the supreme happiness and bliss of the best and most fortunate people.)

PLATO'S AND ARISTOTLE'S THEORIES of art spawned a long history of ideas on the good and evil that art can do. Perhaps the most notorious

TOLSTOY of these were the ideas of Jean-Jacques Rousseau. He commenced his career with the *Discourse on the Moral Effects of the Arts and Sciences* (1750), denouncing the arts and modern culture in general for debasing natural human goodness. Then in his short book *Letter to d'Alembert on the Theatre* (1758) Rousseau echoed Plato as he condemned drama in particular for corrupting public virtue while commending populist festivals and the like for fostering that virtue. Rousseau was a peculiar character who lashed out at everything. But his intellectual genius, piercing perceptions, and folksy eloquence won him a wide following in his times—and many admirers today (see Chapter 6).

Since Rousseau's times no voice has resounded more loudly on the morality and immorality of art than Leo Tolstoy's. Late in life, amid the deepening unorthodox Christianity that possessed him toward the end of the nineteenth century, Tolstoy took up Plato's and Rousseau's themes in a book that moralistically rejected virtually all Western art and all prevailing Western attitudes towards art of the past five hundred years. He called this book *What Is Art?* And it is surely the most provocative and insightful, angry and eccentric book on its subject ever written. It is also among the funniest—its comic version of an opera rehearsal and a performance of Wagner's *Ring of the Nibelungen* will make you laugh and never hear Wagner quite the same again. And if you can resist hurling the book against a wall for its intemperate provocations, and if you take the trouble to meet Tolstoy's arguments head on, you will see art in a new light, and possibly value it differently than you did before. And you will see how Tolstoy's description of the culture of his times in many ways fits the culture of our times like a glove.

To learn from *What Is Art?* we first have to be fair to it. So we should start where Tolstoy did. He wrote the book in response to some conspicuous facts in the culture of his day. Those facts added up to an astounding quantity of human and economic resources consumed, as he says, "to satisfy the demands of art." And he saw more and more of those resources being consumed all the time—in a historical trend that, we must admit, carries us along today.

Running down a long list of institutions and activities devoted to the arts, Tolstoy describes an "artworld," as critics now call it, that sounds very much like our own: "In every large town enormous buildings are erected for museums, academies, conservatories, dramatic schools, and for performances and concerts. Hundreds of thousands of workmen—carpenters, masons, painters, joiners, paperhangers, tailors, hairdressers, jewelers, molders, typesetters—spend their whole lives in hard labor" for art. At the same time, governments and private benefactors subsidize the arts, and the press publicizes "new works of art . . . discussed in the utmost detail by critics and connoisseurs." Only the military, Tolstoy adds, "consumes so much energy as this." Tolstoy might have exaggerated the facts, but he was definitely on to something. The artworld of the twenty-first century, from the proliferation of art schools and performing arts centers to the ubiquity of entertainment, encompasses more of life than even Tolstoy could have imagined.

Whether we judge the growth of this artworld good or bad depends on how we value art. Most people in the West today probably think this growth is a good thing because they value art for bringing many civilized pursuits and pleasures. Not Tolstoy. He looked at his artworld with a sharply critical eye. And he picked up the military allusion again to depict what he saw. "As in war," he declares, "the very lives of men are sacrificed" to art, for "hundreds of thousands of people devote their lives from childhood to learning to twirl their legs rapidly (dancers), or to touch notes and strings very rapidly (musicians), or to draw with paint and represent what they see (artists), or to turn every phrase inside out and find a rhyme to every word." And he concludes: "Is it true that art is so important that such sacrifices should be made for its sake?"

Many people reading these lines will balk and ask: Why does he label these artistic pursuits "sacrifices" and equate them with war? Are they not simply the necessary and admirable activities of art? And that is exactly what Tolstoy wants us to ask. For he knows that this admiration of art has become a reigning assumption of Western culture. It is his very purpose to shake that assumption.

Now that he has got us to take the bait, Tolstoy leads us on. "We have the terrible probability to consider," he says, "that while fearful sacrifices of the labor and lives of men, and of morality itself are being made to art, that some art may not only be useless but even harmful," causing the very "stunting of human life"—a consequence Tolstoy hilariously illustrates with an opera rehearsal whose abusive conductor, brutalizing regimen, and theatrical absurdities reduce the performers to dispirited, bickering, pathetic drudges. With this "terrible probability," Tolstoy brings us to his central issue. It is this: in order to decide whether we should make "these sacrifices of labor, of human life, and even goodness" for art, we must first decide how "important and necessary for humanity" art is, and "whether all that professes to be art is really art." In other words, we must find out: What is the true purpose of art? and What *is* art?

Simple questions? Just try to answer them. Few people do. We merely take the answers for granted. Art is somehow good for us, we tell ourselves, or at all events it gives us a rewarding pleasure. Tolstoy will not let it go at. If we do not know exactly what art should do for us, how can we know if art—or what we call *art*—is doing what it should do, and if we should make "sacrifices" for it. Is he wrong?

Rummaging through books of philosophy and quizzing habitués of the artworld of his day for answers to these questions, Tolstoy did not find much to help him. Only facile claims that art is a good thing, along with vague and often contradictory notions of "what is meant by art and especially what is good art." But then, behind these facile claims and vague notions he detected an implicit value judgment that linked them together. That judgment was the notion that art is somehow good just because it is *art*. Tolstoy did not mean the explicit doctrine of art-for-art's-sake advocated by his contemporaries Walter Pater and Oscar Wilde (see Chapter 25). He rather meant a tradition, originating in the Renaissance, that had divorced art from its previous religious, moral, and social purposes and had sent art out on a life of its own. And increasingly, Tolstoy observed, this life had become nothing but a life of pleasure. Accordingly, he complains, people assume, with absurd circular reasoning, that "artistic enjoyment is a good and important thing because it *is* enjoyment" since they have come to believe that all "enjoyment is good because it is enjoyment." Self-indulgent and self-satisfied as they are, people give art no higher purpose than that.

Theories of aesthetics from the eighteenth century onward had justified this hedonistic trend in art. And Tolstoy didn't approve—although he ignored modern moral conceptions of art, like those of Rousseau, William Wordsworth, and Percy Bysshe Shelley (see Chapter 23). Asserting that "true art" has nothing to do with either *pleasure* or *aesthetics*, Tolstoy blamed these misconceptions on the lassitude and lasciviousness of upper class life and on the ascending late nineteenth-century artistic fashions of Decadence, Symbolism, Impressionism, and aesthetic modernism in general. All of this has bastardized art, he says, making it sensual and sensationalist, exclusive and elitist, hedonistic and aestheticized, altogether depriving art of its true life-serving purposes. For whereas *true art* has nothing to do with pleasure and aesthetics, Tolstoy argued, it has everything to do with morality, society, and humanity at large.

Tolstoy minces no words. "Art is not a pleasure, a solace, or amusement," he cries, "art is a great matter." Pleasure could no more be the true purpose of art, he declares, than "that the purpose and aim of food is the pleasure derived when consuming it." Pleasure is at most a by-product of art, not an end. Any art created for the purpose of "artistic enjoyment" must therefore be "false art." And when we "sacrifice" other things in life for false art of this kind we are sacrificing life to pleasure. That is a depraved sacrifice, Tolstoy rails. So, he has made his mission clear: he will save humankind from the evils of false art by defending the virtues of true art. Tolstoy is nothing if not ambitious—and combative.

To fulfill this ambition, Tolstoy passes quickly through some philosophy and then gets down to the nuts and bolts. Far from a mere pleasure, he asserts, art is "a great matter" because it is "one of the conditions of human life." Specifically, it is "one of two organs of human progress." The other is language. Both of these are "indispensable means of communication" among human beings. "By words man exchanges thoughts," he explains, and "by the forms of art he exchanges feelings." Now, taking a deep breath, Tolstoy pulls these ideas together in a definition of true art, which he spells out with emphasis: *"Art is a human activity consisting in this, that one man consciously, by means of certain external signs . . . movements, lines, colors, sounds, or forms expressed in words . . . hands on to others feelings he has lived through, and that other people are infected by these feelings and also experience them.*" This is Tolstoy's direct answer to the question "What is art?" But that is not all there is to it.

It was hardly path-breaking for Tolstoy to say that art communicates feelings. Thinkers had been saying this in one way or another since the Greeks. But Tolstoy converted this age-old notion into a thumping dogma that he invoked to banish anything else that art might do besides communicate emotions (quite unlike Plato, who condemned art that trafficked in the emotions). He won't win many converts today. He hits, however, on more telling features of our own artworld than you would expect. And despite his dogmatism, he gives us cause to think twice before accepting all that this artworld offers us—and asks of us. He does this by playing out the fundamental differences between true art and false art.

In the first place, Tolstoy explains, true art does not communicate just *any* feelings, since false art can communicate feelings too. True art does not communicate feelings just for their own sake either, since that would smack of self-indulgent pleasure or elitist aestheticism. No, true art communicates only certain feelings, and it does this to a single lofty purpose. Tolstoy puts it this way: "True art" communicates only the "the simple feelings of common life, accessible to everyone without exception." When an artist genuinely feels these emotions and can "hand them on" to other people through art, those people become spontaneously "infected" by the same emotions. This emotional "infection" unites people in a community of shared feelings and humanity. And some day, so Tolstoy hoped, true art will "infect" everyone with these common emotions and advance what he called "the brotherhood of man" (which is his moral ideal of true Christianity).

That, in sum, is true art. Now false art. False art does many things to us, Tolstoy says, but none of them good in the end. It can give pleasure. It can excite thrills. It can breed sophistication. It can provide a career. And so forth. But these purposes of art only prove that it is false. For if an artwork fails to "infect" us spontaneously with universal feelings, Tolstoy contends, it is false. If we have to learn to like it, it is false. If it unites only "habituated" and "perverted" devotees, it is false. If it uses sensationalism or sensuality, it is false. The list goes on and on, stamping most of what we likely think of as art with the label "false art."

These are not mere quibbles over artistic taste. Tolstoy is emphatic about what is at stake here: false art brutalizes human beings and drives humanity and civilization into the ground. For when false art reigns, he complains, human beings do not just sink into its self-indulgent pleasures, they "become continually more savage, more coarse, more cruel," and then social bonds loosen, culture withers, civilization declines, and humanity founders. But when true art reigns, human beings become more humane, social bonds strengthen, civilization flourishes, culture flowers, and humanity thrives amid "the brotherhood of man." Therefore, true art is "indispensable for the life and progress toward wellbeing of individuals and humanity," and without it, Tolstoy goes so far as to say, "mankind could not exist." That is why "art is a great matter"—humankind depends on true art for its very survival.

Despite his gloomy diagnoses of the artworld around him, Tolstoy actually envisions the future optimistically, foreseeing a time when true art will prevail. But this would be a time that not many art lovers today would welcome. "The art of the future," Tolstoy predicts, "will thus be completely distinct, both in subject matter and in form, from what is now called art." Shedding the baggage of the modern artworld—its aestheticism and elitism, its sacrifices and exploitations, its amorality and inhumanity—the art of the future will be "open to everyone" and advance "the highest comprehension of life" as "the brotherhood of man." This art of "brotherhood," Tolstoy continues, will consist only of art deeply rooted in social life, and will communicate the deepest unifying feelings of all people, such as "joy at another's gladness . . . sorrow at another's grief," love, humility, and admiration. These true artworks, he remarks, will include marches, Masses, birthday tunes, and some melodies of Bach, Mozart, and Chopin, as well as edifying moralistic tales like those of Victor Hugo and Charles Dickens. As to his own writings, he sneers, "I consign my own artistic productions to the category of bad art," except for a couple of religious tales.

By this point, most readers have slammed the book shut. Who wants to shackle art with Tolstoy's folksy Christian moralism and gather around the campfire for peasant songs and homiletic tales? And yet, we should not conclude that this resistance dispatches Tolstoy's argument. We should ask ourselves: If Tolstoy is wrong, how is he wrong? And what should art do for us that Tolstoy denies or fails to recognize? To answer these questions, we must come up with a *What Is Art?* of our own. Everyone should do it.

In our own *What Is Art?* we will have to say things like this: art does not exist solely to let us share "spontaneous" and "simple feelings" with everyone else; it should also expand the range of our own imaginations, emotions, senses, and even our intellects (Aristotle had suggested no less). We might also say that this kind of expansiveness makes us better human beings. But what would we say about Tolstoy's criticism of art's place in modern culture and of how the modern artworld works? For, eccentric as he was, Tolstoy saw much here that should give us pause.

For instance, only the most adamant aesthete would deny that when we invite art to challenge and change us as individuals—even for the good that we think it can do by expanding the range of our imaginations and so on—we assure that art will divide us to some degree by taste and judgment. And if we let artistic taste and judgment become a supreme standard of value, it can even do us harm. Oscar Wilde and Thomas Mann wrote classic fiction on that theme. As Mann said in his story "Tonio Krüger"—one of his many excursions into the perils of aesthetics—"What more pitiable sight is there than a life led astray by art?" For all of his excesses, Tolstoy was right: celebrating art for its personal gratifications wholly apart from its social consequences can be risky.

Nor do we have to share Tolstoy's moralism to see in the artworld of our times virtually everything that Tolstoy had reproached in his, and more. In the little more than a century since Tolstoy wrote *What Is Art?*, every social fact and artistic tendency that he bewailed has doubled and redoubled. Art schools, museums, performing arts centers, symphony orchestras, opera companies, theater and dance troupes, arts organizations, and, above all, the popular arts or entertainment, have proliferated, engaging more and more lives and resources, and weaving the arts, and especially entertainment, ever more tightly into the fabric of modern life. We might praise these developments as signs of an advanced civilization. But Tolstoy was not wrong to detect in them many a questionable consequence, and possibly even something like cancerous growths. The insatiable commercialization of the artworld is obviously among these consequences. But Tolstoy also saw both subtler and more egregious consequences of the modern artworld's influence. One of the more subtle and suggestive of these was the rise of that most unemotional, pseudointellectual, and now-ubiquitous aesthetic notion—the *interesting*.

"To speak of an interesting work of art," Tolstoy observes, is a practice of recent times. For the "interestingness" of an artwork, he points out, "has nothing to do with its excellence as a work of art." It only means that the artwork offers "information new to us" or that it is "not fully intelligible." Either way, we feel nothing and must rely on "mental effort" to respond at all. Tolstoy considered this a mark of much false art: if we have to learn to appreciate a work of art, we are merely intellectualizing it and habituating ourselves to it, just as we can habituate ourselves to "bad food . . . and opium." We should think about this the next time we grope for a response to a confusing or unappealing artwork and come up with: "It's, uh, well . . . interesting." That paltry response proves that the artwork does not move us, and that we suspect we must learn how to appreciate it intellectually lest we appear to be a Philistine. Our retreat to the "interesting," more often than not, betrays our confusion and intimidation. Tolstoy damned this retreat as a coward's way of dealing with certain kinds of false art.

If Tolstoy's hostility to the intellectualizing of art goes too far, he had nonetheless detected a telling clue to our artworld. We might say that we should learn to understand art in order to improve ourselves. But we should not let artists, or art critics, or anyone else intimidate us into accepting their versions of what art should do for us. Tolstoy tries to boost our confidence by urging us to trust our common human responses to art. Overwrought as Tolstoy can be, he does us a valuable service here. For he asks us to take seriously our spontaneous and honest responses to an artwork as a measure of its worth. And although Tolstoy would have us stop right there, we ought to see that this is surely where we should begin.

But what about the popular arts? While Tolstoy would disdain the intellectualization, professionalization, and overall cult of high art in our times, we might expect that he would take some cheer from the infectious emotionality of the proliferating popular arts. The communal tears of sadness and bursts of joy in movie theaters, the gratifying familiarity of television soap operas and sitcoms, the collective exuberance at rock concerts, the adoring mass-identifications with celebrities, the moralistic children's fables of Disney, the wholesome thrills of families at theme parks, all seize us emotionally with no mental effort. And these kinds of pop cultural entertainments are also dissolving boundaries of customs, nations, and social classes around the world, promising to produce a truly global culture and "brotherhood of man." Wouldn't Tolstoy applaud?

No, he wouldn't. Our popular arts are not Tolstoy's "art of the future" leading to a Christian "brotherhood of man." Tolstoy commended folk art as the traditional artistic expression of a people's common life, for folk art had ties to enduring ceremonial or other social practices, and always served social ends. The modern popular arts may reflect and appeal to the common life, but they rely on sophisticated technologies, play to cheap sensationalism, and always serve commercial ends. Folk art belongs to human nature and traditional societies. The modern popular arts belong to consumer capitalism and mass society. And Tolstoy wouldn't like that.

He even foresaw this mass popular culture down the road and put up danger signs against it. Sharing Plato's wariness of artistic ingenuity, Tolstoy warned against any artworks that appeal strongly to sensations and emotions through technical artistry itself (although he welcomed such modern technological devices as the telegraph and the telephone for bringing people together). These kinds of artworks do not "infect" us with genuine feelings. They rather captivate our senses with contrived stimulation and arouse artificial and ephemeral emotions. Even before the advent of movies and television, Tolstoy complained about "amusement-art" that is "manufactured to ready-made, prearranged recipes . . . by the armies of professional artists" who use "striking . . . effects" to produce "physiological effects" on audiences. Were Tolstoy to witness the techniques of American popular culture today, which all but bewitch the young and which are casting their spell around the world, he might have to concede that an "art of the future" is indeed "diffused among mankind" and forging a global unity. But he would shudder at it. For it would show him that false art purveying only artistic enjoyment might unify the world after all—in a brotherhood of mass entertainment.

Tolstoy was a dogged opponent of nearly all the art and entertainment of his times. And he gives us in *What Is Art?* a prescription for art that only moralists like himself could embrace. But you cannot read this book thoughtfully without recognizing that for all of his eccentricities and excesses, Tolstoy knows art and our culture remarkably well, and he has seen in them things we should not fail to see. In the end, no one else has given us more pressing reasons to answer the question, What is art?

LOOKING AT MODERN CULTURE TODAY, where the arts and entertainment pervade life, and yet people do not take art very seriously as a molder of character and culture, Plato, Aristotle, and Tolstoy would see much to fault, and much to repair. Plato would surely wag an accusing finger at us for allowing the arts to foster moral decline and social disorder. Aristotle would more likely try to improve the schools. Tolstoy would scold us for accepting the many varieties of false art that have fashioned a culture of shallow pleasures and emotional self-absorption rather than genuine human community. And all of them would warn that wherever our modern world is headed from here, art is certain to help lead us there, for the better or the worse.

On the Morality and Immorality of Art

1. There is no such thing as art for art's sake—art always affects character and social life.
2. Art has the power to do us both good and harm.
3. Art shapes character by bringing instruction or imitation, insight or error, restraint or self-indulgence, morality or immorality.
4. To make art to do more good than harm, we must understand how its powers work on us—emotionally, intellectually, morally.

5. Art reaches us most forcefully through the emotions. (Plato, Tolstoy)

6. Art can bring *katharsis*, which purges strong emotions so they do us no harm. (Aristotle)

7. Art can deceive us by manipulating the emotions and misrepresenting reality.

8. When art becomes "interesting," it has lost its emotional power. (Tolstoy)

9. If we have to learn to like an artwork, it lacks emotional power and is only an intellectual exercise. (Tolstoy)

10. Art can open our eyes to truths about life as it is, and as it might be. (Aristotle)

11. Art should make us better and help complete us as human beings.

12. The meaning of life is to fulfill ourselves as human beings and to use all the good powers of art to that end, while being aware of the harm art can do.

20

All Stories Are True

Islamic Storytelling: *The Arabian Nights*
Ghanaian Folklore: "Why We Tell Stories About Spider"

I will begin to tell a story, and it will cause the King to stop
his practice, save myself, and deliver the people.
Shahrazad

To have stories told about you is a very heavy responsibility.
Ghanaian storyteller

The Arabian Nights, or *The Thousand and One Nights (c. thirteenth
century)**, is the world's most renowned collection of stories. Passed down
orally over many generations by anonymous Indian, Persian, and Arabic
storytellers, some of these stories were probably first brought together and
recorded in the ninth or tenth centuries C.E. But a standard edition of *The
Thousand and One Nights* did not appear in Arabic until the thirteenth
century, and stories continued to be added in various editions even after
that. Because Arabic was the language of the rising religion of Islam and
of its holy book, the Koran, *The Thousand and One Nights* took its place
in world literature as a collection of Islamic tales popularly known as *The
Arabian Nights*. Although Islam sets the stage for the stories of the *Nights*,
the prevailing subject of these stories is none other than storytelling itself.
These stories fall within the overarching tale of Shahrazad, who tells them
to her husband, King Shahrayar, an angry, peerlessly misogynistic man who
has vowed revenge on all women for the unfaithfulness of one of his wives.
Shahrazad married Shahrayar hoping to end his murderous rage by telling
stories that would entertain him and soften his heart. Her first story in the
original edition, "The Demon and the Merchant," reflects her own situation. It tells of a demon bent on bloody revenge, and of how good stories
turn out to change his mind. And this theme runs through the original
Arabian Nights—the power of stories not just to entertain, but to change
people for the better.

The African tale **"Why We Tell Stories About Spider"** is also about
storytelling. It typifies the classic folktales told in oral cultures about clever

371

"tricksters" who cause mischief and become the butt of moral reproach. The story here is one of many told in the West African country of Ghana about the emblematic trickery and malefactions of the creature called Spider. It tells how Spider's clever tricks became a principal subject of Ghanaian stories. No less than Shahrazad the storyteller, Spider as the subject of stories represents the moral uses and imaginative power of stories. And both show how that power makes all stories true.

———————————

STORIES COME in many forms and have many purposes. They come as myths, legends, fables. They come as parables, proverbs, riddles. They comes as yarns, entertainments, lies. They rouse laughter, prompt tears, stir thoughts. They divert. They instruct. They help hold societies together. They can undo societies. Whatever their form or effects, stories have power. And every culture tells them.

We could say that the power of stories acts mainly through pleasure. Or rather, through three interrelated kinds of pleasure. One is the familiar pleasure of fantasy or what we nowadays casually call "escape"—leaving the "real world" for that of the imagination, where anything can happen because there we suspend effort and judgment and get refreshment without risk. This pleasure is like play (Freud took it very seriously—see Chapter 17). The second pleasure comes from something near the opposite of escape. It is the pleasure of learning something new about reality, or seeing our expectations or wishes about reality confirmed (Aristotle found this in the pleasure of imitation—see Chapter 19). The first pleasure is more imaginative, the second more intellectual. The third pleasure shares something with both the first and second. And it is the most important of the three. For it is the pleasure of inventing or discovering possibilities. And therein lies the distinctive kind of truth, or truths, that stories contain. These are the truths of possibilities—what might *be* in reality. Everyone knows these truths of stories. We can hardly live without them. Even though they can be unhappy ones.

"There is no story that is not true," says a wise man in Chinua Achebe's novel *Things Fall Apart* (1959) to a fellow Nigerian who cannot believe the first reports he hears of white men and their slave trade. "There is no story that is not true," the wise man ruefully explains, because "the world has no end, and what is good among one people is an abomination with others." Achebe goes on to reimagine the ravaging of his native Nigerian culture by the European slave trade, reminding us that the truths of possibilities are not always good—because frightful, and hard to imagine, possibilities can come true.

A century after the tragic events of Achebe's novel, another historical horror, the Jewish Holocaust, prompted one of its victims, Elie Wiesel, to become a storyteller dedicated to this very theme: opening people's eyes to frightfully unbelievable events that can happen, and did happen, in reality (see Chapter 16). Achebe and Wiesel both show us that any story can be true because reality is not bound by the past or by what we are used to, or even by what we can easily imagine. As Wiesel says, with knowing sorrow, "anything is possible."

Aristotle said almost the same thing in the *Poetics* when he elevated the truths of poetry (meaning literature in general) over the truths of history (see Chapter 19). History, Aristotle says, deals "with specific facts or events" and "relates what has happened," but poetry deals "with universal truths" of "what might happen" or "possibilities and probabilities." Therefore, poetry "is more akin to philosophy and is a better thing than history." For, like the universal truths of philosophy, those of literature come not from facts but from imagination, transcending known experience to reach imagined possibilities and enable us to envision what *might be*. And when we see what might be, we have the chance to change the world and ourselves, avert dangers, and bring good things to pass—Don Quixote is the fictional model of all those who change themselves to make the world better (see Chapter 22).

It is no wonder that so many of the world's seminal religious and philosophical teachers—like Confucius, Socrates, and Jesus—often spoke in stories, images, parables. These conveyed the universal truths of spiritual and moral possibility. Such teachers, who never wrote a word, also suggest something else about stories: it is that the power of stories has probably been greatest where people have depended on the spoken rather than the written word. For where the spoken word reigns, it tends to tie fact and fiction into a knot. An oral culture might distinguish between, say, poetic accounts of the gods honored as truth and campfire tales told largely as diversion, but the two literary forms readily blend. For in passing from one generation to another through oral repetition, reports of the sacred and tales of the secular cannot help but flow together. That is what makes myths—the very word comes from *mythos*, a Greek term that also meant stories in general. Such were the origins of most ancient religious and philosophical traditions (think of Hinduism, Confucianism, Taoism, Buddhism, Judaism, Platonism, Christianity).

In his novel *The Storyteller* (1989) the Peruvian author Mario Vargas Llosa invents an oral tradition like this, dependent on the truth of stories. The novel's title character spurns a promising career in Lima to enter the jungle, where he becomes a storyteller wandering among scattered, illiterate tribes, telling them stories that not only entertain, but provide threads of a common culture. These threads are the truth of stories—or the *possible* truths. The storyteller underscores this at the end of every tale when he always assures his listeners: "That, anyway, is what I have learned." Fact or fiction, every story he tells repeats something he has "learned": a truth of possibility.

Although the possible truths of stories count most in oral cultures, these truths—happy or sad, hopeful or ominous—reside in every story. And the ability to tell stories, or to find these truths in them with what we might call the imagination of possibility, can give both pleasure and power, as well as the power of pleasure, to anyone. Even Plato, who criticized stories for telling lies, recommended beginning a child's education with the "right kind" of "stories" (*mythos*) because they present images of goodness and teach us what we might become, and should become (see Chapter 19). And there is no greater gift to give children, or for anyone to possess as adults, than to be able to imagine good possibilities, and then bring them to pass.

THE POWER AND TRUTHS OF STORIES nowhere leap more vividly from the page—or from the storyteller's lips—than in that most fabled collection of the storyteller's art, *The*

ARABIAN NIGHTS

Thousand and One Nights, or *The Arabian Nights*. The title conjures up notions of vaporous genies, flying carpets, breathtaking adventures, magical escapes, and memorable heroes like Aladdin, Ali Baba, and Sinbad (although these three came very late to the collection and are of dubious origins). But *The Arabian Nights* is not just a batch of entertainingly tall tales. It is about nothing so much as the truths of possibility that stories tell, and the power of these truths to change us.

Paradoxically, the stories of *The Arabian Nights* and the truths they tell came down to us from an Islamic storyteller. This is paradoxical because the Islamic religious tradition officially opposed storytelling. One reason for this is that the sacred book of Islam, the Koran—unlike many other formative documents of religions, such as the Bible and the *Mahābhārata*—did not take form from an oral tradition. Although it contains arresting images, like those of Paradise and of Allah Himself, it speaks absolute truth in the sacred words of Allah as revealed directly to Mohammed by the Angel Gabriel in the Arabic language said to have been created by Allah for this purpose. Those words were supposed to be read, memorized, and recited by believers without invention or variation.

"Recite in the name of your Lord who created man," were, according to tradition, Allah's first revealed words in the Koran. "Recite! Your Lord is the Most Bountiful One, who by the pen taught man what he did not know." This revelation gave the very name to the book. As translators point out, Koran or *Qur'an* means "recital" or "recitation." Memorizing and reciting Koranic verses were therefore to become the primary acts of Islamic devotion—the chief expression of "submission" (to Allah), which is what the Arabic word *Islām* means. Where literal recitation was pious devotion, storytelling was impiety, if not blasphemy. And the Koran says as much. It denounces storytellers as fabricators and deceivers who "spread frivolous stories to mislead (others) from the way of God, without any knowledge"; and "as for poets, only those who go astray follow them."

And yet, Islam nevertheless inspired some of the world's greatest storytellers and storytelling traditions. Even today, Islamic storytellers ply their trade in Arab marketplaces—like that most famous marketplace for Islamic storytellers, entertainers, and hucksters, as well as for Islamic teachers, the Djma el Fna in Marrakech, Morocco. But Islamic storytelling does not betray a simple paradox or incorrigible impiety. It could be said to arise from the imagination of possibilities at the heart of Islam itself. For even while the Koran denounced storytellers, it also implicitly encouraged them.

In the first place, the very air of mystery and the absence of clear narrative in the Koran actually prompted so much puzzlement and curiosity about Allah and his transcriber-prophet Mohammed that soon teachers began to explain the holy book with allusions and images and—stories. From these beginnings, Islamic teachers and Islamic storytellers often became rolled into one. You can see this every day in the Djma el Fna, where Islamic teachers and storytellers work side by side and sometimes sound much the same.

In the second place, the teachers and storytellers discovered something else in the Koran to inspire their inventive imaginations. This was the very image of Allah Himself—His absolute power, His transcendence, His boundlessness. This image of Allah's supremacy demanded submission from believers, but it also aroused and even sanctioned the storyteller's imagination of possibility. If Allah's power is absolute, He can make anything happen. So, as the pious Arabic phrase *In Sha'Allah* ("God willing") implies—words uttered in Islamic lands whenever possibilities are mentioned—*anything is possible*.

So it was that Islamic storytellers could freely mingle fact and fantasy, morals and marvels, the ordinary and the extraordinary, the possible and the seemingly impossible, while nonetheless always honoring Allah. The

Islamic storyteller's subject is the infinite realm of Allah, where carpets can fly, genies can rise from lamps, and magic can transform things, all proving Allah's infinite powers.

The Arabian Nights belongs to this Islamic tradition. But it is also a monument to the imagination of possibility and to the truth of stories everywhere. We overlook the Islamic content when we read *The Arabian Nights* solely for the pleasures of their engaging fantasies. But while we enjoy those pleasures we should ponder them, too. How they work on us, how they convey the kinds of truths that stories tell, and how they make *The Arabian Nights* what it is. Then we not only enjoy those pleasures, we also feel the power that stories can exert, awakening us to infinite possibilities, Islamic or not.

THE ARABIAN NIGHTS begins where Islamic storytellers are obliged to begin, with dutiful obeisance to Allah (in the Foreword): "In the name of God the Compassionate, the Merciful . . . the Creator of the World and man." But then the unidentified narrator goes on to explain "the purpose of writing this agreeable and entertaining book." And that purpose might surprise you. It is not only to "delight and divert," but to give readers "edifying histories and excellent lessons" that will, among other things, "teach the reader to detect deception and to protect himself from it," as well as teach "the art of discourse," which is nothing less than the art of storytelling itself. *The Arabian Nights* therefore comes to us as a collection of tales about how to understand life, beware of deception, and appreciate how stories tell truths wrapped in fantastic possibilities. And, in one way or another, all of its stories (especially those in the original edition, deftly translated by Husain Haddawy), do that, if we listen to them. That makes *The Arabian Nights* more consequential, and useful, than most people predict.

Before getting down to the storytelling, the narrator gives another obligatory nod to Allah by saying that no storyteller should claim too much knowledge, since "the Supreme God is the True Guide" to all truths and all possibilities. After that pious Islamic demurral, the narrator then launches the renowned story of Shahrazad herself (more commonly known as Scheherazade, thanks to Rimsky-Korsakov's musical suite by that title). This story (sometimes called the Prologue), sets the stage for, or "frames," all the stories that follow. These are told by Shahrazad within the story that is told about her. But the story of Shahrazad not only sets the stage for the stories she tells. Her story has one particular theme echoed by all the others (playing out "the excellent lessons" that the anonymous narrator had promised). This theme is how stories yield pleasures in truths of possibility that can change people for the better. That, above all, is the power of stories in *The Arabian Nights*.

The story about Shahrazad herself opens with yet another humble bow to Allah's omniscience: "It is related—but God knows and sees best what lies hidden in the old accounts of bygone peoples and times—that long ago. . . . " Again, the Islamic storyteller must not presume to know the whole truth of any story that he or she tells. Only Allah knows that. But, the modest narrator reports with the venerable gambit of the world's storytellers, "it is related . . . that long ago. . . . " Did the events "related" actually happen? It is possible.

These events begin with two brothers, Shahrayar and Shahzaman, who ruled Samarkand and parts of India and Indochina. After an unhappy series of events reveal to them both that their wives have been unfaithful, they turn against all women. Shahzaman vows never to marry again, but King Shahrayar, gripped by a darker rage and a crueler resentment against "the wickedness and cunning of women," swears "to marry for one night only and to kill the woman the next morning." True to his vile oath, Shahrayar takes a new wife each night and has her executed the next day—in a practice of calculated misogyny unparalleled in literature (a stream of misogyny runs through many other tales in *The Arabian Nights* as well). When Shahrayar's lustful and unrelenting murderousness eventually threatens to destroy the kingdom, Shahrazad, daughter of the vizier to the king, pleads with her father to arrange her own marriage to Shahrayar. She has a plan, ingenious and simple.

After her wedding, but before the fateful morning comes, she confides to her father, "I will begin to tell a story, and it will cause the king to stop his practice, save myself, and deliver the people." Shahrazad thinks this will work because she believes stories have the power first to captivate any listener and then to change him or her for the better. Once the pleasure, suspense, and enlightenment of her first story have taken hold of Shahrayar, she says, he will want to hear more, and then the pleasures and enlightenment of her stories will dissolve his cruelty, and in time she and her people will be saved.

The ploy works. "Morning overtook Shahrazad, and she lapsed into silence leaving King Shahrayar burning with curiosity to hear the rest of the story." She assures him that "tomorrow night I shall tell you something even lovelier, stranger, and more wonderful if I live, the Almighty willing." He muses grimly: "I will spare her until I hear the rest of the story; then I will have her put to death the next day."

And so it goes for a thousand and one nights, the same seductive promise, the same temporary reprieve. Tradition has it that through those nights of storytelling, King Shahrayar did indeed forsake his distrust of women, abandon his horrid vengeance, and remain happily with Shahrazad thereafter.

That is the overarching story of Shahrazad told by a nameless story-teller, within which come the many tales that Shahrazad herself tells to Shahrayar (and to her sister, who encourages the telling). She tells most of these in the words of other storytellers. And many of these storytellers tell their stories as stories within stories within stories. In the world of *The Arabian Nights*, stories weave a thick fabric of life and fantasy—one flying carpet on top of another, and another. And Shahrayar is not the only listener transformed by stories. Many characters within the stories Shahrazad tells are changed for the better by stories, too—hearts are softened, and cruelty yields to kindness again and again. And that is what Shahrazad intends her stories, and the stories within her stories, to do: not just to entertain, but to take people out of themselves, and to give them pleasures that transform them by revealing "amazing" pos-sibilities. This is not mere escape. Shahrazad uses the power of stories as a weapon—and a wand.

Take the first tale she tells, "The Story of the Merchant and the Demon." This tale displays every power of stories that Shahrazad needs as she en-twines the ordinary and the extraordinary, entertainment and enlight-enment, to bring the benign truths of possibility to life for Shahrayar.

"It is said," Shahrazad begins (following the storytellers' convention that opens virtually all of her tales), "that once there was a prosperous merchant" who accidentally killed the son of a demon on the road by carelessly tossing a date pit. Never mind the implausibility. The consequences are bad for the merchant. The demon suddenly appears and thunders: "You killed my son," so "I must now kill you." Begging forgiveness, the unfortunate merchant invokes Allah and recites some verses on the delusions of happiness and the inevitability of fate. The demon shows no mercy. He "raised his sword to strike." And there Shahrazad stops, "leaving Shahrayar burning with curiosity to hear the rest of the story," which she promises to tell "tomorrow night . . . if I live."

When Shahrazad resumes the next night, she reports that, submitting to his fate, the merchant requests time to go home and arrange his affairs before returning to die. The demon relents. When the merchant duti-fully returns on New Year's Day and awaits the demon's arrival, three travelers happen by, one after the other. He tells his unhappy story to the first, who then tells it to the second, and they both tell it to the third. Captivated by curiosity, and moved by the story, all three decide to stay and find out "what [will] happen between the merchant and the demon." The merchant's story, told over and over within Shahrazad's story about him, is already working some of its effects.

When the demon arrives in a cloud of dust, the first traveler, touched by the merchant's plight, steps up with a proposition. He wants to tell a story of his own to the demon. For a peculiar price. "Fiend and king of demon kings," he says, "if I tell you what happened to me and that deer" standing nearby, "and you find it strange and amazing, indeed stranger and more amazing than what happened to you and the merchant, will you grant me a third of your claim on him for his crime and guilt?"

A sucker for stories—like almost everyone else in *The Arabian Nights*, beginning with Shahrayar, animated as they are by curiosity to learn of "strange and amazing" things—the demon agrees. And the traveler recites how it astonishingly came to pass that the deer is actually his wife. After a childless marriage of thirty years, he reports, he had taken a mistress, who bore him a son. Growing jealous of both the mistress and the child, his wife had cast a spell on them both while he was on a long journey, changing the mistress into a cow and the son into a bull. When the traveler returned, his wife told him that his mistress had died and his son had run away. Then she arranged to have a particular cow and bull slaughtered for the Feast of Immolation. Unsuspecting who these animals really were—although he sensed fright emanating from them—the traveler had allowed the cow to be sacrificed. But when the bull's emotions tugged too hard at his heart, he had spared the animal and given it to a shepherd. The next day the shepherd had returned with remarkable news. "I have a daughter who is fond of soothsaying and magic," the shepherd said, and she had discovered that "the bull was in reality the son put under a spell by his stepmother." Aghast and aggrieved, the traveler had asked the shepherd's daughter to undo the spell; and then she had cast another spell on his wife, turning her into a deer to "taste what she has inflicted on others." And this is how it came to pass that the traveler was accompanied by a deer, his vicious wife—they were going to find his son, who now lived in the land where they stood. "This is my amazing story," he concludes, "my strange and amazing story."

A rapt and delighted listener, the demon concedes that the storyteller has fulfilled his promise to astonish and please with strange possibilities. The demon honorably fulfills his own promise: "I grant you one third of this man's life." The story has not only astonished and pleased the demon, it has also lessened his hunger for revenge on the merchant.

Then the second traveler, accompanied by two dogs, offers the demon a similar proposition. "I too shall tell you what happened to me and these two dogs, and if you find it stranger and more amazing than this man's story, will you grant me one third of [the merchant's] life?" The demon cannot resist. Another tale, another trade.

This story relates how the second traveler had shared his wealth with his two brothers and had happily married a poor waif of a girl who had begged for his "kindness and charity." But the brothers had squandered his gifts, and then they had so resented his wealth and happiness that one night they had seized him and his wife and thrown them into the sea to drown. Suddenly his wife had then revealed herself to be "one of the demons who believe in God," and she had carried him to an island, where he told her about his treacherous brothers. "When she heard my story," he recalls, she had vowed to kill them. But, ever merciful—as Muslims are told to be, following the standard epithet for Allah in the Koran: "The Compassionate and Merciful," and as Shahrazad wants Shahrayar to become—the traveler had asked her not to harm them because you are to "be kind to those who hurt you." Instead of killing them, she had transformed them into dogs for a period of ten years. Then she had vanished. The ten years having now elapsed, the traveler was taking his brothers, the dogs, to find his magical wife and get the spell on them lifted.

"This is my story," he says to the demon. "Isn't it amazing?" "By God," the demon replies, "it is strange and amazing." The story has worked. And again the demon grants that a good story of remarkable events is worth another portion of his claim on the merchant's life.

The third traveler strikes the same deal as his two companions. Shahrazad does not recite his story, but observes that it "was even stranger and more amazing than the first two." And the demon, "very much amazed, and swaying with delight," relinquishes the final part of his claim on the merchant and departs happily. Then the others go on their way. The telling of three "amazing" stories—prompted by the merchant's own story—have softened the demon's heart and supplanted his hunger for revenge with wonder and delight at the truths of possibilities in the stories he has heard, and with gratitude for hearing them.

It takes Shahrazad eight nights to tell "The Story of the Merchant and the Demon" with its several stories within the story (as is common in oral traditions, what was finally written down is probably but a fragment of what had been told by storytellers over time with many variations). And at the end, like the three travelers with the demon, she assures her vengeful listener, Shahrayar, that she has an even more astonishing story to tell. For "this story is not as strange or amazing as the story of the fisherman" to come. Shahrayar is hooked for good.

To be sure, "The Story of the Merchant and the Demon" and Shahrazad's other tales deal in the common moral fare of folklore—conflicts between good and evil, enlightenment and ignorance, prudence and self-indulgence, charity and greed, trust and betrayal, and so on. But besides this, as the anonymous narrator had promised, they deal above all—like her own life story—in "the art of discourse," or how telling "amazing" stories can change people and the course of events. Shahrazad expects her stories to do that with Shahrayar. Through their surprises and delights, their reports of deception and revenge, transformation and compassion, their play upon curiosity, and their imagination of possibilities, they will induce him, like the demon of her tale, to trade his harsh vengeance for pleasure, forgiveness, and generosity. And so again and again she tells Shahrayar tales about how stories pacify demons, assuage kings, quell anger, thwart cruelty, and foster humanity. These are not just amazing stories about amazing storytellers. They are about the power of stories to change anyone for the better (even when they do not end happily for everyone).

Islamic moralists and others going back to Plato have feared the power of stories to change people for the worse. As a scornful cleric in Cervantes' *Don Quixote* puts it when he condemns Don Quixote's library: fiction causes trouble by creating "new ways of life." But Shahrazad, like most storytellers, believed it is the very purpose of literature to do just that by opening our eyes to fresh possibilities, stirring our empathy with others, and giving us higher purposes than we might otherwise have.

We can learn a lot from Shahrazad. For she—or the many voices that originally told her tales—delightfully and inventively and abundantly shows us that, far from being idle entertainments, good stories with their truths of possibilities can change hearts and minds forever. Her stories—with their infinite Islamic possibilities—saved her and the women of her country from a misogynistic, vengeful king. This happened, of course, only in the story of her life. But, true or false, this story and those she tells made Shahrazad the emblematic storyteller not only of Islam but of the world.

SHAHRAZAD'S STORIES, and the story about her, tell how stories change people through the truths of possibility. And that is a common theme of the world's storytelling traditions. Another

GHANAIAN FOLKLORE

of these traditions, in the West African country of Ghana, puts another twist on the theme. Like all folk traditions, this one abounds in tales of nature and morals, usually woven together. West African tribes tell many stories about such things as "why the sky is high," "why hippo wears no coat," "how crab got his shell," "why fowls scratch." Many of these are conventional "trickster" fables featuring clever animals whose precocious cunning and deft deceptions people must learn to detect. The favorite of these creatures in Ghanaian folklore is the Spider. Clever, resourceful, and resilient, Spider often pulls off his trickery, but he also sometimes fails. Either way, he gives lessons in the follies of pride, greed, ignorance, and so forth.

Why Spider? Anthropologists might account for this by pointing to the prevalence of big spiders in Ghana. Some Ghanaian tribes account for it with, what else?—a story. Although only a slight piece of folklore, this story nevertheless says something important about storytelling. Just as the framing story of Shahrazad explains why she tells the stories of *The Arabian Nights* to her husband Shahrayar, this Ghanaian tale explains, as the English title reads, "Why We Tell Stories About Spider." Ghanaian tribes do not seem to care *who* tells their stories. The storytellers are anonymous. Ghanaians care more about the subjects of stories. And this story tells why Spider is chief among those subjects.

"In the olden days," begins "Why We Tell Stories About Spider," "stories were told about God, not about Spider." And Spider "felt a very strong desire to have stories told about him. So he went to God and said, 'Dear God, I want to have your stories told about me.'" This god, being benign and generous and wise, is willing to grant Spider's wish, but on severe conditions. "To have stories told about you is a very heavy responsibility," he cautions. "If you want it, I will let you have it, but first you must prove to me that you are fit to have it."

To prove himself worthy to be the subject of stories, Spider must perform the seemingly impossible tasks of bringing three things to God: a swarm of bees, a live python, and a live leopard. Spider ponders these tasks for days. Then he hits on a plan. Taking a calabash into the forest, he finds a swarm of bees. "They can fill it; they can't fill it," he shouts so that the bees will be sure to hear him. The bees ask what he is doing, and he replies that he has had an argument with someone over whether a swarm of bees can fit into the calabash—his opponent has said they can't; he says they can. Falling for the ruse, the bees boast that they can fit in, and they crowd inside to prove it. Spider then slaps on the top and proudly carries the calabash to God. The first task is done.

Spider goes off to find a python, whom he similarly tricks. This time he persuades the python to be tied to a stick just to prove that he is longer than the stick. Spider hauls the bound python back to God. The second task is completed. He then returns to the forest and digs a pit in the path of the leopard, who falls in and allows himself to be hoisted out in a net. Spider triumphantly delivers the netted leopard to God. The three tasks are accomplished.

Ghanaian Folklore: "Why We Tell Stories About Spider"

"You have done the impossible," God congratulates Spider. "So from today I decree that the stories that were once told about me shall be told about you."

By imagining and then doing the seemingly impossible, Spider, the ambitious and clever trickster, won the right to be the surrogate of God as the subject of Ghanaian stories. We might say that to be the subject of stories is godlike because stories tell truths of the moral life. And Spider represents these truths in stories even when he proves not only his cagey ingenuity, but displays his moral imperfections—greed, pride, impulsiveness, etc. Whatever his tricky actions, Spider plays the godlike role in Ghanaian stories of teaching people things that they should know about truth and deception, good and evil, rewards and punishments, and that they would not know if God, or Spider, did not show them—through stories with their revealing possibilities.

Unlike Shahrazad's stories in *The Arabian Nights,* the Ghanaian stories about Spider do not try to win over listeners and change them with amazing adventures and miraculous events. They do it with folksy imagery closer to everyday life. Perhaps this is because the Ghanaian God who lets Spider represent Him is less magisterial and omnipotent and mysterious than Allah, thereby limiting the range of possibilities that Ghanaian stories can describe. But that would not mean that the Ghanaian stories do not try to do much the same thing as Shahrazad's. For folktales like "Why We Tell Stories About Spider" also tell us about the power of stories. They tell us that through the imaginative pleasures of escape and recognition, and especially the truths of possibilities, stories can change people. And this is often their very purpose.

STORIES COME TO US promising simple and uncomplicated pleasures. And yet they can exercise subtle and irresistible powers. Those powers come in no small part from the vision of new ways of life that stories offer us and that we might not otherwise see. "Life can be other than it is," stories say to us, "imagine the possibilities, and learn from them, even if you do not like what you imagine."

"There is no story that is not true," as the Nigerian character in Achebe's novel says, because, as Elie Wiesel added, "anything is possible." Both of these were cautionary voices, asking us to imagine the worst and to protect against it. But in the world's "sea of stories"—as Salmon Rushdie playfully imagines in *Haroun and the Sea of Stories* (1990)—anything is possible because stories can change the world, for the better as well as the worse. This kind of truth rules in oral cultures. But it exists in all cultures. It lives in our hopes and fears, and in our striving to understand the world and to live well in it. And it thrives on the imagination of possibilities that takes us out of ourselves and shows us what can happen, and what we might become, and how we might enable the future to improve upon the past.

On the Truths of Stories

1. Stories have the power to affect us in many ways.

2. Stories have power because they give us the imaginative pleasures of going outside of this world, learning about this world, and seeing new possibilities for this world.

3. All stories are true because they imagine possibilities—and any possibility could be true.

4. The truths of stories can be good or bad, and can change us.

5. When the truths of stories are bad, we should learn from them how to protect ourselves from harm.

6. When the truths of stories are good, we should learn from them how to live well.

7. When stories change us, they become true in fact as well as in possibility.

8. We cannot understand life or live well without imagining the truths of possibility, both good and bad.

9. The truths of possibility in stories are similar to those in religion.

10. The emblematic stories of history tell how stories change people for the better through the pleasures and truths that stories can provide.

11. The meaning of life is to use the power of stories, with their truths of possibility, to improve our lives and the human world.

21

How Beautiful, How Sad

Murasaki Shikibu: *The Tale of Genji*

The cherry blossoms of spring are loved because they bloom so briefly.
These flowers must fall. It is the way of the world.

Murasaki Shikibu

Murasaki Shikibu (970?–1015?) had the good fortune to live at one of the brightest moments of world artistic culture. It was the Heian period in Japan (794–1186), when the arts, cultivated by the royal court in the new capital of what is now Kyoto, flowered radiantly. And most radiant was the literature written by women. Unconstrained by the Chinese language and the Confucian bureaucracy that reigned among the men at court, women fashioned a vernacular Japanese prose literature possessing subtleties of perception and a grace of expression that remains unexcelled. Rising above the rest of these gifted literary women was Murasaki Shikibu.

We know little about her. Not even her real name. Tradition called her Murasaki, after the prominent female character of that name in her epochal novel, *The Tale of Genji*. Born sometime in the late tenth century and living about forty years, Murasaki was the daughter of a court official (affiliated with the Board of Rites, or Shikibu), and she was attendant to an empress. So she knew the court well, and recorded part of what she knew in a journal of approximately the years 1008–1010. During those same years she was undoubtedly writing *The Tale of Genji*, which first appeared in the 1020s, after her death, immediately capturing a ravenous readership and leaving a lasting imprint on Japanese literary culture.

The Tale of Genji is probably the world's first novel—and none absorbs us more. A complex, allusively told tale of court life and amorous adventures ranging across seventy-five years of Heian society, it revolves around Prince Genji. Handsome and talented, artistic and sensitive, Genji is popular at court and with the ladies, becoming a legendary figure of beauty, artistry, and romance in a world that relished these qualities. Evocative scenes and teary-eyed emotions, along with festivals celebrating the beauties of nature and of art, fill the book's pages, with Genji usually at the center. But Genji also has his troubles as he goes through many love affairs and marriages.

Eventually he settles into his marriage to Lady Murasaki, whom he had educated as a child and who, despite his infidelities, is his true love. Then, shortly after Lady Murasaki dies, Genji himself, beset by grief, dies too. The rest of the novel (almost a third of it) follows the younger generation until the book unceremoniously ends, probably unfinished. *The Tale of Genji* gives us little drama or sweep of events. Instead it indelibly portrays a world marked by a deep, fond, often sad feeling for this transitory life and fleeting beauties, and it teaches us how to find these beauties everywhere.

THE TALE OF GENJI is not only the world's first novel. It is the richest novel of what was once commonly called "sensibility." We do not use this word much nowadays. But it used to mean a lot to the European lasses and lads, the ladies and gentlemen, of the eighteenth and early nineteenth centuries who understood "sensibility" to name the sensory and emotional inclinations that shape our responses to the world. A person of sensibility was much admired in those days for perceiving acutely and feeling deeply. And a person lacking sensibility was disdained for being dull and gross, feeding coarse appetites, and feeling little. Jane Austen brilliantly played upon these attitudes and gently satirized them in her novel *Sense and Sensibility* (1811). But long before Europe celebrated this acute and fine sensibility, *The Tale of Genji* carried sensibility to heights never surpassed.

Written in the early eleventh century by Murasaki Shikibu, that most brilliant literary woman of Japan's Heian period, *The Tale of Genji* is an epic of enlivening sensations awakened by the slightest scene, and of deep emotions aroused by seeming trifles, no less than by tragedies. And so it yields copious pleasures of aesthetics and feeling that have nourished Japanese culture for nearly a thousand years, and that offer an education in sensibility not to be missed.

Imbibing this sensibility will not make you good. Or not morally good as we usually think of it—self-sacrificing, socially responsible, and the like (although this is hardly the only kind of moral good, as Aristotle and Nietzsche, among others, remind us—see Chapters 4, 8). But it is a sensibility that, in some measure, belongs in the repertoire of any civilized life, of anyone, anywhere. For it sharpens the responses of our senses and deepens the well of our emotions, enhancing the vitality of our every waking hour.

The rewards of *The Tale of Genji* have little to do with the actual story or plot of the book. You do not turn its pages wanting to know what happens next. Not much happens at all. Murasaki Shikibu rather tells her tale as a record of aesthetic sensations and bittersweet emotions woven through a web of court life, love affairs, personalities, works of art, and scenes of nature, much of it depicted as obliquely as if in a novel by Henry James. The *story* is the least of it, although some of the characters and incidents will stick in your mind.

That story takes Genji, the son of an emperor and of the emperor's favorite consort (who is of low social rank, thereby denying Genji succession to the throne), from his birth to his death just before he reaches the age of fifty two. Thanks to his physical beauty and artistic talents, he enjoys a precocious youth and a brilliant court life; he also engages in numerous love affairs, goes into voluntary exile for a while over an untoward sexual liaison, marries three women (including his true love, Lady Murasaki, whom he nurtures from the age of ten), fathers three children (one of them, the illegitimate Reizei, becomes emperor), and then quietly passes away—between chapters no less. The twisty skein of amorous and courtly doings goes on from Genji's death to follow the lives of two young men—Kaoru, a melancholy lad erroneously thought to be Genji's son because he was born to Genji's third wife, and Niou, Genji's dashing grandson, who can't leave ladies alone—particularly as these amorous youths competitively woo three rather mysterious and melancholy daughters of Genji's reclusive younger half-brother, eventually provoking the most memorable of these daughters, Ukifune, to take up monastic life. The tale then breaks off unclimactically with the twenty-eight-year-old Kaoru searching for the vanished Ukifune. The book was likely left incomplete when Murasaki Shikibu died.

Keeping track of the large cast of characters, the tangled love affairs, and the court intrigues can be something of a trial. But, again, the heart of *The Tale of Genji* lies elsewhere: in its pervasive sensibility. To make the most of this sensibility, we must open ourselves up to it, letting Murasaki Shikibu lead us slowly through the aesthetic and emotional world of her fabled prince. Then, unless your own sensibility is incorrigibly dull and gross, *The Tale of Genji* will have its way with you. And after reading it, your senses and emotions will be more alive than before. You will see beauty where you had not seen it earlier, and you will likely never see the moon quite the same way again, or the dew in morning light, or cherry blossoms, especially when they fall.

THE TALE OF GENJI starts working its spell by enfolding all existence in a peculiarly beguiling atmosphere. That is the atmosphere of evanescence, the transience of things. Every culture pays some homage to the transience of things, if only in nostalgia for bygone times. In the West an agitated sense of transience arose with the tides of modernity that washed away so much of the past and left an expectation of rapid, incessant change. No one nowadays could ignore this expectation, or be blind to its causes. The accelerating pace of technological innovation, consumer fads, even historical events (which distressed William Wordsworth as early as 1800—see Chapter 23) now cause practically everything in this modern world to literally pass away before our eyes—and much of it is manufactured to do just that. Modern culture thrives on change and obsolescence. As Karl Marx said in *The Communist Manifesto*, "All that is solid melts into air"; and as Marx's contemporary, poet-critic Charles Baudelaire put it in "The Painter of Modern Life" (1863), "Modernity is the ephemeral, the fugitive, the contingent." Where former ages patiently took centuries to build temples and cathedrals and castles to last forever, we now erect skyscrapers in a year or two and tear them down in mere decades. The juggernaut of historical change in the West has brought occasional waves of nostalgia, but more typically it has fueled a restless desire to leave things behind and rush into the future, escaping the present and all but forgetting the past. That is the modern Western way, the Faustian way—energetic, insatiable, never looking back (see Chapter 7).

The sense of evanescence in *The Tale of Genji* is not like this modern Western mentality at all. Quite the contrary. Rather than a hunger for the new, it reflects a sad, appreciative regret for things as they pass, and for those that linger in memory. But this sense of evanescence comes not from a Proustian journey down the byways of memory—although *The Tale of Genji* has clear affinities with Marcel Proust's *In Search of Lost Time*—any more than from the swift pace of material and historical change. It comes from a vision of existence itself, from the belief that everything, every emotion, every sensation, every beauty, every life, is by nature transitory, fugitive, fleeting, here and gone.

This vision came in part from Japanese Shintoism, with its worship of nature. But it had stronger roots in Buddhism—chiefly the late schools that would give rise to Zen and have most influence on Japan—which regarded nothing to be permanent, nothing to last for more than a brief passage from one transitory state to another, from one insubstantial life to another in a cycle of insubstantial lives in an illusory existence on the long path to Nirvana. "Thus shall ye think of this fleeting world," says the seminal Zen Buddhist scripture of the late seventh century known as the *Platform Sutra* or *Sutra of Hui-Neng*, "A star at dawn, a bubble in a stream . . . a phantom, and a dream" (see Chapter 2). This Buddhist idea of cosmic evanescence bequeathed to Chinese and Japanese literature many evocative images of the insubstantiality of things—among them that of life as a "floating bridge of dreams," the title given to *The Tale of Genji*'s final chapter.

The Japanese have a term for this sad, transcendent sense of evanescence, or for certain attributes of it. It is *aware*. *Aware* labels a complex idea, but scholars agree that it broadly signifies the pathos of passing, a pathos uniting the sadness of loss with a poignant affection for the beautiful. It could be described as a melancholy aesthetic perception of life that becomes a way of life. It says: "Ah, how fleeting. How beautiful. How sad. And how beautiful because it is sad."

The Tale of Genji is steeped in *aware*. By scholarly calculations, Murasaki Shikibu uses the word more than a thousand times in it, translated with a variety of English terms connoting pathos, loss, and evanescence. *Aware* infuses *Genji*'s very atmosphere, touching every sensation, breathing through every sigh, lacing every tear—of which there are many. It clings to everyone. "It is a transient world," a lady remarks to Genji, in a phrase echoed again and again. Genji tells another lady in his own refrain: "Life is fleeting, and so is everything in it." An older lady says to Genji's son Yugiri (born to Genji's first wife, Aoi), "Yes, the sad thing is that it should all be so uncertain and fleeting." The mournful Kaoru offers a poetic version: "With flowers that fade, with leaves that turn, they speak / Most surely of a world where all is fleeting." And a princess philosophizes: "These flowers must fall. It is the way of the world."

Genji and Kaoru feel *aware* and its Buddhist transience more consumingly, and philosophically, than any other characters in the novel. Genji is "obsessed with evanescence," Murasaki Shikibu remarks, and she reports that "even the shallowest of the younger women were moved to tears at the awareness he brought of transience and mutability." Kaoru carries the obsession farther: it defines his entire being—and the chapters that tell his story sink into ever deeper melancholy, often occasioned by his relations with the somber daughters of his uncle who dwell on the mountain of Uji. Sometimes Genji and Kaoru suffer a sadness that borders on despair. Grieving over the loss of one lady, Genji spent "the night in thoughts of the evanescence of things" and decided "what a purposeless life was his." In his last days he reflects on how "it has always seemed that I was meant for sad things," so that "I have often wondered whether the Blessed One [Buddha] was not determined to make me see more than others what a useless, insubstantial world it is." Kaoru takes up the same despondent speculations. Overcome by "the knowledge of evanescence" with its "sadness that all is fleeting," he asks if it is "to push a man toward renunciation of the world that the Blessed One sent such afflictions."

The woebegone sadness felt by Genji and Kaoru at the passing of things fits their finely tuned sensibilities. But that sadness is also the dominant emotion in Genji's world. For almost everything arouses it. Because everything brings loss. With the losses come sorrows, and with sorrows come tears. Many of the tears flow from mourning the deaths of loved ones, or from yearning for a lover gone away, or from the ache of hopeless troubles—like Ukifune, torn between Kaoru and Niou. But everyone cries. Often. Openly. We hear of "weeping courtiers" and teary rustics; one emperor frequently has "tears streaming over his face," and "tears came easily" to another; a princess is "blinded by tears"; a court lady "cannot see for tears"; another lady says "the autumn night is too short to contain my tears"; an old woman "collapsed in tears"; a group of nuns "seemed also to be speaking through tears." And no one weeps more than Genji himself.

He cries at the fall of a flower, the sight of the moon, the scent of a lady, the sound of the wind, at every memory, and, above all, at the loss of loved ones. On nearly every page we hear that "Genji was near tears," that "memory following memory, Genji was in tears," that his "tears flowed on," that he "dried his tears and still they flowed on," that "sometimes he would weep aloud," and sometimes, as if throwing in the towel, "Genji spent a tearful day in bed." Genji's tears do not, of course, spell weakness or affectation (any more than do the tears in Homer's *Iliad* —see Chapter 1). They express the deep feelings of the book's revered sensibility. As Murasaki Shikibu says of Genji: "There seemed nothing in the least false about Genji's own tears, which gave an added elegance and fineness of feature."

The abysses of sorrow and oceans of tears shed over the passing of things might seem to make *The Tale of Genji* a pretty lugubrious saga. But it isn't. Its sensibility is too delectable for that. And yet this delectable sensibility arose from a curious irony.

That irony lies in the sadness of *aware* itself. Buddhists are not supposed to be sad. The Buddhist idea of the ephemerality of all things was supposed to be a liberating idea, freeing human beings from attachment to things and from the sorrows that attachments bring. Because everything is fleeting and dream-like, we should not be attached to anything. But in *The Tale of Genji* this Buddhist idea of transience does not bring freedom from attachments and their attendant sorrows. It rather seems to do the opposite. It strengthens the attachments and intensifies the sorrows.

Murasaki Shikibu is not oblivious to this irony. From time to time she lets her characters notice that people care too much about this ephemeral life, even though they know better. "I am told that it is important," says an old woman who has tended Genji during an illness, "to rid oneself of the smallest regret for this world"; yet she and Genji both weep effusively at his departure, while the woman's "children were ashamed for her" because "it would not do to have these contortions taken as signs of a lingering affection for the world." Later, Genji himself reminds a mourner to "try to shake loose" of life, for "We go, we stay, alike of this world of dew. / We should not let it have such a hold upon us." And yet, he admits another time, this is "a world which, for all its trials and uncertainties, is not easy to leave."

To believe a transitory existence unworthy of attachment, and yet not to be able to let it go—that is the emotional irony of the *The Tale of Genji*. We could say this irony comes from adopting the metaphysics of Buddhism, but not its psychology or ethics—that is, believing that human existence is evanescent and unreal and therefore insignificant, but failing to achieve detachment from it. The irony may also reflect a tension between the Shinto veneration of nature and Buddhist dreaminess. In any case, the irony flowered in a sensibility, tinged with sadness, that found the meaning of life to lie in this ephemeral world itself: in moments of sensation and emotion, in the beauty of things, and in the intensity of feelings, even as they pass—and *because* they pass. With this sensibility, *The Tale of Genji* bequeathed an enduring legacy not only to Japan but to the world.

THAT LEGACY COMES MOST VISIBLY from the person of Genji himself. He embodies the sensibility of his tale in all that he does. Preternaturally sensitive to impulses of emotion and nuances of the senses, exuding *aware* at every passing moment, Genji is also himself a work of art, sublimely handsome and artistically gifted without peer. Born "a jewel beyond compare," he grew "into a lad of such beauty that he hardly seemed meant for this world." And "among the more discriminating, indeed, were some who marveled that such a paragon had been born into this world." Soon "people began calling Genji 'the shining one,'" or "the shining Genji." And the honorific stuck (elegantly elaborated upon by the eminent scholar Ivan Morris in *The World of the Shining Prince* [1964]).

Wherever Genji goes he stirs the same awed response. At a country temple where he is recuperating from an illness, "his manner and voice were beautiful beyond description," so the nuns "asked whether he might be a visitor from another world," while the bishop, "brushing away a tear," thinks, "How can it be that such a one has been born into the confusion and corruption in which we live?" Later a group of women "gathered for a look at him," enthusing, "What a marvelous young man. And see how beautifully he carries himself." The emperor (Genji's halfbrother) agrees: "I often say to myself that the word 'radiant' was invented especially for him"; and he sums up Genji with a phrase that follows the Shining Prince to his grave: "There is no one quite like him."

A living work of art, Genji proves himself a masterly artist as well. He plays music, sings, dances, writes poetry, and paints (marrying these last two arts in marvelous calligraphy—"his writing was more beautiful all the time"—a prominent artform in Japan and China reflecting their ideographic languages). "Sometimes," another of Genji's half-brothers, Hotaru, says to Genji during a painting competition, "the best families will suddenly produce someone who seems to do everything well. Father was tutor for all of us, but I thought he took himself seriously only when you were his pupil. There was poetry, of course, and there was music, the flute and the koto [a stringed instrument like a zither], painting seemed less study than play, something you let your brush have its way with when poetry had worn you out. And now see the results. See all of the professionals running off and hiding their faces."

Genji's inborn artistry puts professional artists to shame. And it moves to tears everyone who encounters it. Performing at a royal concert, "Genji scarcely seemed of this world. As he intoned the lyrics, his listeners could have believed they were listening to the Kalavinka bird of paradise. The emperor brushed away tears of delight, and there were tears in the eyes of all the princes and high courtiers as well." Then, "as Genji rearranged his dress at the end of his song and the orchestra took up again, he seemed to shine with an ever brighter light." And when he begins to dance, "a chill as if from another world passed over the assembly," for he brought such "pleasure to the eye and serenity to the heart" that he "made people wonder what beauty of grace might be his from former lives." Genji can effortlessly do anything the arts ask—down to his perfumes, an artform cultivated throughout the court lending a distinctive aromatic identity to each person's lavish robes and accentuating many a sensory and emotional incident, like this one: "The scent of [Genji's] sleeve, as he brushed away a tear, quite flooded the room." Genji is a one-man artistic culture.

With his physical beauty, artistic talents, and exquisite sensibility, it is no surprise that Genji attracts women, and is attracted to them. Genji's story is full of love affairs. They virtually *are* his story, and he pursues them quite recklessly, including one with his own father's favorite consort (after Genji's mother, the previous favorite, had died at the novel's beginning), who secretly bears Genji's illegitimate son, the future emperor Reizei, publicly known as Genji's half-brother. Genji cannot resist the allure of an appealing woman (beautified in the fashion of the day with whitened face, painted eyebrows, and blackened teeth), especially one of good breeding, whose poetry is evocative, calligraphy graceful, robes exquisite, perfumes rich, and sensibility refined. Some of these affairs get Genji into trouble at court, where gossip flourishes amidst incessant jockeying for influence; and one affair even brings scandalous consequences that send him into voluntary exile for a time. This cautions but does not change him. A sensibility like Genji's is not doused by scandal—even in exile he falls in love with another lady and fathers a daughter by her.

And so Genji became the idealized Japanese romantic hero—radiant prince, rapturous lover, consummate artist, and tearful, sensitive soul, who never truly leaves a lady he has loved, and finally brings them all to live under his care. He has enthralled readers for centuries. A generation after *The Tale of Genji* appeared, another talented literary woman of the day, known as Lady Sarashina, recalled in a delightful memoir her own youthful captivation by the Shining Prince. "My sister, my stepmother, and others in the household," she wrote, "would tell me stories from the Tales, including episodes about Genji, the Shining Prince." These stirred her "impatience and curiosity . . . to see the entire *Tale of Genji* from beginning to end," and once she obtained a copy, she "kept reading all day long and as late as possible into the night," fantasizing that "when I grew up, I would surely become a great beauty . . . who was loved by the Shining Prince." Soon she wholly lost herself in these fantasies (anticipating the fate of her Western kindred spirit, Flaubert's Emma Bovary—see Chapter 24), confessing that "I lived forever in a dream world" where "the height of my aspirations was that . . . someone like Shining Genji in the Tale would visit me once a year in the mountain village where he would have hidden me like Lady Ukifune [whom Kaoru conceals for a while in a cottage on the Uji mountain]. There I should live my lonely existence, gazing at the blossoms and the Autumn leaves and the moon and the snow, and wait for an occasional splendid letter from him. This was all I wanted." But eventually Lady Sarashina abandoned her dreams, dejectedly concluding: "How could anyone as wonderful as Shining Genji really exist in this world of ours?" Like Genji himself, Lady Sarashina lives a life of ripe sensations and sad *aware*.

The Shining Genji was perfection itself. And perfection in a time and place that most prized a sensibility capable of sensing, feeling, and savoring beauty and the passing of things everywhere. Within this sensibility, you cannot unravel sensation from emotion, nature from art, metaphysics from aesthetics. They are one, suffused by the bittersweet sense of evanescence.

This sensibility displays itself most often among the sights and sounds of nature (the sense of taste, incidentally, is alone neglected in *Genji*, where food and drink seldom enter). Following Genji and his companions into nature, we encounter a galaxy of sensations and emotions where previously we might have found only routine flora and fauna, days and nights, seasons and weather. We learn to see new shadings in the moon-light, hear fresh melodies in birdsongs, find poignancy in a blossom, and discover metaphor in the dew. And so our senses awaken, and nature comes alive in ways and with beauties we have not known before.

NATURE IS EVERYWHERE in *The Tale of Genji*. Not nature as an agent of the gods, as in, say, Homer's *Iliad,* or as force and energy, as in Goethe's *Faust.* It comes closer to nature as Wordsworth knew it, a source of poignant memories and poetic inspiration. But it is not quite that either. Nature in *Genji* is all "moods" and aesthetics and metaphor. Most of us have felt these moods acting on our own emotions and states of mind from time to time—romance flourishes on warm summer nights, and rainy days are sad. But in *Genji* the "moods of nature" touch everything that happens, concentrating every perception, intensifying every emotion. Especially the moods that elicit *aware*.

First among these is the mood of night under the light of the moon. Nighttime and moonlight so reign in *Genji* that one might think the seventy-odd years that the book records took place after dark. Virtually absent is the midday sun. It is too bright, too revealing for Genji's intimate, sensuous society of curtained privacy and closeted liaisons. Characters talk through the night, or engage in amours ended only by first light. Festivals and nighttime concerts last until dawn. People gather for "moon-viewing" events. And variations in the moon and its light rouse debates over their virtues. Moonlight has a presence in *Genji* probably unmatched elsewhere in literature (not even in the moonlight-obsessed writings of the English preromantic "graveyard" poets). To know the moon in its many moods and its metaphors of love and loneliness and transience is one of the rewards of reading *The Tale of Genji*.

The moon's moods and metaphors affect everyone in the book, and Genji himself above all. "One is always moved by the full moon," Genji observes one night, "but somehow the moon this evening takes me to other worlds," and he slips into reveries about a lost companion who had spoken so well about "the moods of nature." On an early spring night, as "the first rays of 'the moon for which one lies in wait' [the full moon] came forth," Genji says to his son Yūgiri, "the misty moon of spring is not the best, really." And Yūgiri replies: "It is true that on an autumn night there is sometimes not a trace of a shadow over the moon. . . . But the sky can have a sort of put-on look about it, like an artificial setting. . . . It is too pat, too perfect." Genji concedes: since "the ancients were unable to resolve the dispute," he says, "you may be right." But his heart still belongs to cloudless moons and clear nights, like one night when "a radiant moon had come out" and, seeing "that it was the harvest full moon," Genji "could not take his eyes from it" until "he had to turn away to hide his tears."

But best of all, and "unlike most people," Murasaki Shikibu explains, "Genji loved the cold moonlit nights of winter" when, after "a heavy fall of snow . . . the moon turned the deepest recesses of the garden a gleaming white." On one such night, Genji reflects, "People make a great deal of the flowers of spring and the leaves of autumn, but for me a night like this, with a clear moon shining on snow, is the best—and there is not a trace of color in it. I cannot describe the effect it has on me, weird and unearthly somehow." His paintings, for which he is renowned, resemble these same nights. Stark black-and-white scenes devoid of color, they, too, are a little "weird and unearthly."

The mood of these winter nights captivates Genji. And that mood is, of course, sad. One night, as "a clear moon moves into the Western sky" and "the water is stilled among the frozen rocks" and "the scene [is] utterly quiet," Genji hears "the call of a waterfowl" overhead and is moved to voice his emotions in a poem:

> A night of drifting snow and memories
> Is broken by another note of sadness.

Remembering this scene, how could we not see a cold moonlit winter night, even without the call of a lone waterfowl, with a little of this aesthetic sensibility and sweet sadness ourselves?

Although the moonlit nights of winter touch Genji most deeply, all moonlit nights in *The Tale of Genji* are at once beautiful and sad. It could not be otherwise. For "the soft sad light of the moon" always cloaks the landscape in a penumbral melancholy. And the sadness deepens when the moon sets, because then the moon itself is evanescent. "The setting moon is always sad," Murasaki Shikibu remarks, and nature itself seems to mourn the passing: "The moon was sinking over the hills," she says of one scene, "the air was crystal clear, the wind was cool, and the songs of the insects among the autumn grasses would by themselves have brought tears." As we might expect, in his mournful mood (during his exile) Genji identifies himself most with the setting moon, thinking "its situation rather like his own," because "the moon itself seemed to be weeping."

Nighttime and moonlight give the world of Genji its most recurrent scenes and emotions. But nature brings many moods aroused by every sensation. The changing colors of the leaves, the fragrances of flowers, the sight of birds, and sounds of insects—nothing goes unnoticed or unfelt, or unremembered as metaphors of human life and the nature of things.

When "a line of geese flew over in the dawn sky," Genji is reminded of his own loneliness in exile, because "their cries ring sadly through the sky of their journey." Genji also listens to "the waves . . . like moans of helpless longing" and hears "the winds—like messengers from those who grieve." Another time, Genji thinks "the mists that will not let me see . . . the autumn moon . . . are as unkind as people."

Then there is "the scent of blossoms," which "brings thoughts of days now gone" and sometimes intimations of passings to come. Plum blossoms and orange blossoms arouse vague longings; and it is plum blossoms, the first to bloom in the spring, that betoken Genji's own death. But cherry blossoms evoke the poignancy of all transient beauty—"the cherry blossoms of spring are loved because they bloom so briefly."

Flowers arouse similar emotions. Wisteria, perhaps the most prominent of these flowers, suggests human affinities and even love (its color, lavender, or purple, is known in Japanese as "Murasaki"). Carnations hint at the wild. Chrysanthemums, the last flower of the fall, imply resilience. And the morning glory betokens early daylight and swift fading—"the morning glory . . . took on a reddish hew as it withered, and a strange new beauty . . . 'Forlorn the flower that fades with dew upon it.'"

The dew itself, a fugitive visitor of the night, bathing every petal and branch, and wetting sleeves as lovers part at dawn, conspicuously embodies the ephemeral and yet recurrent nature of things. "We go, we stay, alike of this world of dew," Genji says. And Lady Murasaki sighs, "It is a life in which we cannot be sure / Of lasting as long as the dew upon the lotus."

Like the dew, the drake fly, or May fly, that most fragile and insubstantial of creatures—which lives only a few hours, or days, and is classed by biologists among *ephemeroptera*—also bespeaks the mystery of life on a bridge of dreams. "'I see the drake fly,' says Kaoru, 'take it up in my hand. / Ah, here it is, I say—and it is gone.'" Then, "he added softly, as always: 'Here, and perhaps not here at all.'"

To perceive and feel nature in these many and sometimes minute ways, to catch their beauties as they pass, to fathom their metaphors, you can overlook nothing. Or perhaps we should say you must be open to everything. Most of all to the delicate, the suggestive, the understated. "I feel sorry for the man who says that night dims the beauty of things," wrote the sixteenth-century Buddhist monk Yoshida Kenkō in his influential *Essays in Idleness* (acknowledging a debt to *The Tale of Genji*), since "leaving something incomplete makes it interesting." Generations of Japanese poets, gardeners, flower arrangers, and others (many under the influence of Zen, which complemented the aesthetic heritage of *Genji*) have followed the rule—showing that a single branch can be more beautiful than a tree, a garden path scattered with a few flower petals more arresting than when bare (see Chapter 2).

And so in the world of Genji nature not only has many moods, and holds emotional and often metaphysical significance, it also displays artistry, and gives inspiration to artists. In this world the artistry of nature and the artistry of human beings easily become one.

"The evening sky was serenely beautiful," Murasaki Shikibu writes of a typical occasion, "the flowers below the verandah were withered, the songs of the insects were dying, too, and autumn tints were coming over the maples . . . the scene . . . might have been a painting." Another time, she says, "The evening breeze had scattered leaves of various tints to make the ground a brocade as rich and delicate as the brocades along the galleries." And yet another time: "There were heavy mists in the dawn sky, and bird songs came from Genji knew not where. Flowering trees and grasses which he could not identify spread like a tapestry before him." Later he thinks "a sheaf of autumn leaves admired in solitude" is like "damasks worn in the darkness of the night," a beauty regrettably unshared.

The artistry of nature makes of every scene and season an occasion for aesthetic reflection—and artistic competition. (Sei Shōnagon, a contemporary of Murasaki Shikibu, records similar responses to nature in *The Pillow Book*, which factually describes the Heian court that Murasaki fictionalized.) Some of these competitions pit recognized experts against each other in poetry, painting, music, and perfumes. Other contests are more informal, like the sustained and amusing rivalry between Lady Murasaki and Lady Akikonomu (consort of the emperor Reizei, Genji's illegitimate son) over their gardens, designed to capture the qualities of different seasons. Lady Murasaki has a spring garden to catch the beauties of budding trees and flowers in bloom, while Lady Akikonomu has an autumn garden exhibiting the spectacle of golden colors and leaves before they fall. One autumn, Lady Akikonomu sends Lady Murasaki an arrangement of "leaves and flowers" with an autumnal poem:

> Your garden quietly awaits the spring.
> Permit the winds to bring a touch of autumn.

Lady Murasaki replies with a delicate arrangement of pine sprigs, moss, and stones, and a poem invoking spring:

> Fleeting, your leaves that scatter in the wind.
> The pine at the cliffs is forever green with spring.

When springtime comes, Lady Murasaki holds an event in her garden to display its glories. There,

☙

the smallest of the hanging rocks was like a detail of a painting. The branches, caught in the mists . . . were like a tapestry. . . . A willow trailed its branches in a deepening green and the cherry blossoms were rich and sensuous. . . . Along the galleries wisteria was beginning to send forth its lavender. Yellow yambuki reflected on the lake as if about to join its own image. Waterfowl swam by in amiable pairs . . . and one longed to paint the mandarin ducks as they coursed about on the water.

The festivities go on all night, as usual. And when "morning came, from behind her fences Lady Akikonomu listened to the morning birds and feared that her autumn garden had lost the contest."

Nature as art and metaphor, art as nature and metaphor, Genji's world could not have separated them. Reading *Genji*, we may feel the same—and like Lady Sarashina after she read it, we might want to keep "gazing at the blossoms and the Autumn leaves and the moon and the snow." We might also want to have our own Japanese gardens, evoking moods of the seasons and secluded behind wisteria-draped walls like those in Kyoto (the capital of Heian Japan) today, themselves another legacy of the world of the Shining Prince.

And just as everyone in Genji's world sees beauty and art in nature, they prize beauty and nature in art. Like nature, art nurtures the sensibility that makes that world what it so singularly and seductively is.

Genji was himself both a work of art and a consummate artist. But everyone else relishes art and is an artist too—from an emperor who "loved art more than anything," "painted beautifully," and was a connoisseur of poetry, to the courtiers and court ladies, the commoners and even monastics. And some form of art honors every public event, accentuates each private emotion, and occasions many a competition.

Poetry most of all. Hundreds of poems are scattered through *The Tale of Genji*—allusive vignettes (translated as couplets by Edward Seidensticker) anticipating the haiku perfected by the celebrated poet Bashō in the seventeenth century. They punctuate conversations and distill thoughts, capture scenes and convey memories, and almost always they weave together metaphors of people and places, sensations and emotions. And usually they are touched by *aware*.

Lovers exchange poems, as we might expect; but so do nuns and monks and the highest figures of the court, as well as ladies extolling the merits of their gardens. Festivals and ceremonies always feature poetry readings. We are told that "poem followed poem" at Lady Murasaki's spring garden festival. And "poem answered poem" at a painting contest in response to the paintings. The "festival of the cherry blossoms" would not be complete without a poetry contest, where Genji's contribution is "so remarkable that the reader paused to comment on each line." And at a perfume contest, Genji and his companions engage in a typical poetic exchange:

> Hotaru: The voice of the warbler lays a deeper spell
> Over one already enchanted by the blossoms.
> Genji: Honor us by sharing our blossoms this spring
> Until you have taken on their hue and fragrance.
> Kashiwagi: Sound your bamboo flute all through the night
> And shake the plum branch where the warbler sleeps.
> Yūgiri: I thought we wished to protect them from the winds,
> The blossoms you would have me blow upon madly.
> Kōbai: Did not the mists intercede to dim the moonlight
> The birds on these branches might burst into joyous
> blossom.

These poetic conversations go on with ease, meandering through images of nature and metaphors of life.

No occasion more surely elicits poems than farewells, and the sadder the poem the better, calling upon the usual emotive images of nature to wring every feeling and metaphor from the moment. Genji leaves one lady at the end of the night, under "a sky even more beautiful now that the moon was setting," with the poem:

> A dawn farewell is always drenched in dew,
> But sad is the autumn sky as never before.

And she replies, amid a "serenade" of crickets in the trees:

> An autumn farewell needs nothing to make it sadder.
> Enough of your songs, O crickets on the moors.

Appropriately Genji bids farewell to life itself with a poem. It comes at a feast for a holy man held when "the plum trees, just coming into bloom, were lovely in the snow." Foreseeing his own death—while "he was handsomer than ever, indeed almost unbelievably handsome"—Genji says:

> Put blossoms in your caps today. Who knows
> That there will still be life when spring comes around.

The guest of honor replies:

> I pray that these blossoms may last a thousand springs.
> For me the years are as the deepening snowdrifts.

જી

Then Genji composes what turns out to be his last poem, and his last recorded words:

> I have not taken account of the days and months.
> The end of the year—the end of life as well?

Or, as rendered in a more lush translation:

> Lost in my sorrows I never knew months and days were still passing by—is the year really over, and my time, too, in the world?

After this poem Genji speaks no more. When we next hear of him, at the opening of the following chapter, Murasaki Shikibu simply says: "The shining Genji was dead, and there was no one quite like him." He was in the twelfth month of his fifty-second year.

Love and death, joy and loss, nature and art, all have their poems—if only "of the usual trite and fusty sort," Murasaki Shikibu remarks of one batch, with a bit of authorial teasing. Still, good or bad, original or conventional, poetry concentrates those moments of keen perception and rich emotion that Genji's world thrives on. Probably only during the heyday of Romanticism, when Wordsworth, Byron, Keats, Shelley, Goethe, Leopardi, and others put their every mood into verse, has Western culture known anything like the intimate marriage of poetry and life in *The Tale of Genji*.

Then comes music. It, too, gives voice to the moods of nature and touches the sensitive heart. "The most ordinary music can seem remarkable if the time and place are right," Murasaki Shikibu says while Genji plays a koto on the seacoast one night. At an autumn concert, she tells us that the sound of "flutes, mingled with the sighing of the pines, was like a wind coming down from deep mountains," and Genji observes on another occasion that "in the autumn the singing of the insects weaves a fabric with the music," and "the combination is rather wonderful" (elsewhere, Genji even debates "the relative merits of the insect songs"). At a perfume contest succeeded by a concert, fragrances and sounds play together: "The mist-enshrouded moon was weirdly beautiful, and the breeze following gently upon the rain brought a soft perfume of plum blossoms. The mixture of scents inside the hall was magical," where "music did sound all through the night."

The music of nature and art also, of course, carry the strains of sad passing. This is the music of evanescence. The music of *aware*. Genji and his companions listen to it tearfully and perform it feelingly. On one night during his exile along the coast at Suma (near Kobe today), Genji "raised his head from his pillow and listened to the roar of the wind and of the waves. . . . He plucked a few notes on his koto, but the sound only made him sadder. . . . He had awakened the others. They sat up and one by one they were in tears." On another night, "The moon having come forth in all its radiance, [Genji] sat gazing up at it, lost in thoughts of his own. What a changeable uncertain world it is, he was thinking," and "his koto seemed to plead in sadder tones than usual." Over and over Genji plays the koto, sending its mournful sonorities "on a sighing of wind and waves"—and "lowly rustics, though they could not have identified the music, were lured out into the sea winds." Genji's son Yūgiri and a lady also play the music of *aware* on a particularly affecting night:

> The moon had come out in a cloudless sky. And what sad, envious thoughts would the calls of the geese, each wing to wing with its mate, be summoning up? The breeze was chilly. In the autumn sadness she played a few notes, very faintly and tentatively, on a Chinese koto. He was deeply moved. . . . Taking up a lute he softly played the Chinese lotus song with all its intimate overtones. . . . She added a poem: "I feel the sadness, in the autumn night. / How can I speak of it if not through the koto."

Genji's world would be unthinkably quiet without music, less beautiful and less sad. The most emotional of the arts, music resonates through *The Tale of Genji*, where it has a wealth of emotions to express and share.

The sensations and emotions stirred by the arts—from poetry and music to gardening and perfumes—join those aroused by nature to imbue all experience in the novel with profound, if peculiar, human meaning. That meaning resides in moments of beauty and sweet sorrow, and in a kind of gratitude for those moments, cherished as they pass. And this is a meaning given to life that only a singular sensibility can bestow. But a sensibility everyone can learn from.

WE MIGHT BE TEMPTED to see in the sensibility of *The Tale of Genji* the signs of sappy sentimentality. We could say that the obsession with fleeting sensations, the aching woe at every loss, and the rivers of tears betray feelings excessive to their cause with shallow exhibitions of emotional self-indulgence. How, we might ask, could life truly be so incessantly moving and profoundly sad—particularly for the Uji mountain sisters and Kaoru in the last part of the book? How could people care so much about the passing of things, about the light of the moon and insects' songs, about the fall of a blossom and the fragrance of a robe, about the lines of a poem and the notes of a flute? Is it not affectation? We might also think of the sentimental European novels of the eighteenth century, like Samuel Richardson's *Clarissa*, all weepy heartache, or of Flaubert's

Madame Bovary a century later, whose heroine is sentimentally enraptured by the emotions found in novels and by the aesthetics of the church. This kind of emotionality beggars its source, feeds on itself, and likes to parade itself as virtue. It has little authentic connection to real life, or genuine emotion. It is sentimentality.

But the people in the world of Genji are not creatures of mere sentimentality. Their sensibility is more authentic than that. Although, as Murasaki Shikibu observes, ladies of the court adore sentimental "old romances," this is more a diversion of the prevailing sensibility—"to relieve our boredom," Genji speculates—than an expression of its heart. And while Genji chides the young Lady Murasaki for being "addicted to romances," he delivers a lengthy discourse on the "uses of fiction"—Murasaki Shikibu's own historically surprising defense of fiction—in which he grants that perhaps "nothing is empty and useless" in fiction since "the difference between enlightenment and confusion" is about the same in literature and life, and even the Buddha himself told stories to point "obliquely at the truth" that everything is fleeting. Thanks largely to this Buddhist view of life, *The Tale of Genji* is not a novel of sentimentality (however many its tears or however sentimental some of its readers, like Lady Sarashina, might be). Its sensibility is honest. That honesty goes beneath the tears and the sorrows (where sentimentality lies empty) into solemn beliefs about the evanescent nature of things.

This sensibility actually comes closer to European aestheticism than to sentimentality. The European aesthetes of the late nineteenth century, such as Walter Pater and Oscar Wilde, exalted aesthetic experience beyond all others for its sensory and emotional intensity (see Chapter 25). Pater even had a theory of human life akin to that in *Genji*, contending that our lives consist of nothing but momentary sensations, and so we should give "the highest quality to [our] moments as they pass, and simply for those moments' sake." And he was convinced that the "highest quality" came with the enjoyment of "art for art's sake." This kind of aestheticism not only celebrates art and beauty, it elevates aesthetic sensations and emotions above all other human experiences. And this makes aesthetics superior to ethics, or, rather, it lets aesthetics define ethics—the beautiful *is* the good.

The aesthetic sensibility of Genji's world approaches Pater's aestheticism in both its vision of human life and its tendency to prize what we would call aesthetic experience as the highest good (reflecting, scholars say, Murasaki Shikibu's artistic reaction against the stuffy moral constraints of the Confucianism dominant in the court). This tendency shows up even in the practice of reading Buddhist scriptures. Although *The Tale of Genji* contains frequent readings of Mahayana Buddhist scriptures, or sutras (the only religious observances in the book and evidently confined to the influential *Lotus Sutra*), we hear nothing much of these scriptures' message of self-sacrificing Buddhist compassion. Instead, we get emotive artistic performances. For instance, on one occasion during his exile, "Genji came out, when the evening flowers were at their best," and "the loneliness of the setting made him seem like a visitor from another world. . . . He brushed away a tear induced by the splashing of oars and the calls of geese overhead," then "he announced himself as 'a disciple of the Buddha' and slowly intoned a sutra, and his men thought they had never heard a finer voice." No spiritual religious piety or selfless Buddhist ethics here. Aesthetic sensation and delectable feelings are everything.

And yet, despite its similarities to European aestheticism, the sensibility of *The Tale of Genji* does not boil down to that. For unlike the European aesthetes, who proudly, and whimsically, took the pleasures of beauty to be an end in themselves, the sensibility of *The Tale of Genji* embraces beauty not for its own sake, or for the pleasure it brings. That sensibility embraces beauty in nature and art as a metaphysical no less than an aesthetic experience. Where all life is a fleeting passage on a bridge of dreams, where nothing is more substantial than the dew—or than a drake fly that is "here, and perhaps not here at all"—human beings must find opportunities everywhere to intensify each moment, and to fill life, however sad it may be, with human meaning. This is not mere aestheticism. It is the enveloping sense of *aware* translated into an aesthetically acute and emotionally enlivening philosophy of life.

The Tale of Genji will not teach us how to be morally good. But it can teach us something equally important. It can teach us how to cultivate our sensations and emotions so that we can appreciate the subtlest beauties of nature and art, and savor the sweet sorrows of the passing of things. This is not cheap sentimentality or elitist aestheticism. It is a love of life in every cherished moment, graced with gratitude for those moments. And it is as encompassing and profound as any love of life that we can know.

On the Evanescence of Beauty and Life

1. Everything in life is evanescent.
2. The evanescence of things brings sadness.
3. The evanescence of things actually enhances the value of every poignant, precious moment.

4. Because everything is evanescent, we should capture and savor poignant, precious moments.

5. To capture these moments we must cultivate our senses, imagination, and emotions.

6. We find some of the most poignant, precious moments of life in sensations of beauty that have emotional resonance for us.

7. We can learn to find sources of beauty and emotional resonance anywhere if we cultivate the proper sensibility.

8. Many of the finest beauties and richest emotional resonances come from the most incidental of things—a phrase, a melody, a blossom, a fragrance, the light of the moon, a line of geese across the sky.

9. When we learn to find and create sources of beauty and emotional resonance everywhere, we gain a love of life and a gratitude for every cherished moment, despite, and because of, the evanescence of things.

10. The meaning of life is to find and create delectable, poignant, precious moments of beauty and emotional resonance, and to savor and share them along with our bittersweet feelings for life's evanescence.

22

The Uses of Idealism

Miguel de Cervantes: *Don Quixote*

*God knows whether Dulcinea exists on earth or no, or whether
she is fantastic or not fantastic. These things are not matters whose
verification can be carried out to the full. I neither engendered
not bore my lady, though I contemplate her in her ideal form.
. . . In my imagination I draw her as I would have her be.*
Cervantes

No great writer lived a more troubled life than **Miguel de Cervantes Saavedra (1547–1616)**. Son of a penurious Spanish surgeon who drifted around
Spain, Cervantes left his homeland for Italy in his early twenties. It proved
to be a misadventure. In Italy he became a soldier, suffered a permanent
arm injury, and fell into the hands of enemy Turks who sold him into slavery. Five years later he was ransomed and wound up back in Spain. But
somehow he managed to read widely, and now he made his own first forays
into literature. After a few undistinguished plays, he took a stab at a pastoral
novel, *La Galatea* (1585), which he never finished, but which displayed his
bent for narrative. Unable to live from writing, Cervantes tried a series of
careers in public service. But nothing worked out. He was plagued by debt
and several times imprisoned. His marriage went from bad to worse. And
an illegitimate daughter went after what few financial resources he had.
Amid these troubles, Cervantes found time to write *Don Quixote* (published as *El Ingenioso Hidalgo* [The Ingenious Nobleman] *Don Quixote de la
Mancha* in 1605), a batch of short fiction entitled *Novelas ejemplares* (1613),
some plays, and *Don Quixote*, Part II (1615). His final novel, *Los trabajos de
Persiles y Sigismunda* (1617), came out posthumously.

All of Cervantes' writings exhibit a penchant for romance, adventure,
intrigue, history, edification, and a hint of the absurd. *Don Quixote* combined these qualities (it also incorporated a number of Cervantes' earlier
tales). Regarded by many critics as both the first Western novel and the
greatest, it records the saga of a learned Spanish gentleman who has read
too many books about the glories and virtues of chivalry and who then
decides to become a knight-errant and live out such glories and virtues for
himself. The laughable consequences make him seem ridiculous and even

mad. But the comedy also makes you think about how ideas and ideals shape our lives. And in Part II (written to refute a fraudulent sequel to the original *Don Quixote* published by another author after the success of what Cervantes now called Part I), the story takes on a distinctly philosophical and ultimately melancholy tone, without losing its humor. We laugh at the beginning. We cry at the end. And we never forget Don Quixote. And more than his comic adventures, we should remember his uses of idealism.

THEY SAY HE IS MAD. Sometimes he is violent. At heart he is good. No doubt he is comical. Always he is irresistible. We know him as Don Quixote. And he rises from the book that bears his name to become one of those literary characters who is so grandly and utterly himself, who embodies an idea so singularly and fully, that he belongs neither to his book, nor to his author, nor to his times. Don Quixote belongs to everyone. He lives in our childish fantasies and in our loftiest ideals, in our stubborn follies and in our finest virtues, especially when those ideals and virtues, and even those fantasies and follies, make our lives more worth living.

Don Quixote actually seems to have escaped his own author's intentions. And we have to suspect that Cervantes saw this happening. The book starts off as something of a burlesque, with Don Quixote appearing to be rather daft and acting like a buffoon. But by the time the book ends, Don Quixote has won over most of the characters in the novel who have ridiculed him, as well as nearly every reader. Along the way, Cervantes frequently meddles with whether Don Quixote is himself fiction or fact, an author's invention or a historian's discovery. These and many other playful confusions of illusion and reality pervade the book. In Don Quixote's world many things are not what they seem, and what turns out to be real can surprise you—as Don Quixote probably surprised Cervantes. And that is the enduring delight and a lasting truth of *Don Quixote*: it shows us how, amid the tangles of fantasy and fact, the ideal and the real, fantasies can become fact, ideals can become real. And so much the better.

This formative power of ideals suggests what the psychologist and philosopher William James later called "the will to believe" (in an essay of that name). Ideas or beliefs become true, James said, when we embrace them fervently enough and act on them consistently enough to make them true in the lives we live (James was thinking mainly of religion, but that doesn't matter here). Karl Marx would say that this never happens because ideas only reflect our material needs, having no influence of their own (see Chapter 15). But only an incorrigible Marxist could think that of Don Quixote. For if ever there was a persuasive proof of the "will to believe," Don Quixote is it. In both his inspired life and his sorrowful death, Don Quixote embodies how we shape our lives with ideals, and how we must do this or our lives (literally in his case) might not be worth living.

We use ideals to shape our lives in many ways. Perhaps the first of these comes in the making of our "identity," or self. We fashion this identity or self out of our innate aptitudes and our temperament, as well as the aspirations—or fantasies, beliefs, and ideals—that take hold of our minds and imaginations. We do this of necessity in youth when we are naively molding our lives and characters, or as the modish phrase says, "searching for ourselves"—Flaubert's *Madame Bovary,* sharing much with *Don Quixote,* dramatizes the dangers that can lie in this youthful quest for an ideal self (see Chapter 24). Later on we might take up a variation on this psychological idealism when our ambitions or our circumstances change and we seek to reinvent ourselves from a perennial need for rejuvenation. For these reasons we should read *Don Quixote* when we are young and want to believe that we can do anything. Then we should come back to it again and again for the rejuvenation that a dose of *Don Quixote* can deliver at any age.

If you find yourself laughing at Don Quixote and then dismissing him as a dotty fantasist who bumbles through ridiculous incidents and survives as no more than an endearing icon of misbegotten dreams and foredoomed failure, think again. Don Quixote is laughable, to be sure. But he is no mere joke. For he not only gave us "quixotic" as a name for apparently hopeless aspirations. He also showed us the very best use of idealism—which is just this: whatever else ideals (or beliefs or fantasies) may be and do for us, they can give us the very highest meanings of our lives. This is not just psychological idealism, it is also moral idealism—the vision of reality and goodness that we create and live by at our best. Don Quixote proves this comically as he lives out his ideal of himself as a knight-errant, to the bafflement of his friends and the mockery of strangers. And he proves it philosophically and morally as he lives for ideals of goodness, to the enduring inspiration of readers through whom Don Quixote's idealism will live on and on.

WE COULD SAY THAT Don Quixote's story starts with an act of psychological idealism—inventing an identity. To set the stage, Cervantes, or his narrator, tells us that a person who called himself "Don Quixote" did in fact exist, although no one knows for certain what his real name was. But Cervantes adds a few pertinent details about this person before he became "Don Quixote." He was, Cervantes reports, "a gentleman . . . verging on fifty" from an unidentified village on the plain of Montiel in La Mancha, Spain. "They say that his surname was Quixada or Quesada," Cervantes goes on, but "by very reasonable conjecture we may take it that he was called Quexana." Whatever his original name, the "gentleman" from La Mancha "gave himself up to the reading of books of knight-errantry" brimming with "enchantments, quarrels, battles, challenges, wounds, wooings, loves, torments, and other impossible nonsense." Eventually, Cervantes says, "these writings . . . wrecked his reason . . . his brain dried up and he lost his wits." In this deranged state he fell into "the belief that all the fanciful stuff he read was true." And then he took up "the strangest fancy that ever a madman had in the whole world": he decided to act out his readings, "to turn knight-errant and travel through the world with horse and armor in search of adventures, following in every way the practice of the knights-errant he had read of, redressing all manner of wrongs, and exposing himself to the chances and dangers, by the overcoming of which he might win eternal honour and renown."

Was the "gentleman" from La Mancha mad? Cervantes doesn't equivocate about that—"his brain dried up and he lost his wits." But Cervantes is unfair to him. Deciding to invent a new identity is not in itself a symptom of madness. It tells the world who we want to be. And if we can live up to that invented identity, we are not mad. We are someone new. Our fantasy has become our reality. It is who we are. Señor Quexana, or whoever he was, looks upon his action that way—as pure self-reinvention. Perhaps he was suffering a midlife crisis—although that would be anachronistic for a man "verging on fifty" in his times, when few people lived beyond that age (although Dante suffered a similar crisis at a slightly earlier age, leading to his spiritual journey through hell, purgatory, and paradise—see Chapter 5). Whatever the cause, the gentleman from La Mancha fashions a new identity for himself out of fertile fantasies and moral ideals, inventive imagination and determined will, as anyone can. Shedding the person he had become, he tries to be someone else, the person *he wants to be*, a person born of an idea. Does he know what he is doing? Does he live up to the new identity? These are the measures of madness and sanity. Every reader will judge.

It takes the gentleman eight days to settle on a new name. Finally "he resolved to call himself Don Quixote de la Mancha," a dignified knightly title honoring his native land. He renames his horse, too, since a knight must have a knightly steed. After rejecting many possibilities, he picks "Rosinante, a name which seemed to him grand and sonorous" befitting "the first and the foremost of all hacks in the world." Everything in Don Quixote's life must be reinvented and renamed for Don Quixote to start life anew.

One thing remains: "To find a lady to be enamoured of. For a knight-errant without a lady is like . . . a body without a soul." In her name he will do his valiant deeds. He picks out Aldonza Lorenzo, a "good-looking farm girl" from El Toboso, "whom he had been taken with at one time." And he chooses to call her Dulcinea del Toboso, "a name which seemed to him as musical, strange, and significant as those others that he had devised for himself and his possessions." Reinvented and renamed, Don Quixote, his horse, and his lady are poised, at least in Don Quixote's mind, for a new life of knight-errantry to begin.

Equipped with an old suit of armor and a makeshift helmet held together with green ribbons, Don Quixote sets out on Rosinante to put "his ideas into effect" and win knightly honor by finding "the wrongs to right, the injuries to amend, the abuses to correct" that are his duty. And through these "deeds worthy to be engraved in bronze, carved in marble and painted on wood, as a memorial for posterity," he will demonstrate to the world that he is who he wants to be.

But wait! Something is still missing. As Don Quixote strikes out across the open country, "he suddenly remembered that he had never received the honour of knighthood," that is, the formal anointing of himself as a knight. This lapse must be rectified at once. But the honor cannot be bestowed by the knight himself. The act must be performed by someone else who witnesses the knight's valor. Don Quixote cannot be the person he wants to be without recognition of his new identity by other people—nor can anyone.

The occasion he picks for acquiring this honor is pure comedy. Perceiving everything he encounters to be the makings of knightly adventure, he happens upon a nondescript inn—the first of many in his adventures. Immediately he identifies the inn as "a castle," he sees a local hog caller as the requisite "dwarf giving notice of his approach," he judges the innkeeper to be the castle warden, and he views harlots at the door as graceful ladies-in-waiting. But astonishingly—again, for the first of many times—these characters do not try to disabuse him of his illusions. Instead they play the very roles his knightly fantasy expects of them. Wanting "to make some sport for that night," and not wishing to provoke the wrath of this strange visitor brandishing sword and shield who clearly "was wrong in the head," the innkeeper receives Don Quixote deferentially. He and the women help him off with his armor and serve him dinner (laughably feeding him through openings in the helmet, which he keeps on his head lest it fall apart). The innkeeper then agrees to perform the knighting, remarking in veiled jest that he had himself once pursued the knightly life and had then "retired to this castle . . .

welcoming all knights-errant." After a nightlong vigil of watching over his armor to prove his knightly valor, Don Quixote solemnly kneels before the innkeeper, who pronounces his impromptu honorific ritual "as if he were reciting some devout prayer." Then, with a stroke of hand and sword, he dubs Don Quixote a knight, while one of the ladies, controlling her laughter, archly proclaims: "God make your worship a fortunate knight and give you good luck in your battles."

Don Quixote de la Mancha is now officially, by public authority, a knight-errant readied to right the wrongs of the world. With such a formal endorsement, how could Don Quixote have failed to believe in his new identity? He leaves the inn in search of honorable adventures with that identity secure.

What he meets instead are comic misadventures. Within days he is all but undone. During an attack on some traveling merchants—whom he fancies to be a band of knights defying his demand that they declare Dulcinea to be the most "beauteous maiden" in the world—Rocinante stumbles and throws Don Quixote clattering to the ground, where the merchants batter him. When they leave, he describes the episode as "a disaster peculiar to knights-errant," and issues a recitation of knightly adversities, like his own, reported in books he has read. When a neighbor from his village comes along and escorts him home, Don Quixote continues the harangue, treating the neighbor as a part of his adventure. "Look you, your worship," the man says exasperatedly, "I am not" someone in a book "but your neighbor Pedro Alonzo. And your worship is not" one of those characters either, "but that worthy gentleman Master Quixada" [sic]. Don Quixote will hear none of this. He snaps back: "I know who I am," adding: "I know, too, that I am capable of being not only the characters I have named but" others as well, "for my exploits are far greater."

I know who I am (*yo sé quién soy*). Don Quixote knows who he is! A knight-errant. His ideal identity has become real. Is he deluded? William Wordsworth, the romantic poet, declared in his autobiographical poem *The Prelude* that personal identity, or "the consciousness" of who we are, is "the highest bliss that flesh can know" (see Chapter 23). Don Quixote claims to possess this consciousness—even if it is not bliss that he feels as he goes home to heal his wounds. Before long he will leave home again to take to the field on his second expedition, even more confident of who he is, thanks largely to the misguided efforts of people who strengthen his new identity while trying to cure him of it. The gentleman from La Mancha becomes more fully "Don Quixote" all the time—later taking on the epithets Knight of the Sad Countenance and Knight of the Lions to confirm this new identity as he proceeds.

ℰ

BUT BEFORE FOLLOWING these further adventures in the making of Don Quixote's identity, we need to pause for a few clarifying observations. We need to do this because as Don Quixote sallies about, being the knight-errant he wants to be, Cervantes keeps readers guessing what in his story is real and what is invention, what is truth and what is fantasy, what is fact and what is fiction. This can make for some confusing moments and tax your patience trying to sort things out. But Cervantes is not just playing idle literary games. His trickery actually draws us into the romance of fantasy and reality that at once drives Don Quixote's story and helps elevate Don Quixote into a figure with a life of his own beyond the pages of the book. To head off confusion—or to make the most of it—we can pluck the skein of Cervantes' trickery from the plot and trace it from beginning to end. This will untangle the tangles and make clear what Cervantes is up to. Then we can go back to the story itself and let the romance of fantasy and reality have its way with us.

The tricks and playful confusions begin even before the beginning, in the Prologue. There Cervantes blows smoke in our faces to make us unsure of what we are seeing. He says he took up writing the "history of the famous Don Quixote de la Mancha" with the encouragement of a "friend" who told him to "keep your aim steadily fixed" on "destroying the authority and influence which books of chivalry have in the world." But while the book is therefore "the child of my brain," Cervantes continues, the character of Don Quixote is really a stepchild, for "though in appearance Don Quixote's father, I am really his step-father." Right away we do not know what we have before us, fact or fiction, or who the author truly is—and whether the intention to discredit books of chivalry comes from Cervantes or from someone else. Pretending to allay uncertainties, Cervantes reports that "the inhabitants of the district around the plain of Montiel" regard Don Quixote as "the chastest lover and most valiant knight seen in those parts for many a year," even if "authors" dispute who he originally was. We are left with the implication that the book is indeed a "history," less fiction than fact, and that Cervantes is merely recording someone else's account of Don Quixote. But who knows?

Amidst these ambiguities, the unidentified "gentleman" from la Mancha takes on his new identity as "Don Quixote" and embarks on his first adventures. But only eight short chapters later—after Don Quixote has healed his wounds and returned to the field on his second expedition, the story abruptly stops. In the heat of battle, no less, with Don Quixote's sword raised to skewer an accused villain on the road. "The unfortunate thing," Cervantes steps in to say, "is that the author of this history left the battle in suspense at this critical point with the excuse that he could find no more records of Don Quixote's exploits." Now we see how Cervantes (or rather the nameless narrator he has created; but let us not stray farther into that morass) can be the "step-father" of Don Quixote: he is indeed reporting *someone else's* historical record of the knight. As "the second author of this work," he says that he now felt "great annoyance" at the first author for cutting off the adventure, for "I really could not bring myself to believe such a gallant history could be left maimed and mutilated." Cervantes goes to find the rest of the "history."

He discovers it by chance among some old parchments sold on the street. Curiously, the writing on these parchments is in Arabic, seemingly written by yet *another* author, "Cide Hamete Benengeli, Arabic Historian." After he has a Spanish-and-Arabic-speaking Moor translate the manuscript for him, Cervantes eagerly presents "this delightful history" to the world, adding the cautionary note: "If any objection can be made against the truth of this history, it can only be that its narrator was an Arab" (long the enemies of Christians in Spain, Arabs were not to be trusted, "being ready liars"). We never learn who wrote the earlier part of the book, but now Don Quixote's story resumes where it had so unceremoniously ended—in the midst of battle—as recorded from here on by the Arab historian Cide Hamete Benengeli and translated by the Spanish Moor, then reported third hand by Cervantes, or his anonymous narrator.

The maze of fact and fiction only gets worse. For Cide Hamete's record also trails off when the Arabic manuscript itself runs out. Cervantes steps in again to say that he has searched for more of it, this time without success. "Anxiously and diligently" he had "inquired after Don Quixote's exploits" on future expeditions, but he could find only a few parchments, written this time in Gothic Castilian script. These evidently contained accounts of further adventures, Cervantes explains, but all that could be reliably deciphered were some poems, as well as, surprisingly, a batch of epitaphs for the deceased "dunderheaded" Don Quixote. Cervantes quotes these epitaphs, and there he concludes the history of Don Quixote de la Mancha, who is now dead and buried.

At least Cervantes seemed to think it would conclude there—notwithstanding a tantalizing hint that the "author" might yet "discover other histories" of Don Quixote "as ingenious and entertaining" as this one. That is the entire book originally published as *El Ingenioso Hidalgo Don Quixote de la Mancha*. But today we turn the page to begin what is headed Part II. This was published ten years after what is now known as Part I. And in Part II—again recorded by the Arabic historian Cide Hamete Benengeli (presumably from those parchments, but we never know)—Cervantes lets the muddles of fact and fiction double and redouble. Many of these play on the actual historical facts that Part I had previously been published and that Spaniards had been reading it with delight.

The Don Quixote we see in Part II is pleased that reports of his early exploits had been published. Although a bit troubled that an Arab had reported them, he nonetheless glows "to see himself, in his life-time, printed and in the Press"—a recent influence at the time, by the way, hence a novelty. And now he will start meeting characters who know him from reading his published history, and who treat him exactly as he expects to be treated—as a knight-errant—so he will grow ever more certain that he is who he thinks he is. He will also discuss his history with people who are reading about him, and he asks at one point: "Does the author by any chance promise a second part?" "Yes, he does," a reader asserts, "but he says he has not found it, and does not know who has it." "What is the author up to then?" Don Quixote intently inquires. "As soon as he has found the history which he is taking extraordinary pains to search for," the reader assures Don Quixote, "he will give it straight to the Press." At this, Sancho Panza (who had joined Don Quixote as his squire for the second adventure in Part I) bursts out: "Let this Master Moor, or whoever he is, take care and look what he is doing, for I and my master will provide him with enough rubble in the way of adventures and different things for him to be able to make up not only a second part but a hundred more."

What is this? Have the events in Part II of *Don Quixote* already occurred or is the author waiting for them to happen? Either way, fact and fiction are hopelessly snarled, and Don Quixote himself is leaving the pages of the book to become a character on his own, the embodiment of an idea, a maker of history, the bearer of truth in illusion.

Cervantes' sleight-of-hand and Don Quixote's gathering independence of his author take a strikingly quirky turn in Part II owing to another historical fact. It happens that after Cervantes thought he had finished with Don Quixote and buried him in Part I, someone else published a book claiming to fill in the missing adventures before Don Quixote's death. Cervantes heaps scorn in the Prologue to his own Part II on the "author of the second *Don Quixote*," who wants "to deprive me of my profits by means of his book." And he proclaims that in his own book alone "an honest man has told the story" of Don Quixote to its conclusion (has Cide Hamete gained stature in Cervantes' eyes?). Therefore, no one should "presume to raise fresh testimonies to him" after this.

Cervantes then goes on in Part II to debunk the *false* Don Quixote as he reports the adventures of the *true* Don Quixote. When, for instance, the true Don Quixote learns from some readers that the spurious version of his story tells of him visiting the city of Saragossa—where he had said in Part I that he planned to go—he defiantly decides to head in the other direction. "I will not set foot in Saragossa," he announces, and "thus I will publish this modern historian's lie to the world, and people will see that I am not the Don Quixote he writes of."

And in a final turn of the screw, as Don Quixote returns home for the last time near the end of the novel, Cervantes has him meet a person named Don Alvaro Tarfe. Don Alvaro, not knowing to whom he is speaking, begins talking about events in the false history. He does not know it is false. But he has not only read it, he is a character in it. "This same Don Quixote," Don Alvaro boasts, "was a very great friend of mine." And, he adds, "it was I who . . . persuaded him to go to . . . Saragossa" (and later "left him shut up in a madhouse in Toledo," as the false history reports). The true Don Quixote recoils. A false version of his story in print is bad enough. But a false version of *himself* in existence, complete with a false Sancho Panza for a companion? That is too much! Don Quixote hastens to persuade Don Alvaro that he had in fact been duped, for the Don Quixote he had known was an imposter, and the authentic Don Quixote stands before him. Don Alvaro agrees: it must have been not the true "Don Quixote the good," but the false "Don Quixote the bad" whom he had known.

Cervantes is having fun with us. But by this time, we are used to his tricks entangling fact and fiction (tricks anticipating those of later writers like Luigi Pirandello, Vladimir Nabokov, and Jorge Luis Borges, who even wrote a story, "Pierre Menard: Author of Don Quixote," about a character who writes *Don Quixote* exactly like the original and calls it his own). And yet, again, the tricks Cervantes plays are more than literary devices. For they help give the book and its hero the powers of fantasy and invention that make Don Quixote who he is. And they remind us of the inextricable ties between truths and illusions, fantasy and reality, which give ideals their uses not only in *Don Quixote* but anywhere.

To LEARN MORE about these uses of idealism, we return to where we left Don Quixote limping home to recuperate after his first misadventure, but confident of *who he is*. When he arrives home, Don Quixote finds himself the object of concerted strategies to cure him of his delusions—or of his newly forged identity. But the cures only compound the disease, for they fortify Don Quixote's conviction that everything he thinks about himself is true.

Convinced that "books of chivalry" have driven a sane man insane, Don Quixote's niece and housekeeper, along with the local priest and barber, torch his books and wall up his library. Unable to find the books or even the room where they were shelved, Don Quixote asks what has happened. "What room?" the housekeeper answers. "There is no room and no books in this house," she continues, adding provocatively that "the Devil himself has carried everything off." Jumping in, his niece offers a captivatingly weird explanation of the mystery. There was "an enchanter," she says, "who came one night on a cloud, after you went away, and getting down from the dragon he was riding on, went into the room." Then "he went flying out through the roof and left the house full of smoke," shouting about "a secret grudge he bore the owner of those books," and afterwards "there was no room and not a book to be seen." Without a pause, Don Quixote knows: "Freston," he cries. "He is a learned enchanter and a great enemy of mine."

If Don Quixote needed more encouragement to be the knight-errant he wants to be, he got it here. Now he has unequivocal evidence from people he has long known that the world of knight-errantry lives not in himself alone, but in the form of an enchanter who is his sworn enemy.

With the entrance of this enchanter, Don Quixote's story takes a decisive turn. No longer just a comedy of invented, perhaps deranged, identity and deluded perceptions, it now enters a wider realm of enchantment itself, where anything can happen. Matter and spirit, appearances and reality freely merge and separate, separate and merge in Don Quixote's visionary eyes. This makes for plenty of laughs. But now we also learn that nothing in Don Quixote's world happens without a moral purpose, and Don Quixote knows what that purpose is. At the same time, the uses of idealism become more complex and ever more revealing.

Secure in who he is, with the enchanter as his enemy and the world of enchantment before him, Don Quixote embarks on his second series of adventures. This time he takes a companion, Sancho Panza, a local laborer he has enticed to join him as his squire with the promise of adventures and the prospect of winning an island to govern. They steal away in darkness, the ramshackle knight on his rickety Rocinante, the dumpy squire on his donkey, a sight to bring smiles—and inspiring the many evocative illustrations by Honoré Daumier in the nineteenth century.

The most renowned of Don Quixote's adventures occurs the next day. It is the incident that fixes the mad knight and his quixotic folly in everyone's mind. But it is not simply an episode in madness and folly. It reveals Don Quixote's way of thinking, mad or not, and the genius of one kind of his idealism.

"They caught sight of some thirty or forty windmills," Cide Hamete Benengeli records, and Don Quixote alerts his squire: "Look over there, friend Sancho Panza, where more than thirty monstrous giants appear. I intend to do battle with them and take all their lives." Sancho, always down-to-earth and plainspoken, calmly replies: "What giants?" Then, contradicting Don Quixote's repeated insistence, he explains, "Those things over there are not giants but windmills, and what seem to be the arms are the sails." Don Quixote firmly persists, "It is quite clear you are not experienced in this matter of adventures." And with no further ado he attacks, "at full gallop," thrusting his lance into the sail of the nearest windmill. "But the wind turned it with such violence that it shivered his weapon in pieces, dragging the horse and his rider with it, and sent the knight rolling badly injured across the plain."

That is virtually the entire episode. It lasts about a page. And it gave us the definition of "quixotic" as a futile, delusory tilting at windmills. But that definition does Don Quixote an injustice. His own explanation of his failed act is indeed ingenious. He does not dispute that he has clashed with windmills. Instead he deftly contends that they were originally giants that were suddenly transformed into windmills by the dreaded enchanter who had stolen his library. "The same sage Friston [sic] who robbed me of my room and my books," he exclaims, "has turned those giants into windmills, to cheat me of the glory of conquering them. Such is the enmity he bears me."

Don Quixote does not expect Sancho to understand this. He does not even expect Sancho to see anything the way a knight does. "Matters of war are more subject than most to continual change," he explains, warning Sancho that sharing in the adventures of a knight-errant, "you will witness things which will not be credited." In the realm of enchantment anything can happen, but only knights-errant can perceive accurately what is going on. And what they see—like all idealists of this type—is the reality behind appearances.

Don Quixote exhibits this kind of idealism again and again as he sees things to be other than what they seem to be. And he expounds upon it to Sancho in the fabled incident of Mambrino's helmet. Traveling the roads in search of more knightly adventures, he and Sancho see a man approaching "with something glittering on his head." Sancho does not make much of it. But to Don Quixote what glitters is "Mambrino's helmet" sitting on the head of a pagan villain. He urges Rocinante forward, lance couched for a kill, cursing the foe, who leaps from his donkey and flees terrified, leaving the gleaming object behind, resting on the ground. Picking it up and examining it, Sancho remarks that it looks "like nothing so much as a barber's basin"—which, in fact, it is, Cide Hamete Benengeli confirms, owned by the barber who had donned it to shield himself from the rain. Don Quixote does not deny that it looks like a basin. But, as usual, he points out that appearances can deceive. The "helmet must have fallen into the hands of someone who did not esteem it at its true value," he speculates, and so it was melted down for the gold and otherwise remade into "what looks like a barber's basin." But, typical of the knightly idealist he has become, Don Quixote assures Sancho, "its metamorphosis is of no consequence to me, who knows what it really is."

Just as Don Quixote knows who *he really is*, he knows what *things really are*, notwithstanding appearances. This gives him not only remarkable powers of perception, but peculiar interpretations of experience, which baffle Sancho the more. Don Quixote elucidates the principle, with some exasperation, to the still unpersuaded Sancho, who stubbornly sees only a barber's basin:

> Is it possible that all this while you have been with me you have not discovered that everything to do with knights-errant appears to be chimera, folly and nonsense, and to go all contrariwise? This is not really the case, but there is a crew of enchanters always amongst us who change and alter all our deeds, and transform them according to their pleasure and their desire either to favour us or injure us. So what seems to you to be a barber's basin appears to me to be Mambrino's helmet, and to another as something else. It shows a rare foresight in the sage who is on my side to make what is really and truly Mambrino's helmet seem to everyone a basin. For, as it is of such great value, the whole world would persecute me in order to get it from me. However, as they see that it is nothing more than a barber's basin, they do not trouble about it.

As a knight-errant in a world of enchantment, Don Quixote knows that things may not be what they seem to be to the ordinary eye. "Spells transform all things and change them from their natural shapes," he observes. "I do not mean that they actually change them, but they appear to." A benign enchanter had therefore altered the appearance of Mambrino's helmet to protect it, but the real helmet had remained true to itself. So, in Don Quixote's enchanted world, while appearances can deceive by being changed through both good and evil forces, the good or evil of things in themselves stays the same. And only knights-errant can see through the malleable and deceptive appearances to the true reality behind. Is this madness? It can be.

And yet, every believer in a spiritual reality shares some of this way of looking at things. Hinduism and Buddhism made an entire creed of it (see Chapter 2). And in the West thinkers beginning with Plato have fashioned whole philosophies of idealism out of it. But you do not have to see a reality behind appearances in order to be an idealist. You can simply believe that the ideas and ideals in your mind give meaning to your life. That is the difference between metaphysical idealism and both psychological idealism and moral idealism. Metaphysical idealists claim that an ideal realm actually exists somewhere out there and that only the mind or spirit can perceive it (we might think of Plato here—see Chapter 19). Psychological and moral idealists make the lesser claim that ideals exist only in our minds to give us an uplifting sense of ourselves and our highest purposes in life (we might think more of Socrates here—see Chapter 3). This is the idealism of William James's "will to believe." Don Quixote is a metaphysical idealist when he sees through the variable appearances of things to a fixed metaphysical reality behind. But in his heart and mind he is a psychological and, even more, a moral idealist with the "will to believe."

To be sure, psychological and moral idealism, like any other type, carries the risks of self-deception, imperious arrogance, blinkered fanaticism, and even madness. Don Quixote got accused of them all. But short of these unsavory excesses, these two kinds of idealism give the ordinary life extraordinary purposes. And notwithstanding his tendency to excess, and his periodic nuttiness, Don Quixote lived such a life. This is what takes *Don Quixote* from a burlesque comedy, with its wacky metaphysics, to the human truth of a reinvented life lived for noble ideals. And it is what makes Don Quixote what he most inspiringly and irresistibly is, to himself and to anyone.

We saw the gentleman of La Mancha first take up his idealism when he invented the identity of Don Quixote. Later, as Don Quixote, he articulates and celebrates that idealism when he speaks of Dulcinea. She is the emblem of his knightly self and moral vision. But does Dulcinea exist in the "real world" as Don Quixote imagines her? Does it matter?

Don Quixote candidly, and surprisingly, answers these questions himself. He does this first when he tells Sancho that his celestial Dulcinea is actually none other than the common peasant girl Aldonza Lorenzo, whom he has seen only in passing, if at all. When Sancho reacts dumbfoundedly, Don Quixote explains that who Dulcinea is in ordinary life, and what others see in her, have no importance. "I am quite satisfied," he says, "to imagine and believe that the good Aldonza Lorenzo is lovely and virtuous," for "I imagine all I say to be true, neither more nor less, and in my imagination I draw her as I would have her be, both as to her beauty and her rank." That is the secret of Don Quixote's moral idealism: "In my imagination I draw her as I would have her be" (*Y pintola en mi imaginación como la deseo*). She need not exist in the world at all. Don Quixote knows the truth of moral ideals: they live within us, and then we try to live them out.

Later Don Quixote elucidates this truth for a duke and duchess who have read Part I of his history and are lavishly, and mockingly, hosting him. Curious about Dulcinea and Don Quixote's description of her, the Duchess prods Don Quixote. "We gather from . . . the history of Don Quixote," she says, that "this same lady does not exist on earth, but is a fantastic mistress, whom your worship engendered and bore in your mind, and painted with every grace and perfection you desired." Don Quixote responds philosophically. "There is much to say on that score," he explains. "God knows whether Dulcinea exists on earth or no, or whether she is fantastic or not fantastic. These are not matters whose verification can be carried out to the full. I neither engendered nor bore my lady, though I contemplate her in her ideal form [or "as befits who she truly is"—*como conviene que sea*], as a lady with all the qualities needed to win her fame in all quarters of the world."

Here is the heart of the quixotic at its best—not bumbling folly and inexorable failure, not tilting at windmills, not seeing things that are not there, but the idealism of the heart and mind that gives us the will to believe. Can ideals exist on earth like facts in the everyday world? Don Quixote answers wisely: *These are not matters whose verification can be carried out to the full.* Whether ideals can come to exist outside the mind in reality, whether they are fantastic or not fantastic, is of no ultimate importance. What counts is that they exist in the mind and give direction to life—*I contemplate her in her ideal form . . . as I would have her be.* That is good enough.

The father of Western moral idealism, Socrates, said the same thing about Plato's ideal state in the *Republic*: "It makes no difference whether it exists now or ever will come into being," he confessed; it exists to believe in, and to live for; and to serve as a model for life; for if we "contemplate it," we can become "its citizens" in our souls. Socrates made the same point about the immortality of the soul itself shortly before he died: "No reasonable man ought to insist that the facts are exactly as I have described them" about "our souls and their future," he concluded, but it is "a belief worth risking, for the risk is a noble one" (see Chapter 3). Like Socrates, Don Quixote does not demand to live in an ideal world. He is satisfied to live in a real world given meaning by ideals in his mind. He knows that this is how ideals can best become real: not by our expecting to make the real world itself live up to the ideal (as Flaubert's Emma Bovary did), but by our living lives in the real world inspired by ideals.

The Duchess cannot resist Don Quixote. She laughs, but she also becomes a kind of believer. "Henceforth, I shall believe, and make my whole household believe," she declares, "that there is a Dulcinea del

Toboso, and that she lives today, and is beautiful, nobly born and deserving that such a knight as Don Quixote should serve her, which is the highest compliment I know how to pay her." The Duchess may not mean all she says. She is no doubt teasing Don Quixote and preparing for fun-making to come at his expense. But she bows to Don Quixote's philosophy with a certain undeniable affection. And this points to Don Quixote's ultimate and lasting victory. For Don Quixote not only lives up to his idealized identity and moral ideals, he induces other people to play along with him, then to believe in him. And then he changes them, despite themselves.

No wonder Don Quixote's most devoted modern disciple, the Spanish philosopher Miguel de Unamuno, linked Don Quixote with Jesus Christ (in *The Life of Don Quixote and Sancho* [1905]). Both of them, Unamuno said, were determined to live, and willing to die, for a moral ideal. Their ideals seemed absurd to many people and impossible to fulfill in the physical world. But those ideals and the lives they lived for them also inspired people, and changed the world. And is that not the making of morality itself, ideals of goodness and the lives lived for them? Where do morals come from if not from ideals of goodness, of perfection, and of the life that is alone worth living?

Don Quixote further presses his case for this idealism in a debate with a clergyman, or canon, over the merits of books of chivalry during an episode when he is being transported back again to his village for another attempted cure. "Books of chivalry," the canon says, are nothing but "liars and imposters, beyond the realm of common sense" that can "confuse the minds of intelligent and well born gentlemen." And worse, they can become "founders of new sects and new ways of life." He would "pitch them in the fire"—already the fate of Don Quixote's own books. Reacting to this indictment, Don Quixote defends the books that had supposedly done him much harm and turned his brain. They had indeed, he grants, helped make him the person he is by giving him a new way of life. But this is not the life of a lunatic or an outlaw. It is, he insists, that of a noble and virtuous human being. "I can say of myself that since I became a knight-errant I have been valiant, courteous, liberal, well-bred, generous, polite, bold, gentle, and patient, and an endurer of toils, imprisonment, and enchantments." Most readers would agree. However laughable and hard on his enemies he can be (for which Vladimir Nabokov faulted him in *Lectures on Don Quixote* [1983]), Don Quixote is good, decent, honorable, and unwaveringly faithful to his principles—and a loyal friend to Sancho, "the best man in the world," he calls him; and Sancho says of Don Quixote, "I love him dearly." Who could ask much more of morality?

In addition to high-minded moral ideals, Don Quixote's new way of life also gave him some practical wisdom. Look at the advice he offers Sancho for governing an island (which the Duke, in another conversion of Don Quixote's fantasies into reality, has given Sancho in order to fulfill the promise Don Quixote had made to him in Part I). Above all, Don Quixote advises, "you must consider what you are, seeking to know yourself, which is the most difficult task conceivable." For "from self-knowledge you will learn not to puff yourself up," and lose perspective on the "duties of governing." Also, "never be guided by arbitrary law," or by "personal passion," for these deny justice. And, perhaps most difficult, do not be deceived by appearances, since the truth is often hidden—"try to discover the truth behind the rich man's promises as well as behind the poor man's sobbings and importunities." Who knows the clash of appearances and realities better than Don Quixote?

Don Quixote's advice goes on and on. All of it is wise. And Sancho proves a worthy disciple, governing ably, if briefly. Cervantes even has Cide Hamete Benengeli remark: "Could anyone hear this last discourse of Don Quixote and not take him for a person of singular intelligence and excellent intentions?" The mad knight is not so mad after all. Thanks to his knightly ideals, he has become a sage.

NOTHING SHOWS THE POWER of Don Quixote's idealism more dramatically and poignantly than the events that bring the story to an end. Like Don Quixote's whole life, its ending is full of surprises. But by this time, the burlesque comedy of the early misadventures has long since given way to more complex doings, and to a character we do not so much laugh at as feel warmly towards and think hard about.

The climactic events follow from Don Quixote's final adventure in the field. This adventure has Don Quixote engaging in battle with the Knight of the White Moon, who is actually an educated young man from Don Quixote's village named Samson Corrasco. Samson had previously appeared as the Knight of the Mirrors in a plot like this one devised by the priest and the barber to defeat Don Quixote and send him home. But Don Quixote had vanquished him in that episode. Now Samson is trying again as the Knight of the White Moon. He incites the supposedly mad knight to battle by insulting Dulcinea, then he extracts from Don Quixote the promise that if he loses the battle he will retire from knight-errantry for at least a year. The scheme works. The Knight of the White Moon defeats Don Quixote, and, true to his pledge, Don Quixote heads home in retirement. His knightly code requires it. "When I was a knight-errant," he tells Sancho as they slump away, "daring and valiant, my arms brought credit to my exploits, and now that

I am a common squire I will bring credit on my words by fulfilling the promise I made." Knight-errant or not, Don Quixote will live up to his knightly ethics; he will abide by "the virtue of keeping my word." The gentleman from La Mancha has become a knight in his soul.

The beaten Don Quixote heads home for a sorrowful year, expecting later to "return to the honorable calling" and "win a kingdom" for his dear friend Sancho. But a change starts to come over him. First, he declines to blame his ill fortune on the machinations of an enchanter or on any other malevolent forces, as he had always done before. "Every man is the architect of his own destiny," he affirms, and "I have been so of mine." "I did what I could" in fighting the Knight of the White Moon, he concludes. "I was overthrown," that is all.

Then, when he and Sancho reach an inn (where they meet Don Alvaro and learn of the false Don Quixote), Don Quixote sees it as nothing but that: an inn. It is not the first that he had recognized as an inn, but Cide Hamete Benengeli notes that this time he "did not take [the inn] for a castle with a deep moat" because "since his defeat he spoke on all subjects with a sounder judgment"—although Don Quixote still insists to Don Alvaro that he himself is the *true* Don Quixote.

Finally, a couple of days later when the two companions enter their village, they hear some boys quarreling. "Don't worry," one boy says to another, "you won't see it in all the days of your life." Without knowing what the boy is talking about, Don Quixote mournfully remarks to Sancho: "Did you not hear, friend, what that boy said: —'You'll never see it again, never.' . . . If you apply that saying to myself, it means that I shall never see Dulcinea again." It is one of the saddest moments in the book. Don Quixote has lost Dulcinea, and he seems to be abandoning hope. (He believes, by the way, that Dulcinea has been in the grips of an enchanter ever since Sancho had falsely reported much earlier to have recognized her on the road as a person whom Don Quixote had perceived only as an unsightly peasant, prompting Don Quixote to conclude at the time that an evil enchanter must have altered her appearance for him alone.)

Once Don Quixote is home, the change in him becomes complete. He falls ill for no discernable reason, and everyone around him agrees the cause must be "grief at his overthrow and the disappointment of his hopes for Dulcinea's deliverance and disenchantment." A doctor confirms the worst: "Melancholy and despondency were bringing him to his end." Then his condition takes a sharp and shocking turn. The ailing Don Quixote renounces knight-errantry. From his sickbed, he proclaims to everyone's astonishment: "My judgment is now clear and free from misty shadows of ignorance with which my ill-starred and continuous reading of those detestable books of chivalry had obscured it. Now I know their absurdities and their deceits, and the only thing that grieves me is that this discovery has come too late." "Congratulate me, good sirs," he says to Samson Corrasco and to the barber and the priest who had burned his library, "for I am Don Quixote de la Mancha no longer, but Alonso Quixano [sic]. . . . Now all profane histories of knight-errantry are odious to me. . . . Now, by God's mercy, I have learnt from my own bitter experience and I abominate them."

Immediately the sane Alonso Quixano puts these sentiments into his will, bequeathing his estate to his niece on the single condition that she marry a man who "does not even know what books of chivalry are." And he adds regrets over the book that was written about his exploits as Don Quixote: "I quit this life with an uneasy conscience," he laments, for giving the author of that book "an excuse for writing" about those "gross absurdities" (although, retaining his affection for Sancho, he says, "I would give him a kingdom, were I able").

But startling as this transformation is, the reaction of those around the former Don Quixote is more unexpected still. For as Alonso Quixano renounces his identity as Don Quixote and all the "absurdities" of knight-errantry, some of the very people who have tried so hard to cure him of his "delusions" fail to react with relief and gratitude. Quite the contrary. They get sad, and Samson Corrasco even tries to change his mind. Despite Samson's victory in the field, which had sent the broken Don Quixote home at last, Samson now switches sides and invents a brash bit of fantasy. "Must you come out with that, Don Quixote," he asks, "just now when we have news that the Lady Dulcinea is disenchanted. . . . No more of that . . . return to your senses." Buoyed by these unexpected words, the loyal Sancho cries: "Oh, don't die, dear master! . . . get out of bed, and let's go into the fields dressed as shepherds as we decided to. Perhaps we shall find the lady Dulcinea behind some hedge, disenchanted and pretty as a picture." Sancho goes on to remind Don Quixote that he should not to suffer "grief at being beaten" because, as "your books of chivalries" show, "it's a common thing for one knight to overthrow another, and the one that's conquered to-day may be the conqueror to-morrow." Samson chimes in: "That's right. Honest Sancho has hit the truth of the matter."

The truth of the matter? Return to your senses? Dulcinea disenchanted? What is going on here? Has Samson gone mad? Of course not. It is just that neither he nor Sancho, nor anyone else really, wants to lose Don Quixote. But it is no use. Alonso Quixano holds firm. "I was mad, but I am sane now." And it is with his original identity as the sane Alonso Quixano, not that of the mad Don Quixote de la Mancha, that the "gentleman" from La Mancha dies.

Here Cervantes—or Cide Hamete Benengeli, or the original anonymous narrator—pronounces the tale of Don Quixote de la Mancha finished for good. Then he proudly asserts, in the last line, that the stated intention of the book has now been fulfilled: "For my sole object has been to arouse men's contempt for all fabulous and absurd stories of knight-errantry, whose credit this tale of my genuine Don Quixote has already shaken, and which will, without a doubt, soon tumble to the ground. Farewell."

Did Cervantes truly believe these closing words? What reader would agree with him? Don Quixote's cure through the renunciation of his knightly identity and his transformation back into Alonso Quixano cannot possibly have the effect on readers that the narrator assumes they have. Don Quixote has won over too many people, both within the book and outside of it, with his good nature, his virtues, and his infectious idealism. Cervantes virtually conceded the point. Near the end he says that whether the gentleman of La Mancha was "plain Alonso Quixano the Good, or Don Quixote de la Mancha, he was always of an amiable disposition and kind in his behavior, so that he was well beloved . . . by everyone who knew him." Hasn't Don Quixote the Good made a believer of his author, too?

By the time Don Quixote renounces knight-errantry, he has left his author no less than Alonso Quixano behind. He has become the embodiment of an idea. That idea is this: that our lives gain their highest meaning through the ideals and beliefs, purposes and passions, and even the inspiriting fantasies, that we envision and adopt to shape our lives. Alonso Quixano does not really convince us that his life as Don Quixote was altogether a bad thing, does he? He rather convinces us that being Don Quixote had made his life worth living. So, when he ceased believing in himself as Don Quixote, it is no surprise that he dies of "melancholy and despondency." He has nothing left to live for. No longer possessing the will to believe in himself as Don Quixote, and in the glorious, honorable career of knight-errantry that had charged his new life with extraordinary purpose, he has no will to live.

Alonso Quixano dies from the melancholy of losing an idealized identity and the life that went with it. But Don Quixote does not die. He lives on in our minds, where, as he himself had learned, ideas and ideals do their work. For that is where they act on us, invigorating, rejuvenating, ennobling us, and pointing to life-giving ends, whether we can live them out to the full or not. And that is why Don Quixote should live always in our minds as the image, above all, of the ideas and ideals and beliefs that we use, and must use, to lend our ordinary lives

extraordinary purposes, and to make those lives intensely worth it
whoever we are—or choose to become.

On the Uses of Idealism

1. Ideals make life most worth living.

2. Idealism comes in many varieties and has many uses.

3. Metaphysical idealism shows us a perfect reality beyond appearances in this world.

4. Psychological idealism gives us an ideal image of who we want to be.

5. Moral idealism offers us a vision of the highest good to live for in this world.

6. Idealism serves us best when it gives us an ideal image of ourselves and a vision of the highest good to live for that exist in our minds, but that we do not expect to be absolutely true or to find completely in the real world.

7. Idealism should give us practical wisdom, generous humanity, and courage, while it gives us purpose in our lives.

8. We can begin life anew at any time by imagining and adopting a new ideal of ourselves.

9. Ideals can be dangerous if they misdirect our lives and do more harm than good in this world.

10. When we lose our ideals, we might have nothing left to live for.

11. We should live for ideals, but live in this world.

12. The meaning of life is to live for ideals of who we want to be and of what is good, without expecting them to be absolutely true or ever to fit entirely into the world.

23

he Gifts of Imagination

am Wordsworth: Preface to *Lyrical Ballads, The Prelude*
Percy Bysshe Shelley: "A Defense of Poetry"

*Imagination, in truth, is but another name for absolute
power and clearest insight, amplitude of mind,
and Reason in her most exalted mood.*

Wordsworth

*Poets . . . are not only the authors of language and of music, of
the dance, and architecture, and statuary, and painting;
they are the institutors of laws, and the founders of
civil society, and the inventors of the arts of life.*

We want the poetry of life.

Shelley

Born in the lake country of northern England, **William Wordsworth** (1770–1850) gained early fame for his lyric poems exuding affection for nature, innocence, and poignant emotions. His first collection of poems—including the now-renowned "Lines Composed a Few Miles Above Tintern Abbey"—appeared in *Lyrical Ballads* (1798), to which Wordsworth added a Preface for the second edition (1800) explaining the purpose of poetry, how the imagination works, and why the modern world needs both poetry and the imagination more than ever. Then came *Poems in Two Volumes* (1807) and *The Excursion* (1814). After that, although he continued to write poetry, Wordsworth shed much of his romantic enthusiasm—and he aroused disillusionment in the young Robert Browning for becoming a staid poet laureate, expressed in Browning's poem "The Lost Leader." And yet flames of that enthusiasm still burned in the long autobiographical poem *The Prelude*, written in three versions beginning in 1798 and left unpublished at Wordsworth's death in 1850. Covering his first twenty-nine years, this remarkable poem evocatively records how Wordsworth discovered the powers of feeling and imagination that shaped his life and work. Together, *The Prelude* and the Preface to *Lyrical Ballads* stand as monuments above all to how the imagination can show us the most important meanings of our lives.

Percy Bysshe Shelley (1792–1822) was another English Romanticist who celebrated the imagination and the power of poetry. The son of a wealthy landowner, Shelley rebelled against his family and all constraints on human freedom, becoming politically radical, philosophically idealistic, and lyrically poetic. He wrote prolifically on these themes from his juvenilia and the early *Queen Mab* (1813) to the ambitious lyrical drama *Prometheus Unbound* (1820)—he also had a tempestuous love life, including his marriage to Mary Wollstonecraft Godwin, author of *Frankenstein* (1817). When he drowned in a boating accident off the coast of Italy at the age of twenty-nine, Shelley left a legacy in ideas as well as poetry. In "A Defense of Poetry" (an essay written in 1821, but not published until 1840), he laid out part of this legacy with a theory of the imagination. Ambitious and argumentative, Shelley's essay—like Wordsworth's Preface and *Prelude*—exalts the imagination for giving us not only poetry, but all good things in life.

T HE IMAGINATION as we know it is not very old. It was born not much more than a couple of centuries ago as a child of European Romanticism. People had used the imagination before then, of course. But traditionally in Western culture, they had thought of the imagination mainly as a faculty that produces "images" in the mind mirroring things outside, whether or not it mirrored them accurately. Or sometimes they had thought of it as a wayward "fancy" that conjures up fears and illusions and induces us to believe in them—writing in the late sixteenth century, Michel de Montaigne faulted it for this in his essay "The Power of the Imagination." Romanticism changed all that. Romanticists exalted the imagination as a power of free creation, more of a "lamp" than a "mirror," as the literary critic Meyer Abrams memorably put it in *The Mirror and the Lamp* (1953). And they celebrated it as the path to truth, a light of transcendental revelation, and the source of life's highest meanings.

This idea of the imagination was possibly Romanticism's most enduring gift to us. And it was the Romantic poets who presented this gift most "enthusiastically"—a favorite Romantic term previously derided by the more sober-minded thinkers of the Enlightenment, like Voltaire in his *Philosophical Dictionary*. They also implied, where they did not state, that poetry was itself the preeminent art of Romanticism and of truth—the German Romantic philosopher Hegel asserted this outright in his *Lectures on Aesthetics*, although the German Romantic poet Johann von Goethe gave the idea a more ambiguous twist in his autobiography, *Poetry and Truth (Dichtung und Wahrheit)*.

Among the Romantic poets, none displayed more enthusiasm for the imagination than the English. Lord Byron, William Blake, William Wordsworth, Samuel Taylor Coleridge, John Keats, and Percy Bysshe Shelley, all reveled in the imagination's powers. And they believed everyone should do that. Their enthusiasm arose in part from their zest for escaping from the constraints of the dominant British philosophical tradition, empiricism, which limited knowledge to "sense experience" and verifiable data. The most fervent of these anti-empiricist poets was William Blake. He wanted to blast the founders of the empiricist tradition—Francis Bacon, John Locke, and Isaac Newton—out of the water, or sink them under it, where one of Blake's paintings shows a glum Newton beneath the sea fiddling with a compass in the sand. Truth does not come from the passive senses, Blake insisted, it comes from the creative imagination, which sees with the mind's eye; and the mind's eye can see anything it wants to see—angels in the sunshine, demons in the dark—for, as Blake hymned in *The Marriage of Heaven and Hell* (1790): the "imagination is eternal delight." At a celebrated dinner in 1817 at the home of the painter Benjamin Haydon, John Keats and Charles Lamb echoed Blake, condemning Newton for having "destroyed all the poetry of the rainbow" with his empiricist theory of optics. And then, as Haydon reports in his autobiography, the whole party, including Wordsworth (who generally admired Newton), sarcastically drank to "Newton's Health, and the confusion of mathematics."

But among the Romantic poets' enthusiasm for the imagination, the ideas of William Wordsworth and Percy Bysshe Shelley surpass the rest for their sustained and searching speculations on how the imagination works and what it can do for us. Wordsworth and Shelley spelled out these ideas in a pair of essays—Wordsworth's Preface to his *Lyrical Ballads* and Shelley's "A Defense of Poetry." Although these two essays do not always agree, they nonetheless make complementary and classic cases for how the imagination helps us find the meaning of anything, most of all our own lives. Wordsworth then went on to demonstrate this most invaluable use of the imagination in his poetic autobiography, *The Prelude*. Wordsworth's greatest achievement, *The Prelude* is an illuminating record of the poet's youth and early adulthood, and it is an adventurous exploration of the inner world of the thoughts and feelings, perceptions and memories that shaped his life. And more, it tells us that everyone contains such an inner world, and that exploring it can indeed reveal what is most important to us.

Wordsworth sat down to write about the imagination in 1800 because he and his friend Samuel Taylor Coleridge were preparing a new edition of their *Lyrical Ballads*, comprised of poems by both of them. Coleridge had urged Wordsworth to explain in a preface to the second edition how the kind of poetry that the two of them wrote differed from more traditional verse. Although Wordsworth's poems in *Lyrical Ballads* were mainly short, simple lyrics, and Coleridge's were long, mysterious narratives—notably "The Rime of the Ancient Mariner"—their poetry was new for its day, and very much their own. As it turned out, the preface Wordsworth wrote accounted chiefly for his own style of poetry, not Coleridge's. But he also described how he believed the imagination works in general, and how it discovers the most important things in life—Coleridge later offered his own complementary version of the imagination in his *Biographia Literaria*. Wordsworth also warned that modern culture was threatening the imagination and humanity from every side. And this warning, no less than Wordsworth's idea of the imagination, is as germane today as it was then, if not more.

It is true that some of Wordsworth's terms and concepts belong more to his era than to ours. But when we see what he is getting at, we see how timeless—and not merely late eighteenth-century English and Romantic—his ideas are. And when we use the imagination as Wordsworth advises, we find that it can do everything for us that he says it can.

Here, in short, is how Wordsworth says the imagination works. When the "imagination" sees "ordinary things . . . in an unusual way," it puts us "in a state of excitement." This "excitement" brings "our feelings and ideas" together, and when this happens we see life anew and discover its true meanings, or "what is really important." That is a *very* short version. Now some illuminating details.

Wordsworth was drawing here on what he regarded one of the "primary laws of our nature," which he had learned from eighteenth-century theories of "the association of ideas." Those theories, popular at the time thanks to the British empiricists, said that we gain knowledge when our senses stimulate ideas by bringing sensations into our minds, and then our minds connect or "associate" those ideas with each other. That "association of ideas" is knowledge. William Blake scorned exactly this empiricist version of knowledge for making the mind too dependent on the senses, too passive, too inert, and devoid of creative powers. Wordsworth could make fun of empiricism for similar reasons. But he also detected in the "association of ideas" a key to the imagination itself—as had, in a different way, the more empiricist-minded Joseph

Addison in "The Pleasures of the Imagination" (1712). At the same time, Wordsworth added something new to give the "association of ideas" more juice. That was a shot of emotional "excitement." This converted the empiricists' intellectual "association of ideas" into a Romantic fusion of feelings and ideas. And this fusion, Wordsworth believed, brings us our highest joys and the most important revelations in life.

That fusion and those revelations, Wordsworth explains, happen rather like this: a spark of "excitement" stirs "powerful feelings" in us, then these feelings prompt "thoughts, which are representatives of all of our past feelings"; then "by contemplating the relation of these general representatives to each other we discover what is really important to men." In other words, when we have strong emotions and think about them, our emotions and thoughts become joined, and then *we discover what is really important*. Wordsworth later called this unity of thoughts and emotions the "feeling intellect," which is, in essence, the imagination.

But we needn't labor Wordsworth's knotty theories. Most of us know what Wordsworth is talking about because we have experienced something like it. Our strongest feelings do sometimes give rise to thoughts, and when this occurs our thoughts and feelings do sometimes come together, and then we do sometimes discover meanings in our lives that neither our feelings nor our thoughts alone could have revealed. We might sum it up this way: the meaning of life is the feeling that our lives have meaning, and we get that feeling when we think about our emotions and find the ones that move us most, and understand why. Wordsworth could have said that. He didn't quite. But he implied it. At all events, it is true.

Marcel Proust discovered something close to this when he tasted a madeleine dipped in a cup of tea and found himself flooded with emotions and memories that threw open the secret of his life. Sigmund Freud derived psychoanalysis from a kindred discovery—he learned that we must find the emotions that lie hidden in our psyches, and then bring them to the surface and consciously recognize them in order to truly understand ourselves. Wherever we pick up this idea, we should use it.

Wordsworth put his discovery to most conspicuous use in poetry. For he decided that the very purpose of poetry is to spark the "excitement" that ignites strong feelings and fuses them with thoughts in the "feeling intellect." "Poetry," he wrote in a now-familiar line, "is the spontaneous overflow of powerful feelings: it takes its origin from emotion recollected in tranquillity." For, he went on, when a poet contemplates "powerful feelings," an "emotion . . . is gradually produced that does itself actually exist in the mind," and "in this mood successful composition generally begins." Here the fusion of thoughts and emotions in the "feeling intellect" creates the *poetic* imagination. And the aim of the imagination in poetry is nothing less than to yield "truth, not individual and local, but general," about "what is really important to men." That makes poetry, so Wordsworth says, tipping his hat to Aristotle, "the most philosophical of all writing" (see Chapter 19).

This is a very Romantic boast for the poetic imagination. But Wordsworth also grants that the "feeling intellect" has much the same purpose in life at large as it does in poetry—that is, to show us "what is really important." When we ask what Wordsworth means by "what is really important," we do not get a direct answer. Instead we get another rather vague idea. And yet, it is a good idea.

When emotions and thoughts converge in the "feeling intellect," Wordsworth tells us, "the mind upon the whole will be in a state of enjoyment." This is not an idle notion. It had roots in eighteenth-century philosophies of pleasure common in Wordsworth's youth. But Wordsworth goes beyond these theories, just as he goes beyond the empiricist "association of ideas." He exalts "the grand elementary principle of pleasure" as the very "native and naked dignity of man . . . by which he knows, and feels, and lives and moves." The "state of enjoyment" aroused by the "feeling intellect" therefore not only reveals what is really important in life. It *is* what is really important in life.

We might not want to limit the most important things in life to a "state of enjoyment," since we can also learn from sacrifice and pain. Still, in the calculus of our lives, we likely make enjoyment or happiness at least a portion of what we live for (Aristotle and Freud took happiness to be the natural goal of human beings—see Chapters 4, 17), even if we have to await that happiness in the next life. To be sure, most Hindus and Buddhists strive not for happiness in this life or in any other, but only for an escape from pain. But Wordsworth would say that they deny "the grand elementary principle of pleasure" that is the "native and naked dignity of man." And if he possibly identified the meaning of life too much with feelings of pleasure and joy, Wordsworth nonetheless made a good case for how our highest joys can indeed give meaning to our lives, and how our lives would lack meaning without them.

Poet that he was, Wordsworth figured that poetry in particular should stir this kind of joy in us. "The Poet writes under one restriction only," he claims, "namely, that of the necessity of giving immediate pleasure to a human being . . . not as a lawyer, a physician, a mariner, an astronomer or a natural philosopher, but as a Man." And because of this, poetry "binds together by passion and knowledge the vast empire of human society, as it is spread over the whole earth, and over all time." Finding what is most important to us through pleasure and joy, and sensing our common humanity—these discoveries lift human beings to the heights, Wordsworth believed, and poetry makes that happen.

These are heady claims for poetry, or for any art. But anyone who has been moved deeply by any work of art knows that Wordsworth was at least partly right. Art can give us moments of intense "enjoyment," uniting feelings and thoughts that awaken us to new meanings in life (art can also deceive us in the same way, as critics of art's emotional powers have warned since Plato—see Chapter 19—but that was not Wordsworth's concern). And Wordsworth saw a greater need for this kind of awakening in his day than ever before. For he observed that the rapid pace and multiplying distractions of modern times were making it ever harder for people to experience those moments when thoughts and feelings converge in the "feeling intellect" to stir elation and reveal "what is really important." And although he wrote the Preface to *Lyrical Ballads* over two hundred years ago, what he said on this theme could have been written today.

"A multitude of causes, unknown to former times," Wordsworth says, "are now acting with a combined force to blunt the discriminating powers of the mind" and reduce people "to a state of savage torpor," deadening the genuine "excitement" and revelatory "enjoyment" that human beings need to thrive. He saw this occurring through a vicious cycle of modern life—which is more conspicuous today than it was in Wordsworth's day. This cycle arises from the fact that modern life can be achingly dull in its everyday routine and yet ephemerally stimulating in its keen sensations. To escape from the dullness we often seek those sensations. But the more of these sensations we get, the duller we wind up feeling. As Wordsworth puts it, "the increasing accumulation of men in cities" and the "uniformity of their occupations . . . produces a craving for extraordinary incident, which the rapid communication of intelligence hourly gratifies." This fleeting gratification breeds a craving for more of the "extraordinary" that people try to satisfy through more stimulation, including the sensationalism of "frantic novels" and "idle and extravagant stories." But this "degrading thirst after outrageous stimulation" can only lead to overstimulation and then to a "savage torpor" in which people feel and think almost nothing at all. Sound familiar?—and Wordsworth said that long before the mass popular culture of our times with its overamplified sounds and wowing "special effects." Wordsworth was right. Shallow sensationalism deadens while it thrills, causing life to become less satisfying even as it grows more sporadically "stimulating."

Worried over these baleful consequences of modernity, Wordsworth took it upon himself "to counteract . . . the general evil" by demonstrating that "the human mind is capable of being excited without the application of gross and violent stimulants." What modern culture needs, he argued, is less superficial stimulation and more genuine feelings. And he vowed to ignite these feelings. He would do this by writing poetry in the "language really used by men," and by enfolding the "common life" and "elementary feelings" with the "imagination, whereby ordinary things should be presented to the mind in an unusual way." This imaginative poetry would excite the "feeling intellect" in readers, putting them in the state of enjoyment that reveals what is most important, and leaving each one "in some degree enlightened and his affections ameliorated." That was Wordsworth's theory, and his hope.

Most readers of Wordsworth's poetry today probably do not respond to it as he had desired. It sounds too sweet and sentimental to our ears. But that may be more a symptom of our times than a failure of the poetry. For in his day Wordsworth's lyrics did in fact bring about some of the very effects that Wordsworth had predicted. A nice example of this came in the life of the philosopher John Stuart Mill. After a youth of extraordinary intellectual accomplishments and steely dedication to his father's philosophy of Utilitarianism (which had its own social theory linking "pleasure with all things beneficial to the whole," and which Charles Dickens parodied in the character of Mr. Gradgrind in *Hard Times*—see Chapter 13), Mill reports in his autobiography that at the age of twenty, in 1826, he fell into a "mental crisis." Suddenly he "seemed to have nothing to live for," he confesses, because "all feeling was dead within me." But over time he found a cure. And what was it but—poetry. And Wordsworth's poetry more than any other.

Mill discovered in Wordsworth's poetry, which he first read in 1828, just what Wordsworth had promised: how the "feeling intellect" can bring joy and reveal "what is really important." "What made Wordsworth's poems a medicine for my state of mind," Mill writes, "was that they expressed not mere outward beauty, but states of feeling, and of thought coloured by feeling, under the excitement of beauty." And through them "I seemed to draw from a source of inward joy, of sympathetic and imaginative pleasure, which could be shared in by all human beings." After reading Wordsworth, Mill concludes, "I gradually, but completely, emerged from my habitual depression, and was never again subject to it."

Mill's account of his "cure" fulfilled all of Wordsworth's hopes for poetry and the imagination. "Thought colored by feeling"—"excitement of beauty"—"inward joy"—"imaginative pleasure" to "be shared in by all human beings." All of these Wordsworthian ideals came together through poetry to release Mill from his despair. And not only that. Wordworth's poetry changed the course of Mill's life. For Mill had now discovered what was "really important." And that was not—as he had previously assumed by virtue of his Utilitarian philosophy—the "analysis" of facts and the "ordering of outward circumstances," but rather "the internal culture of the individual" and "the common feelings and the common destiny of human beings." From that time onward, Mill became more of a humanist, embarking on a new life animated by a mission to advance the "inward joy" of "all human beings." His classic book *On Liberty*, written with the woman Harriet Taylor, who helped nourish his emotions and came to share his life, would be a lasting monument to the human spirit born of this new life (see Chapter 14).

Mill's testimonial to the healing powers of the "feeling intellect" in poetry would no doubt have pleased Wordsworth had he lived to read it. And if Wordsworth's lyrics no longer display those powers today as once they did, that is our loss. Nevertheless, Wordsworth's ideas can still remind us of what art and the imagination can, and should, do for us. Amidst the mushrooming overstimulation of our twenty-first-century world, we need such ideas more all the time.

The Preface to *Lyrical Ballads* lays out Wordsworth's ideas of how the imagination works and what it can do for us. *The Prelude* (which Wordsworth started writing shortly before the Preface and kept writing on and off until his death) records, among other things, how these ideas arose in him, and how he used them, and how the "feeling intellect" showed him what was most important to him. The Preface is theory, *The Prelude* is life—Wordsworth's life, and in many ways ours as well.

Wordsworth announces that *The Prelude* speaks "not of outward things," but of "what passed within me," for it is "the history of a Poet's Mind." But in fact, *The Prelude* knits Wordsworth's outer and inner lives together. It recreates the life of a young man who lived among nature and among friends, who passed through rousing expectations and painful disillusionments, who cultivated the powers of imagination, and who later discovered in looking back over his life again and again what was "really important" to him. *The Prelude* therefore steeps us—like Proust's *In Search of Lost Time*—in "remembrances . . . and the power they had left behind." It explores the kinds of moments that give our past its texture and meaning, and that bring understanding of ourselves and lend purpose to our lives.

Wordsworth calls these revelatory moments "spots of time." "Such moments," he says, "are scattered everywhere, taking their date from our first childhood." And they stay with us always, even if not consciously. Then, when recalled, they have an "efficacious spirit" and "renovating" power "by which pleasure is enhanced, / That penetrates, enables us to mount, / When high more high, and lifts us up when fallen." In other words, these spots of time come alive through the acts of imagination that Wordsworth had described in the Preface to *Lyrical Ballads*, and which he now shows are not limited to poetry. For when we "recollect" and "contemplate" our emotions, they come to "exist in the mind" as the "feeling intellect," and this brings the joy of recognizing "what is really important" to us. That is the drift.

And the drift is good enough. We should not get pedantic about it. We can easily see how Wordsworth's "spots of time" can arise in anyone from moments of strong emotions, how these emotions can seize our minds as the "feeling intellect," and how these "spots of time" can then leave lasting residues in memories. So, as we open *The Prelude* we should expect to find many emotions wrapped in memories. Exuberance and longing, enthusiasm and dejection, passion and sorrow, and many more are here, all animated by recollection. But one emotion stands out for the frequency of its appearance, the intensity of its expression, and the importance of its role in Wordsworth's life, although it seems almost quaint today. This is none other than *joy*.

Joy pervades *The Prelude*, heightening all other good emotions and eclipsing the bad ones. For joy, as Wordsworth had said in the Preface to *Lyrical Ballads*, betokens the "grand elementary principle of pleasure" through which humankind "knows, and feels, and lives and moves." Here he restates this idea with poetic enthusiasm: The "deep enthusiastic joy" that we can feel, he effuses, proves a "bond of union between life and joy" that can burst forth in a "rapture of the hallelujah sent / From all that breathes and is."

Wordsworth's rhapsodic words might prompt more smiles than assent in our irony-besotted postmodern era. But it would be a mistake to dismiss Wordsworth's joy as trite Romanticism or easy sentimentality. For the joys of *The Prelude* should prompt us to seek our own joys in those vital spots of time that reveal what is really important to us.

Wordsworth found those spots of time and those joys for himself in many places, just as anyone can. First among these places was wild nature, which he lauded as an antidote to the "savage torpor" that cities breed, and that he celebrated in poem after poem and regaled throughout *The Prelude*. But he found other spots of time and other joys in places of the heart and mind common to us all, although we might not use them as as he did. Most important of these places to Wordsworth were love, hope, and the imagination itself. These usually flowed together in Wordsworth's life. And Wordsworth's account of how he discovered his highest joys and the meanings of his life in them can ring true for anyone.

Wordsworth begins *The Prelude* with a salute to the reigning emotion, joy. "O there is a blessing in this gentle breeze," he sings, "a visitant that while it fans my check / Doth seem half-conscious of the joy it brings." He goes on to hymn how his youth had brimmed "With a heart / Joyous," and with "the hope / Of active days," and "A cheerful confidence in things to come." This cheery mood did not always stay with him. How could it have? But recollecting it taught Wordsworth how moments of joy can give meaning to life.

He recollected first feeling this joy as a child amidst nature, as in that first line. And this joyfulness grew into the "feeling intellect." He records a moment in his "seventeenth year" when that intellect came fully to life in him. "From Nature and her overflowing soul," he recalls, "I had received so much that all my thoughts / Were steeped in feeling." And then he goes on, "To every natural form, rock, fruit or flower, / Even the loose stones that cover the high-way, / I gave a moral life: I saw them feel, / Or linked them to some feeling; . . . and all / That I beheld respired with inward meaning." That sensation gave him a rush of exhilaration that seemed to pervade both himself and nature, and to unite everything as one—that "rapture of the hallelujah sent from all that breathes and is." A "bliss ineffable," he gushes, "spread / O'er all that moves and all that seemeth still. . . . / O'er all that leaps and runs, and shouts and sings, / Or beats the gladsome air; o'er all that glides / Beneath the wave, yea, in the wave itself." If Wordsworth sounds a bit drunk on nature here, his recollections had nevertheless found some of the most joyous "spots of time" that gave meaning to his life. "O Nature!" he cries, "Thou hast fed / My lofty speculations; and in thee . . . I find / A never-failing principle of joy / And purest passion." The intoxication never entirely passed.

Wordsworth felt this jubilant passion for nature most in his youth, but he never lost it. "Some called it madness," he admits. But he dubbed it the "sentiment of Being." And he meant by this phrase a sensation that most of us have known at least fleetingly now and then. It is the feeling of being at one with the universe, as he was with nature. And it is a kind of mysticism—Taoism made a creed of such a feeling (see Chapter 10), and every religious mystic has lived for it. For Wordsworth it was more a kind of pantheism—the divinity that breathes through all things. It was also a kind of Romantic *love*.

Wordsworth thought so, anyway. For true Romantic love, as he and many of his contemporaries idealized it, brought the complete and blissful union of lover and beloved—although many a Romantic lover, such as Heathcliff and Cathy in Emily Brontë's *Wuthering Heights*, came to believe this possible only after death. Wordsworth celebrated this kind of love again and again. The word "love" appears in *The Prelude* probably more frequently than any other except "joy." But love and joy were inextricable in Wordsworth's heart and life. Not for him the anguished passion of love, at least not in *The Prelude*. Wordsworth was no Byron.

Wordsworth felt this joyous love in nature as the "sentiment of Being." Then he carried it into the human world, where he merged himself with other human beings almost as enthusiastically as he did with nature. He did this not through erotic love affairs (he married during the events he records in *The Prelude*, and you would hardly know it), but through intense friendships and a generic affection for all humankind.

Wordsworth's devotion to friendship appears in *The Prelude* most conspicuously in Wordsworth's feelings for Coleridge. Wordsworth wrote the poem specifically for him. "Coleridge!" Wordsworth exclaims, "O capacious Soul! / Placed on this earth to love and understand, / And from thy presence shed the light of love . . . to thee the work shall justify itself." This was no formulaic dedication. It was a profession of genuine love. For, like so many of his Romantic contemporaries, Wordsworth thought of friendship as far more than congenial companionship. Friendship approached Romantic love in its near-mystical union of two human beings. We hardly know this kind of friendship today—any more than we know the emotional power once exercised by Romantic poetry. And we are the poorer for it.

More prominently than the love of friends, though, *The Prelude* glows with Wordsworth's love of humankind. This, too, started amidst nature. "My heart was early introduced / To an unconscious love and reverence / Of human nature," he says, by a single shepherd in the hills who embodied the "sanctity of Nature given to man" and thus made "man / Ennobled outwardly in my sight." This innocent and noble shepherd might be a Wordsworthian cliché—and Wordsworth would in time come to see another side of human nature, fraught with "meanness, selfish cares, / Coarse manners, vulgar passions, that beat in / On all sides from the ordinary world." But Wordsworth would never forget the love he learned when "first I looked / At Man" in the form of that shepherd. And he would later be grateful that he had learned to love humanity in general before he got to know many human beings.

He took that generic affection, as well as the joy it stirred, with him on his ventures into France during the great revolution. There he found the best of times in the early revolutionary exuberance of 1790, although he would later come to see the worst of times in the horrendous terror and destructive wars that followed. "Europe at that time was thrilled with joy," he exults; "human nature seeming born again . . . when joy of one / Is joy for tens of millions." He wanted to be part of it. Traveling on foot through the countryside, he eagerly joined a "merry crowd . . . gaudy and gay as bees," dancing and drinking to liberty "in the unruliness of joy." Recollecting these thrilling days in the light of the revolution's bloody excesses, Wordsworth wrote one of his most often-quoted lines: "Bliss was it in that dawn to be alive, / But to be young was very heaven." Has anyone ever penned a more loving and joyous description of political revolution? Idealized no doubt. But in France Wordsworth saw human nature born again in the unity of a nation forged together by the common joy of newfound liberty. He saw this as a type of love, for sure, and he loved it.

Wordsworth also saw something else to love in the joy of a people united through political and social revolution. This was optimism, or hope in the future—the "cheerful confidence in things to come," as he had said of his own youthful joys. "O pleasant exercise of hope and joy!" he enthuses, when, during the early stages of the revolution, "the whole Earth, / The beauty wore of promise—that which sets . . . / The budding rose above the rose full blown." Wordsworth would later suffer some of his deepest disappointments and bleakest moments when—during a later stay in France for a year beginning the fall of 1791—he saw the French Revolution's rosy "promise" succumb to rapacious violence in a time when "the soil of common life" was "too hot to tread upon." Yet in those early days, he recalls fondly, nothing "could overthrow my trust / In what we *may* become." And that optimism gave him a joy to remember in itself, and taught him why we relish "promise," and why we may prize "the budding rose above the rose full blown."

Wordsworth is surely correct to see that many of the "spots of time" that give meaning to our lives do indeed display a joyous "confidence in things to come" rather than a satisfaction over things in hand. Hope in the future gives purpose to the present. That is one reason that we cling to our hopes as long as we can, and why we must find new ones when the old ones die—and why Dante inscribed over the entrance to hell: "Abandon all hope, you who enter here." This is also why we tend to feel more exuberance at beginnings than at endings, even when endings fulfill those beginnings and satisfy us. For the spark and the energies and the élan of life come from beginnings, not endings. No wonder *The Prelude* is a poem much more about youth and beginnings and hopes than it is about age and endings and fulfillment—more about "the budding rose" than "the rose full blown." And it suggests that the most rewarding feat of our lives may well be to keep the spark of beginnings aglow and the flame of hope burning in us always to the very end (like Gabriel García Márquez' Florentino Ariza in *Love in the Time of the Cholera*—see Chapter 26).

While Wordsworth found many joys in nature, in love, and in hope, he also found them, as we would expect, in the creative powers of the imagination itself. For he discovered that the imagination is not only a "gift that consecrates the joy" in revelatory "spots of time." It is also a gift that brings the "redundant energy" of "creation." Together, these gifts of the imagination made Wordsworth the person and poet he became. He tells us how.

"Imagination," he says, "that awful Power rose from the mind's abyss" and "revealed / The invisible world" of creativity, which, he adds, "whether we be young or old," enfolds "Our destiny, our being's heart and home" with a "hope that can never die." For this "glorious faculty," he continues, enables us at once to "converse with the spiritual world" of the unknown, and to "build up greatest things / From least suggestions" in the lives we live. We might take this to mean that the imagination opens our eyes to both hidden meanings and everyday possibilities, just as it creates new meanings and fresh possibilities. Buoyed by this "power," Wordsworth wanted to pursue every "Effort, and expectation, and desire" with a vision of "something evermore about to be" that he could himself create. So he became a poet.

A hope that can never die for something evermore about to be. That is the joyous creative power of the imagination. All of us, not only poets, can use this to keep "the budding rose" alive in ourselves. From where could we get more "confidence in things to come" than that?

"Imagination," Wordsworth goes on, ratcheting up his claims, "in truth / Is but another name for absolute power / And clearest insight, amplitude of mind, / And Reason in her most exalted mood." That is to say, the imagination stretches our minds as far as they can go, and makes everything possible that we can ever know. The imagination is also, Wordsworth adds with a rush of Romantic zeal, a kind of "spiritual Love" or "intellectual Love" of life, since the imagination gives us the joys of discovering and creating life's meanings for us with "a hope that can never die."

When we have all of this, Wordsworth winds up, we reach "the highest bliss / That flesh can know." This bliss comes in "the consciousness / Of [who we] are, habitually / Infused through every image and through every thought, / And all affections." In short, the imagination awakens our most vital selves. And with this consummate and joyous self-consciousness we gain the "peace that passeth understanding." And so,

Wordsworth concludes about the imagination: "Oh, joy to him who here hath sown" and "hath laid here the foundations / Of his future years!" For in him the "budding rose" will live on, the "highest bliss" will thrive, and hope will never die.

Wordsworth has been criticized for excessive self-absorption. Perhaps he deserves the criticism. But *The Prelude* is, after all, "the history of a Poet's mind." And even if we do not share Wordsworth's conviction that "the highest bliss that flesh can know" comes from the consciousness of who we are, we will likely agree with him that a full awareness of ourselves can give a resilient purpose and an energizing confidence to our lives. In the same vein, if we find that Wordsworth's excursions into himself, and his effusions about how to find joy in life, smack too much of a prescription for therapy, we should remember that this prescription cured John Stuart Mill of his depression, and that Wordsworth believed it would cure an ailing civilization. For besides his occupation with his own life, Wordsworth expected his art and ideas to remedy the modern cultural malaise of "savage torpor." That expectation expressed Wordsworth's highest hopes for the imagination.

This brings us to the end of *The Prelude*. Wordsworth finishes up with an exuberant affirmation of the imagination as the energy of life itself, so needed in these enervating modern times. "What we have loved, / Others will love," he writes of what he and Coleridge hoped to achieve, "and we will teach them how, / Instruct them how the mind of man becomes / A thousand times more beautiful than the earth / On which he dwells." Or, as he had put it a bit earlier, "Imagination having been our theme . . . from its progress have we drawn / Faith in life endless." *A faith in life endless*, like a budding rose that never dies. What more could we ask of the imagination?

Our lives have many meanings, as Wordsworth knew. Some of these are common to us all, others differ from person to person, and from era to era in history. How to find the best of these meanings has occupied thinkers ever since human beings have had the time to think. At the dawn of the nineteenth century, Wordsworth concluded that we find the best of these meanings through the imagination as it touches on our emotions, memories, and the joys of life. This makes him much more than an effusive Romantic poet of nature, childhood, and sentimentality. It makes him the poet-philosopher of the imagination as the secret of life. For Wordsworth saw how the imagination works to reveal what is most important to us and to enable us to create the future with a "hope that can never die." This is Wordsworth's gift of the imagination to us. It is a gift to cherish, and to use for all it is worth.

PERCY BYSSHE SHELLEY celebrated the imagination every bit as much as Wordsworth did, and possibly more. For Shelley credits the imagination with virtually every noble achievement of human

SHELLEY

beings in history. An enthusiast of the imagination if ever there was one, Shelley nevertheless gets it right when he points to certain powers of the imagination that both individuals and civilizations depend upon to flourish.

Shelley laid out his notions of the imagination in the essay called "A Defense of Poetry," which he wrote in response to a flamboyant historical excursion by his friend Thomas Love Peacock entitled "The Four Ages of Poetry" (1820). A game fellow, Peacock was actually baiting Shelley by claiming that in modern times poetry had ceded its formerly eminent cultural role to more "useful studies" like science. As evidence of this decline in poetry's stature, Peacock contended that poetry was now in the hands of mere "drivellers and mountebanks" who purvey the "puling sentimentality . . . and promiscuous rubbish of the present time." Taking the bait, Shelley set out in "A Defense of Poetry" to prove that poetry has as much stature in modern times as ever—and it is even more necessary precisely because of the rise of science.

As it turned out, Shelley did not defend just the art of poetry itself. And so much the better. He made "poetry" a metaphor for all creations of the imagination. "Poetry, in a general sense," he says, "may be defined to be 'the expression of the Imagination.'" And since Shelley believed that every good thing that human beings do or ever have done is an "expression of the Imagination," he declared that all of these good things are "poetry." An odd usage, perhaps, but it gives "A Defense of Poetry" pertinence to all human life at any time. For whether we accept Shelley's expansive definition of poetry or his account of the imagination—in what occasionally bogs down in some rather opaque theorizing—Shelley has several enduringly true and useful things to say about the uses of the imagination for everyone.

Shelley starts out with theory. The imagination, he says, is one of two types of "mental action." The other type is "reason." Reason, he explains, is the "mental action" of "analysis," and imagination is the "mental action" of "synthesis." Through reason we analyze "quantities already known" to find "the relations" and "differences" among them. But through the imagination we synthesize the known and unknown to find "similitudes" and "the value" of things. Therefore reason does not *judge* or *discover* or *create* anything. It just identifies things. The imagination does the hard work. Through synthesis, or by combining ideas into "other thoughts," the imagination judges, discovers, creates, and ultimately leads us to the "universal." "Reason is to the imagination," Shelley confidently asserts, "as the body to the spirit, as the shadow to the substance," or as arid intellect is to the pulse of life. That gives the imagination all the marbles.

We could easily protest that Shelley was not fair to reason here because analysis can be as imaginative as synthesis, requiring both judgment and creativity—and we could quote Wordsworth to that effect, since he united reason and imagination in the "feeling intellect" and even pronounced the imagination to be "Reason in her most exalted mood." But Shelley was correct to strike a certain distinction between one activity of mind (whether we call it "reason" or "analysis" or something else) that gives us knowledge of facts as they are, and another activity of mind (whether we call it "imagination" or "synthesis" or something else) that judges experience and creates values. For example, we can assemble the factual knowledge to do all kinds of things, but that knowledge cannot tell us whether we *should* do those things, because the decision requires a value judgment that the knowledge of facts in itself cannot give. The judgment of value is always more creative than factual, or in Shelley's terms, it is more an act of imaginative synthesis than of rational analysis. This is why we cannot live by factual knowledge alone. We have to create values to live by, or not live at all (as Dickens' Mr. Gradgrind notably failed to see until too late—see Chapter 13).

This is also why Shelley can make the surprising claim that we should all be poets "in a general sense." Not that we write poetry. But we use the imagination to create and judge values and to shape the lives we live. "Poets," he says, "imagine and express" the "order" and value and meaning of things. Therefore they "are not only the authors of language and of music, of the dance, and architecture, and statuary, and painting; they are the institutors of laws, and the founders of civil society, and the inventors of the arts of life."

Inventors of the arts of life. A nice phrase. We should indeed all become poets in this sense, for that is how we create what Shelley calls "the poetry of life." The poetry of life amounts to the "new materials of knowledge and power and pleasure" formed by the imagination to bring "the beautiful and the good" into the world through the highest achievements of all cultures. So it was, for instance, that "the true poetry of Rome lived in its institutions," for these institutions were the supreme imaginative creation of Roman culture. And among the highest creations of the poetry of life in all cultures, Shelley says, is the "moral good."

A long tradition from Plato (whose idealism Shelley much admired) to many contemporary moralists has accused the imagination and its artistic inventions of often warring with morality. A contrary tradition, common in modern times under the name aestheticism, has insisted that the imagination and its inventions have nothing to do with morality, or they are superior to morality (see Chapter 25). Shelley, along with Wordsworth and other Romanticists, rather stands between these two traditions. Like his Romantic contemporaries, Shelley believed that the imagination is the very fount of morality. And he made a good case for this belief. He said morality comes from the imagination because the imagination takes us beyond ourselves and gives us *empathy* with others (part of the "mental action" of synthesis). "To be greatly good," he asserts, a person "must imagine intensely and comprehensively; he must put himself in the place of another and of many others; the pains and pleasures of his species must become his own." That imaginative empathy makes morality, and therefore civilization, possible in the form of respect for the elemental humanity that all human beings share (Jean-Jacques Rousseau had also set empathy at the root of morals, but he divorced it from the imagination, whose powers he distrusted—see Chapter 6).

Good Romanticist that he was, Shelley also saw this empathy and respect as a version of love. This was the same Romantic love that Wordsworth had espoused, uniting people through bonds of deep affinity and affection. "The secret of morals is love," Shelley says, for it is "a going out of our own nature, and an identification of ourselves with the beautiful which exists in thought, action, or person, not our own." And because it is the imagination that makes this kind of "love" possible, Shelley can conclude: "The great instrument of moral good is the imagination."

Most of us would probably agree with Shelley that to imagine like this, to get out of ourselves and to empathize with others, and to love like this is the heart of the moral life, whatever abstract moral principles we may espouse. If we do not agree with him, we should give our own morality another look.

No less than Wordsworth, Shelley also thought that modern culture was threatening this moral use of the imagination, as well as everything else the imagination does. Shelley saw these threats coming mainly from the ascendancy of the "sciences" with their reliance on reason and analysis. He grants that these sciences, have "enlarged the . . . empire of man over the external world," but he nevertheless complains that the spread of their "calculating processes" and "accumulation of facts" has "proportionally circumscribed . . . the internal world" of "the poetical faculty"—or the imagination—to where it can atrophy. And that spells doom for humanity. For the hegemony of science will eventually produce a "barren world," he predicts, where "man, having enslaved the elements, remains himself a slave." There is only one way to head off that fate. We must, Shelley declares, cultivate anew the "creative faculty to imagine." In short, he cries: "We want the poetry of life."

We want the poetry of life created by the *inventors of the arts of life* who use the imagination to bring the beautiful and the good into the world in every form. Shelley was right.

Shelley concludes his essay with the well-known but offbeat assertion that "poets are the unacknowledged legislators of the world." He had in mind here the idea that poets who actually write poems provide "the highest wisdom, pleasure, virtue and glory" because they use the imagination to express "less their spirit than the spirit of the age" and to see "the gigantic shadows which futurity casts upon the present." That gives these poets a lot of credit. But we also might read Shelley's words to imply that anyone can be a "legislator of the world" by being a poet in the general sense of an "inventor of the arts of life," imaginatively creating everything from art to law. That is the spirit of "A Defense of Poetry" anyway. And that spirit gives Shelley's ideas of poetry and the imagination good uses for everyone.

Both Wordsworth and Shelley saw the world around them growing ever more occupied with facts and the factitious, incidents and incidentals, arid intellect and dulled emotions, to the detriment of human life. We could say they worried too much because the modern world is not that bad—and we should note that Shelley slighted the uses of the imagination in the sciences that he ridiculed, although he conceded in passing that "poetry in the universal sense" actually "comprehends all science." But their concerns have become commonplace among critics who find modern culture becoming less human all the time.

Whether we share those concerns, now more than ever we could surely use the imagination as Wordsworth and Shelley defined it. For amidst the deadening routine and numbing stimulations, galloping materialism and global anxieties, overreaching intellectualization and wayward emotionalism of our times, we greatly need all of the powers that they said the imagination can give us—powers to discover and to create, to synthesize and to judge, to form values and to live by them, to understand ourselves and to empathize with others, to nurture abiding love and to feel intense joy, to bring the beautiful and the good into the world, and to have hopes for the future that can never die. This all comes down to seeing "what is really important" and creating "the poetry of life." The imagination could give us no greater gifts than these.

On the Imagination

1. The imagination is the highest human power.

2. The imagination includes the powers of intellect and emotion, perception and judgment, discovery and creativity, empathy and possibility.

3. We must keep the powers of imagination alive to fend off the savage torpor of modern life caused by dull routine, trivial overstimulation, and deadening overintellectualization.

4. The imagination takes flight when our thoughts and feelings merge. (Wordsworth)

5. The imagination creates morality by taking us out of ourselves and giving us empathy with others. (Shelley)

6. The imagination shows us what is really important to us in life by awakening us to spots of time in our lives that brought us our most memorable joys. (Wordsworth)

7. The imagination makes us inventors of the arts of life and creators of the poetry of life by enabling us to make everything beautiful and good, from art to laws. (Shelley)

8. The powers of the imagination can give us a hope that can never die for something ever more about to be. (Wordsworth)

9. We get many of our greatest joys at the beginnings of things—from the budding rose, not the rose full blown. (Wordsworth)

10. We should keep life as full of new beginnings as we can.

11. The meaning of life is to feel that our lives have meaning, and we get that feeling by discovering what is most important to us in moments of joy and in imaginatively living out our own *poetry of life*.

24

Fantasies of Seduction and the Seductions of Fantasy

Gustave Flaubert: *Madame Bovary*

Why then was life so inadequate?

What was making her so unhappy?

Flaubert

Gustave Flaubert (1821–1880) lived to write. The son of a doctor in Rouen, France, north of Paris, he never married or pursued a conventional profession, and except for some travels, erotic liaisons, and socializing with other authors, he stayed put in Rouen and neighboring Croisset—writing. Obsessed with artistic objectivity and finding the exact word for every detail, Flaubert let his writing cost him blood. But the agony paid off. He became an eminent novelist in a century of great novels, revered especially for his exquisitely crafted style and for his razor-sharp renderings of contemporary society and culture. Nurtured on Romanticism, and an idealist by temperament, Flaubert readily suffered disillusionment, and heartily deplored what he took to be the clod-hopping vulgarity and gross hypocrisies of his times. Although he wrote one novel on a philosophical-religious theme, *The Temptation of Saint Anthony* (1874), and another set in an exotic locale, *Salammbô* (1862), as well as a few delicate tales, *Three Stories* (1877), Flaubert's fame rests on the novels fired by his loathing of stupidity, sham, and hypocrisy: *Madame Bovary* (1857), and the autobiographical *Sentimental Education* (1864), and the angry, satiric, unfinished *Bouvard and Pécuchet* (1881).

The most renowned of these novels, *Madame Bovary*, records the troubled lives of Emma Bovary and her husband Charles. Seized in her youth by romantic fantasies born largely of literature, the vivacious Emma later finds herself stifling as the wife of a doltish village doctor who cannot do anything right. At first disillusioned and then determined, she pursues her fantasies in ill-fated love affairs and then in shopping sprees, which crush her under debt and impel her to suicide, leaving Charles destitute and soon to die. But these lamentable events unfold in an atmosphere of provincial doldrums and hypocrisy, ignorance and fraud, that can arouse as much sympathy for

Emma Bovary's yearnings and pains as contempt for her unsavory actions. And this sympathy holds clues to both the uses and abuses of fantasy, in Emma Bovary and everyone.

SHE IS ONE of the wretchedest characters in literature. And one of the best. Daughter of a provincial official, student of nuns, wife of a country doctor (whom she ruins financially and drives to the grave), mother of a hapless child (whom she neglects and leaves to the workhouse), ravenous reader, celebrated dreamer, desperate lover, pathetic suicide. She is Emma Bovary. And her sad story is a warning—and a mirror. Or so it was for Gustave Flaubert, who seems to have identified himself with Emma even while he gave her a tormented life. But her story could be a warning and a mirror for anyone. It is surely a story you cannot forget.

That story takes Emma from her early schooling in a convent through her misbegotten marriage to the unfortunate Charles Bovary (whom we meet as a dull-witted schoolboy long before we meet Emma), and on through her seductive fantasies, destructive love affairs, lust for luxury, and sordid decline down to her self-inflicted death. The novel goes on from there to trace poor Charles's grim descent, and then it ends with a jarring note on the ironies of success and failure in this sorry world. It is not a pretty tale, although it is beautifully told. And it is a warning to anyone who wants to avoid a fate like Emma's. And everybody does.

Madame Bovary signals a warning to us, and holds a mirror to our faces, by depicting an inclination, a fallibility perhaps, to which we all succumb occasionally—if not, like Emma Bovary, for a lifetime. Under the sway of this inclination, we want our lives to be better than they are, and we fantasize about the ideal life, and we try to make our fantasies come true. A bit of this is a good thing, stirring us to change our lives, expand ourselves, and maybe improve the world—like Goethe's Faust and Don Quixote, as well as many a storyteller and zealous champion of the imagination (see Chapters 7, 20, 22, 23). All visionaries and revolutionaries have a large dose of this inclination. If we had none of it, our lives would hardly be worth living. But if we give ourselves over to it altogether, life as it is can be hard to take. Emma Bovary discovers this all too painfully.

Emma Bovary's troubles might call to mind the many female sufferers in nineteenth-century literature—Anna Karenina, Hedda Gabler, Maggie Tulliver, Effi Briest, and others. Are these women victims of circumstance, or of themselves? For Emma Bovary, the specific question is: Does she embrace fantasies to escape an abject life, or do her fantasies make her life abject? Or, put another way, does Emma Bovary dream because she suffers, or does she suffer because she dreams?

This question goes to the heart of Emma's story. The answer lays open that heart, exposing not only the source of Emma's character, but the nature of fantasy itself—what it can do *for* us and what it can do *to* us. And here we see that, however we judge Emma Bovary, she is one of us. Her wishes and her sorrows haunt *our* dreams.

Emma has her own interpretation of her troubles, of course. She thinks she dreams because she suffers. And she thinks she suffers because she is trapped in the confining social roles of a provincial middle-class woman. Constantly rattling her cage, she complains that if only she were a man, she could do what she wants. "A man at least is free," she wails. "He can explore passions and countries, surmount obstacles, taste the most exotic pleasures. But a woman is continually held back. Inert and flexible at the same time, she has both the susceptibilities of the flesh and legal restrictions against her. Her will, like the veil of her hat that is tied by a ribbon, reacts to every wind; there is always some desire to respond to, some convention that restricts action." Feeling helplessly constrained as a woman, she hates her woman's life.

So heated is her anger at her sex that it erupts in astonishing, not to say unconventional, attitudes and actions—which, along with her adulteries, provoked condemnation of the book for immorality and got Flaubert put on trial. The oddest of these involves motherhood. When she discovers she is pregnant, Emma prays to give birth to a male child "as anticipatory revenge for all her earlier helplessness." But in this, as in so many things, she loses out: "She gave birth one Sunday, at about six A.M., as the sun rose. 'It's a girl,' said Charles. She turned her head away and fainted." A few years later, after the child, christened Berthe, has taken a fall and hurt her head, Emma watches her go to sleep. "Great big tears were hovering in the corners of her half-closed eyelids," Flaubert says of the poor innocent. What does Berthe's mother feel? "'Strange,' Emma thought, 'how ugly this child is.'" Emma never forgives her daughter for being female—just as she never forgives her husband for being an ineffectual male.

There is some truth to Emma's complaints. She is unquestionably bound by social and economic constraints, like many other stifled women of her times in literature and life. But Emma's discontents come not from her circumstances alone—our discontents never do. They come from how she looks at her circumstances. And she looks at them bitterly in the light of expectations that would be hard to fulfill no matter what. Emma Bovary is not simply a victim of circumstances. She is more interesting and significant than that. She is the quintessential victim of fantasy. Not just a dreamer, Emma Bovary is a creature, and a casualty, of her dreams.

ENTICEMENTS TO FANTASY surround us nowadays—movies, television, theme parks, consumer products, advertising, and so on. We grow up on fantasies, and the temptation can be strong to prefer their pleasures to everything else. Emma Bovary falls victim to fantasy just like that. Her enticements came first from fanciful stories, maudlin songs, and romantic books mainly about love and religion—later they would also come from "the sensualities of luxury," which she confused with "the joys of the heart." Tutored in a convent, she made a daily diet of the emotional religiosity and lush romanticism of writers like Walter Scott, Chateaubriand, and Lamartine, as well as the aesthetics of the Catholic Mass and of the moonlight. She devoured them, and her appetites grew. Love and religion, the two attractions that Virginia Woolf denounces in *Mrs. Dalloway* for destroying "the privacy of the soul" (see Chapter 18), were the very nutrients of Emma Bovary's being.

Her absorption in fantasies born of literature puts Emma Bovary in the company of many other figures in fiction—such as her kindred spirit, the eleventh-century Japanese girl known as Lady Sarashina, who fell in love with the hero of *The Tale of Genji* and dreamed of a life with him (see Chapter 21), and, of course, Don Quixote, who acts out tales of chivalry. She also resembles most adolescents today, who live on fantasies taken from the culture around them. Adolescence—especially in our era—is a time for trying out ideal selves modeled on fantasies or fiction or other sources in quest of one that fits. These are "identifications," in psychological parlance. The extremities of the adolescent's moods, the elations and dejections, illusions and disillusionments, reflect that quest. Eventually most people shuck off their youthful identifications with fictional heroes and ideal lovers, thrilling adventures and endless ecstasies, to settle on an identity of their own that is not only what they imagine themselves to be, but also what others recognize them to be. This becomes who they are as adults. And adults have less need than do adolescents for fantasy to supply their satisfactions; adults have reality to do that for them, for the better or the worse—although adults may still indulge in fantasies, consciously or unconsciously (which inspired Freud's theory of psychoanalysis—see Chapter 17), as well as in the escapes of entertainment, alcohol, and drugs.

But this passage from identification to identity, from fantasy to reality, Emma Bovary could not travel. Instead of growing out of the fantasies she derived from books and stories and songs, she let them tighten their grip on her, shaping her every perception, fueling her every desire, guiding her every response. At first enticed by fantasy, then seduced by it, Emma Bovary is ultimately betrayed and destroyed by it.

Fantasy betrays Emma Bovary by leading her to believe more fervently in the pure pleasures of fantasy than in the prosaic facts of actuality. Fantasy becomes the measure of reality for her. And compared to fantasy, reality will almost always be found wanting. "I hate everyday heroes and restrained emotions," Emma confesses, "like the ones in real life," or in "nature" *(Je deteste les héros communs et les sentiments tempérés, comme il y en a dans la nature)*. This is the danger of fantasy for anyone. Because fantasy lives in the imagination, it is free from the confines of the real world. It can go anywhere, do anything, with nothing standing in its way to say: "Stop! That's impossible." Impossibilities belong to reality, not to fantasy. The pleasures of fantasy are unconditional and instantaneous. You only have to imagine them to enjoy them. That is the danger. The realm of fantasy is so wonderful a place that we might never want to leave it, or, if we must leave it, we might expect the real world to play by the rules of fantasy, which amount to almost no rules at all. So instead of preparing us to live in the real world—as youthful fantasies should do by inventing possibilities and stretching our imaginations—or granting a temporary escape from it, fantasy can mis-prepare us, keeping us in perpetual childhood, chasing perfect, spontaneous pleasures. This it does to Emma Bovary.

Like a child, Emma could not wait for any pleasure, and she "rejected as useless everything that could not contribute to the immediate gratification of her heart." The more intense the delights of her fantasies, the more inadequate everyday reality was bound to appear, and the more attractive would life at a distance become. A brief sojourn in Paris, where she attends a ball and revels in the grandeur and opulence far from her provincial married life, only heightens her yearnings. "The closer things were," Flaubert writes, "the more she turned her thoughts from them. Everything that immediately surrounded her, the dull countryside, imbecile petty-bourgeois people, the mediocrity of existence, seemed to her an exception in the world, an unusual accident in which she found herself trapped, while beyond it the immense world of happiness and passion extended itself as far as the eye could see" in regions "full of ideal ambitions and fantastic dreams."

No wonder Emma hates real life as she knows it. Her education in fantasy has left her incapable of comprehending, much less appreciating, reality in its prosaic particularities, its compromised satisfactions, its honorable sacrifices. "Why then was life so inadequate?" (*D'où venait donc cette insuffisance de la vie?*), Emma asks bewilderedly.

The pains of failed expectations set in not long after Emma's marriage, with a mood that foreshadows her fate. Emma wonders why she does not feel about this marriage as she had expected to feel. "Before she had married she thought she was in love," Flaubert reports, "but the happiness that should have resulted from this love had never come; she must have deceived herself, she thought." Then Flaubert explains why: "Emma sought to learn what was really meant in life by the words 'happiness,' 'passion,' and 'intoxication'—words that had seemed so beautiful to her in books." She was bound for disappointment, as readers of romance novels today could easily have predicted.

In Emma's overwrought imagination, emotional elation knows no bounds: the words that label emotions have no limits, no ambiguities, no relativity, no vagaries of conventional usage. "Happiness," "passion," "intoxication," and the like, are absolute terms promising all that she can imagine in immediate, untempered ecstasy. She could hardly accept what they "really meant in life."

Her insistence on the pure meaning of words shows Emma Bovary to be something of a philosopher. She is one of those metaphysical idealists, going back to Plato, who believe that words are not just useful, if imprecise, devices fashioned for communication, they are instead absolute names for absolute realities. But Emma departs from such idealists at a decisive point. They believed these absolute realities exist only in a realm of ideas where everything is immaterial and changeless, eternal and perfect, by contrast to the real world where everything is material and mutable, transitory and imperfect. Emma expected to find in the real world the perfection she associates with words in her mind. She was sure to fail. And she never understands why.

Emma's illicit lover, Rodolphe, understands, or thinks he understands. Jaded, egocentric, predatory, Rodolphe seduces Emma as unfeelingly as she submits to him passionately. "I'll have her," he tells himself, casually wondering, "how would I get rid of her later?" And in one of the funniest seduction scenes in literature he wins her over during an agricultural fair where his soft seductive words are punctuated by loud speeches in the background on the merits of hogs and manure. Rodolphe takes the seduction and all that follows it in stride. He is not impressed, much less bewitched, like Emma, by ideas or emotions or words. Unlike Emma, who had learned the language of thought and feeling from fiction and fantasy, Rodolphe had learned it from a life of debauchery and worn-out passions. And compared to actual thoughts and feelings, which are sometimes intense, but frequently fleeting, the words of romance strike Rodolph as "exaggerated speeches that mask lack of feeling." The exalted words that inspire and torment Emma are to Rodolphe merely predictable and trite clichés that echo emptily. They bore him—although Flaubert, the exacting and anguished author, remarks that the cynical Rodolphe failed to recognize that "the fullness of soul" can "sometimes overflow into the emptiest of metaphors" because "the human language is like a cracked kettle on which we beat out a tune for a dancing bear, when we hope with our music to move the stars."

How sadly fitting that the idealist Emma Bovary should fall for a cynic like Rodolphe—"I have a lover!" she cries. "Realizing the long dream of her adolescence, seeing herself as one of those amorous women she had so long envied . . . in the books she had read . . . she herself was becoming a part of those fantasies." Fantasies of perfect pleasures will throw anyone into the arms of predatory seducers, lying hucksters, and false prophets, more often than not. Emma could not have resisted Rodolphe. Like an evangelist appealing to lost and yearning spirits, or a salesman pitching products for self-fulfillment, he supplies the intoxicants her fantasies craved. Then he leaves her.

Rodolphe's rejection shatters Emma's naive fantasies of love. She will love again, but never like that. "How impossible it seemed!" she will lament during a subsequent affair. "Nothing was worth looking for; everything was a lie. Each smile hid a yawn of boredom, each joy a curse, each pleasure its aftermath of disgust, and the best of kisses left on your lips only the unattainable desire for a higher delight." This despondent mood recalls Goethe's insatiably unsatisfied Faust. But it lacks Faust's overarching ambitions and energetic defiance. In truth, Emma's state of mind comes closer to the mentality of a demanding child having become a narcissistic adult. Forever self-absorbed. Forever unfulfilled. Forever resentful. Foredoomed.

This is also the mentality of one who will plunder every experience for nothing but emotional booty. "Incapable as she was of understanding that which she did not feel," Emma subjects every experience to her emotional appetites. Fantasy and feeling join forces in Emma to mount claims on life that finally drive her to the grave—and that bequeathed to the world the name for a life of unquenchable, self-destructive, fantasies: *Bovaryisme*. *Bovaryisme* is quite different from *Quixotism*, although Emma Bovary and Don Quixote have much in common. The quixotic person lives purposefully, if sometimes absurdly, for noble ideas and causes. But anyone infected by *Bovaryisme* lives desperately for fantasies of selfish pleasure that can never be fulfilled. Don Quixote's fantasies lead him hopefully into the world to change it; Emma Bovary's fantasies take her irretrievably, and hopelessly, out of it.

WHEN FANTASIES OF LOVE FAIL HER, Emma Bovary turns to other closely related psychic pleasures, principally the fantasies of faith and the sentimentalities of religion that have nourished her since childhood. Who among us does not tilt in that direction when lovers desert us, or any disillusionment hits? We might not turn to religion, but we seek consoling beliefs or recuperative therapies. We are ripe for conversion. That is the time to be most wary not only of seducers, hucksters, and false prophets, but of beguiling self-deceptions. Those deceptions can go deep, tainting every thought and feeling with spuriously gratifying convictions. Let Emma Bovary be a lesson here, too.

Emma had always drawn from religion and the church only what she had wanted from them. She "loved the church for its flowers" and its sympathies. And, picturing "the sweet face of the Virgin in bluish clouds of incense," she would find "a tender emotion" to "suffuse her" and become "all limp and abandoned like the down of a bird swirling in the tempest." When her life goes very bad, she tightens her spiritual wraps.

After Rodolphe abandons her, Emma falls gravely ill. Convinced she is dying, she summons a clergyman to administer Communion. Then she has an epiphany: "She could hear the far-off song of heavenly harps, and God the Father on a golden throne" appears to her "in an azure sky, in the midst of saints bearing green palms, a God radiant in majesty signaling to angels with flaming wings to descend to earth and take her off in their arms." With this "most beautiful dream imaginable" in her eye, Emma discovers—what else?—the perfect cure for a broken heart: a "love above all other loves, with neither interruption nor end." Namely, the eternal love of God. In this benighted state, Emma decides that she "wanted to become a saint." She surrounds herself with rosaries, reliquaries, and devotional books, and performs the appropriate pious gestures. Then the illness abates. The delicious visions fade. And the suspicion dawns on her that, alas, her spiritual transport "was all a huge fraud." Another fantasy has betrayed her.

Yet Emma's religious histrionics do not end there. Later, when she lies dying for good, she relapses into them again. Although barely able to move, she reaches out to clutch a crucifix held by the priest granting absolution. And "pressing her lips to the body of the Man-God, she placed on it, with all her fading strength, the most passionate kiss of love she had ever given." The act is downright obscene.

Emma Bovary's religion is typical of her—and not untypical of some other worshipers. It is a religion of the senses and the emotions barely veiling the profane inspiration behind it. It has nothing to do with authentic faith or morals. Erotic, exotic, neurotic, it borders on sacrilege. At most, it is the sentimentalization of faith and morality—the bliss of feeling righteous and at one with God.

Most of us know this feeling at some time. It is aroused by the aesthetics of the church, by images of purity, by sympathy for suffering. And although this feeling easily masquerades as true conviction, it does not often lead to deep devotion or self-sacrificing action. It mainly gives rise to ritualistic performances and pious tears. These make us feel that we are good, and we let it go at that. So it is for Emma Bovary. Submission to the spirit? Service to humankind? Hardly. Not for Emma the strictures of conscience, the demands of ecclesiastical rules, or the moral rigor of sincere belief. Emma "rebelled before the mysteries of faith in proportion to her . . . irritation against the discipline, which was antipathetic to her nature." Her religion is all sensuosity and sensuality, aesthetics and sentiment, feeling and fantasy. It is a lusty hunger for spiritual romance. How seductive sentimentality can be.

Besides her entwined fantasies of love and religion, Emma indulges in similar fantasies of art. She knows them all only as reservoirs of sentimental emotion. "Her temperament was more sentimental than artistic," Flaubert explains; "she sought emotions and not landscapes . . . the attractive fantasy [*fantasmagorie*] of sentimental realities," not the prosaic facts of life. A rush of unalloyed feeling, delectable pleasures, moral exaltation, ready tears—these are the stuff of sentiment in art no less than in love and religion. For however emotionally satisfying art might be, a truly aesthetic response to art demands discrimination, judgment, and some notion of how an artwork affects us as it does. An aesthetic response challenges easy emotions; sentimentality feeds on them. An aesthetic response stimulates intellect and imagination; sentimentality induces passive pleasure. An aesthetic response asks for psychological honesty; sentimentality invites psychological denial. Nowadays the popular arts exploit sentimentality wherever they can. But most artworks can arouse sentiment if we let them. For sentimentality comes from us, not from the artwork itself—no matter how sentimental an artist tries to be. Sentimentality lives in our responses, which are learned or are rooted in our temperaments. However we get it, sentimentality debases all it touches—love, religion, morality, and art alike—with saccharine and self-righteous emotions.

Even Emma herself discerns, momentarily at least, the menacing seductions of sentimentality, and of the fantasies that abet them. During a performance of Donizetti's opera *Lucia di Lammermoor*, based on a novel by one of her favorite authors, Walter Scott, she longs to be loved as the hero, Edgar, loves the heroine, Lucia—passionately, tenderly, virtuously—and she fantasizes about marriage and the happiness that should have been hers. Then in a rare moment of detachment, she admits the futility of her longing and thinks her illusions of happiness are only "a lie invented to cause the despair of all desire." And, for the first time, she "knew the petty quality of the passions that art exaggerated," art that gives us "nothing but a colorful fantasy, an entertaining spectacle for the eyes."

At this moment Emma Bovary rises above herself, discerning both a secret of art and the cunning of sentimentality. But, like her passing questions about religious ecstasy, these suspicions about art vanish as swiftly as they had arrived. Soon Emma is lost in fantasy and sentimentality again, first imagining a life with Edgar, then believing his eyes are locked on her, and finally yearning to "run into his arms" and "cry out: 'Take me away, take me with you, let us go! I am yours, yours, all my passion and all my dreams are yours.'" Emma has reduced the opera to a sentimental fantasy of her own emotions. The curtain falls. Within days Emma's fateful liaison with her second lover, the mediocre fellow-dreamer Leon, begins. With this new love affair, Emma starts on the downward path that leads through ever more frenzied desires, acquisitive excesses, and pathetic failures ending in suicide.

AND YET FOR ALL OF EMMA'S regrettable failings and inexorable doom, Flaubert himself reportedly confessed enigmatically, unsettlingly: *"Emma Bovary, c'est moi"*—"Emma Bovary, that is me." This telling confession—possibly intended to put off pesky questions about his factual source for Emma, and echoing what Cervantes is said to have remarked about his own relation to Don Quixote—also suggests that, if there was a lot of Emma in Flaubert, there is probably some of Emma in everyone.

Flaubert could identify himself with Emma because he, too, was a dreamer and an idealist who continually rued the inadequacy of life. As he wrote in a letter while working on *Madame Bovary*, "mediocrity is creeping in everywhere . . . imitation cloth, imitation luxury, imitation pride," even "the stones under our feet are becoming dull." Now "we are all fakes and charlatans. Pretense, affectation, humbug everywhere." So "we must take flight into the ideal" and "employ every means to stem the flood of trash invading us. . . . Oh! our ivory towers! Let us climb them in our dreams."

Flaubert's life and literary career chart the tortured history of his own idealism—his illusions and disillusionments, resentments and rage against "pretense, affectation, humbug everywhere." And in Emma Bovary he created a portrait not only of himself, but of anyone at those times when ideals, fantasies, wishes, and dreams go unfulfilled, leaving disillusionment and dejection in their wake.

Flaubert saved his sharpest barbs on this theme for the novel's conclusion. This takes place well after Emma's suicide, which is followed by the bizarre decline and eventual demise of Charles and the pathetic fate of Berthe, who, poor and neglected, is "sent to work in a cotton mill to earn her living," a life suited to a Dickens novel. The last words of *Madame Bovary* concern none of them. These words center on another character: Homais, the local pharmacist. And they add new color to the story.

A self-righteous, self-important consumer of superficial learning and a purveyor of pseudoscientific fads, Homais has disseminated all kinds of misinformation and perpetrated egregious medical malpractices throughout the novel, giving Flaubert occasion for some sickening accounts. But Homais will not pay for the ignorance he lives by or the hypocrisy he practices or the agony he causes. To the contrary. Since the death of the failed village doctor, Charles Bovary, whose career he helped ruin, Homais has managed to keep any new doctor from establishing a practice, insuring himself "an enormous clientele." And in the novel's last line Flaubert coldly states the cutting irony of Homais's ultimate triumph with the fulfillment of Homais's own dream: "He has just received the Legion of Honor."

Homais is a fraud, a charlatan, as pernicious as he is stupid. But he cannot be found out in a land of fraud. Instead he is rewarded with the French nation's highest honor for service and accomplishment. Flaubert, the disillusioned idealist, lets this conclusion of fraudulence acclaimed as excellence stand as an indictment of a world of sham.

Compared to Homais's grotesque worldly success, Emma Bovary's foolish fantasies and arch sentimentality seem almost benign. Flaubert did, after all, identify himself with Emma and her failed dreams, not with Homais and his bogus triumph. Emma Bovary *is* Flaubert—and everyone who has enticing, soaring, wishful fantasies; Homais is the prosaic world of earthbound stupidity and deadening deceptions.

Yet the climactic irony of Homais's wrongful glory should not obscure a harsh, deeper truth of the novel. This is the truth that disillusioned idealism like Emma's, and perhaps Flaubert's, is never entirely benign. It usually gives rise, as it did in them, to resentment and rage. Flaubert himself put this to artistic uses, first in *Madame Bovary*, then in the novel of his own youthful disillusionment, *Sentimental Education*; and finally he poured his loathing of Homais and the society that engendered him into the novel that occupied Flaubert's last years—except for a few excursions into moralistic tales—*Bouvard and Pécuchet*, a satiric, choleric tribute to specious learning, false honors, and the wholesale depravity of modern culture.

Disillusioned idealism can go even farther than provoking resentment and rage. It can dissolve the value of everything. Love, art, morality, society, culture—everything. "Nothing was worth looking for," Emma had said, "everything was a lie." Idealizing too loftily, losing ourselves in fantasy, expecting too much of reality, we can, like Emma Bovary and unnumbered other thwarted dreamers, turn our disappointment against existence itself. Then instead of serving life, fantasy and idealism breed nihilism, an attitude that denies value to all existence—the character of Bazarov in Ivan Turgenev's novel *Fathers and Sons* (1862) gave the name to this attitude (Goethe's Mephistopheles and Dickens' James Harthouse are nihilists, too, but of different kinds—see Chapters 7, 13). W. B. Yeats caught the twisted psychology of this attitude in a memorable couplet of "Meditations in Time of Civil War": "We had fed the heart on fantasies, / The heart's grown brutal from the fare."

Let Emma Bovary be a warning against this perverse consequence of fantasy. And yet, let her be a mirror too, affectionately reminding us of our own irrepressible, unfulfillable, bittersweet wishes for a perfect world. Let us also learn from her to use those wishes to improve our lives in this world, and not just to live in our fantasies.

On Fantasy and Reality

1. Fantasy can be better than reality.

2. Fantasy can be better than reality because it immediately fulfills wishes in our minds.

3. Fantasy can be dangerous because it can keep us from living in the real world.

4. If we expect to live out our fantasies—or ideals—to the full, we will likely be disappointed because fantasy does not fit well into the real world.

5. Frustrated fantasies and disillusioned idealism can lead to nihilism—the conclusion that nothing has meaning.

6. Fantasy gives us many pleasures, but we should be wary of its seductions.

7. Sentimentality is a variation on fantasy.

8. Sentimentality is a sweet feeling of goodness that takes the place of actual goodness.

9. We sentimentalize morality, religion, and art when we enfold them in feelings divorced from judgment, action, and responsibility.

10. If we live for fantasy and sentimentality, we cannot see truth or reality.

11. A culture that feeds fantasy and sentimentality will deny reality, breed hypocrisy, and honor people for the wrong reasons.

12. The meaning of life is to use fantasy to help us live well in the real world, and to avoid the seductions of fantasy that take us too far out of this world.

25
Art for Life's Sake

Théophile Gautier: Preface to *Mademoiselle de Maupin*
Walter Pater: Conclusion to *The Renaissance*
Oscar Wilde: *The Picture of Dorian Gray*
Thomas Mann: "Death in Venice"

*Someone has said somewhere that literature and the arts influence
morals. Whoever he was, he was a undoubtedly a great ass.*
Gautier

*To burn always with a hard, gemlike flame, to maintain this
ecstasy, is success in life.*
Pater

It is better to be beautiful than to be good.
Wilde

*Has not [aesthetic] form two aspects? Is it not moral and immoral at
once: moral insofar as it is the expression and result of discipline,
and immoral—yes, actually hostile to morality—in that of its very
essence it is indifferent to good and evil, and deliberately concerned to
make the moral world stoop beneath its proud and undivided scepter?*
Mann

Théophile Gautier (1811–1872) won notoriety as a young Parisian Romanticist who wore garish waistcoats and rebelled against literary traditions. A
gifted poet and able novelist, he became an influential literary figure mainly
through his voluminous journalism and adroit criticism. But he gained a
lasting place in history as the first to proclaim—in the Preface to his narrative poem *Albertus* (1832) and then more boldly in the Preface to his novel
Mademoiselle de Maupin (1835)—that art has nothing to do with morals, or
with anything else except the aesthetic pleasures of beauty. With this brash
idea Gautier launched modern aestheticism as the exaltation of those pleasures above everything else.
   Walter Pater (1839–1894) turned Gautier's glib aesthetic manifestos into

a thoroughgoing philosophy. An Oxford don with an Epicurean bent, Pater lived a quiet, inward life and wrote learned essays on artists and thinkers, as well as a philosophical novel about the love of beauty set in ancient Rome, *Marius the Epicurean* (1885). But his most enduring and influential work is the "Conclusion" to his collection of essays now known as *The Renaissance* (1873). There he spells out a theory of why we should pursue "art for art's sake," or rather for the moments of intensity that art and beauty—among other things—provide. And he shows us the highest rewards that a life lived for such moments can give us.

Oscar Wilde (1854–1900) made aestheticism a way of life and a subject of comedy. Born in Ireland and educated at Oxford, Wilde became celebrated for ridiculing Victorian proprieties in the name of beauty and pleasure. Then he ran afoul of Victorian sexual mores and was imprisoned for homosexuality in 1895. His time in the limelight lasted about fifteen years as he conversed scintillatingly, lectured widely, wrote brilliant essays, and enjoyed a brief but dazzling career in the theater with *Lady Windermere's Fan* (1892), *A Woman of No Importance* (1893), *An Ideal Husband* (1895), and *The Importance of Being Earnest* (1895). He also wrote some notable children's stories and, after prison, the somber *Ballad of Reading Gaol* (1898). In his most unconventional vein he wrote the scandalous play *Salomé* (1892) and the wittily shocking novel *The Picture of Dorian Gray* (1891). This infamous novel imaginatively and irreverently plays upon the enticements and dangers of aestheticism as it tells the tale of a young man who lives for beauty and pleasure, and who does not age physically while a portrait of him mysteriously deteriorates. Dorian Gray is an amoral aesthete and the emblematic victim of aestheticism.

Thomas Mann (1875–1955), son of a merchant in Lübeck, Germany, became one of the twentieth century's most respected authors. For half a century (including a long residence in the United States) he wrote essays, stories, and lengthy novels—for example, *Buddenbrooks* (1901), *The Magic Mountain* (1924), *Joseph and His Brothers* (1933–43), *Doctor Faustus* (1947). He received the Nobel Prize for Literature in 1929. And no theme occupied him more frequently, from the beginning of his long career to the end, than the effects of art on life, and of aesthetics on ethics. His story "Death in Venice" (1911) is surely the most profound and thought-provoking exploration in literature of the most ambiguous and troublesome of these effects, as it shows an artist becoming enraptured by the love of beauty, and finally literally dying for it.

FOR MOST OF human history, art was not "art." Artworks pointed beyond themselves to other things. They honored the gods, or the king, or the tribe, or the harvest, or the hunt, or fertility, or death, and so forth. They also possessed powers to influence these things, or so people probably believed. Artistry has, of course, always served lesser purposes, too, such as decorating domestic wares and the human body to please the eye, playing music to lighten the heart, and telling tales to delight the mind and imagination. But even these humble uses of artistry likely also had higher ends in a world pervaded by myth and superstition. At all events, none of this was labeled "art" as we use that English term today. Most cultures have not even had a word for "art" at all.

The closest words to our "art" have traditionally been terms for the various "arts" of "making" things, like weaving fish nets or carving spears or molding clay pots. The English word "art" comes from the Latin *ars*, for technical skill in making things—preceded by the kindred Greek terms *ararisko*, for fitting something together; *technē*, for the skill and rules in making something; and *poiein*, for making or bringing something to pass (hence our words "technique" and "poetry"). Traditional cultures have therefore tended to view the activities we label "art" as what we would call "craft." Requiring specific skills, the crafts, or technical "arts," would likely have been known only by their own names, like poetry, dance, music, and painting—which became loosely linked under the *muses* in ancient Greece and collectively taught as *mousikē*—but never as "art."

At the same time, traditional cultures typically entwined the "crafts" so thoroughly with the rest of life, from religion to the social order, that no one could think of them as a separate and unique kind of experience. That is why the productions of the crafts, which we now call "artworks," pointed beyond themselves. Just look, for instance, at the culture of Bali, where the lack of a word for "art" goes unnoticed by the Balinese amidst an unsurpassed abundance of activities in the name of Hindu worship that Westerners deem "artistic," and where almost everyone is to Western eyes an "artist" of some kind—and where Western tourists nowadays flock to enjoy it all as "art," or as art's dim-witted child, "entertainment." Or remember Plato and Aristotle, who put art education (*mousikē*) at the center of their political theories (see Chapter 19). But for all of the importance that traditional cultures have assigned to the technical "arts" or "crafts" in the past and the present, through most of human history no one could have imagined, much less extolled, the idea of "art for art's sake."

Then things changed. The traditional "arts" or "crafts" became "art." At least in the West. The Renaissance foreshadowed this by elevating certain artists to the new rank of "genius." But it was not until the eighteenth century that the arts or crafts started truly leaving their traditional religious, moral, social, and political roles behind to become prized as "art" on their own. This passage began with the rise of some new ideas, along with new uses of some old ideas.

One of these new ideas was the notion of "taste." It gained wide currency in the eighteenth century as something of a novelty—prompting many a philosophical meditation, such as David Hume's "Of the Standard of Taste" (1757)—and gave new uses to an old idea. As one early eighteenth-century Englishman said, nothing could refine a person's character better than acquiring "a just and delicate *taste*" in art through the "new science" of the "connoisseur." The claim that the delicate taste of the connoisseur could improve character made "good taste" a mark of cultural and social status that remains with us today—recycling the ancient Greek assumption that an appreciation of good artworks forms good moral character. And the idea of good taste helped crack open the door to "art for art's sake."

That door opened wider with eighteenth-century theories on how art and beauty can uniquely affect us. Many of these theories arose from efforts to separate the "fine arts," or *beaux arts*, from the crafts, or practical, technical arts. In an influential foray entitled *The Fine Arts Reduced to a Single Principle* (1746) the Abbé Batteau identified the *"beaux arts par excellence"* as music, poetry, painting, sculpture, and dance, because these all "have pleasure as their object." Batteau had no yen to laud aesthetic pleasure. He was only trying to indicate the difference between the fine arts and the more practical arts, and he concluded with a description of how the theater unites both types. On the same theme, the German intellectual Karl Philippe Moritz remarked in his treatise "On the Unification of All the Fine Arts" (1785) that the "beautiful object is valuable to me more for its own sake" and "provides me with a higher and more disinterested pleasure than the merely useful object." Moritz viewed beauty as a sign of God's sublime creativity, but he implied that the pleasure of beauty could be valued for itself, apart from morality or truth, God's creation or not.

In the light of these novel ideas of taste, the fine arts, and the "disinterested pleasure" of beauty, it should come as no surprise that the term "aesthetics" also made its first appearance in the eighteenth century. The German philosopher Alexander Baumgarten gets credit for it with his book *Aesthetica* (1750–1758). Baumgarten coined "aesthetics" to denote what he called a "science" of perception and feeling, or a "logic of sensuous thinking," that would account for both artistic creativity and our "aesthetic" response to art. Baumgarten's so-called science is now forgotten, but the term "aesthetics" stuck as the name for a new type of human experience—or new in the sense that people could now think that it stood outside of everything else. And before long, aesthetics would take on a vigorous life of its own.

The great philosopher Immanuel Kant helped this trend along with his influential *Critique of Judgment* (1790). Drawing on contemporary ideas about art and beauty—and leaving out Moritz' reference to God—Kant described how the "aesthetical judgment" identifies what is "beautiful" through the "entirely disinterested satisfaction" that beauty brings us unrelated to practical usefulness or moral purposes. Here was aesthetics in philosophy. But it was not yet a philosophy of aestheticism. That would come later, thanks to Romanticism.

The early generations of Romantic artists and thinkers proclaimed the superiority of art and aesthetics to most other pursuits as the very energy of life, the path to truth, and the source of our highest joys. But this was not aestheticism. The early Romanticists, such as William Wordsworth and Percy Bysshe Shelley, were too earnest and moralistic for that, despite their artistic "enthusiasm" (see Chapter 23). But their leanings toward a cult of art made aestheticism all but inevitable. The later Romantic French poet and critic Théophile Gautier took the cue.

Gautier brashly flung open the door to aestheticism as the love of art for its own sake. After that, others would rush through, most notably the British intellectual Walter Pater and the Irish wag Oscar Wilde. Pater did it with theory and Wilde did it with literary genius and brilliant wit. But both fashioned full-fledged doctrines of aestheticism that divorced art and aesthetics from the rest of life—or, rather, they made the pleasures of art and aesthetics the supreme value in life. And yet, Wilde also recognized the perversities that aestheticism can breed, and he made these the subject of his timeless novel *The Picture of Dorian Gray*.

Taking up this darker theme, the German novelist Thomas Mann penned reams of fiction about how art and aesthetics can at once elevate us and lead us astray. Drawn by the allure of aesthetics himself, and yet troubled by some of the consequences, Mann gave us in the story "Death in Venice" a classic version of what can happen when aesthetics becomes ethics, or ethics becomes aesthetics.

These four literary figures—Gautier, Pater, Wilde, Mann—more penetratingly than any others, reveal the nagging paradox of "art for art's sake" in modern times. That paradox is: by granting art and aesthetics a purpose and value divorced from the rest of life, Western culture has allowed art and aesthetics to become at once useless to the ordinary life and yet prized more highly than anything else. These authors also show how this paradox touches us in many ways, for the better and the worse, and why we should take it very seriously indeed.

Poet, novelist, critic, flamboyant Romantic character, Théophile Gautier was the first to come right out and proclaim that art has one purpose and one purpose only, and that this is to give us

GAUTIER

pleasure, and that this pleasure is the crowning experience of life. He did this with his typical panache in a few vivid passages of the Preface to his novel *Mademoiselle de Maupin*. Annoyed at contemporary moralists who—like many others from Plato onward—blamed "immoral books" for causing immoral behavior, Gautier snapped: "Someone has said somewhere that literature and the arts influence morals. Whoever he was, he was undoubtedly a great ass." At most, he adds, "books follow morals, and not morals books."

From there, Gautier goes on to spin a plucky argument against anyone who has ever assigned art a moral or social purpose, especially the "utilitarian critics" of his day. Not only does art have no influence on morals, he asserts, but it has no influence on society, for good or ill. Those who ask, "What purpose does this book serve?" in satisfying "the needs of society . . . civilization and progress" amount to nothing but "fools" and "goitrous cretins," he cries. Art does not work like that. "A book does not make a gelatin soup; a novel is not a pair of seamless boots." Soup and boots are "useful" things. Art is the opposite of the useful. It has no *use* at all. "What is the good of music? of painting?" Gautier asks. Certainly they are not useful—unless, he cracks, we include as useful that it earns money for artists, sparing them from doing vulgarly useful things.

To see the true purpose of art, Gautier explains, we must first get over our preoccupation with *usefulness*. In fact, he says, we have to overturn our entire value system and see that the true worth of all artistic activities and objects stands "in an inverse ratio to the services they render" to society and morals. Once we understand this, we discover that "everything useful is ugly, for it is the expression of some need"—for instance, "the most useful place in a house is the water closet"—and that "there is nothing truly beautiful but that which can never be of any use whatsoever."

This might sound eccentric today, when people in Western culture have come to expect all kinds of useful objects to possess "good design," and they aspire to "decorate" every room in their homes in "good taste"(the telling subject of Oscar Wilde's early lectures in America). It was also never true among the aristocratic nobility who surrounded themselves with beautiful things. But Gautier was writing a manifesto against the ascending, moralistic, acquisitive, and to him tasteless middle class, so he needed outlandish assertions. These assertions vividly made the point that art and beauty should have no practical use outside themselves.

But where does the *uselessness* of art and beauty take us than to the paradox that their uselessness makes them more valuable than every-thing else? And that is because they deliver only aesthetic pleasure, which is both good for its own sake and the best thing in life. "Enjoy-ment appears to me," Gautier declares, playing with the paradox, "to be the end of life and the only useful thing in the world." For this reason, he announces, "I should be more willing to go without boots than without poems," and "would sell my breeches for a ring." He would even "gladly renounce my rights as a Frenchman and a citizen to see an authentic pic-ture by Raphael." The pleasures of art and beauty are so superior to the practical life, Gautier concludes, that "the most fitting occupation for a civilized man is to do nothing" except to revel in them.

Gautier is something of a jester, but his passions are clear. With a broad swipe he brushes away the long tradition—including much of Romanticism—that had revered art as a sign of God, or the source of morals, or the ground of education, or the way to truth, or the bond of humanity. Art, he insists, is none of these things. All it can do is give us aesthetic pleasure. And that is enough. For this is the highest rung on the ladder of life that human beings can reach.

Leo Tolstoy would later rail in *What Is Art?* against the entire modern tradition of aesthetic ideas that had engendered the likes of Gautier's manifesto (see Chapter 19). But Gautier had caught a rising tide that would largely pass over Tolstoy. Nowadays, owing to the aesthetics of modernism and to the exploitation by commerce of "good taste," "good design," and their ilk, that tide has washed over Western culture and shows no signs of abating. We are living out Gautier's pioneering ideas whether we agree with them or not. Is that a good thing?

WALTER PATER would say it is. Although a reclusive intellectual who watched life more than he lived it, Pater went on from Gautier's feisty and jocular pronouncements to articulate a theory of aes-

PATER

theticism that gave us the very phrase "art for art's sake." But, to his credit, Pater also turned aestheticism into a useful prescription for living life overall. He did these things in a dimin-utive essay that he attached as the conclusion to his book of essays on art and artists originally entitled *Studies in the History of the Renaissance* (1873), known in later editions as *The Renaissance*. There, in a few pages, Pater lays out how art and beauty help us live life to the fullest, and why otherwise we hardly live at all.

Pater starts off his essay with an ambitious theory of nothing less than "what is real in our life." "What is *real*," he states, is not the external world around us, but the "inward world" of "impressions, images, sensations" that "burn and are extinguished with our consciousness of them." That means our lives consist of nothing but a series of "flickering," "flamelike" moments of "sensations" and "consciousness" that are continually "vanishing away" in a "perpetual weaving and unweaving of ourselves." Capacious—if brief—as it is, this theory makes our lives and our selves sound peculiarly insubstantial. It suggests the Buddhist idea that all existence is evanescent, even illusory (which inspired the shimmering aesthetic atmosphere of fleeting beauty in the Japanese classic, *The Tale of Genji*—see Chapter 21). But Pater has more to say. And it is good.

Instead of letting this life of flickering sensations and consciousness fade away into Buddhist illusion, Pater turns up the heat. He says that because our lives consist of "flickering," "flamelike" moments of "consciousness," the more frequent and intense those moments are, the more vital our lives will be. "A counted number of pulses is given to us" in our "variegated, dramatic life," he observes. So we should try to put "as many [of these] pulsations . . . of a quickened, multiplied consciousness . . . as possible into the given time." After all, he concludes, "not the fruit of experience, but experience itself, is the end." And by "experience" Pater means consciousness itself.

We could argue that Pater gets it wrong here by reducing human life to consciousness. There is a real world out there, we might say. If we did not live in it we would never need to get out of bed. And what about professional accomplishments or service to others or parenthood? Surely such "fruits of experience" count for something outside of our consciousness.

Pater does not deny this commonsense view of life. He just thinks it misses the point of what makes life worth living. And, playing upon his metaphor of the flickering flame of consciousness, he captures in a vivid image what he thinks makes life *most* worth living: "To burn always with a hard, gemlike flame, to maintain this ecstasy, is success in life." It is a splendid image. One to remember. Even a creed to live by. For it can enhance anyone's life in many ways. And these go well beyond aesthetics, as Pater himself points out. But before getting there, we should first see how Pater uses this image to celebrate beauty and art.

Pater believed that nothing makes this flame of consciousness burn more brightly than the "sensations" or "impressions" of beauty, and that nothing gives us more of these than art. In fact, this is art's sole purpose: to give us the sensations or impressions of beauty that brighten our flame. "Art comes to you," Pater declares, "professing frankly to give nothing but the highest quality to your moments as they pass, and simply for those moments' sake." Therefore, he concludes, because art and beauty give "the highest quality" possible to our "moments as they pass" by fueling our flame to its whitest heat, "the wisest" among us live for "the desire of beauty, the love of art for its own sake." And that is all.

We find the highest meaning of life in moments of beauty because these give us the most intense "ecstasy" we can have. This makes Pater's theory of art for art's sake, or of *art for life's sake*, about as plain as it can be. But Pater does not limit the ecstasy of life to the experience of art and beauty. He carries his credo beyond aesthetics. For Pater says that we can find ecstatic moments everywhere in life, if we know how to look for them. "Every moment," he tells us, "some tone on the hills or sea is choicer than the next, some mood of passion or insight or intellectual excitement is irresistibly real and attractive to us—for that moment only." So we should seek those ecstatic moments everywhere, in perceptions, emotions, ideas, no less than in art and beauty, and let them burn in us with that "hard gemlike flame." For that is success in life.

Anyone can do this, but it is not easy. It takes passion and power. Passivity will not do. "Great passions may give us this quickened sense of life," Pater emphasizes, "only be sure it is passion." The routine life wars against this. The superficiality of our sensations wars against it. Our own inertia wars against it. But when we experience a passionate intensity of life, no matter how we get it, we know that Pater is right. For then we do feel in our deepest selves that "to burn always with a hard, gemlike flame, to maintain this ecstasy, is success in life."

And yet, we should also see that a life lived for that *hard gemlike flame* alone can have consequences that are not altogether good. For if we live solely for moments of ecstasy within us we can wind up neglecting the real world outside of us, to the detriment of ourselves and of those around us. Pater might have dismissed these consequences while sitting among his books and fanning the flame of his own consciousness. But no one ever portrayed these consequences more dramatically than Pater's most prominent disciple, and history's most legendary devotee of art for art's sake, Oscar Wilde.

OSCAR WILDE LEARNED to revere art from the moralistic Victorian art critic John Ruskin as well as from the amoral aesthetes Gautier and Pater. Ruskin taught him that art has profound moral

WILDE

significance, but Gautier and Pater went the other way and claimed that art's importance has nothing to do with morals. Wilde had his own natural bent toward amoral aestheticism, to be sure, and he voiced this in clever and irreverent phrases whenever he opened his mouth or put his pen to paper. His first reported bon mot, from his student days at Oxford, could even be an aesthete's parody of Ruskin. "I find it harder and harder every day," he quipped, "to live up to my blue china."

Wilde's witty aestheticism made him a celebrated figure in his twenties. He lectured widely on beauty and art in those years—including a tour of the U.S. promoting good taste and the "Ethics of Art" that took him as far as the silver-mining town of Leadville, Colorado, where his spirited account of Renaissance artists moved locals to brandish pistols in the streets, hailing Benvenuto Cellini as a hero, and to name a new ore deposit "The Oscar." He would later write a series of brilliant and provocative essays in the late 1880s and early 1890s on his aesthetic vision of life, including "The Decay of Lying," "The Truth of Masks," "The Soul of Man Under Socialism," and the taunting philosophical dialogue "The Critic as Artist." But it was the novel *The Picture of Dorian Gray* (first published as a magazine story in 1890, then revised and expanded into the novel published in 1891), followed by a string of comic plays, that gave Wilde his lasting fame.

Everything Wilde wrote glittered with his genius for making light comedy of weighty things. As he said of his most famous play, *The Importance of Being Earnest*, it showed that "we should treat all trivial things very seriously, and all the serious things of life with sincere and studied triviality." But Wilde was not merely going for laughs. He acutely sensed the paradoxes and the ironies that can turn life topsy-turvy, making good things bad, and bad things good, causing us sometimes to laugh through our tears, and other times to cry through our laughter (he admired the eccentric Taoist Chuang Tzu—see Chapter 10—for philosophizing on the same theme, as he wrote in an essay called "A Chinese Sage"). These paradoxes and ironies pervade Wilde's every work. This made for many lighthearted laughs in his comedies. But it also made for darker humor, and even tragedy, in *The Picture of Dorian Gray*.

The Picture of Dorian Gray is one of those books that almost everybody knows and almost nobody reads. That is because it tells such a unique, striking, and readily graspable story that we hardly need to read the book to get the point. The story is about a dashing young man named Dorian Gray who wishes that a beautiful portrait of himself will age and wither instead of himself—and he gets his wish: the figure in the portrait grows old and ugly, while his own appearance remains young and handsome. It is an extraordinary literary image. We do not forget it. We may even joke to friends who appear young despite their years that they must have a portrait of themselves decaying in an attic.

But the novel is not as simple as that image. Dorian Gray's portrait does not decay from age alone. It decays from Dorian's corrupting love of beauty and pleasure. And that makes *The Picture of Dorian Gray* a classic cautionary tale on aestheticism, punctuated with Wilde's usual scintillatingly irreverent wit. We can use its witty lines to enliven our cocktail conversation, but we should not ignore the dangers that lie behind Dorian's, or anyone's, consuming love of beauty and its pleasures. Laugh and learn.

Wilde opens *The Picture of Dorian Gray* with a preface of epigrams (many of them taken from his responses to critics who had reviewed the earlier magazine version of the story) setting the tone with echoes of Gautier: "All art is quite useless." – "No artist has ethical sympathies." – "There is no such thing as a moral or immoral book." And so on. Wilde could never resist a clever line puncturing conventions with snappy irony. Even as he neared his end in a seedy Paris hotel he would joke: "My wallpaper and I are fighting a duel to the death. One or the other of us has to go." And, "I am dying beyond my means."

Wilde generously sprinkles such epigrams throughout *The Picture of Dorian Gray*. And he gives nearly all of them to the cynical Lord Henry Wotton. Philosopher, aesthete, aphorist, Lord Henry is Walter Pater as a moralist, or Friedrich Nietzsche in the drawing room. And he is one of Wilde's most deliciously wicked creations. It is Lord Henry who persuades young Dorian Gray to live for beauty and pleasure, and to damn everything else as dehumanizing vulgarity.

"Beauty is the wonder of wonders," he tells Dorian. "It needs no explanation.... It cannot be questioned. It has its divine right of sovereignty." He does not mean an abstract Platonic ideal of beauty to be contemplated in its perfection with the mind's eye. He means the ripe physical beauty of visual "appearances," because, he says, "the true mystery of the world is the visible, not the invisible." Hence he advises Dorian to "be always searching for new sensations" to delight in, and even to create "a new Hedonism—that is what our century wants." Dorian himself, Lord Henry adds, "might be its visible symbol" in his own beauty and taste for pleasures. But, Lord Henry also warns, "when your youth goes, your beauty will go with it, and then you will suddenly discover that there are no triumphs left for you." So he urges his protégé, "Live! Live the wonderful life that is in you! Let nothing be lost upon you." And do it now.

Live the wonderful life that is in you. Let nothing be lost upon you. These are galvanizing words, recalling Pater's entreaty to "burn always with a hard, gemlike flame" (and echoing Henry James's advice to literary artists in *The Art of Fiction* [1884] that they become persons "on whom nothing is lost"). They are good words to live by—up to a point. Dorian Gray discovers that point too late. He follows Lord Henry too far.

What about morality? Posh! Lord Henry would respond. "It is better to be beautiful than to be good." Or look at it another way, he adds philosophically. "When we are happy we are always good," for "to be good is to be in harmony with oneself." After all, he goes on, "the aim of life is self-development," nothing more. "One's own life—that is the important thing," and "as for the lives of one's neighbors," he sniffs, "they are not one's concern."

Good-bye to conscience. Farewell to self-restraint. If we deny ourselves any desire, Lord Henry insists, we inhibit our "self-development" and languish in resentment and self-hatred, because "every impulse that we strive to strangle broods in the mind, and poisons us." Therefore, as he says in one of Wilde's most familiar lines, "the only way to get rid of a temptation is to yield to it. Resist it, and your soul grows sick with longing for the things it has forbidden itself." In his philosophical dialogue "The Critic as Artist" Wilde speculated that "if we lived long enough to see the results of our actions, it may be that those who call themselves good would be sickened with dull remorse, and those the world calls evil stirred by a noble joy." This is why Lord Henry can say, in another wry epigram: "No civilized man ever regrets a pleasure, and no uncivilized man ever knows what a pleasure is." Pleasure, self-development, and civilization go together. Everything else is barbarism.

We laugh at Lord Henry's glibly perverse philosophizing. Who could take it seriously? And yet, don't Lord Henry's words actually fit our own culture quite well when we take the physical beauty of people as the measure of their human worth, or when we make a cult of good taste, or when we become enslaved to fashion, or when we adulate the glamour of show business and celebrity as we do? We might not speak Lord Henry's words, but we often come close to living them out.

Dorian Gray lives them out for sure. This begins when he first casts his eyes on the portrait of him by the painter Basil Hallward. After falling under the sway of Dorian's beauty with an "aesthetic idolatry," Hallward had poured that idolatry into the painting. Now, as Dorian looks at it, "the sense of his own beauty came on him like a revelation," and he falls in love with that beauty. "How sad it is!" he muses, recalling Lord Henry's warning about aging: "I shall grow old, and horrible, and dreadful. But this picture will remain always young." Then he makes his fateful, Faust-like wish: "If only it were the other way! If it were I who was to be always young, and the picture that was to grow old! For that—for that—I would give everything! . . . I would give my soul for that."

Lord Henry's aestheticism and Hallward's "aesthetic idolatry" have done their job. Dorian Gray has decided that it is indeed "better to be beautiful than to be good." And he gets his Faustian wish without knowing it. But he also gets more than he bargained for. Not only will the painting age, it will also reveal the corruption that his soul suffers from his consuming love of himself and pursuit of pleasure.

This begins to dawn on him after he humiliates and spurns his fiancée, Sybil Vane, an actress whom he has adored for her artistry, but whom he rejects when she lets her love for him eclipse her art and she gives a bad performance: "Without your art," he jeers, "you are nothing." That very night as he glances at the picture, he thinks he detects a slight change in it. "The expression looked different. One would have said there was a touch of cruelty in the mouth." Then he remembers his rash wish in the painter's studio. Shuddering that it might be coming true, he vows to mend his ways and listen no more to Lord Henry's "subtle poisonous theories."

But it is too late. Aestheticism already owns his soul. He admits as much when, upon learning that his disconsolate fiancée has committed suicide, he remarks coldly: "This thing that has happened does not affect me as it should." Instead of remorse, he feels a fresh and awful pleasure. It "seems to me to be simply like a wonderful ending to a wonderful play," he says to himself. "It has all the terrible beauty of a Greek tragedy."

The "terrible beauty" of his lover's suicide brings Dorian Gray a strange thrill. It is the thrill of perceiving life, and even death, as nothing but aesthetics. "To become a spectator of one's own life," he reflects, drawing on more of Lord Henry's pernicious wisdom, "is to escape the suffering of life." This new insight emboldens him. Concluding that "life itself was the first, the greatest of the arts," he can now live for "eternal youth, infinite passion, pleasure subtle and secret, wild joys and wilder sins" without hesitation or regret. "The portrait was to bear the burden of his shame: that was all." But it would not be all.

From here, Dorian Gray pursues "wild joys" everywhere. He savors all of the familiar arts, and, under the influence of a strange book that Lord Henry has given him, he goes farther, taking up the "study of jewels," steeping himself in the "psychology of perfumes," collecting lush tapestries and lavish textiles, and reveling in every affectation of "Fashion" and "Dandyism." This book is not named, but it is unmistakably a variation on Karl Joris Huysmans' Á *Rebours*, or *Against Nature* (1884), which had become the bible of late nineteenth-century decadence with its tale of a dissolute aristocrat who lives for nothing but the pleasures of the senses.

All the while, Dorian grows more indifferent to everyone else and "more and more enamoured of his own beauty," which does not dim. He even acquires a malevolent aesthetic pleasure "in the corruption of his own soul" and its visual expression in the portrait. A spectator of his life from the outside, he has also become a spectator of it from the inside, which appears before him now in this work of art and fascinates him as he wonders "which were the more horrible, the signs of sin or the signs of age." In a moment of reckless curiosity and perverse pride, he shows the transformed painting to its painter, who recoils in horror and urges Dorian to pray for salvation. Offended by Hallward's reaction, Dorian grabs a knife and stabs to death the unsuspecting painter of his soul.

Before long, Dorian Gray has claimed other victims as well—his fiancée's vengeful brother in a shooting incident, and a man who commits suicide after Dorian has blackmailed him into disposing of poor Basil Hallward's body. But ultimately Dorian Gray's accumulating villainies do begin to weigh on him. A spark of conscience has somehow stayed alive. To lighten the weight, he blames these villainies on the pernicious powers of the mysterious portrait, along with Lord Henry and the evil novel Lord Henry had given him. But when he discloses this change of heart to Lord Henry he receives only disdain. "You are really beginning to moralize," Lord Henry scoffs. "You will soon be going about . . . warning people against all the sins of which you have grown tired." Remember, Lord Henry says, "life has been your art," don't spoil it now with sentimental guilt and pedestrian morality. As to art impairing life, Lord Henry repeats, this is impossible: "Art has no influence upon actions. . . . It is superbly sterile."

By this time Dorian Gray can no longer believe that. His own life proves the opposite. His obsessive love of beauty and pleasure, along with the influence of that poisonous book and the sinister mystery of Basil Hallward's painting, have devoured his life. And now he has lost delight in everything. As he looks at the portrait again, with its grotesque reflections of his own depravity—a depravity that has involved secret visits to opium dens, where one night Sybil Vane's brother almost killed him—he is disturbed to detect new traces of "cunning" in the eyes and hints of a "hypocrite" in the "curved wrinkle of the mouth." For he suspects where these telltale signs came from. They came from his "one good deed," which was recently to spare an innocent young country girl from his own predatory desires. Now he recognizes that he had performed this deed not from honest virtue or genuine concern for the girl, but from "vanity" and "curiosity" about what a selfless act would feel like. The painting knows. Suddenly he decides he must destroy the picture so that "he would be free" from the cruel conscience it has become for him—a Freudian superego that inescapably punishes the ego for its guilty wishes and selfish actions (see Chapter 17). Grasping the same knife he had used to murder the picture's painter, he plunges it into the canvas to kill his conscience, "this monstrous soul-life" that knows him better than he knows himself.

A cry, "horrible in its agony," pierced the air. When the servants who had heard the sound get into the room, they find the portrait just as Basil Hallward had painted it, radiant with "youth and beauty." And on the floor beneath it, with a dagger through his heart, lies an unrecognizably "withered, wrinkled, and loathsome" figure who would later be identified as Dorian Gray.

Oscar Wilde is not very subtle here. Dorian Gray dies from moral degeneration (in the prominent *fin de siècle* book *Degeneration* [1892], the loquacious German critic Max Nordau accused Wilde of exemplifying that disorder himself; and Wilde, after his imprisonment for homosexual crimes, actually cited Nordau's authority in a letter of July 1896 to the British Home Secretary appealing for an early medical release from jail). In fact, the moral message of Wilde's novel turns out to be quite conventional—namely, that a self-indulgent and wicked life can thoroughly corrupt a person's character (just as in Dante's *Inferno*—see Chapter 5). Wilde even told a critic that "the real trouble I experienced in writing the story was that of keeping the extremely obvious moral subordinate to the artistic and dramatic effect." But Dorian did not succumb to self-indulgence and wickedness for conventional reasons. At Lord Henry's urging, he had acted on a high-minded ideal—the love of beauty, or aesthetic pleasure.

"To have ruined oneself over poetry is an honour," Lord Henry had told him. Well, perhaps. But it is to ruin oneself all the same. As Oscar Wilde knew, *The Picture of Dorian Gray* is not about the love of aesthetic pleasure for its own sake wholly divorced from the moral life. It is about the love of that pleasure *as the moral life itself.* This means the book is about how aesthetics can become ethics.

When Lord Henry declared, "it is better to be beautiful than to be good," he was restating a moral principle that Wilde had proclaimed in "The Critic as Artist": "Aesthetics are higher than ethics," so "to discern the beauty of a thing is the finest point to which we can arrive." But that does not remove aesthetics from ethics. It makes aesthetics the highest ethics possible for those who believe that beauty is the highest good. Lord Henry gave Dorian a backhanded compliment for acknowledging this when, in a moment of stricken conscience, Dorian had vowed to be good because "I can't bear the idea of my soul being hideous." That, Lord Henry says, is "a very charming artistic basis for ethics, Dorian! I congratulate you on it." Here Dorian clearly had let aesthetics define both good and evil—good is beautiful, and beauty is good; evil is ugly, and ugliness is evil. Lord Henry had encouraged him to do this, of course, as when he cracked, after Sybil Vane's bad theatrical performance, "It's not good for one's morals to see bad acting." (In some of this same spirit, by the way, Friedrich Nietzsche, who shared many of Wilde's ideas on art and artistry, remarked in *The Gay Science*: "The sight of the ugly makes one bad and gloomy"—see Chapter 8.) This is not Plato's ideal of the union of the Beautiful and the Good. It is the aesthete's creed of beauty in itself as the highest good irrespective of any other moral ideals. And, although Dorian comes to feel remorse for his sins, he still acts on this creed to the end by attacking the portrait of his soul for being, what else but—ugly.

Oscar Wilde got loads of laughs from the ironies of exalting beauty as the highest good, and from turning aesthetics into ethics, and ethics into aesthetics. But funny as it can be, *The Picture of Dorian Gray* is a tragic parable against doing just these things. Ironically, Wilde himself ignored his own warnings, or he willfully neglected to see that some of his contemporaries might not only laugh when he boasted that he lived for beauty, not morals, or for aesthetics, not ethics—or that he had made aesthetics into his ethics. He certainly did not see this when he defiantly carried his vaunted love of beauty into homosexual love for a beautiful and narcissistic boy whose father decided to ruin Wilde. Wilde paid the price for his defiance with imprisonment, followed by the premature end of his literary career and his early death. Like Dorian Gray, Oscar Wilde suffered an aesthete's tragedy.

Wilde would not have to pay that price today. But the temptations and the dangers of turning aesthetics into ethics are perhaps more abundant in our culture of art, entertainment, consumer commerce, and celebrity than ever. Although few people may succumb to these temptations as far as Oscar Wilde did, and certainly not as far as Dorian Gray did, we should not treat those temptations or their dangers lightly. We might even look into *The Picture of Dorian Gray* for signs of ourselves.

OSCAR WILDE GIVES US many chuckles amidst his tragic tale of aestheticism gone wrong. Thomas Mann seldom raises a smile. But no one has looked into the ethics of aesthetics, or the aesthetics of

MANN

ethics, more deeply, or depicted them more frequently and more hauntingly, than he. He wrote tale after tale exploring the subject, beginning with his first novel, *Buddenbrooks*—about a family that declines over generations into a wan aestheticism—on through numerous stories about artists, such as "The Infant Prodigy," "Tonio Krüger," "Felix Krull," "Death in Venice," "Mario the Magician," down to the long philosophical novel *Doctor Faustus*, about a composer who trades his soul to the devil for spontaneous creativity. And the particular idea that occupied Mann throughout these works was the paradox of modern aestheticism. That is: art and aesthetics set standards of value for artists and art lovers that can bring either exaltation or ruin—or both. Oscar Wilde could joke about this down to his death-bed battles with his wallpaper. Thomas Mann rarely saw anything funny about it (although he could amusingly satirize human follies, as he did in *The Magic Mountain*).

In the early story "Tonio Krüger," for instance, Mann tells of an artist who decides that "one must die to life in order to be utterly a creator" because "a properly constituted, healthy, decent man never writes, acts, or composes." Drained by the sacrifices that he himself has made for his art, Tonio Krüger laments: "What more pitiable sight is there than life led astray by art." In another story, "Felix Krull," one of his few overtly comic tales (later expanded into the novel *Felix Krull, Confidence Man*), Mann created a more upbeat artist. Instead of bemoaning the life-deny-ing demands of art, Felix Krull takes pride in the "self-conquest" that art requires, especially the self-conquest of his own art, which is none other than deceiving people as a "confidence man." Felix even judges his mas-tery of this "art" to be "a moral achievement of a high order." Deception as art? And the art of deception as "a moral achievement"? In Mann's world they can be. For aesthetics and ethics become tightly tangled in a thicket of ironies.

"Death in Venice" brilliantly puts these ironies on disturbing display through its profound, sad understanding of why we value art and aes-thetics as we do, and how we can let that value become our ethics, and why we should be wary of doing that. This makes "Death in Venice" indispensable reading for anyone who prizes the pleasures of beauty and art, as probably everyone does, and particularly for anyone who judges those pleasures to be the crowning experience of life.

Mann weaves his probing ideas of how aesthetics became ethics into this story of a writer who, like Tonio Krüger, had "sacrificed to art" the energies and gratifications of a normal life. With fierce self-discipline this writer had created literary works of increasingly severe formalism, marked by "an almost exaggerated sense of beauty, a lofty purity, sym-metry, and simplicity" as a "rebuke to the excesses of a psychology-ridden age." These works had won him high honors, including the honorific "von" in his name: Gustave von Aschenbach. But he had paid dearly. As "the poet spokesman of all those who labor at the edge of exhaustion," Mann says, Aschenbach had grown cold and "got no joy" from either his reputation or his writings with their "cynic utterances on the nature of art and the artistic life." In this bleak and enervated state of mind, Aschen-bach decides that he needs a change of scene. He heads for Venice.

In Venice, Aschenbach undergoes wondrous changes that have terrible consequences. His dispassionate reverence for pure aesthetic form turns into an impassioned love of beauty in the form of a fourteen-year-old boy. And for this love of physical beauty he becomes willing to die.

When Aschenbach first sees this boy in a hotel restaurant, he thinks "he had never seen, either in nature or in art, anything so utterly happy and consummate" as "the lad's perfect beauty." Then, as he wonders how "form and art" can be so fully embodied in "human beauty," he falls under the boy's unintended spell, which deepens every time he sees the boy—who is named Tadzio and is vacationing with his family—thereafter. And when the boy smiles at him one day, Aschenbach collapses on a bench whispering to himself, "I love you."

This is obviously homosexual erotic love. And Aschenbach knows it, admitting that from his first frisson upon seeing the boy, the attraction he feels belongs to Eros. But there is more than sexual attraction here. As Aschenbach ponders what is happening to him he discovers several unsettling things about aesthetics and beauty that he had not known before. And everyone should come to know them.

In the first place, Aschenbach "told himself that what he saw" in the boy "was beauty's very essence; form as divine thought, the single and pure perfection which resides in the mind." This is beauty as an aesthetic ideal, like that celebrated in Plato's *Symposium*. But Aschenbach also discovers—as Plato suggests in the *Symposium* and elaborates in the *Phaedrus* (see Chapter 19), which Aschenbach paraphrases—that ideal beauty does not reside wholly in the mind as a pure, emotionless idea or form. Ideal beauty ignites feelings. Some of these feelings are erotic, but that is not Mann's primary point. As Aschenbach goes on to say, beauty, or perfect aesthetic form, arouses "the artist's highest joy" because it gives rise to a "thought that can merge wholly into feeling" and a "feeling that can merge wholly into thought." In short, beauty fuses mind and emotions.

William Wordsworth had said almost exactly these words in describing the joyous union of thought and feeling that art and the imagination can forge (see Chapter 23). And, like Wordsworth, Aschenbach concludes that this joyous union reveals what is most important in life. But Aschenbach lets this revelation take him to a place where Wordsworth would not have gone. For Aschenbach decides that because beauty brings "the artist's highest joy" through the union of thoughts and feelings, he should live for the ecstatic love of beauty itself alone. Wordsworth wanted more from life than that.

Mann's explanation of how this sequence can occur should stick in the mind of every artist and art lover. For it shows us how aesthetics can become ethics, leading us to live for aesthetics above all. What serious artist or art lover has not known at least moments of wanting to do this? But Mann's explanation also shows us how this *aesthetic ethics* can lead anyone's life astray.

Here is the core of Mann's account. "Has not [aesthetic] form two aspects?" he asks. "Is it not moral and immoral at once: moral in so far as it is the expression and result of discipline," but "immoral—yes, actually hostile to morality—in that of its very essence it is indifferent to good and evil, and deliberately concerned to make the moral world stoop beneath its proud and undivided scepter?" In other words, aesthetics becomes ethics by elevating the discipline of artistic excellence and the aesthetic qualities of art, good taste, and so on, into the supreme standard of value in life—that is, as Oscar Wilde had suggested, we should try to live up to the beauties of our blue china more than anything else. We forgive great artists many a sin, and we probably sacrifice a few virtues ourselves, in the service of this aesthetic ethics (Leo Tolstoy memorably blasted modern culture as a whole in *What Is Art?* for doing both—see Chapter 19). But we pay a price too. Aschenbach pays with his life.

Aschenbach had lived by one version of this aesthetic ethics before going to Venice when he had imposed the rigid artistic discipline of austere form on his writings. Now he gives himself over to another version of it by yielding to the irresistible emotional power of beauty in the physical form of the boy. Abandoning the very "dignity and self-control" that he used to take pride in, Aschenbach now sees his former "stern cult of the beautiful" transmuted into "intoxication and desire" as his own moral world stoops beneath the scepter of the boy's physical beauty. Entangled in the paradox that perfect aesthetic form can enflame unruly passions, Aschenbach lives out this new aesthetic ethics through a bizarre sequence of events to a blissfully self-destructive end.

First, he begins furtively following Tadzio everywhere. Then he tries to become more youthful himself by having a barber dye his hair and rouge his cheeks (like a dissolute old character he had noticed with disgust earlier). When he hears reports of cholera in the city, he declines to warn the boy's family, fearing that Tadzio will leave and deprive Aschenbach of his life-giving aesthetic and erotic thrills. And as the disease spreads, he observes the boy at every opportunity. Even after contracting cholera himself, Aschenbach stays on, conceding that "the whole cultural structure of a lifetime" was being "trampled on, ravaged, and destroyed," but that he was powerless to do anything about it. For "in his infatuation he cared for nothing" but to savor Tadzio's aesthetic perfection. Beauty and Eros have Aschenbach in their deathly grip.

Finally, learning that the boy's family is departing at last, Aschenbach goes to see Tadzio one more time on the beach of the Lido. And there, sprawled in a chair, with the physical image of ideal beauty poised in the sunshine before him at the edge of the glistening water, Aschenbach takes his last breath. Even more surely than Dorian Gray, Gustave von Aschenbach dies for the love of beauty.

GAUTIER AND PATER freed aesthetics from the long tradition that had subordinated aesthetics and art to ethics. Then they promoted aesthetics over ethics. Wilde and Mann went on to play out the ironic and tragic implications of this moral revolution that gave aesthetics a victory over ethics. Together, these four writers tell us some complicated and often disturbing truths about what aesthetics and the love of beauty can do *for* us, and *to* us.

They say that, at best, aesthetic pleasures give us some of our most intense moments of being alive, so we should seize those moments for *life's sake*. They also imply—and Pater states outright—that we can learn to find such moments in anything that intensifies our "consciousness" through our senses or imagination, our mind or emotions. And they say, in Pater's words again, that whatever we do, we should try "to burn always with a hard, gemlike flame, to maintain this ecstasy," for that "is success in life." These are the uses and the virtues of aestheticism. And life can be gray without them.

But our quartet of writers also lays bare the moral paradox of aesthetics: if we allow aesthetics to set the highest standard of value in human life so that we *"stoop beneath its proud and undivided scepter,"* we may lose more than we gain. For despite the exaltation we might feel, we become insensitive to the common good of human beings, and we sacrifice a portion of our humanity—succumbing, as George Eliot wrote in *Middlemarch*, to "that softening influence of the fine arts which makes other people's hardships picturesque." That is the abuse and the vice of aestheticism.

So, let us by all means use aestheticism well and try to burn always with a hard, gemlike flame of ecstasy. But let us not forget that we live in a real world of other human beings. Let us live for them, too, and share the flame.

On Aesthetics and Ethics

1. Anyone who thinks art must always serve morality is wrong.

2. If we require art to serve morality, we risk sacrificing the good that art can do.

3. The highest good that art can do is to intensify our lives by giv-

ing us unique aesthetic pleasures of the senses, the emotions, and the imagination.

4. Art comes to us professing to give us nothing but the highest quality to our moments as they pass, and simply for those moments' sake—that is why we can love art for its own sake. (Pater)

5. We should make the fleeting moments of our lives as intense and pleasurable as possible. (Pater)

6. We can learn to make our lives intense in anything we do—through the senses, the imagination, the emotions, the mind. (Pater)

7. "To burn always with a hard, gemlike flame, to maintain this ecstasy, is success in life." (Pater)

8. Aesthetics is both moral and amoral. (Mann)

9. Aesthetics is moral when it sets high standards of discipline and value. (Mann)

10. Aesthetics is amoral when it reduces all standards of value to its own. (Mann)

11. Aesthetics can become ethics, and ethics can become aesthetics.

12. It is dangerous to let aesthetics become ethics or ethics become aesthetics—these are moral self-deceptions that conceal amorality.

13. When aesthetics becomes ethics, we make the discipline and value of aesthetic objects our highest moral standard, and we dismiss the morality of actions.

14. When ethics becomes aesthetics, we make the aesthetic refinements of social appearance, style, and manners our highest morality and dismiss other moral actions.

15. Anyone who thinks art serves nothing but aesthetics is wrong.

16. A life without keen aesthetic pleasures is empty, but a life with nothing but keen aesthetic pleasures is dangerous.

17. The meaning of life is to burn always with a hard, gemlike flame of aesthetic intensity and ecstasy in any pursuit, without letting aesthetics become ethics or ethics become aesthetics.

26
Of Love and Marriage,
Passion and Aging

Gabriel García Márquez: *Love in the Time of the Cholera*

It is life, more than death, that has no limits.

Márquez

Gabriel García Márquez (1928–) has been troubled by Latin American politics and haunted by ghosts almost all his life. Born in Aracataca, Colombia, to a couple whose peculiar courtship would inspire the novel *Love in the Time of the Cholera*, Márquez was reared by his maternal grandparents because his own parents lacked money. The times were tumultuous in Colombia, as they had been for most of the country's hundred years of independence. This tumult would form the political backdrop of Márquez' fiction, beginning with his first short stories and his early novels, *No One Writes to the Colonel* (1961) and *In Evil Hour* (1962). But it was not politics that made Márquez the great writer he became. It was the ghosts.

Márquez' grandparents' home echoed with stories of ghosts and mysteries and bizarreries told by Márquez' grandmother with unquestioning acceptance and a matter-of-fact manner that seeped into Márquez' consciousness and eventually (along with Kafka and Faulkner) gave him his own literary voice as a leader of "magic realism." This voice first sounded in the celebrated novel *A Hundred Years of Solitude* (1967), a saga of historical turmoil, cultural isolation, self-destructive cycles of life, and weird events spanning a century in Colombia. The novel made Márquez famous and earned him financial security for the first time in a peripatetic existence badgered by political enemies. Then came *Erendira and Other Stories* (1972), *Autumn of the Patriarch* (1975), *Love in the Time of the Cholera* (1986), *Strange Pilgrims* (1992), *Love and Other Demons* (1994), the memoir *To Live to Tell It* (2003), and the short novel *Memoirs of My Melancholy Whores* (2005).

Márquez received the Nobel Prize for Literature in 1982 before he wrote the novel that likely moves readers most, *Love in the Time of the Cholera*. It tells a remarkable love story—two, really. One is about a marriage, the other is about a passion outside marriage that gives a singular purpose, lasting hope, and ultimate elation to an unusual character all his life. Strange and surprising, *Love in the Time of the Cholera* is also beautiful, inspiriting,

and wise, a great book about love and marriage, passion and old age, culminating in an exuberant affirmation of the will to live life to the very end
with hope and joy.

———————

THEY SAY OLD AGE is not for sissies. Gabriel García Márquez
knows this well. In *Love in the Time of the Cholera* he sees old age in
all of its nascent and impending infirmities and discouragements. But
that is not all he sees. He also finds a fire of life and energy in the human
spirit that can blaze so fiercely it will never die as long as there is breath
in the body. He calls to mind Walter Pater's memorable line: "To burn
always with a hard, gemlike flame, to maintain this ecstasy, is success in
life." Pater meant having a passion for beautiful and enlivening things,
adding, "only make sure it is passion" (see Chapter 25). Such a passion is
a form of love. And that love is Márquez' favorite subject.

Plato had hinted at this kind of love as a philosophical-erotic desire
that attracts us to the Beautiful, the Good, and the True (see Chapter
19). William Wordsworth later discovered another version of it in the
joyous moments that give meaning to life (see Chapter 23). Plato, Wordsworth, and Pater all implied that anyone can find things to love in these
ways. Everyone should find them. For to feel that love, to pulse with that
passion, to "burn always with a hard, gemlike flame," is surely "success
in life," whatever other kinds of successes we might achieve. And in old
age, difficult as it can be to keep that flame alight, it might be more life-
giving than ever to do it—if only in intensely cherished memories, or in
happy expectations for a younger generation.

In *Love in the Time of the Cholera* Gabriel García Márquez spins the
central tale of a man who burned with such a passion from adolescence
to old age, and who vowed to keep it burning to the end. His passion,
his love, was for a girl, who became a woman, and then a matron, and
then a widow, and whom he adored at a distance for over half a century
until he won her heart at last when he was seventy-six years old and she
was seventy-two.

Márquez gives this man the name Florentino Ariza. He is a curious
character whose passion flamed secretly within an outward life of professional accomplishments, personal eccentricities, and a persistent bach-
elorhood abounding with sexual liaisons. And he is a quixotic character.
For he shows how a life lived for an ideal, or for an idealized love, never
loses animating purpose and energizing hope. But unlike Don Quixote,
who forsook his ideals as illusions at the end of his life, Florentino Ariza
never abandons his ideal, his love. Florentino carries these through to

the end of the novel, where he tells a riverboat captain, who has piloted him and his beloved up and down a river, that after waiting over half a century to win her, he will now happily travel along that river with her for his "whole life," or even "forever." Only a reader with a heart of stone could read Márquez' ending without feeling that Florentino Ariza has a passion worth respecting, and possibly emulating.

Florentino Ariza lives his quixotic life for those fifty-odd years largely ignored by the object of his undying love, Fermina Daza. Their two lives intersect only occasionally in a nameless South American town on the Caribbean coast, as Florentino secretly nurtures his love while Fermina goes through a publicly exemplary, privately complicated, and overall quite admirable marriage. Both of these lives have much to tell us about how any life can take unexpected turns, and how we find meaning in our lives in unexpected ways. And when the lives of Florentino and Fermina come together at last, hardly a reader can fail to wish for a love like theirs to flower in the deepening dusk of his or her own life.

So LET US BEGIN at the beginning of this dense and winding, astonishing and inspiring story of Florentino Ariza's unquenchable love for Fermina Daza. This beginning is not, however, where Márquez opens the novel. He starts with the circumstances surrounding the death of Fermina Daza's husband, Dr. Juvenal Urbino, who, at the age of eighty-one, after fifty years of marriage, fatally tumbles from a ladder while chasing his pet parrot up a tree. But the chronology of the book actually starts long before this odd and unfortunate incident. It starts with the adolescent romance of Florentino Ariza and Fermina Daza, which we learn about only after Fermina becomes a widow.

Florentino had fallen consumingly in love with Fermina when he was about nineteen and she was only fifteen (Márquez is not altogether consistent with such chronological details, even though he makes a point of identifying certain ages of people and passages of time). Florentino had first caught sight of Fermina while delivering a telegram to her father, who had moved to the town a couple of years earlier. Thin, myopic, with an "air of weakness"—and suffering from "chronic constipation, which forced him to take enemas throughout his life"—Florentino nonetheless possessed a romantic spirit that led him to learn "the latest dances and recite sentimental poetry" and "to play violin serenades to his friends' sweethearts." This attracted girls who even vied with each other for his company. But then he lost his heart to Fermina Daza and "began his secret life as a solitary hunter."

First he stalked the young Fermina, lurking in a park waiting for her to pass by on her way to school or to church. Then he composed a letter

that grew into a seventy-page epistle before he finally gained the courage
to deliver it to Fermina one day while she was sitting outside her house
under an almond tree in the company of her aunt—who had previously
alerted her to Florentino's daily presence in the park and to his probable
intentions, and had ignited her curiosity about this strange young man.
But Florentino did not give Fermina the seventy pages. Instead he had
condensed them into a half-page simply professing "his perfect fidelity
and his everlasting love." Those last words would become a refrain.

Florentino goes home that day besieged by nausea, diarrhea, de-
lirium, "fainting spells," and "the weak pulse, the hoarse breathing, and
the pale perspiration of a dying man." His mother fears "the devastation
of cholera," which was endemic in the region and periodically erupted
in epidemics. But an old physician called in to diagnose Florentino finds
no illness. Instead he concludes that "the symptoms of love were the
same as those of cholera." Now Florentino's mother understands. And
with the wry nature that endeared her to Florentino she tells him to
"take advantage of it now, while you are young, and suffer all you can
. . . because these things don't last your whole life" (*toda la vida*). How
wrong she proves to be.

When Florentino finally receives a reply from Fermina weeks later,
their romance flowers. But it is almost entirely epistolary. For two years
they exchange letters virtually every day via Fermina's romantic and mis-
chievous aunt, who facilitates the clandestine correspondence behind
Fermina's father's back. Florentino's letters exude the ardor of first love,
many of them echoing poetry he had read, and some "inscribed with
the point of a pin on camellia petals," whereas hers are more restrained,
"intended to keep the coals alive without putting her hand in the fire."
Florentino also serenades Fermina on his violin in the moonlight at
anyplace in the town or on the surrounding hills from where the winds
could carry his melodies to her ears. Eventually he proposes marriage,
and she accepts, because her aunt advises her: "You will be sorry all the
rest of your life if you say no."

But it is an ill-fated betrothal. Fermina's father won't allow it. He banishes Fermina's beloved aunt for her complicity in the romance. And he
threatens to shoot Florentino if the young man refuses to leave Fermina
alone. When Florentino defies him with the words, "there is no greater
glory than to die for love," he takes Fermina away to make her forget.
They are gone for a year and a half.

But Fermina does not forget. Florentino uses his position at the telegraph office to track her, and he surreptitiously keeps their correspondence and their romance alive, unbeknownst to her father, with the help
of cooperative telegraph operators. When her father finally becomes

confident that at age eighteen Fermina has forgotten Florentino, the two of them return home, where Fermina assumes responsibility for running their house (Fermina's mother had died long ago). But Fermina secretely resolves to give herself to Florentino "as the certain husband to whom she belonged heart and soul."

Learning of her arrival, Florentino grows feverish with expectation and nervous with desire. Then, when he sees her walking across the Plaza of the Cathedral, he shyly follows her as she moves from place to place revisiting the town she has missed so much. She is taller now, more dignified, more assured, and more beautiful. Finally, in the Arcade of the Scribes, crowded with vendors, he approaches her from behind and whispers "crowned goddess" in her ear, an epithet he had used for her in his letters. She turns around. Their eyes meet. "But now," Márquez writes, "instead of the commotion of love, she felt the abyss of disenchantment," wondering how "she could have nurtured such a chimera in her heart for so long." Immediately "she erased him from her life." She goes home and writes him a letter saying, "Today when I saw you, I realized that what is between us is nothing more than an illusion."

Florentino Ariza never sees or speaks to Fermina Daza alone again until the day that Dr. Juvenal Urbino topples to his death. During those years Florentino would live an eventful life, but not one single day would pass without his thinking of Fermina Daza and of his "everlasting love."

Márquez first shows us Florentino's life over this half century as something of a shadow in the background of Fermina Daza's life. In fact, on the rare occasions when Fermina encounters Florentino by chance in the city, she thinks that "it is as if he were not a person but only a shadow." That is how little she thinks or knows of him over those fifty years. But no one else really knows him either. Florentino keeps his "everlasting love" to himself. And when he reenters Fermina's life in his mid-seventies on the day her husband dies, "he was convinced in the solitude of his soul that he had loved in silence for a much longer time than anyone else in this world ever had."

ACROSS THOSE NEARLY fifty-two years, Fermina Daza and Florentino Ariza had lived very different lives. Hers was the more conventional, but it nonetheless had had a portion of passion and vitality. For Fermina's story is that of her marriage to Dr. Juvenal Urbino, and of how these two intelligent, civilized, and independent people find in this marriage, despite its troubles, more happiness, and in more disparate ways, more love than they had ever imagined possible.

Dr. Juvenal Urbino enters Fermina Daza's life not long after the young Fermina casts Florentino aside. Dr. Urbino is twenty-eight years old at the time, and Fermina is said to be eighteen when he comes to treat her for what her father fears is cholera, but turns out to be a minor stomach ailment. Dr. Urbino's own father had died fighting a cholera epidemic several years earlier, and this had spurred the young doctor to strive to defeat the disease once and for all. At the time he meets Fermina, he has succeeded in staving off further epidemics by promoting the innovations of better hygiene and clean water, although cholera recurs in the country along the rivers and the coast. Mature, accomplished, respected, and attractive, Dr. Urbino is a most desirable bachelor. Soon he is drawn to the beautiful, intelligent, and tempestuous Fermina Daza, who coquettishly rejects his attentions until her cousin Hildebranda Sanchez comes to visit. Hildebranda "thrust[s] Fermina Daza into life" by chastising her for being too removed from it, and by flirting with Dr. Urbino, gushing over what an appealing man he is. The next thing we know, Fermina Daza and Dr. Juvenal Urbino are getting married.

This marriage turns out to be one of sharp conflicts, emotional upheavals, aching resentments, and the gradual nurturing over fifty years of a love more heartfelt than anything that either Fermina or Dr. Urbino had felt for each other in the first place. "The truth is," Márquez writes, "Juvenal Urbino's suit had never been undertaken in the name of love." He had brought to the marriage "only worldly goods: security, order, happiness," which, "added together, might resemble love, almost be love. But they were not love." And "he was aware that he did not love her. He had married her because he liked her haughtiness, her seriousness, her strength, and also because of some vanity on his part." For her part Fermina had originally seen Dr. Urbino "as the creature of a paternal plot"—a proper husband selected for her. But "she was also not convinced that love was really what she most needed to live." And yet, despite the loveless origins of this marriage, it lasted, and it became a marriage that more than a few people might wish was theirs.

That is the paradox of this marriage and of many others. It was not born of love. And it did not depend on conjugal happiness. It thrived on the resilience of spouses living together through the routine of daily life and the vicissitudes of emotions, becoming changed in ways that neither of them had expected or would have chosen, growing closer to each other along the way, and being the better for it all. Many a good marriage works just like this. And of all the things that Fermina Daza and Dr. Juvenal Urbino learned about marriage during their fifty years together, the discovery that came hardest was this: "It was easier to avoid great matrimonial catastrophes than trivial everyday miseries." These "everyday miseries" almost ended their marriage after thirty years over nothing more than a missing bar of soap in the bathroom.

Returning from the bath one morning, Dr. Urbino complained to his wife that he had been "bathing for almost a week without any soap." Nettled at the complaint of this husband who often made her feel like a servant, Fermina snarled, "there's always been soap." The dispute then mushroomed into a shared rage that dredged up "other trivial quarrels from many other dim and turbulent dawns. Resentments stirred up other resentments, reopened old scars," until both husband and wife "were dismayed at the desolating proof that in so many years of conjugal battling they had done little more than nurture their rancor." Shaken by the discord, Dr. Urbino moved into quarters at the hospital, and it was four months before he would move back. And "even when they were old and placid they were careful about bringing it up, for the barely healed wounds could begin to bleed again." All of this happened because Dr. Urbino had complained of no soap in the bathroom. Yes, "trivial miseries" can threaten a marriage more than "catastrophes," for everyday life is loaded with trivialities, and these can irritate like a rash that gets scratched until blood flows.

But this marriage also has a catastrophe. It occurred at about the same time as the soap incident—Márquez reports these events in different places, but says they both took place thirty years into the marriage. Dr. Urbino causes this catastrophe by having a love affair with a patient. He slides into this affair inadvertently, but he gives himself over to it zestfully. When Fermina finds her suspicions of his infidelity confirmed, she leaves her husband and goes to live with Hildebranda on a ranch. She remains there for two years, until Dr. Urbino, driven by guilt, regret, and yearning, comes to plead for her return. And "she thought she would die of joy." This marriage turns out to be too strong to break over either "trivial everyday miseries" or a "catastrophe."

Here we see the paradox of marriage again: the compromises and sacrifices that make a marriage survive over decades can also bring surprising satisfactions. "In the long run," Márquez says of Fermina and Dr. Urbino, "neither of them had made a mistake" in marrying each other. And by the time of their fiftieth wedding anniversary, "they were not capable of living for even an instant without the other, or without thinking about the other." For "together they had overcome the daily incomprehension, the instantaneous hatred, the reciprocal nastiness and fabulous flashes of glory in the conjugal conspiracy," and, above all, they had become "conscious of and grateful for their incredible victories over adversity." Márquez adds, "Over the years they had both reached the same conclusion by different paths: it was not possible to live together in any other way, or love in any other way, and nothing in this world was more difficult than love."

The marriage of Fermina Daza and Dr. Juvenal Urbino is one to ponder and to admire, especially, perhaps, for making them "grateful for their incredible victories over adversity" (*agradecidos de sus victorias inverosímiles contra la adversidad*). This is a gratitude everyone should cultivate. Fermina and Dr. Urbino also might remind us of another notable fictional marriage that passes through unforeseen, if not so treacherous, terrain to reach equanimity. This is the marriage of Levin and Kitty in Leo Tolstoy's *Anna Karenina*. "Levin had been married for three months," Tolstoy writes, and "he was happy, but not at all in the way he had expected. At every step he found disenchantment with his old dream and a new, unexpected enchantment." His wife's "trifling preoccupation" with the mundane "was one of his disenchantments," yet it also became "one of his new enchantments," just as "their quarrels were another disenchantment and enchantment." How could love allow and endure such quarrels, he wondered, and then he discovered that "not only was she close to him, but that he no longer knew where she ended and he began."

Levin and Kitty's marriage, like that of Fermina Daza and Dr. Juvenal Urbino, could exemplify the familiar first line of *Anna Karenina*, which says, "All happy families are alike," but "each unhappy family is unhappy in its own way." For happiness in marriages and families might be the same for everyone as a kind of calm contentment, whereas unhappiness might differ owing to the myriad conflicts that can disrupt any marriage. But the marriage of Fermina Daza and Dr. Juvenal Urbino also invites us to look at marriages from another angle. This angle discloses a truth that is the opposite of Tolstoy's, and possibly higher and more useful. It is this: *All unhappy marriages are alike, and all happy marriages are happy in their own ways*. This is because unhappy marriages come from spouses succumbing to the conflicts that beset every marriage, but happy marriages—or happy families or enduring friendships—are created by people who learn to overcome those conflicts and to adapt in their own ways to the differences that divide them. In any case, Fermina Daza and Dr. Urbino surely find happiness in their own way, through their "incredible victories over adversity." And when Fermina Daza becomes a widow after fifty years of marriage, she even wonders "how one can be happy for so many years in the midst of so many squabbles, so many problems." But she had been happy after all.

When we first meet Fermina Daza and Dr. Juvenal Urbino at the beginning of the novel, they have been married for that half-century. They have both gained social prominence—he as a distinguished doctor and patron of the arts, she as a lady of elegance and public service. But he is growing senile at the age of eighty-one, and she attends to him with affectionate care, dressing and undressing him, compensating for his lapses of memory, and helping him deal with his diminishing powers as he descends into the infirmities of old age. It happens that a friend of his, Jeremiah de Saint-Amour, has just committed suicide at age sixty to avoid that descent, having vowed, "I will never be old." This death from "Gerontophobia," which actually opens the novel, surprises and saddens Dr. Urbino. But he understands it.

Dr. Urbino also has a parrot. He had acquired it when, after grumbling for years about Fermina's obsession with animals—she had populated the house with countless dogs, cats, birds, monkeys, turtles, and a snake—and after one of Fermina's dogs had slaughtered the other animals in a rabid rampage, he had declared: "Nothing that does not speak will come into this house" again. Submitting to his edict, Fermina had resourcefully brought home a parrot who could speak with a human voice and imitate any sound it heard. Her husband was defeated. He even grew fond of the bird. And when it escapes to the top of a mango tree on the day of Jeremiah de Saint-Amour's funeral, he goes after it, first cajoling it in several languages, which it repeats back to him, then summoning the fire department, who almost destroy the tree but fail to retrieve the bird, and finally scaling a precarious ladder and seizing the parrot by the neck just before the ladder slips and he falls. Lying fatally injured on the ground, he mutters with his last breath to Fermina, who is bending over him: "Only God knows how much I loved you." Silently she prays to God that her husband "not go without knowing how much she had loved him despite all their doubts, and she felt an irresistible longing to begin life with him over again so that they could say what they had left unsaid and do everything right that they had done badly in the past." That is how their marriage ends—with a love they had earned with effort and resilience, and had come to feel to the depths of their hearts.

Half a century is a long time to be married. Those years would change anyone. And as Fermina, at the age of seventy-two, says farewell to her husband with the promise, "We will see each other very soon," her story would seem to be over. She thinks it is. Then among the visitors paying respects to the distinguished doctor, there lingers until the end the peculiar personage of Florentino Ariza. Now a refined gentleman, if still a little odd in appearance (always wearing black), he had kindly volunteered to help to manage the flow of people at the doctor's wake, and when "the fugitive parrot" showed up, he had calmly apprehended it and carried it to the barn. Fermina had hardly recognized him at first. Now she wants to thank him for coming and for being so helpful. He speaks first.

But his words do not express condolence. Instead they repeat to her his youthful "vow of eternal and everlasting love."

Taken aback at this profession of romantic devotion "on her first night of widowhood," Fermina curses Florentino for his tasteless indiscretion and expels him from her house. He had misjudged her heart.

FLORENTINO HAD MISJUDGED Fermina's heart because during the fifty-one years of Fermina's marriage to Dr. Juvenal Urbino, Florentino Ariza had been only a shadow to her. But she had been the sun, moon, and stars to him.

In fact, Florentino's life from the day the fifteen-year old Fermina had first rejected him until he appears at her door over half a century later is a life that reveals not only the perdurable power of romantic love—or perhaps romantic obsession—but how a quixotic zeal to live for an ideal or a passion can give an invigorating meaning to everything we do. For Florentino Ariza lives for the hope that one day his passion will find a home in the heart of Fermina Daza, his Dulcinea, and that they will end their lives together. Inspired by this hope, he becomes a prominent businessman and respected citizen to be worthy of her—while also becoming a prodigious lover. He leads a peculiar bachelor's life, but aglow with love.

Here is how that peculiar, impassioned life evolves. When Florentino had first learned that Fermina was going to marry a distinguished and prosperous doctor not long after she had cast him aside, "he had lost his speech and appetite" and spent his nights "in constant weeping." Concerned for his health, his mother had tenderly cared for him, and when he recovered she had arranged through an uncle to get him a job as a telegraph operator in a village twenty days' journey up the river where he could start a new life and heal his broken heart. The journey did change his life, but not as his mother had intended.

In the first place, while on the boat Florentino is seduced by an unknown woman who literally snatches him into her cabin. She not only strips him of the virginity he had preserved so reverently for Fermina Daza, but she gives him "a revelation that he could not believe." This revelation showed him that his consuming love for Fermina Daza "could be replaced by an earthly passion." Or, if not replaced, his love for Fermina could at least be channeled into a substitute sexual pleasure. But the discovery also brings new pain. For it enflames Florentino's jealousy as he pictures Fermina's wedding and her honeymoon. He suddenly wishes she would fall dead in her wedding gown. Then, revising the wish, he fantasizes that someday she will "suffer one moment . . . when the phantom of the sweetheart she had scorned, humiliated, and insulted would appear in her thoughts, and all her happiness would be destroyed."

Before long, though, Florentino's angry resentments and tormenting fantasies give way to a new vision: he decides to return home and "never again would he abandon the city of Fermina Daza." His life as a solitary lover observing his beloved from a distance is about to begin.

But more hurt awaits him when he arrives home. He learns that the newlyweds have gone to Paris, where Dr. Urbino will practice medicine and they will remain for no one knows how long. To smother the disappointment, Florentino turns to the newfound pleasures of sex. He even becomes something of an artist at them. By the time he reenters Fermina's life a half-century later he has filled some twenty-five notebooks with accounts of 622 long-term sexual relationships, not including the occasional interludes that did not warrant mention. But in his heart he was always making love to Fermina Daza.

When Florentino sees Fermina again, as the happy couple returns from Paris two years after the wedding, she is worldly and pregnant. But instead of lapsing into another bout of dejected agony, this time Florentino resolves "to win fame and fortune in order to deserve her" once Dr. Urbino dies, which Florentino convinces himself will one day open the door for him. Florentino is willing to wait for this "ineluctable event" until "the end of time."

From that day forward, Florentino "was another person." Now "winning back Fermina Daza was the sole purpose of his life." And through his many sexual liaisons, and his successful professional career, he waits.

Leaving his job as a telegraph operator, and bent on rising to wealth and social prominence, Florentino secures a position in his uncle's River Company of the Caribbean. But the work does not come easily. Assigned the responsibility of preparing official documents, he finds that everything he writes expresses the passions of his heart. His "routine business letters had a lyrical spirit" and even "his bills of lading were rhymed . . . because the only convincing document he could write was a love letter." That wouldn't do in business, so he learns to discipline himself on the job. But he finds a suitable outlet for his epistolary skills. After each working day he goes to the Arcade of the Scribes to write letters for lovers who seek his expertise—two of these lovers even marry each other thanks to the letters he has written for each of them unknown to the other; and when they later discover this fact, they make Florentino godfather of their first child. Florentino's love letters accumulate to fill three volumes. And, like his many erotic affairs and the journals in which he records them, these letters all bespeak his "everlasting love" for Fermina Daza.

Over time Florentino manages to rise in the riverboat company, and he takes it over when his uncle retires. Meanwhile he watches Fermina wherever he can. Occasionally they meet briefly in society—and he has lunch once with Dr. Urbino, who knows nothing of Florentino's obsession, much less of Florentino's thoughts at the time, which are that for Florentino to be happy the doctor sitting across the table from him must die—but she treats him indifferently. Florentino excuses her indifference "with his infinite capacity for illusion," which leads him to believe she might be concealing her true feelings for him. In one flight of fancy, to be near Fermina he persuades a restaurateur to sell him a mirror in which Florentino had watched Fermina's reflection for two hours one evening while Fermina had dined in the restaurant across the room, and she had not even known that he was there.

As the years pass, Florentino also watches Fermina age—her hair graying, her eyes dimming, her steps faltering. He sees himself age, too. By his late fifties he has lost his teeth and most of his hair. And as intimations of morality bubble up, he begins to fear that death or the humiliations of his own decrepitude might take her from him. So he "faced the insidious snares of old age with savage temerity" and resolved "with fierce determination to be alive and in good health at the moment he would fulfill his destiny." Just as he had vowed to "win fame and fortune" to become worthy of Fermina, he now fought physical decline in order to be ready for the day when Dr. Juvenal Urbino would breathe no more.

Finally that day comes. As Florentino rides in a taxi with the adolescent girl for whom he has long served as guardian—and with whom he has nonetheless carried on an amorous affair—he learns from the driver that the bells he hears outside are tolling for a doctor who had died in a fall while chasing his parrot up a tree. Florentino's heart throbs, and he tells the driver to deliver the young girl to school, then head for Dr. Urbino's house. There, after the crowds have left, with a dauntless hope born of an undying passion, with a will strengthened over decades, and with a courage braced by knowing that his lifelong rival is dead at last, he repeats "his vow of eternal fidelity and everlasting love to Fermina Daza on the first night of her widowhood."

FERMINA REACTS to Florentino's renewed profession of love not just by throwing him out of the house, but by writing him a scathing letter. She wants to reproach him further for his act of insensitivity in the hour of her grief, when she had felt so bereft of the man who had shared her life. But grief and rage over Florentino's insensitivity are not all she feels as she writes the letter. Her response to Florentino's act had more complicated causes—and consequences. For Fermina had also heard in Florentino's words a dual affront that had nothing to do with the death of her husband.

In the first place, those words had shattered an expectation: Fermina had thought that, although only a shadow to her all of these years, Florentino had resented her for the hurt she had done him long ago, and that now he had perhaps come to her husband's wake as "an act of forgiving and forgetting." She had welcomed him with this expectation in mind. His shocking words had therefore struck her not as a genuine profession of love, but as an ironic expression of persistent bitterness. That angered her. And "the more she thought about him the angrier she became."

But Fermina had also heard something else in Florentino's words. And, although she says little about it, this was more poignant, and it cut deeper than the other affront. This is what she had heard: Florentino was deliberately trying to mock her sorrows by proclaiming an "everlasting love" for her "at an age when Florentino Ariza and she could expect nothing more from life." Fermina, at age seventy-two, had just lost her husband of fifty-one years. She felt that her life was over. Florentino had seemingly taunted her about that.

How wrong Fermina was on both scores. Florentino's profession of "everlasting love" contained neither bitterness over an old wound nor mockery over her age and loss. Florentino had simply stated a reality that Fermina could not understand. It was the reality that a love like Florentino's can last a lifetime. Far from reaching an age at which *they could expect no more from life*, Florentino wanted to prove to Fermina that because of this love, they both had much more to live for indeed.

Even though Florentino does not know the full range of Fermina's feelings when she throws him out and writes the insulting letter, he soon sets out to show her the truth of his feelings and how misplaced her anger is. But now he tries a new strategy.

Without mentioning "the terrible letter," Florentino writes Fermina a "meditation on life based on his ideas about, and experience of, relations between men and women." It is unlike anything he had written to her before—and written on a typewriter, lending it stature in those early days of the twentieth century when typewriters were still a novelty. For he wanted to pacify Fermina and yet "teach her to think of love as a state of grace: not the means to anything but the alpha and omega, an end in itself." That is what his love for her had become for him—the meaning of life itself. Many of us may love in this way, at least for a while, if we are lucky. But not many of us can live for this love so long.

Florentino receives no reply to his letter, but he takes consolation from not getting it back unopened, as he had feared would happen. So he writes another, and then another. Within weeks he is sending Fermina a new "meditation" every day. He continues to do this for a full year, still with no reply. Finally he concludes that Fermina had discarded all of the letters without opening them. But even this does not daunt him. It rather emboldens him to attend the anniversary memorial Mass for Dr. Juvenal Urbino in hopes of meeting Fermina and gauging her feelings. He gets his wish. And more.

When Fermina sees Florentino at the Mass, she approaches him, reaches our her hand, and "with a very sweet smile" says, "Thank you for coming." That is all she says to him. But it is more than Florentino had allowed himself to expect. Two days later he sends her another letter with a "simple paragraph of gratitude for the courtesy of her greeting."

Actually Fermina had been grateful to Florentino for more than attending the memorial service. She did not say so at that time, but she was also grateful for his letters. She had not only opened and read them, she had found in them reflections "on life, love, old age, death" by "a wise old man." And they "had helped her to recover her peace of mind," given her "serious and thoughtful reasons to go on living," and made it possible for her "to understand her own life and to await the designs of old age with serenity." Fermina felt that she owed Florentino for all of these things. Moved by this deeper gratitude, she had warmly thanked Florentino for coming to honor her husband, prompting him to thank her for her graciousness to him. A nice touch: Márquez has Florentino Ariza and Fermina Daza bring half a century of estrangement to a close with an exchange of gratitude.

We should see these expressions of gratitude as more than mere social conventions. For Florentino and Fermina had discovered the virtue, the wisdom, and the power of gratitude as an emotion. Neither Florentino nor Fermina makes an issue of it, and Márquez does not dwell on it. But their shared gratitude deserves notice. For no emotion, or attitude of mind, brings more equanimity to old age—and none brings more humanity to us at any age—than gratitude. It can be gratitude to our contemporaries for their kindnesses and for the lives they help us live. It can be gratitude to our forebears for their legacies and for the lives they made possible for us. It can be gratitude to life itself for the opportunities it offers us, for the rewards we can gain from it, and for the joys it yields. It can even be, as Fermina Daza and Dr. Juvenal Urbino had discovered on the threshold of old age, gratitude for victories over adversity. There is more wisdom in this last idea than in shelves of self-help books. To become conscious of and grateful for our victories over adversity, like Fermina and Dr. Urbino, is a high achievement. It gives us both a rich appreciation for the lives we have lived and a resilient confidence in the future. Parents who cultivate this gratitude in their children plant seeds of a strong character, a humane spirit, and a happy life. And anyone who learns this gratitude has gained a kind of success in life that eclipses many other kinds. This gratitude for victories over adversity—which Fermina surely felt toward Florentino for giving her "serious and thoughtful reasons to go on living" and for teaching her "to understand her own life and to await old-age with serenity," and which he felt toward Fermina for her unexpectedly gracious greeting—make *Love in the Time of the Cholera* in no small part a tale of this generous and humane emotion taking flight from a long, tempestuous marriage, from a lover's obsessive passion, and from a widow's sorrows. And these flights of gratitude hold a clue to both a serene old age and to a good life at any age.

Florentino brings his gratitude for Fermina's greeting with him as he knocks on the door to see his beloved alone for the first time in their entire lives. The visit is cut short, however, when, in a typical shot of Márquez' unpredictable realism, Florentino is gripped by the pangs of diarrhea and rushes home. But he returns another day. And now, sitting together, Florentino and Fermina see "each other for what they were: two old people, ambushed by death, who had nothing in common except the memory of an ephemeral past that was no longer theirs but belonged to two young people who had vanished and who could have been their grandchildren." Of course there is more in Florentino's heart than that. Still, their conversation goes rather awkwardly. Then, when Fermina gratefully tells Florentino that his letters "have helped me a great deal," he gets the confidence to ask if he can come again. Despite her wary reply that "I don't see what sense so many visits would make," he returns the next week, and every week. She begins to depend on his visits almost as much as he delights in them, if for different reasons. In time, her son and daughter-in-law join them regularly for games of cards. And at a private lunch with Florentino her son thanks him "for the good companionship" he has given Fermina "in the solitude of her widowhood." Florentino glows, thinking that one day soon he will ask this solicitous son for his mother's hand in marriage.

When an accident following that lunch lays Florentino up for two months with a broken ankle, he resorts to letters again. Missing his visits, Fermina replies, and they begin to use the familiar form of "you," *tu*. Then she gets "new reasons to be grateful to Florentino." For he writes a forceful letter to a scandal-mongering newspaper condemning its publication of two scurrilous articles about Fermina's father and her late husband. Those stories had been lies, but they had nonetheless wounded Fermina—particularly the report that her husband had had a fling with her best friend, one of the lies that she found herself believing. And Florentino's letter had consoled and heartened her.

Fermina suffers another emotional blow when her own daughter assails her for socializing with the "pervert" Florentino and sneers that love at her age is "revolting." But this attack brings Fermina "back to life." She banishes her daughter from the house for being so "insolent and evil-minded." Then she confides to her sympathetic daughter-in-law: "A half-century ago life screwed that poor man and me because we were too young, and now they want to do the same thing because we are too old." Insulted and fuming, she adds: "They can all go to hell." Shortly afterwards, she tells Florentino, "what I would like is to walk out of this house, and keep going, going, going, and never come back." Florentino jumps at the thought. "Take a boat," he says. And so she does.

On the deck of one of the boats belonging to Florentino's company, Fermina bids her son farewell as she embarks on the first riverboat cruise of her life—booked into the Presidential Suite that Florentino had constructed years earlier for public officials, but with the secret hope that it would "be the joyous refuge of his wedding trip with Fermina Daza." Surprised to discover that Florentino will be on the voyage too, Fermina's son could not help thinking, like his sister had earlier, that "there was an age at which love began to be indecent." But he holds his tongue. And the boat pulls away in the twilight.

It is to be an eight-day trip up the river and a five-day journey back. The first evening passes with Fermina and Florentino enjoying a ceremonial dinner with the captain, followed by music and dancing. Then, after Florentino escorts Fermina to her cabin, she invites him to join her on the private deck outside. They sit quietly. And in the soft light he could see "that she was crying in silence." He doesn't know why, and it is just as well. For she was "longing to understand . . . what she should do with the love that had been left behind without a master," her deceased husband, even if she does "not really know if it was love or not." Florentino politely asks if he should leave her alone, but she tells him to stay. Encouraged, he inched his hand toward hers "and found it waiting for him." These "hands made of old bones were not the hands" that these two old people "had imagined before touching." But "in the next moment . . . they were." Age has altered the young lovers, but it has not altogether robbed them of their youthful selves.

As Florentino leaves Fermina that night, he attempts to kiss her, but she turns away with the words, "Not now. I smell like an old woman." Yet she thinks of him through the night and prays "that Florentino Ariza would know how to begin again the next day." He is not a shadow to her now. Nor is he a sentimental romantic lover. He is, she reflects, "old and lame, but real." And she likes that.

When Florentino appears the next day, he is dressed for the first time ever in white clothes instead of black. She feels a "fiery blush," and they both get a twinge of embarrassment sensing that they are "behaving as if they were sweethearts." Later that night, on the public observation deck under a cloudy, moonless sky, "it was she who reached for his hand in the darkness." Florentino had not expected this. But "now it seemed to her that she knew him as well as if she had lived with him all her life." This night she lets him kiss her on the cheek, and, "with a profound trembling," on the lips. He feels a happiness "so intense it frightened him." But he also detects "the sour smell of old age" that they both emit—"the smell of human fermentation." Márquez does not idealize old age. He lets his aging lovers feel elation despite it, and, in their own way, because of it.

In the days that follow—some of them passing while the boat is delayed to await fuel wood from the largely depleted forests—the intimacy between Fermina and Florentino ripens. "They spent unimaginable hours holding hands in the armchairs by the railing, they exchanged unhurried kisses, they enjoyed the rapture of caresses without the pitfalls of impatience." Finally they decide to take the last step and make love, notwithstanding his flagging masculinity and her "decaying bones," "aging veins," and "flabby skin"—and her painful temporary loss of hearing in one ear during the voyage upriver. They approach this step with more seasoned hesitation and knowing amusement than erotic anticipation. They talk "of themselves, of their divergent lives," and "of the incredible coincidence of their lying naked in a dark cabin on a stranded boat when reason told them they had time only for death." Fermina is learning how wrong she had been on her first day of widowhood to think that they were "at an age when Florentino Ariza and she could expect nothing more from life."

Even when Florentino fails to respond sexually to her touch—"It's dead," he sighs—he does not give up. The next day they try again, but this time he gets too excited, hurried, and clumsy. It does not go well. And yet, "despite the disappointment that each of them felt," they are still amused, and "satisfied with the simple joy of being together." On subsequent nights they would make love more successfully, but it would hardly matter anymore.

It is in this mood of serene affection that Florentino and Fermina reach La Dorada, the last stop up river. And there, as the boat crew begins reloading cargo and passengers for the return voyage, Florentino gets an idea. "Would it be possible," he asks the captain, "to make a trip without stopping, without cargo or passengers, without coming into any port, without anything?" The captain replies that it would be possible without breaking contracts under one condition: hoist a yellow flag signaling cholera on board. "Let's do that," Florentino responds—an order that, as owner of the company, he has the authority to give. And so they head back down the river, the boat empty but for the crew and its two passengers, with "the yellow cholera flag waving jubilantly from the mainmast."

The river they have sailed up and are now sailing back down is not a thing of beauty. Its shores have been deforested by woodcutters to fuel riverboats like this one, and the landscape has been denuded of wildlife by hunters and by the loss of natural habitat. "The Great Magdelena River" is dying, Márquez writes, to be claimed by the sand and waste of a "ravaged land." Swollen corpses float past, victims of accidental drowning, not of the recurrent civil wars or epidemics, so the captain hastily explains, but without conviction. It is a surreal setting of desolation, where few living things can be seen.

One apparently living thing had caught Fermina's eye on the voyage up river. It was a woman in white standing on the shore beckoning the boat with a handkerchief. When the captain had refused to stop for her, Fermina had asked why and was told that the figure was only the "ghost of a drowned woman" attempting to lure the boat to destruction on the treacherous bank. As they had passed by, Fermina "saw her in sharp detail" and "had no doubt that she did not exist." The woman in white was real, but did not exist. This is the world that Márquez' characters inhabit—a world of "magic realism," which Márquez had discovered in his own grandmother's stories, mingling the mundane and the mystical, the commonplace and the bizarre with a matter-of-factness that defies common sense. Or it defies common sense unless, like Márquez' grandmother and many of his characters, you have seen many uncommon things, and you believe in a "holy spirit" that can work miracles and mysteries anywhere, making strangeness ordinary.

As they now sail on down the river under the cholera flag, the two lovers deepen their intimacy. "It was as if they had leapt over the arduous calvary of conjugal life and gone straight to the heart of love." For they "understood each other" with an ease of instinctive and uninhibited union. "She helped him take his enemas," she brushed his false teeth, she shared his spectacles, and "they made the tranquil, wholesome love of experienced grandparents." Possibly they sensed, Márquez says, that love "was more solid the closer it came to death." But it is not death that they have on their minds, or in their hearts. It is life.

Florentino starts playing the violin for her again, and Fermina dreams of taking other journeys with him, "mad voyages, free of trunks, free of social commitments: voyages of love." When they reach the port on the Caribbean that they had left about three weeks ago, "Fermina Daza felt in her blood the wild beating of her free will," and "neither of them felt capable of capitulating" to the journey's end. Good fortune comes to their rescue.

The port officials refuse to allow the boat to dock because of the cholera flag, and they insist that it depart the bay to wait outside for the formal quarantine and inspection. The captain curses. Florentino does not hesitate. "Let us keep going, going, going," he says (repeating Fermina's words that had prompted the voyage), "back to La Dorada." The captain balks. He stares at Florentino. And now he sees in him something he had not heeded before—Florentino's "intrepid love" and his "invincible power." Then the captain finds himself becoming "overwhelmed by the belated suspicion that it is life, more than death, that has no limits."

It is life, more than death, that has no limits—(es la vida, más que la muerte, la que no tiene límites). This idea, as a metaphor for overcoming adversity and affirming life, resonates throughout *Love in the Time of the Cholera* (quite unlike the aching futility that permeates, and the hopeless desolation that ends, *One Hundred Years of Solitude*). It sustains Florentino's passion. It takes Fermina Daza and Dr. Urbino through their long marriage. It overcomes Fermina's widowed desolation. It breathes energy and contented bliss into Florentino's and Fermina's old age. And it leads the story of Florentino Ariza and Fermina Daza to its unforgettable end.

"How long do you think we can keep up this goddamned coming and going?" the captain, still irked at their plight, asks Florentino. With Florentino's answer, Márquez brings the novel to a close. It is perhaps the most hauntingly romantic conclusion in literature:

"Florentino Ariza had kept his answer ready for fifty-three years, seven months, and eleven days and nights.

"'Forever,' he said."

Forever, he said. In fact, the words Márquez has Florentino say here are *toda la vida*—"my whole life," or "all of life," the same words his mother had spoken long ago when telling him that no consuming passion, such as he was suffering over his adolescent rejection by Fermina Daza, lasts *toda la vida*. Ignoring that allusion, the translator Emily Grossman nevertheless captures Florentino's élan with "Forever." We might even wish Márquez had used that term—*para siempre*. For we can imagine that Florentino thinks of his love as lasting not just his whole life, but forever. After all, Florentino's passion has given him, even at an age when most people expect no more of life, what the riverboat captain had seen in him as an intrepid love and invincible power revealing that *it is life, more than death, that has no limits*. William Wordsworth had dubbed such a power "a faith in life endless," born of an imagination that can transcend all limitations. To be sure, Florentino has a passion that transcends the ordinary life. That is his nature, and his blessing.

And here we see this passion, and Florentino's quixotic spirit, at their best. For they lead him to live intensely for an animating purpose and an infrangible ideal. Old age therefore becomes for him chiefly a troublesome physical condition that, if anything, strengthens his purpose and vivifies that ideal. How strikingly does Florentino's memorable affirmation of life in his old age at the end of the novel contrast with the suicide of Jeremiah de Saint-Amour from "Gerontophobia" that opens it. Florentino declares that he will go on happily traveling up and down the Magdelena river with his beloved for all of life, and maybe forever. He knows much better than Jeremiah de Saint-Amour how to pass across the threshold of old age, and how to live life with a Wordsworthian *faith in life endless*. He deserves a place in our hearts for that alone.

Not that Florentino Ariza is an altogether admirable character. Obsession takes a toll on him and many people around him. For one thing, "clouded by his passion for Fermina Daza," he had never bothered himself with the "alarming reports on the state of the river" caused in part by his own riverboats whose boilers were consuming the forests. Even when he travels amidst the desolation of the river and the landscape during his voyage with Fermina, he hardly notices it. He is too caught up in his bliss.

Florentino also betrays a cavalier disregard for the welfare of the adolescent girl, América Vicuña, for whom he serves as guardian and with whom he shamelessly engages in an erotic relationship, and from whom he withdraws his attentions as soon as Fermina becomes a widow, and who later commits suicide. After he learns of América's suicide while on the journey with Fermina, he weeps over "how much he had loved her." But that was not true love. True love he felt for only the one with whom he wants to sail up and down the river *toda la vida*.

Should we forgive Florentino for his negligence and irresponsibility because his love for Fermina Daza is so profound? Probably not. People who hurt those close to them, or the world at large, even if inadvertently, for the sake of a singular ideal or a passion, do not deserve our ready forgiveness. Still, let us not be too harsh on Florentino either. He has too much to offer us with his life-giving passion, his quixotic spirit, and his power to reveal that *it is life, more than death, that has no limits*.

THAT IS THE GENIUS of *Love in the Time of the Cholera*. Márquez gives us here an affirmation of the human will to live and love and find joy despite—and sometimes because of—the vicissitudes of life and depredations of old age. This affirmation echoes, in its way, much of the

Western humanistic tradition (and that of the rest of the world) beginning with Homer in the *Iliad*. For from the *Iliad* at the dawn of Western civilization to *Love in the Time of the Cholera* in the late twentieth century—and beyond—this tradition demonstrates one thing more compellingly than any other. It is this: how human beings can find inspiriting and ennobling meanings in our lives in this world if we have the imagination and the will and the passion to do it, whatever tragedies and sorrows and losses we suffer. The *Iliad* shows this through the valiant and also tender humanity that human beings wrested from an ancient world of capricious gods, inexorable fate, and tragic war. *Love in the Time of the Cholera* shows it through a human gratitude for victories over adversity, and through a kind of passion that can keep us jubilantly burning with a hard, gemlike flame our whole lives, *toda la vida*, to the end, and possibly *forever*. There is worldly wisdom in all of this, from beginning to end.

On Passion, Marriage, and Aging

1. To live for an enduring passion can give meaning to life—to the very end.

2. We should never let ourselves believe that we have reached an age when we can expect no more from life.

3. We can create love from marriage as much as we create marriage from love.

4. The banalities of married life can threaten marriage more than can catastrophes.

5. All happy marriages are different; all unhappy marriages are alike.

6. Happy marriages differ because each one adapts in its own way to the varieties of human personalities and to the conflicts these varieties can cause; unhappy marriages are alike because they all succumb to the conflicts that the varieties of human personalities can cause.

7. We should have gratitude for our victories over adversity, as well as for life's benefactions.

8. Gratitude is a necessary virtue for living well.

9. We should approach old age with humor, gratitude, and an enduring passion.

10. An enduring passion can show us that *it is life, more than death, that has no limits.*

11. The meaning of life is to adapt to life's surprises, have gratitude for victories over adversity, and live with a passion to the very end—and possibly forever.

Notes

The Notes identify the sources of quotations in *Worldly Wisdom* (except for a few incidental quotations). They cite these sources by page number, unless otherwise indicated in the first citation of a source. Generally, the Notes give the opening words of a quotation, followed by that quotation's location in its source. However, where several quotations appear sequentially in one or more sentences or paragraphs—sometimes extending across pages—and come from a single location in a source uninterrupted by quotations from anywhere else, the Notes give only the opening words of the first quotation. Therefore, if a quotation in the text does not appear in the Notes, its source and location are those of the nearest quotation previously cited (unless, as occasionally happens, it is a quotation that appeared earlier). And where a note gives no title for the source of a quotation, that title is the nearest one previously cited. The Selected Bibliography gives full bibliographic references for the primary works (and a few others) discussed in the text.

Preface

Page

xiv "knowledge of how," Michel de Montaigne, "Of Experience," *The Complete Essays*, 852.

xv "the uses and ends," Montaigne, "Of the Education of Children," Ibid., 117; "Have you been able," Montaigne, "Of Experience," Ibid., 850.

xvi "Have you read Voltaire?" Honoré de Balzac, *Lost Illusions*, trans. Herbert J. Hunt (New York: Penguin Books, 1971), 654; "terrible simplifiers" [*terrible simplificateurs*], quoted in James Hastings Nichols, "Jacob Burckhardt," in Jacob Burckhardt, *Force and Freedom: Reflections on History*, ed. James Hastings Nichols (Boston: Beacon Press, 1964), 43.

Chapter 1

4 "the tragic sense of life," Miguel de Unamuno, *The Tragic Sense of Life* [*Del Sentimento trágico de la vida en los hombres y en los pueblos* (1913)], trans. J. Crawford Flitch (New York: Curier Dover Publications, 1954).

6 Quotations come primarily from *The Iliad of Homer*, trans. Richmond Lattimore, cited as L by book and page number, but a few come from *The Iliad*, trans. Robert Fagels, cited as F by book and page number. "As a heavy surf," F: IV, 159; "the screaming and the shouts," L: IV, 124–25, *passim*; "as when an oak," L: XVI,

343; "thunderously," L: IV, 126; "screaming a terrible cry," L: XVI, 351; "swept about his powerful shoulders," L: XVIII, 380–81.

7 "Sing, goddess," L: I, 59; "anger came on," L: I, 64; "blazing with anger," F: I, 81; "angered in his heart," L: I, 60; "weeping went and sat," L: I, 68.

8 "Bent on outrage," F: XXII, 554; "the heart within," L: I, 62; "the delusion of Paris," L: XXIV, 476; "Paris in all his madness," F: XXIV, 589; "hatred for sacred Ilion," L: XXIV, 476; "the anger of Hera," L: V, 152.

9 "Father Zeus," L: V, 151; "the most hateful of all gods," L: V, 152; "I wish that strife," L: XVIII, 378.

10 "an urn of evils," L: XXIV, 489; "You are only my third slayer," L: XVI, 353; "knew the truth," L: XXII, 443; "Die: and I will take my death," L: XXII, 445; "It is decreed," L: XVIII, 377; "As for fate," L: VI, 166; "Among all creatures," L: XVII, 366.

11 "Such is the way," L: XXIV, 489; "In the house of Hades," L: XXIII, 453.

12 "is destined," L: XVI, 342.

13 "The father balanced," L: VIII, 184; "one for Achilleus," L: XXII, 440; "death day was heaviest," L: VIII, 184; "Hector's death-day," L: XXII, 440–41.

14 "his priest whom Agamemnon," L: I, 61; "a new prize," L: I, 62; "Agamemnon has dishonored," L: I, 68. Greek definitions come from *A Lexicon*, Abridged from Liddell and Scott's *Greek-English Lexicon* (Oxford: Oxford University Press, 1963).

15 "worthy of honor . . . ," Aristotle, *Ethics*, IV, iii, 154–55.

16 "Let me at least," L: XXII, 443; "Achilleus delighting his heart," L: IX, 203.

17 "The black cloud," L: XVIII, 375–77 *passim*; "wept still as he remembered," L: XXIV, 475; "We will let all this," L: XVIII, 378; "held out his arms," L: VI, 165–66 *passim*.

18 "I wish only," L: XXII, 444; "In the words," L: XXIV, 488–93 *passim*.

19 "whoever begs," F: XXIV, 594; "the sands . . . and their armour," L: XXIII, 450–57 *passim*.

20 "sweet sleep," L: XXIV, 475; "Singers chanted," L: XXIV, 494–96 *passim*.

21 "two cities of mortal men," L: XVIII, 388–89 *passim*; "a prize for the judge," F: XVIII, 484; "I wish that strife," L:XVIII, 378.

Chapter 2

27 Quotations from the *Bhagavad-Gita* come from *The Song of God: Bhagavad-Gita*, trans. Swami Prabhavananda and Christopher Isherwood, cited as PI by chapter and page number, and from *The Bhagavad-Gita*, trans. S. Radhakrishnan, in *Sourcebook in Indian Philosophy*, cited as R by chapter and paragraph number. "My face is everywhere," PI: X, 90; "Nothing animate," PI: X, 89–90 *passim*; "I am the syllable," PI: X, 89; "absolute knowledge," PI: IX, 82.

28 "When the mind," R: 2, #67; "for the uncontrolled," R: 2, #66.

29 "withdraw all their senses," PI: IV, 53; "practice breathing," PI: IV, 54; "Shutting off sense," PI: V, 61; "Others mortify the flesh," PI: IV, 53–54 *passim*; "steady concentration," PI: VIII, 76; "The sage who has controlled," R: V, #27–28; "free from attachment," PI: XII, 99; "a man of disciplined mind," R: II, #64; "this is the divine state," R: II, #72.

31 "any ascetic," "The Sermon at Benares," in *The Teachings of the Compassionate Buddha*, 32; "Our life is the creation," *The Dhammapada: The Path to Perfection* (cited by chapter and section number), I, #1.

32 "The mind is fickle," III, #35; "impure mind," I, #1; "pure mind," I, #2; "good is the control of the mind," XXV, #361; "This mind of mine," XXIII, #326.

33 "the four great truths," XIV, #190; "The followers of Buddha," XXI, #297; "Find joy in watchfulness," XXIII, #327; "the wise man," II, #28; "Those who in high thought," II, #23.

34 "Neither nakedness," X, #141; "master of yourself," XXV, #380; "free from whatever may darken," VI, #88; "Even his manner," Yoshida Kenkō, *Essays in Idleness*, section 137; "Although a man," *Dhammapada*, X, #142; "he whose mind is well-trained," VI, #89.

35 "self-control, calmness of mind," Emperor Ashoka, "The Edicts," in *World of the Buddha*, 239.

36 "When both myself and others," Acharaya Shantideva, *A Guide to the Bodhisattva's Way of Life* (cited by chapter and section number), III, #96; "Hence I should dispel," III, #94; "This intention," I, #25; "If we never let our mind," *The Sutra of Hui-Neng*, in *The Diamond Sutra and the Sutra of Hui-Neng*, 96.

37 "Truth is uncontainable," *The Diamond Sutra*, in Ibid., 24; "We should get rid of pairs," *Hui-Neng*, 97; "A bodhisattva," *Diamond*, 28; "the mind should be kept," *Diamond*, 33; "idea-lessness," *Hui-Neng*, 96; "nothing is knowable," *Hui-Neng*, 118; "Free from the idea," *Diamond*, 32; "are merely figures," *Diamond*, 52; "All things—good or bad," *Hui-Neng*, 96; "in all things," *Hui-Neng*, 146.

38 "this world as a bubble," *Dhammapada*, XIII, #170; "Thus shall ye think," *Diamond*, 53; "preoccupation with worldly desires," Kenkō, section 7; "Better than a thousand," *Dhammapada*, VIII, #100–102.

39 "Hard by the forest," Buddhist teacher in Horst Hammitzsch, *Zen in the Art of the Tea Ceremony*, trans. Peter Lemesurier (New York: E. P. Dutton, 1988), 49; "When you're both alive," Bunan poem in *World of the Buddha*, 355.

Chapter 3

43 "new gods," Plato, *The Last Days of Socrates* [*Euthyphro, Apology, Crito, Phaedo*], trans. Hugh Tredennick, rev. ed. (cited by individual work and/or page number), *Euthyphro*, 20. For Greek words I have consulted the bilingual edition Plato, *Euthyphro, Apology, Crito,* and *Phaedo*, trans. Harold North Fowler.

44 "Do you really believe," *Euthyphro*, 23; "Tell me that my beliefs," 24; "describe the actual feature," 26.

45 "they all love," 31; "because it is pious," 32.

46 "Whatever we put forward," 33; "because it is pious," 32; "make a fresh start," 33; "I myself will help you," 34; "tendance," 36; "service to the gods," 37; "sacrifice and prayer," 39; "honor and esteem," 40; "is pleasing to the gods," 38–39; "Don't you see," 40–41; "I am a passionate admirer," 39; "if you didn't know," 41.

47 "an urgent engagement," 41; "the unexamined life" (see p. 50 in text); "independent thinking," *Apology*, 23; "guilty of corrupting," 54.

48 "he inquires into things," 47; "skillful speakers," 45; "try to educate," 48; "I do not think," 50; "private mission," 65; "stinging fly," 63.

49 "I do this intentionally," 56; "I set myself," 70; "to persuade each one," 60.

50 "let no day pass," 71–72; "I spend all my time," 62; "long as I draw breath," 61; "What do I deserve," 70; "To be afraid," 60.

51 "all the dead," 75; "It is still not too late," *Crito*, 81; "you profess to have made," 83; "some opinions," 84.

52 "expert knowledge," 85; "the part of us," 86; "the really important thing," 87;

"Do we say," 88.

53 "It should be our first care," Plato, *Republic*, X, 618c, 452; "lies not with God," Ibid., X, 617e, 452.

54 "One must not even," *Crito*, 88; "continue to exist," 90; "with suspicion," 94.

55 "so loudly in my head," 96; "It seems to me," 107; "the release of the soul," 108.

56 "true philosophers," 113; "real nature of any given thing," 110.

57 "The body is most like," *Phaedo*, 132; "if we are ever," 111; "takes nothing with it," 170.

58 "no reasonable man," 178; "it makes no difference," Plato, *Republic*, IX, 592b, 420; "sing more loudly and sweetly," *Phaedo*, 138; "Crito, we ought to offer," 183.

Chapter 4

62 Quotations come primarily from Aristotle, *Ethics*, trans. J. A. K. Thompson, rev. Hugh Tredennick, cited by book, section, and page number, but a few come from Aristotle, *Ethics*, trans. H. Rackman, rev. ed., cited by translator's name, book, section, and page number. "prudence," VI, v, 209; "we must be satisfied," I, iii, 64; "the subject matter," I, iii, 65; "we are studying," II, ii, 93; "practical aim," Rackman, II, ii, 75.

63 "The Good," I, i, 63; "the highest of all," I, iv, 66.

64 "when it comes," I, iv, 66; "what is known to us," I, iv, 67; "in medicine is health," I, vii, 73; "Any kind of excellence," II, vi, 99.

65 "The excellence of a horse," II, vi, 99–100; "human excellence," II, vi, 100; "function of human beings," I, vii, 75; "activity of the soul," I, vii, 75; "implying a rational principle," I, vii, 76; "life is a form," X, iv, 322; "our virtues," II, v, 99; "in accordance with its proper excellence," I, vii, 76.

66 "supreme good," I, i, 63; "knows what he is doing," II, iv, 97; "Anything that we have to learn," II, i, 91; "we wish to be healthy," III, i, 116; "invalids who listen," II, iv, 98; "Our characters are determined," III, ii, 117.

67 "moral virtues," II, i, 91; "slight modification," II, i, 91 (Hugh Tredennick discusses the relations among these the Greek words on pages 27, 91n., 92n.); "It is a matter," II, i, 92; "Could the young," William James, *Principles of Psychology*, Authorized edition (New York: Dover Publications, 1950 [1890]), vol. I, Ch. IV, 127.

68 "lack of exercise," III, v, 124; "for in matters," X, i, 312; "(a) external," I, viii, 78; "good birth," Aristotle, *Rhetoric*, Book I, Ch. 5, p. 1340.

69 "A man is scarcely happy," *Ethics*, I, viii, 80; "Our definition seems to include," I, viii, 78; "exercise and care," III, v, 124; "pleasure is very closely bound," X, i, 312; "pleasure perfects the activities," X, vi, 321; "closely connected," X, vi, 322.

70 "Pleasant amusements," X, vi, 326; "Amusement," X, vi, 327; "taking a nap," Aristotle, *The Politics* (cited by book, section, and page number), VIII, v, 463; "it would be paradoxical," *Ethics*, X, vi, 327; "are destroyed by excess," II, ii, 94.

71 "Both excessive and insufficient exercise," II, ii, 94; "Temperance," II, vii, 103–06 *passim.*

72 "Every knowledgeable person," II, vi, 100; "What is possible," *Politics*, VIII, vii, 475; "the happy man," VIII, vii, 476; "failure is possible," *Ethics*, II, vi, 101.

73 "greatness of soul," IV, iii, 153; "claims much," Rackman, IV, iii, 215; "extreme as regards the greatness," IV, iii, 154; "his gait is measured," IV, iii, 158; "self-love," IX, vii, 301; "It is right," IX, viii, 302; "what makes existence desirable," IX, viii, 306; "because it is beneath," IV, iii, 157.

74 "happiness . . . is found," I, vii, 74; "naturally constituted," IX, ix, 304; "to fulfill our own lives," IX, ix, 307; "The happy man needs friends," IX, ix, 304; "not only a necessary thing," VIII, i, 259; "A friend," IX, iv, 294; "become better . . . ," IX, xii, 311; "good men and friends," VIII, i, 259; "friendship also seems," VIII, i, 258.

75 "Assuming that we have," X, ix, 335; "the best system," X, ix, 342; "the art of politics," X, ix, 341; "what is good," I, ii, 64; "the blessed life," *The Politics*, VIII, iii, 456.

Chapter 5

80 Quotations come primarily from Dante Alighieri, *Inferno*, trans. Robert and Jean Hollander, bilingual edition, cited by canto and page number, but a few come from *The Divine Comedy: Hell*, trans. Dorothy L. Sayers—whose notes are particularly suggestive for Dante's allegories—cited by the translator's name, canto, and page number. "Abandon all hope," III, 47; "Midway in this journey," I, 3.

81 "through an eternal place," I, 9; "lost the good of intellect," III, 47; "truth is the good," Sayers, III, 90n.

82 "Let us not speak," III, 49; "Among these," IV, 69; "the master of those who know," IV, 75; "the sound of sighing," Sayers, IV, 92.

83 "incontinence offends God," XI, 209; "More than once," V, 99.

84 "Love," V, 97; "For pity," V, 99; "Why hold so tight?" VII, 133; "the fair world," VII, 135; "more piteous," Sayers, VII, 113; "sullen in the sweet air," VII, 139.

86 "gambles away," XI, 207.

87 "hold God in disdain," XIV, 263.

88 "art" (Sayers' translation: "Art and Nature"), Sayers, XII, 136–37 *passim*; "bread and prosper," XI, 211.

89 "the vice of fraud," XI, 205; "severs the bonds," XI, 207; "special kind of trust," XI, 209.

90 "horned demons, XVIII, 331; "fancy [or polished] words," XVIII, 335.

91 "magic tricks," XX, 367; "because he aspired," XX, 363.

92 "gilded and dazzling," XXIII, 423.

93 "the stratagem of the horse," XXVI, 481; "could overcome the fervor," XXVI, 483– 85 *passim*; "a con artist," Hollander, Notes, 493.

94 "sowed scandal," XXVIII, 517; "Sowers of Discord," Sayers, XXVIII, 246.

95 "the lying Greek," XXX, 555–57 *passim*.

96 "vile traitor," XXXII, 593; "Extend your hand," XXXIII, 615.

98 "Emperor of the woeful kingdom," XXXIV, 629.

Chapter 6

101 "I have received," Voltaire, Letter to Jean-Jacques Rousseau, August 30, 1755, in *The Portable Voltaire*, 493.

102 Quotations come primarily from Jean-Jacques Rousseau, *Emile*, trans. Barbara Foxley, but a few come from *Emile, or On Education*, trans. Allan Bloom. The Foxley translation is more vivid, but since the Bloom translation is more literal I cite locations of all quotations in both translations, identified as F and B, by page number. "God makes all things good," F: 5; "Everything is good," B: 37.

103 "I call nature," F: 7/B: 39; "Man's first state," F: 37/B: 65; "natural man," F: 7/B: 39; "an imaginary pupil," F: 18/B: 50.

104 "harmony with these," F: 7/B: 40; "When I want to train," F: 217/B: 255; "Emile is no savage," F: 167/B: 208; "We begin to learn," F: 9/B: 42; "is forged the first link," F: 32/B: 65.

105 "The child's first tears," F: 33/B: 66; "can think of people," F: 34/B: 68; "is flung upon the world," F: 16/B: 48.

106 "By imposing on," F: 55/B: 91.

107 "what does it all," F: 55/B: 91; "All wickedness," F: 33/B: 67; "Attracted by self-ishness," F: 54/B: 90.

108 "Do not try," F: 58/B: 94; "Foolish teachers," F: 56/B: 92; "The apparent ease," F: 71/B: 107; "With every piece," F: 56/B: 92; "What is the use," F: 142/B: 179; "present interest," F: 81/B: 117.

109 "I hate books!" F: 147/B: 184; "reading is the curse," F: 80/B: 116.

110 "man's natural curiosity," F: 130/B: 167; "Self-love," F: 173/B: 212; "concerns itself only," F: 174/B: 213.

111 "the first feeling," F: 197/B: 235; "the help and attention," F: 174/B: 213; "Selfishness, which is always comparing," F: 174–75/B: 214; "The man of the world," F: 191/B: 230.

112 "It's human nature," *Wall Street Journal*, July 10, 1998, p. 1; "to know how to live," F: 16/B: 48; "That man is truly free," F: 48/B: 84; "enjoy our whole being," F: 44/B: 80; "Society has enfeebled," F: 48/B: 84.

113 "are dependent," F: 47/B: 83; "Do you know," F: 51/B: 87; "As they cannot do," F: 52/B: 88; "true happiness," F: 44/B: 80.

114 "discriminate between those desires," F: 35/B: 68; "Let there be no comparison," F: 146/B: 184; "Oh man," F: 47/B: 83.

115 "Let [them] know that man," F: 198/B: 237; "Such is man," F: 56/B: 92; "external causes" F: 199/B: 237; "passions and prejudices," F: 217/B: 255; "specious appearance," F: 198/B: 236; "what forces move [people]," F: 212/B: 249; "by nature, men are neither," F: 183/B: 222.

116 "Man's weakness makes him sociable," F: 182/B: 221.

117 "Rich or poor," F: 436/B: 472; "Give me my Sophy," F: 437/B: 473.

118 "to fight against himself," F: 437/B: 473.

119 "I am showing," F: 59/B: 95.

Chapter 7

123 Quotations come from Johann von Goethe, *Goethe's Faust*, trans. Walter Kaufmann, bilingual edition, cited by part, scene title, and page number. Because Part I is divided into scenes, not acts, and quotations from Part II all come from Act V, no act numbers are given; the two scenes entitled "Study" are distinguished as (1) and (2). "For all our science and art," I, Night, 93; "secret," I, Night, 95.

124 "mysterious potency," I, Night, 99; "your peer," I, Night, 103; "Not yours?" I, Night, 105; "I am not like the gods!" I, Night, 111–113 *passim*; "You must renounce!" I, Study (2) 175; "had tears to drown," I, Study (2), 175.

125 "Deep in the heart," I, Night, 113; "sneaks . . . in," II, Midnight, 455; "In all forms," II, Midnight, 457; "I wield," II, Midnight, 459; "you persecute," II, Midnight, 461.

126 "It is inborn," I, Before the City Gate, 143; "the god who dwells," I, Study (2), 175; "two souls," I, Before the City Gate, 145; "I now curse all," I, Study (2), 177–79.

127 "existence is . . . ," I, Study (2), 175; "tear open the eternal portals," I, Night, 117; "I am the spirit" I, Study (1), 161.

128 "Man errs so long," Prologue in Heaven, 87; "dark urge," Prologue in Heaven, 89; "In the beginning," I, Study (1), 153.

129 "What will you bet?" Prologue in Heaven, 87; "Man's activity," Prologue in Heaven, 89.

130 "What would you," I, Study (2), 183; "You are welcome," I, Study (2), 189; "the time comes," I, Study (2), 183; "Do you not hear?" I, Study (2), 189; "Plunge into time's whirl," I, Study (2), 187; "I grow stagnant," I, Study (2), 185; "cured from the craving," I, Study (2), 189; "passions drink," I, Study (2), 187.

131 "Show me the fruit," I, Study (2), 183; "restless activity," I, Study (2), 187; "worthy," Johann Wolfgang von Goethe, *The Sorrows of Young Werther and Selected Writings*, trans. Catherine Hutter (New York: New American Library, 1962), 30.

132 "Which is better?" Fyodor Dostoevsky, *Notes from Underground*, 128; "stormed through life," *Faust*, II, Midnight, 459; "My realm is endless," II, Palace, 439; "that are not mine," II, Palace, 445; "inside me there shines," II, Midnight, 463; "many millions," II, Large Outer Court of the Palace, 467–69 *passim*.

133 "Why have eternal," II, Large Outer Court of the Palace, 471.

134 "the traces of my earthly days," II, Large Outer Court of the Palace, 469; "Whoever strives," II, Mountain Gorges, Forest, Rock, and Desert, 493; "What is passing," II, Mountain Gorges, Forest, Rock, and Desert, 503.

Chapter 8

137 "People like my sister," quoted in H. F. Peters, *Zarathustra's Sister: The Case of Elisabeth and Friedrich Nietzsche* (New York: Crown Publishers, 1976), 82; "almost the opposite," Friedrich Nietzsche, letter to Elisabeth Nietzsche, December, 1888, in *Selected Letters of Friedrich Nietzsche*, 339; "entire philosophy," quoted in Peters, 82.

138 "to philosophize," Friedrich Nietzsche, *Ecce Homo*, in *On the Genealogy of Morals* [and] *Ecce Homo*, page following Preface; "I am challenging," Friedrich Nietzsche, letter to Elisabeth Nietzsche, December, 1888, *Selected Letters*, 340; "I hold, quite literally," Ibid., 339; "Our ideas, our values," Friedrich Nietzsche, *On the Genealogy of Morals*, in *On the Genealogy of Morals* [and] *Ecce Homo* (cited as GM by preface or part and section number), GM, Preface, #2.

139 "What really was that," GM, Preface, #1; "There are no moral phenomena," Friedrich Nietzsche, *Beyond Good and Evil* (cited as BGE by section number), BGE, #108; "the reverse were true?" GM, Preface, #6.

140 "a powerful physicality," GM, I, #7; "It was on the soil," GM, I, #6; "develops from a triumphant affirmation," GM, I, #10.

141 "there is a soft," GM, I, #14; "According to master morality," BGE, #260; "different from the evil," GM, I, #13.

142 "The slave revolt," GM, I, #10.

143 "I suffer," GM, III, #15; "the Evil One," GM, I, #10; "Whoever is dissatisfied," Friedrich Nietzsche, *The Gay Science*, in *The Portable Nietzsche* (cited as GS by section number), GS, #290; "the sublime self-deception," GM, I, #13; "A real lie," GM, III, #19.

144 "the man of *ressentiment*," GM, I, #10; "active forgetfulness," GM, II, #1.

145 "the right to make promises," GM, II, #1–#2 *passim*; "the institution of law,"

GM, II, #11; "artists of violence," GM, II, #18; "piece of perfection," GM, II, #11.

146 *mercy,* GM, II, #10; "everything that dominates," GM, II, #12; "misarchism," GM, II, #12; "What gives greater offense," GM, II, #24; "morality of the common man," GM, I, #9.

147 "a bold recklessness," GM, I, #10; "indifference to and contempt for," GM, I, #11; "there is indeed too much," GM, I, #10; "this is how things are," GM, I, #12.

148 "Who would not a hundred times," GM, I, #11; "Here precisely is what," GM, I, #12.

149 "all signs that a more manly," GS, #283; "the beast of prey," GM, I, #11; "the great nausea," GM, II, #24; "Grant me the sight," GM, I, #12; "severity and respect," GM, II, #24; "One thing is needful," GS, #290.

150 "One must have chaos," Friedrich Nietzsche, *Thus Spoke Zarathustra,* in *The Portable Nietzsche* (cited as Z by book or section title and section number), Z, Prologue, #5; "This secret self-ravishment," GM, II, #18; "imaginative phenomena," GM, II, #18; "a bridge," GM, II, #16; "maggot man," GM, I, #11; "Superman," Z, IV, #13, subsection 2 (Walter Kaufman translates *Übermensch* as "Overman" rather than "Superman," but that seems too literal); "preparatory," GS, #283; "higher men," Z, IV, #13, subsection 2; "characterized by cheerfulness," GS, #283; "possessed of keen and free judgment," GS, #283; "The Higher Man," Z, IV, #131; "The secret of the greatest fruitfulness," GS, #283.

151 "A human being," GS, #290.

Chapter 9

154 "anti-hero," *Notes from Underground,* 129.

155 "rational self-interest" (or "reason and profit"), Ibid., 25; "piano key," Ibid., 24, 31.

156 "the most evil of heretics," Fyodor Dostoevsky, "The Grand Inquisitor," in *The Brothers Karamazov.* "The Grand Inquisitor" constitutes Chapter 5 of Part II, Book Five, pp. 246–64 of this novel; because all quotations here come from pages 252–62, no individual page numbers are cited.

161 "condemned to be free," Jean-Paul Sartre, "Existentialism," 23.

162 "human nature," 38; "thrown into the world," 23; "universal human condition," 38.

163 "the first principle," 15; "you are nothing else," 33; "we are alone," 23; "rejects the hypothesis," Jean-Paul Sartre, "Existential Psychoanalysis," from *Being and Nothingness,* trans. Hazel Barnes, in *Existentialism and Human Emotions,* 72; "recognizes nothing *before,*" "Existential Psychoanalysis," 70; "The existentialist does not believe," "Existentialism," 23.

164 "Choice always remains," 44.

165 "What art and ethics," 43; "You are free," 28; "want but one thing," 45; "may choose anything," 48; "man is nothing else," 15; "responsible for everything," 23.

166 "determinism," 45; "existentialism's first move," 16; "When we say," 16; "in creating the man," 17; "existence precedes essence," 15; "In choosing myself," 18; "for every man," 20.

167 "His fate belongs," Albert Camus, "The Myth of Sisyphus," in Albert Camus, *The Myth of Sisyphus and Other Essays,* 91; "optimistic . . . doctrine," "Existentialism," 51; "there is no doctrine," 35; "you are nothing else," 33; "action is the

only thing," 36; "You are free," 28; "There is no universe," 50; "before you come alive," 49.

168 "man's destiny is in himself," 36; "things will be," 31; "man makes himself," 43; "will fulfill himself," 51; "human universe," 50; "existentialist humanism," 51.

Chapter 10

176 "There is nothing I can do," Confucius, *The Analects (Lun yü)*, trans. D. C. Lau, (cited as A by book and section number), A, XV, #16.

177 "Men are close," A, XVII, #2; "Those who wished," *The Great Learning*. Because the entire text of *The Great Learning* appears on pages 86–87 of *Sourcebook in Chinese Philosophy*, no individual page numbers are cited here; but quotations from the commentary by Chu Hsi that follows the text are cited as TGL/CH by page number.

178 "When equilibrium and harmony," *The Doctrine of the Mean* (cited as DM by section and page number), DM, #1, 98; "once the roots are established," A, I, #2; "He cultivates himself," A, XIV, #42; "Devote yourself to learning," A, VIII, #13.

179 "the principles of all things," TGL/CH, 89; "Learn without flagging," A, VII, #2; "When there is anything," DM, #20, 107; "To love benevolence," A, XVII, #8; "when one is affected," TGL/CH, 90.

181 "To think how," DM, #20, 107; "only those who are absolutely sincere," DM, #22, 107; "There is no greater joy," *Mencius* (cited as M by book, part, and section number), M, VII, A-6; "sincerity means the completion," DM, #25, 108; "It is due to our nature," DM, #21, 107; "Shall I tell you," A, II, #17; "always be watchful," TGL/CH, 89.

182 "The intelligent mind," TGL/CH, 89; "Fraud," Voltaire, *Dictionaire philosophique*, 243–45.

183 On "goodness" (*jen*) and "superior person" (*chün-tzu*), see Arthur Waley, Introduction to *The Analects of Confucius*, 27–29, 34–38.

184 "It is these things," A, VII, #3; "the gentleman," A, XV, #19; "superior men have got hold," A, XIX, #22; "gentleman" is "easy of mind," A, VII, #37; "what the gentleman seeks," A, XV, #21; "the gentleman is at ease," A, XIII, #26; "Make it your guiding principle," A, XII, #10; "Do not impose," A, XV, #24; "Not to enter public life," A, XVIII, #7; "the proper regulation of old," A, XVIII, #7.

185 "What the gentleman," M, VII, B-32; "in administering," A, XII, #19; "Rule over them," A, II, #20; "when the prince is benevolent," M, IV, B-5.

186 "with a long body," *Chuang Tzu, Basic Writings* (cited as CT by title of essay and page number), CT/"Eternal Things," 135; "Get rid of your proud bearing," Ibid., 134; "Can the Way," CT/"Great and Venerable Teacher," 78. Quotations from *Tao Te Ching* come from [Lao Tzu] *Tao Te Ching*, trans. Arthur Waley, *The Way and Its Power: A Study of the Tao Te Ching and Its Place in Chinese Thought*, cited as TTC-W by section number, and from Lao Tzu, *The Way of Life. A New Translation of the Tao Te Ching*, trans. R. B. Blakney, cited as TTC-B by section number. "If one looks for Tao," TTC-W, #35.

187 "The Way has its reality," CT/"Great and Venerable Teacher," 77; "The Way itself," TTC-B, #21; "Suppose I try saying," CT/"Discussion on Making All Things Equal" (cited as "Discussion"), 41; "there must be some distinction," 45; "a man . . . has no way," A, XX, #3; "The way I see it," CT/"Discussion," 41; "If right were really right," 44; "The stupid believe," 43; "Perception and under-

standing," CT/"Secret of Caring for Life," 46–47.

188 "Forget distinctions," CT/"Discussion," 44; "Touch ultimate emptiness," TTC-B, #16; "The world may be known," TTC-B, #47; "just let things be," CT/"Sign of Complete Virtue," 72; "Cultivate the Way yourself," TTC-B, #54; "So long as I do nothing," TTC-W, #57.

189 "a good swimmer," CT/"Mastering Life," 121.

Chapter 11

193 Quotations come primarily from Niccolò Machiavelli, *The Prince*, trans. George Bull, cited by chapter and page number, but a few come from *The Prince*, trans. Luigi Ricci, rev. E. R. Vincent, cited by translator's name, chapter, and page number. "things as they are," XV, 90; "the gulf between," XV, 91.

195 "All the states," I, 33.

197 "Machiavelli's teaching," Leo Strauss, *Thoughts on Machiavellli* (Seattle: University of Washington Press, 1969 [1958]), 12; "The Machiavellian principle," 14.

198 "One can make this generalization," XVII, 96; "the qualities of a ferocious lion," XIX, 110; "I know no better precepts," VII, 55; "Men must be either pampered," III, 37–38.

199 "The wish to acquire," III, 42; "Whoever is responsible," III, 44; "One can be hated," XIX, 108; "The bond of love," XVII, 96–97; "use persuasion," VI, 52; "This is why," VI, 52.

200 "A prince must learn," XV, 91; "good deeds are your enemies," XIX, 108; "The common people," XVIII, 101; "A prince, therefore," XVIII, 100.

202 "cope not only," III, 39; "circumstances change," XXV, 132; "mode of procedure," Ricci, XXV, 93; "one of those violent rivers," XXV, 130; "fortune is a woman," XXV, 133; "Men prosper," XXV, 133; "are successful so long," Ricci, XXV, 94; "the demands of the times," XXV, 131; "better to be impetuous," XXV, 133.

203 "Men use various methods," XXV, 131.

Chapter 12

207 "All the world," Erving Goffman, *The Presentation of Self in Everyday Life*, 72.

208 Quotations from Shakespeare come from *William Shakespeare: The Complete Works*, cited first by the title of the play, then by act and scene number only. "Why seems it so peculiar," *Hamlet*, I, ii; "Smiling, damned villain!" I, v.

209 "something like the murder," II, ii; "Observe my uncle" III, ii; "compelled even to the teeth," III, iii; "They had begun," V, ii.

210 "To thine own self," I, iii.

211 "Though I do hate him," *Othello*, I, i; "honest Iago," I, iii; "Men should be," III, iii; "To get [Cassio's] place," I, iii; "When devils will," II, iii; "did deceive her father," III, iii.

212 "villain," V, ii; "Which of you," *King Lear*, I, i.

214 "I do profess," I, iv; "I pray you, father," II, iv.

215 "under covert and convenient seeming," III, ii; "Never, never, never," V, iii.

217 "By God, you ought to die," Jean Baptise Poquelin de Molière, *The Misanthrope*, in *The Misanthrope and Tartuffe* (cited by act and scene number), I, i.

218 "there's no evil," Molière, *Tartuffe*, IV, v (see note for p.217); "To bring you, as your friend," *Misanthrope*, III, v; "This artificial style," I, ii.

219 "I take men," I, i.

220 "Man's a beastly creature," V, i; "it's no more a matter," I, i; "If honesty shone," V, i; "not mask themselves," I, i.

221 "is in truth a wedding," Goffman, 36.

222 "My one great talent," *Misanthrope*, III, vii; "love's irrational and blind," IV, iii.

223 "fly with me," V, vii; "flee this bitter world," V, viii.

Chapter 13

229 "metaphysico-theologo-cosmolonigology," François-Marie Arouet de Voltaire, *Candide, or Optimism*, trans. Richard Aldington, rev. and ed. Norman L. Torrey (cited by chapter and page number), I, 2. This standard translation, without Torrey's editing, also appears in Voltaire, *Candide and Other Writings*, ed. Haskell M. Block (New York: Random House, The Modern Library, 1956).

230 "Doctor Pangloss was right," III, 9; "love," IV, 11; "It was all indispensable," IV, 12; "had been expressly created," V, 14; "This earthquake is not a new thing," V, 15.

231 "it is impossible," V, 16; "accidents are not always fatal," VII, 20; "to a new world," X, 28.

232 "palace of sciences," XVIII, 59; "three thousand learned scientists," XVIII, 60.

233 "to infuriate us," XXI, 72; "work keeps at bay," XXX, 113; "You are right," XXX, 114; "All events are linked up," XXX, 114–15.

234 "'Tis well said," XXX, 115; "whatever [the] mind seizes," Francis Bacon, *Novum Organum*, Book I, Section LVIII, in *Selected Writings of Francis Bacon*, 477.

236 "Now, what I want is, Facts," Charles Dickens, *Hard Times. For These Times* (cited by book, chapter, and page number), I, i, 47; "a man of realities," I, ii, 48; "girl number twenty," I, ii, 49; "Quadruped," I, ii, 50.

237 "Would you paper," I, ii, 51; "From their tenderest years," I, iii, 53; "replete with facts," I, iii, 57; "by means of addition," I, viii, 89; "Ologies of all kinds," II, ix, 225; "educating the reason," I, viii, 89; "never wonder," I, iii, 54; "like an indifferently executed transparency," I, iv, 60; "Go and be somethingological," I, iv, 61.

238 "to view everything," I, xv, 132–37 *passim*; "the excellence of the whole system," II, ii, 158; "National Prosperity," I, ix, 97; "Coketown," I, v, 65; "Fact, fact, fact," I, v, 66; "severely workful," I, v, 65; "the healthiest things in the world," II, ii, 159; "analogy between the case," I, v, 67.

239 "iron cage," Max Weber, *The Protestant Ethic and the Spirit of Capitalism*, 181; "the modern economic order," 180; "The peculiarity of modern culture," Max Weber, "Bureaucracy," in *From Max Weber: Essays in Sociology*, 215–16; "The fate of our times," Max Weber, "Science as a Vocation," Ibid., 155.

240 "The question I have to ask," *Hard Times*, I, xv, 136; "I wish I could collect," I, viii, 92.

241 "So many people," III, vii, 300; "It was very remarkable," II, iii, 165; "This night," II, xii, 242.

242 "face was ashy white," II, xii, 242; "Indifferent and purposeless," II, viii, 207; "Whither he tended," II, viii, 195; "I am not a moral sort," III, ii, 254; "what will be will be," II, viii, 207; "a new sensation," II, vii, 196.

243 "the hard Fact fellows," II, vii, 195; "in any moral sort," III, ii, 254; "*virtue or benevolence*," II, vii, 195.

244 "It is known," I, xi, 108; "closely imprisoned forces," III, i, 247; "there is a wis-

dom," III, i, 246; "Have you a heart?" III, viii, 302; "No man, sir," III, viii, 303.

245 "Faith, hope," III, ix, 313; "People mutht be amuthed," III, ix, 308; "I lay down the philosophy," I, vi, 83; "immaterial part of my life," II, xii, 240; "the graces of my soul," II, xii, 239; "There ith a love," III, viii, 308.

246 "something in her," I, xiv, 128; "happy Sissy's happy children," III, ix, 313.

247 "the growing good of the world," George Eliot, *Middlemarch* (Boston: Houghton Mifflin, Riverside Editions, 1956), Book VIII, Finale, 613.

Chapter 14

253 "in the nature of man," James Madison, *Federalist #10*, in Alexander Hamilton, James Madison, John Jay, *The Federalist Papers*. Because this work comprises only pages 50–58 and is widely available, no individual page numbers are cited here.

256 Quotations from Alexis de Tocqueville's *Democracy in America* come primarily from the eloquent nineteenth-century translation by Henry Reeve, revised by Francis Bowen and edited by Phillips Bradley, cited as RB by part and page number, which follows the pagination of the original, published in two volumes. But some quotations come from the recent translation by Harvey C. Mansfield and Delba Winthrop, cited as MW by page number. I cite both translations for all quotations, with the first one cited being the source of the quotation. "A custom is becoming," RB: I, 255/MW: 3.

258 "In America I saw more," RB: I, 14/MW: 13.

259 "fundamental fact," RB: I, 3/MW: 3; "development of the principle," RB: I, 6/MW, 6.

260 "Although men cannot become," RB II, 95/MW, 479–80; "Democratic peoples," RB: II, 97/MW: 482; "*Individualism*," MW: 482/RB: II, 98.

261 "as old as the world," MW: 483/RB: II, 98; "Individualism proceeds," MW, 482–83 *passim*/RB: II, 98–99 *passim*; "aristocratic peoples," RB: II, 228/MW: 587.

262 "variety" . . . "is disappearing," RB: II, 229/MW: 588; "When I survey," RB: II, 332/MW: 674.

263 "distinctions of ranks," RB: II, 129/MW: 507; "hypocrisy of luxury," RB: II, 48–51 *passim*/MW: 439–42 *passim*.

265 "a sole tutelary," RB: II, 318–19 *passim*/MW: 662–64 *passim*.

266 "I firmly believe," MW: 672/RB: II, 329; "with that salutary fear," MW: 673/RB: II, 330; "I say," MW: 488/RB: II, 105.

267 "Americans of all ages," RB: II, 106/MW: 489; "As men become more equal," RB: II, 111/MW: 493; "equality isolates," MW: 668/RB: II, 324; "wandering minds," RB: II, 112/MW: 493; "The empire of newspapers," MW: 495/RB: II, 114; "freedom of the press," MW: 668/RB: II, 324; "the press is the chief," RB: II, 325/MW: 668; "maintain civilization," RB: II, 111/MW: 493.

268 "self-interest rightly understood," RB: II, 21–24 *passim*/MW: 500–03 *passim*; "The nations of our time," RB: II, 334/MW: 676.

269 "The subject of this essay," John Stuart Mill, *On Liberty* (cited by chapter and page number), I, 3; "protection against political despotism," I, 6.

270 "The vital question of the future," I, 3; "individual independence," I, 6; "The object of the Essay," I, 10–11.

271 "The only part of the conduct," I, 11; "No person is an entirely isolated being," I, 13; "When I say only himself," IV, 74; "To individuality should belong," IV, 70;

"perceptible hurt to any assignable individual," IV, 76.

272 "the inward domain," I, 13; "different opinions," III, 54; "lead different lives," III, 60; "different experiments," III, 54; "they neither obtain," III, 64; "It is good there should be differences," III, 69.

273 "It is only by the collision," III, 50; "The initiation of all wise," III, 63; "desires and impulses," III, 55–63 *passim*.

274 "social rights," IV, 83; "there is no violation," IV, 84; "moral police," III, 79; "In our time," III, 58.

275 "robbing the human race," I, 18; "whether the general welfare," IV, 70; "lie on the exact boundary line," V, 92.

276 "states should require," V, 97; "should be free," V, 95; "the activity and powers," V, 106.

Chapter 15

282 Unless otherwise noted, quotations from Karl Marx come from *The Marx-Engels Reader*, cited by the title of the individual work and by page number in that volume. "Life is not determined," Karl Marx and Friedrich Engels, *The German Ideology 1845–46* (cited as GI), 155; "reflexes and echoes . . . ," GI, 159; "morality, religion," GI, 155.

283 "Does it require," Karl Marx and Friedrich Engels, *The Manifesto of the Communist Party* (or *The Communist Manifesto*), (cited as CM by section number as well as by page number), II, 489; "All I know," Friedrich Engles, letter to C. Schmidt, August 5, 1890, in *Marx-Engels Works in Two Volumes*, vol. 1, 486.

285 "The proletarians have nothing," CM, IV, 500; "The history of all," CM, I, 473; "oppressor and oppressed," CM, I, 474.

286 "The bourgeoisie historically," CM, I, 475; "It has been the first," CM, I, 476.

287 "Religion is the expression," Karl Marx, Introduction to "Contribution to a Critique Of Hegel's Philosophy of Right," 54; "the criticism of religion," 53; "The abolition of religion," 54; "idyllic relations," CM, I, 475–76 *passim*.

288 "money is the supreme good," Karl Marx, *Economic and Philosophical Manuscripts of 1844*, 103; "What the bourgeoisie," CM, I, 483.

289 "are but the outgrowth," CM, II, 487; "By individual," CM, II, 486.

290 "The theory of the Communists," CM, II, 484; "Communism," *Economic and Philosophical Manuscripts*, 84; "*human, i.e., social*, mode," 85; "individuality and freedom," CM, II, 485; "The middle-class owner," CM, II, 486; "identical with the disappearance," CM, II, 487; "eternal truths," CM, II, 489; "transform[ed] into eternal laws," CM, II, 487; "a mere training ground," CM, II, 487.

291 "In place of the old," CM, II, 491.

Chapter 16

296 "I do not remember," Frederick Douglass, *Narrative of the Life of Frederick Douglass. An American Slave. Written by Himself* (cited by chapter and page number), I, 21; "a common custom," I, 22; "a sense of my own identity," XI, 114.

297 "A single word," VIII, 60; "part and parcel," X, 84; "to carry off," X, 85; "evidence of their contentment," II, 31–32 *passim*.

298 "to escape punishment," IV, 39; "to take great pleasure," I, 24–25 *passim*; "artful, cruel, and obdurate," IV, 38; "his mangled body," IV, 40; "Killing a slave," IV, 41.

299 "He was a cruel man," I, 24; "some training," VII, 52; "men and women," VIII,

59– 60; "At this moment," VIII, 60.

300 "relied upon his own depravity," IX, 67; "of all slaveholders," X, 87; "One of the many," IX, 69; "tie up . . . and whip," IX, 68; "I assert most unhesitatingly," X, 86; "*slaveholding* religion," Appendix, 120; "I am filled," Appendix, 120–21.

301 "Learning would *spoil*," VI, 49.

302 "To make a contented slave," X, 103–04; "I understood the pathway," VI, 49; "Sabbath school," X, 90; "We were linked," X, 91.

303 "the idea of speaking," XI, 119.

304 "Anything is possible," Elie Wiesel, *Night*, 30; "no longer any joy," 4.

305 "What an imagination," 4–5; "Why are you so anxious," 5; "weary of speaking," 6; "but not for long," 7; "the Jews of Sighet," 8; "The general opinion," 9–10; "Surely it was all a nightmare," 28; "flames were leaping up," 30.

306 "I pinched my face," 30; "Never shall I forget," 32; "What have you come here for?" 28.

307 "wild beasts of prey," 95.

308 "My eyes were open," 65.

309 "the bondage of myths," Martin Luther King, Jr., "Letter from the Birmingham Jail," April 16, 1963, in *The Norton Reader*. Because this letter comprises only pages 455–69 of that volume and is widely available, no individual page numbers are cited here.

Chapter 17

314 "conquistador by temperament," Sigmund Freud, quoted in Peter Gay, *Freud: A Life for Our Times* (New York: W. W. Norton, 1988), xvi; "I am not basically interested," Sigmund Freud, quoted in Russell Jacoby, *Social Amnesia* (Boston: Beacon Press, 1975), 123; "My discoveries," Sigmund Freud, quoted in Jacoby, 124.

315 "the true source of religious sentiment," Sigmund Freud, *Civilization and Its Discontents*, 11; "show by their behavior," 24; "A feeling can only be the source," 20; "what we call happiness," 25.

316 "strong feelings of pleasure, 24; "We are so made," 25; "an unrestricted satisfaction," 26; "Why [is it] so hard," 36; "One feels inclined," 25; "avoidance of unpleasure," 26; "moderate [our] claims," 25.

317 "The Pleasure Principle," 15; "Life, as we find it," 23; "We are threatened," 25; "happiness in the reduced sense," 33.

319 "internal, psychical processes," 29; "psychical intellectual work," 28; "special dispositions," 29; "No feature seems better," 45.

320 "mild," 28.

322 "Men are not gentle," 65; "constitutes the greatest impediment," 77; "reveals man as a savage," 65; "psychical reaction-formations," 66; "man is wholly good," 66–67; "paths the development of civilization," 68; "really justified," 66.

323 "sense of guilt," 91; "a sort of malaise," 93.

324 "the most important problem," 91.

325 "If civilization imposes," 69; "In the severity," 101.

Chapter 18

329 "knew nothing," Virginia Woolf, *Mrs. Dalloway*, 11; "could not think," 185.

330 "My party tonight!" 72; "Suppose Peter said," 184; "these parties . . . ," 116; "She

frittered her time away," 118; "It was a very odd thing," 180; "childish," 183; "the Albanians," 182; "But—but—why did she suddenly feel," 182–83 *passim*.

331 "What a lark!" 3; "waves of that divine vitality," 9; "Heaven only knows," 5.

332 "the veriest frumps," 5; "I love walking," 7; "She enjoyed practically everything," 118; "Nothing could be slow enough," 282; "what she loved," 12; simply life," 183; "how unbelievable," 185; "People would say," 182; "Oh if she could have lived," 13–14.

333 "Could any man understand," 184; "she had the oddest sense," 14.

334 "With Peter," 10; "What's your love?" 184; "horrible passion!" 192; "Love . . . that monster," 67; "Had not that, after all," 48; "kissed her on the lips," 52; "It had a quality," 50; "she could not resist," 46; "she did undoubtedly then feel," 47; "she could never dispel," 46; "Richard gave her," 10; "It was a miracle," 175.

335 "to tell Clarissa," 176; "(But he could not bring himself," 179; "Love and religion!" 191; "love and religion would destroy," 192; "health is largely a matter," 138; "sense of proportion," 150; "health is proportion," 149; "Conversion is her name," 151; "under some plausible disguise;" 152; "her blessing on those," 151.

336 "Conversion," 151; "worshipping proportion," 150; "naked, defenseless," 154; "have said (indeed she felt)," 281; "What business had the Bradshaws," 280; "She felt somehow very like him," 283.

337 "There was in the depths," 281; "This late age," 13; "There! the old lady," 283; "She always had the feeling," 11; "The sin for which human nature," 137.

338 "Sylvia's death," 117–18; "Possibly she said," 117; "Not for a moment," 43; "She evolved this atheist's religion," 118.

339 "They thought," 183; "both of them criticised her," 183–84 *passim*; "Oh, it was very queer," 184–85; "the supreme mystery," 193; "transcendental theory," 231; "the unseen part of us," 232; "somehow in the streets," 12; "to kindle," 6; "it was her gift," 185; "pay back from this secret deposit," 43; "an offering," 185.

340 "She made her drawing room," 116; "Here he was starting to go," 247–48; "Cabs were rushing," 250; "For there she was," 296; "prancing, sparkling," 264; "an inexpressible dignity," 265; "the perfect hostess," 93; "art which does not seem," Baldesar Castiglione, *The Book of the Courtier*, trans. Charles S. Singleton (Garden City, N.Y.: Doubleday, Anchor Books, 1959), Book I, p. 43; "She did it genuinely," *Mrs. Dalloway*, 117; "Every time she gave a party," 259–60.

341 "The world, in truth," Goffman, *Presentation of Self*, 72; "courage and endurance," *Mrs. Dalloway*, 13.

342 "the growing good" (see note to p. 247).

Chapter 19

347 "educating mind and character," Plato, *The Republic* (cited by book, section, and page number—Lee also divides *The Republic* into Parts not indicated here), II, 376e – 378e, 130–33 *passim*. For the Greek text, I have consulted the bilingual edition Plato, *The Republic*, trans. Paul Shorey (Cambridge, Mass.: Harvard University Press, Loeb Classical Library, 1935), 2 vols.

349 "If our young men," III, 388d, 143; "We must therefore put a stop," III, 392a, 148; "We must issue similar orders," III, 401b, 162.

350 "no grasp of truth," X, 597e–600e, 425–29 *passim*; "So great is the natural magic," X, 601b, 429; "scene painter and conjurer," X, 602d, 432.

351 "On what part," X, 602c, 432; "irrational," X, 604d–605a, 435 *passim*; "difficult to understand," X, 604e, 435.

352 "gratifies and indulges," X, 605b–607a, 436–37 *passim*; "innovation," IV, 424b–c, 191; "disorder" . . . "morals and manners," IV, 424d–e, 192.

353 "brings lasting benefits," X, 607d–e, 438; "for happiness in this life," X, 619e, 453; "tale," X, 621c, 455; "It doesn't matter," X, 592b, 420.

354 "rightly dislike and condemn," III, 401e–402a, 163; "object of education," III, 403e, 165; "The person who sees absolute beauty," Plato, *Symposium*, 95.

355 "practice and cultivate the arts," Plato, *Phaedo*, 60e–61b *passim* (see note for p. 43).

356 "a certain kind of character," Aristotle, *Politics* (see note to p. 70), VIII, v, 462; "kinds of stories," VII, xvii, 445; "unseemly talk," VII, xvii, 446; "tunes and modes," VIII, vii, 474; "orgiastic and emotional," VIII, vii, 475; "hearing such sounds," VIII, v, 465; "Amusement," VIII, v, 462–63 *passim*; "make amusements an end," VIII, v, 464; "civilized pursuits," VIII, iii, 456.

357 "completely immune," VII, xvii, 447; "a way of working off," VIII, vi, 469; "pity and fear, for example," VIII, vii, 473–74 *passim*.

358 "discovery," Aristotle, *On the Art of Poetry* [*Poetics*], in Aristotle, Horace, Longinus, *Classical Literary Criticism* (cited only by chapter number), Ch. 11; "tragic pleasure," Ch. 14; "purgation of such emotions," Ch. 6; "The instinct for imitation," Ch. 4.

359 "action and life," Ch. 6; "By universal truths," Ch. 9; "enjoying oneself," *Politics*, VIII, v, 465; "the best kinds of enjoyment," VIII, iii, 456.

360 "professional education," VIII, v, 471; "the mind preoccupied," VIII, ii, 454; "requires the skill," VIII, vi, 469.

361 "the blessed life," VIII, iii, 456.

362 "to satisfy the demands of art," Leo Tolstoy, *What Is Art?* (cited by chapter and page number), I, 10.

363 "Is it true," I, 14; "We have the terrible probability," II, 16; "stunting of human life," I, 10; "these sacrifices of labor," II, 16; "what is meant by art," I, 15.

364 "artistic enjoyment is a good," IV, 47; "Art is not a pleasure," XX, 189; "that the purpose and aim," IV, 46; "one of the conditions," V, 49; "one of two organs," XVII, 159; "indispensable means of communication," V, 53; "By words man exchanges," XVII, 159; *Art is a human activity*," V, 51.

365 "True art," VIII, 67; "the simple feelings of common life," XVI, 150; "habituated," X, 96; "perverted," XIV, 133; "become continually more savage," XVII, 160.

366 "indispensable for the life," V, 52; "mankind could not exist," V, 53; "The art of the future," XIX, 179; "open to everyone," VI, 54; "joy at another's gladness," XIV, 138; "I consign my own artistic productions," XVI, 155n.

367 "To speak of an interesting work," XI, 106; "bad food . . . ," X, 96.

369 "amusement-art," XVII, 162; "manufactured to ready-made," XI, 109; "by the armies of professional artists," XVII, 162; "striking . . . effects," XI, 100; "physiological effects," XI, 105.

Chapter 20

372 "There is no story that is not true," Chinua Achebe, *Things Fall Apart* (New York: Ballantine Books, Fawcett Crest, 1983), 130.

375 Quotations from the Koran come from *The Koran*, trans. N. J. Dawood, cited as D by verse or page number, and from *Al-Qur'an*, trans. Ahmed Ali, cited as A by verse number. "Recite in the name of your Lord," D: #96 (Ahmed Ali uses

"read" instead of "recite" in this verse); "recital," D: Introduction, p. 111; "spread frivolous stories," A: #31; "as for poets," A: #26.

376 "In the name of God the Compassionate," *The Arabian Nights*. Because all quotations come from pages 2–29 of this edition, consisting of "Foreword" (p. 2), "Prologue: Story of King Shahrayar and Sharazad, His Vizier's Daughter" (pp. 3–16), and "Story of the Merchant and the Demon" (pp. 17–29), no individual page numbers are cited.

382 "In the olden days," "Why We Tell Stories About Spider," *West African Folk Tales*. Because the entire story comprises pages 1–16 of this volume, no individual page numbers are cited.

Chapter 21

388 "All that is solid" (see p. 287 in the text); "Modernity is the ephemeral," Charles Baudelaire, "Le Peintre de la Vie Moderne," in Baudelaire, *Oeuvres complètes*, Bibliothéque de la pléiade ([Paris], Gallimard, 1961), 1163.

389 Quotations from Murasaki Shikibu's *The Tale of Genji* come from the translation by Edward Seidensticker, cited only by page number, except for one quotation from the recent translation by Royall Tyler, cited by Tyler's name and the page number. Although Tyler's translation may be truer to the original in the length of its sentences and the absence of personal names, the Seidensticker translation is often more lucid and arresting, bringing out the sense of evanescence more consistently and evocatively. "It is a transient world," 555; "Life is fleeting," 870; "Yes, the sad thing," 652; "With flowers that fade," 854; "These flowers must fall," 761; "obsessed with evanescence," 316; "even the shallowest," 220; "the night in thoughts," 199; "it has always seemed," 724; "the knowledge of evanescence," 867; "sadness that all is fleeting," 1029; "to push a man," 867.

390 "weeping courtiers," 6; "tears came easily," 642; "blinded by tears," 177; "cannot see for tears," 8; "the autumn night," 10; "collapsed in tears," 59; "seemed also to be speaking," 89; "Genji was near tears," 59; "memory following memory," 217; "tears flowed on," 59; "dried his tears," 725; "sometimes he would weep," 78; "Genji spent a tearful day," 99; "There seemed nothing," 177; "I am told," 59.

391 "try to shake loose," 173; "a world which, for all its trials," 675; "a jewel beyond compare," 4; "into a lad of such beauty," 13; "among the more discriminating," 5; "people began calling Genji," 16; "the shining Genji," 19; "his manner and voice," 93; "asked whether he might be a visitor," 95; "brushing away a tear," 96; "gathered for a look," 540; "There is no one quite like him," 541.

392 "his writing was more beautiful," 176; "Sometimes," 316; "Genji scarcely seemed of this world," 132; "a chill as if from another world," 134; "pleasure to the eye," 135; "The scent of [Genji's] sleeve," 59.

393 "My sister, my stepmother," Lady Sarashina, *As I Crossed a Bridge of Dreams*, 31; "impatience and curiosity . . . ," 46; "kept reading all day long," 47; "I lived forever," 64; "How could anyone as wonderful," 79–80.

394 "moods of nature," *Genji*, 672; "the first rays of the moon," 603; "a radiant moon," 238.

395 "unlike most people," 598; "a heavy fall of snow . . . ," 357; "A clear moon," 359; "the soft sad light," 225; "The moon was sinking," 10; "its situation rather like his own," 225.

396 "a line of geese," 244; "their cries ring sadly," 238; "the waves . . . like moans," 236; the mists that will not let me see," 203; "the scent of blossoms," 878; "the

cherry blossoms of spring," 736; "the morning glory . . . ," 894; "We go, we stay," 173; "It is a life," 621; "I see the drake fly," 1042; "I feel sorry for the man," Kenkō, *Essays in Idleness*, section 191; "leaving something incomplete," section 82.

397 "The evening sky," *Genji*, 79; "The evening breeze," 536; "there were heavy mists," 93; "a sheaf of autumn leaves," 202; "leaves and flowers," 386.

398 "the smallest of the hanging rocks," 419; "morning came," 420; "loved art more than anything," 310; "Poem followed poem," 419; "Poem answered poem," 313; "festival of the cherry blossoms," 151.

399 "Hotaru: The voice of the warbler," 515; "a sky even more beautiful," 188; "the plum trees," 734.

400 "Lost in my sorrows," Tyler, 779; "The shining Genji was dead," 735; "of the usual trite and fusty sort," 930; "The most ordinary music," 255; "flutes, mingled with the sighing," 133; "in the autumn," 603; "the relative merits," 672; "The mist-enshrouded moon," 514; "music did sound," 515; "raised his head," 235; "He plucked a few notes," 236.

401 "The moon having come forth," 672; "on a sighing of wind," 254; "The moon had come out," 661; "She added a poem," 662.

402 "old romances," 437; "addicted to romances," 438.

403 "Genji came out," 237.

Chapter 22

407 "a gentleman . . . verging on," Miguel de Cervantes Saavedra, *The Adventures of Don Quixote* (cited by part, chapter, and page number), I, i, 31–35 *passim*.

409 "his ideas into effect," I, ii, 35; "deeds worthy to be engraved," I, ii, 36; "a castle," I, ii–iii, 37–46 *passim*.

410 "beauteous maiden," I, iv, 51; "a disaster peculiar to knights errant," I, iv, 52; "Look you, your worship," I, v, 54.

411 "history of the famous Don Quixote," I, Prologue, 30; "the child of my brain," I, Prologue, 25; "the inhabitants of the district," I, Prologue, 30; "authors," I, i, 31; "The unfortunate thing," I, viii, 74.

412 "great annoyance," I, ix, 75; "Cide Hamete Benengeli," I, ix, 77; "this delightful history," I, ix, 75; "If any objection," I, ix, 78; "Anxiously and diligently," I, lii, 457; "dunderheaded," I, lii, 458.

413 "to see himself," II, iii, 486; "Does the author," II, iv, 494; "the author of the 'second *Don Quixote*'," II, Prologue, 467; "to deprive me," II, Prologue, 469; "an honest man," II, Prologue, 470.

414 "I will not set foot," II, lix, 853; "This same Don Quixote," II, lxxii, 926–27 *passim*; "books of chivalry," I, v, 56.

415 "What room?" I, vii, 64–65 *passim*; "They caught sight," I, viii, 68–69 *passim*.

416 "with something glittering," I, xxi, 162–63 *passim*.

417 "Is it possible that all this," I, xxv, 204; "Spells transform all things," II, xxix, 659–60.

418 "I am quite satisfied," I, xxv, 210.

419 "We gather from . . . ," II, xxxii, 680; "Henceforth, I shall believe," II, xxxii, 681.

420 "Books of chivalry," I, xlix, 436; "I can say of myself," I, l, 442; "I love him dearly," II, xxxiii, 687.

421 "you must consider what you are," II, xlii, 738–39 *passim*; "Could anyone hear

this last discourse," II, xliii, 740; "When I was a knight-errant," II, lxvi, 896.

422 "return to the honorable calling," II, lxv, 893; "Every man is the architect," II, lxvi, 896; "did not take [the inn]," II, lxxi, 924; "Don't worry," II, lxiii, 930; "grief at his overthrow," II, lxxiv, 935–36 *passim.*

423 "does not even know," II, lxxiv, 938; "I would give him," II, lxxiv, 937; "Must you come out with that," II, lxxiv, 936–38 *passim.*

424 "For my sole object," II, lxxiv, 940; "plain Alonso Quixano," II, lxxiv, 937.

Chapter 23

428 "destroyed all the poetry," quoted in Marjorie Hope Nicolson, *Newton Demands the Muse: Newton's Optics and the Eighteenth-Century Poets* (Princeton, N.J.: Princeton University Press, 1946, 1966), 1.

429 "imagination" sees "ordinary things," William Wordsworth, Preface to *Lyrical Ballads,* in William Wordsworth, *Selected Poetry and Prose.* This edition is a slightly abridged version of the edition of 1802, and because it comprises only pages 410–24 of this volume no individual page numbers are cited.

430 "feeling intellect," William Wordsworth, *The Prelude. The Four Texts. (1798, 1799, 1805, 1850)* (cited by book and page number from the text of 1850), XIV, 523.

433 "mental crisis," John Stuart Mill, *Autobiography,* Chapter 5 *passim.*

434 "not of outward things," *The Prelude,* III, 113 (see note to p. 430); "The history of a Poet's mind," XIV, 535; "remembrances . . . ," XII, 483; "spots of time," XII, 479.

435 "deep enthusiastic joy," XIV, 527; "bond of union," I, 69; "rapture of hallelujah," XIV, 527.

436 "O there is a blessing," I, 37; "the hope / Of active days," I, 39; "A cheerful confidence," I, 41; "seventeenth year," II, 97; "To every natural form," III, 109–11; "bliss ineffable," II, 97; "O Nature!" II, 99; "Some called it madness," III, 111.

437 "sentiment of Being," II, 97; "Coleridge!" XIV, 525; "to thee the work," XIV, 535; "My heart was early introduced," VIII, 319; "sanctity of Nature," VIII, 321; "man / Ennobled outwardly," VIII, 319; "meanness, selfish cares," VIII, 321.

438 "Europe at that time," VI, 227–29 *passim;* "Bliss was it," XI, 441; "O pleasant exercise," XI, 441; "the soil of common life," IX, 355; "could overthrow my trust," VIII, 343.

439 "gift that consecrates the joy," I, 39; "Imagination . . . that awful power," VI, 241; "glorious faculty," XIV, 515; "Effort, and expectation," VI, 241; "Imagination . . . in truth," XIV, 521; "the highest bliss," XIV, 517.

440 "Oh, joy to him," XIV, 523; "What we have loved," XIV, 537; "Imagination having been our theme," XIV, 521.

441 "Poetry, in a general sense," Percy Bysshe Shelley, "A Defense of Poetry," *Selected Poetry and Prose of Shelley.* Because all quotations here come from pages 416–25 and 441–48, no individual page numbers are cited.

Chapter 24

448 "A man at least is free," Gustave Flaubert, *Madame Bovary,* trans. Mildred Marmur (cited by part, chapter, and page number), II, iii, 101; "Great big tears," II, vi, 124; "'Strange,' Emma thought," II, vi, 124.

449 "the sensualities of luxury," I, ix, 76.

450 "I hate everyday heroes," II, ii, 97; "rejected as useless," I, vi, 56; "The closer

things were," I, ix, 76; "full of ideal ambitions," I, ix, 75.

451 "Why then was life so inadequate?" III, vi, 267; "Before she had married," I, v, 55; "I'll have her," II, vii, 137.

452 "exaggerated speeches," II, xii, 188; "I have a lover!" II, ix, 163; "How impossible it seemed!" III, vi, 267; "Incapable as she was," I, vii, 62.

453 "loved the church," I, vi, 59; "the sweet face of the Virgin," II, vi, 120; "She could hear the far-off song," II, xiv, 207–08 *passim*; "pressing her lips," III, viii, 301.

454 "rebelled before the mysteries of faith," I, vi, 59; "Her temperament was more sentimental," I, vi, 56–57.

455 "a lie invented," II, xv, 217; "run into his arms," II, xv, 218; "mediocrity is creeping in," Gustave Flaubert, letter to Louise Colet, January 29, 1854, in *Letters of Gustave Flaubert, 1830–1857*, 212–14 *passim*.

456 "sent to work in a cotton mill," *Madame Bovary*, III, x, 322; "an enormous clientele," III, x, 322.

457 "Nothing was worth looking for," II, vi, 267.

Chapter 25

462 "*a just and delicate taste*," Jonathan Richardson, "A Discourse on the Science of a Connoisseur" (1719), quoted in M. H. Abrams, "Art-as-Such: The Sociology of Modern Aesthetics," in M. H. Abrams, *Doing Things With Texts: Essays in Criticism and Critical Theory* (New York: W. W. Norton, 1989), 143; "*beaux arts par excellence*," Abbé Batteau, *Les beaux arts réduits à un même principe* (1746), quoted in Paul Oskar Kristeller, "The Modern System of the Arts," in Paul Oskar Kristeller, *Renaissance Thought II: Papers on Humanism and The Arts* (New York: Harper and Row, Torchbooks, 1965), 200n; "beautiful object is valuable," Karl Philippe Moritz, quoted in M. H. Abrams, "From Addison to Kant: Modern Aesthetics and the Exemplary Art," in *Doing Things*, 165; "logic of sensuous thinking," Alexander Baumgarten, quoted Ibid., 178.

463 "aesthetical judgment," Immanuel Kant, *Critique of Judgment*, 47; "beautiful . . . entirely disinterested," 45.

464 "Someone has said somewhere," Théophile Gautier, Preface to *Mademoiselle de Maupin*. Because all quotations here come from pages xxi–xxvi, no individual page numbers are cited.

465 "what is real in our life," Walter Pater, Conclusion, *The Renaissance*. Because the Conclusion comprises only pages 150–53 of the book, no individual page numbers are cited.

468 "I find it harder and harder," quoted in Richard Ellman, *Oscar Wilde* (New York, Alfred A. Knopf, 1988), 45; "Ethics of Art," Oscar Wilde, "Impressions of America," in *The Artist as Critic: Critical Writings of Oscar Wilde*, 9; "we should treat all trivial things," quoted in H. Montgomery Hyde, *Oscar Wilde* (New York: Farrar, Straus and Giroux, 1975), 177.

469 "All art is quite useless," Oscar Wilde, Preface, *The Picture of Dorian Gray* (London: Penguin Books, Penguin Classics, 2000), 2–3; "My wallpaper and I," quoted in Ellman, *Oscar Wilde*, 581; "I am dying," Ibid., 580; "Beauty is the wonder of wonders" to "Live!," Oscar Wilde, *The Picture of Dorian Gray* in *Collected Works of Oscar Wilde* (cited by chapter and page number—all quotations, except those from the Preface, come from this edition, which lacks the Preface), II, 118.

470 "It is better to be beautiful," XVII, 226; "When we are happy," VI, 153; "the

aim of life," II, 115; "One's own life," VI, 153; "Every impulse that we strive to strangle," II, 115–16; "the only way to get rid," II, 116; "if we lived long enough," Oscar Wilde, "The Critic as Artist," in *The Artist as Critic*, 360; "No civilized man ever regrets," *Dorian Gray*, VI, 153; "aesthetic idolatry," I, 111; "the sense of his own beauty," II, 120.

471 "Without your art," VII, 159; "The expression looked different," VII, 160; "subtle poisonous theories," VII, 162; "This thing that has happened," VIII, 167; "To become a spectator," IX, 173; "life itself was the first," XI, 185; "eternal youth," VIII, 170; "study of jewels," XI, 185–91 *passim*; "more and more enamoured," XI, 184.

472 "You are really beginning," XIX, 240–41 *passim*; "cunning" . . . "hypocrite," XX, 243.

473 "horrible in its agony," XX, 243; "youth and beauty," XX, 244; "the real trouble I experienced," Oscar Wilde, letter to the Editor of the *Daily Chronicle*, June [30], 1890, in *Artist as Critic*, 245 (see note for p. 270); "To have ruined oneself," *Dorian Gray*, IV, 137; "Aesthetics are higher," Oscar Wilde, "Critic as Artist," in *Artist as Critic*, 406; "I can't bear the idea," *Dorian Gray*, VIII, 165; "It's not good for one's morals," VII, 157.

475 Quotations from Thomas Mann's stories come from Thomas Mann, *Stories of Three Decades*, cited by story title and/or page number in this volume. "one must die to life," "Tonio Kröger," 100; "a properly constituted," 103; "What more pitiable sight," 109; "self-conquest," "Felix Krull," 362; "sacrificed to art," "Death in Venice," 384; "an almost exaggerated sense of beauty," 386; "the poet spokesman," 385; "got no joy," 381; "cynic utterances," 386.

476 "he had never seen," 396; "form and art," 398; "I love you," 418; "told himself," 412; "the artist's highest joy," 413.

477 "Has not [aesthetic] form," 386; "dignity and self-control," 431; "stern cult of the beautiful," 435; "the whole cultural structure," 430; "in his infatuation," 420.

478 "that softening influence," George Eliot, *Middlemarch*, Book IV, Chapter 39, 288 (see note to p. 247).

Chapter 26

482 "air of weakness," Gabriel García Márquez, *Love in the Time of the Cholera*, 54; "began his secret life," 56.

483 "his perfect fidelity," 61; "fainting spells," 62; "inscribed with the point of a pin," 69; "You will be sorry," 71; "there is no greater glory," 82.

484 "as the certain husband," 98; "crowned goddess," 102; "it is as if," 204; "he was convinced," 48.

485 "thrust[s] Fermina Daza into life," 32; "The truth is," 205; "he was aware," 159; "as the creature of a paternal plot," 205; "it was easier to avoid," 26.

486 "bathing for almost a week," 28; "even when they were old," 29–30; "she thought she would die," 254; "In the long run," 159; "they were not," 26; "together they had overcome," 224; "Over the years," 223.

487 "Levin had been married," Leo Tolstoy, *Anna Karenina*, trans. Richard Pevear and Larissa Volokhonsky (New York: Penguin Books, 2001), 479–82 *passim*; "how can one be happy," *Love in the Time of thr Cholera*, 329.

488 "I will never be old," 23; "Only God knows," 43; "not go without knowing," 47; "We will see each other," 47; "the fugitive parrot," 48.

489 "vow of eternal and everlasting love," 277; "he had lost his speech," 137; "a revelation that he could not believe," 143; "suffer one moment . . . ," 146.

490 "never again would he abandon," 147; "to win fame and fortune," 165; "ineluctable event," 165; "was another person," 173; "routine business letters," 167; "because the only convincing document," 171.

491 "with his infinite capacity," 230; "faced the insidious snares of old age," 260; "with fierce determination," 268–69; "his vow of eternal fidelity," 277.

492 "an act of forgiving," 284; "the terrible letter," 293.

493 "with a very sweet smile," 298; "simple paragraph," 303; "on life, love," 299; "had helped her," 302; "serious and thoughtful reasons," 298; "to understand her own life," 302.

494 "each other for what they were," 305–06; "have helped me," 308; "I don't see what sense," 309; "for the good companionship," 312; "new reasons to be grateful," 322.

495 "pervert," 323; "They can all go to hell," 324; "Take a boat," 325; "be the joyous refuge," 326; "there was an age," 327; "that she was crying," 328; "longing to understand . . . ," 329; "that Florentino Ariza would know," 330.

496 "fiery blush," 331; "it was she," 334; "now it seemed," 335; "They spent unimaginable hours," 338; "flabby skin," 339; "It's dead," 340; "despite the disappointment," 341; "Would it be possible," 342.

497 "Let's do that," 343; "The Great Magdelena River," 328; "ravaged land," 336; "ghost of a drowned woman," 332; "It was as if they had leapt," 345; "understood each other," 344; "they made the tranquil, wholesome love," 345; "Fermina Daza felt in her blood," 347.

498 "neither of them felt capable," 346; "Let us keep going," 348.

499 "clouded by his passion," 337; "how much he had loved her," 346.

Selected Bibliography

Aristotle. *Ethics*. Translated by J. A. K. Thompson, and revised by Hugh Tredennick. New York: Penguin Books, 1976.

———. *Ethics*. Translated by H. Rackman. Revised edition. Cambridge: Harvard University Press, Loeb Classical Library, 1934.

———. *On the Art of Poetry*. In *Aristotle, Horace, Longinus. Classical Literary Criticism*. Translated by T. S. Dorsch. New York: Penguin Books, 1965.

———. *The Politics*. Translated by T. A. Sinclair, and revised by Trevor J. Sanders. Harmondsworth, Middlesex, England: Penguin Books, 1981.

———. *Rhetoric*. Translated by W. Rhys Roberts. *The Basic Works of Aristotle*. Edited and introduction by Richard McKeon. New York: Random House, 1941.

The Arabian Nights. Translated by Husain Haddawy. Edited by Muhsin Mahdi. New York: W. W. Norton, 1990.

Bacon, Francis. *Selected Writings of Francis Bacon*. Introduction and notes by Hugh G. Dick. New York: Random House, Modern Library, 1955.

The Bhagavad-Gita. Translated by S. Radhakrishnan. In *A Sourcebook in Indian Philosophy*, edited by Sarvepalli Radhakrishnan and Charles Moore. Princeton: Princeton University Press, 1957.

Camus, Albert. *The Myth of Sisyphus and Other Essays*. Translated by Justin O'Brien. New York: Random House, Vintage Books, 1955.

Cervantes Saavedra, Miguel de. *The Adventures of Don Quixote*. Translated by J. M. Cohen. Baltimore: Penguin Books, 1950.

Chuang Tzu. *Basic Writings*. Translated by Burton Watson. New York: Columbia University Press, 1984.

Confucius. *The Analects (Lun yü)*. Translated by D. C. Lau. London: Penguin Books, 1979.

———. *The Analects of Confucius*. Translated and annotated by Arthur Waley. New York: Random House, Vintage Books, 1989.

Dante Alighieri. *The Divine Comedy: Hell*. Translated by Dorothy L. Sayers. New York: Penguin Books, 1949, 1980.

————. *Inferno.* Translated by Robert and Jean Hollander. Bilingual edition. New York: Random House, 2000.

The Dhammapada: The Path to Perfection. Translated by Juan Mascaro. New York: Penguin Books, 1973.

The Diamond Sutra and the Sutra of Hui-Neng. Translated by A. F. Price and Wong Mou-Iam. Boston: Shambhala, 1990.

Dickens, Charles. *Hard Times. For These Times.* Edited by David Craig. London: Penguin Books, 1985.

The Doctrine of the Mean. In *Sourcebook in Chinese Philosophy.* Translated and compiled by Wing-Tsit Chen. Princeton: Princeton University Press, 1963.

Dostoevsky, Fyodor. *The Brothers Karamazov.* Translated by Richard Pevear and Larissa Volkhonsky. New York: Random House, Vintage Classics, 1991.

————. *Notes from Underground.* Translated by Richard Pevear and Larissa Volkhonsky. New York: Random House, Vintage Classics, 1994.

Douglass, Frederick. *Narrative of the Life of Frederick Douglass. An American Slave. Written by Himself.* New York: Penguin, Signet Books, 1968.

Flaubert, Gustave. *Madame Bovary.* Translated by Mildred Marmur. New York: New American Library, Signet Classics, 1964.

————. *Madame Bovary.* Translated by Francis Steegmuller. New York: Random House, Vintage Books, 1957, 1992.

————. *Letters of Gustave Flaubert, 1830–1857.* Selected, edited, and translated by Francis Steegmuller. Cambridge: Harvard University Press, 1979.

Freud, Sigmund. *Civilization and Its Discontents.* Standard edition. Translated and edited by James Strachey. New York: W. W. Norton, 1961.

Gautier, Théophile. *Mademoiselle de Maupin.* Translation anon. New York: Random House, Modern Library, n.d.

Goethe, Johann Wolfgang von. *Goethe's Faust.* Translated by Walter Kaufmann. Bilingual edition. New York: Doubleday, Anchor Books, 1968.

Goffman, Erving. *The Presentation of Self in Everyday Life.* New York: Doubleday, Anchor Books, 1959.

The Great Learning. In *Sourcebook in Chinese Philosophy.* Translated and compiled by Wing-Tsit Chen. Princeton: Princeton University Press, 1963.

Homer. *The Iliad.* Translated by Robert Fagels. New York: Penguin Books, 1990.

————. *The Iliad of Homer.* Translated by Richmond Lattimore. Chicago: University of Chicago Press, 1951.

Kant, Immanuel. *Critique of Judgment*. Translated by J. H. Bernard. New York: Hafner Publications, 1951.

Kenkō, Yoshido. *Essays in Idleness*. Translated by Donald Keene. New York: Columbia University Press, 1967.

King, Martin Luther, Jr. "Letter from the Birmingham Jail" (April 16, 1963). In *The Norton Reader: An Anthology of Expository Prose*. Sixth edition. Edited by Arthur M. Eastman et al. New York: W. W. Norton, 1984.

The Koran. Translated by N. J. Dawood. London: Penguin Books, 1990.

[Lao Tzu]. *Tao Te Ching*. Translated by Arthur Waley. In *The Way and Its Power. A Study of the Tao Te Ching and Its Place in Chinese Thought*. New York: Grove Press, 1958.

———. *The Way of Life. A New Translation of the Tao Te Ching*. Translated by R. B. Blakney. New York: New American Library, Mentor Books, 1955, 1983.

Machiavelli, Niccolò. *The Prince*. Translated by George Bull. New York: Penguin Books, 1961, 1975.

———. *The Prince*. Translated by Luigi Ricci. Revised by E. R. Vincent. New York: Random House, Modern Library, 1940, 1950.

Madison, James. *Federalist #10*. In Alexander Hamilton, James Madison, John Jay. *The Federalist Papers*. New York: Random House, Bantam Classics, 1982.

Mann, Thomas. *Stories of Three Decades*. Translated by H. T. Lowe-Porter. New York: Alfred A. Knopf, 1936.

Márquez, Gabriel García. *Love in the Time of the Cholera*. Translated by Edith Grossman. New York: Penguin Books, 1989.

The Marx-Engels Reader. Edited by Robert C. Tucker. Second edition. New York: W. W. Norton & Co., 1978.

Marx-Engels Works in Two Volumes. Moscow: Foreign Languages Publishing House, 1955.

Mencius. Translated by D. C. Lau. London: Penguin Books, 1970.

Mill, John Stuart. *On Liberty*. Edited by David Spitz. New York: W. W. Norton, Critical Editions, 1975.

———. *Autobiography*. New York: New American Library, Signet Classics, 1964.

Molière [Jean-Baptiste Poquelin]. *The Misanthrope and Tartuffe*. Translated by Richard Wilbur. New York: Harcourt, Brace and World, Harvest Book, 1965.

Montaigne, Michel de. *The Complete Essays of Montaigne*. Translated by Donald M. Frame. Stanford: Stanford University Press, 1958.

Murasaki Shikibu. *The Tale of Genji*. Translated by Edward G. Seidensticker. New York: Alfred A. Knopf, 1976, 1993.

————. *The Tale of Genji*. Translated by Royall Tyler. New York: Penguin Books, 2003.

Nietzsche, Friedrich. *Beyond Good and Evil*. Translated by R. J. Hollingdale. Harmondsworth, Middlesex, England: Penguin Books, 1973.

————. *On the Genealogy of Morals* [and] *Ecce Homo*. Edited by Walter Kaufmann. New York: Random House, Vintage Books, 1969.

————. *The Portable Nietzsche*. Translated and edited by Walter Kaufmann. New York: Viking Press, 1954.

————. *Selected Letters of Friedrich Nietzsche*. Translated and edited by Christopher Middleton. Chicago: University of Chicago Press, 1969.

Pater, Walter. *The Renaissance*. Oxford–New York: Oxford University Press, World Classics, 1986.

Plato. *Euthyphro, Apology, Crito, Phaedo*. In *The Last Days of Socrates*. Translated by Hugh Tredennick. Revised edition. New York: Penguin Books, 1969.

————. *Euthyphro, Apology, Crito, Phaedo*. Translated by Harold North Fowler. Cambridge: Harvard University Press, Loeb Classical Library, 1914, 1968.

————. *The Republic*. Translated by Desmond Lee. Second edition, revised. London: Penguin Books, 1974.

Ibid. Translated by Paul Shorey. Cambridge: Harvard University Press, Loeb Classical Library, 1935.

————. *Symposium*. Translated by Walter Hamilton. New York: Penguin Books, 1951.

Al-Qur'an. Translated by Ahmed Ali. Princeton: Princeton University Press, 1988.

Rousseau, Jean-Jacques. *Emile*. Translated by Barbara Foxley. London: Dent, Everyman Library, 1911, 1966.

————. *Emile or On Education*. Translated by Allan Bloom. New York: Basic Books, 1979.

Sarashina, Lady. *As I Crossed a Bridge of Dreams*. Translated by Ivan Morris. London: Penguin Books, 1975.

Sartre, Jean-Paul. "Existentialism." Translated by Bernard Frechtman. In *Existentialism and Human Emotions*. New York: Citadel Press, Philosophical Library, 1957, 1985.

Shakespeare, William. *The Complete Works*. Edited by Alfred Harbage. Baltimore: Penguin Books, 1969.

Shantideva, Acharya. *A Guide to the Bodhisattva's Way of Life*. Translated by Stephen Batchelor. Dharamshala: Library of Tibetan Works and Archives, 1979.

Shelley, Percy Bysshe. "A Defense of Poetry." In *Selected Poetry and Prose of Shelley*. Edited by Harold Bloom. New York: New American Library, Signet Modern Classics, 1966.

The Song of God: Bhagavad-Gita. Translated by Swami Prabhavananda and Christopher Isherwood. New York: New American Library, Mentor Books, Vedanta Society of Southern California, 1972.

The Teachings of the Compassionate Buddha. Edited by E. A. Burtt. New York: New American Library, Mentor Books, 1955, 1982.

Tocqueville, Alexis de. *Democracy in America*. Translated by Henry Reeve. Revised by Francis Bowen. Edited by Phillips Bradley. New York: Alfred A. Knopf, Everyman Library, 1994.

Ibid. Translated by Harvey C. Mansfield and Delba Winthrop. Chicago: University of Chicago Press, 2000.

Tolstoy, Leo. *What Is Art?*. Translated by Almyer Maude. Indianapolis: Bobbs-Merrill, Library of Liberal Arts, 1960.

Voltaire [François-Marie Arouet]. *Candide, or Optimism*. Translated by Richard Aldington. Revised and edited by Norman L. Torrey. New York: Appelton Century Crofts, Inc, 1946.

————. *Candide and Other Writings*. Edited by Haskell M. Block. New York: Random House, Modern Library, 1956.

————. *Dictionaire philosophique*. Translated by Peter Gay. In *The Enlightenment. A Comprehensive Anthology*. Edited by Peter Gay. New York: Simon and Schuster, 1993.

————. *The Portable Voltaire*. Edited by Ben Ray Redman. New York: Viking Press, 1949, 1968.

Weber, Max. "Bureaucracy." In *From Max Weber: Essays in Sociology*. Translated and edited by C. Wright Mills. New York: Oxford University Press, 1946.

————. *The Protestant Ethic and the Spirit of Capitalism*. Translated by Talcott Parsons. New York: Charles Scribner's Sons, 1958.

"Why We Tell Stories About Spider." In *West African Folk Tales*. Collected and translated by Jack Berry. Edited by Richard Spears. Evanston: Northwestern University Press, 1991.

Wiesel, Elie. *Night*. Translated by Stella Rodway. New York: Farrar, Straus & Giroux, 1960.

Wilde, Oscar. *The Picture of Dorian Gray*. In *Collected Works of Oscar Wilde*. New York: Graystone Press, n.d.

————. "The Critic as Artist." In *The Artist as Critic. Critical Writings of Oscar Wilde*. Edited by Richard Ellman. New York: Random House, 1968.

World of the Buddha. An Introduction to Buddhist Literature. Edited by Lucien Stryk. New York: Grove Press, 1968.

Woolf, Virginia. *Mrs. Dalloway*. New York: Harcourt, Brace, Jovanovich, Harvest Book, n.d.

Wordsworth, William. Preface to *Lyrical Ballads*. In *Selected Poetry and Prose*. Edited by Jeffrey Hartman. New York: New American Library, Signet Books, 1970.

———. *The Prelude. The Four Texts (1798, 1799, 1805, 1850)*. Edited by Jonathan Wordsworth. London: Penguin Books, 1955.

Index

Titles of works that appear in parentheses next to an author's name indicate separate index entries for those works. Page numbers in **boldface** type signal the extended discussion of a work or subject.

Index

This book was composed in Adobe Garamond Pro by the Nangle Type Shop in Meriden, Connecticut. This cutting of the typeface was created by Adobe's Robert Slimbach, who T retained, with rakishly tilted serifs on the capital I crossbar, the tradition of other designers, notably Jean Jannon and Frederic Goudy, who adapted the letterforms developed in early sixteenth-century Paris by Claude Garamond (roman) and Robert Granjon (*italic*). It was Garamond who built on the work of Francesco Griffo and helped to form the alphabet in use today.